AMSCO®

ADVANCED PLACEMENT® EDITION

UNITED STATES HISTORY

JOHN J. NEWMAN
JOHN M. SCHMALBACH

PERFECTION LEARNING®

Advanced Placement® and AP® are trademarks registered and/or owned by the College Board, which was not involved in the production of, and does not endorse, this product.

Authors

John J. Newman, Ed.D., served for many years as an Advanced Placement® U.S. History teacher and the Department Coordinator of Art, Foreign Language, and Social Studies at Naperville North High School, Naperville, Illinois. He continued his career as Adjunct Professor of History at the College of DuPage and Adjunct Assistant Professor of History Education at Illinois State University.

John M. Schmalbach, Ed.D., taught Advanced Placement® U.S. History and was Social Studies Department head at Abraham Lincoln High School, Philadelphia, Pennsylvania. He continued his career as Adjunct Assistant Professor at Temple University.

This book is dedicated to our wives,
Anne Newman and Rosemarie Schmalbach;
our children, Louise Newman, and
John, Suzanne, and Robert Schmalbach; and
our students, who share our study of America's past.

Reviewers and Consultants

Chris Averill, Former Member of the AP® U.S. History Development Committee
  Cosby High School | Midlothian, Virginia

Paul Faeh, AP® U.S. History Exam Leader
  Hinsdale South High School | Darien, Illinois

Kamasi Hill, AP® U.S. History Teacher
  Evanston Township High School | Evanston, Illinois

John P. Irish, Former Co-Chair of the AP® U.S. History Development Committee
  Carroll Senior High School | Southlake, Texas

Michael Kim, AP® U.S. History Exam Table Leader
  Schurr High School | Montebello, California

Susan Pingel, AP® U.S. History Exam Table Leader
  Skaneateles High School (retired) | Skaneateles, New York

James Sabathne, Former Co-Chair of the AP® U.S. History Development Committee
  Hononegah Community High School | Rockton, Illinois

Contents

UNIT 3—Period 3: 1754–1800

UNIT 4—Period 4: 1800–1848

UNIT 7—Period 7: 1890-1945

UNIT 9—Period 9: 1980–Present

Preface

This new edition of *AMSCO® Advanced Placement® United States History* involved a major revision based on the 2019 College Board Course and Exam Description (CED). The recent CED divided the course into 105 topics. Eighteen of these topics focused on historical thinking skills and reasoning processes. This new edition also includes updated review questions and activities at the end of each topic and the units to increase practice of skills, such as "Think As an Historian" and "Write As a Historian" features.

The other 87 topics provide the essential historical content and accessible explanations of events that have been the heart of this textbook. The topics from the new CED are not equal in length or depth, and therefore the amount of time needed for each one will vary. Many can be treated in one class period or less, but others may take two or more class periods. The College Board recommends that treatment of each topic should be at the pace best suited to the needs of the students and school. There is also a separate teacher resource book that includes an answer key and additional activities on race and justice that is available exclusively for teachers and schools.

Since 1997, this textbook has been used by more than a million students in various ways. Many teachers have successfully used it as a core textbook in conjunction with college-level resources and supplemental materials. Others have used it as a supplemental text to bridge the gap between a college-level textbook and the needs of their AP® high school students. In addition, students have effectively used it on their own to support their study of the content. Given the diverse instructional settings across the nation, the most effective use of this textbook is an instructional decision best made by the educators responsible for their students' performance.

We continue to be committed to keep this textbook current and to incorporate revisions from the College Board. Teachers and students should also check the College Board websites for the latest updates: AP® Central site (apcentral.collegeboard.com) and the Advances in AP® section (advancesinap. collegeboard.org). We appreciate your feedback on the new edition and how it works for students and teachers during these challenging times.

The authors want to thank the staff of Perfection Learning Corporation for their support and the tireless effort they have put into this new edition. We also appreciate the continued opportunity to support the efforts of high school students and teachers as they strive to meet the challenges of the Advanced Placement® U.S. History examination.

John Newman and John Schmalbach, June 2020

Introduction

Studying Advanced Placement® United States History

Since 1998, the number of high school students taking the Advanced Placement® exam in United States History has more than tripled. Students enroll in AP® U.S. History classes for many reasons. Some of these are related to doing well on the AP® exam:

- to demonstrate one's ability to succeed as a college undergraduate
- to become eligible for scholarships
- to save on college expenses by earning college credit
- to test out of introductory college courses

The College Board's website provides a list of colleges and universities that normally use AP® exam grades for determining placement and credits. However, the placement and credit offered vary from school to school. To find out a particular college's or university's policy on AP® exams, see that school's website.

Even within high school, AP® U.S. History classes are beneficial because they enrich a student's experience. They teach students how to read complex passages, to write clearly and persuasively, and to develop higher level thinking skills. Most students who have taken AP® courses report that these courses are more difficult than regular ones but are worth the extra effort because they are more engaging. The rewards of these challenging classes can foster lifelong reading, thinking, and writing skills and, for many students, an increased interest in and enjoyment of history.

Overview of the AP® U.S. History Exam

This edition of this textbook was revised to address the most recent changes to the *AP® United States History Course and Exam Description* (CED). The revision places a greater focus on the historical thinking skills and reasoning processes used by historians and on historical themes and related concepts in order to deepen a student's understanding of U.S. history. The 3-hour-and-15-minute exam relies heavily on excerpts, images, and other data sources.

The AP® exam includes the following components, along with the amount of time allotted for each and the percentage each is weighted in the final grade:

- 55 Multiple-Choice Questions (MCQs)   55 minutes   40%
- 3 Short-Answer Questions (SAQs)   40 minutes   20%
- 1 Document-Based Question (DBQ)   60 minutes   25%
- 1 Long Essay Question (LEQ)   40 minutes   15%

The multiple-choice section still has the greatest weight in a student's final grade, but students' performances on recent exams suggest that working on writing skills may offer the greatest opportunity for improvement. Each of these components, along with a guide to sequential skill development, will be explained in this Introduction.

The College Board grades student performance on Advanced Placement® examinations, including the AP® U.S. History exam, on a five-point scale:

- 5: Extremely well qualified
- 4: Well qualified
- 3: Qualified
- 2: Possibly qualified
- 1: No recommendation

An AP® grade of 3 or higher is usually considered evidence of mastery of course content similar to that demonstrated in a college-level introductory course in the same subject area. However, since the requirements of introductory courses may vary from college to college, some colleges may accept a 2 on the AP® History exam, while others may require a score of 4.

How This Book Can Help

The goal of this textbook is to provide U.S. history students with the essential content and instructional materials to develop the knowledge, the mastery of historical thinking skills and reasoning processes, and the writing skills needed to understand U.S. history and to approach the past as historians do. The book includes these elements:

Introduction This section introduces students to the historical thinking skills and reasoning processes, course themes, and nine periods of the AP® U.S. History program. A step-by-step skill development guide explains how to answer the four types of questions found on the exam: (1) multiple-choice, (2) short-answer, (3) long essay, and (4) document-based.

Concise History The organization of the content into topics within each unit/period reflects the new Fall 2019 *AP® U.S. History Course and Exam Description*. Each of the nine units/periods is divided into a number of topics based on the new CED. These topics provide the essential historical content and accessible explanations of events that form the heart of this textbook. Each unit begins with an overview of the context of the period and concludes with the practice of one of the three reasoning processes used in argumentation.

Maps and Graphics Maps, charts, graphs, cartoons, photographs, and other visual materials are integrated into the text to help students practice their analytical skills.

Historical Perspectives Certain topics include a Historical Perspective section that introduces students to conflicting interpretations about significant historical issues. These are integral to the content of the book.

Key Terms by Themes Each of the 87 narrative topics includes a list of key names, places, and words, organized by theme, as an aid for student review of the topic.

Multiple-Choice Questions Each of the 87 narrative topics contains at least one set of source-based, multiple-choice questions to evaluate students' historical knowledge and skills using sources.

Short-Answer Questions Each of the 87 narrative topics contains at least one set of short-answer questions for review of the topic and opportunities to apply AP® historical thinking skills and reasoning processes.

Long Essay Questions Periods 2 through 9 conclude with a review section that includes four to eight long essay questions. The long essay questions prompt students to deal with significant issues and to apply course reasoning and writing skills.

Document-Based Questions The reviews for periods 2 through 8 each include one DBQ.

Practice Examination Following the final unit is a complete practice examination using the current format.

Index The index is included to help locate key terms for review.

Answer Key A separate Answer Key is available from the publisher for teachers and other authorized users of the book.

The Study of AP® U.S. History

Historians attempt to give meaning to the past by collecting historical evidence and then explaining how these "facts" are connected. Historians interpret and organize a wide variety of evidence from both primary and secondary sources in order to understand the past. Students should develop their ability to analyze and use historical sources, to answer probing questions about past events, and to demonstrate these abilities in their writing. For many historical questions, no one "answer" is accepted by all historians, nor can one find all answers in any one historical source. AP® teachers and exam readers are looking for a student's ability to think about history and to support ideas with evidence.

AP® students should appreciate how both participants and historians differ in their interpretations of critical questions in U.S. history. The Historical Perspectives feature introduces readers to some of the issues raised by historians over time. AP® U.S. History does not require an advanced knowledge of historiography, sometimes described as "the history of history." Nevertheless, prior knowledge of the richness of historical thought can add depth to a student's analysis of historical questions.

The study of AP® U.S. History includes three basic components that shape the course: (1) the thinking skills and reasoning processes of history, (2) thematic analysis, and (3) the concepts and understandings of the nine periods that organize the content. These three components are explained below for orientation and future reference.

How Historians Think

The Advanced Placement® History courses encourage students to think like historians. The practices and skills that historians use in researching and writing about historical events and developments are the foundation of the AP® U.S. History course and exam. Learning these skills and reasoning processes can be developed over a course of study, but an introduction to them is a good place to start.

- Historians need to be able to **analyze historical evidence** found in a wide variety of **primary sources** from written records to historical images and artifacts. Historians also need to explain and evaluate the evidence from **secondary sources**, especially the work of other historians with differing points of view.

- As historians research the evidence, they look for **connections** and patterns among historical events and developments. They use reasoning processes, such as making **comparisons**, studying **causation**, and analyzing **continuity and change** to find and test possible connections.

- Most historians communicate their findings through publications and presentations. This creative process takes the additional practice of **argument development**, which includes making a defensible claim and marshaling relevant and persuasive evidence to support an argument. Writing about history also challenges one to clarify and refine one's thinking about the subject or the question under study.

Historical Thinking Skills

The study of history includes the use of many thinking skills. Of these, AP® courses focus on six.

1. Developments and Processes The ability to identify and explain historical concepts, developments, and processes is fundamental to the analysis of historical evidence. For example, "salutary neglect" has proved a useful concept to describe and explain British behavior toward the American colonies before the 1750s. During that period colonists were relatively autonomous. That is, the British allowed colonies to govern themselves with minimal interference. Students need to be able to explain the historical concepts and developments and provide specific historical evidence to illustrate or support such a historical concept or development. For example, a multiple-choice question on the AP® exam might ask "Which of the following is the best example of British salutary neglect in the American colonies before 1750?"

2. Sourcing and Situations The use of historical evidence involves the ability to explain and evaluate diverse kinds of primary and secondary sources, including written works, data, images, and artifacts. Students need to be able to explain (1) the historical setting of a source, (2) its intended audience, (3) its purpose, and (4) the point of view of the original writer or creator. For example, an AP® exam question might ask "Which of the following best reflects the point of view expressed by the author?" Another possible question is "Briefly explain ONE characteristic of the intended audience for this image."

For secondary sources, this skill also involves understanding how particular circumstances might influence authors. Historians can "rewrite" history because their personal perspective or society's perspective changes, because they discover new sources and information, and, above all, because they ask new questions.

3. Claims and Evidence in Sources The analysis of either primary or secondary sources also includes the ability to identify the author's argument and the evidence used to support it. For example, an AP® question might provide short quotations from two secondary sources about the causes of the American Revolution. The reading might be evaluated by a multiple-choice question such as "Which of the following would best support the argument of historian A?" A short-answer question might ask "Briefly explain ONE major difference between historian A's and historian B's historical interpretations." Questions can also ask students to discover patterns or trends in quantitative data found in charts and graphs.

4. Contextualization The skill of contextualization involves the ability to accurately and explicitly explain how a historical event, policy, or source fits into the broader historical picture, often on the regional, national, or global level. Placing the specifics of history into their larger context gives them additional usefulness and significance as historical evidence. Contextualization is evaluated through questions such as this: "(The excerpt) best reflects which of the following developments in U.S. foreign policy?" or "The conditions shown in the image depict which of the following trends in the late 19th century?"

5. Making Connections This skill involves identifying and analyzing patterns and connections between and among historical developments and processes, and how one development or process relates to another. Making connections on the AP® exam will use the three reasoning processes of comparisons, causation, and continuity and change (see below). For example, the developments of large-scale industrial production, concentration of wealth, and the labor movement were taking place during the same period from 1865 to 1900. Are any patterns and connections common among these developments? The exam could ask an essay question such as this: "To what extent was the rise of labor unions related to the development of large corporations during the period from 1865 to 1900?"

6. Argumentation Developing an argument includes the skill of using evidence effectively to make a point. Students need to recognize that not all evidence has equal value in support of a position. Writers need to select examples that are accurate and relevant to their argument. Making judgments about the use of relevant historical evidence is an essential skill in free-response questions on the AP® exam.

Again, the focus of the question will be not on the simple recall of facts but on a conceptual understanding of the evidence and the ability to link that understanding to the argument. For example, to support the argument about the impact of technology from 1865 to 1900, it is not enough to describe the technologies of the period. In addition, one should explain the connection of specific new technologies, such as railroads or electric power, to the changes in the economy. The AP® exam also values the use of diverse and alternative evidence to qualify or modify an argument in order to develop a more complex insight into history.

Reasoning Processes

The study of history includes the use of several reasoning processes. Of these, AP® courses focus on three very important ones.

1. Comparison Thinking about comparison involves the ability to describe and evaluate similarities and differences between two or more historical developments. The developments might be in the same era or in different ones. This process also asks one to explain the relative significance of similarities and differences between historical developments and to study a given historical event or development from multiple perspectives.

The ability to make a comparison is evaluated in questions such as "The ideas expressed in the excerpt were most similar to those of which of the following?" or "Compare and contrast views of the United States' overseas expansion in the late 19th century." Expect AP® questions to test similarities and differences of conceptual understandings rather than simple recall.

2. Causation The study of causation is the primary tool of historians to explore the connections—both causes and effects—among events. Historians are often challenged to make judgments between primary and secondary causes and between short-term and long-term effects for developments such as the American Civil War or the Great Depression.

Students will need to not only identify causes or effects but also explain the relationship between them. For example, it will not be enough to state that either imperialist attitudes or idealistic beliefs led to U.S. involvement in the War in Vietnam. One must be able to explain the connections of specific evidence to one's position. At the AP® level, a causation question might ask "Which of the following most strongly influenced A?" or "B contributed most directly to which of the following trends?" The use of causation as a reasoning process is used with all historical thinking skills.

3. Continuity and Change The study of history also involves the ability to describe and explain patterns that reveal both continuity and change over time. The study of themes especially lends itself to discovering continuity and change in varying lengths of time from a few decades to hundreds of years.

For example, one might argue that President Washington's foreign policy from the 1790s continued as the standard for American foreign policy into the mid-20th century. The AP® exam might evaluate the understanding of continuity and change by asking "Which of the following developments best represents the continuation of A?" or "Which of the following best represents a later example of the change B?" A more complex essay question can ask "Evaluate the extent to which C contributed to maintaining continuity as well as fostering change in D." Responding to this item involves understanding not only an event but also its significance in longer trends in United States history.

Thematic Learning Objectives

Just as historians combine the use of multiple historical thinking skills and reasoning processes, they address multiple themes in their work. Questions on the AP® exam will focus on one or more of eight themes that recur throughout U.S. history. Following are analyses of each of the eight. The quotations are from the *AP® U.S. History Course and Exam Description*.

1. American and National Identity (NAT) "This theme focuses on how and why definitions of American and national identity and values have developed among the diverse and changing population of North America as well as on related topics, such as citizenship, constitutionalism, foreign policy, assimilation, and American exceptionalism." Students should be able to explain how identities related to American values and institutions, regions, and societal groups developed in response to events and how they have affected political debates. For example, the American Revolution changed the identity of Americans from British colonial subjects to citizens of a free and independent republic.

2. Work, Exchange, and Technology (WXT) "This theme focuses on the factors behind the development of systems of economic exchange, particularly the role of technology, economic markets, and government." Students should understand how the economy has shaped society, labor systems, government policy, and innovation. For example, the transportation revolution in the 1800s transformed the economy and the lives of farmers, workers, and consumers.

3. Geography and the Environment (GEO) "This theme focuses on the role of geography and both the natural and human-made environments in the social and political developments in what would become the United States." Students need to examine how geography and climate have contributed to regional differences and how debates over the use and control of natural resources have impacted different groups and government policies. For example, how did the frontier experience shape early settlers' attitudes toward the natural environment?

4. Migration and Settlement (MIG) "This theme focuses on why and how the various people who moved to and within the United States both adapted to and transformed their new social and physical environments." Students should be able to answer questions about the peoples who have moved to and lived in the United States. For example, they should be able to explain how Irish and German Catholics in the 19th century, southern and eastern Europeans in the early 20th century, and Hispanics and Asians in recent decades have each affected U.S. society.

5. Politics and Power (PCE) "This theme focuses on how different social and political groups have influenced society and government in the United States, as well as how political beliefs and institutions have changed over time." Students need to understand the debates over power between branches of government, between the national and state governments, and among voters and special interest groups. For example, the debate over government policies in Congress during the 1790s led to the development of political parties in the United States.

6. America in the World (WOR) "This theme focuses on the interactions between nations that affected North American history in the colonial period and on the influence of the United States on world affairs." Students need to understand key developments in foreign policy as well as domestic debates over these policies. For example, they need to understand how the French Revolution and the Napoleonic Wars challenged U.S. efforts to remain neutral and ultimately contributed to U.S. involvement in the War of 1812.

7. American and Regional Culture (ARC) "This theme focuses on how and why national, regional, and group cultures developed and changed as well as how culture has shaped government policy and the economy." It also addresses how various identities, cultures, and values have shaped the lives of citizens, politics, and the economy. Students should be able to explain why and how cultural components both hold constant and change over time, as well as the conflicts between traditional and modern values. For example, "In what ways did artistic expression change in response to war and to the growth of industry and cities from 1865 to 1898?"

8. Social Structures (SOC) "This theme focuses on how and why systems of social organization develop and change as well as the impact that these systems have on the broader society." It involves the study of the roles of men, women, and other categories of family and civic units, and how they have been maintained, challenged, and transformed throughout American history. This theme could be evaluated with questions such as "To what extent were the roles of women in the United States transformed during the period from 1890 to 1945?" Another question might ask "In what ways did government policies change the role of children in American society during the Progressive Era?"

Using the Themes The tracing of multiple themes through each period of U.S. history is an effective way to study and review content throughout the course. A thematic approach encourages one to think about specific events in a larger framework and to make judgments about comparison, causation, and continuity and change over time. A theme also provides a frame in which to view issues. Students can use themes to organize an essay.

Historical Periods

The content of AP° U.S. History is also organized by the AP° unit framework of nine chronological periods.

Period 1: 1491–1607 The period from before Columbus arrived in the Americas to the founding of the English colony at Jamestown covers the interaction of Native American, European, and African cultures to create a "new" world.

Period 2: 1607–1754 The mixtures of people from various heritages living in different geographic settings created colonies with distinctive cultures, economies, and populations.

Period 3: 1754–1800 Wars over empires provided the context for the American Revolution and the founding of the United States, including the political struggles to form a "more perfect union."

Period 4: 1800–1848 The promise of the new republic played out during a period of rapid economic, territorial, and population growth that tested the political institutions that held the nation together.

Period 5: 1844–1877 A war with Mexico intensified the conflict over slavery and states' rights, which led to the Civil War and then to struggles to reconstruct the Union and address the legacy of slavery.

Period 6: 1865–1898 Industrialization, the rapid growth of cities, and a large new wave of immigration transformed the American economy, society, culture, and regional identities.

Period 7: 1890–1945 While the United States responded to the impact of industrialization during the Progressive Era and New Deal years, it also became deeply involved in world affairs during World Wars I and II.

Period 8: 1945–1980 The United States assumed a world leadership role during the Cold War while society became more divided over issues of economic and social justice, especially for minorities and women.

Period 9: 1980–Present A renewed conservative movement challenged the efficacy of government at home while the end of the Cold War, the spread of globalization, and the increase in terrorism prompted the federal government to redefine its policies.

The text does not attempt to cover every historical fact, but it includes all of the essential evidence and understandings needed to address the challenges of the AP° U.S. History exam.

The College Board provides a key to the amount of emphasis to be put on each period of history, but it also recognizes that the allocation of time will vary from class to class. Usually the emphasis will fall within these ranges:

- Period 1, 1491–1607: between 4% and 6%
- Period 2, 1607–1754: between 6% and 8%
- Periods 3 to 8, 1754 to 1980: each between 10% and 17%
- Period 9, 1980–Present: between 4% and 6%

In the AP® U.S. History exam, some multiple-choice and short-answer questions will be based on periods 1 and 9, and content from these periods may be used in the long essays and DBQs. However, no long essay or DBQ will focus exclusively on these two periods of history.

History, like any other field of study, is a combination of subject matter and methodology. The practices, skills, and themes are methods or tools to explore the subject matter of history. One cannot practice these skills without knowledge of the historical situation and understanding of specific historical evidence. The following section provides suggestions for development of another set of skills useful for answering the questions on the exam. Again, the "mastery" of these skills, particularly writing answers to AP® questions, takes practice.

Keeping Perspective

The skills and understandings required for learning AP®-level U.S. history may strike many students as overwhelming at first. Mastering them takes time. Working on the AP® U.S. History skills and understandings will take an ongoing step-by-step effort throughout the course of study. While the effort may seem challenging, what keeps students and teachers in the program is the impressive intellectual growth that can be achieved during an AP® course.

Some students also may become discouraged with the difficult level of AP® exams. AP® exams are unlike most classroom tests. They are not designed to measure mastery of a lesson or unit on which 90 percent or more correct may receive an "A," 80 percent a "B," etc. Rather, the AP® exams are more difficult than most classroom tests. Only a small percentage of students will gain more than 80 percent of the possible points. Further, they are deliberately constructed to provide a wider distribution of scores and higher reliability (the likelihood that a test-taker repeating the same exam will receive the same score). AP® students who are having difficulty with a large number of the questions on the practice AP® exams should not be discouraged.

A specific grade on the AP® exam is also not the main purpose of the course. What is most important in the long run are the thinking and writing skills, understandings of the complexities of historical developments, and habits and appreciation of lifelong learning. Students' educational and personal development during the course will have a greater impact on their futures than a number.

To the Student: The Course and Exam Description

The CED describes the four types of questions on the AP® U.S. History exam: (1) multiple-choice, (2) short-answer, (3) long essay, and (4) document-based. On the exam, the long essay questions are last. Once you have developed the long essay writing skills, you are more than halfway to writing a competent answer to the DBQ. For this reason, in the following section, the long essay is presented before the DBQ.

Answering the Multiple-Choice Questions

The AP® exam asks 55 multiple-choice questions (MCQ), and you will have 55 minutes to answer them. The value of the MCQs is 40 percent of your score. Each question is related to the analysis of a stimulus, which is a primary or secondary source such as a text excerpt, image, chart, graph, or map. Three or four questions will be asked about each stimulus. Each MCQ assesses one or more historical thinking skills but also requires historical knowledge you have learned studying U.S. history.

Each question will have one BEST answer and three distractors. Compared to most history tests, the AP® exam will place less emphasis on simple recall and more emphasis on your ability to analyze primary and secondary sources and to use history reasoning processes.

This book includes 87 topics that are each followed by MCQs based on sources. The MCQs in the topic reviews are similar to ones on the AP® exam but are also designed to review the content and understanding of the topic. In addition to the MCQs in the topics, the practice AP® exam includes 55 multiple-choice questions.

Analyzing Historical Evidence   Below is one example of a primary source, a political cartoon from 1934. Your first step in analyzing this kind of evidence, whether an image or a reading, is to ask these questions: What was the historical situation in which it was created? Who was the intended audience? What was the point of view of the author? What was the author's purpose? The development of these four skill-building questions is part of the foundation of studying U.S. history at the AP® level.

You might recognize the patient in the cartoon as Uncle Sam, a characterization used by political cartoonists since the early 19th century as a stand-in for the United States. The doctor (President Franklin D. Roosevelt) is clearly under pressure from "Old Lady" Congress to cure the ills of the United States. However, in order to interpret and use the evidence in this cartoon, you need knowledge about the 1930s. You need to understand both the economic problems of the era known as the Great Depression and about Roosevelt's New Deal program that were a response to these problems. A source by itself will not reveal the answers to the MCQs: You will also need to call upon your knowledge and skills to effectively unlock and use the evidence.

Source: C.K. Berryman, *Washington Star*, 1934. Library of Congress

Below are examples of the kinds of MCQs that might be asked on the AP® exam about a source and the skills being assessed. Each would be followed by four possible answers:

- *Analyzing Historical Evidence:* Which of the following statements most directly supports the argument in the cartoon?

- *Causation:* Which of the following events most clearly explains what caused the cartoonist to take the point of view reflected in the cartoon?

- *Comparison:* Which of the following ideas most closely resembles the point of view of the cartoon?

- *Contextualization:* Which of the following developments most clearly provided the context for the cartoonist's point of view?

- *Continuity and Change:* Which of the following events represents a continuation of the ideas expressed in the source?

Making a Choice Read the stem of the question and all four choices carefully before you record your answer. A number of choices may appear to be correct, but you should select the BEST answer. Choices that reflect absolute positions, such as "always," "never," and "exclusively," are seldom correct because historical evidence rarely offers such complete certainty. Keep in mind the need to make judgments about the significance of a variety of causes and effects.

Should you guess on the AP® exam? The current format does not penalize guessing. Obviously, the process of first eliminating a wrong answer or two increases your chances of guessing correctly.

Budgeting Your Time The AP® History exam gives you 55 minutes to answer the 55 questions. You will not have enough time to spend two or three minutes on difficult questions. Follow a relaxed but reasonable pace rather than rushing through the exam and then going back and second-guessing your decisions. Avoid skipping questions and be careful changing answers.

Recommended Activity Become familiar with the type of multiple-choice questions on the exam before taking it. This will reduce the chance of surprises over the format of the questions.

However, for many students, reviewing content through multiple-choice questions is not the most productive way to absorb the information. The purpose of the content in this textbook is to provide a useful and concise presentation of the essential concepts and evidence needed for the exam. By reviewing the essential facts in their historical situations, you will better recall and understand the connections between events—so important for applying the history reasoning processes.

Answering the Short-Answer Questions

The short-answer questions (SAQ) section of the AP® U.S. History exam will have three sets of questions and allow you 40 minutes to answer them. They will count for 20 percent of your final score. The first two sets of questions are **required**, but in the third set, you can **choose** between question 3 from periods 1–5 and question 4 from periods 6–9. This option gives students an opportunity to write in an area of their strength. Each question consists of three tasks, and you receive one point for a successful response to each task, so each question is worth three points.

In the format for the current exam, question 1 will involve analyzing a secondary source. Question 2 will involve analyzing a primary source and the reasoning process of either causation or comparison. Questions 3 and 4 will involve the reasoning process of either causation or comparison without a reference to a source.

Below is an example of how an SAQ without a source could be structured. It consists of three tasks, labeled (a), (b), and (c). All involve the reasoning process of comparison.

1. Answer (a), (b), and (c).

   (a) Briefly describe ONE difference between the economies of the British North American colonies in the Chesapeake region and in New England in the period from 1607 to 1754.

   (b) Briefly describe ONE similarity between the economies of the British North American colonies in the Chesapeake region and in New England in the period from 1607 to 1754.

(c) Briefly explain ONE reason for the difference between the economy of the Chesapeake colonies and the economy of the New England colonies.

Writing Short Answers

SAQs, unlike DBQs and long essay questions, do not require the development of a thesis statement. However, they do need to be answered in complete sentences. An outline or bulleted list alone is not acceptable. Students have a total of 40 minutes to answer three questions, each of which consists of three tasks. "Briefly" is a key direction in most short-answer questions. The number of sentences that it will take to answer the question will depend on the task in the question. As you write responses to SAQs, work on your ability to write clear and complete sentences supported with specific and accurate evidence. If the question calls for specific evidence, try to provide it using the proper names of persons, places, and events.

While the College Board does not give specific directions, most exam readers recommend labeling the three tasks in your answer A, B, and C. You will have one page in the exam booklet that includes approximately 23 lines on which to write your answers to the three tasks of each SAQ.

Recommended Activity Each of the 87 topics in this textbook contains short-answer questions based on the models provided by the College Board. Some questions contain greater emphasis on reviewing content than the questions found on the AP® exam. As you answer the SAQs, first identify the reasoning process used in the question. This will help orient you to the purpose of the question, whether it involves comparison, causation, or continuity and change. To evaluate your progress in answering these short-answer questions, use this simple scoring standard:

- 1 point for accomplishing the task identified in the prompt

- 0 points for each task that is not accomplished or completed

You might need to answer many short-answer questions over several weeks to learn how to budget the 12 to 14 minutes available to answer each of the three-point questions.

Answering the Long Essay Question

In the current format of the AP® U.S. History exam, students choose ONE long essay question (LEQ) from among THREE options. Each option will focus on the same theme and same reasoning process, but the options will be about different sets of periods. This means that students choose to answer a question from periods 1–3 (1491–1800), from periods 4–6 (1800–1898), or from periods 7–9 (1890–2001). The suggested writing time is 40 minutes. The long essay represents 15 percent of the final grade on the exam. An edited copy of the current format released by the College Board is reproduced below:

Students will choose one of the three long essay questions to answer. The long essay requires students to demonstrate their ability to use historical evidence in crafting a thoughtful historical argument.

Question from periods 1–3: Evaluate the extent to which transatlantic interactions fostered change in the labor systems in British North American colonies from 1600 to 1763.

Question from periods 4–6: Evaluate the extent to which new technology fostered change in the United States economy from 1865 to 1898.

Question from periods 7–9: Evaluate the extent to which globalization fostered change in the United States economy from 1945 to 2000.

In the sample above, all three essays are based on the same theme—Work, Exchange, and Technology (WXT)—and the same reasoning process—Continuity and Change. Much like the SAQ format, the LEQ format gives students the choice to answer a question from a period that best reflects their understanding of the relevant examples from that period.

Requirements of the Long Essay Question The AP® exam is very specific in what is expected in answering an LEQ. The grading rubric is based on a six-point scale, which is worth 15 percent of one's final grade. While the traditional model of writing an essay with an introduction, body, and conclusion is still useful in the overall organization of your essay, the AP® U.S. History exam rubrics for the LEQ clearly define what you need to do to gain each point.

- **Point 1: Thesis** Earn one point for making a historically defensible thesis or claim that establishes a line of reasoning and how it will be argued. This thesis must do more than restate the question. It must create an argument. The thesis must consist of one or more sentences in either the introduction or the conclusion.

- **Point 2: Contextualization** Earn one point for describing a broader historical context that is relevant to the question. This context might be events or development before, during, or after the time frame of the question. This requires more elaboration than a mere reference.

- **Points 3 and 4: Evidence** Earn one point for describing at least two specific examples that are relevant to the question. For two points, you must explain how the specific examples support your arguments stated in the thesis.

- **Points 5 and 6: Historical Reasoning and Complexity** Earn one point for using the reasoning process in the question (comparison, causation, or continuity and change) to frame your arguments that address the question. To gain a second point, you must demonstrate a complex understanding that uses evidence to corroborate, qualify, or modify your argument, such as using an additional historical reasoning process.

The next section on writing long essay question answers explains how to achieve each of these points.

Practice Writing Long Essay Question Answers The long essay question (LEQ) and the document-based question (DBQ) have proven to be the two parts of the exam on which students need to improve the most. Although the DBQ is worth more than the LEQ, it is better to start with learning how to master the LEQ skills, because they include the fundamental skills for writing the DBQ and also have fewer elements to handle. For many students, writing an AP® history essay is much different from writing an essay for an English or literature class.

The skills you need to write AP® history essays take time and practice to master, so you will benefit from starting to work on them as early as possible. Instead of writing and rewriting complete essays until all elements are mastered, break down the essay writing into sequential steps to develop the skills needed for each point. The following steps have proven useful in developing the skills needed to answer the AP® long essay question:

1. Analyze the Question

2. Organize the Evidence

3. Write the Thesis Statement

4. Provide Context

5. Use Evidence

6. Address Historical Reasoning and Complexity

7. Evaluate a Long Essay Answer

Let's look at the sequential steps that you can use to develop your skill at writing long essays.

1. Analyze the Question Students who rush to start writing risk overlooking what the question is asking. Take time to fully understand the question in order to avoid the mistake of writing an excellent essay that receives little or no credit because it answered a question that was not asked. Consider this sample long essay question:

> Evaluate the extent to which transatlantic interactions fostered change in the labor systems in British North American colonies from 1600 to 1763.

Before writing, ask yourself, "What are the key words in the question? What is the targeted history reasoning process in the question?" Underline words related to the reasoning process and the time frame, such as "evaluate the extent," "change," and "from 1600 to 1763." Next, circle the content words, such as "transatlantic interactions," "labor systems," and "British North American colonies." During this step, identify all parts of the question. In the answer to the above essay question, the writer should apply the reasoning process of continuity and change over time.

Simply describing transatlantic interactions and labor systems in the colonies is not enough for a good essay. You must also explain and evaluate how interactions, such as trade and migration, contributed to continuity and change in labor systems such as free labor, indentured servitude, and slavery.

Recommended Activity As an initial skill-building activity, analyze the LEQs in the period review sections throughout this book.

- *Underline* the key words that indicate the targeted reasoning process. These say what the writer should do.

- *Circle* the words that indicate the specific aspects of the content that need to be addressed. These say what the writer should write about.

2. Organize the Evidence Many students start writing their answers to an essay question without first thinking through what they know, and they often write themselves into a corner. Directions for the AP® History exam suggest you spend some time reading and planning before starting to write. Take a few minutes to identify what you know about the question and organize your information by making a rough outline in the test booklet, using abbreviations and other memory aids. This outline is not graded. Taking a few minutes to organize your knowledge can help you answer an important question: Do you have enough evidence to select a certain essay or to support your argument?

Below is a sample list of items that could be used in answering the long essay question about the impact of transatlantic interactions on the continuity and changes in the labor systems in the British North American colonies.

Transatlantic Interactions	Labor Systems	British North American Colonies
• Migration over time	• Adventurers	• Plantation system
• Mercantilism	• Free labor	• Raw materials for export
• Triangular trade	• Family units	• New England
• Navigation Acts	• Indentured servants	• Middle Colonies
• Slave trade	• Headright system	• Chesapeake region
• Racial prejudices	• Slavery	• Carolina and Georgia
• Cash crops such as tobacco	• Native Americans	
	• Labor shortages	

Facts are important. However, the key to writing an effective long essay answer is that your thesis and arguments drive your writing so that you do not simply list information.

Recommended Activity Create a list of the kinds of relevant information that could be incorporated into the responses to the long essay questions found in the period reviews. Organize the information under headings that reflect the major parts of the question. This activity parallels the lists developed by AP® consultants before readers start scoring essays. It is a very useful prewriting activity.

3. Write the Thesis Statement The development of a strong claim or thesis is an essential part of every AP® History essay answer. Some students have difficulty taking a position because they are afraid of making a mistake. Remember, understanding different interpretations of events is part of the study of history. AP® readers are looking not for the "right answer." Rather, they want to see a writer's ability to interpret the historical evidence and marshal it into a persuasive argument.

A thesis must be more than a restatement of the question. The AP® scoring guide requires that the thesis address the history reasoning process in the question, such as causation, comparison, or continuity and change over time. The following thesis is one effort to address the long essay question presented earlier:

> Transatlantic interactions fostered continuity in the demand for labor in the British North American colonies from 1600 to 1783 but also fostered change in the kinds of labor systems in use.

This statement is straightforward, and it takes a position on the question and the reasoning process of continuity and change, but does it provide a well-developed line of reasoning? Below is an example of how to extend and develop the short thesis statement from the question about labor systems:

> Not surprisingly, the colonies from New England to Georgia tried different labor systems, such as indentured servitude, slavery, and free labor. Changes in these labor systems were affected by changes in trade and migrations, but the racial attitudes of the period also hardened the institution of slavery against change, especially in the Southern colonies.

By developing and extending a thesis statement, one both clarifies the thesis and provides the organizing ideas and arguments that will guide the development of the essay.

An effective introductory paragraph should also introduce the main arguments of the essay. The above example of an extended thesis does that by identifying three labor systems, which will be evaluated for continuity and change. This second feature of the introduction is sometimes called the essay's "blueprint" or "organizing ideas." By the end of the first paragraph, a reader should not only know your thesis but also have a clear idea of the main arguments to be developed in support of the thesis.

The AP® exam rubric states that the thesis must be "located in one place, either in the introduction or in the conclusion." Based on experience, most teachers and readers of the exam recommend putting your thesis in the introductory paragraph. While it might seem to create more drama to reveal the thesis in the last paragraph, you are not writing a "who-done-it" mystery.

Recommended Activity Practice writing an introductory paragraph with a thesis statement and introduction of main arguments to support it. Use LEQs from this text and from prior AP® exams. Use the following criteria to assess your work:

- Does the thesis consist of one or more sentences?
- Does the thesis make a historically defensible claim?
- Does the thesis address the history reasoning process?
- Does the thesis address all parts of the question?
- Does the introduction provide a framework for understanding the main arguments that will be used to support the thesis?
- How could you improve the thesis and supporting arguments?

4. Provide Context The AP® program describes the context requirement as "describe a broader historical context relevant to the prompt." For the above essay question about continuity and change in the "labor systems," an explanation of the competition among European powers, such as Britain, France, and Spain, could provide context for "transatlantic interactions" and what was happening in the colonies. Explaining the growing political conflicts over slavery after independence could also provide the context for the significance of this question.

Context could become a separate second introductory paragraph, since the AP® exam expects "more than a mere phrase or reference." However, the placement for the contextualization point should be determined by the logical flow of the essay. Explaining the context from after the time frame of the question may make more sense at the end of the essay than the beginning.

Recommended Activity The first step is to think about the possible historical context that you can provide for the question. It can be historical events or developments before, during, or after the time frame of the question. Next, write a separate paragraph for the context point. For practice use LEQs from this text and from prior AP® exams. Use these criteria to assess your work:

- Is the context more than a phrase or reference?
- Is the context passage or paragraph relevant to the topic of the question?
- Does the response explain broader historical events, developments, or processes that occur before, during, or after the time frame of the question?
- How can the explanation of context for the question be improved?

5. Use Evidence As explained above, to receive at least one point for use of evidence, you should try to describe at least two specific examples of evidence (such as proper nouns, historical terms, and developments) relevant to the topic of the question. However, two examples are the minimum. Most teachers and graders recommend more. What if one example is wrong? For the above LEQ about impact of trade on labor systems in the colonies, a writer could receive one point for describing the three labor systems of free labor, indentured servitude, and slavery in the colonies supported with specific historical facts.

Recommended Activity Before your first efforts to write paragraphs for the evidence points, practice outlining three paragraphs of evidence to back up your thesis and arguments. Incorporate historical terms, such as proper names or terms in each paragraph. Once you understand the reasoning process involved, practice writing complete paragraphs. Use the following criteria to assess your work:

- Does the response earn one point by providing at least two specific examples of historical evidence relevant to the question?

- Does the response earn two points by using examples of specific historical evidence to support the arguments made to support the thesis?

- How effectively is the evidence linked to the arguments?

- How can the variety, depth, and analysis of the evidence be improved?

6. Address Historical Reasoning and Complexity To receive one point for historical reasoning, one must use the appropriate reasoning process (causation, comparison, or continuity and change over time) to structure the argument used to address the question. In the question above on changes in colonial labor systems, the writer should frame the argument using continuity and change over time.

For example, one argument might explain how the growing demand for cash crops from the Britain's American colonies promoted the growth of a plantation system that depended on a large supply of low-cost labor to be profitable. The landowners' desire for labor was then satisfied by slavery. This requirement does not demand writing a separate paragraph for the point, but the historical reasoning process can and should be integrated into your use of evidence.

The second point for complexity is often the hardest one for students to earn. It is not given out just for good essays that are clearly written and organized with no historical errors. The response needs to show a deeper, more complex understanding of the question. The AP® exam rubrics from the College Board state the following ways to demonstrate a complex understanding:

- Explaining nuance of an issue by analyzing multiple variables

- Explaining both similarities and differences, or explaining both continuity and change, or explaining multiple causes, or explaining both causes and effects

- Explaining relevant and insightful connections within and across periods

- Confirming the validity of an argument by corroborating multiple perspectives across themes

- Qualifying or modifying an argument by considering diverse or alternative views or evidence

For example, a point for a complex understanding of historical developments for this LEQ could be gained by explaining both change and continuity. As another example of complexity, one could explain that the institution of slavery developed in the colonies not only for economic causes but also for social or racial reasons.

However, to receive two points one must explain the relationship of evidence to the arguments used to support the thesis. For example, it is not enough to simply describe the labor systems used in the colonies. You must explain and evaluate, for example, how changes in voluntary and involuntary migration were linked to the growth of free labor and slavery and the decline of indentured servitude. Linking the evidence to your arguments also helps you avoid writing out a "laundry list" of unrelated facts.

Recommended Activity The demonstration of the targeted reasoning process (causation, comparison, or change and continuity over time) and the complex understanding can be integrated into paragraphs using evidence to support one's arguments. However, for initial practice, write a separate paragraph for each process that demonstrates the use of it to frame the argument and a complex understanding of the question using one of the various ways outlined above. Use the following criteria to assess your work:

- Does the essay use historical reasoning to frame or structure the argument made?
- How could the targeted reasoning process be better analyzed in the arguments?
- Does the response demonstrate a complex understanding of the question using evidence to corroborate, qualify, or modify an argument that addresses the question?
- How could a complex understanding of the question be better demonstrated?

7. Evaluate a Long Essay Answer The feedback from your practice essays—whether from teachers, peers, or self-evaluation—is essential for making the practice produce progress and for learning to master the exam requirements. You might find teacher evaluation and self-evaluation of essays less threatening than peer evaluation. However, once you establish more confidence, peer evaluation is a useful form of feedback. The comments you receive from your peers, as well as the comments you make on their essays, will help you become a better writer.

Recommended Activity Before writing out your first practice essay, it helps to first organize your arguments by outlining each paragraph for the essay. The first effort for writing a complete AP® History essay will be a more positive experience if it is an untimed assignment. After you gain some confidence in writing the long essay, you should apply these skills in a timed test, similar to that of the AP® exam (e.g., 40 minutes for the long essay). The purpose of this practice is to become familiar with the time restraints of the AP® exam.

Use the following practice scoring guide for the LEQ or the most recent rubric released by the College Board to evaluate your own work and to help you internalize the grading standards used on the AP® exam. While the AP® exam booklet will list what needs to be done to gain each point, with effective practice you should know going into the exam what you need to write before opening the booklet.

Scoring Guide for a Long Essay Question Answer

A. Thesis/Claim: 0–1 Point

❏ 1 point for a historically defensible thesis/claim that establishes a line of reasoning to address the question and not merely restate it. The thesis must be at least one sentence and located in one place, either in the introduction or in the conclusion.

B. Contextualization: 0–1 Point

❏ 1 point to describe the broader historical context of the question, such as developments either before, during, or after its time frame. Describing the context requires more than a mere phrase or reference.

C. Evidence: 0–2 Points

❏ 1 point for identifying specific historical examples of evidence relevant to the question.

OR (Either the 1 point above or the 2 points below, but not both.)

❏ 2 points for using specific and relevant historical examples of evidence that support the arguments used to address the question.

D. Analysis and Reasoning: 0–2 Points

❏ 1 point for using historical reasoning to frame or structure the arguments that address the question, such as causation, comparison, or continuity and change over time. Reasoning may be uneven or not as complex as needed to gain 2 points.

OR (Either the 1 point above or the 2 points below, but not both.)

❏ 2 points for using historical reasoning and demonstrating a complex understanding of the historical developments by analyzing the multiple variables in the evidence. This can include analyzing more than one cause, both similarities and differences, both continuity and change, and/or the diversity of evidence that corroborates, qualifies, or modifies an argument used to address the question.

Other Suggestions for Writing Essay Questions

The following suggestions, while not part of the formal rubrics for grading essays, can help or detract from the impact of your essay writing in AP® history.

Be accurate and clear. AP® readers realize that students are writing a first draft under pressure. However, accuracy and clarity become problems when they interfere with the overall quality of the work. Does the historical content of the essay demonstrate accurate knowledge? Do grammar mistakes obscure the demonstration of the content knowledge and thinking skills in the essay? The scoring guidelines allow for some errors in content and grammar, unless they detract from the students' overall demonstration of knowledge and skills.

Follow the writing style used by historians. Avoid use of the first person ("I," "we"). Rather, use the third person ("he," "she," "they"). Write in the past tense, except when referring to documents or sources that currently exist (e.g., "the document implies"). Use the active voice rather than the passive voice because it states cause and effect more strongly (e.g., "Edison developed a practical light bulb" is in the active voice; "a practical light bulb was created" is in the passive voice). The AP® long essays do not call for a narrative style of historical writing or "stories." Rather, they should be analytical essays that support the writer's argument with specific knowledge and historical reasoning.

Remain objective. Avoid emotional appeals, especially on social or political issues. The AP® test is not the place to argue that a group was racist or that some people were the "good guys" and others the "bad guys." Avoid absolutes, such as "all" and "none." Rarely in history is the evidence so conclusive that you can prove that there were no exceptions. Do not use slang terms!

Communicate awareness of the complexity of history. Distinguish between primary and secondary causes, short-term and long-term effects, and the more and less significant events. Use verbs that communicate judgment and analysis, such as "reveal," "exemplify," "demonstrate," "imply," and "symbolize."

Communicate the organization and logical development of your argument. Each paragraph should develop one main point that is clearly stated in the topic sentence. Provide a few words or a phrase of transition to connect one paragraph to another.

Use words that are specific. Clearly identify persons, factors, and judgments. Replace vague verbs such as "felt" and "says" with more precise ones. Do not use words such as "they" and "others say" as vague references to unidentified groups or events.

Define or explain key terms. If the question deals with terms (such as "liberal," "conservative," or "Manifest Destiny"), an essential part of your analysis should include an explanation of these terms.

Anticipate counterarguments. Consider arguments that are against your thesis, not to prove them but to show that you are aware of opposing points of view. Doing so demonstrates your complex understanding of a question.

Recognize the role of a conclusion. An effective conclusion should focus on the thesis. Some teachers also recommend that this is fine place to demonstrate your complex understanding (see above rubric). However, if you are running out of time and have written a well-organized essay supporting your argument, do not worry about omitting the conclusion.

Model for Organizing Answers to Essay Questions This model for a five-paragraph expository essay illustrates how an introductory paragraph relates to a well-organized essay. An essay should not always consist of five paragraphs. The total number of paragraphs is for the writer to determine. What the model does suggest is that the introductory paragraph is crucial because it should shape the full essay. An effective introduction tells the reader the arguments you will develop in the body of the essay and then explains how you will develop that view, identifying the main points you will be making in the body of your essay. If your introductory paragraph is properly written, the rest of the essay will be relatively easy to write, especially if you have already organized your information.

Paragraph 1: Introduction Background and context to the question
_____ Thesis statement
_____ Development of the
thesis with preview of main arguments _____
_____

Paragraph 2: First Argument Topic sentence explaining first
argument related to the thesis _____
Evidence to support argument using the targeted reasoning process
_____

Paragraph 3: Second Argument Topic sentence explaining
second argument related to the thesis _____
_____ .
Evidence to support argument using the targeted reasoning process
_____

Paragraph 4: Third Argument Topic sentence explaining third
argument related to the thesis _____ .
Evidence to support argument using the targeted reasoning process
_____

Paragraph 5: Conclusion and Complex Understanding
_____
_____

Answering the Document-Based Question

This part of the AP® exam comes closest to the challenges and work of practicing historians. The AP® exam's document-based question (DBQ) will be drawn from the concepts and content of periods 3 through 8 (1754–1980). Students have no choice of questions, but they are given 60 minutes to write their answers. Directions suggest that students use the first 15 minutes to read and study the seven documents because they are the essential focus for this kind of question. These documents include mostly texts, but they will usually include one or more images, such as cartoons, maps, or graphs. These sources will include differing points of view and often contradictory evidence.

Requirements of the Document-Based Question The rubric used to grade the DBQ includes seven possible points, and the question counts for 25 percent of one's overall exam grade. Many of the DBQ requirements are the same or similar to ones for the LEQ. However, in addition students need to be able to analyze at least six of the seven historical documents provided and use them to support the arguments of the essay.

- **Point 1: Thesis** Respond to the prompt with a historically defensible thesis or claim that establishes a line of reasoning.

- **Point 2: Contextualization** Describe a broader historical context relevant to the prompt.

- **Points 3 and 4: Evidence from the Documents** Earn one point for using the content of at least three documents to address the question. For two points you must use at least six documents and must also explain how the documents are related to the thesis arguments.

- **Point 5: Evidence Beyond the Documents** Use at least one additional piece of specific historical evidence, beyond the evidence found in the documents, that is relevant to your arguments.

- **Point 6: Analysis of the Sources** For at least three documents, one must explain how or why the document's point of view, purpose, historical situation, or audience (or more than one of these) is relevant to your arguments.

- **Point 7: Complexity** Demonstrate a complex understanding of the question by using the evidence to corroborate, qualify, or modify an argument that addresses the question.

Practice Writing the Document-Based Question Keep in mind that writing a DBQ answer is similar to writing an effective long essay and that many of the same skills apply. As with an LEQ, a DBQ answer needs an effective thesis that addresses all parts of the question and uses a historical reasoning process, usually causation. As in a long essay, you need to make persuasive arguments supported by evidence.

However, in a DBQ much of the evidence can be drawn from the seven documents. You must still utilize your knowledge of history to help you analyze the documents. The better you understand the concepts and evidence from the historical periods used in the question, the greater understanding you are likely to gain from the documents and the less likely you are to misinterpret them.

Below is a sample DBQ prompt. Use the steps following it to develop the skills for writing an effective DBQ answer.

Analyze major changes in the social and economic experiences of African Americans who migrated from the rural South to urban areas in the North in the period 1910 to 1930.

1. Analyze the Question and the Documents Besides analyzing the question, as explained under the LEQ section, the preparation for answering a DBQ must include analyzing the seven documents. This is why the directions for the DBQ on the exam recommend taking 15 minutes to read the documents before you begin writing. Use the first 15 minutes not only to read the documents but also to underline and make notes on them in the margin. While reading the documents, note what side of possible arguments each document could be used to support. Also identify at least three documents that you could use to explain the relevance of the source's point of view, purpose, historical situation, or audience to your arguments.

2. Organize the Evidence Unlike the LEQ, the DBQ provides much of the evidence to support a thesis and arguments. The poorest approach to answering a DBQ is to write about just the seven documents from 1 to 7 and hope for the best. Instead, much like with the LEQ, take time during the reading of the documents to organize them into categories such as northern experiences versus southern experiences. You might create a chart or matrix that uses a combination of rows and columns to organize information. For example, you might have one row for each region (South and North). Each column might be a type of information (economic conditions such as jobs) and social conditions (such as degree of prejudice and segregation). If time allows, add short notes about relevant knowledge from outside the documents to support your arguments.

3. Write a Thesis Statement The requirement for gaining the one point for a thesis or claim is the same as the LEQ. The thesis must be historically defensible and establish a line of reasoning. (See the LEQ section for details.)

4. Provide Context As with the LEQ, the DBQ essay also requires you to describe a broader historical context for the question. This involves explaining a relevant historical development not found in the documents. For example, in the response to the sample DBQ, you could broaden the discussion of the African American migrant experience by explaining a context not found in the documents, such as the race riots in northern cities like Chicago during and after World War I. This contextualization point also requires an explanation of multiple sentences or a full paragraph. Most AP® teachers recommend that contextualization should be addressed in the essay's introduction or second paragraph as part of the background to the question.

5. Use Evidence from the Documents You must use six of the seven documents in writing the essay to gain two points for use of evidence. To use the documents well, link the evidence in them to your arguments. Your thesis and arguments, not the arrangement of the documents in the exam booklet, should control the organization of the essay.

To receive two points, it is not enough to accurately explain the content from six documents. You also need to integrate the content into a persuasive argument to support your thesis.

In the use of documents as evidence, you must do more than just quote or paraphrase the documents. The readers already know the content of the documents, so there is no need to quote them. Another novice mistake is to write no more than a description of each document. "Document 1 says . . . Document 2 says . . ." This approach can gain you only one point.

Below is a sample document for the above AP® sample DBQ. It is just one of seven documents that a DBQ would include.

> Document 2. Letter from a prospective African American migrant, April 27, 1917, New Orleans, Louisiana
>
> > "Dear Sirs:
> >
> > Being desirous of leaving the South for the betterment of my condition generally and seeking a Home Somewhere in Ill' Chicago or some other prosperous town, I am at sea about the best place to locate having a family dependent upon me for support. I am informed by the *Chicago Defender* a very valuable paper which has for its purpose the Uplifting of my race, and of which I am a constant reader and real lover, that you were in position to show some light to one in my condition.
> >
> > Seeking a Northern Home. If this is true, Kindly inform me by next mail the next best thing to do. Being a poor man with a family to care for, I am not coming to live on flowery Beds of ease for I am a man who works and wish to make the best I can out of life. I do not wish to come there hoodwinked not knowing, where to go or what to do, so I Solicit your help in this matter and thanking you in advance for what advice you may be pleased to Give. I am yours for success."

The sample below illustrates a couple of ways to integrate documents in support of an argument and how to reference them in an essay. Documents 3 and 7 (not included in this book) describe discrimination in employment and housing:

> The southern reader of the northern African American newspaper, Chicago Defender (Doc. 2), had cause for being suspicious that moving his family North would not be an easy escape from conditions in the South. During this period, black migrants to the North faced racial barriers in finding a place to live in segregated cities like Chicago (Doc. 7) and discrimination on the job in northern industries (Doc. 3).

The documents should influence your arguments to the extent that you will have to deal with the complexity, contradictions, and limitations found in them. Realize that not all documents will have equal weight. Communicate to the reader your awareness of the contradictions or limitations of a document or how a document might not support your thesis but fits into the historical situation relevant to the question.

6. Use Evidence Beyond the Documents Much like the LEQ, the DBQ does require at least one example of historical evidence to support your arguments, but it should not duplicate the evidence in the documents or their analysis. For example, the documents provided for the sample DBQ might not explicitly address the impact of African American music during the Harlem Renaissance in the North. Explaining how African American music enhanced the image of black artists and changed their experience in northern cities after migration would be going beyond the documents.

You could establish that you understand the era by setting the historical scene early in the essay using "outside" information. However, do not "double-dip" by using the same example from your outside information in the explanation of context. If you do, you will not receive credit for both.

7. Source the Documents One additional point is gained for analyzing at least three of the documents in one or more of the following aspects: a) historical situation for the document, b) intended audience for the document, c) purpose of the document, and/or d) point of view of the author. Identifying one of the sourcing elements, such as historical situation, is not enough to get over the threshold for sourcing. To receive a point, you must also explain how or why this element of the source is relevant to an argument. In the example, for the 1917 letter from a reader of the *Chicago Defender*, you could explain the historical situation of the letter, that it was written during World War I. This was significant because labor shortages in the North encouraged employers to recruit workers from the South, which contributed to the great migration of African Americans.

In this text, you will find dozens of excerpts, cartoons, and other kinds of documents that provide you opportunities to practice sourcing documents as a prewriting activity. In writing the DBQ, the sourcing requirement can be accomplished in the same paragraph in which the document is used as evidence. To explain the historical situation for a document, you need not take more than one sentence or modifying phrase in the paragraph that uses the document as evidence. The readers are looking for the sourcing of three documents for the one point.

8. Provide Complexity As explained before, an essay needs to show a deeper, more complex understanding of the question to gain this point. Refer back to the AP® Guidelines for complexity under "Writing the LEQ" for the many ways to demonstrate a complex understanding. The options are the same for both the LEQ and the DBQ. In recent exams, few students have received the complexity point for their DBQ answers. This suggests that most students should focus on linking the document evidence to their arguments and on achieving both the contextualization and outside evidence points before tackling complexity.

9. Evaluate a DBQ Answer At this point, some students may ask, how can one possibly juggle all the requirements to write a strong DBQ essay? First remember that in writing a DBQ, you apply many of the same skills you learned in writing a strong LEQ answer, such as writing an effective thesis, providing context for the question, and using outside knowledge to support your arguments. As recommended for development of LEQ writing, use a step-by-step skill development approach to the DBQ. It will take time to master each new skill, such as the use of documents as evidence. Only practice can prepare you to answer a challenging DBQ successfully.

After writing your first untimed and timed DBQ essays, use the DBQ practice scoring guide, or the rubrics released by the College Board, to evaluate your essays. Using the scoring guide will help you to internalize the criteria for writing an effective DBQ. Samples of recent DBQ rubrics, scoring guidelines, and graded essays can be found at https://apcentral.collegeboard.org.

Finally, AP® readers counsel students to "take ownership of the question." This means to address the LEQ and DBQ directly and commit your writing to supporting your arguments, rather than just describing documents and other evidence like isolated bits of information. Again, the time you spend on the front end thinking about the question and organizing the documents and other evidence into categories can give your essay purpose, direction, and clarity while you write.

Recommended Activity In this textbook, you will have dealt with more than a dozen excerpts, cartoons, and other forms of sources before practicing the first DBQ. There are DBQs in the reviews at the ends of period 2 through period 8 and in the practice exam. As a prewriting activity, identify and discuss each document's point of view, historical situation or context, intended audience, and purpose.

In writing a DBQ answer, apply the same skills you use in writing a strong long essay answer. In addition, use the documents to support your thesis. After writing your first DBQ answers, use the scoring guide that follows or the DBQ exam rubrics released by the College Board to help you internalize the criteria for writing a strong DBQ answer.

Scoring Guide for a Document-Based Question Answer

A. Thesis/Claim: 0–1 Point

❑ 1 point for a historically defensible thesis/claim that establishes a line of reasoning to address the question and does not merely restate it. The thesis must be at least one sentence and located in one place, either in the introduction or in the conclusion.

B. Contextualization: 0–1 Point

❑ 1 point to describe the broader historical context of the question, such as developments either before, during, or after its time frame. Describing the context requires more than a mere phrase or reference.

C. Evidence: 0–3 Points

Evidence from the Documents: 0–2 Points

❑ 1 point for accurately describing the content of three documents that address the question.

OR (Either the 1 point above or the 2 points below, but not both.)

❑ 2 points for accurately describing the content of six documents and using them to support the arguments used in response to the question. Using the documents requires more than simply quoting them.

Evidence Beyond the Documents: 0–1 Point

❑ 1 point for using at least one additional piece of specific historical evidence beyond those found in the documents that is relevant to the arguments for the question. The evidence must be different from evidence used for the contextualization point and more than a mere phrase.

D. Analysis and Reasoning: 0–2 Points (Unlike the LEQ scoring, both points can be gained)

❑ 1 point for using at least three documents to explain how or why the document's point of view, purpose, historical situation, and/or audience is relevant to an argument used to address the question.

❑ 1 point for demonstrating a complex understanding of the historical developments by analyzing the multiple variables in the evidence. This can include analyzing more than one cause, both similarities and differences, both continuity and change, and/or the diversity of evidence that corroborates, qualifies, or modifies an argument used to address the question.

Review Schedule

Under the best conditions, preparation for the AP® U.S. History exam takes place within the context of an Advanced Placement® or Honors course. However, whether this text is used in conjunction with the course or as a review book before the exam, the teacher or students will benefit from organizing a review schedule before the exam. Many AP® candidates find that study groups are helpful, especially if the students bring to the group a variety of strengths.

Following is a sample of a six-week review schedule using this text that either teachers or students might construct to organize their preparation.

Proposed Review Schedule		
Week	Time Period	Content
1	1491 to 1754	Units 1–2
2	1800 to 1848	Units 3–4
3	1844 to 1898	Units 5–6
4	1890 to 1945	Unit 7
5	1945 to the Present	Units 8–9
6	Final Review	Practice Exam

Staying with such a schedule requires discipline. This discipline is greatly strengthened if a study group chooses a specific time and place to meet and sets specific objectives for each meeting. For example, students might divide up the material and prepare outline responses to key terms and review questions. Some individuals may find it more productive to review on their own. Either way, the essential content presented in and the reasoning processes developed through the use of this book should make it a convenient and efficient tool for understanding U.S. history.

UNIT 1 — Period 1: 1491–1607

Topic 1.1

Contextualizing Period 1

Learning Objective: Explain the context for European encounters in the Americas from 1491 to 1607.

Today, the United States is a synthesis, or combination, of people from around the world. The first people arrived in the Americas at least 10,000 years ago. A survey of how these indigenous people lived before the arrival of Christopher Columbus in the Americas in 1492 provides the context for understanding the interaction of the Europeans and Native Americans and the impact this had on both groups. Columbus's first voyage was a turning point in world history because it initiated lasting contact between people on opposite sides of the Atlantic Ocean. His voyages, followed by European exploration and settlement in the Americas, had profound results on how people on every continent lived.

Another landmark change came in 1607 with the founding of the first permanent English settlement at Jamestown, Virginia. The Jamestown settlement marked the beginning of the framework of a new nation.

Cultural Diversity in the Americas When Columbus reached the Americas, the existing cultures varied greatly, partially because of differences in geography and climate. Each culture developed distinctive traits in response to its environment, from tropical islands where sugar grew to forests rich in animal life to land with fertile soil for growing corn (maize). Native Americans also transformed their environments. For example, people in dry regions created irrigation systems, while those in forested regions used fire to clear land for agriculture.

Motives for Exploration The European explorers in the Americas—first the Spanish and Portuguese, then the French and Dutch, and later the English—competed for land in the Americas. Some were motivated by desires to spread Christianity. Others hoped to become wealthy by finding an all-water route to Asia, establishing fur-trading posts, operating gold and silver mines, or developing plantations. Europeans often relied on violence to subdue or drive away native inhabitants.

Transatlantic Exchange Contact between Europeans and the natives of America touched off a transatlantic trade in animals, plants, and germs known as the Columbian Exchange that altered life for people around the globe.

Crops originally from America such as corn (maize), potatoes, and tomatoes revolutionized the diet of Europeans. However, germs that had developed in Europe caused epidemics in the Americas. Typically, the native population of a region declined by 90 percent within a century after the arrival of Europeans.

Addition of Enslaved Africans Adding to the diversity of people in the Americas were enslaved Africans. They were brought to the Americas by Europeans who desired low-cost labor to work in mines and on plantations. Africans, like Native Americans, resisted European domination by maintaining elements of their cultures. The three groups influenced the others' ideas and ways of life.

European Colonies Within a century of the arrival of Columbus, Spanish and Portuguese explorers and settlers developed colonies that depended on natives and enslaved Africans for labor in agriculture and mining precious metals. In particular, mines in Mexico and South America produced vast amounts of silver that made Spain the wealthiest European empire in the 16th and 17th centuries.

ANALYZE THE CONTEXT

1. Describe a historical context for understanding the diverse Native American cultures that had developed in the Americas by the 1490s.

2. Explain a historical context for the European exploration in the Americas from the 1490s to early 1600s.

3. Explain a historical context for the interactions between Europeans and Native Americans in the period from 1491 to 1607.

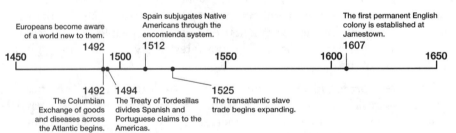

LANDMARK EVENTS: 1450–1650

Europeans become aware of a world new to them. **1492**

Spain subjugates Native Americans through the encomienda system. **1512**

The first permanent English colony is established at Jamestown. **1607**

1450 | 1500 | 1550 | 1600 | 1650

1492 The Columbian Exchange of goods and diseases across the Atlantic begins.

1494 The Treaty of Tordesillas divides Spanish and Portuguese claims to the Americas.

1525 The transatlantic slave trade begins expanding.

Native American Societies Before European Contact

The American Indian is of the soil, whether it be the region of forests, plains, pueblos, or mesas. He fits into the landscape, for the hand that fashioned the continent also fashioned the man for his surroundings.

Luther Standing Bear, Oglala Lakota Chief, 1933

Learning Objective: Explain how various native populations interacted with the natural environment in North America in the period before European contact.

The original discovery and settlement of North and South America began at least 10,000 and maybe up to 40,000 years ago. Migrants from Asia might have crossed a **land bridge** that once connected Siberia and Alaska (land now submerged under the Bering Sea). Over time, people migrated southward from near the Arctic Circle to the southern tip of South America. As they adapted to the varied environments they encountered, they evolved into hundreds of tribes speaking hundreds of languages. By 1491, the population in the Americas was probably between 50 million and 100 million people.

Cultures of Central and South America

The native population was concentrated in three highly developed civilizations.

- Between the years 300 and 800, the **Mayas** built remarkable cities in the rain forests of the Yucatán Peninsula (present-day Guatemala, Belize, and southern Mexico).

- Several centuries after the decline of the Mayas, the **Aztecs** from central Mexico developed a powerful empire. The Aztec capital, Tenochtitlán, had a population of about 200,000, equivalent in population to the largest cities of Europe.

- While the Aztecs were dominating Mexico and Central America, the **Incas** based in Peru developed a vast empire in western South America.

All three civilizations developed highly organized societies, carried on an extensive trade, and created calendars that were based on accurate scientific observations. All three cultivated crops that provided a stable food supply, particularly **corn (maize)** for the Mayas and Aztecs and potatoes for the Incas.

Cultures of North America

The population in the region north of Mexico (present-day United States and Canada) in the 1490s may have been anywhere from under 1 million to more than 10 million.

General Patterns Native societies in this region included fewer people and had less complex social structures than those in Mexico and South America. One reason for these differences was how slowly the cultivation of corn (maize) spread northward from Mexico. The nutrition provided by corn allowed for larger and more densely settled populations. In turn, this led to more socially diversified societies in which people specialized in their work.

Some of the most populous societies in North America had disappeared by the 15th century for reasons not well understood. By the time of Columbus, most people in the Americas in what is now the United States and Canada lived in semipermanent settlements in groups seldom exceeding 300 people. In most of these groups, the men made tools and hunted for game, while the women gathered plants and nuts or grew crops such as corn (maize), beans, and tobacco.

Language Differences Beyond these broad similarities, the cultures of American Indians were very diverse. For example, while English, Spanish, and almost all other European languages were part of just one language family (Indo-European), American Indian languages constituted more than 20 language families. Among the largest of these were **Algonquian** in the northeast, **Siouan** on the Great Plains, and Athabaskan in the southwest. Together, these 20 families included more than 400 distinct languages.

Southwest Settlements In the dry region that now includes New Mexico and Arizona, groups such as the **Hohokam, Anasazi,** and **Pueblos** evolved multifaceted societies. Many people lived in caves, under cliffs, and in multistoried buildings. The spread of maize cultivation into this region from Mexico prompted economic growth and the development of irrigation systems. The additional wealth allowed for a more complex society to develop, one with greater variations between social and economic classes.

By the time Europeans arrived, extreme drought and other hostile natives had taken their toll on these groups. However, their descendants continue to live in the region, and the arid climate helped preserve some of the older stone and masonry dwellings.

Northwest Settlements Along the Pacific coast from what is today Alaska to northern California, people lived in permanent longhouses or plank houses. They had a rich diet based on hunting, fishing, and gathering nuts, berries, and roots. To help people remember stories, legends, and myths, they carved large totem poles. However, the high mountain ranges in this region isolated tribes from one another, creating barriers to development.

Great Basin and Great Plains People adapted to the dry climate of the Great Basin region and the grasslands of the Great Plains by developing mobile ways of living. Nomadic tribes survived on hunting, principally the buffalo, which supplied their food as well as decorations, crafting tools, knives, and clothing. People lived in tepees, frames of poles covered in animal skins, which were easily disassembled and transported. Some tribes, though they also hunted buffalo, lived permanently in earthen lodges often along rivers. They raised corn (maize), beans, and squash while actively trading with other tribes.

Not until the 17th century did American Indians acquire horses by trading or stealing them from Spanish settlers. With horses, tribes such as the Lakota Sioux could more easily follow buffalo herds. The plains tribes would at times merge or split apart as conditions changed. Migration also was common. For example, the Apaches gradually migrated southward from Canada to Texas.

NATIVE PEOPLES OF THE AMERICAS, 1491

Mississippi River Valley East of the Mississippi River, the Woodland American Indians prospered with a rich food supply. Supported by hunting, fishing, and agriculture, people established permanent settlements in the Mississippi and Ohio River valleys and elsewhere. The Adena-Hopewell culture, centered in what is now Ohio, is famous for its large earthen mounds, some 300 feet long. One of the largest settlements in the Midwest was Cahokia (near present-day East St. Louis, Illinois), with as many as 30,000 inhabitants.

Northeast Settlements Some descendants of the **Adena-Hopewell** culture spread from the Ohio Valley into New York. Their culture combined hunting and farming. However, their farming techniques exhausted the soil quickly, so people had to move to fresh land frequently. Multiple families related through the mother's lineage lived together in **longhouses** that were up to 200 feet long.

Several tribes living near the Great Lakes and in New York—the Seneca, Cayuga, Onondaga, Oneida, Mohawk, and later the Tuscaroras—formed a powerful political union called the **Iroquois Confederation**, or Haudenosauanee. From the 16th century through the American Revolution, this powerful union battled rival American Indians as well as Europeans.

Atlantic Seaboard Settlements In the area from New Jersey south to Florida lived the people of the Coastal Plains such as the Cherokee and the Lumbee. Many were descendants of the **Woodland mound builders** and built timber and bark lodgings along rivers. The rivers and the Atlantic Ocean provided a rich source of food

Overall Diversity The tremendous variety of landforms and climate prompted people in North America prior to 1492 to develop widely different cultures. While Europeans often grouped these varied cultures together, each tribe was very conscious of its own distinctive systems and traditions. Not until much later in history did they develop a shared identity as Native Americans.

REFLECT ON THE LEARNING OBJECTIVE

1. Describe the influence of the natural environment on the society and culture that various Native Americans had developed.

KEY TERMS BY THEME

Migration (MIG, ARC)	Identity and Politics (NAT, POL)	American Indians (MIG, POL, ARC)
land bridge	Mayas	Algonquian
Hohokam, Anasazi, and Pueblos	Aztecs	Siouan
Adena-Hopewell	Incas	longhouses
Woodland mound builders	corn (maize)	Iroquois Confederation
		Woodland mound builders

Questions 1–2 refer to the following excerpt.

"During the thousands of years preceding European contact, the Native American people developed inventive and creative cultures. They cultivated plants for food, dyes, medicines, and textiles; domesticated animals; established extensive patterns of trade; built cities; produced monumental architecture; developed intricate systems of religious beliefs; and constructed a wide variety of systems of social and political organization. . . . Native Americans not only adapted to diverse and demanding environments, they also reshaped the natural environments to meet their needs. . . . No society had shaped metal into guns, swords, or tools; none had gunpowder, sailing ships, or mounted warriors."

"Overview of First Americans," *Digital History,* 2016

1. According to the excerpt, one contrast between Native Americans and Europeans before contact between the two groups of people was that
   (A) all Native Americans shared a common political system
   (B) most Native Americans had little trade with other groups
   (C) some Native Americans had metal tools they used in farming
   (D) no Native Americans had certain military technologies that were common in Europe

2. What does the source imply was the cause of the "wide variety of systems of social and political organization"?
   (A) Variations in the moral code
   (B) Variations in the natural environment
   (C) Variations in religious beliefs
   (D) Variations in styles of architecture

SHORT-ANSWER QUESTION

1. Answer (a), (b), and (c).
   (a) Briefly describe ONE specific difference between the cultures of the indigenous peoples of North America and those in Central and South America in the period 1491–1607.
   (b) Briefly describe ONE specific similarity between the cultures of the indigenous peoples of North America and those in Central and South America in the period 1491–1607.
   (c) Briefly explain ONE specific contrast between language families among Native Americans and Europeans in the period 1491–1607.

Topic 1.3

European Exploration in the Americas

Thirty-three days after my departure . . . I reached the Indian Sea, where I discovered many islands, thickly peopled, of which I took possession without resistance in the name of our illustrious monarch, by public proclamation and with unfurled banners.

Christopher Columbus, *Select Letters*, 1493

Learning Objective: Explain the causes of exploration and conquest of the New World by various European nations.

Until the late 1400s, the people of the Americas carried on extensive trade with each other but had no connection to the people of Europe, Africa, and Asia. Similarly, Europeans, Africans, and Asians traded among themselves without knowing of the Americas. However, starting in the 1400s, religious and economic motives prompted Europeans to explore more widely than before. As a result, they brought the two parts of the world into contact with each other.

The European Context for Exploration

While Vikings from Scandinavia had visited Greenland and North America around the year 1000, these voyages had no lasting impact. Columbus's voyages of exploration finally brought people into ongoing contact across the Atlantic. Several factors made sailing across the ocean and exploring distant regions possible and desirable in the late 15th century.

Changes in Thought and Technology

In Europe, a rebirth of classical learning prompted an outburst of artistic and scientific activity in the 15th and 16th centuries known as the Renaissance. Several of the technological advances during the Renaissance resulted from Europeans making improvements in the inventions of others. For example, Europeans began to use **gunpowder** (invented by the Chinese) and the **sailing compass** (adopted from Arab merchants who learned about it from the Chinese). Europeans also made major improvements in shipbuilding and mapmaking. In addition, the invention of the **printing press** in the 1450s aided the spread of knowledge across Europe.

Religious Conflict

The later years of the Renaissance were a time of intense religious zeal and conflict. The Roman Catholic Church and its leader, known as the pope, had dominated most of Western Europe for centuries. However, in the 15th and 16th centuries, their power was threatened by both Ottoman Turks, who were Muslims, and rebellious Christians who challenged the pope's authority.

Catholic Victory in Spain In the 8th century, Islamic invaders from North Africa, known as Moors, rapidly conquered most of what is now Spain. Over the next several centuries, Spanish Christians reconquered much of the land and set up several independent kingdoms. Two of the largest of these kingdoms united when **Isabella**, queen of Castile, and **Ferdinand**, king of Aragon, married in 1469. In 1492, under the leadership of Isabella and Ferdinand, the Spanish conquered the last Moorish stronghold in Spain, the city of Granada. In that year, the monarchs also funded **Christopher Columbus** on his historic first voyage. The uniting of Spain under Isabella and Ferdinand, the conquest of Granada, and the launching of Columbus's voyage signaled new leadership, hope, and power for Europeans who followed the Roman Catholic faith.

Protestant Revolt in Northern Europe In the early 1500s, certain Christians in Germany, England, France, Holland, and other northern European countries revolted against the authority of the pope in Rome. Their revolt was known as the **Protestant Reformation**. Conflict between Catholics and Protestants led to a series of religious wars that resulted in many millions of deaths in the 16th and 17th centuries. The conflict also caused the Roman Catholics of Spain and Portugal and the Protestants of England and Holland to want to spread their own versions of Christianity to people in Africa, Asia, and the Americas. Thus, a religious motive for exploration and colonization was added to political and economic motives.

Expanding Trade

Economic motives for exploration grew out of a fierce competition among European kingdoms for increased trade with Africa, India, and China. In the past, merchants had traveled from the Italian city-state of Venice and the Byzantine city of Constantinople on a long, slow, expensive overland route all the way to eastern China. This land route to Asia had become blocked in 1453 when the Ottoman Turks seized control of Constantinople.

New Routes So the challenge to finding a new way to the rich Asian trade appeared to be by sailing either south along the West African coast and then east to China, or sailing west across the Atlantic Ocean. The Portuguese realized the route south and east was the shortest path. Voyages of exploration sponsored by Portugal's Prince **Henry the Navigator** eventually succeeded in opening up a long sea route around South Africa's Cape of Good Hope. In 1498, the Portuguese sea captain Vasco da Gama was the first European to reach India via this route. By this time, Columbus had attempted what he mistakenly believed would be a shorter route to Asia.

Slave Trading Since ancient times people in Europe, Africa, and Asia had enslaved people captured in wars. In the 15th century, the Portuguese began trading for enslaved people from West Africa. They used the enslaved workers on newly established sugar plantations on the Madeira and Azores islands off the African coast. Producing sugar with enslaved labor was so profitable that when Europeans later established colonies in the Americas, they used a similar system there.

Developing Nation-States

Europe was also changing politically in the 15th century.

- Small kingdoms were uniting into larger ones. For example, Castile and Aragon united to form the core of the modern country of Spain.

- Enormous multiethnic empires, such as the sprawling Holy Roman Empire in central Europe, were beginning to break up. For example, most of the small states that united to form the modern country of Germany in 1871 were once part of the Holy Roman Empire.

Replacing the small kingdoms and the multiethnic empires were **nation-states**, countries in which the majority of people shared both a common culture and common loyalty toward a central government. The monarchs of the emerging nation-states, such as Isabella and Ferdinand of Spain; Prince Henry the Navigator of Portugal; and similar monarchs of France, England, and the Netherlands depended on trade to bring in needed revenues and on the church to justify their right to rule.

Dividing the Americas

The Western European monarchs used their power to search for riches abroad and to spread the influence of their version of Christianity to new overseas dominions. This led to competition for control of land in the Americas.

Spanish and Portuguese Claims Spain and Portugal were the first European kingdoms to claim territories in the Americas. Their claims overlapped, leading to disputes. The Catholic monarchs of the two countries turned to the pope to resolve their differences. In 1493, the pope drew a vertical, north-south line on a world map, called the *line of demarcation*. The pope granted Spain all lands to the west of the line and Portugal all lands to the east.

In 1494, Spain and Portugal moved the pope's line a few degrees to the west and signed an agreement called the **Treaty of Tordesillas**. The line passed through what is now the country of Brazil. This treaty, together with Portuguese explorations, established Portugal's claim to Brazil. Spain claimed the rest of the Americas. However, other European countries soon challenged these claims.

English Claims England's earliest claims to territory in the Americas rested on the voyages of John Cabot, an Italian sea captain who sailed under contract to England's King Henry VII. Cabot explored the coast of Newfoundland in 1497.

EUROPEAN LAND CLAIMS IN NORTH AMERICA IN THE 1600s

England, however, did not immediately follow up Cabot's discoveries with other expeditions of exploration and settlement. Other issues preoccupied England's monarchy in the 1500s, most importantly the religious conflict that followed Henry VIII's break with the Roman Catholic Church.

Later in the 16th century, England took more interest in distant affairs. In the 1570s and 1580s, under Queen Elizabeth I, England challenged Spanish shipping in both the Atlantic and Pacific Oceans. Sir Francis Drake, for example, attacked Spanish ships, seized the gold and silver that they carried, and even attacked Spanish settlements on the coast of Peru. Another English adventurer, Sir Walter Raleigh, attempted to establish a colonial settlement at **Roanoke Island** off the North Carolina coast in 1587, but the venture failed.

French Claims The French monarchy first showed interest in exploration in 1524 when it sponsored a voyage by an Italian navigator, Giovanni da Verrazzano. Hoping to find a northwest passage leading through the Americas to Asia, Verrazzano explored part of North America's eastern coast, including the New York harbor. French claims to American territory were also based on the voyages of Jacques Cartier (1534–1542), who explored the St. Lawrence River extensively.

Like the English, the French were slow to develop colonies across the Atlantic. During the 1500s, the French monarchy was preoccupied with European wars as well as with internal religious conflict between Roman Catholics and French Protestants known as Huguenots. Only in the next century did France develop a strong interest in following up its claims to North American land.

REFLECT ON THE LEARNING OBJECTIVE

1. Explain what supported and motivated European exploration and colonization in the New World.

KEY TERMS BY THEME

Atlantic Trade (WOR)
gunpowder
sailing compass
printing press
Isabella and Ferdinand
Christopher Columbus

Henry the Navigator
Treaty of Tordesillas
Roanoke Island
Identity & Politics (NAT, PLC)
Protestant Reformation
nation-states

MULTIPLE-CHOICE QUESTIONS

Questions 1–3 refer to the following excerpt.

"I marvel not a little, right worshipful, that since the first discovery of America (which is now full four score and ten years), after so great conquests and plannings of the Spaniards and Portuguese there, that we of England could never have the grace to set fast footing in such fertile and temperate places as are left as yet unpossessed of them. But . . . I conceive great hope that the time approacheth and now is that we of England may share and part stakes . . . in part of America and other regions as yet undiscovered. . . .

Yea, if we would behold with the eye of pity how all our prisons are pestered and filled with able men to serve their country, which for small robberies are daily hanged up in great numbers, . . . we would hasten . . . the deducting [conveying] of some colonies of our superfluous people into these temperate and fertile parts of America, which being within six weeks' sailing of England, are yet unpossessed by any Christians, and seem to offer themselves unto us, stretching nearer unto Her Majesty's dominions than to other parts of Europe."

Richard Hakluyt, *Divers Voyages Touching the Discovery of America and the Islands Adjacent*, 1582

1. Which of the following would best explain the British failure to follow the Spanish and Portuguese in exploring the New World?
   (A) Lack of British explorers
   (B) Development of British colonies in Asia
   (C) Domestic challenges to the crown within England
   (D) Establishment of the Church of England

2. Which of the following would eventually become a more important motivation for colonists than the ones suggested in the excerpt?
   (A) The desire for religious freedom
   (B) The hope of finding gold and silver
   (C) The loyalty of members of the nobility
   (D) The success of merchants and traders

3. According to the excerpt, which of the following areas is the most likely region that the British would colonize?
   (A) North Atlantic coast
   (B) West Indies
   (C) Southern Florida
   (D) Central America

SHORT-ANSWER QUESTION

Use complete sentences; an outline or bulleted list alone is not acceptable.

1. Answer (a), (b), and (c).
   (a) Briefly explain ONE specific cause that led to European colonization in the Americas during the 15th and 16th centuries.
   (b) Briefly explain ONE additional cause that led to European colonization in the Americas during the 15th and 16th centuries.
   (c) Briefly explain ONE specific effect that resulted from European colonization in the Americas during the 15th and 16th centuries.

Columbian Exchange, Spanish Exploration, and Conquest

In 1491, the world was in many of its aspects and characteristics a minimum of two worlds—the New World, of the Americas, and the Old World, consisting of Eurasia and Africa. Columbus brought them together, and almost immediately and continually ever since, we have had an exchange.

Alfred W. Crosby, historian and geographer, 2011

Learning Objective: Explain causes of the Columbian Exchange and its effect on Europe and the Americas during the period after 1492.

Columbus's purpose in sailing westward in the 1490s was to find a sea route to the lucrative trade with Asia, which had been limited by a long and dangerous land route. The eventual impact of what Columbus found was of far greater importance.

Christopher Columbus

As mentioned in the previous topic, 1.3, changing economic, political, and social conditions in Europe combined to support new efforts to expand. Exploration across the seas was specifically supported by the improvements in shipbuilding and in navigation with better compasses and mapmaking. These factors all helped shape the ambitions of many to explore.

Plans to Reach Asia One of these explorers was from the Italian city of Genoa, Christopher Columbus. He spent eight years seeking financial support for his plan to sail west from Europe to the "Indies." Finally, in 1492, he succeeded in winning the backing of Isabella and Ferdinand. The two Spanish monarchs were then at the height of their power, having just defeated the Moors in Granada. They agreed to outfit three ships and to make Columbus governor, admiral, and viceroy of all the lands that he would claim for Spain.

After sailing from the Canary Islands on September 6, Columbus landed on an island in the Bahamas on October 12. His success in reaching lands on the other side of the ocean brought him a burst of glory in Spain. But three subsequent voyages across the Atlantic were disappointing—he found little gold, few spices, and no simple path to China and India.

The Columbian Exchange

Europeans and the original inhabitants of the Americas had developed vastly different cultures over the millennia. The contact between them resulted in the Columbian Exchange, a transfer of plants, animals, and germs from one side of the Atlantic to the other for the first time. These exchanges, biological and cultural, permanently changed the entire world. Never again would people live in isolation from the other hemisphere.

Europeans learned about many new plants and foods, including beans, corn, sweet and white potatoes, tomatoes, and tobacco. These food items transformed the diet of people throughout Eurasia and touched off rapid population growth in regions from Ireland to West Africa to eastern China. Europeans also contracted a new disease, syphilis.

People in the Americas learned about sugar cane, bluegrasses, pigs, and **horses**, as well as new technology, such as the wheel, iron implements, and guns. But while the Columbian Exchange led to population growth in Europe, Africa, and Asia, it had the opposite effect in the Americas. Native Americans had no immunity to the germs and the **diseases** brought by Europeans, such as **smallpox** and **measles**. As a result the native population declined rapidly in the first century after contact. In Mexico, the native population declined from around 22 million in 1492 to around 4 million by the mid-16th century.

The Rise of Capitalism

In Europe, population growth and access to new resources encouraged trade, which led to economic, political, and social changes. The medieval system of feudalism, a system in which monarchs granted land to nobles in exchange for military service, declined. In its place rose **capitalism**, an economic system in which control of capital (money and machinery) became more important than control of land. As trade increased, commerce became increasingly important, and political power shifted from large landowners to wealthy merchants.

One reason trade increased was that Europeans were eager to gain access to the riches of the Americas, Africa, and Asia. A single successful trade expedition could make the individual who financed the voyage very wealthy. However, ocean voyages were expensive and dangerous. One bad storm could destroy all the ships in an expedition. To finance trade voyages more safely, Europeans developed a new type of enterprise, the **joint-stock company**, a business owned by a large number of investors. If a voyage failed, investors lost only what they had invested. By reducing individual risk, joint-stock companies encouraged investment, thereby promoting economic growth.

HISTORICAL PERSPECTIVES: *WAS COLUMBUS A GREAT HERO?*

When Columbus died in 1506, he still believed that he had found a western route to Asia. However, many Spaniards realized he had not. Nor had he found gold and spices. They viewed him as a failure. Even the land that he had explored was named for someone else, Amerigo Vespucci.

Columbus then became more honored. Scholars praised his skills as a navigator and his daring. He traveled where nobody else had ever dared to venture. As early as 1828, Washington Irving wrote a popular biography extolling the explorer's virtues. The apex of Columbus's heroic reputation was reached in 1934 when President Franklin Roosevelt declared October 12 a national holiday.

Since the 1990s, however, historians have become more aware of the strength and diversity of indigenous cultures and the devastating impact of contact with Europeans. As a result, several biographies have revised their view of Columbus, taking a more critical look at him.

A Fortunate Navigator Some have argued that Columbus was simply at the right place at the right time. Europeans at the end of the 15th century were eager to find a water route to Asia. If Columbus had not run into the Americas in 1492, some other explorer—perhaps Vespucci or Cabot—would have done so a few years later.

A Conqueror Some revisionists take a harsh view of Columbus, regarding him not as a discoverer but as a conqueror. They portray him as a religious fanatic who sought to convert the American natives to Christianity and kill those who resisted.

Response to the Critics Arthur M. Schlesinger Jr. argued that Columbus's chief motivation was neither greed nor ambition—it was the challenge of the unknown. Others pointed out that, while Columbus brought deadly diseases to the Americas, the costs of contact were partially offset by positive results such as the development of democracy.

Historians will continue to debate the nature of Columbus's achievement. As with other historical questions, distinguishing between fact and fiction and separating a writer's personal biases from objective reality are difficult. One conclusion is inescapable: As a result of Columbus's voyages, world history took a sharp turn in a new direction. People are still living with the consequences of this interaction.

Support an Argument *Explain two perspectives on Columbus's role in the European expansion in the Americas.*

REFLECT ON THE LEARNING OBJECTIVE

1. How did the Columbian Exchange develop, and what was its impact on both sides of the Atlantic Ocean?

KEY TERMS BY THEME

Exchange & Interaction (WXT, GEO)	smallpox, measles
horses	capitalism
diseases	joint-stock company

Questions 1–2 refer to the following excerpt.

"Apart from his navigational skills, what most set Columbus apart from other Europeans of his day were not the things that he believed, but the intensity with which he believed in them and the determination with which he acted upon those beliefs. . . .

Columbus was, in most respects, merely an especially active and dramatic embodiment of the European—and especially the Mediterranean—mind and soul of his time: a religious fanatic obsessed with the conversion, conquest, or liquidation of all non-Christians; a latter-day Crusader in search of personal wealth and fame, who expected the enormous and mysterious world he had found to be filled with monstrous races inhabiting wild forests, and with golden people living in Eden."

David E. Stannard, historian, *American Holocaust: Columbus and the Conquest of the New World*, 1992

1. According to Stannard, which of the following most accurately describes the context in which Columbus lived?

   (A) Europeans believed they should spread Christianity to people in other parts of the world.

   (B) Europeans viewed their culture and the cultures of other people as very similar.

   (C) Europeans were the wealthiest people in the world and considered themselves "golden."

   (D) Europeans assumed that a continent existed that they had no contact with.

2. Evidence that would modify or refute the view of Columbus expressed by Stannard in this excerpt would include

   (A) statements by Spaniards in the late 16th century who believed that they should not try to convert people to Christianity

   (B) excerpts from letters by Columbus indicating that he hoped his ventures would make him wealthy

   (C) descriptions of Native Americans by other European explorers that were negative

   (D) examples of long-term benefits for people in Europe and Asia that resulted from the voyages by Columbus

1. "The New World provided soils that were very suitable for the cultivation of a variety of Old World products, like sugar and coffee. The increased supply lowered the prices of these products significantly, making them affordable to the general population for the first time in history. The production of these products also resulted in large inflows of profits back to Europe, which some have argued fueled the Industrial Revolution and the rise of Europe. . . .

   The exchange also had some extremely negative impacts. Native American populations were decimated by Old World diseases. This depopulation along with the production of valuable Old World crops . . . fueled the demand for labor that gave rise to the transatlantic slave trade. The result was the forced movement of over twelve million slaves from Africa to the Americas and devastating political, social, and economic consequences for the African continent."

   Nathan Nunn and Nancy Qian, The Columbian Exchange, 2010

   "Most dramatically, the Columbian Exchange transformed farming and human diets. This change is often so culturally ingrained that we take it for granted…

   Despite the transport of new killer diseases, including the emergence of deadly syphilis in Europe and Asia, which was linked to trade with the Americas, the Columbian Exchange eventually allowed more people to live off the land. These newly available plants and animals led to the single largest improvement in farm productivity since the original agricultural revolution. The results of different peoples' efforts in domesticating and refining crops over thousands of years were now available and being adopted worldwide."

   Simon L. Lewis and Mark A. Maslin, Atlantic, August 24, 2018

   Using the excerpts above, answer (a), (b), and (c).

   (a) Briefly describe ONE important difference between Nunn and Qian's and Lewis and Maslin's historical interpretations of the Columbian Exchange.

   (b) Briefly explain how ONE specific historical event, development, or circumstance from the period 1491–1607 that is not specifically mentioned in the excerpts could be used to support Nunn and Qian's argument.

   (c) Briefly explain how ONE specific historical event, development, or circumstance from the period 1491–1607 that is not specifically mentioned in the excerpts could be used to support Lewis and Maslin's argument.

Labor, Slavery, and Caste in the Spanish Colonial System

Know ye that I have given permission . . . to take to the Indies, the islands and the mainland of the ocean sea already discovered or to be discovered, four thousand negro slaves both male and female, provided that they be Christians.

Emperor Charles V of Spain, colonial charter, August 18, 1518

Learning Objective: Explain how the growth of the Spanish Empire in North America shaped the development of social and economic structures over time.

Spanish dominance in the Americas was based on more than a papal ruling and a treaty. The new empire began with ambitious and skilled leaders in Ferdinand and Isabella. With its adventurous explorers and conquerors (called **conquistadores**) and the labor provided by Indians and enslaved Africans, Spain rapidly expanded its wealth and power.

Spanish Exploration and Conquest

Feats such as the journey across the Isthmus of Panama to the Pacific Ocean by Vasco Núñez de Balboa, the circumnavigation of the world by one of Ferdinand Magellan's ships (Magellan died before completing the trip), the conquests of the Aztecs in Mexico by **Hernán Cortés**, and the conquest of the Incas in Peru by **Francisco Pizarro** secured Spain's initial supremacy in the Americas.

The conquistadores sent ships loaded with gold and silver back to Spain from Mexico and Peru. They increased the gold supply in Spain, making it the richest and most powerful kingdom in Europe. Spain's success encouraged other states to turn to the Americas in search of gold and power.

Indian Labor In Mexico and Peru, the Spanish encountered the well-organized and populous Aztec and Inca empires. Even after diseases killed most natives, millions survived. The Spanish incorporated the surviving Indians into their own empire. To control them, the Spanish used the **encomienda** system in which Spain's king granted natives who lived on a tract of land to individual Spaniards. These Indians were forced to farm or work in the mines. The fruits of their labors went to the Spanish, who in turn had to "care" for the Indians.

Enslaved African Labor On their sugar plantations on islands off the African coast, the Portuguese had already shown that using enslaved Africans to grow crops could be profitable. They provided a model for other Europeans. The Spanish, to add to their labor force and to replace Indians who died from diseases and brutality, began trading with African partners who could supply enslaved people. The Spanish imported people under the **asiento** system, which required colonists to pay a tax to the Spanish king on each enslaved person they imported to the Americas.

As other Europeans established American colonies, they also imported enslaved Africans in large numbers. During the colonial era, more Africans than Europeans crossed the Atlantic to the Americas. Before the transatlantic **slave trade** ended in the late 1800s, slave traders sent between 10 million and 15 million enslaved people from Africa. Between 10 percent and 15 percent died on the voyage across the Atlantic Ocean, called the **Middle Passage**.

African Resistance Though transported thousands of miles from their homelands and brutally repressed, Africans resisted slavery in multiple ways. They often ran away, sabotaged work, or revolted. Further, they maintained aspects of African culture, particularly in music, religion, and folkways.

Spanish Caste System

The combination of Native Americans, Europeans, and Africans made the Spanish colonies ethnically diverse. In addition, since most Spanish colonists were single men rather than families, many had children with native or African women. The result was that the Spanish colonies included many people with mixed heritage. In response, the Spanish developed a caste system that defined the status of people in the colonies by their heritage:

- At the top were pure-blooded Spaniards.

- In the middle were several levels of people ordered according to their mixture of European, Native American, and African heritage.

- At the bottom were people of pure Indian or Black heritage.

REFLECT ON THE LEARNING OBJECTIVE

1. How was the society and economy of North America affected by the expansion of the Spanish Empire?

KEY TERMS BY THEME

Labor Systems (WXT)	Identity and Politics (POL)	Atlantic Trade (WXT)
encomienda	conquistadores	slave trade
asiento	Hernán Cortés	Middle Passage
slavery	Francisco Pizarro	

MULTIPLE-CHOICE QUESTIONS

Questions 1–3 refer to the following excerpt.

"The province of Quivira is 950 leagues from Mexico. Where I reached it, it is in the fortieth degree [of latitude]. The country itself is the best I have ever seen for producing all the products of Spain. . . . I have treated the natives of this province, and all the others whom I found wherever I went, as well as was possible, agreeably to what Your Majesty had commanded, and they have received no harm in any way from me or from those who went in my company. I remained twenty-five days in this province of Quivira, so as to see and explore the country and also to find out whether there was anything beyond which could be of service to Your Majesty, because the guides who had brought me had given me an account of other provinces beyond this. And what I am sure of is that there is not any gold nor any other metal in all that country."

Francisco Coronado, Spanish conquistador,
Travels in Quivira, c. 1542

1. Which of the following best summarizes Coronado's goal in exploring Mexico as expressed in this excerpt?

   (A) To inform the natives about Spain and its culture

   (B) To learn from the native inhabitants in the region

   (C) To spread Roman Catholic Christianity in the region

   (D) To find natural resources that might enrich the king

2. The activities described in this excerpt were similar to those of other Spanish and Portuguese explorers in the Americas in the 16th century because they depended primarily on the support of

   (A) merchants and fur traders

   (B) the Catholic Church

   (C) monarchs

   (D) impoverished Europeans

3. Based on the excerpt, one difference between Coronado and many European explorers was that he expressed little interest in

   (A) enriching the king

   (B) finding gold and silver

   (C) converting the native people to Christianity

   (D) increasing the power of his country

SHORT-ANSWER QUESTIONS

Use complete sentences; an outline or bulleted list alone is not acceptable.

1. "I want the natives to develop a friendly attitude toward us because I know that they are a people who can be made free and converted to our Holy Faith more by love than by force. I therefore gave red caps to some and glass beads to others. They hung the beads around their necks, along with some other things of slight value that I gave them. . . . I warned my men to take nothing from the people without giving something in exchange."

Christopher Columbus, Log, October 12, 1492

   Using the excerpt above, answer (a), (b), and (c).

   (a) Briefly explain ONE expectation about Native Americans that caused Columbus to issue this statement to his men.

   (b) Briefly explain ONE effect that this statement by Columbus would likely have on a powerful group in Spain, other than the monarchy.

   (c) Briefly explain ONE effect of contact between Europeans and the first inhabitants of America that is not consistent with the above passage.

2. Answer (a), (b), and (c).

   (a) Briefly explain ONE specific example of how the Spanish managed their American colonial empire during the 15th and 16th centuries.

   (b) Briefly explain ONE specific example of how a non-Spanish individual or country influenced Spain's American colonial empire during the 15th and 16th centuries.

   (c) Briefly explain ONE specific example of the diversity that developed in Spain's American colonial empire during the 15th and 16th centuries.

3. Answer (a), (b), and (c).

   (a) Briefly explain ONE specific example of a benefit that the Native Americans gained from the Spanish settlements during the 15th and 16th centuries.

   (b) Briefly explain ONE specific example of a negative effect on Native Americans caused by the Spanish settlements during the 15th and 16th centuries.

   (c) Briefly explain ONE specific factor that influenced the Spanish in their treatment of Native Americans during the 15th and 16th centuries.

Topic 1.6

Cultural Interactions in the Americas

The Spanish have a perfect right to rule these barbarians of the New World and the adjacent islands, who in prudence, skill, virtues, and humanity are as inferior to the Spanish as children to adults, or women to men.

Juan Ginés de Sepúlveda, Spanish theologian, 1547

Learning Objective: Explain how and why European and Native American perspectives of others developed and changed in the period.

History is filled with experiences of contact between diverse people, such as the Romans and Africans in the Classical Era, or the Christians and Muslims in the Middle Ages. Often these conflicts were violent, but they were in small regions and lasted no more than a couple centuries. The contact between Native Americans, Europeans, and Africans in the Americas also featured violence, but the interaction was on a much larger scale for a much longer time.

Europeans and Native Americans held conflicting worldviews. For example, most Europeans believed in a single god, while most Native Americans honored many deities. European women had little role in public life, while Native American women in some tribes held decision-making positions. Europeans used legal documents to establish the right to plow a field or hunt in a forest. Native Americans relied more on tradition to make land use decisions.

European Treatment of Native Americans

The Europeans who colonized North and South America generally viewed Native Americans as inferior people who could be exploited for economic gain, converted to Christianity, and used as military allies. However, Europeans used various approaches for ruling Native Americans and operating colonies.

Spanish Policy

The Spanish overwhelmingly subjugated Native Americans. However, Spanish scholars also debated the status of Native Americans and the treatment of them.

Bartolomé de Las Casas One European who dissented from the views of most Europeans toward Native Americans was a Spanish priest named

Bartolomé de Las Casas. Though he had owned land and slaves in the West Indies and had fought in wars against the Indians, he eventually became an advocate for better treatment for Indians. He persuaded the king to institute the **New Laws of 1542**. These laws ended Indian slavery, halted forced Indian labor, and began to end the encomienda system that kept the Indians in serfdom. Conservative Spaniards, eager to keep the encomienda system, responded and successfully pushed the king to repeal parts of the New Laws.

Valladolid Debate The debate over the role for Indians in the Spanish colonies came to a head in a formal debate in 1550–1551 in Valladolid, Spain. On one side, Las Casas argued that the Indians were completely human and morally equal to Europeans, so enslaving them was not justified. On the other side, another priest, **Juan Ginés de Sepúlveda**, argued that Indians were less than human. Hence, they benefited from serving the Spaniards in the encomienda system. Neither side clearly persuaded the entire audience. Though Las Casas was unable to gain equal treatment for Native Americans, he established the basic arguments on behalf of justice for Indians.

English Policy

Unlike the Spanish, the English settled in areas with no large native empires that could provide forced labor. Further, when English colonists arrived in the 1600s, European diseases had already dramatically reduced the indigenous population. In addition, many English colonists came in families rather than as single young men, so marriage with natives was less common.

Initially, at least in Massachusetts, the English and the American Indians coexisted, traded, and shared ideas. American Indians taught the settlers how to grow new crops such as corn (maize) and showed them how to hunt in the forests. They traded furs for an array of English manufactured goods, including iron tools and weapons, that they found useful.

But peaceful relations soon gave way to conflict and warfare. Most English showed no respect for American Indian cultures, which they viewed as "savage." American Indians saw their way of life threatened as the English seized land to support their growing population. The English occupied the land and forced the small, scattered tribes they encountered to move away from the coast to inland territories. They expelled the natives rather than subjugating them.

French Policy

The French, looking for furs and converts to Catholicism, viewed American Indians as potential economic and military allies. Compared to the Spaniards and the English, the French maintained good relations with the tribes they encountered. Seeking to control the fur trade, the French built trading posts throughout the St. Lawrence Valley, the Great Lakes region, and along the Mississippi River. At these posts, they exchanged French goods for beaver pelts and other furs collected by American Indians. Because the French had few colonists, farms, or towns, they posed less threat to the native population than did other Europeans. In addition, French soldiers assisted the Huron people in fighting their traditional enemy, the Iroquois (Haudenosaunee).

Survival Strategies by Native Americans

As European settlements expanded, Native Americans responded to protect their cultures. One strategy was to ally with one European power or another. For example, in Mexico, several tribes allied with the Spanish to help them win their freedom from the Aztecs in the 16th century. Later, in the Ohio River Valley, the Delawares and the Shawnees allied closely with the French against English encroachment on their land.

Other tribes simply migrated west to get away from settlers, though this often led them into conflict with Native Americans already living in a region. The conflicts reflected the strong tribal loyalty that Native Americans felt. Since they did not identify as part of a larger group that included all tribes, European settlers pushing westward rarely faced a unified response from Native Americans. Only later would the shared desire to resist European power lead people to identify as Native Americans as well as members of a particular tribe. Regardless of how they dealt with the European invasion, Native Americans would never be able to return to the life they had known prior to 1492.

The Role of Africans in America

Africans contributed a third cultural tradition in the Americas. Their experience growing rice resulted in rice becoming an important crop in the colonies of South Carolina and Louisiana. They brought musical rhythms and styles of singing that shaped the development of music throughout the Americas. They also introduced European settlers to the banjo. By the 19th century, the banjo would be closely associated with the culture of the southeastern United States.

Europeans justified slavery in many ways. Some cited passages from the Bible to support their belief that slavery had always existed and was approved by God. As slavery became exclusively for Africans, Europeans began to argue that Africans were biologically inferior, so enslaving them was acceptable. This was similar to the argument used by de Sepúlveda regarding Native Americans.

REFLECT ON THE LEARNING OBJECTIVE

1. Describe the evolution in the views of the Europeans and Native Americans toward each during the period of European colonization.

KEY TERMS BY THEME

Identity and Politics (NAT, POL)	Values and Attitudes (SOC)	
New Laws of 1542	Bartolomé de Las Casas	Valladolid Debate Juan Ginés de Sepúlveda

Questions 1–2 refer to the following excerpt.

"Concerning the treatment of Native American workers: When they were allowed to go home, they often found it deserted and had no other recourse than to go out into the woods to find food and to die. When they fell ill, which was very frequently because they are a delicate people unaccustomed to such work, the Spaniards did not believe them and pitilessly called them lazy dogs, and kicked and beat them; and when illness was apparent they sent them home as useless, giving them some cassava for the twenty- to eighty-league [about 60 to 240 miles] journey. They would go then, falling into the first stream and dying there in desperation; others would hold on longer, but very few ever made it home. I sometimes came upon dead bodies on my way, and upon others who were gasping and moaning in their death agony."

Bartolomé de Las Casas, *In Defense of the Indian*, c. 1550

1. How did Las Casas's attitudes compare to those of most Europeans?

   (A) He was more sympathetic toward the suffering of Indians.

   (B) He was more critical of Indians for causing their own problems.

   (C) He was more focused on how Indians treated Europeans.

   (D) He was very typical in his attitudes toward Indians.

2. Las Casas was primarily trying to influence

   (A) the monarchs of Spain who shaped colonial policies

   (B) the religious leaders in Europe who were not Roman Catholics

   (C) the conquistadores in the colonies who were moving into new areas

   (D) the Native Americans who were reacting to the Spanish colonists

SHORT-ANSWER QUESTION

Use complete sentences; an outline or bulleted list alone is not acceptable.

1. Answer (a), (b), and (c).

   (a) Briefly explain ONE specific effect of Spain's policy toward Native Americans during the period 1492–1607.

   (b) Briefly explain ONE specific effect of a policy of a European country other than Spain toward Native Americans during the period 1492–1607.

   (c) Briefly explain ONE specific reaction of Native Americans to European policies during the period 1492–1607.

Topic 1.7

Causation in Period 1

Learning Objective: Explain the effects of the development of transatlantic voyages from 1491 to 1607.

The reasoning skill of "causation" is the suggested focus for evaluating the content of this period. As explained in the contextualization introduction to Period 1, there are many factors to consider in the broad topic of European encounters in the Americas in the 15th and 16th centuries. One needs to be able to *describe what caused* the Native Americans to develop diverse societies across the enormous and varied lands of North America. This appreciation of the status of Native Americans during this period will help to *explain the specific developments* when the Europeans came to explore what they saw as a "new world."

A number of factors had come together to explain the causes of the European explorations during this particular period. For example, both desires to spread Christianity and desires for economic gain. However, not all causes are equally significant. One task of a historian is to weigh the evidence to decide how much emphasis to place on each of these various causes. Among the most common differences among historians are debates over whether one cause was more important than another.

Note that causation implies that an event or development had an effect. The results of the contact are viewed by some as the Columbian Exchange, which *explain both the short- and long-term* impact not only on both sides of the Atlantic but on people throughout the world. Given the many factors involved, one can argue as to the *historically significant effects* on the various peoples involved on both sides of the Atlantic.

QUESTIONS ABOUT CAUSATION

1. Explain the factors that resulted in various Native American groups developing their own unique cultures.

2. Explain a significant development in Europe by the 15th and 16th centuries that caused a surge in exploration.

3. Explain the extent to which the Columbian Exchange had beneficial effects on both the Native Americans and Europeans.

Below are models of a step-by-step process for analyzing a primary source and a secondary source. As you study the italicized questions and answers, consider alternate answers based on your own knowledge and skill as a historical thinker.

Analyzing a Primary Source

"Being earnestly requested by a dear friend to put down in writing some true relation of our late performed voyage to the north parts of Virginia [Massachusetts] I resolved to satisfy his request. . . .

"Coming ashore, we stood awhile like men ravished at the beauty and delicacy of this sweet soil. For besides diverse clear lakes of fresh water . . . meadows very large and full of green grass. . . .

"[This climate so agreed with us] that we found our health and strength all the while we remained there so to renew and increase as, notwithstanding our diet and lodging was none of the best, yet not one of our company (God be thanked) felt the least grudging or inclination to any disease or sickness but were much fatter and in better health than when we went out of England."

John Brereton, *The Discovery of the North Part of Virginia*, 1602

Content

- *What is the key point?* New England has a healthy environment.
- *What content is useful?* It states one early impression of New England, which can help explain why Europeans wanted to colonize the region.

The Author's Point of View

- *Who was the author?* John Brereton, an Englishman
- *How reliable is the author?* Answering this requires additional research.
- *What was the author's point of view?* New England is a wonderful place.
- *What other beliefs might the author hold?* He believes in God.

The Author's Purpose

- *Why did the author create this document at this time?* Others expressed interest in his experiences in land that was new to them.
- *How does the document's purpose reflect its reliability?* The author could be biased to encourage investment in colonization.

Audience

- *Who was this document created for?* people in England
- *How might the audience affect the document's content?* The audience was looking for opportunities for success in the Americas.
- *How might the audience affect its reliability?* It might emphasize positive information.

Historical Context

- *When and where was this produced?* England in the early 17th century
- *What concurrent events might have affected the author?* the desire of many to encourage and profit from the new colonies

Format/Medium

- *What is the format?* a first-person narrative

Limitations

- *What is one limitation of the excerpt or the author's view?* The document says nothing about the indigenous people living in the region.

Analyzing a Secondary Source

"Why did the English found colonies and make them stick? For most the goal was material. . . . For some the goal was spiritual. . . . But all the colonists who suffered perilous voyages and risked early death in America were either hustlers or hustled. That is, they knew the hardships beforehand and were courageous, desperate, or faithful enough to face them, or else they did not know what lay ahead but were taken in by the propaganda of sponsors. . . . In every case colonists left a swarming competitive country that heralded self-improvement but offered limited opportunities for it."

Walter A. McDougall, *Freedom Just Around the Corner,* 2004

Content and Argument

- *What is the main idea of the excerpt?* English settlers came to America for diverse reasons.
- *What information supports this historian?* The author gives examples of both the religious Puritans and adventurers as settlers.
- *What information challenges this historian?* Many people were forced to settle in America because they were enslaved or convicts.
- *What is the interpretation of events argued for in this excerpt?* The opportunities for prosperity and religious freedom were far greater in the colonies than those they left behind in Europe.

The Author's Point of View

- *How could the author's perspective have been shaped by the times in which he wrote?* The author was writing in 2004, long after the English colonies had become the United States. The size and power of the United States might have led him to focus on the lack of these traits in the colonies.
- *Why might another historian view the same events differently?* Another historian might emphasize a single factor instead of multiple factors.

UNIT 1 — Period 1 Review: 1491–1607

The long essay question will require you to develop an *argument*, which requires asserting a *defensible claim* and backing it up with *evidence*. (For more on arguments, claims, and evidence, see page xxx–xxxi.) The process for developing your argument is described in the checklist below. (See also pages xli–xlvii.) Each stage of the process will be the focus of a writing activity at the end of units 3–8. These activities will help you apply to each stage the historical thinking skills you must demonstrate in your essay.

1. **Carefully read and analyze the task.** Read the question carefully. Within your argument, you will be asked to evaluate the extent to which subjects show similarity or difference, continuity or change, or causation. Look for key words defining the task. Note the geographic area(s) and time period(s) framing the task.

2. **Gather and organize the evidence you will need to complete the task.** Write down everything you know that is *directly* related to the topic. Include both broad ideas and specific incidents or events. Then review your information looking for patterns and connections. Also determine a way to organize the evidence to fulfill the task.

3. **Develop a thesis—a defensible claim—that lays out a line of reasoning.** You should be able to defend your claim using the evidence you collected and express your thesis in one or more sentences in the same location in your essay, typically in the introduction.

4. **Write an introductory paragraph.** Use the introduction to relate your thesis statement to a broader historical context. Explain how it fits into larger or divergent historical trends.

5. **Write the supporting paragraphs.** Use information you gathered in step 2 to support the argument expressed in your thesis statement with corroboration (support), modification (slight change), or qualification (limitation). Use transitional words to tie ideas together.

6. **Write the conclusion.** To unify your essay, return to the ideas in your introduction. Instead of restating your thesis statement, however, extend it to draw a nuanced conclusion that follows from your evidence.

7. **Reread and evaluate your essay.** Become familiar with the scoring rubric. Check your essay to make sure you have included everything needed to earn the maximum number of points.

Application: Follow the steps above as you develop a long essay in response to one of the prompts below.

For current free-response question samples, visit: https//apcentral.collegeboard.org/ courses/ap-united-states-history/exam

LONG ESSAY QUESTIONS

Directions: The suggested writing time for each question is 40 minutes. In your response, you should do the following:

- Respond to the prompt with a historically defensible thesis or claim that establishes a line of reasoning.
- Describe a broader historical context relevant to the prompt.
- Support an argument in response to the prompt using specific and relevant examples of evidence.
- Use historical reasoning (e.g., comparison, causation, continuity or change) to frame or structure an argument that addresses the prompt.
- Use evidence to corroborate, qualify, or modify an argument that addresses the prompt.

1. Evaluate the extent to which the environment fostered variations in Native American societies by the year 1491.

2. Evaluate the extent to which differences in European nations fostered differences in how these nations explored the Western Hemisphere.

3. Evaluate the extent of the similarities in the impact of the Columbian Exchange in the Western Hemisphere and in other areas of the world.

4. Evaluate the extent of the differences in the approaches of various European nations in relations with Native Americans in the period from 1491 to 1607.

Topic 2.1

Contextualizing Period 2

Learning Objective: Explain the context for the colonization of North America from 1607 to 1754.

The period in the Americas from 1491 to 1607 was a time of European exploration, dominated by the Spanish. In the period from 1607 to 1754, exploration began giving way to expanding colonization. In North America, the Spanish, French, Dutch, and British established colonies, with the British dominating the region from Canada to the Caribbean islands. In particular, the British established 13 colonies along the Atlantic coast. Most of these provided a profitable trade and a home to a diverse group of Native Americans, Europeans, and Africans.

From the establishment of the first permanent English settlement in North America in 1607 to the start of a decisive war for European control of the continent in 1756, the colonies evolved. At first, they struggled for survival. Over time, they became a society of permanent farms, plantations, towns, and cities. European settlers brought various cultures, economic plans, and ideas for governing to the Americas. In particular, with varying approaches, they all sought to dominate the native inhabitants.

Early Settlements

The earliest Europeans in the Americas, the Spanish and Portuguese, settled in Central and South America. The Spanish slowly migrated into North America. Subsequently, the French, Dutch, and British settled along the Atlantic coast of North America and gradually migrated westward and developed various types of colonial systems and relationships with Native Americans.

The first two successful British colonies along the Atlantic coast of North America were Jamestown and Plymouth. They served as the starting points that would lead to 13 colonies as far south as Georgia. Depending on the environmental conditions and settlement patterns, each colony developed its own economic and cultural system. For many, transatlantic trade was important, with tobacco, timber, and rice being important products. Trade, along with ties of religion and language, created strong bonds between the colonies and Great Britain. However, in the mid-1700s, trade also became a point of conflict. Colonies increasingly resisted British control over their trade.

Trade was also the mainstay of early contact between the Europeans and Native Americans. The colonists wanted a dependable food supply and the Native Americans were drawn to the iron tools and guns of the newcomers. But the Europeans generally treated the Native Americans as inferiors to be used or pushed aside. Trade also led to competition for resources among colonists and natives. In particular, the British and the French fought a series of wars for control of land. Native Americans such as the Iroquois and the Huron allied with Europeans or each other to advance their own interests.

Sources of Labor

As Europeans seized land from Native Americans, they looked for a source of labor to make the lands profitable. They first tried to enslave Native Americans. This failed because the Native Americans could escape too easily. Europeans then tried to employ indentured servants, individuals who agreed to work for a master for a set number of years (often seven) in exchange for transportation from Europe to the Americas. Indentured servants became common in the colonies, but they did not provide sufficient labor for people who owned land.

The British, following the example of the Spanish and others, soon began importing enslaved laborers from Africa. Given the steady flow of support and families from Britain, the various 13 colonies gradually developed societies that both mirrored and varied from British society. From 1607 to the 1750s, the growth of these 13 British colonies would lead them to use trade and war to dominate both the Native Americans and the other European colonists.

ANALYZE THE CONTEXT

1. Explain a historical context for understanding the interaction between the Native Americans and the Europeans as colonies were established in North America in the period from 1607 to 1754.

2. Explain a historical context for the development of slavery in the European colonies in North America in the period from 1607 to 1754.

3. Explain a historical context for the development of society and culture in the 13 British colonies in the period from 1607 to 1754.

LANDMARK EVENTS: 1600–1800

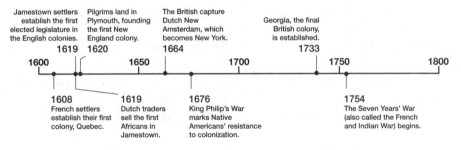

European Colonization in North America

If they desire that Piety and godliness should prosper; accompanied with sobriety, justice and love, let them choose a Country such as this is . . . which may yield sufficiency with hard labour and industry.

Reverend John White, *The Planter's Plea,* 1630

Learning Objective: Explain how and why various European colonies developed and expanded from 1607 to 1754.

Migration to the Americas during the 17th century and the first half of the 18th century was both influenced by the environment and had a lasting impact on it. The many different peoples that settled in North America from Europe, together with the Native Americans already living on the continent and the enslaved Africans brought there, would ultimately form a society unlike any previously seen.

Exploration in the new world by Europeans was quickly followed by colonization. The primary motivations for settling in the Americas in the 17th century were the desires for wealth, to spread Christianity, and to escape persecution.

Spanish Colonies

Spanish settlements developed slowly in North America as a result of limited mineral resources and strong opposition from American Indians. Missionary zeal was an important motivator as Roman Catholic Spain worked to counter the expanding influence of the Reformation and Protestantism. These colonies were largely populated by men, and they would gradually include Native Americans and Africans in their society.

Florida Juan Ponce de Leon claimed these lands for Spain in 1513. After a number of failures and the strong resistance of American Indians in the region, the Spanish established a permanent settlement at St. Augustine in 1565, more than 50 years before the English founded Jamestown. St. Augustine became the oldest city founded by Europeans in what became the mainland of the United States. Only a few small settlements developed as the Spanish found little silver and gold, a declining native population due to wars and disease, and periodic hurricanes.

New Mexico and Arizona In a region that had been settled by American Indians for about 700 years, Spanish colonists began arriving in 1598. They established Santa Fe as the capital of New Mexico in 1610.

Texas Between Florida and New Mexico, the Spanish established settlements in Texas. These communities grew in the early 1700s as Spain resisted French efforts to explore the lower Mississippi River.

California With Russians exploring from Alaska, the Spanish started a settlement at San Diego in 1769. By 1784, the Franciscan order and Father Junípero Serra had established missions along the California coast.

French Colonies

Similar to the Spanish, the French colonizers were mainly men. However, there were few French. Some came as Christian missionaries. Those who came for economic reasons mostly worked in the lucrative fur trade, traveling throughout the interior of North America purchasing furs gathered by American Indians. Many traders married American Indian women, who then provided valuable services as guides, translators, and negotiators with other American Indians. The reliance of the French on trade made rivers particularly important in their colonies.

- Quebec, the first French settlement in America was located on the St. Lawrence River. It was founded by Samuel de Champlain, the "Father of New France," in 1608.

- In 1673, Louis Jolliet and Father Jacques Marquette explored the upper Mississippi River. Nine years later, Robert de La Salle explored the Mississippi basin, which he named Louisiana (after the French king, Louis XIV).

- By 1718, the French had moved southward down the Mississippi River and established a permanent settlement, New Orleans, where the river entered the Gulf of Mexico. New Orleans became a prosperous trade center.

Dutch Colonies

During the 1600s, the Netherlands sponsored voyages of exploration. The government hired Henry Hudson, an English sailor, to seek westward passage to Asia. In 1609, while searching for a northwest passage, Hudson sailed up a broad river that was later named for him, the Hudson River. This expedition established Dutch claims to the surrounding area, New Amsterdam (and later New York). The Dutch government granted a private company, the Dutch West India Company, the right to control the region for economic gain.

Like the French colonies, the Dutch colonies consisted of small numbers of traders who built strong trade networks among American Indians. However, the Dutch were more likely to settle in trading posts near the coast or along major rivers and less likely to intermarry with American Indians.

British Colonies

In the early 1600s, England was in a position to colonize the lands explored a century earlier by **John Cabot**. England's population was growing more rapidly than its economy, so its number of poor and landless families was increasing. They were attracted to opportunities in the Americas. Using **joint-stock companies** to finance the risky enterprise of colonization, the English began settling colonies in the Americas.

Compared to other European colonists, those from England included a higher percentage of families and single females, and they were more interested in farming. As a result, English settlers were more likely to claim American Indian land and less likely to intermarry with Indians. In addition, the English colonies attracted a more diverse group of European settlers than did other colonies. Most of these settlers migrated in search of better lives or religious freedom.

REFLECT ON THE LEARNING OBJECTIVE

1. Explain what the motivations and methods were that supported European colonial growth during the period from 1607 to 1754.

KEY TERMS BY THEME

Settlements (ARC)	Authority (WOR)
John Cabot	joint-stock company

MULTIPLE-CHOICE QUESTIONS

Questions 1–2 refer to the following excerpt.

> "As touching the quality of this country, three thinges there bee, which in fewe yeares may bring this Colony to perfection; the English plough, Vineyards, & Cattle. . . .
>
> All our riches for the present doe consiste in Tobacco, wherein one man by his owne labour hath in one yeare, raised to himself to the value of 200 sterling; and another by the means of six servants hath cleared at one crop a thousand pound english. These be true, yet indeed rare examples, yet possible to be done by others. Our principall wealth (I should haue said) consisteth in servants: but they are chargeable to be furnished with armes, apparel, & bedding, and for their transportation, and casuall both at sea, & for their first yeare commonly at lande also: but if they escape, they proove very hardy, and sound able men."

John Pory, Secretary of Virginia, Letter to Sir Dudley Carlton, 1619

1. The excerpt illustrates which of the following visions for Virginia?
   (A) A land that would provide agricultural products that would enrich England
   (B) A settlement designed to reproduce England's social structure and economy
   (C) A haven where servants could escape bondage and live as free individuals
   (D) A colony that would help expand England's empire and diplomatic power

2. Which of the following developments in the 17th century could best be used as evidence to support or modify the references to servants in the second paragraph?
   (A) Colonists became more dependent on raids of Native American settlements to obtain workers.
   (B) Europeans from outside of England became the majority of colonists who settled in Virginia.
   (C) Large numbers of English citizens emigrated to the colonies as indentured laborers.
   (D) The king started wars against other European powers to capture their citizens and send them to Virginia.

SHORT-ANSWER QUESTION

Use complete sentences; an outline or a bulleted list alone is not acceptable.

1. "[This colony] was for the most part at first peopled by persons of low circumstances. . . . Nor was it hardly possible it should be otherwise; for 'tis not likely that any man of a plentiful estate should voluntarily abandon a happy certainty to roam after imaginary advantages in a New World. Besides which uncertainty, must have proposed to himself to encounter the infinite difficulties and dangers that attend a new settlement. These discouragements were sufficient to terrify any man that could live easy in England from going to . . . a strange land."

   Robert Beverly, historian, *The History and Present State of Virginia*, 1705

   Using the excerpt above, answer (a), (b), and (c).
   (a) Briefly explain Robert Beverly's perspective in the excerpt.
   (b) Briefly explain ONE example of historical evidence that supports Beverly's position.
   (c) Briefly explain ONE example of historical evidence that challenges Beverly's position.

The Regions of British Colonies

Liberty of conscience . . . we ask as our undoubted right by the law of God, of nature, and of our own country.

William Penn, "The Great Case of Liberty of Conscience," 1670

Learning Objective: Explain how and why environmental and other factors shaped the development and expansion of various British colonies that developed and expanded from 1607 to 1754.

The English colonies developed regional or sectional differences based on many influences including topography, natural resources, climate, and the background of their settlers. Starting with Jamestown (Virginia) in 1607 and ending in 1733 in Georgia, 13 distinct colonies developed along the Atlantic coast of North America. Every colony received its authority to operate by a charter granting special privileges from the monarch. Each charter described the relationship between the colony and the crown. Over time, three types of charters—and three types of colonies—developed:

- **Corporate colonies**, such as Jamestown, were operated by joint-stock companies, at least during these colonies' early years.
- **Royal colonies**, such as Virginia after 1624, were to be under the direct authority and rule of the king's government.
- **Proprietary colonies**, such as Maryland and Pennsylvania, were under the authority of individuals granted charters of ownership by the king.

The British took pride in free farmers working the land. Unlike the French and Spanish colonists, the English had a tradition of representative government. They were accustomed to elections for representatives speaking for property owners and deciding important measures, such as taxes, proposed by the king's government. While political and religious conflicts dominated England, feelings for independence grew in the colonies. Eventually, tensions emerged between the king and his colonial subjects.

Early English Settlements

The earliest English colonies were founded for very different reasons and hundreds of miles apart in Virginia and Massachusetts.

Jamestown

England's King James I chartered the **Virginia Company**, a **joint-stock company** that founded the first permanent English colony in America at **Jamestown** in 1607.

Early Problems The first settlers of Jamestown suffered greatly, mostly from their own mistakes. The settlement's location in a swampy area along the James River resulted in fatal outbreaks of dysentery and malaria. Many of the settlers were gentlemen unaccustomed to physical work or gold hunters who refused to hunt or farm. A source of goods came from trade with American Indians, but conflicts between settlers and the natives stopped trade and settlers starved.

Through the leadership of **Captain John Smith**, Jamestown survived its first five years. Through the efforts of **John Rolfe** and his Indian wife, **Pocahontas**, the colony developed a variety of tobacco that became popular in Europe and a profitable crop. To recruit White settlers, Virginia provided 50 acres of land, called a *headright*, to any settler or to anyone who paid for passage for a settler to the colony. While the headright system helped many Europeans move to Virginia, it mostly aided landowners who added to their holdings by sponsoring indentured servants. During the first several decades of colonization, planters mostly used White laborers. However, by the end of the 17th century, landowners relied more on enslaved Africans.

Transition to a Royal Colony Despite tobacco, by 1624 the Virginia colony remained near collapse. More than 5,000 people had settled in it, but death from disease and conflicts with Indians was so high that the population was only 1,300. Further, the Virginia Company was nearly bankrupt. King James I finally revoked the company charter and took direct control. Now known as **Virginia**, the colony became England's first royal colony.

Plymouth and Massachusetts Bay

About 500 miles to the north of Jamestown, English settlers founded two other colonies, Plymouth and Massachusetts Bay, in the region that became known as New England. While many of the settlers in these colonies came as indentured servants in search of economic opportunity, the distinctive force that set the tone for these colonies was religious motivation, the search for wealth. Both were settled by English Protestants who dissented from the government-supported Church of England, known as the Anglican Church. The Church of England, lead by the English king, had broken away from the Roman Catholic Church in 1534. However, it had kept most of the Catholic rituals and governing structure. The dissenters, influenced by the teachings of Swiss theologian John Calvin, charged that the Church of England should break completely with Rome. England's King James I, who reigned from 1603 to 1625, viewed the religious dissenters as a threat to his religious and political authority and ordered them arrested and jailed.

The Plymouth Colony The radical dissenters, the **Separatists**, wanted to organize a completely separate church that was independent of royal control. Several hundred Separatists left England for Holland in search of religious freedom. Because of their travels, they became known as **Pilgrims**. Economic hardship and cultural differences with the Dutch led many of the Pilgrims to seek another haven for their religion. They chose the new colony in America, then operated by the Virginia Company of London. In 1620, a small group of Pilgrims set sail for Virginia aboard the *Mayflower*. Fewer than half of the 100 passengers on this ship were Separatists; the rest were people who had economic motives for making the voyage.

After a hard voyage that lasted 65 days, the *Mayflower* dropped anchor off the Massachusetts coast, 600 miles north of Virginia. Rather than sail to Jamestown as planned, the Pilgrims established a new colony at Plymouth.

After a first winter that saw half the settlers perish, the survivors were helped by local American Indians to adapt to the land. They celebrated a good harvest at a thanksgiving feast (the first Thanksgiving) in 1621. Strong leaders, including Captain Miles Standish and Governor William Bradford, grew Plymouth slowly. Fish, furs, and lumber became the mainstays of the economy.

Massachusetts Bay Colony A group of more moderate dissenters, called **Puritans**, believed that the Church of England could be reformed, or purified. The persecution of Puritans increased when a new king, Charles I, took the throne in 1625. Seeking religious freedom, a group of Puritans gained a royal charter for the Massachusetts Bay Company (1629).

In 1630, a thousand Puritans led by **John Winthrop** sailed for Massachusetts and founded Boston. Religious and political conflict in England in the 1630s drove some 15,000 settlers to the Massachusetts Bay Colony—a movement known as the **Great Migration** (The same term is used for the movement of African Americans from southern to northern states in the 20th century.)

Puritans from Massachusetts Bay founded several settlements in New England. In contrast to the plantations in Virginia, these New England settlements were mixtures of small towns and family farms that relied on a blend of commerce and agriculture.

Religious Issues in Maryland

In 1632, King Charles I split off part of Virginia to create a new colony, Maryland. He granted control of it to George Calvert (Lord Baltimore), a Catholic noble, for his service to the king. Maryland was the first proprietary colony. The king expected proprietors to carry out his wishes faithfully, thus giving him control.

The first Lord Baltimore died and Maryland passed to his son, **Cecil Calvert**—the second Lord Baltimore. The son set about implementing his father's plan in 1634 to provide a haven for his fellow Catholics, who faced persecution from Protestants in Britain.

Act of Toleration To avoid persecution in England, several wealthy Catholics emigrated to Maryland and established plantations. However, they were quickly outnumbered by Protestant farmers who held a majority in Maryland's assembly. In 1649, Calvert persuaded the assembly to adopt the **Act of Toleration**, the first colonial statute granting religious freedom to all Christians. However, the statute also called for the death of anyone who denied the divinity of Jesus.

Protestant Revolt In the late 1600s, Protestants angered by a Catholic proprietor ignited a civil war. The Protestants triumphed, and they repealed the Act of Toleration. Catholics lost the right to vote in elections for the assembly. In the 18th century, Maryland's economy and society was like that of Virginia, except that Maryland tolerated more diversity among Protestant sects.

Development of New England

Strong religious convictions sustained settlers in their struggle to establish the Plymouth and Massachusetts Bay colonies. However, Puritan leaders showed intolerance of anyone who questioned their religious teachings, often banishing dissidents from the Bay colony. These dissidents formed settlements that became Rhode Island and Connecticut.

NEW ENGLAND AND ATLANTIC COLONIES
1600s

Rhode Island One well-respected Puritan minister who moved from England to Boston was **Roger Williams,** who arrived in 1631. He believed that the individual's conscience was beyond the control of any civil or church authority. His teachings placed him in conflict with other Puritan leaders, who ordered his banishment. Leaving Boston, Williams fled southward to Narragansett Bay, where he and a few followers founded the community of **Providence** in 1636, and Williams started one of the first Baptist churches in America. The government allowed Catholics, Quakers, and Jews to worship freely. Further, the new colony was unique in that it recognized the rights of American Indians and paid them for the use of their land.

Another dissident who questioned the doctrines of the Puritan authorities was **Anne Hutchinson**. She believed in *antinomianism*—the idea that since individuals receive salvation through their faith alone, they were not required to follow traditional moral laws. Banished from the Bay colony, Hutchinson and her followers founded Portsmouth in 1638. A few years later, Hutchinson migrated to Long Island and was killed in an American Indian uprising.

In 1644, Roger Williams was granted a charter from the Parliament that joined Providence and Portsmouth into a single colony, **Rhode Island**. Because this colony tolerated diverse beliefs, it served as a refuge for many.

Connecticut To the west of Rhode Island, the Connecticut River Valley attracted others who were unhappy with the Massachusetts authorities. The Reverend **Thomas Hooker** led a large group of Boston Puritans into the valley and founded Hartford in 1636. The Hartford settlers then drew up the first written constitution in American history, the *Fundamental Orders of Connecticut* (1639). It established a representative government with a legislature elected by popular vote and a governor chosen by that legislature.

South of Hartford, a second settlement in the Connecticut Valley was started by **John Davenport** in 1637 and given the name New Haven. In 1665, New Haven joined with Hartford to form **Connecticut**. The royal charter for Connecticut granted it a limited degree of self-government, including election of the governor.

New Hampshire The last colony to be founded in New England was **New Hampshire**. Hoping to increase royal control over the colonies, King Charles II separated New Hampshire from the Massachusetts Bay colony in 1679 and made it a royal colony, subject to the authority of an appointed governor.

Halfway Covenant To be a full member of a Puritan congregation, individuals needed to have a confirmed religious experience, a conversion. However, fewer members of the new native-born generation were having such experiences. To maintain the church's influence and membership, a *halfway covenant* was offered by some clergy so that people could become partial members even if they had not felt a conversion. Nevertheless, as the years passed, strict Puritan practices weakened in most New England communities in order to maintain church membership.

Restoration Colonies

New American colonies were founded in the late 17th century during a period known as the Restoration. The name refers to the restoration of the monarchy under King Charles II in 1660 following a brief period of republican rule under a Puritan leader, Oliver Cromwell.

The Carolinas

As a reward for helping him gain the throne, Charles II granted a huge tract of land between Virginia and Spanish Florida to eight nobles. In 1663, these nobles became the lord proprietors of the Carolinas. In 1729, two royal colonies, South Carolina and North Carolina, were formed from the original grant.

THE THIRTEEN ENGLISH COLONIES AROUND 1750

South Carolina In 1670, a few colonists from England and some planters from the island of Barbados founded Charleston, named for their king, Charles II. Initially, the southern economy was based on trading furs and providing food for the West Indies. By the middle of the 18th century, South Carolina's large **rice-growing plantations**, worked by enslaved Africans, resembled the economy and culture of the West Indies.

North Carolina Unlike South Carolina, the region that became North Carolina had few good harbors and poor transportation. As a result, it developed few large plantations and little reliance on slavery. It attracted farmers from Virginia and New England who established small, self-sufficient **tobacco farms**. Some made use of indentured servants and enslaved Africans. North Carolina in the 18th century earned a reputation for democratic views and autonomy from British control.

The Middle Colonies

The four colonies between New England and Virginia—**New York, New Jersey, Pennsylvania, and Delaware**—are often called the Middle Colonies. They had fertile land that attracted a relatively diverse group of European immigrants, good harbors where cities developed, and tolerant attitudes toward religion.

New York Charles II wished to consolidate holdings along the Atlantic coast and close the gap between the New England and the **Chesapeake colonies**. This required compelling the Dutch to give up New Amsterdam on Manhattan Island and the Hudson River Valley.

In 1664, the king granted his brother, the Duke of York (the future James II), the lands lying between Connecticut and Delaware Bay. James dispatched a force that easily took control of the Dutch colony from its governor, Peter Stuyvesant. He ordered his agents to rename the colony New York, but to treat the Dutch settlers well by allowing them the freedom to worship as they pleased and to speak their own language.

James also ordered new taxes, duties, and rents without the consent of a representative assembly. He insisted that no assembly should be allowed in his colony. Taxation without representation met strong opposition from the English-speaking settlers. In 1683, James did yield by allowing New York's governor to grant broad civil and political rights, including a representative assembly.

New Jersey Believing that the territory of New York was too large, James split it in 1664. He gave the section located between the Hudson River and Delaware Bay to Lord John Berkeley and Sir George Carteret. In 1674, one received West New Jersey and the other East New Jersey. To attract settlers, both made generous land offers and allowed religious freedom and an assembly. Eventually, they sold their interests to groups of Quakers. Land titles in the Jerseys changed hands often, and inaccurate property lines added to the general confusion. To settle matters, the crown decided in 1702 to combine the two Jerseys into a single royal colony: New Jersey.

Pennsylvania, "The Holy Experiment" To the west of New Jersey lay a broad expanse of forested land that the royal family gave to a military and political leader, William Penn, in payment for a debt. The land became known as Penn's woods, or Pennsylvania.

When Penn died, he left the land to his son, also named **William Penn**. The son had joined a group of Christians who called themselves the Religious Society of Friends. Commonly known as **Quakers**, they were considered radical by most people in Britain and the colonies. They believed that religious authority was found within each person and not in the Bible nor in any outside source. This led them to support equality among all men and women and to reject violence and resist military service. Because their beliefs challenged authority, the Quakers of England were persecuted and jailed for their beliefs.

Penn hoped his colony would provide a religious refuge for Quakers and other persecuted people as well as generate income and profits for himself. He put his Quaker beliefs to the test by enacting liberal ideas in government. He provided a **Frame of Government** (1682–1683), which guaranteed a representative assembly elected by landowners, and a written constitution, the **Charter of Liberties (1701)**, which guaranteed freedom of worship for all and unrestricted immigration. Unlike other colonial proprietors, who governed from England, Penn crossed the ocean to supervise the founding of Philadelphia on the Delaware River. He brought a plan for a grid pattern of streets, which was later imitated by other cities. He also attempted to treat the American Indians fairly and to not cheat them when purchasing their land.

To attract settlers, Penn hired agents and published notices throughout Europe promising political and religious freedom and generous land terms. Penn's lands along the Delaware River had previously been settled by several thousand Dutch and Swedish colonists, who eased the arrival of the newcomers.

Delaware In 1702, Penn granted the lower three counties of Pennsylvania their own assembly. In effect, Delaware became a separate colony, even though its governor was the same as Pennsylvania's until the American Revolution.

Georgia, The Last Mainland Colony

In 1732, **Georgia**, the thirteenth and final British colony between Canada and the Caribbean, was chartered. It was the only colony to receive direct financial support from the government. The British had two reasons to start a new southern colony:

- They wanted to create a defensive buffer to protect South Carolina plantations from the Spanish Florida.

- They wanted a place to send the thousands of people in England imprisoned for debt. Sending debtors to a colony would both relieve the overcrowded jails and provide a chance for people to start life over.

Given a royal charter for a proprietary colony, a group of philanthropists led by **James Oglethorpe** founded Savannah in 1733. Oglethorpe, the colony's first governor, put into effect a plan for making the colony thrive. There were strict regulations, including bans on drinking rum and slavery. Nevertheless, partly because of the constant threat of Spanish attack, the colony did not prosper.

By 1752, Oglethorpe's group gave up. Georgia was taken over by the British government and became a royal colony. Restrictions on rum and slavery were dropped. The colony grew slowly, adopting the plantation system of South Carolina. In 1776, Georgia was the smallest of the 13 colonies that rebelled against the British.

Early Political Institutions

Britain had difficulty exerting tight control over the colonies. The distance across the Atlantic was great enough that communication was slow. Further, Britain was often consumed by domestic upheavals and wars with France, so it paid little attention to the colonies. Because of these factors, self-rule began early in the colonies.

A Representative Assembly in Virginia The Virginia Company encouraged settlement by guaranteeing to settlers the same rights as residents of England had, including representation in lawmaking. In 1619, Virginia's colonists organized the first representative assembly in America, the **House of Burgesses**. It was dominated by elite planters.

Representative Government in New England Aboard the *Mayflower* in 1620, the Pilgrims drew up and signed a document in which they pledged to make decisions by the will of the majority. Known as the **Mayflower Compact**, this was an early form of self-government and a rudimentary written constitution.

Throughout New England, then, communities held town meetings to debate local decisions and to elect members to colonial legislatures. Voting rights were relatively broad for the time. In Massachusetts Bay Colony, all freemen—male members of the Puritan Church—had the right to elect the colony's governor and a representative assembly.

Limits to Colonial Democracy Despite these steps, most colonists other than male property owners were excluded from the political process. Females and landless males had few rights, indentured servants had practically no rights, and enslaved people had none. Many colonial governors ruled with autocratic or unlimited powers, answering only to the king or to those who provided the colonies' financial support. Thus, the gradual development of democratic ideas in the colonies coexisted with antidemocratic practices such as slavery and the widespread mistreatment of American Indians.

REFLECT ON THE LEARNING OBJECTIVE

1. Explain the forces, including the environment, that played a role in the growth of the British colonies during the period from 1607 to 1754.

KEY TERMS BY THEME

Religion (SOC)
Cecil Calvert, Lord
  Baltimore
Act of Toleration
Roger Williams
Providence
Anne Hutchinson
antinomianism
Rhode Island
halfway covenant
Quakers
William Penn
Holy Experiment
Charter of Liberties (1701)

Crops (GEO)
rice-growing plantations
tobacco farms

Settlements (ARC)
Jamestown

Captain John Smith
John Rolfe
Pocahontas
Virginia
Plymouth Colony
Separatists
Pilgrims
Mayflower
Massachusetts Bay Colony
Puritans
John Winthrop
Great Migration
Thomas Hooker
John Davenport
Connecticut
New Hampshire
the Carolinas
New York
New Jersey

Pennsylvania
Delaware
Georgia
James Oglethorpe

Self-Rule (PCE)
Fundamental Orders of
  Connecticut (1639)
Frame of Government
  (1682–1683)
Virginia House of
  Burgesses
Mayflower Compact

Authority (WOR)
corporate colonies
royal colonies
proprietary colonies
Virginia Company
Chesapeake colonies
joint-stock company

MULTIPLE-CHOICE QUESTIONS

Questions 1–3 refer to the following excerpt.

"Be it therefore ordered and enacted. . . . That whatsoever person or persons within this Province . . . shall henceforth blaspheme God, that is, curse Him or shall deny our Savior Jesus Christ to be the Son of God, or shall deny the Holy Trinity . . . or the Godhead of any of the said Three persons of the Trinity or the Unity of the Godhead . . . shall be punished with death and confiscation or forfeiture of all his or her lands. . . . And whereas . . . that no person or persons whatsoever within this province, or the islands, ports, harbors, creeks, or havens thereunto belonging, professing to believe in Jesus Christ, shall from henceforth be any way troubled, molested or discountenanced for or in respect of his or her religion nor in free exercise thereof within this province or the islands thereunto belonging nor any way compelled to the belief or exercise of any other Religion against his or her consent."

The Maryland Act of Toleration, 1649

1. The authors of the Maryland Act of Toleration were primarily trying to protect which of the following religious groups?
   (A) Jews who faced antisemitism in Europe and in other colonies
   (B) Quakers who were being attacked for their support of nonviolence and other beliefs
   (C) Anglicans who had been persecuted in New England
   (D) Roman Catholics who felt threatened by the growing number of Protestant settlers

2. Which of the following best summarizes the attitude toward religious beliefs expressed in this document?
   (A) Individuals should be free to believe or not believe in God as they wish.
   (B) Religion should be a personal matter that the government should not try to influence.
   (C) Christians should be able to practice their faith without fear of persecution.
   (D) The colony should be reserved for the one specific type of Christianity approved by the local government officials.

3. Which of the following colonies practiced greater religious toleration than the excerpt about Maryland calls for?
   (A) Roger William's Rhode Island
   (B) Thomas Hooker's Connecticut
   (C) Anne Hutchinson's Portsmouth
   (D) John Winthrop's Massachusetts

SHORT-ANSWER QUESTION

Use complete sentences; an outline or bulleted list alone is not acceptable.

1. Answer (a), (b), and (c).
   (a) Briefly explain ONE way in which Puritanism influenced the development of New England from 1630 to 1685.
   (b) Briefly explain another way in which Puritanism influenced the development of New England from 1630 to 1685.
   (c) Briefly explain how ONE specific new colony in New England developed differently as a result of Puritanism during the period from 1630 to 1685.

Transatlantic Trade

The sad truth is that without complex business partnerships between African elites and European traders . . . the slave trade to the New World would have been impossible.

Henry Louis Gates Jr., "Ending the Slavery Blame-Game," *New York Times*, 2010

Learning Objective: Explain the causes and effects of transatlantic trade over time.

While the colonists had various reasons for settling in the Americas, such as an opportunity to practice their religious faith or an opportunity to search for wealth, the European nations that controlled the colonies looked at them to increase their power. A principal way to become stronger was through transatlantic trade.

Triangular Trade

Merchant ships regularly followed a triangular, or three-part, route, that connected North America, Africa, and Europe in various ways. A typical voyage might begin in New England:

- A ship would leave a port in New England carrying rum across the Atlantic to West Africa. There the rum would be traded for hundreds of captive Africans.

- Next, the ship would set out on the horrendous Middle Passage. Those Africans who survived the voyage would be traded in the West Indies for sugarcane.

- Third, completing the last side of the triangle, the ship returned to a New England port where the sugar would be sold to be made into rum.

Variations on the route included stops in England or Spain. Every trade provided the slave-trading entrepreneur a substantial profit.

In the 17th century, English trade in enslaved Africans was first monopolized by the Royal African Company. However, by the late 17th century, the RAC could not supply as many enslaved Africans as demanded by colonial planters. Parliament ended the company's monopoly on the slave trade, and New England merchants entered the lucrative business.

COLONIAL TRIANGULAR TRADE ROUTES

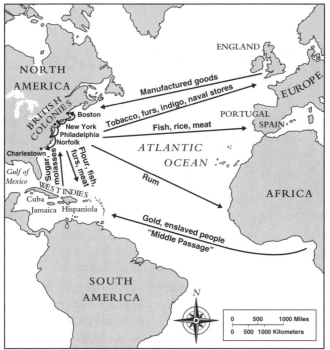

Mercantilism and the Empire

Most European kingdoms in the 17th century believed in *mercantilism*, the economic theory that a country's wealth was determined by how much more it exported than it imported. Hence, governments tried to promote the sales of goods to other countries and to discourage purchases through tariffs. In a mercantilist system, colonies existed for one purpose only: to enrich the parent country. They were to provide raw materials to the parent country to promote that country's industries. Spanish and French rulers had followed mercantilist policies from the start of colonization. England began applying them after the end of the English Civil War in 1651.

Acts of Trade and Navigation England's government implemented a mercantilist policy with a series of **Navigation Acts** between 1650 and 1673, which established three rules for colonial trade:

- Trade to and from the colonies could be carried only by English or colonial-built ships, operated only by English or colonial crews.

- All goods imported into the colonies, except for some perishables, had to pass through ports in England.

- Specified or "enumerated" goods from the colonies could be exported to England only. Tobacco was the original "enumerated" good, but over the years, the list was greatly expanded.

Impact on the Colonies The Navigation Acts had mixed effects on the colonies. The acts aided New England shipbuilding, provided Chesapeake tobacco a monopoly in England, and provided English military forces to protect the colonies from any attacks by the French and Spanish. The triangular slave trade that connected the colonies and Africa was largely unaffected by increased regulations.

However, the acts also severely limited the development of the colonial economy. Since colonists could not manufacture their own goods, they had to pay high prices for manufactured goods from England. Since Chesapeake farmers could sell their crops only to England, they had to accept low prices for their crops. For example, in the 1660s, low tobacco prices that resulted from high production brought hard times to the Chesapeake colonies, Maryland and Virginia. When Virginia's House of Burgesses tried to raise tobacco prices, the merchants of London retaliated by raising their prices on goods exported to Virginia.

Besides trading with Great Britain, colonists also continued to trade with American Indians for furs, food, and other goods. This created ongoing contact between settlers and the indigenous population, leading to cultural exchanges, particularly along the western frontier of the colonies. For example, some Indians adopted Christianity and some colonial men married Indian women. While intermarriage was uncommon, the resulting couple almost always lived in the Indian rather than the settler community. The famous marriage between Pocahontas and John Rolfe in Virginia was a rare exception of an Indian-settler couple who lived in Jamestown.

Enforcement of the Acts While the theory of **mercantilism** called for strict enforcement of trade regulations, the practice was quite different. England was normally very lax in enforcing regulations, a policy known as **salutary neglect.** Several factors made enforcement difficult:

- The Atlantic Ocean separated the British government from the colonies, so exerting any authority from London over its distant possessions was challenging.

- England faced larger problems than regulating trade. Between 1642 and 1763, it was in constant turmoil. It went through the English Civil War, a revolution that replaced the monarch, and four wars with France.

- Britain's colonial agents were often corrupt. As a result, colonial merchants could evade regulations easily with well-placed bribes to those in charge of enforcing regulations.

In retrospect, regulation might not have been necessary. Because of their close economic and cultural ties, England and its colonies were natural trading partners. The colonies had abundant natural resources that they probably would have sold mostly to the English with or without regulation.

The Dominion of New England

Occasionally, though, the crown would attempt to overcome resistance to its trade laws. In 1684, it revoked the charter of Massachusetts Bay because it had been the center of smuggling activity. Whatever economic advantages this and other efforts brought England were offset by their harm to English-colonial relations. Colonists resented the regulatory laws imposed by the government in London. Especially in New England, colonists defied the acts by smuggling goods from other countries.

A New King A new king, James II, succeeded to the throne in 1685. He was determined to increase royal control over the colonies by combining them into larger administrative units and doing away with representative assemblies. In 1686, he combined New York, New Jersey, and the various New England colonies into the **Dominion of New England**. **Sir Edmund Andros** was sent from England to serve as governor of the dominion. The new governor made himself instantly unpopular by levying taxes, limiting town meetings, and revoking land titles.

Overthrow of the King James II did not remain in power for long as his attempts at asserting his powers led to an uprising. The **Glorious Revolution** of 1688 succeeded in deposing James and replacing him with William and Mary. James's fall from power brought the Dominion of New England to an end, and the colonies again operated under separate charters.

Ongoing Trade Tensions

After the Glorious Revolution, mercantilist policies remained in force, but the efforts to enforce them were never sustained enough to be effective. Until 1763, salutary neglect and colonial resistance to regulation continued. Regulation of trade, while not the only source of friction, would remain the fundamental problem between the colonists and England.

REFLECT ON THE LEARNING OBJECTIVE

1. Explain what brought about transatlantic trade and what its long-term impact was.

KEY TERMS BY THEME

Royal Authority (WOR)   Dominion of New England
triangular trade   Sir Edmund Andros
mercantilism   Glorious Revolution
Navigation Acts

MULTIPLE-CHOICE QUESTIONS

Questions 1–2 refer to the following excerpt.

> "Whereas the welfare and prosperity of Your Majesty's sugar colonies in America are of the greatest consequence and importance to trade, navigation, and strength of this Kingdom. . . .
>
> There shall be raised, levied, collected, and paid into and for the use of His Majesty, His Heirs, and Successors upon all rum or spirits of produce or manufacture of any colonies or plantations in America, not in the possession or under the dominion of His Majesty . . . which at any time or times within or during the continuance of this act shall be imported or brought into any of the colonies or plantations in America . . . the sum of 9d [9 pennies]."

Molasses Act of 1733

1. The intentions of the English government in passing the Molasses Act were most similar to the intentions motivating which of the following?

    (A) Theocratic laws passed by the Puritan leaders of New England

    (B) Ordinances passed by Virginia's governors during the 17th century

    (C) Regulations imposed by the Dominion of New England

    (D) Actions by colonial customs officials during the period of salutary neglect

2. The immediate response to the action described in the excerpt was most likely an increase in

    (A) sugar production in France's colonies in the West Indies

    (B) rum production in Spain's colonies in the West Indies

    (C) smuggling by New England merchants

    (D) trade between England and its colonies

SHORT-ANSWER QUESTION

1. Answer (a), (b), and (c).

    (a) Briefly describe ONE specific historical benefit the colonies received under British mercantilism in the period from 1607 to 1754.

    (b) Briefly describe ONE specific historical disadvantage the colonies had under British mercantilism in the period from 1607 to 1754.

    (c) Briefly describe ONE specific historical action the colonies took in response to British mercantilism in the period from 1607 to 1754.

Interactions Between American Indians and Europeans

Fifty-six years after the sailing of the Mayflower, the Pilgrims' children had not only defeated the Pokanokets . . . they had taken conscious, methodical measures to purge the land of its people.

Nathaniel Philbrick, *Mayflower: A Story of Courage, Community, and War*, 2006

Learning Objective: Explain how and why interactions between various European nations and American Indians changed over time.

From the very beginning Europeans saw each other as rivals for power in the Americas. In general, they viewed American Indians as inferior people who could be used as forced labors or pushed off their land, but also as potential allies in conflicts with other Europeans or other American Indians.

In response, Native Americans who survived the devastation of European diseases defended themselves and their cultures. Sometimes various tribes joined together to resist Europeans. Other times, a particular tribe allied with one group of Europeans to fight another or to fight against a traditional tribal rival. For example, in 1626 in southern New York, the Mahican Indians persuaded Dutch settlers to join in an attack on the Mohawk Indians.

Conflict in New England

In the 1640s, the New England colonies faced the constant threat of attack from American Indians, the Dutch, and the French. With England in the midst of a civil war, the colonists expected little assistance.

New England Confederation In 1643, four New England colonies (Plymouth, Massachusetts Bay, Connecticut, and New Haven) organized for their mutual protection. They formed a military alliance known as the **New England Confederation**. The confederation was directed by a board composed of two representatives from each colony. It had limited powers to act on boundary disputes, the return of runaway servants, and dealings with American Indians.

The confederation lasted until 1684, when colonial rivalries and renewed control by the English monarch brought this first experiment in colonial cooperation to an end. Though it lasted only four decades, it established an important precedent for colonies taking unified action for a common purpose.

Metacom's War (King Philip's War) Only a few years before the confederation's demise, it helped the New England colonists win a vicious war. In response to English settlers encroaching on the American Indians' lands, a chief of the **Wampanoag, Metacom**, known to the colonists as King Philip, united many tribes in southern New England. Some tribes, such as the Mohegans and the Pequots, supported the colonists because of their long-standing rivalry with the Wampanoag. The resulting conflict was called Metacom's War (1675–1676). In it, several villages were burned to the ground, hundreds of people were killed, and thousands of people were injured. Eventually, the colonial forces and their Indian allies prevailed, killing Metacom and ending most American Indian resistance in New England.

Conflict in Virginia

Sir William Berkeley, the royal governor of Virginia (1641–1652; 1660–1677), used dictatorial powers to govern on behalf of the large planters. He antagonized small farmers on Virginia's western frontier because he failed to protect them from Indian attacks.

Bacon's Rebellion Nathaniel Bacon, an impoverished gentleman farmer, seized upon the grievances of the western farmers to lead a rebellion against Berkeley's government. Bacon and others resented the control exercised by a few large planters in the Chesapeake area. He raised an army of volunteers and, in 1676, conducted a series of raids and massacres against American Indian villages on the frontier, including some who had friendly relationships with the colonial government. Berkeley's government in Jamestown accused Bacon of rebelling against royal authority. Bacon's army defeated the governor's forces and burned the Jamestown settlement. Soon afterward, Bacon died of dysentery, and the rebel army collapsed. Governor Berkeley suppressed the remnants of the insurrection, executing 23 rebels.

This drawing of Bacon (center, left) confronting Berkeley (center, right) was created for a history textbook written in 1895.
Source: Susan Pendleton Lee, *A School History of the United States* (1895). Wikimedia.org.

Lasting Problems Though it was short-lived, Bacon's Rebellion, or the Chesapeake Revolution, highlighted long-lasting disputes in Virginia and most of the colonies:

- sharp class differences between the wealthy and landless or poor farmers
- conflict on the frontiers between settlers and American Indians
- colonial resistance to royal control

These problems would continue into the next century, even after conditions in the Chesapeake and other colonies became more stable and prosperous.

Spanish Rule and the Pueblo Revolt

Spain's economic policy for its colonies was based on forcing Native Americans to labor for them through the encomienda system (see Topic 1.5). In religion, Spain's Roman Catholic missionaries followed an aggressive, sometimes harsh, program to convert Native Americans to Christianity. The pressure of these efforts led to the Pueblo Revolt of 1680. Various tribes of Pueblo Indians, including the Hopi and Zuni, united against the Spanish. Hundreds of people died in the fighting, and the Spanish were driven from the area until 1692. However, after the Spanish regained control in 1692, they made some accommodations to the American Indians in the region. By ruling less harshly, the Spanish found greater stability.

REFLECT ON THE LEARNING OBJECTIVE

1. Explain the nature of the relationship between the Europeans and Native Americans and the reasons it evolved over time.

KEY TERMS BY THEME

Conflict (MIG)	Authority (PCE)
Wampanoag	Sir William Berkeley
Metacom	Bacon's Rebellion
King Philip's War	New England Confederation

Questions 1–3 refer to the following excerpt.

"These at the heads of James and York rivers . . . grew impatient at the many slaughters of their neighbors and rose for own defense, who choosing Mr. Bacon for their leader, sent oftentimes to the Governor, . . . beseeching a commission to go against the Indians at their own charge; which His Honor as often promised, but did not send. . . .

During these protractions and people often slain, most or all the officers, civil and military, . . . met and concerted together, the danger of going without a commission on the one part and the continual murders of their neighbors on the other part. . . . This day lapsing and no commission come, they marched into the wilderness in quest of these Indians, after whom the Governor sent his proclamation, denouncing all rebels who should not return within a limited day; whereupon those of estates obeyed. But Mr. Bacon, with fifty-seven men, proceeded. . . . They fired and . . . slew 150 Indians."

Samuel Kercheval, Virginia lawyer,
"On Bacon's Rebellion in Virginia," 1833

1. Based on this excerpt, what is Samuel Kercheval's perspective toward Bacon and his followers?
   (A) They were dangerous men who threatened colonial stability and prosperity.
   (B) They were frustrated men who were taking action because the government did not.
   (C) They were allies of the governor who carried out actions that he supported.
   (D) They were a primarily political movement that wanted Bacon to become governor.

2. Bacon's Rebellion was initiated by a group of farmers who felt most directly threatened by
   (A) an increase in royal taxes
   (B) the power of large planters
   (C) conflicts with American Indians
   (D) the growth of the slave trade

3. Which of the following groups led the opposition to Bacon's Rebellion?

(A) The British Army

(B) The House of Burgesses

(C) The governor of Virginia

(D) The leaders of the Church of England

SHORT-ANSWER QUESTION

Use complete sentences; an outline or bulleted list alone is not acceptable.

1. "As to the natives of this country, I find them entirely savage and wild, strangers to all decency, yea, uncivil and stupid as garden stakes, proficient in all wickedness and ungodliness, devilish men who serve nobody but the devil. . . . They have so much witchcraft, divination, sorcery, and wicked arts that they can hardly be held in by any bands or locks. They are as thievish and treacherous as they are tall, and in cruelty they are altogether inhuman."

> Jonas Michaelius, pastor, Dutch Reformed Church,
> Letter to Reverend Andrianus Smoutius, 1628

"I confess I think no great good will be done till they [Indians] be more civilized. But why may not God begin with some few to awaken others by degrees? Nor do I expect any great good will be wrought by the English . . . because God is wont ordinarily to convert nations and peoples by some of their own countrymen who are nearest to them and can best speak, and, most of all, pity their brethren."

> John Eliot, Puritan, "The Day-Breaking
> of the Gospel with the Indians," 1646

Using the excerpts above, answer (a), (b), and (c).

(a) Briefly describe ONE major difference between Michaelius's and Eliot's views of the Native Americans.

(b) Briefly describe how ONE historical event or development in the period from 1607 to 1754 that is not explicitly mentioned in the excerpts could be used to support Michaelius's interpretation.

(c) Briefly explain how ONE historical event or development in the period from 1607 to 1754 that is not explicitly mentioned in the excerpts could be used to support Eliot's interpretation.

Topic 2.6

Slavery in the British Colonies

In every human Breast, God has implanted a Principle,
which we call Love of Freedom.

Phillis Wheatley, "A Principle Which We Call Love of Freedom," 1774

Learning Objective 1: Explain the causes and effects of slavery in the various British colonial regions.

Learning Objective 2: Explain how enslaved people responded to slavery.

With the colonial emphasis on agriculture came a demand for labor. Since the Native Americans could escape too easily and the supply of indentured servants was too small, landowners looked for another source of workers. They turned to the labor of enslaved Africans, especially in the southern colonies. The transatlantic slave trade (see Topic 2.4) was important to the economy, and much of the trade was financed or conducted by people in the northern colonies.

Demand for Labor

In Maryland and Virginia, landowners saw great opportunities for profit because of the European demand for tobacco. They could get land by taking it or trading for it from the American Indians. But they could not find enough laborers willing to work for low wages. The high death rate from disease, food shortages, and battles with American Indians meant that the population of colonists grew slowly. Landowners tried several ways to find the workers they wanted.

Indentured Servants The early colonists of the Virginia Company were struggling to survive and too poor to purchase enslaved Africans as the owners of sugar plantations in the West Indies did. Instead, the Virginia Company hoped to meet the desire for labor using indentured servants. Under contract with a master or landowner who paid for their passage, those from the British Isles agreed to work for a specified period—usually four to seven years—in return for room and board. Indentured servants were under the absolute rule of their masters until the end of their work period. At the end of that period, they gained their freedom and could work for wages or obtain land of their own. For landowners, the system provided laborers, but only temporarily.

Headright System Virginia attempted to attract immigrants through offers of land. It offered 50 acres of land to each immigrant who paid for his own passage and to any plantation owner who paid for an immigrant's passage.

The Institution of Slavery

In 1619, an English ship serving the Dutch government sold an unusual group of about 25 **indentured servants** to Virginia: the servants were Black Africans. These first Africans in Virginia were not in life bondage, and children born to them were free. However, this soon changed. By the end of the 1660s, the Virginia House of Burgesses enacted laws that kept Africans and their offspring in permanent bondage. They were enslaved.

By the early 18th century, the number of enslaved people and laws to control them had greatly expanded. All British colonies included at least some enslaved laborers. The fewest were in New England, where small farmers had little demand for additional workers. More were in the Middle Colonies, particularly in the port cities, where African Americans often worked loading and unloading ships and as sailors. Most were in the southern colonies, working on plantations. By 1750, half of Virginia's population and two-thirds of South Carolina's population were enslaved.

The British colonies with the highest number of enslaved people were the West Indian sugar islands. During the course of American **slavery**, about 95 percent of enslaved Africans were delivered to the West Indies or Brazil. Less than 5 percent went to the British colonies in North America.

Increased Demand for Enslaved Africans Several factors explain why slavery became increasingly important, especially in the southern colonies:

- *Reduced migration:* Increases in wages in England reduced the supply of immigrants to the colonies.

- *Dependable workforce:* Large plantation owners were disturbed by the political demands of small farmers and indentured servants and by the disorders of Bacon's Rebellion (see Topic 2.5). They thought that slavery would provide a stable labor force totally under their control.

- *Low-cost labor:* As tobacco prices fell (see Topic 2.4), rice and indigo became the most profitable crops. To grow such crops required a large land area and many inexpensive, relatively unskilled field hands.

This increased demand also supported the active, profitable, and ruthless triangular trade (see Topic 2.4).

Slave Laws As the number of enslaved workers increased, White colonists adopted laws to ensure that they would be held in bondage for life and that slave status would be inherited. In 1641, Massachusetts became the first colony to recognize the enslavement of "lawful" captives. Virginia in 1661 enacted legislation that children automatically inherited their mother's enslaved status for life. By 1664, the English law that people baptized as Christians could not be enslaved was being overturned. Maryland declared that baptism did not affect the enslaved person's status and that White women could not marry African American men. As slavery became common, Whites began to regard all Blacks as inferior. Racism and slavery evolved into integral parts of colonial society.

Resistance to Slavery Although very difficult, many Africans challenged enslavement. They struggled to maintain family ties, even though slaveowners could break up a family by selling off a husband or a wife or a child at any time. Even as many adopted Christianity, they kept elements of the African religious practices they had brought with them. They used songs and storytelling to maintain traditions and customs. They resisted slavery through direct action such as going on hunger strikes, breaking tools, refusing to work, or fleeing—even if they knew they would likely be caught and punished harshly. The owners' concern over slave resistance was reflected over the years in the enactment of new laws to control them.

REFLECT ON THE LEARNING OBJECTIVE

1. Explain the reasons for slavery in the various British colonies and its impact on them.

KEY TERMS BY THEME

| **Labor (WXT)** | headright system | Middle Passage |
| indentured servants | slavery | |

MULTIPLE-CHOICE QUESTIONS

Questions 1–2 refer to the following excerpt.

"These are the reasons we are against the traffic of mens-body. . . . Now, though they are black, we cannot conceive there is more liberty to have them slaves as it is to have other white ones [slaves]. There is a saying that we shall do to all men like as we will be done ourselves, making no difference of what generation, descent, or color they are. And those who steal or rob men, and those who buy or purchase them, are they not alike. . . .

In Europe there are many oppressed for conscience sake; and here there are those oppressed which are of a black color . . . This makes an ill report in all those countries of Europe, where they hear of that the Quakers do here handle men like they handle there the cattle. And for that reason some have no mind or Inclination to come hither."

Mennonite Community, Germantown, Pennsylvania, 1688

1. The most direct cause of the practice objected to in the source was that
   (A) landowners wanted more workers than were arriving from Europe
   (B) investors thought English settlers were unwilling to work hard
   (C) settlers wanted Africans to come to Virginia to learn Christianity
   (D) colonists from European spoke too many different languages

2. Which of the following reasons does the excerpt suggest best explains why the group took the stance it did?
   (A) They were defending their economic interests.
   (B) They were opposed to increasing the colony's population.
   (C) They felt that the colony should accept only settlers from England.
   (D) They were motivated by their religion beliefs.

SHORT-ANSWER QUESTION

Use complete sentences; an outline or bulleted list alone is not acceptable.

1.

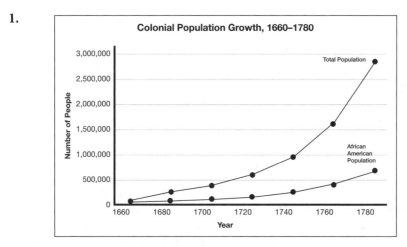

Colonial Population Growth, 1660–1780

Source: U.S. Bureau of the Census.
Historical Statistics of the United States, Colonial Times to 1970

Using the graph above, answer (a), (b), and (c).

(a) Briefly explain ONE specific historical development or circumstance between 1660 and 1780 that led to the changes in the African American population as depicted in the graph.

(b) Briefly explain ONE specific effort made by the British authorities during the 17th and early 18th centuries to increase the population levels as depicted in the graph.

(c) Briefly explain ONE specific cause for the periodic shortages of labor in the colonies during the period between 1660 and 1780.

Topic 2.7

Colonial Society and Culture

I assert that nothing ever comes to pass without a cause.

Jonathan Edwards, *The Freedom of Will*, 1754

Learning Objective 1: Explain how and why the movement of a variety of people and ideas across the Atlantic contributed to the development of American culture over time.

Learning Objective 2: Explain how and why the different goals and interests of European leaders and colonists affected how they viewed themselves and their relationship with Britain.

The struggling English colonial villages at the start of the 17th century evolved by the middle of the 18th century to develop a culture distinct from any in Europe. If Americans in the 18th century constituted a new kind of society, what were its characteristics and what forces shaped its "new people"?

Population Growth

In 1701, the English colonies on the Atlantic coast consisted of barely 250,000 Europeans and Africans. By 1775, the population was 2,500,000 people. Among African Americans, the increase was more dramatic: from about 28,000 in 1701 to 500,000 in 1775. The spectacular gains in population resulted from two factors: immigration of almost 1 million people and a sharp natural increase, caused by a high birthrate among colonial families. An abundance of fertile land and a dependable food supply attracted thousands of Europeans and supported the raising of large families.

European Immigrants

Newcomers to the British colonies came not only from England, Scotland, Wales, and Ireland, but also from western and central Europe. Many **immigrants**, most of whom were Protestants, came from the kingdom of France and various German-speaking states. Many were fleeing religious persecution and wars, while others were searching for economic opportunity as farmers, artisans, or merchants. Most immigrants settled in the middle colonies (Pennsylvania, New York, New Jersey, Maryland, and Delaware) and on the western frontier of the southern colonies (Virginia, the Carolinas, and Georgia). Few headed for New England where land was limited and Puritans dominated.

English Settlers from England continued to come to the American colonies. However, with fewer problems at home, their numbers were relatively small.

Germans This group settled chiefly on the farmlands west of Philadelphia, an area that became known as Pennsylvania Dutch country. They maintained their German language, customs, and religious beliefs as Lutherans, Amish, Brethren, or Mennonites. They obeyed colonial laws but took little interest in English politics. By 1775, people of German stock comprised 6 percent of the colonial population.

Scotch-Irish These English-speaking people were Protestants who came from northern Ireland. Their ancestors had moved to Ireland from Scotland, and they were known as the Scotch-Irish or Scots-Irish. They had little respect for the British, who had pressured them to leave Ireland. Most settled along the frontier in western Pennsylvania, Virginia, the Carolinas, and Georgia. By 1775, they comprised 7 percent of the population.

Other Europeans Other groups included French Protestants (known as **Huguenots**), the **Dutch**, and the **Swedes**. These groups made up 5 percent of the population.

Enslaved Africans

The largest single group of people entering the English colonies did not come to America by choice. They were **Africans** who had been taken captive, forced onto European ships, and sold as enslaved laborers. They worked a range of occupations, such as laborer, bricklayer, or blacksmith, but the most common work was as field laborers on plantations. By 1775, African Americans (enslaved and free) made up 20 percent of the colonial population. Most lived in the southern colonies, and enslaved people formed a majority of the population in South Carolina and Georgia.

A few Africans obtained their freedom. They were either emancipated by their owner or allowed to work for money and to purchase their freedom. However, every colony passed laws that discriminated against African Americans.

American Indians

Colonial population growth created conflicts between settlers and American Indians already living in a region. Some American Indians formed alliances to protect their land, such as the Powhaten Confederation in Virginia and the Iroquois Confederation in the Great Lakes region. Others used European settlers as allies in their conflicts with rival tribes. Among the most peaceful relations between American Indians and settlers were those in Pennsylvania. William Penn often obtained land through treaties rather than violence.

This frieze showing William Penn signing a treaty with the Delaware Indians in 1683 appears on a wall in the U.S. Capitol.
Source: Architect of the Capitol. Wikimedia.org.

The Structure of Colonial Society

Each of the 13 British colonies developed distinct patterns of life. However, they all also shared a number of characteristics. For example, most of the population was English in origin, language, and tradition. In all colonies, both Africans and non-English immigrants brought diverse influences that modified the culture of the majority in significant ways.

Liberty and Opportunity

The colonies also offered people more self-determination than they found in Europe. This was evident in both religion and the economy.

Religious Toleration All of the colonies permitted the practice of different religions, but with varying degrees of freedom. Massachusetts, the most restrictive, accepted several types of Protestants, but it excluded Roman Catholics and all non-Christians. Rhode Island and Pennsylvania were the most open. Pennsylvania accepted all who believed in God, including Jews. However, only Christians could participate in government.

No Hereditary Aristocracy The extremes of Europe, with very wealthy nobility and masses of hungry poor, were missing in the colonies. A narrower class system, based on economics, was developing. Wealthy landowners were at the top; craft workers and small farmers made up the majority of people.

Social Mobility In all colonies, White residents had an opportunity to improve their standard of living and status by hard work. Acquiring land was much easier than in Europe.

The Family

The family was the center of colonial life. With an expanding economy and ample food supply, people married younger and reared more children than in Europe. More than 90 percent of the people lived on farms. While life was hard, most colonists had a higher standard of living than did most Europeans.

Men Besides working as farmers or artisans, men could own property and participate in politics. The law gave the husband almost unlimited power in the home, including the right to beat his wife.

Women A colonial woman bore an average of eight children, many of whom would die at birth or in infancy. She performed multiple tasks including cooking, cleaning, making clothes, providing medical care, and educating children. She often worked next to her husband in the shop, on the plantation, or on the farm. Divorce was legal but rare, and women had limited legal and political rights. Yet the shared labors and mutual dependence with their husbands gave most women protection from abuse and an active role in decision making.

The Economy

By the 1750s, half of Britain's world trade was with its American colonies. The government limited colonial manufacturing, such as making textiles. The rich American land and British mercantilist policy produced colonies almost entirely engaged in agriculture, forestry, and fishing.

As communities grew, more people became ministers, lawyers, doctors, and teachers. The quickest route to wealth was land, although regional geography often provided distinct opportunities for hardworking colonists.

New England Rocky soil and long winters limited most people to **subsistence farming**, producing just enough for the family. Most farms were small—less than 100 acres—and work was done by family and an occasional hired laborer. The descendants of the Puritans profited from logging, shipbuilding, fishing, trading, and rum-distilling.

Middle Colonies Rich soil produced an abundance of wheat and corn for export to Europe and the West Indies. Farms of up to 200 acres were common. Often indentured servants and hired laborers worked with the farm families. A variety of small manufacturing efforts developed, including iron-making. Trading led to the growth of cities such as Philadelphia and New York. In 1750, Philadelphia was the largest city in the colonies, with a population of about 25,000 people.

Southern Colonies Because of the diverse geography and climate in these colonies, agriculture varied greatly. Most people lived on small subsistence family farms without slaves. A few lived on large plantations of more than 2,000 acres relying on slave labor. Colonial plantations were self-sufficient, growing their own food and using enslaved craftworkers. Products were tobacco in the Chesapeake and North Carolina colonies, timber and naval stores (tar and pitch) in the Carolinas, and rice and indigo in South Carolina and Georgia. Most plantations were located on rivers so they could ship exports to Europe.

Monetary System One way the British controlled the colonial economy was to limit the use of money. These limits forced colonies to use their limited gold and silver to pay for British imports that exceeded the value of colonial exports. To provide currency for domestic trade, many colonies issued paper money. However, they often issued too much money, causing it to decline in value, a process called inflation. The British government also claimed the right to veto any colonial laws that might harm British merchants.

Transportation Transporting goods by water was easier than over land on poor roads. Trading centers such as Boston, New York, Philadelphia, and Charleston were located on the sites of good harbors and navigable rivers. Gradually overland travel by horse and stagecoach became more common in the 18th century. Taverns provided food and lodging for travelers and served as social centers where people exchanged news and discussed politics. By the mid-18th century, the colonies ran a postal system using horses and small ships.

Religion

Most colonists were Protestants, but each region had some religious diversity:

- In New England, most people were Congregationalists (Puritans) or Presbyterians.
- In New York, people of Dutch descent often attended the Reformed Church. Most others belonged to the Church of England and were known as Anglicans (and later, Episcopalians).
- In Pennsylvania, Lutherans, Mennonites, and Quakers were common.
- In Virginia and other southern colonies, Anglicans were dominant. Maryland included many Catholics and some Jews.

Challenges Each religious group, even the Protestants who dominated, faced problems. Jews, Catholics, and Quakers suffered from intense discrimination. Congregationalist ministers were criticized as domineering. Many people resented the Church of England and saw it as a symbol of English control because it was headed by the king.

Established Churches In the 17th century, most colonial governments taxed the people to support a particular Protestant denomination, an **established church**. As various immigrants increased the religious diversity, governments gradually reduced their support of churches. However, some direct tax support of some New England churches remained until the 1830s.

The Great Awakening

By the early 18th century, sermons in Protestant churches tended to portray God as the creator of a perfect universe. Ministers gave less emphasis than their ancestors to human sinfulness and damnation. In the 1730s and 1740s, however, a dramatic change swept the colonies. This was the **Great Awakening**, a movement of fervent expressions of religious feeling among the masses.

Jonathan Edwards Among the best-known leaders of the Great Awakening was a Congregational minister from Massachusetts, Reverend **Jonathan Edwards**. When he first gave his sermon "Sinners in the Hands of an Angry God" to his own congregation, it excited little emotion. However, as he traveled and delivered it elsewhere it generated a fervent response. Invoking the vivid language of the Old Testament, Edwards presented a God that was angry with human sinfulness. Individuals who deeply repented would be saved, but those who ignored God's commandments would suffer eternal damnation.

George Whitefield Beginning in 1739, **George Whitefield** spread the Great Awakening throughout the colonies, attracting audiences of 10,000 people. In barns, tents, and fields, he stressed that God was all-powerful and would save only those who openly professed belief in Jesus Christ. Those who did not would be damned to hell. Whitefield taught that ordinary people with faith and sincerity could understand the gospels without ministers to lead them.

Religious Impact The Great Awakening had a profound effect on religious practice. As sinners confessed their guilt and then joyously exulted in accepting salvation, emotionalism became more common in Protestant services. This caused splits in some denominations, such as the Congregationalists and Presbyterians, between supporters ("New Lights") and opponents ("Old Lights") of the new expressiveness of feeling. As people studied the Bible in their homes, ministers lost some authority over them. As a consequence, evangelical sects such as the Baptists and Methodists that often relied on traveling ministers attracted large numbers of new members. As the Great Awakening spread, new denominations challenged the Congregationalists and Anglicans. One result was that people called for stricter separation of church and state.

Political Influence The Great Awakening was one of the first common experiences shared by colonists as Americans. It had a democratizing effect by changing the way people viewed authority. If people made their own religious decisions without the "higher" authority of ministers, then could they also make their own political decisions without deferring to others? This revolutionary idea was not expressed in the 1740s, but 30 years later it would challenge the authority of a king and his royal governors.

Cultural Life

In the early 1600s, the chief concern of most colonists was survival. However, 100 years later, the colonial population had grown enough that the arts could flourish, at least among the well-to-do southern planters and northern merchants.

Achievements in the Arts and Sciences

In the coastal areas, as fear of American Indians faded, people displayed their prosperity by adopting architectural and decorative styles from England.

Architecture The Georgian style of London was widely imitated in houses, churches, and public buildings. Brick and stucco homes were built in this style along the eastern seaboard. On the frontier, a one-room log cabin was the common shelter.

Painting Many colonial painters were itinerant artists who traveled the country in search of families who wanted their portraits painted. Shortly before the Revolution, two American artists, **Benjamin West** and **John Copley**, went to England where they established themselves as prominent artists.

Literature With only a few printing facilities available, most authors wrote on serious subjects, chiefly religion and politics in the 18th century. These authors included **Cotton Mather** and Jonathan Edwards on religion. Political writings highlighting the conflict between American rights and English authority came from John Adams, James Otis, John Dickinson, Thomas Paine, and Thomas Jefferson, among others. The most popular writer was **Benjamin Franklin**. His witty aphorisms and advice were collected in *Poor Richard's Almanack,* a best-selling book that was annually revised from 1732 to 1757.

The lack of support for fiction and poetry did not stop everyone. **Phillis Wheatley** was born in West Africa, enslaved, and living in Boston when she published a collection of her poems in 1773. She was freed soon after this. Her work is noteworthy both for her triumph over slavery and the quality of her verse. Charles Brockden Brown, a Quaker who was born in Philadelphia in 1771, was one of the first novelists to set his stories in North America.

Science Most scientists, such as the botanist **John Bartram** of Philadelphia, were self-taught. Benjamin Franklin won fame for his work with electricity and his developments of bifocal eyeglasses and the Franklin stove.

Education

Basic education was limited and varied among the colonies. Formal efforts were directed to males, since females were trained only for household work.

Elementary Education In New England, the Puritans' emphasis on reading the Bible led them to create the first tax-supported schools. A Massachusetts law in 1647 required towns to establish primary schools for boys. In the middle colonies, schools were either church-sponsored or private. In the southern colonies, parents gave their children whatever education they could. On plantations, tutors provided instruction for the owners' children.

Higher Education The first colonial colleges were **sectarian**, promoting the doctrines of a particular religious group. The Puritans founded Harvard in 1636 to prepare ministers. The Anglicans opened William and Mary in Virginia in 1694, and the Congregationalists started Yale in Connecticut in 1701. During this period the only **nonsectarian** college founded was the College of Philadelphia. Founded in 1765, it later became the University of Pennsylvania. Benjamin Franklin was among its founders.

Ministry During the 17th century, the Christian ministry was the only profession to enjoy widespread respect among the common people. Ministers were often the only well-educated people in a small community.

Physicians Colonists who fell prey to epidemics of smallpox and diphtheria were often treated by "cures" that only made them worse. A doctor's training was as an apprentice to an experienced physician. The first medical college was begun in 1765 as part of Franklin's idea for the College of Philadelphia.

Lawyers During the 1700s, as trade expanded and legal problems became more complex, people felt a need for expert assistance in court. The most able lawyers formed a bar (committee or board), which set rules and standards for young lawyers. **Lawyers** gained respect in the 1760s and 1770s when they argued for colonial rights. John Adams, James Otis, and Patrick Henry were lawyers whose legal arguments would ultimately provide the intellectual underpinnings of the American Revolution.

The Press

News spread mainly through a postal system and local printing firms.

Newspapers By 1776, there were more than 40 newspapers issued weekly in the colonies. They provided month-old news from Europe, various ads for goods and services and for the return of runaway indentured servants and enslaved people, and pious essays giving advice for better living.

The Zenger Case Newspaper printers in colonial days ran the risk of being jailed for libel if any article offended the authorities. English common law at the time stated that it was a crime to criticize the governor, no matter whether the criticism was true or false. In 1735, **John Peter Zenger**, a New York publisher, was tried on a charge of libelously criticizing New York's royal governor. Zenger's lawyer, **Andrew Hamilton**, argued that his client had printed the truth. Ignoring the law, the jury acquitted Zenger. While this case did not guarantee freedom of the press, it encouraged newspapers to criticize the government.

The Enlightenment

In the 18th century, some educated Americans felt attracted to a European movement in literature and philosophy known as the **Enlightenment**. The leaders of this movement believed that the recent past was a "dark" era in which people relied too much on tradition and God's intervention in human life. They believed that the "light" of reason could solve most of humanity's problems.

A major influence on the Enlightenment and American thinking was John Locke, a 17th-century English philosopher. Locke, in his *Two Treatises of Government,* reasoned that while the state (the government) is supreme, it is bound to follow "natural laws" based on the rights that people have simply because they are human. He argued that sovereignty ultimately resides with the people rather than with the state. Furthermore, citizens had a right and obligation to revolt against a government that failed to protect their rights. Other Enlightenment philosophers adopted and expounded on Locke's ideas. His stress on natural rights would provide a rationale for the American Revolution and the principles of the U.S. Constitution.

The Colonial Relationship with Britain

For all their diversity, in some ways, the colonies were becoming more like England. They built on English political traditions to develop self-governing local communities. Most colonists spoke English and could read the books and newspapers in the colonies. Many had commercial ties with England, either exporting tobacco or importing manufactured goods. Most colonists, including Puritans, Quakers, and Anglicans, were connected to England by religion.

Colonial Identity At the same time, the colonists were developing a distinctly American viewpoint and way of life. Their motivations for leaving Europe, the English political heritage, the diverse mixture of people, the emergence of writers and painters, and the influence of the American natural environment combined to create a culture unlike any in Europe. The colonists —especially White male property owners—exercised the rights of free speech and a free press, became accustomed to electing representatives to colonial assemblies, and tolerated a variety of religions. Observers were beginning to think of Americans as restless, enterprising, practical, and forever seeking to improve their circumstances.

Mistrust of the British Development of a colonial identity reflected diverging interests between the colonies and Great Britain. Colonists were eager to push westward, while the British desired peace on the frontier with American Indians. Colonists were comfortable with salutary neglect, while the British sometimes tried to enforce trade regulations. Colonists took pride in governing themselves according to English traditions of liberty, while the British claimed sovereignty over them as part of the empire. Finally, colonies were more ethnically and religiously diverse than England, which meant that many colonists did not identify from birth with the country that ruled them. These differences would become stronger after 1763.

Politics and Government

By 1750, the colonies had similar systems of government, with a **governor** as chief executive and a **legislature** voting to adopt or reject the governor's proposed laws. In every colony, the legislature consisted of two houses:

- Members of the lower house, or assembly, were elected by White male property owners. It voted for or against new taxes. Colonists thus became accustomed to paying taxes only if their chosen representatives approved.

- Members of the upper house in the two self-governing colonies were also elected. In the other colonies, members were appointed by the king or the proprietor, and were also known as the council.

- Governors were either appointed by the crown, elected by the people (Rhode Island and Connecticut), or appointed by a proprietor (Pennsylvania and Maryland).

Local Government Colonists in New England established towns and villages. In these, the local government was the town meeting in which people would regularly come together to vote directly on public issues. In the southern colonies, where farms and plantations were more widely separated, towns were less common. Local government was carried on by a law-enforcing sheriff and other officials who served a large territory called a *county*.

Voting If democracy is defined as the participation of all people in the making of government policy, then colonial democracy was limited. Laws barred most people—White women, poor White men, slaves of both sexes, and most free Blacks—from voting. Nevertheless, the government was beginning to remove some barriers to voting in the 18th century. In particular, religious restrictions were declining. Property qualifications often remained.

Another variable in the development of democracy was who could serve in the assemblies and councils. In Virginia, the House of Burgesses was restricted to a small group of wealthy landowners. However, in Massachusetts, the legislature was open to small farmers. Even there, the educated, propertied elite held power for generations. The common people everywhere tended to defer to their "betters" and depend upon the privileged few to make decisions.

Political life in the colonies was restricted to landowning White males only. Yet, compared with Europe, the English colonies allowed greater self-government. This made the colonial political system unusual for its time.

HISTORICAL PERSPECTIVES: *WAS COLONIAL SOCIETY DEMOCRATIC?*

Was colonial America "democratic" or not? The question is important for its own sake and also because it affects one's perspective on the American Revolution and on the subsequent evolution of democratic politics in the United States.

Democracy in Action Many historians have focused on the politics of colonial Massachusetts. Some have concluded that colonial Massachusetts was indeed democratic, at least for the times. By studying voting records and statistics, they determined that the vast majority of White male citizens could vote and were not restricted by property qualifications. According to these historians, class differences between the elite and the masses of people did not prevent the latter from participating fully in colonial politics.

Consensus over Conflict Other historians question whether broad voting rights by themselves demonstrate the existence of real democracy. The true test of democratic practice, they argue, would be whether different groups in a colonial town felt free to debate political questions in a town meeting. In the records of such meetings, they found little evidence of true political conflict and debate. Instead, they found that the purpose of **town meetings** in colonial days was to reach a consensus and to avoid conflict and real choices. These historians believe that consensus-forming limited the degree of democracy.

The Maritime Elite A third historical perspective is based on studies of economic change in colonial Boston. According to this view, a fundamental shift from an agrarian to a maritime economy occurred in the 18th century. In the process, a new elite emerged to dominate Boston's finances, society, and politics. The power of this elite prevented colonial Massachusetts from being considered a true democracy.

The question remains: To what extent were Massachusetts and the other colonies democratic? The answer depends on the definition of democracy.

Support an Argument *Explain two perspectives on the degree of democracy practiced in the British colonies.*

1. Explain how the contributions of various migrant groups crossing the Atlantic influenced the growth of an American culture.

KEY TERMS BY THEME

Arts & Science (SOC)
Benjamin West
John Copley
Benjamin Franklin
Poor Richard's Almanack
Phillis Wheatley
John Bartram
ministry
physicians
lawyers

Religion (SOC)
religious toleration
established church
Great Awakening
Jonathan Edwards
George Whitefield
Cotton Mather
sectarian
nonsectarian

The Land (GEO)
subsistence farming

Ethnicity (NAT)
Germans
Scotch-Irish
Huguenots
Dutch
Swedes
Africans

People (MIG)
immigrants
social mobility

Government (POL)
hereditary aristocracy
John Peter Zenger
Andrew Hamilton
Enlightenment
governor
legislature
town meetings

MULTIPLE-CHOICE QUESTIONS

Questions 1–3 refer to the following excerpt.

"To understand political power . . . we must consider what estate all men are naturally in, and that it is a state of perfect freedom to order their actions and dispose of their possessions . . . within the bounds of the law of nature, without asking leave, or depending upon the will of any other man. . . .

Whosoever therefore out of a state of nature unite into a community must be understood to give up all the power necessary to the ends for which they unite into society, to the majority of the community . . . And this is done by barely agreeing to unite into one political society. . . . And thus that which begins and actually constitutes any political society is nothing but the consent of any number of freemen capable of a majority to unite. . . . And this is that . . . which did or could give beginning to any lawful government in the world."

John Locke, *Second Treatise of Government,* 1690

1. Increases in which of the following contributed most directly to the ideas expressed in the excerpt?
   (A) The frequency of floods, droughts, and other problems related to nature
   (B) The criticism of the idea of absolute monarchy
   (C) The influence of competing religious groups in politics
   (D) The support of government for merchants who wanted to import goods

2. Locke's writings had the most direct influence on the
   (A) American Revolution through his ideas on government
   (B) Great Awakening through his ideas on religion
   (C) Mayflower Compact through his ideas on community
   (D) Zenger case through his ideas on defining what is true

3. Which of the following groups in the English colonies represented ideas most directly opposed to those expressed in the excerpt?
   (A) Owners of plantations who kept people enslaved
   (B) Church leaders who advocated for religious toleration
   (C) Merchants who wanted more freedom to trade
   (D) Women who believed that all people were born with certain rights

SHORT-ANSWER QUESTION

Use complete sentences; an outline or bulleted list alone is not acceptable.

1. Answer (a), (b), and (c).
   (a) Briefly explain how ONE specific ethnic group contributed to the development of culture and society in the colonies during the period from 1607 to 1754.
   (b) Briefly explain ONE specific cause of religious revivalism in the mid-18th century.
   (c) Briefly explain ONE specific reason for the difference in economic developments between colonial regions during the period from 1607 to 1754.

Comparisons in Period 2

Learning Objective: Compare the effects of the development of colonial society in the various regions of North America.

The reasoning skill of "comparison" is the suggested focus for evaluating the content of this period. Historians often compare various European colonial systems or various British colonies. As explained in Topic 2.1, there are many factors to consider in the broad topic of the influences on the development of society in the 13 colonies from 1607 to 1754. On the AP exam, a question might be focused on any one factor such as migration, the North American environment, interaction with Native Americans, or British expectations to list but a few of the factors.

In an effort to "Explain the extent to which the British colonies were involved in political, cultural, and economic exchanges with Great Britain," one could show that from the very beginning the colonialists questioned the British government's control while asking for their support and mirroring much of their culture.

One could show that, economically, the British policy of mercantilism dictated what the colonies could produce and with whom they could trade. This is specific evidence of an economic factor that negated colonial use of all their available resources that produced "enumerated" goods. One can take other specific evidence to demonstrate the complexity of the relationship between Britain and the colonies. For example, one could compare the colonial desire for government support to drive away the Native Americans to the colonial view of mercantilism.

Further evidence can support the argument that in the 17th century the colonies had an evolving relationship with Britain. One element that could be compared is religion. How did the influence of the British-led Church of England compare with that of the Puritans, Quakers, and Catholics who played active roles in starting specific colonies? One might consider several plausible arguments and then decide which one is best supported by the evidence:

- Colonial culture was more tolerant of religious diversity than was British culture.

- People in the colonies carried on the same religious conflicts that existed in Great Britain.

- Colonists held similar ideas about religious toleration as the British did, but circumstances led them to act more tolerantly.

COMPARING COLONIAL REGIONS			
Characteristic	**New England**	**Middle Atlantic**	**Southern**
Colonies	• New Hampshire • Massachusetts • Rhode Island • Connecticut	• New York • Pennsylvania • New Jersey • Delaware	• Maryland • Virginia • North Carolina • South Carolina • Georgia
Population Groups	• English	• English • German • Dutch	• English • Scotch-Irish • African American
Religious Groups	• Puritans • Dissenters • Baptists	• Anglicans • Roman Catholics • Quakers • Jews	• Anglicans • Roman Catholics • Baptists
Commercial Centers	• Boston • Providence	• New York • Philadelphia	• Charleston • Savannah
Exports	• Fish • Lumber • Ships	• Grain	• Tobacco • Rice • Indigo
Education	• Tax-supported schools	• Private religious schools	• Tutors and parents
Environment	• Rock soils • Long winters	• Rich soil • Moderate climate	• Diverse soils • Diverse climate
Representative Government	• Town meetings	• Colonial assemblies	• Virginia House of Burgesses

QUESTIONS ABOUT COMPARISON

1. Explain the extent to which the 13 colonies developed differently during the 17th century. For example, compare the people who settled the specific colonies as well as the available resources and support they had.

2. Explain the influence of British political, cultural, and economic views on the development of the 13 colonies. For example, compare how the British and colonists viewed mercantilism, representative government, and religion among many possible areas of interaction.

3. Explain the extent to which the various conditions in the English colonies led to the development of a unique system of slavery. For example, compare the influence of the colonial economy, geography, and population on the enslaving of Africans.

Historians do more than repeat facts and quotations. They also develop arguments. Argumentation means using reasons and evidence effectively to make a point. The first part of an argument is making a claim. That means making a statement that can be proved or disproved.

You may have made claims in English class or speech class. For example, maybe you argued "Schools should require students to wear uniforms." Or perhaps your topic was "The city should ban single-use plastic bottles."

Historians' claims are more robust and demanding than these. A historian's claim must be historically defensible. That means there are specific and relevant facts, statistics, records, or accounts that support the claim.

Evaluate this claim: "The original thirteen colonies were based on republican ideals that persist in the United States to this day." Is this claim historically defensible? To decide, you'll need to evaluate the evidence. Then you will need to consider whether the claim can be proved or disproved.

On one hand, colonial governments included elections. On the other hand, most people today would not consider any of those colonies to be very inclusive. That's because the colonies excluded most people from voting—including women, men who did not own property, indentured servants, and enslaved people.

Historians consult secondary sources, including works by other historians, to help them make claims and develop arguments. However, only primary sources provide the actual words of people who were alive at the time.

How could a historian prove the claim that the colonies were based on republican ideals? He or she might quote from documents such as the *Fundamental Orders of Connecticut,* the first written constitution in American history. To disprove that same claim, a historian might quote from letters by indentured servants or women. Voting records would be valuable sources to historians on either side of the issue.

For each claim listed below, tell whether it is historically defensible and describe sources you would search for to prove or disprove the claim.

1. Native Americans' escape from enslavement changed not only the colonies' economies but also world history.

2. Britain's salutary neglect ended up having negative outcomes for its colonies.

3. Metacom's War marked the end of most Native American resistance in New England. However, it was not the end of Native American influence on that region.

4. The large numbers of children that colonial women bore affected the wealth and development of colonial economies.

5. In the 13 colonies, owning land was the likeliest way to become wealthy.

UNIT 2 — Period 2 Review: 1607–1754

WRITE AS A HISTORIAN: *HISTORICAL THINKING SKILLS AND LONG ESSAYS*

Writing answers to long essay questions requires using historical thinking skills. Different stages of the process call for using different historical thinking skills. Study the chart below. The page numbers in parentheses indicate places where the skill is practiced in this book.

Stages in the Writing Process	Historical Thinking Skills
Analyze the question by identifying the exact task and the geographic and chronological framework.	Identify, describe, and explain a historical concept, development, or process. (See pages xli–xlii.)
Gather and organize the evidence you will need to complete the task.	Identify, describe, and explain patterns or connections among historical concepts, developments, and processes. These patterns and connections provide the key to organizing your evidence. Make sure your organization supports the task in the prompt. (See pages xlii, 28, and 156.)
Develop a thesis that lays out a line of reasoning.	Make a historically defensible claim related directly to the task and your evidence as the basis for your argument. Use historical reasoning (comparison, continuity and change, or causation) to frame your argument. (See pages xliii–xliv and 77.)
Write an introductory paragraph.	Identify and describe a broader historical context for your argument, and explain how the development or process you are examining is situated within that context. (See page 431.)
Write the supporting paragraphs.	Support an argument using specific and relevant evidence, explaining how the evidence ties to the argument. Explain relationships among various pieces of evidence. (See page xliv–xlvi, 254, 340, 685, and 747.)
Write the conclusion.	Reinforce and extend relevant and insightful connections within and across periods as you tie together your complex argument. (See page 573.)
Reread and evaluate your essay.	Be sure it demonstrates a complex understanding of the question and uses historical evidence to corroborate, qualify, or modify an argument. (See pages xlvi–xlvii.)

Application: Find the scoring rubric and sample essays for U.S History on the College Board website. Work in a small group to prepare a presentation explaining how to earn the most possible points on a long essay question. Share your presentation with the rest of the class.

For current free-response question samples, visit: https://apcentral.collegeboard.org/courses/ap-united-states-history/exam

LONG ESSAY QUESTIONS

Directions: The suggested writing time for each question is 40 minutes. In your response, you should do the following:

- Respond to the prompt with a historically defensible thesis or claim that establishes a line of reasoning.
- Describe a broader historical context relevant to the prompt.
- Support an argument in response to the prompt using specific and relevant examples of evidence.
- Use historical reasoning (e.g., comparison, causation, and continuity or change) to frame or structure an argument that addresses the prompt.
- Use evidence to corroborate, qualify, or modify an argument that addresses the prompt.

1. Evaluate the extent of the differences in the role of religion in the founding of the Spanish colonies in the 16th century and in the founding of the English colonies in the 17th century.

2. Evaluate the extent to which freedom of religion fostered the founding of the English colonies.

3. Evaluate the extent to which the environment influenced the development of different regions of the English colonies along the Atlantic coast in the 17th and 18th centuries.

4. Evaluate the extent to which the Great Awakening had an influence on the development of a democratic society in the English colonies during the period from 1607 to 1745.

Directions: Question 1 is based on the accompanying documents. The documents have been edited for the purpose of this exercise. You are advised to spend 15 minutes planning and 45 minutes writing your answer. In your response you should do the following:

- Respond to the prompt with a historically defensible thesis or claim that establishes a line of reasoning.
- Describe a broader historical context relevant to the prompt.
- Support an argument in response to the prompt using at least six documents.
- Use at least one additional piece of specific historical evidence (beyond that found in the documents) relevant to an argument about the prompt.
- For at least three documents, explain how or why the document's point of view, purpose, historical situation, and/or audience is relevant to an argument.
- Use evidence to corroborate, qualify, or modify an argument that addresses the prompt.

1. Evaluate the extent to which different factors fostered unity throughout the English colonies between 1620 and 1754.

Document 1

Source: The Mayflower Compact, 1620

This day before we came to harbor, observing some not well affected to unity and concord, but gave some appearance of faction, it was thought good there should be an association and agreement that we should combine together in one body, and to submit to such government and governors as we should be common consent agree to make and choose, and set out hands to this that follows word for word. . . . [We] do by these present, solemnly and mutually, in the presence of God and one another, covenant and combine ourselves together into a civil body politic, for our better ordering and preservation and furtherance of the ends aforesaid; and by virtue hereof to enact, constitute, and frame such just and equal laws, ordinances, acts, constitutions, offices from time to time as shall be thought most meet and convenient for the general good of the colony.

Document 2

Source: Fundamental Orders of Connecticut, 1639

As it has pleased the Almighty God . . . we, the inhabitants and residents of Windsor, Hartford, and Wethersfield are now cohabiting and dwelling in and upon the river of Conectecotte [Connecticut] and the lands thereunto adjoining; and well knowing where a people are gathered together the Word of God requires that, to maintain the peace and union of such a people, there should be an orderly and decent government established according to God, to order and dispose of the affairs of the people at all seasons as occasion shall require; do therefore associate and conjoin ourselves to be as one public state or commonwealth, and do, for ourselves and our successors and such as shall be adjoined to us at any time hereafter, enter into combination and confederation together, to maintain and preserve the liberty and purity of the Gospel of our Lord Jesus which we now profess.

Document 3

Source: The New England Confederation, 1643

The Articles of Confederation between the Plantations under the Government of the Massachusetts . . . New Plymouth . . . Connecticut and . . . New Haven with the Plantations in Combination therewith. . . .

The said United Colonies . . . hereby enter into a firm and perpetual league of friendship and amity for offence and defence, mutual advice . . . upon all just occasions . . . and for their own mutual safety and welfare. . . .

It is by these Confederates agreed that the charge of all just wars, whether offensive or defensive, upon what part or member of this Confederation soever they fall . . . be borne by all the parts of this Confederation . . .

It is further agreed that if any of these Jurisdictions or any Plantation under or in combination with them, be invaded by any enemy whatsoever, upon notice and request of any three magistrates of that Jurisdiction so invaded, the rest of the Confederates without any further meeting or expostulation shall forthwith send aid to the Confederate in danger.

Document 4

Source: William Penn, Plan of Union, 1697

A brief and plain scheme how the English colonies in the North parts of America... Boston, Connecticut, Rhode Island, New York, New Jerseys, Pennsylvania, Maryland, Virginia, and Carolinas—may be made more useful to the crown and one another's peace and safety. . . .

1. That the several colonies before mentioned do meet . . . at least once in two years in times of peace . . . to debate and resolve of such measures as are most advisable for their better understanding and the public tranquillity and safety.

2. That, in order to it, two persons . . . be appointed by each province as their representatives or deputies, which in the whole make the congress. . . .

3. That their business shall be to hear and adjust all matters of complaint or difference between province and province . . . to consider the ways and means to support the union and safety of these provinces against the public enemies.

Document 5

Source: The Albany Plan of Union, 1754

It is proposed that humble application be made for an act of Parliament of Great Britain, by virtue of which one general government may be formed in America, including all the said colonies, within and under which government each colony may retain its present constitution, except in the particulars wherein a change may be directed by the said act, as hereafter follows:

1. That the said general government be administered by a President-General, to be appointed and supported by the crown; and a Grand Council, to be chosen by the representatives of the people of the several Colonies met in their respective assemblies. . . .

2. That they raise and pay soldiers and build forts for the defense of any of the colonies. . . .

3. That for these purposes they have power to make laws, and lay and levy such general duties, imposts, or taxes, as to them shall appear most equal and just.

Document 6

Source: Pennsylvania *Gazette*, 1754. Library of Congress

J O I N,   or   D I E.

Document 7

Source: Ben Franklin, "The Problem of Colonial Union," 1754

[On] the subject of uniting the colonies more intimately with Great Britain by allowing them representatives in Parliament, I have something further considered that matter and am of opinion that such a union would be very acceptable to the colonies, provided they had a reasonable number of representatives allowed them; and that all the old acts Parliament restraining the trade or cramping the manufacturers of the colonies be at the same time repealed. . . .

I should hope, too, that by such a union the people of Great Britain and the people of the colonies would learn to consider themselves as not belonging to different community with different interests but to one community with one interest, which I imagine, would contribute to strengthen the whole and greatly lessen the danger of future separations.

Topic 3.1

Contextualizing Period 3

Learning Objective: Explain the context in which America gained independence and developed a sense of national identity.

In the 150 years after 1607, the 13 British colonies in North America began to develop an identity distinct from Great Britain. In the following 50 years, these colonies helped fight a war against France, won their own independence, wrote a constitution, and established a democratic republic. The transformation from colonies to a new country resulted from a change in how the British ruled their colonies, the impact of European affairs and ideas on the colonists, and the development of American leaders and people who wanted self-government.

British-French Wars During the colonial period, the British and the French fought a series of wars for control of territory in Europe, the Americas, and South Asia. The last of these, the Seven Years' War, began in North America in 1756. Because American Indians were heavily involved in defending their interests, and most allied with the French, this event is also known as the French and Indian War. The British victory in 1763 consolidated their control of North America and freed colonists from fear of French attacks. In addition, the contributions by the colonies reflected their political maturity. They became more confident of their ability to stand up for their interests.

Colonial Independence To pay for the war, the British tried to collect more taxes from the colonies they were protecting. In contrast, many American colonists saw themselves as self-sufficient and were emboldened by "enlightened" thinking to call for greater self-governance. These clashing views caused the colonies to found a new nation.

The Articles of Confederation and the Constitution Inspired by the republican ideals of the American Revolution, the new country was initially governed by the Articles of Confederation. However, the national government was so weak that people soon replaced it with a new constitution with a stronger federal government but reserved certain powers for the states. With the addition of the Bill of Rights, it protected basic individual liberties. This Constitution still provides the basis of the U.S. government today.

Conflicting Views of Government Debates over the new constitution continued as policy debates under the first president, George Washington.

Truly "Founding Fathers," the leaders of the new government argued over the economy, individual rights, foreign affairs, relations with Native Americans, and the roles of the federal and state governments.

By the end of Washington's eight years in office, two political parties had emerged. The Democratic-Republicans argued for stronger state governments. The Federalists argued for a stronger federal government. After the Democratic-Republicans defeated the Federalists in the election of 1800, the young country faced a test of political stability. When the Federalists peacefully transferred power to their political rivals, the country passed the test. By 1820, the Federalists had disappeared as a party. However, their ideas continued to have influence through judges and later politicians.

Changes in Economics, Politics, and Culture In the new country, immigrants continued to arrive. As people migrated westward in search of land and economic opportunities, they caused conflicts with the Native Americans living on those lands. The British, French, and Spanish who also claimed North American territory provided additional challenges. The United States had to defend its borders on land and its ships at sea in order to protect its economic and diplomatic interests.

As the United States established its place as a new country, people began to form their own cultures. While the United States declared independence in 1776 and ratified the Constitution in 1788, it was not until after 1800 that a national identity could be recognized.

ANALYZE THE CONTEXT

1. Explain a historical context for the changing relationship between the American colonists and the British government following the Seven Years' War (the French and Indian War).

2. Explain a historical context for the development of new constitutions and declarations of rights by American political leaders after 1776.

3. Explain a historical context for understanding the regional differences over economic, political, social, and foreign issues that continued along with the formation of the new U.S. cultural and political institutions.

LANDMARK EVENTS: 1750–1800

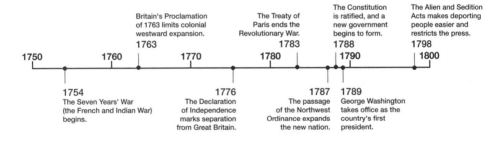

The Seven Years' War

It is truly a miserable thing that we no sooner leave fighting our neighbors, the French, but we must fall to quarrelling among ourselves.

Reverend Samuel Johnson, minister in Connecticut, 1763

Learning Objective: Explain the causes and effects of the Seven Years' War (the French and Indian War).

Historic European rivalries, particularly between Great Britain, France, and Spain, had been brought to North America by the earliest immigrants from those nations. While the basis for the conflict between these nations may be found in Europe, disputes between them in their colonies served to intensify their differences. While Britain eventually triumphed in a series of 18th century wars, victory was at a cost that they never could have imagined: the rebellion and the loss of their Atlantic coast colonies.

Empires at War, 1689–1763

Late in the 17th century, a series of wars broke out involving Great Britain, France, and Spain. They were worldwide in scope, with battles in Europe, India, and North America, and they often involved other Europeans and natives of India and North America. The stakes were high for power in Europe and for control of colonies and their lucrative trade. In North America, the most valuable possessions were sugar-producing islands in the Caribbean Sea and the fur-trading network with American Indians in the interior of North America.

The First Three Wars

These conflicts occurred between 1689 and 1748 and were named after the British monarch under whose reign they occurred:

- In King William's War (1689–1697), the British launched expeditions to capture Quebec from the French, but they failed. American Indians supported by the French burned British frontier settlements.

- In Queen Anne's War (1702–1713), the British had more success. They gained both Nova Scotia from France and trading rights in Spanish America.

- King George's War (1744–1748) was named for George II. In Georgia, James Oglethorpe led a colonial army that repulsed Spanish attacks. New Englanders captured Louisbourg in Canada, a major French fortress on Cape Breton Island that controlled access to the St. Lawrence River. In the peace treaty ending the war, however, Britain returned Louisbourg to the French in exchange for political and economic gains in India. New Englanders were furious about the loss of a fort that they had fought so hard to win.

The Decisive Conflict

In the first three wars, European powers saw little value in committing regular troops to America. They relied on "amateur" colonial forces. Further, most of the fighting was in Europe. However, by 1754, when the fourth and decisive conflict began, conditions had changed. Great Britain and France recognized the great value of their colonies for the raw materials they produced. Only about 60,000 settlers lived in the French colonies, but they worked with Native Americans to carry on a valuable fur trade. The British colonies were more densely populated, with about 1.2 million people. They produced grain, fish, tobacco, lumber and other products that fueled British industry.

The final war in this series was known in Europe as the **Seven Years' War**. The North American phase of this war is often called the **French and Indian War**. It began in 1754 and ended in 1763.

Beginning of the War From the British point of view, the French provoked the war by building a chain of forts in the Ohio River Valley. One reason the French did so was to halt the westward growth of the British colonies. Hoping to stop the French from completing work on Fort Duquesne (Pittsburgh) and thereby win control of the Ohio River Valley, the governor of Virginia sent a small militia (armed force) under the command of a young colonel named **George Washington**. After gaining a small initial victory, Washington's troops surrendered to a superior force of Frenchmen and their American Indian allies on July 3, 1754. With this military encounter in the wilderness, the final war for empire began.

At first the war went badly for the British. In 1755, another expedition from Virginia, led by General **Edward Braddock**, ended in a disastrous defeat, as more than 2,000 British regulars and colonial troops were routed by a smaller force of both French troops and American Indians near Fort Duquesne. The Algonquin allies of the French ravaged the frontier from western Pennsylvania to North Carolina. The French repulsed a British invasion of French Canada that began in 1756.

The Albany Plan of Union Recognizing the need for coordinating colonial defense, the British government had called for representatives from several colonies to meet in a congress at Albany, New York, in 1754. The delegates from seven colonies adopted an agreement—the **Albany Plan of Union**—developed by Benjamin Franklin that provided for an intercolonial government and a system for recruiting troops and collecting taxes from the various colonies for their common defense. Each colony was too concerned about preserving its own taxation powers to accept the plan, however, and it never took effect. The Albany congress was significant, however, because it set a precedent for later, more revolutionary, congresses in the 1770s.

British Victory The British prime minister, William Pitt, concentrated the government's military strategy on conquering Canada. This objective was accomplished with the retaking of Louisbourg in 1758, the surrender of Quebec to General James Wolfe in 1759, and the taking of Montreal in 1760. After these British victories, the European powers negotiated a peace treaty (the **Peace of Paris**) in 1763. Great Britain acquired both French Canada and Spanish Florida. In compensation for Spain's loss of Florida, France ceded (gave up) to Spain its huge territory west of the Mississippi River known as Louisiana. With this treaty, the British extended their control of North America, and French power on the continent virtually ended.

Immediate Effects of the War Britain's victory in the Seven Years' War was a turning point in the military and diplomatic conflict for control of North America among the British, the French, the colonists, and various tribes of American Indians:

- It gave Great Britain unchallenged supremacy among Europeans in North America.
- It challenged the autonomy of many American Indians.
- It established the British as the dominant naval power in the world.
- It meant that the American colonies no longer faced the threat of concerted attacks from the French, the Spanish, and their American Indian allies.

More important to the colonies, though, was a change in how the British and the colonists viewed each other.

The British View of the War The British came away from the war with a low opinion of the colonial military abilities. They held the American militia in contempt as a poorly trained, disorderly rabble. Furthermore, they noted that some of the colonies had refused to contribute either troops or money to the war effort. Most British were convinced that the colonists were both unable and unwilling to defend the new frontiers of the vastly expanded British empire.

The Colonial View of the War The colonists took an opposite view of their military performance. They were proud of their record in all four wars and developed confidence that they could successfully provide for their own defense. They were not impressed with the British troops or leadership, as their methods of warfare seemed badly suited to the densely wooded terrain of eastern America.

Reorganization of the British Empire

More serious than the resentful feelings stirred by the war experience was the British government's shift in its colonial policies. Previously, Britain had exercised little direct control over the colonies and had not enforced its navigation acts regulating colonial trade. This earlier policy of **salutary neglect** was abandoned as the British adopted more forceful policies for taking control of their expanded North American dominions.

All four wars—and the last one in particular—had been extremely costly. In addition, Britain now felt the need to maintain a large British military force to guard its American frontiers. Among British landowners, pressure was building to reduce the heavy taxes that the government had levied to fund the colonial wars. To pay for troops to guard the frontier without increasing taxes at home, King George III and the dominant political party in Parliament (the Whigs) wanted the American colonies to bear more of the cost of maintaining the British empire.

Pontiac's Rebellion The first major test of the new British imperial policy came in 1763 when Chief Pontiac led an attack against colonial settlements on the western frontier. The American Indians were angered by the growing westward movement of European settlers onto their land and by the British refusal to offer gifts as the French had done. Pontiac's alliance of American Indians in the Ohio River Valley destroyed forts and settlements from New York to Virginia. Rather than relying on colonial forces to retaliate, the British sent regular British troops to put down the uprising.

Pontiac im Kriegsrath.

Source: Getty Images.

This engraving, made in 1876, portrays Chief Pontiac speaking to other Native American leaders about the need to unite to resist European settlements.

Proclamation of 1763 In an effort to stabilize the western frontier, the British government issued a proclamation that prohibited colonists from settling west of the Appalachian Mountains (see map in Topic 3.3). The British hoped that limiting settlements would prevent future hostilities between colonists and American Indians. But the colonists reacted to the proclamation with anger and defiance. After the British victory in the Seven Years' War, colonists hoped to reap benefits in the form of access to western lands. For the British to deny such benefits was infuriating. Defying the proclamation, thousands streamed westward past the imaginary boundary line drawn by the British.

Growing British-Colonial Tensions The divergent views on the war and the changes in British imperial policies provided the context for conflict between Great Britain and its North American colonies. These conflicts would become more intense as the two sides debated issues of taxation and representation.

REFLECT ON THE LEARNING OBJECTIVE

1. Explain the causes and effects of the Seven Years' War (French and Indian War).

KEY TERMS BY THEME

Empire (WOR, GEO)
Seven Years' War (French and Indian War)
George Washington
Edward Braddock
Albany Plan of Union (1754)

Peace of Paris (1763)
salutary neglect

American Indians (MIG)
Pontiac's Rebellion
Proclamation of 1763

MULTIPLE-CHOICE QUESTIONS

Questions 1–3 refer to the following excerpt.

"We apprehend [believe] that as freemen and English subjects, we have an indisputable title to the same privileges and immunities with His Majesty's other subjects who reside in the interior counties . . . , and therefore ought not to be excluded from an equal share with them in the very important privilege of legislation. . . . We cannot but observe with sorrow and indignation that some persons in this province are at pains to extenuate [excuse] the barbarous cruelties practiced by these savages on our murdered brethren and relatives . . . by this means the Indians have been taught to despise us as a weak and disunited people, and from this fatal source have arisen many of our calamities. . . . We humbly pray therefore that this grievance may be redressed."

The Paxton Boys, to the Pennsylvania Assembly, 1764

1. The sentiments exhibited in this excerpt were most directly influenced by which of the following historical developments?
   (A) The Great Awakening
   (B) The Albany Plan of Union
   (C) The Seven Years' War
   (D) The Enlightenment

2. The British had earlier attempted to solve the problem expressed in this excerpt most directly by
   (A) signing the treaty to end the French and Indian War
   (B) establishing a boundary between Indian lands and lands open for colonial settlement
   (C) passing a law that required colonists to house British soldiers
   (D) enforcing regulations on colonial trade after a period of not enforcing them

3. Which of the following individuals led a group that was in the most similar situation to the Paxton Boys?
   (A) John Smith because his supporters also wanted an equal share of privileges with other colonists
   (B) Roger Williams because his supporters also relied on prayer to have their problems solved
   (C) Nathaniel Bacon because his supporters also wanted stronger government action against American Indians
   (D) Edmund Andros because his supporters also disputed the power of the British monarch

SHORT-ANSWER QUESTION

Use complete sentences; an outline or bulleted list alone is not acceptable.

1. Answer (a), (b), and (c).
   (a) Briefly explain ONE historical event or development during the Seven Years' War that demonstrated a fundamental change in the British view of its relationship with its American colonies.
   (b) Briefly explain ONE historical event or development during the Seven Years' War that demonstrated a fundamental change in the colonial view of its relationship with its British government.
   (c) Briefly describe ONE historical event or development resulting from the changing views by either the British or the colonists.

Topic 3.3

Taxation Without Representation

The people, even to the lowest ranks, have become more attentive to their liberties, more inquisitive about them, and more determined to defend them.

John Adams, 1765

Learning Objective: Explain how British colonial policies regarding North America led to the Revolutionary War.

What caused American colonists in the 1760s to become, as John Adams expressed, "more attentive to their liberties"? The chief reason for their discontent in these years was a dramatic change in Britain's colonial policy. Britain began to assert its power in the colonies and to collect taxes and enforce trade laws much more aggressively than in the past. While some colonists accepted these changes, others grew angry in defense of what they viewed as violations of their political rights and their ability to carry on trade and commerce freely. As anger spread, colonists from Massachusetts to Georgia began to unite in protest of British actions.

British Actions and Colonial Reactions

The Proclamation of 1763 was the first of a series of acts by the British government that angered colonists. From the British point of view, the acts were justified as a fair, proper method for protecting its colonial empire and making the colonies pay their share for such protection. From the colonists' view, each act represented an alarming threat to their liberties. Colonists combined a desire to defend long-established practices in Britain of representative government, local self-rule, and individual rights with the influence of the newer ideas of the Enlightenment (see Topic 3.4). One of the core issues dividing the British and the colonists was the idea of representation:

- Colonists pointed out that they could not directly elect representatives to **Parliament**, so they had no way to consent to or oppose British actions.

- The British responded that the colonists, like all British citizens, had virtual representation in the government. According to this theory, all members of Parliament represented the interests of the entire empire, not just the small district that chose them.

New Revenues and Regulations

In the first two years of peace, King **George III**'s chancellor of the exchequer (treasury) and prime minister, Lord George Grenville, successfully pushed through Parliament three measures that aroused colonial suspicions of a British plot to subvert their liberties.

The Sugar Act (1764) This act (also known as the Revenue Act of 1764) placed duties on foreign sugar and certain luxuries. Its supporters wanted to regulate the sugar trade and to raise revenue. A companion law also provided for stricter enforcement of the Navigation Acts to stop smuggling. Those accused of smuggling were to be tried in admiralty courts by crown-appointed judges without juries.

The Quartering Act (1765) This act required the colonists to provide food and living quarters for British soldiers stationed in the colonies.

The Stamp Act In an effort to raise funds to support British military forces in the colonies, Lord Grenville turned to a tax long in use in Britain. The **Stamp Act**, enacted by Parliament in 1765, required that revenue stamps be placed on most printed paper in the colonies, including all legal documents, newspapers, pamphlets, and advertisements. This was the first direct tax—collected from those who used the goods—paid by the people in the colonies, as opposed to the taxes on imported goods, which were paid by merchants.

Reaction to the Stamp Act

People in every colony reacted with indignation to news of the Stamp Act. A young Virginia lawyer named **Patrick Henry** spoke for many when he stood up in the House of Burgesses to demand that the king's government recognize the rights of all citizens—including the right not to be taxed without representation. In Massachusetts, James Otis initiated a call for cooperative action among the colonies to protest the Stamp Act. Representatives from nine colonies met in New York in 1765 to form the so-called **Stamp Act Congress**. They resolved that only their own elected representatives had the legal authority to approve taxes.

The protest against the Stamp Act took a violent turn with the formation of the **Sons and Daughters of Liberty**, a secret society organized for the purpose of intimidating tax agents. Members of this society sometimes destroyed revenue stamps and tarred and feathered revenue officials.

Economic Pressure Boycotts against British imports were the most effective form of protest. It became fashionable in the colonies in 1765 and 1766 for people not to purchase any article of British origin. For example, instead of buying imported British cloth, colonial women proudly made their own. Faced with a sharp drop in trade, London merchants put pressure on Parliament to repeal the controversial Stamp Act.

Declaratory Act In 1766, Grenville was replaced by another prime minister, and Parliament voted to repeal the Stamp Act. When news of the repeal reached the colonies, people rejoiced. Few colonists at the time noted that Parliament had also enacted a face-saving measure known as the **Declaratory Act** (1766). This act asserted that Parliament had the right to tax and make laws for the colonies "in all cases whatsoever." This declaration of policy would soon lead to renewed conflict between the colonists and the British government.

Second Phase of the Crisis, 1767–1773

The British government still needed new revenue. To obtain it, the newly appointed chancellor of the exchequer, Charles Townshend, proposed another tax measure.

The Townshend Acts In 1767, Parliament enacted new duties, known as the **Townshend Acts**, to be collected on colonial imports of tea, glass, and paper. The revenue would be used to pay crown officials in the colonies, thus making the officials independent of the colonial assemblies that had paid their salaries. The Townshend Acts also provided for the search of private homes for smuggled goods. All that an official needed to conduct such a search would be a **writ of assistance** (a general license to search anywhere) rather than a judge's warrant to search a specific property. A related act suspended New York's assembly for its defiance of the Quartering Act.

At first, most colonists accepted the taxes because they were indirect, meaning they were paid by merchants who then raised their prices to cover the additional costs. They were not direct taxes that consumers paid on their purchases.

However, leaders soon protested the new duties. While they accepted Parliament's right to regulate trade as legitimate, they rejected taxation without representation as a violation of an essential principle of English law. In 1767 and 1768, **John Dickinson** made these points in *Letters From a Farmer in Pennsylvania*. He argued that Parliament could regulate colonial commerce, but if it wanted to tax colonists, it had to have the approval of assemblies that included colonial representatives.

In 1768, **James Otis** and **Samuel Adams** jointly wrote the *Massachusetts Circular Letter* and sent copies to every colonial legislature. It urged the colonies to petition Parliament to repeal the Townshend Acts. British officials in Boston ordered the letter retracted, threatened to dissolve the legislature, and increased the number of British troops. Responding to the circular letter, the colonists again conducted boycotts of British goods. Merchants increased their smuggling to avoid the Townshend duties.

Repeal of the Townshend Acts Meanwhile, in London, there was another change in the king's ministers. **Lord Frederick North** became the new prime minister. He urged Parliament to repeal the **Townshend Acts** because they damaged trade and generated a disappointingly small amount of revenue. The repeal of the Townshend Acts in 1770 ended the colonial boycott and, except for an incident in Boston (the "massacre" described below), there was a three-year respite from political troubles as the colonies entered into a period of economic prosperity. However, Parliament retained a small tax on tea as a symbol of its right to tax the colonies.

Boston Massacre Most Bostonians resented the British troops quartered in their city to protect customs officials from attacks by the Sons and Daughters of Liberty. On a snowy day in March 1770, a crowd of colonists harassed the guards near the customs house. The guards fired into the crowd, killing five. Among them was Crispus Attucks, a dockworker of mixed African and American Indian heritage, who would later become a symbol for the antislavery movement. At their trial for murder, the six soldiers were defended by colonial lawyer John Adams. They were acquitted of murder, but two were convicted on the less serious charge of manslaughter. Adams' radical cousin, Samuel Adams, angrily denounced the shooting incident as a "massacre" and used it to inflame anti-British feeling.

Renewal of the Conflict

Even during the relatively quiet years of 1770–1772, Samuel Adams and a few other Americans kept alive the view that British officials were undermining colonial liberties. A principal device for spreading this idea was by means of the **Committees of Correspondence** initiated by Samuel Adams in 1772. In Boston and other Massachusetts towns, Adams began the practice of organizing committees that would regularly exchange letters about suspicious or potentially threatening British activities. The Virginia House of Burgesses took the concept a step further when it organized intercolonial committees in 1773.

The *Gaspee* One incident frequently discussed in the committees' letters was that of the *Gaspee*, a British customs ship that had caught several smugglers. In 1772, it ran aground off the shore of Rhode Island. Seizing their opportunity to destroy the hated vessel, a group of colonists disguised as American Indians ordered the British crew ashore and then set fire to the ship. The British ordered a commission to investigate and bring guilty individuals to Britain for trial.

Boston Tea Party The colonists continued their refusal to buy British tea because the British insisted on their right to collect tax on it. Hoping to help the British East India Company out of its financial problems, Parliament passed the **Tea Act** in 1773, which made the price of the company's tea—even with the tax included—cheaper than that of smuggled Dutch tea.

Many Americans refused to buy the cheaper tea because to do so would, in effect, recognize Parliament's right to tax the colonies. A shipment of East India Company tea arrived in Boston harbor but found no buyers. Before the royal governor could bring the tea ashore, a group of Bostonians, mostly artisans and laborers, took action. Disguised as American Indians, they boarded the British ships and dumped 342 chests of tea into the harbor. Colonial reaction to this incident (December 1773) was mixed. While many applauded the Boston Tea Party as a defense of liberty, others thought the destruction of private property too radical.

Intolerable Acts

In Great Britain, news of the Boston Tea Party angered King George III, Lord North, and members of Parliament. In retaliation, the British government enacted a series of punitive acts (the Coercive Acts), together with a separate act dealing with French Canada (the Quebec Act). The colonists were outraged by these various laws, which were given the epithet "**Intolerable Acts**."

The Coercive Acts (1774) There were four **Coercive Acts**, directed mainly at punishing the people of Boston and Massachusetts and bringing them under control.

- The **Port Act** closed the port of Boston, prohibiting trade in and out of the harbor until the destroyed tea was paid for.
- The Massachusetts Government Act reduced the power of the Massachusetts legislature while increasing the power of the royal governor.
- The **Administration of Justice Act** allowed royal officials accused of crimes to be tried in Great Britain instead of in the colonies.
- The Quartering Act was expanded to enable British troops to be quartered in private homes. It applied to all colonies.

Quebec Act (1774) When it passed the Coercive Acts, the British government also passed a law organizing the Canadian lands gained from France. To satsify the French-speaking Canadians, the act established Roman Catholicism as the official religion of Quebec. It also set up a government without a representative assembly and extended Quebec's boundary to the Ohio River. The plan, accepted by French Canadians, was resented in the 13 colonies.

The colonists viewed the **Quebec Act** as a direct attack on the American colonies because it took away lands that New York, Pennsylvania, Virginia, Massachusetts, and Connecticut claimed along the Ohio River. They also feared that the British would attempt to enact similar laws in America to take away their representative government. Further, the predominantly Protestant Americans resented the recognition given to the Roman Catholic Church.

The Demand for Independence

Britain's intensifying crackdown on resistance to its policies forced more and more colonists to take sides. Supporters of the British response included many wealthy merchants in New York and Philadelphia and planters in the southern colonies. Opponents, from Virginia to Massachusetts, challenged the British with harsh criticisms. These words were supported by hostile actions towards the British throughout the colonies, but particularly in Boston and New England. As violence increased, enough people were willing to speak out publicly, participate in mass protests, and donate money that the movement for independence grew stronger.

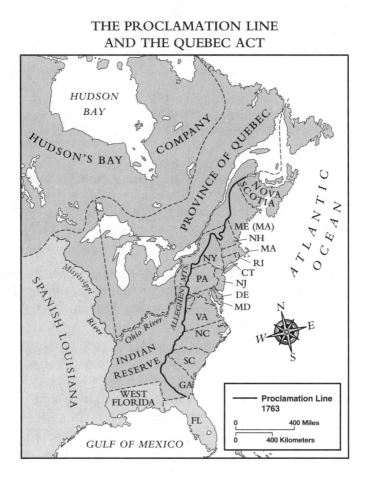

THE PROCLAMATION LINE AND THE QUEBEC ACT

HUDSON BAY

HUDSON'S BAY COMPANY

PROVINCE OF QUEBEC

NOVA SCOTIA

ME (MA)
NH
MA
NY
RI
CT
PA
NJ
DE
MD
VA
NC
SC
GA
WEST FLORIDA
FL

INDIAN RESERVE

SPANISH LOUISIANA

Mississippi River
Ohio River
ALLEGHENY MTS

ATLANTIC OCEAN

GULF OF MEXICO

N E W S

—— Proclamation Line 1763

0   400 Miles
0   400 Kilometers

REFLECT ON THE LEARNING OBJECTIVE

1. Explain how the changes in British policies toward the colonies led them to rebellion.

KEY TERMS BY THEME

Colonial Unrest (NAT, POL)
Patrick Henry
Stamp Act Congress
Sons and Daughters of Liberty
John Dickinson; *Letters From . . .*
James Otis
Samuel Adams
Massachusetts Circular Letter

Committees of Correspondence
Intolerable Acts

Rulers & Policies (WXT)
Parliament
George III
Whigs
Lord Frederick North

Empire (POL, GEO)
Sugar Act (1764)
Quartering Act (1765)

Stamp Act (1765)
Declaratory Act (1766)
Townshend Acts (1767)
writ of assistance
Tea Act (1773)
Coercive Acts (1774)
—Port Act
—Massachusetts Government Act
—Administration of Justice Act
Quebec Act (1774)

Questions 1–2 refer to the following excerpt.

"The unhappy disputes between Great Britain and her American colonies . . . have proceeded to lengths so dangerous and alarming as to excite just apprehensions in the minds of His Majesty's faithful subjects of this colony. . . .

It cannot admit of a doubt but that British subjects in America are entitled to the same rights and privileges as their fellow subjects possess in Britain; and therefore, that the power assumed by the British Parliament to bind America by their statutes in all cases whatsoever is unconstitutional, and the source of these unhappy differences. . . .

To obtain a redress of these grievances, without which the people of America can neither be safe, free, nor happy, they are willing to undergo the great inconvenience that will be derived to them from stopping all imports whatsoever from Great Britain."

Statement by the Virginia Convention, formerly known as the
House of Burgesses , 1774

1. Which of the following actions by the colonists is most similar to the one recommended in the excerpt above?
   (A) The actions taken by the Massachusetts legislature in response to the passing of the Townshend Acts
   (B) The colonists' actions in Boston that led to the Boston Massacre
   (C) The formation of the Committees of Correspondence because it fostered colonial unity against the British
   (D) The Boston Tea Party because it involved destroying property that was a symbol of British authority

2. The statement that "British subjects in America are entitled to the same rights and privileges as their fellow subjects possess in Britain" indicates that the writers of this document believed that colonists should
   (A) purchase more goods from British merchants
   (B) declare independence before the British took any futher actions
   (C) have representation in setting their own internal economic policies
   (D) demand that Parliament reduce their overall level of taxes

1. "The colonists believed they saw . . . what appeared to be evidence of nothing less than a deliberate assault launched surreptitiously by plotters against liberty both in England and in America. The danger to America, it was believed, was in fact only the small immediately visible part of the greater whole whose ultimate manifestation would be the destruction of the English constitution with all the rights and privileges embedded in it. . . .

   It was this—the overwhelming evidence, as they saw it, that they were faced with conspirators against liberty determined at all costs to gain ends which their words dissembled [portrayed falsely]—that was signaled to the colonists after 1763, and it was this above all else that in the end propelled them into Revolution."

   Bernard Bailyn, historian, The Logic of Rebellion, 1967

   "The Americans, 'born the heirs of freedom,' revolted not to create but to maintain their freedom. American society had developed differently from that of the Old World. . . . While the speculative philosophers of Europe were laboriously searching their minds in an effort to decide the first principles of liberty, the Americans had come to experience vividly that liberty in their everyday lives. . . . The Revolution was thus essentially intellectual and declaratory: it 'explained the business to the world, and served to confirm what nature and society had before produced.' 'All was the result of reason. . . .' The Revolution had taken place not in a succession of eruptions that had crumbled the existing social structure, but in a succession of new thoughts and new ideas that had vindicated that social structure. . . . The Americans revolted not out of actual suffering but out of reasoned principle."

   Gordon S. Wood, historian, The Idea of America, 2011

   Using the excerpts, answer (a), (b), and (c).

   (a) Briefly explain ONE major difference between Wood's and Bailyn's historical interpretations of why the American colonies rebelled against the British.

   (b) Briefly explain how ONE historical event or development in the period 1754 to 1776 that is not explicitly mentioned in the excerpts could be used to support Bailyn's interpretation.

   (c) Briefly explain how ONE historical event or development in the period 1754 to 1776 that is not explicitly mentioned in the excerpts could be used to support Wood's interpretation.

Topic 3.4

Philosophical Foundations of the American Revolution

*Government even in its best state is but a necessary evil;
in its worst state an intolerable one.*

Thomas Paine, *Common Sense* 1776

Learning Objective: Explain how and why colonial attitudes about government and the individual changed in the years leading up to the American Revolution.

For Americans, especially those who were in positions of leadership, there was a long tradition of loyalty to the king and Great Britain. As the differences between the colonists and the leaders of Great Britain increased, many Americans tried to justify the diverging directions. As discussed in Topic 2.7, the **Enlightenment**, particularly the writings of John Locke, had a profound influence on the colonies.

Enlightenment Ideas

The era of the Enlightenment was at its peak in the mid-18th century. These were the very years that future leaders of the American Revolution (Washington, Jefferson, Franklin, and Adams) were coming to maturity, and their ideas reflected the influence of Enlightenment thought.

Deism Many Enlightenment thinkers in Europe and America were Deists. They believed in God, but in one who had established natural laws in creating the universe and then rarely or never intervened directly in human affairs. God set the rules but then allowed people to make choices. This view of God contrasted with the belief held by most Christians of their time that God regularly intervened in everyday life, often to reward or punish individuals or groups for their actions.

Rationalism In general, Enlightenment thinkers trusted human reason to understand the natural world and to respond to the many problems of life and society. While most were Christians, their trust in reason led them to emphasize studying science and human behavior rather than following traditional interpretations of the Bible.

Social Contract In politics, one important Enlightenment idea was the **social contract**, the concept of an agreement among people to form a government to promote liberty and equality. This idea represented a sharp break from the prevailing assumption that monarchs ruled by divine right—because God had chosen them. Under the social contract, power came from "below," not from "above." This philosophy, derived from **John Locke** and others, had been developed further by the French philosopher **Jean-Jacques Rousseau.** Support for a social contract had a profound influence on educated Americans in the 1760s and 1770s—the decades of revolutionary thought and action that finally culminated in the American Revolution.

Thomas Paine's Argument for Independence

In January 1776, one of the most important pieces of writing by an American colonist was published. The author, **Thomas Paine**, had been born in England before moving to the colonies. His pamphlet, *Common Sense,* argued in clear and forceful language that the colonies should become independent states and break all political ties with the British monarchy. Paine argued that it was contrary to common sense for a large continent to be ruled by a small and distant island and for people to pledge allegiance to a king whose government was corrupt and whose laws were unreasonable.

The pamphlet spread rapidly throughout the colonies and ignited public demands for independence. Unlike earlier writers, who focused their anger on Parliament and the ministers, Paine directly attacked King George III and even the ideas of a monarchy. Paine's success was based largely on his ability to make complicated, abstract ideas understandable for common readers. *Common Sense* became a key factor in widening the divide between the colonies and Great Britain.

HISTORICAL PERSPECTIVES: *WHY DID THE COLONIES REBEL?*

Did America's break with Great Britain in the 18th century signify a true revolution with radical change, or was it simply the culmination of evolutionary changes in American life?

Revolution as a Radical Break For many years, the traditional view of the founding of America was that the American Revolution was based on the ideas of the Enlightenment and had fundamentally altered society. In the early 20th century, Progressive historians believed that the movement to end British dominance had provided an opportunity to radically change American society. A new nation was formed with a republican government based on a division of powers between a national and state government and an emphasis on equality and the rights of the individual. The revolution was social as well as political.

Revolution Before the War During the second half of the 20th century, some historians argued that American society had been more democratic and changed long before the war with Great Britain. The war reflected these changes. Historian Bernard Bailyn has suggested that the changes that are viewed as revolutionary—representative government, expansion of the right to vote, and written constitutions—had all developed earlier during the colonial period. According to this perspective, what was significant about the break from Great Britain was the recognition of an American philosophy based on liberty and democracy that would guide the nation.

Support an Argument *Explain two perspectives on how revolutionary the colonial separation from Britain was.*

REFLECT ON THE LEARNING OBJECTIVE

1. Explain the new colonial views of the individual and government and the reasons for this in the times leading to the American Revolution.

KEY TERMS BY THEME

Philosophy (NAT, SOC)
Enlightenment
Deism
rationalism

social contract
John Locke
Jean-Jacques Rousseau
Thomas Paine

MULTIPLE-CHOICE QUESTIONS

Questions 1–3 refer to the following excerpt.

> "It is inseparably essential to the freedom of a People, and the undoubted Right of Englishmen, that no taxes be imposed on them, but with their own Consent, given personally, or by their representatives. . . . That it is the indispensable duty of these colonies, to the best of sovereigns . . . to procure the repeal of the act for granting and applying certain stamp duties, of all clauses of any other acts of Parliament . . . for the restriction of American commerce."
>
> Resolutions of the Stamp Act Congress, 1765

1. The above excerpt was primarily directed to which person or group?
   (A) Colonial merchants
   (B) The king
   (C) Leaders in Parliament
   (D) Residents of England

2. The philosophical basis behind the excerpt was that the writers

(A) accepted Parliament's authority generally but not for direct taxation

(B) accepted Parliamentary actions only in specific, limited cases

(C) rejected only how Parliament was spending tax revenues

(D) rejected Parliament's entire authority as violating the social contract

3. The Enlightenment idea most clearly reflected in this passage was that

(A) God rarely intervened in human affairs directly

(B) reason was the best guide to understanding the world

(C) governments needed popular consent to rule legitimately

(D) kings received their authority to rule from God

SHORT-ANSWER QUESTION

Use complete sentences; an outline or bulleted list alone is not acceptable.

1. "I wish I knew what mighty things were fabricating. If a form of government is to be established here, what one will be assumed? Will it be left to our assemblies to choose one? And will not many men have many minds? And shall we not run into dissensions among ourselves?

I am more and more convinced that man is a dangerous creature; and that power, whether vested in many or a few, is ever grasping. . . .

How shall we be governed so as to retain our liberties? Who shall frame these laws? Who will give them force and energy. . . .

When I consider these things, and the prejudices of people in favor of ancient customs and regulations, I feel anxious for the fate of our monarchy or democracy, or whatever is to take place."

Abigail Adams, Letter to John Adams, November 27, 1775

Using the excerpt, answer (a), (b), and (c).

(a) Briefly explain ONE specific perspective expressed by Abigail Adams in the excerpt above.

(b) Briefly explain ONE historical event or development in the period leading up to independence that led to the view expressed here by Abigail Adams.

(c) Briefly explain ONE historical event or development in the period leading up to independence that challenged the views expressed here by Abigail Adams.

The American Revolution

What do we mean by the revolution? The war? That was no part of the revolution; it was only an effect and consequence of it. The revolution was in the minds of the people.

John Adams, Letter to Thomas Jefferson, August 24, 1815

Learning Objective: Explain how various factors contributed to the American victory in the Revolution.

Parliament's passage of the **Intolerable Acts** in 1774 intensified the conflict between the colonies and Great Britain. In the next two years, many Americans reached the conclusion—unthinkable to most colonists only a few years earlier—that the only solution to their quarrel with the British government was to sever all ties with it. How did events from 1774 to 1776 lead to revolution?

The First Continental Congress

The punitive Intolerable Acts drove all the colonies except Georgia to send delegates to a convention in Philadelphia in September 1774. The purpose of the convention—later known as the **First Continental Congress**—was to respond to what the delegates viewed as Britain's alarming threats to their liberties. Most Americans had no desire for independence. They simply wanted to protest parliamentary infringements of their rights and restore the relationship with the crown that had existed before the Seven Years' War.

The Delegates Those attending the congress were outwardly similar: all were wealthy White men. But they held diverse views about the crisis, from radical to conservative. Leading the radicals—those demanding the greatest concessions from Britain—were **Patrick Henry** of Virginia and **Samuel Adams** and **John Adams** of Massachusetts. The moderates included **George Washington** of Virginia and **John Dickinson** of Pennsylvania. The conservative delegates—those who favored a mild statement of protest—included **John Jay** of New York and **Joseph Galloway** of Pennsylvania. Unrepresented were the **Loyalists**, the colonists who would not challenge the king's government in any way.

Actions of the Congress The delegates voted on a series of proposed measures, each of which was intended to change British policy without offending moderate and conservative colonists. Joseph Galloway proposed a plan, similar to the Albany Plan of 1754, that would have reordered relations with Parliament and formed a union of the colonies within the British Empire. By only one vote, Galloway's plan failed to pass. Instead, the convention adopted these measures:

- It endorsed the **Suffolk Resolves**, a statement originally issued by Massachusetts. The Resolves called for the immediate repeal of the Intolerable Acts and for colonies to resist them by making military preparations and boycotting British goods.

- It passed the Declaration and Resolves. Backed by moderate delegates, this petition urged the king to redress (make right) colonial grievances and restore colonial rights. In a conciliatory gesture, it recognized Parliament's authority to regulate commerce.

- It created the Continental Association, a network of committees to enforce the **economic sanctions** of the Suffolk Resolves.

- It declared that if colonial rights were not recognized, delegates would meet again in May 1775.

Fighting Begins

Angrily dismissing the petition of the First Continental Congress, the king's government declared Massachusetts to be in a state of rebellion and sent additional troops to put down further disorders. The combination of colonial defiance and British determination to suppress it led to violent clashes in Massachusetts—what would be the first battles of the American Revolution.

Lexington and Concord On April 18, 1775, General Thomas Gage, the commander of British troops in Boston, sent a large force to seize colonial military supplies in the town of **Concord**. Warned of the British march by two riders, **Paul Revere** and **William Dawes**, the militia (or **Minutemen**) of **Lexington** assembled on the village green to face the British. The Americans were forced to retreat under heavy British fire with eight killed in the brief encounter. Who fired the first shot of this first skirmish of the American Revolution? The evidence is ambiguous, and the answer will probably never be known.

Continuing their march, the British entered Concord and destroyed some military supplies. Marching back to Boston, the long column of British soldiers was attacked by hundreds of militiamen firing from behind stone walls. The British suffered 250 casualties—and also humiliation at being so badly mauled by "amateur" fighters.

Bunker Hill Two months later, on June 17, 1775, a true battle was fought between opposing armies on the outskirts of Boston. A colonial militia of Massachusetts farmers fortified Breed's Hill, next to **Bunker Hill**, for which the ensuing battle was wrongly named. A British force attacked the colonists' position and managed to take the hill, suffering over a thousand casualties. Americans claimed a victory of sorts, having succeeded in inflicting heavy losses on the attacking British army.

The Second Continental Congress

Soon after the fighting broke out in Massachusetts, delegates to the **Second Continental Congress** met in Philadelphia in May 1775. The congress was divided. One group of delegates, mainly from New England, thought the colonies should declare their independence. Another group, mainly from the middle colonies, hoped the conflict could be resolved by negotiating a new relationship with Great Britain.

The congress adopted a **Declaration of the Causes and Necessities for Taking Up Arms** and called on the colonies to provide troops. George Washington was appointed the commander-in-chief of a new colonial army and sent to Boston to lead the Massachusetts militia and volunteer units from other colonies. Congress also authorized a force under Benedict Arnold to raid Quebec in order to draw Canada away from the British empire. An American navy and marine corps were organized in the fall of 1775 for the purpose of attacking British ships.

Peace Efforts

At first the congress adopted a contradictory policy of waging war while at the same time seeking a peaceful settlement. Many in the colonies valued their heritage and Britain's protection, so they did not want independence. They did, however, want a change in their relationship with Britain. In July 1775, the delegates voted to send an "**Olive Branch Petition**" to King George III, in which they pledged their loyalty and asked the king to intercede with Parliament to secure peace and the protection of colonial rights.

King George angrily dismissed the congress's plea and agreed instead to Parliament's **Prohibitory Act** (August 1775), which declared the colonies in rebellion. A few months later, Parliament forbade all trade and shipping between Britain and the colonies.

The Declaration of Independence

After meeting for more than a year, the congress gradually and somewhat reluctantly began to favor independence rather than reconciliation. On June 7, 1776, Richard Henry Lee of Virginia introduced a resolution declaring the colonies to be independent. Five delegates, including **Thomas Jefferson**, formed a committee to write a statement in support of Lee's resolution. The declaration drafted by Jefferson listed specific grievances against George III's government and also expressed the basic principles that justified revolution: "We hold these truths to be self-evident: That all men are created equal; that they are endowed by their Creator with certain unalienable rights; that among these are Life, Liberty, and the pursuit of Happiness."

The congress adopted Lee's resolution calling for independence on July 2. It adopted Jefferson's work, the **Declaration of Independence**, on July 4, 1776.

The Revolutionary War

From the first shots fired in Lexington and Concord in 1775 to the final signing of a peace treaty in 1783, the American War for Independence, or Revolutionary War, was a long and bitter struggle. As Americans fought, they also laid the foundations for a new national identity, as the former colonies became a new country, the United States of America.

The Competing Sides

About 2.6 million people lived in the 13 colonies in 1775. Maybe 40 percent of them actively joined the struggle against Britain. They called themselves American **Patriots**. Around 25 percent sided with the British as Loyalists. All others remained neutral, with many paying little attention to the struggle.

British Strength The British entered the war with far greater resources than the colonists. They had three times the population, a wealthy economy that could finance a war, a large and well-trained army, and the most powerful navy in the world. From previous conflicts with French, they had experience fighting overseas in North America, the West Indies, and South Asia.

Patriots The largest number of Patriots were from the New England states and Virginia. Most soldiers were reluctant to travel outside their own region. They would serve in local militia units for short periods, leave to work their farms, and then return to duty. Thus, even though several hundred thousand people fought on the Patriot side in the war, General Washington never had more than 20,000 regular troops under his command at one time. His army was chronically short of supplies, poorly equipped, and rarely paid. However, many colonists had a strong commitment to independence, so they provided a solid core of people resilient enough to undergo hardships.

African Americans Initially, George Washington rejected the idea of African Americans serving in the Patriot army. However, when the British promised freedom to enslaved people who joined their side, Washington and the congress quickly made the same offer. Approximately 5,000 African Americans fought as Patriots. Most of them were free citizens from the north, who fought in mixed racial forces, although there were some units composed entirely of African Americans. These troops took part in most of the military actions of the war, and a number, including Peter Salem, were recognized for their bravery.

Tories The Revolutionary War was in some respects a civil war in which anti-British Patriots fought pro-British Loyalists. Those who maintained allegiance to the king were also called **Tories** (after the majority party in Parliament). Almost 60,000 American Tories fought next to British soldiers, supplied them with arms and food, and joined in raiding parties to pillage Patriot homes and farms. The war divided some families. For example, while Benjamin Franklin was a leading Patriot, his son William joined the Tories and served as the last royal governor of New Jersey.

How many American Tories were there? They were often strongest in major port cities, except in Boston. In New York, New Jersey, and Georgia, they were probably in the majority. Toward the end of the war, about 80,000 Loyalists emigrated from the states to settle in Canada or Britain rather than face persecution at the hands of the Patriots.

Although Loyalists came from all groups and classes, they tended to be wealthier and more conservative than the Patriots. Most government officials and Anglican clergy in America remained loyal to the crown.

American Indians At first, American Indians tried to stay out of the war. Eventually, however, attacks by colonists prompted many American Indians to support the British, who promised to limit colonial settlements in the west.

Initial American Losses and Hardships

The first three years of the war, 1775 to 1777, went badly for Washington's poorly trained and equipped revolutionary army. It barely escaped complete disaster in a battle for New York City in 1776, in which Washington's forces were routed by the British. By the end of 1777, the British occupied both New York and Philadelphia. After losing Philadelphia, Washington's demoralized troops suffered through the severe winter of 1777–1778 camped at **Valley Forge** in Pennsylvania.

Economic troubles added to the Patriots' bleak prospects. British occupation of American ports resulted in a 95 percent decline in trade between 1775 and 1777. Goods were scarce, and inflation was rampant. The paper money issued by Congress, known as **continentals**, became almost worthless.

Alliance with France

The turning point for the American revolutionaries came with a victory at Saratoga in upstate New York in October 1777. British forces under General John Burgoyne had marched from Canada in an effort to join forces marching from the west and south. Their objective was to cut off New England from the rest of the colonies (or states). Burgoyne's troops were attacked at Saratoga by troops commanded by American generals Horatio Gates and Benedict Arnold. The British were forced to surrender.

The diplomatic outcome of the **Battle of Saratoga** was even more important than the military result. News of the surprising American victory persuaded France to join the war against Britain. France's king, Louis XVI, an **absolute monarch**, had no interest in aiding a revolutionary movement. But he did see a chance to weaken his country's traditional foe, Great Britain, by undermining its colonial empire. France had secretly provided money and supplies to the American revolutionaries as early as 1775. After Saratoga, in 1778, France openly allied itself with the Americans. (A year later, Spain and Holland also entered the war against Britain.) The French alliance proved decisive in the American struggle for independence as it widened the war, forcing the British to divert military resources away from America.

Victory

Faced with a larger war, Britain decided to consolidate its forces in America. British troops were pulled out of Philadelphia, and New York became the base of British operations. In a campaign through 1778–1779, the Patriots, led by **George Rogers Clark**, captured a series of British forts in the Illinois country to gain control of parts of the vast Ohio territory. In 1780, the British army adopted a southern strategy, concentrating its military campaigns in Virginia and the Carolinas, where Loyalists were especially numerous and active.

Yorktown In 1781, the last major battle of the Revolutionary War was fought near Yorktown, Virginia, on the shores of Chesapeake Bay. Strongly supported by French naval and military forces, Washington's army forced the surrender of a large British army commanded by General Charles Cornwallis.

Treaty of Paris News of Cornwallis's defeat at Yorktown was a heavy blow to the Tory Party in Parliament that was conducting the war. The war had become unpopular in Britain, partly because it placed a heavy strain on the economy and the government's finances. Lord North and other Tory ministers resigned and were replaced by Whig leaders who wanted to end the war.

In Paris, in 1783, the belligerents finally signed a peace treaty. The **Treaty of Paris** provided for the following: (1) Britain would recognize the existence of the United States as an independent nation. (2) The Mississippi River would be the western boundary of that nation. (3) Americans would have fishing rights off the coast of Canada. (4) Americans would pay debts owed to British merchants and honor Loyalist claims for property confiscated during the war.

REFLECT ON THE LEARNING OBJECTIVE

1. Explain the factors that resulted in the American success against Britian.

KEY TERMS BY THEME

Separation (NAT)
Intolerable Acts
First Continental Congress
Patrick Henry
Samuel Adams
John Adams
George Washington
John Dickinson
John Jay
Joseph Galloway
Suffolk Resolves
economic sanctions
Second Continental
   Congress (1775)

Declaration of the Causes
   and Necessities for
   Taking Up Arms
Olive Branch Petition
Thomas Jefferson
Declaration of
   Independence

War (POL)
Concord
Paul Revere
William Dawes
Lexington
Bunker Hill
Battle of Saratoga

George Rogers Clark
Yorktown

Final Break (WOR)
Prohibitory Act (1775)
absolute monarch
Treaty of Paris (1783)

A New Nation (SOC)
Loyalists (Tories)
Patriots
Minutemen
continentals
Valley Forge

MULTIPLE-CHOICE QUESTIONS

Questions 1–2 refer to the following excerpt.

> "I have not the least doubt that the Negroes will make very excellent soldiers, with proper management. . . .
>
> I foresee that this project will have to combat much opposition from prejudice and self-interest. The contempt we have been taught to entertain for the black makes us fancy many things that are founded neither in reason nor experience; and an unwillingness to part with property of so valuable a kind will furnish a thousand arguments to show the impracticability or pernicious tendency of a scheme which requires such a sacrifice. But it should be considered that if we do not make use of them in this way, the enemy probably will. . . . An essential part of the plan is to give them their freedom with their muskets."

> Alexander Hamilton, "A Proposal to Arm and Then Free the Negroes," 1779

1. This excerpt suggests that Hamilton saw the conflict with Great Britain as also a conflict among colonists over
   (A) whether to trust reason or experience more
   (B) whether colonists had adequate skills to manage soldiers
   (C) the views of plantation owners about the enemy
   (D) the views of White Americans toward enslaved Black Americans

2. The excerpt supports the claim that the use of Black troops during the Revolutionary War was likely motivated by which of the following?
   (A) Awareness that the French were using Black soldiers in their army
   (B) Fear that the British would recruit African Americans
   (C) Concern that state militias were short of troops
   (D) Belief that the Declaration of Independence called for equality

SHORT-ANSWER QUESTION

1. Answer (a), (b), and (c).
   (a) Briefly explain ONE specific strength that Patriots had in the American Revolution in the period 1774 to 1783.
   (b) Briefly explain ONE specific way that France influenced the American Revolution in the period 1774 to 1783.
   (c) Briefly explain ONE specific role that Native Americans played in the American Revolution in the period 1774 to 1783.

Topic 3.6

The Influence of Revolutionary Ideals

How is the one exalted, and the other depressed, by the contrary modes of education which are adopted! The one is taught to aspire, and the other is early confined and limited. . . . The sister must be wholly domesticated, while the brother is led by the hand through all the flowery paths of science.

Judith Sargent Murray, "On the Equality of the Sexes" (1779)

Learning Objective 1: Explain the various ways the American Revolution affected society.

Learning Objective 2: Describe the global impact of the American Revolution.

Revolutionary ideas impacted American society before, during, and after the war that brought the colonies freedom from British control. These ideas shaped the new state governments that replaced the colonial ones (see Topic 3.7), and they had particular significance for women, enslaved workers, and Native Americans.

Women in the Revolutionary Era

Both prior to and during the war, groups of women such as the **Daughters of Liberty** organized to oppose British actions. Before the war, they took direct action by boycotting British goods. During the war, they provided supplies to the fighting forces. Some women followed men into the armed camps and worked as cooks and nurses. In a few instances, women fought in battle, either taking their husband's place, as **Mary McCauley** (also known as **Molly Pitcher**) did at the Battle of Monmouth, or passing as a man and serving as a soldier, as **Deborah Sampson** did for a year. Similarly, female Loyalists also provided support to colonial and British troops.

Economic Role The most important contribution of women during the war was maintaining the colonial economy. While fathers, husbands, and sons were away fighting, women ran family farms and businesses. They provided much of the food and clothing necessary for the war effort.

Political Demands The combination of hearing the revolutionary rhetoric and being actively engaged in the struggle influenced how many women viewed their role in society. A new view of their status in society evolved, a change referred to as **Republican Motherhood**. This new role called for educating women so that in the home they could teach their children the values of the new republic and their roles as citizens. This gave women a more active role in shaping the new nation's political life. However, it was still a role carried out in the home, not in public, and it did not imply equality with men. Few people, male or female, advocated full equality.

Despite their contributions, women continued in their second-class status. Unsuccessful were pleas such as those of **Abigail Adams** to her husband, John Adams: "I desire you would remember the ladies and be more generous and favorable to them than your ancestors."

The Status of Enslaved African Americans

The institution of slavery contradicted the spirit of the Revolution and the idea that "all men are created equal." For a time, the leaders of the Revolution recognized this and took some corrective steps. The Continental Congress abolished the importation of enslaved people, and most states went along with the prohibition. Several northern states ended slavery, while in the south, some owners voluntarily freed their enslaved laborers. Slavery was in decline. Many leaders, including slave owners such as James Madison, wanted it to end. However, he could not envision a society in which White and free Black people lived together. So, he hoped that freed people would simply return to Africa.

However, this changed dramatically with the development of the cotton gin in 1793 (Topic 3.12). By making cotton production more efficient, it quickly increased the demand for low-cost labor. Slave owners came to believe that enslaved labor was essential to their prosperity and that the ideals of the Revolution did not apply to the people they owned. By the 1830s, they developed a rationale for slavery that found religious and political justification for continuing to hold human beings in lifelong bondage.

Native Americans and Independence

American Indians generally supported the British in the Revolutionary War, so they did not benefit from the success of the colonies' independence. Further, colonists' racism and greed for land caused most of them to view American Indians as obstacles to settlement that should be removed. Very few colonists believed that the ideas of liberty and equality applied to American Indians.

International Impact of the American Revolution

Just as the American Revolution was shaped by ideas imported by the European Enlightenment, so it influenced events elsewhere. The ideas that people have a right to govern themselves, that all people are created equal, and that individuals have inalienable rights have had wide appeal. Leaders of the French

Revolution (1789–1799) that overthrew the monarchy, the United Irishmen who rebelled against British rule (1798), the Haitian Revolution (1791–1804) that ended slavery, and numerous Latin American revolutions against European control in the 19th century all cited the Declaration of Independence as inspiration. In the 20th century, the impact of these ideas appeared in countries as diverse as Zimbabwe in central Africa and Vietnam in southeast Asia.

One of the leaders inspired by the American Revolution was Toussaint L'ouverture of Haiti. He lead the largest successful revolution by enslaved people in history.
Source: Engraving (1802). John Carter Brown Library, Wikipedia.org

HISTORICAL PERSPECTIVES: *HOW UNUSUAL WAS THE REVOLUTION?*

Was the American Revolution similar to or different from other revolutions in history. Historians have provided different answers to this question.

Similarities with Other Revolutions In *Anatomy of a Revolution* (1965), historian Crane Brinton was struck by how alike the America Revolution, the French Revolution (1789–1794), and the Russian Revolution (1917–1922) were. According to Brinton, each one passed through similar stages and became increasingly radical.

Other historians have noted similarities between the American Revolution and the colonial rebellions in Africa and Asia after World War II. All were against distant Europe imperial powers. Many featured guerrilla forces (the colonies in the 1770s, Cuba in the 1950s, and Vietnam in the 1960s) and were weaker in the cities but stronger in the surrounding rural territories.

Differences with Europe Other historians have focused on the differences between American and European revolutions. For example, the French and Russians reacted to feudalism and aristocratic privilege that did not exist in the American colonies. In their view, Americans did not revolt against outmoded institutions but merely carried to maturity a liberal, republican movement that had been gaining force for years.

Impact Historians also disagree on whether the American Revolution shaped later revolutions. Using the insights from comparisons has helped historians better understand the American Revolution in its historical context.

Support an Argument: *Explain two perspectives on the radical nature of the American Revolution.*

REFLECT ON THE LEARNING OBJECTIVE

1. Explain different ways that the American Revolution affected society and the world.

KEY TERMS BY THEME

A New Nation (SOC)		Separation (NAT)
Mary McCauley (Molly Pitcher)	Deborah Sampson	Daughters of Liberty
	Republican Motherhood	
	Abigail Adams	

MULTIPLE-CHOICE QUESTIONS

Questions 1–3 refer to the following excerpt.

"A Declaration of Rights made by the representatives of the good people of Virginia . . .

Section 1. That all men are by nature equally free and independent and have certain inherent rights. . . .

Section 2. That all power is vested in and consequently derived from the people. . . .

Section 4. That no man, or set of men, is entitled to exclusive or separate . . . privileges from the community. . . .

Section 5. That the legislative and executive powers of the state should be separate and distinct from the judiciary. . . .

Section 6. That elections of members . . . as representatives of the people, in assembly, ought to be free; and that all men, having sufficient evidence of permanent common interest with and attachment to the community, have the right of suffrage. . . .

Section 12. That freedom of the press is one of the great bulwarks of liberty. . . .

Section 16. All men are equally entitled to the free exercise of religion."

Virginia Declaration of Rights, 1776

1. Which of the following sections was the most direct reason for conflicts between Virginia and the British government?

   (A) Section 1: all people are by nature equal

   (B) Section 2: legitimate government power comes from the people

   (C) Section 4: no person deserves special privileges

   (D) Section 16: people should be able to worship freely

2. Which of the following sections most clearly reflected a belief in the social contract theory of government?

   (A) Section 2: origins of governmental power

   (B) Section 5: separation of government powers

   (C) Section 6: right to vote

   (D) Section 12: freedom of the press

3. The group most likely to oppose the ideas expressed in this excerpt would have been

   (A) the Minutemen of Lexington, because they were from New England

   (B) the Daughters of Liberty, because they were women

   (C) Tories such as William Franklin, because they supported the British

   (D) African Americans, because most of them were enslaved

SHORT-ANSWER QUESTION

Use complete sentences; an outline or bulleted list alone is not acceptable.

1. "In the decades following the Revolution, American society was transformed.... The Revolution resembled the breaking of a dam, releasing thousands upon thousands of pent-up pressures. . . . It was as if the whole traditional structure, enfeebled and brittle to begin with, broke apart, and the people and their energies were set loose in an unprecedented outburst.

   "Nothing contributed more to this explosion of energy than did the idea of equality. Equality was in fact the most radical and most powerful ideological force let loose in the Revolution. Its appeal was far more potent than any of the revolutionaries realized. Once invoked, the idea of equality could not be stopped, and it tore through American society and culture with awesome power. . . . Within decades following the Declaration of Independence, the United States became the most egalitarian nation in the history of the world, and it remains so today, regardless of its great disparities of wealth."

   Gordon S. Wood, *Radicalism of the American Revolution*, 1993

"Today, 'equality' is generally interpreted to include protection for the rights of minorities; during the Revolution, 'the body of the people' referred exclusively to the majority. . . .

It is one of the supreme ironies of the American revolution that the assumption of authority by "the body of the people"—probably its most radical feature—served to oppress as well as to liberate. This was a real revolution: the people did seize power, but they exercised that power at the expense of others—loyalists, pacifists, merchants, Indians, slaves—who, although certainly people, were not perceived to be part of the whole. This was, after all, a war. It would not be the last time Americans sacrificed notions of liberty and equality in the name of the general good.

Our Revolutionary heritage works both ways. 'The body of the people,' the dominant force during the 1770s, has empowered and deprived."

Ray Raphael, *A People's History of the American Revolution,* 2001

Using the excerpts, answer (a), (b), and (c).

(a) Briefly explain ONE major difference between Wood's and Raphael's historical interpretations of how radical the American Revolution was.

(b) Briefly explain how ONE historical event or development in the period 1774 to 1787 that is not explicitly mentioned in the excerpts could be used to support Wood's interpretation.

(c) Briefly explain how ONE historical event or development in the period 1774 to 1787 that is not explicitly mentioned in the excerpts could be used to support Raphael's interpretation.

Topic 3.7

The Articles of Confederation

The source of the evil is the nature of the government.

Henry Knox to George Washington, December 17, 1786

Learning Objective: Explain how different forms of government developed and changed as a result of the Revolutionary Period.

Having declared independence, the 13 colonies were faced with the task of fighting for it. To win such a war of independence, the colonists realized that they needed some form of government. The challenge was bringing together 13 distinct colonies united largely by a distrust and fear of a tyrannical British government. This led to an intentionally weak form of central government under a document, the **Articles of Confederation**, that was written by the Second Continental Congress during the Revolutionary War.

Organization of New Governments

While the Revolutionary War was being fought, leaders of the 13 colonies worked to change them into independently governed states, each with its own constitution (written plan of government). At the same time, the revolutionary Congress that originally met in Philadelphia tried to define the powers of a new central government for the nation that was coming into being.

State Governments

By 1777, ten of the former colonies had written new constitutions. Most of these documents were both written and adopted by the states' legislatures. In a few states (Maryland, Pennsylvania, and North Carolina), a proposed constitution was submitted to a vote of the people for ratification (approval).

Each state constitution was the subject of heated debate between conservatives, who stressed the need for law and order, and liberals, who were most concerned about protecting individual rights and preventing future tyrannies. Although the various constitutions differed on specific points, they had the following features in common:

List of Rights Each state constitution began with a "bill" or "declaration" listing basic rights and freedoms. Common provisions identified the right to a jury trial and the freedom of religion. These rights and freedoms belonged to all citizens, and state officials could not infringe (encroach) on them.

Separation of Powers With a few exceptions, the powers of state government were given to three separate branches: (1) legislative powers to an elected two-house legislature, (2) executive powers to an elected governor, and (3) judicial powers to a system of courts. The principle of separation of powers was intended to be a safeguard against tyranny—especially against the tyranny of a too-powerful executive.

Voting The right to vote was extended to all White males who owned some property. The property requirement, usually for a minimal amount of land or money, was based on the assumption that property owners had a larger stake in government than did the poor and property-less.

Office-holding Those seeking elected office usually had to meet a higher property qualification than the voters.

The Articles of Confederation

At Philadelphia in 1776, as Jefferson was writing the Declaration of Independence, John Dickinson drafted the first constitution for the United States as a nation. Congress modified Dickinson's plan to protect the powers of the individual states. The Articles of Confederation, as the document was called, was adopted by Congress in 1777 and submitted to the states for ratification.

Ratification Approval of the Articles was delayed by a dispute over state claims to the vast American Indian lands west of the Alleghenies. Some states, such as Rhode Island and Maryland, insisted that states give up these claims and the lands be under the jurisdiction of the new central government. When Virginia and New York finally agreed to cede their claims to western lands, the Articles were ratified in March 1781.

Structure of Government The Articles established a central government that consisted of just one body, a congress. In this unicameral (one-house) legislature, each state was given one vote, with at least nine votes out of 13 required to pass important laws. There was no separate executive, nor a separate judiciary (court system). Amending the Articles required a unanimous vote. A Committee of States, with one representative from each state, could make minor decisions when the full Congress was not in session.

Powers The Articles gave Congress the power to wage war, make treaties, send diplomatic representatives, and borrow money. However, Congress did not have the power to regulate commerce or to collect taxes. To finance any of its decisions, Congress had to rely upon taxes voted by each state. Neither did the government have executive power to enforce its laws.

The United States Under the Articles, 1781–1789

The 13 states intended the central government to be weak—and it was. It consisted of a weak Congress and no executive or judicial branch.

Accomplishments

Despite its weaknesses, Congress under the Articles did have some lasting accomplishments:

- Independence: The U.S. government could claim some credit for the ultimate victory of Washington's army and for negotiating favorable terms in the treaty of peace with Britain.

- **Land Ordinance of 1785**: Congress established a policy for surveying and selling the western lands. The policy set aside one square-mile section of land in each 36 square-mile township for public education.

- **Northwest Ordinance of 1787**: For the large territory lying between the Great Lakes and the Ohio River, Congress passed an ordinance (law) that set the rules for creating new states. The Northwest Ordinance granted limited self-government to the developing territory and prohibited slavery in the region.

THE UNITED STATES IN 1783

By reserving land for schools and banning slavery, the government made the Northwest Territory attractive to both White and free Black settlers. However, the government auctioned land by the square mile (640 acres). So, even though the starting price per acre was a low $1 per acre, the benefit of the system went first to those rich enough to spend at least $640 at once. The purchasers, then, sold off the land in smaller parcels to less wealthy Americans.

Weaknesses of the Articles

These accomplishments were overshadowed by the difficulties the country faced in addressing certain problems without a strong government.

Foreign Affairs Relations between the new United States and the European powers were troubled. European nations had little respect for a nation that could neither pay its debts nor take united action in a crisis. For example, the country could not enforce the Treaty of Paris that ended the Revolutionary War. The U.S. government was too weak to stop Britain from maintaining military outposts on the western frontier and restricting trade. It was also too weak to force states to restore property to Loyalists and repay debts to foreigners as the treaty required. Britain and Spain threatened to take advantage of U.S. weakness by expanding their interests in the western lands.

Economic Problems The underlying problem was that Congress had no taxing power and could only request that the states donate money for national needs. It had no dependable source of revenue to repay the money it borrowed to fight the war. Similarly, states had large unpaid debts as well. The unpaid debts resulted in limited credit and reduced foreign trade. The printing of worthless paper money by many states added to the problems. These problems combined to cause an economic depression.

Internal Conflicts The 13 states treated one another as rivals and competed for economic advantage. They placed tariffs and other restrictions on the movement of goods across state lines. A number of states faced boundary disputes with neighbors that increased interstate tension. The national government had no power to settle these disputes.

Shays's Rebellion In the summer of 1786, Captain Daniel Shays, a Massachusetts farmer and Revolutionary War veteran, led other farmers in an uprising against high state taxes, imprisonment for debt, and lack of paper money. The rebel farmers stopped the collection of taxes and forced the closing of debtors' courts. In January 1787, when Shays and his followers attempted to seize weapons from the Springfield armory, the state militia of Massachusetts broke Shays's Rebellion.

REFLECT ON THE LEARNING OBJECTIVE

1. Explain how during the American Revolution different forms of government arose and adjusted to the ideals and demands of the Revolution.

MULTIPLE-CHOICE QUESTIONS

Questions 1–3 refer to the following excerpt.

> "Let us see what will be the consequences of not authorizing the federal government to regulate the trade of the states. Besides the want [lack] of revenue and of power, besides the immediate risk to our independence, the dangers of all the future evils of a precarious Union. . .
>
> There is something noble and magnificent in the perspective of a great federal republic, closely linked in the pursuit of common interest—tranquil and prosperous at home, respectable abroad. But there is something proportionably diminutive and contemptible in the prospect of a number of petty states, with the appearance only of union."
>
> Alexander Hamilton, "Arguments for Increasing the Power of the Federal Government," July 1782

1. Hamilton's comment that "there is something proportionably diminutive and contemptible in the prospect of a number of petty states, with the appearance only of union" is most directly a criticism of
   (A) the British form of government
   (B) the ideals of the Enlightenment
   (C) the Declaration of Independence
   (D) the Articles of Confederation

2. Hamilton's comments in the excerpt were similar to his concerns about
   (A) the rapid expansion by settlers onto the lands of American Indians
   (B) the slowness of the negotiations over the Treaty of Paris
   (C) the need to repay state debts after the Revolutionary War
   (D) the importance of passing the Northwest Ordinance

3. This excerpt provides support for the argument that Hamilton believed that the Articles of Confederation should be
   (A) kept as they are because they were working well
   (B) amended to protect the rights of states better
   (C) discarded so states could act independently
   (D) replaced with a new constitution

Use complete sentences; an outline or bulleted list alone is not acceptable.

1. "The government designed by the Articles of Confederation made it easy for relatively small groups of people—especially individual states or sections of the country—to block any change. There was a requirement for every single state to agree to alter the powers of the Confederation...

From the beginning the Union had been a pretty loose alliance, so people felt relatively free about saying they just didn't feel like going along with a particular policy... The result was stalemate. I can tell you that the people who wrote the Constitution thought a stalemated government could not survive."

George William Van Cleve, interview, The Nation, 2017

"The conventional view is that American political history from the Declaration of Independence to the Constitution was dominated by 'the complete inability of the government set up by the Articles of Confederation to function.' This view ignores effective exercises of national power that took place during this period and the evolution of institutions extending beyond the text of the articles. Congress and the state judiciaries often read the Articles broadly and expansively in response to the practical needs of the country. The institutions created by Congress exercise wide powers that furthered national unity, and the states acquiesced."

Eric M. Freedman, "The United States and the Articles of
Confederation: Drifting Toward Anarchy or Inching Toward
Commonwealth?" Yale Law Journal, November 1978

Using the excerpt, answer (a), (b), and (c).

(a) Briefly explain ONE major difference between Van Cleve's and Freedman's interpretations of the value of the Articles of Confederation.

(b) Briefly explain how ONE historical event or development in the period 1754 to 1800 that is not explicitly mentioned in the excerpts could be used to support Van Cleve's interpretation.

(c) Briefly explain how ONE historical event or development in the period 1754 to 1800 that is not explicitly mentioned in the excerpts could be used to support Freedman's interpretation.

The Constitutional Convention and Debates Over Ratification

Thus I consent, sir, to this Constitution, because I expect no better, and because I am not sure that it is not the best.

Benjamin Franklin, 1787

Learning Objective: Explain the differing ideological positions on the structure and function of the federal government.

With these words, Benjamin Franklin, the oldest delegate at the **Constitutional Convention** in Philadelphia, attempted to overcome the skepticism of other delegates about the document that they had created. Would the new document, the Constitution, establish a central government strong enough to hold 13 states together in a union that could prosper and endure? Several problems led to a convention that wrote a new constitution, which was followed by intense debates on whether to ratify the new plan of government.

The Annapolis Convention

To review what could be done about the country's inability to overcome critical problems, George Washington hosted a conference at his home in **Mount Vernon**, Virginia (1785). Representatives from Virginia, Maryland, Delaware, and Pennsylvania agreed that the problems were serious enough to hold further discussions at a later meeting at Annapolis, Maryland, with all the states invited. Only five states sent delegates to the **Annapolis Convention** in 1786. After discussing ways to improve commercial relations among the states, **James Madison** and **Alexander Hamilton** persuaded the others that another convention should be held in Philadelphia for the purpose of revising the Articles of Confederation.

Drafting the Constitution at Philadelphia

After a number of states elected delegates to the proposed Philadelphia convention, Congress consented to give its approval to the meeting. It called upon all 13 states to send delegates to Philadelphia "for the sole and express purpose of revising the Articles of Confederation." Only Rhode Island, not trusting the other states, refused to send delegates.

The Delegates

Of the 55 delegates who went to Philadelphia for the convention in the summer of 1787, all were White, all were male, and most were college-educated. As a group, they were relatively young (averaging in their early forties). With few exceptions, they were far wealthier than the average American of their day. They were well acquainted with issues of law and politics. A number of them were practicing lawyers, and many had helped to write their state constitutions.

The first order of business was to elect a presiding officer and decide whether or not to communicate with the public at large. The delegates voted to conduct their meetings in secret and say nothing to the public about their discussions until their work was completed. George Washington was unanimously elected chairperson. Benjamin Franklin, the elder statesman at age 81, provided a calming and unifying influence. The work in fashioning specific articles of the Constitution was directed by James Madison (who came to be known, despite his objections, as the Father of the Constitution), Alexander Hamilton, **Gouverneur Morris**, and **John Dickinson**. While they represented different states, these convention leaders shared the common goal of wanting to strengthen the young nation.

Several major leaders of the American Revolution were not at the convention. John Jay, Thomas Jefferson, and John Adams were on diplomatic business abroad, and Thomas Paine was also in Europe. Samuel Adams and John Hancock were not chosen as delegates. Patrick Henry, opposing any growth in federal power, refused to take part.

James Madison kept detailed notes on the debates at the convention. Since the convention did not allow outside observers and delegates were prohibited from talking to the press, his notes have shaped how historians interpret what happened during the convention. This engraving was probably made when Madison was in his 60s.
Source: David Edwin, c. Library of Congress.

Key Issues at the Convention

The convention opened with the delegates disagreeing sharply on its fundamental purpose. Some wanted to simply revise the Articles. Strong nationalists, such as Madison and Hamilton, wanted to draft an entirely new document. They argued that the confederate model of government, in which the states were loosely united under a weak central government, was unworkable. They believed in **federalism**, a system with a strong but limited central government. The nationalists quickly took control of the convention.

Americans in the 1780s generally distrusted government and feared that officials would seize every opportunity to abuse their powers, even if they were popularly elected. Therefore, Madison and other delegates believed in the **separation of powers**, dividing power among different branches of government. They wanted the new constitution to be based on a system of **checks and balances**, in which the power of each branch would be limited by the powers of the others. (For more on federalism and separation of powers, see Topic 3.9.)

Representation Especially divisive was the issue of whether the larger states such as Virginia and Pennsylvania should have proportionally more representatives in **Congress** than the smaller states such as New Jersey and Delaware. Madison's proposal—the **Virginia Plan**—favored the larger states. It was countered by the **New Jersey Plan**, which favored the smaller states. The issue was finally resolved by a compromise solution. Roger Sherman of Connecticut proposed the **Connecticut Plan** or the **Great Compromise**. It provided for a bicameral (two-house) Congress. In the **Senate**, states would have equal representation, but in the **House of Representatives**, each state would be represented according to the size of its population.

Slavery Two contentious issues grew out of slavery. Should enslaved people be counted in the state populations? Southerners argued they should. northerners said that since they did not have the rights of citizens, they should not. The delegates agreed to the **Three-Fifths Compromise**, which counted each enslaved individual as three-fifths of a person for the purposes of determining a state's level of taxation and representation. Should the slave trade be allowed? Some delegates wanted to ban it for humanitarian reasons. Others were concerned about maintaining a supply of labor. The delegates decided to guarantee that enslaved people could be imported for at least 20 years longer, until 1808. Congress could vote to abolish the practice after that date if it wished.

Trade The northern states wanted the central government to regulate interstate commerce and foreign trade. The south was afraid that export taxes would be placed on its agricultural products such as tobacco and rice. The **Commercial Compromise** allowed Congress to regulate interstate and foreign commerce, including placing tariffs (taxes) on foreign imports, but it prohibited placing taxes on any exports.

The Presidency The delegates debated over the president's term of office. Some argued that the chief executive should hold office for life. The delegates limited the president's term to four years but with no limit on the number of terms. They also debated the method for electing a president. Rather than having voters elect a president directly, the delegates decided to assign to each state a number of electors equal to the total of that state's representatives and senators. This **Electoral College system** was instituted because the delegates feared that too much democracy might lead to mob rule. Finally, the delegates debated what powers to give the president. They finally decided to grant the president considerable power, including the power to veto acts of Congress.

Ratification Procedure On September 17, 1787, after 17 weeks of debate, the Philadelphia convention approved a draft of the Constitution to submit to the states for ratification. Anticipating opposition, the Framers (delegates) specified in Article VII that a favorable vote of only nine states out of 13 was required for ratification. Each state would hold popularly elected conventions to debate and vote on the proposed Constitution.

Federalists and Anti-Federalists

Ratification was fiercely debated for almost a year, from September 1787 until June 1788. Supporters of the Constitution and its strong federal government were known as **Federalists**. Opponents who feared that that new government would be too strong were known as **Anti-Federalists**. Federalists were most common along the Atlantic Coast and in the large cities, while Anti-Federalists tended to be small farmers and settlers on the western frontier.

DEBATING THE CONSTITUTION		
Issue	**Federalists**	**Anti-Federalists**
Position on Constitution as Proposed	• Supported ratification	• Opposed ratification
Arguments	• A stronger central government was needed to maintain order and preserve the Union	• A stronger central government would destroy the work of the Revolution, limit democracy, and restrict states' rights
Strategies	• Emphasized the weaknesses of the Articles of Confederation • Portrayed Anti-Federalists as merely negative opponents with no solutions	• Argued that the proposed Constitution contained no bill of rights to protect individual freedoms • Claimed the proposed Constitution gave the central government more power than the British ever had
Advantages	• Strong leaders • Well-organized • Widespread concern about the problems under the Articles	• Widespread distrust of government power because of experiences as colonists
Disadvantages	• The Constitution was new and untried • The original Constitution lacked a bill of rights	• Less united than the Federalists

The Federalist Papers

A key element in the Federalist campaign for the Constitution was a series of highly persuasive essays written for a New York newspaper by James Madison, Alexander Hamilton, and John Jay. The 85 essays, later published in book form as *The Federalist Papers*, presented cogent reasons for believing in the practicality of each major provision of the Constitution.

The Path to Ratification

The Federalists won early victories in the state conventions in Delaware, New Jersey, and Pennsylvania—the first three states to ratify. However, the Federalists were not confident of victory in enough other states for ratification.

Debate on a Bill of Rights One of the main objections expressed by the Anti-Federalists was that the proposed Constitution lacked a list of specific rights that the federal government could not violate. They argued that Americans had fought the Revolutionary War to escape a tyrannical government in Britain. What was to stop a strong central government under the Constitution from acting similarly? Only by adding a bill of rights could Americans be protected against such a possibility.

Federalists responded that since members of Congress would be elected by the people, they did not need to be protected against themselves. Furthermore, people should assume that all rights were protected rather than create a limited list of rights that might allow unscrupulous officials to assert that unlisted rights could be violated. However, to win support for the Constitution, the Federalists promised to add to it a bill of rights as the first order of business for a new Congress. (For the language of the Bill of Rights, see Topic 3.9.)

Ratification Achieved With this promise, the Federalists successfully addressed the Anti-Federalists' most significant objection. With New Hampshire voting yes in June 1788, the Federalists won the necessary nine states to achieve ratification of the Constitution. Even so, the large states of Virginia and New York had not yet acted. If they failed to ratify, any chance for national unity and strength would be in dire jeopardy.

Final States In 1788, Virginia was by far the most populous of the original 13 states. There, the Anti-Federalists rallied behind two strong leaders, George Mason and Patrick Henry, who viewed the Constitution and a strong central government as threats to Americans' hard-won liberty. Virginia's Federalists, led by Washington, Madison, and John Marshall, managed to prevail by a close vote only after promising a bill of rights.

News of Virginia's vote had enough influence on New York's ratifying convention (combined with Alexander Hamilton's efforts) to win the day for the Constitution in that state. North Carolina in November 1789 and Rhode Island in May 1790 reversed their earlier rejections and thus became the last two states to ratify the Constitution as the new "supreme law of the land."

REFLECT ON THE LEARNING OBJECTIVE

1. Explain the competing philosophical views on the organization and tasks of the new government.

KEY TERMS BY THEME

Founders (NAT, SOC)	A Constitution (POL, ARC)	
James Madison	Constitutional Convention	Virginia Plan
Alexander Hamilton	Mount Vernon Conference	New Jersey Plan
Gouverneur Morris	Annapolis Convention	Connecticut Plan; Great Compromise
John Dickinson	federalism	Senate
Federalists	separation of powers	House of Representatives
Anti-Federalists	checks and balances	Three-Fifths Compromise
The Federalist Papers	Congress	Commercial Compromise
		Electoral College system

MULTIPLE-CHOICE QUESTIONS

Questions 1–3 refer to the following excerpt.

> "The plan of government now proposed is evidently calculated totally to change, in time, our condition as a people. Instead of being 13 republics under a federal head, it is clearly designed to make us one consolidated government. . . .
>
> The essential parts of a free and good government are a full and equal representation of the people in the legislature. . . .
>
> There are certain rights which we have always held sacred in the United States, and recognized in all our constitution, which, by adoption of the new Constitution in its present form, will be left unsecured. . . . I am fully satisfied that the state conventions ought most seriously to direct their exertions to altering and amending the system proposed before they shall adopt it."

Richard Henry Lee, *On the Rights that Must Be Preserved in the New Constitution*, 1787

1. Richard Henry Lee's concerns expressed in this excerpt would have been supported most by people in which of the following groups?

(A) Merchants who wanted stronger support of commerce

(B) Slave owners who opposed the three-fifths compromise

(C) Quakers who advocated for greater freedom of conscience

(D) Politicians who philosophically favored more local autonomy

2. People who advocated for ratification of the Constitution responded to Lee and others who shared his views by
   (A) agreeing to add of a bill of rights
   (B) meeting with Lee at the Mount Vernon Conference
   (C) renegotiating the Commercial Compromise
   (D) rejecting the Great Compromise

3. Based on the excerpt, Lee would have most likely advocated for which of the following types of changes?
   (A) Strengthening the power of the chief executive
   (B) Replacing the compromise on slavery taxation and representation
   (C) Protecting the independence of the judiciary
   (D) Eliminating one house in the two-house legislature

SHORT-ANSWER QUESTION

Use complete sentences; an outline or bulleted list alone is not acceptable.

1. Answer (a), (b), and (c).
   (a) Briefly explain how ONE compromise passed at the Constitutional Convention altered the development of the United States.
   (b) Briefly explain ONE specific criticism of a compromise passed at the Constitutional Convention that would have altered the development of the United States.
   (c) Briefly explain ONE specific criticism brought forth by the Anti-Federalists concerning the power of the new federal government.

Topic 3.9

The Constitution

The Constitution is the guide which I never will abandon.

George Washington, letter to the Boston city leaders, 1795

Learning Objective: Explain the continuities and changes in the structure and functions of the government with the ratification of the Constitution.

The men who wrote the newly ratified Constitution hoped it would both follow the ideals of the Enlightenment and provide a working system to guide the new republic. They wanted to correct the weaknesses of the Articles of Confederation without creating a government with excessive power. To guard against tyranny, they divided power vertically—between the federal and state levels. The also divided federal power horizontally—among three branches. As a further step toward keeping government power in check, and to fulfill a promise made during the ratification debates, one of the first tasks of the new Congress was to propose a Bill of Rights.

Federalism

The writers of the Constitution (or Framers) divided power between the federal government and state governments. The federal government would handle issues that affected the entire country, such as national defense and foreign affairs, and issues that crossed state boundaries, such interstate commerce and a postal service. States would be in charge of issues that affected only their state, such as schools and local elections.

As changes in transportation, communication, and the economy have increased the interactions among people across state lines, the federal government has become more powerful. Further, constitutional amendments added specific powers to the federal government. For example, the 19th Amendment, ratified in 1920, gave Congress the power to protect the right of women to vote.

By the 21st century, the government accounted for around 40 percent of the gross domestic product of the country. The federal goverment was usually responsible for over half of all public expenditures, paying for programs such as Social Security, Medicare, and the military, and transferring money to state and local governments. However, most public employees worked for state or local governments, with the largest number employed in schools and universities.

Separation of Powers

The Framers also divided powers among three main branches of government:

- legislative: Congress makes laws, passes taxes, and allocates spending
- executive: led by the president, it recommends and carries out laws and federal programs
- judicial: it consists of the Supreme Court and all lower federal courts; it interprets the laws and the Constitution

The Constitution provided each branch of government ways to limit the power or at least influence the other two branches:

- Congress can pass laws, but the president can veto laws and the Supreme Court can rule them unconstitutional.
- The president can make treaties, but they must be ratified by Congress.
- The president can enforce the laws, but the Supreme Court can stop those actions if it finds that they violate the Constitution.
- The Supreme Court interprets the laws, but Congress can write new laws.
- The Supreme Court can order a president to enforce a law, but a president has the power to appoint justices.

The Bill of Rights

In 1789, the first Congress acted quickly to approve **amendments** to defend individual liberty. Drafted largely by James Madison, the ten ratified by the states in 1791 are known as the **Bill of Rights**. Originally, they protected against abuses by the central (or federal) government. Since the ratification of the 14th Amendment in 1868, most of the protections have been extended to apply to abuses by state governments as well. Below is the text of the Bill of Rights.

First Amendment "Congress shall make no law respecting an establishment of religion, or prohibiting the free exercise thereof; or abridging the freedom of speech, or of the press, or the right of the people peaceably to assemble, and to petition the Government for a redress of grievances."

Second Amendment "A well regulated Militia, being necessary to the security of a free State, the right of the people to keep and bear Arms, shall not be infringed."

Third Amendment "No Soldier shall, in time of peace be quartered in any house, without the consent of the Owner, nor in time of war, but in a manner prescribed by law."

Fourth Amendment "The right of the people to be secure in their persons, houses, papers, and effects, against unreasonable searches and seizures, shall not be violated, and no Warrants shall issue, but upon probable cause, supported by Oath or affirmation, and particularly describing the place to be searched, and the persons or things to be seized."

Fifth Amendment "No person shall be held to answer for a capital, or otherwise infamous crime, unless on a presentment or indictment of a Grand Jury, except in cases arising in the land or naval forces, or in the Militia, when in actual service in time of War or public danger; nor shall any person be subject for the same offence to be twice put in jeopardy of life or limb; nor shall be compelled in any criminal case to be a witness against himself, nor be deprived of life, liberty, or property, without due process of law; nor shall private property be taken for public use without just compensation."

Sixth Amendment "In all criminal prosecutions, the accused shall enjoy the right to a speedy and public trial, by an impartial jury of the State and district wherein the crime shall have been committed; which district shall have been previously ascertained by law, and to be informed of the nature and cause of the accusation; to be confronted with the witnesses against him; to have compulsory process for obtaining witnesses in his favor, and to have the assistance of counsel for his defense."

Seventh Amendment "In suits of common law, where the value in controversy shall exceed twenty dollars, the right of trial by jury shall be preserved, and no fact tried by a jury shall be otherwise re-examined in any Court of the United States, than according to the rules of the common law."

Eighth Amendment "Excessive bail shall not be required, nor excessive fines imposed, nor cruel and unusual punishments inflicted."

Ninth Amendment "The enumeration in the Constitution of certain rights shall not be construed to deny or disparage others retained by the people."

Tenth Amendment "The powers not delegated to the United States by the Constitution, nor prohibited by it to the States, are reserved to the States respectively, or to the people."

REFLECT ON THE LEARNING OBJECTIVE

1. Explain what stayed the same and what changed in the form and the workings of the government under the new Constitution compared to government under the Articles of Confederation.

KEY TERMS BY THEME

Founders (NAT, SOC)	amendments	Founders (NAT, SOC)
federalism	Bill of Rights	James Madison
separation of powers		

MULTIPLE-CHOICE QUESTIONS

Questions 1–3 refer to the following excerpt.

"It is not denied that there are implied [existing but not clearly stated] as well as express [clearly stated] powers, and that the former are as effectually delegated as the latter.

It is conceded that implied powers are to be considered as delegated equally with express ones. Then it follows, that as a power of erecting a corporation [such as a bank] may as well be implied as any other thing, it may as well be employed as an instrument or means of carrying into execution any of the specified powers. . . . But one may be erected in relation to the trade with foreign countries, or to the trade between the States . . . because it is the province of the federal government to regulate those objects, and because it is incident to a general sovereign or legislative power to regulate a thing, to employ all the means which relate to its regulation to the best and greatest advantage."

Alexander Hamilton, Letter on the National Bank, 1791

1. Hamilton's constitutional argument was based on which of the following types of powers?
   (A) Employed
   (B) Expressed
   (C) Implied
   (D) Regulated

2. Hamilton's position expressed in the excerpt most clearly reflected his dissatisfaction with which of the following?
   (A) The Declaration of Independence
   (B) The Articles of Confederation
   (C) The Northwest Ordinance
   (D) The Bill of Rights

3. Which of the following would best serve as the basis for modifying or refuting Hamilton's position expressed in the excerpt?
   (A) The ideals of the Enlightenment, such as the emphasis on reason
   (B) The theory of the separation of powers, which divided power among three branches of government
   (C) The purpose of the 10th Amendment, which reserves powers to the states
   (D) The writings of Thomas Paine, which supported revolution

1. "The contest over the Constitution was not primarily a war over abstract political ideals, such as states' rights and centralization, but over concrete economic issues, and the political division which accompanied it was substantially along the lines of the interests affected—the financiers, public creditors, traders, commercial men, manufacturers, and allied groups, centering mainly in the larger seaboard towns, being chief among the advocates of the Constitution, and the farmers, particularly in the inland regions, and the debtors being chief among its opponents. That other considerations, such as the necessity for stronger national defense, entered into the campaign is, of course, admitted, but with all due allowances, it may be truly said that the Constitution was a product of a struggle between capitalistic and agrarian interests."

Charles A. Beard, historian, *Economic Origins of Jeffersonian Democracy,* 1915

"It is easy to accept the general proposition that ideas and interests are somehow associated. . . . But there are some dangers in working with any such formula. The first is that ideas—or all those intangible emotional, moral, and intellectual forces that may roughly be combined under the rubric of ideas—will somehow be dissolved and that we will be left only with interests on our hands. . . Then there is the danger that interests will be too narrowly construed: that we will put too much emphasis on the motives and purposes of individuals and groups, not enough on the structural requirements of a social system or on the limitations imposed on men by particular historical situations . . . that the way in which men perceive and define their interests is in some good part a reflex of the ideas they have inherited and the experiences they have undergone. . .

For the generation of the Founding Fathers, the central, formative, shattering, and then reintegrating experience of civic life was the Revolution, which recast the pattern of their interests and galvanized their inherited store of ideas."

Richard Hofstadter, historian, *The Progressive Historians,* 1968

Using the excerpts, answer (a), (b), and (c).

(a) Briefly explain ONE major difference between Beard's and Hofstadter's interpretations of the influences on the Constitution.

(b) Briefly explain how ONE historical event or development in the period 1776 to 1789 that is not explicitly mentioned in the excerpts could be used to support Beard's interpretation.

(c) Briefly explain how ONE historical event or development in the period 1776 to 1789 that is not explicitly mentioned in the excerpts could be used to support Hofstadter's interpretation.

Topic 3.10

Shaping a New Republic

There is nothing which I dread so much as a division of the republic into two great parties. . . . [It] is to be dreaded as the greatest political evil under our Constitution.

John Adams, letter to Jonathan Jackson, 1780

Learning Objective 1: Explain how and why competition intensified conflict among peoples and nations from 1754 to 1800.

Learning Objective 2: Explain how and why political ideas, institutions, and party systems developed and changed in the new republic.

Having faced the challenges of declaring independence, fighting a Revolutionary War, agreeing on a Constitution, and forming a functioning government, the new nation's continued existence was not guaranteed. Under the leadership of the first two presidents, George Washington and John Adams, the Republic dealt with a multitude of challenges, both foreign and domestic.

Washington's Presidency

Members of the first Congress under the Constitution were elected in 1788 and began their first session in March 1789 in New York City (then the nation's temporary capital). People assumed that George Washington would be the electoral college's unanimous choice for president, and indeed he was.

Organizing the Federal Government

Washington took the oath of office as the first U.S. president on April 30, 1789. From then on, what the Constitution and its system of checks and balances actually meant in practice would be determined from day to day by the decisions of Congress as the legislative branch, the president as the head of the executive branch, and the Supreme Court as the top federal court in the judicial branch.

Executive Departments As chief executive, Washington's first task was to organize new departments of the executive (law-enforcing) branch. The Constitution authorizes the president to appoint chiefs of departments, although they must be confirmed, or approved, by the Senate. Washington appointed four heads of departments: Thomas Jefferson as secretary of state, Alexander Hamilton as secretary of the treasury, **Henry Knox** as secretary of war, and **Edmund Randolph** as attorney general. These four men formed a **cabinet** of advisers with whom President Washington met regularly to discuss major policy issues. Today, presidents still meet with their cabinets to obtain advice and information.

Federal Court System The only federal court mentioned in the Constitution is the **Supreme Court**. Congress, however, was given the power to create other **federal courts** with lesser powers and to determine the number of justices making up the Supreme Court. One of Congress' first laws was the **Judiciary Act of 1789**, which established a Supreme Court with one chief justice and five associate justices. This highest court was empowered to rule on the constitutionality of decisions made by state courts. The act also provided for a system of 13 district courts and three circuit courts of appeals.

Hamilton's Financial Program

One of the most pressing problems faced by Congress under the Articles had been the government's financial difficulties. Alexander Hamilton, secretary of the treasury, presented to Congress a plan for putting U.S. finances on a stable foundation. Hamilton's plan included three main actions. (1) Pay off the **national debt** at face value and have the federal government assume the war debts of the states. (2) Protect the young nation's "infant" (new and developing) industries and collect adequate revenues at the same time by imposing high tariffs on imported goods. (3) Create a **national bank** for depositing government funds and printing banknotes that would provide the basis for a stable U.S. currency. Support for this program came chiefly from northern merchants, who would gain directly from high tariffs and a stabilized currency.

Opponents of Hamilton's financial plan included the Anti-Federalists, who feared that the states would lose power to the extent that the central government gained it. Thomas Jefferson led a faction of southern Anti-Federalists who viewed Hamilton's program as benefiting only the rich at the expense of indebted farmers. After political wrangling and bargaining, Congress finally adopted Hamilton's plan in slightly modified form. For example, the tariffs were not as high as Hamilton wanted.

Debt Jefferson and his supporters agreed to Hamilton's insistence that the U.S. government pay off the national debt at face value and assume payment of the war debts of the states. In return for Jefferson's support on this aspect of his plan, Hamilton agreed to Jefferson's idea for the nation's capital to be in the south along the Potomac River (an area that, after Washington's death, would be named Washington, D.C.).

National Bank Jefferson argued that the Constitution did not give Congress the power to create a bank. But Hamilton took a broader view of the Constitution, arguing that the document's "necessary and proper" clause authorized Congress to do whatever was necessary to carry out its enumerated powers. Washington supported Hamilton on the issue, and the proposed bank was voted into law. Although chartered by the federal government, the Bank of the United States was privately owned. As a major shareholder of the bank, the federal government could print paper currency and use federal deposits to stimulate business.

Foreign Affairs Under Washington

Washington's first term as president (1789–1793) coincided with the outbreak of revolution in France, a cataclysmic event that was to touch off a series of wars between the new French Republic and the monarchies of Europe. Washington's entire eight years as president, as well as the four years of his successor, John Adams, were taken up with the question of whether to give U.S. support to France, France's enemies, or neither side.

French Revolution

Americans generally supported the French people's aspiration to establish a republic, but many were also horrified by reports of mob hysteria and mass executions. To complicate matters, the U.S.–French alliance remained in effect, although it was an alliance with the French monarchy, not with the revolutionary republic. Jefferson and his supporters sympathized with the revolutionary cause. They also argued that because Britain was seizing American merchant ships bound for French ports, the United States should join France in its defensive war against Britain.

Proclamation of Neutrality (1793) Washington, however, believed that the young nation was not strong enough to engage in a European war. Resisting popular clamor, in 1793 he issued a proclamation of U.S. neutrality in the conflict. Jefferson resigned from the cabinet in disagreement with Washington's policy.

"Citizen" Genêt Objecting to Washington's policy, "Citizen" Edmond Genêt, the French minister to the United States, broke all the rules of diplomacy by appealing directly to the American people to support the French cause. So outrageous was his conduct, even Jefferson approved of Washington's request to the French government that they remove Genêt. Recalled by his government, Genêt chose to remain in the United States, where he married and became a U.S. citizen.

The Jay Treaty (1794) with Great Britain

Washington sent Chief Justice John Jay on a special mission to Britain to talk about two issues. One was Britain's continued occupation of posts on the U.S. western frontier. The other was Britain's offensive practice of searching and seizing American ships and impressing seamen into the British navy. After a year of negotiations, Jay brought back a treaty in which Britain agreed to evacuate its posts but included nothing about impressment. Narrowly ratified by the Senate, the unpopular **Jay Treaty** angered American supporters of France, but it did maintain Washington's policy of neutrality, which kept the United States at peace.

The Pinckney Treaty (1795) with Spain

Totally unexpected was the effect that the Jay Treaty had on Spain's policy toward its territories in the Americas. Seeing the treaty as a sign that the United States might be drawing closer to Spain's longtime foe Britain, Spain decided to consolidate its holdings in North America. The Spanish influence in the Far West had been strengthened by a series of Catholic missions along the California coast, but they were concerned about their colonies in the southeast. Thomas Pinckney, the U.S. minister to Spain, negotiated a treaty with these provisions:

- Spain opened the lower Mississippi River and New Orleans to American trade.

- The **right of deposit** was granted to Americans so that they could transfer cargoes in New Orleans without paying duties to the Spanish government.

- Spain accepted the U.S. claim that Florida's northern boundary should be at the 31st parallel (not north of that line, as Spain had formerly insisted).

Domestic Concerns under Washington

In addition to coping with foreign challenges, stabilizing the nation's credit, and organizing the new government, Washington faced a number of domestic problems and crises.

PINCKNEY'S TREATY, 1795

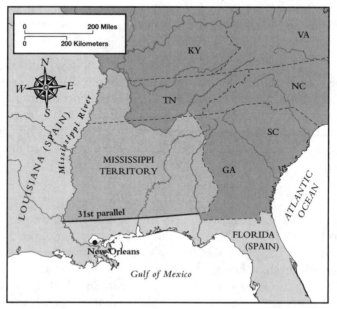

American Indians Through the final decades of the 18th century, settlers crossed the Alleghenies and moved the frontier steadily westward into the Ohio Valley and beyond. In an effort to resist the settlers' encroachment on their lands, a number of the tribes formed the Northwest (or Western) Confederacy. The Shawnee, Delaware, Iroquois, and other tribes allied under the Miami war chief Little Turtle. Initially, they won a series of bloody victories over the settler militias.

In some cases, the British were supplying the American Indians with arms and encouraging them to attack the settlers. Hearing this incensed the Americans. In 1794, the U.S. army, led by General Anthony Wayne, defeated the Confederacy tribes at the **Battle of Fallen Timbers** in northwestern Ohio. The next year, the chiefs of the defeated peoples agreed to the **Treaty of Greenville**, in which they surrendered claims to the Ohio Territory and promised to open it up to settlement.

The Whiskey Rebellion (1794) Hamilton, to make up the revenue lost because tariffs were lower than he wanted, persuaded Congress to pass excise taxes, particularly on the sale of whiskey. In western Pennsylvania, the refusal of a group of farmers to pay the federal tax on whiskey seemed to pose a major challenge to the viability of the U.S. government under the Constitution. The rebelling farmers could ill afford to pay a tax on the whiskey that they distilled from surplus corn. Rather than pay the tax, they defended their "liberties" by attacking the revenue collectors.

Washington responded to this crisis by federalizing 15,000 state militia and placing them under the command of Alexander Hamilton. The show of force had its intended effects. The Whiskey Rebellion collapsed with almost no bloodshed and the federal government solidified its authority. Some Americans applauded Washington's action, contrasting it with the previous government's helplessness to do anything about Shays's Rebellion. Among westerners, however, the military action was widely resented and condemned as an unwarranted use of force against the common people. The government's chief critic, Thomas Jefferson, gained in popularity as a champion of western farmers.

Western Lands In the 1790s, the Jay Treaty and the victory at the Battle of Fallen Timbers gave the federal government control of vast tracts of land. Congress encouraged the rapid settlement of these lands by passing the **Public Land Act** in 1796, which established orderly procedures for dividing and selling federal lands at moderate prices. The process for adding new states to the Union, as set forth in the Constitution, went smoothly. While the first new state was in New England (Vermont in 1791), the next two reflected the country's push westward: Kentucky in 1792 and Tennessee in 1796.

The First Political Parties

Washington's election by unanimous vote of the Electoral College in 1789 underscored the popular belief that political parties were not needed. The Constitution itself did not mention political parties, and the framers assumed none would arise. They were soon proven wrong. The debates between Federalists and Anti-Federalists in 1787 and 1788 were the first indication that a two-party system would emerge as a core feature of American politics.

Origins

In colonial times, groups of legislators commonly formed temporary factions and voted together either for or against a specific policy. When an issue was settled, the factions would dissolve. The dispute between Federalists and Anti-Federalists over the ratification of the Constitution closely resembled the factional disputes of an earlier period. What was unusual about this conflict was that it was organized—at least by the Federalists—across state lines and in that sense prefigured the national parties that emerged soon afterward.

In the 1790s, sometimes called the **Federalist era** because it was dominated largely by Federalist policies, political parties began to form around two leading figures, Hamilton and Jefferson. The **Federalist Party** supported Hamilton and his financial program. In opposition, the **Democratic-Republican Party** supported Jefferson and tried to elect candidates in different states who opposed Hamilton's program. The French Revolution further solidified the formation of national **political parties**. Americans divided sharply over whether to support France. A large number followed Jefferson's lead in openly challenging President Washington's neutrality policy.

Differences Between the Parties

The Federalists were strongest in the northeastern states and advocated the growth of federal power. The Democratic-Republicans were strongest in the southern states and on the western frontier and argued for states' rights. By 1796, the two major political parties were taking shape and becoming better organized. In that year, President Washington announced that he intended to retire to private life at the end of his second term.

COMPARISON OF FEDERALIST AND DEMOCRATIC-REPUBLICAN PARTIES		
Trait	**Federalists**	**Democratic-Republicans**
Leaders	· John Adams · Alexander Hamilton	· Thomas Jefferson · James Madison
View of the Constitution	· Interpret loosely · Create a strong central government	· Interpret strictly · Create a weak central government
Foreign Policy	· Pro-British	· Pro-French
Military Policy	· Develop a large peacetime army and navy	· Develop a small peacetime army and navy
Economic Policy	· Aid business · Create a national bank · Support high tariffs	· Favor agriculture · Oppose a national bank · Oppose high tariffs
Chief Supporters	· Northern business owners · Large landowners	· Skilled workers · Small farmers · Plantation owners

Washington's Farewell Address

Assisted by Alexander Hamilton, the retiring president wrote a speech known as his Farewell Address for publication in the newspapers in late 1796. This message had enormous influence because of Washington's prestige. The president spoke against policies and practices that he considered unwise:

- Do not get involved in European affairs.
- Do not make **"permanent alliances"** in foreign affairs.
- Do not form political parties.
- Do not fall into sectionalism.

For the next century, future presidents would mostly heed Washington's first two warnings against foreign entanglements. However, in the case of political parties, Washington was already behind the times. By the time he spoke, political parties were well on their way to becoming a vital part of the American political system and sectional differences were growing stronger.

One long-term consequence of Washington's decision to leave office after two terms was that later presidents followed his example. Presidents elected to two terms (including Jefferson, Madison, Monroe, and Jackson) would voluntarily retire even though the Constitution placed no limit on a president's tenure in office. The **two-term tradition** continued unbroken until 1940 when Franklin Roosevelt won election to a third term. Then, the 22nd Amendment, ratified in 1951, made the two-term limit a part of the Constitution.

John Adams' Presidency

Even as Washington was writing his Farewell Address, political parties were working to gain majorities in the two houses of Congress and to line up enough electors from the various states to elect the next president. The vice president, **John Adams**, was the Federalists' candidate, while former secretary of state Thomas Jefferson was the choice of the Democratic-Republicans.

Adams won by three electoral votes. Jefferson became vice president, since the original Constitution gave that office to the candidate receiving the second highest number of electoral votes. (Since the ratification of the 12th Amendment in 1804, the president and vice president have run as a team.)

The XYZ Affair Troubles abroad related to the French Revolution presented Adams with the first major challenge of his presidency. Americans were angered that French warships and privateers were seizing U.S. merchant ships. Seeking a peaceful settlement, Adams sent a delegation to Paris to negotiate with the French government. Certain French ministers, known only as X, Y, and Z because their names were never revealed, requested bribes as the basis for entering into negotiations. The American delegates indignantly refused. Newspaper reports of the demands made by X, Y, and Z infuriated many Americans, who now clamored for war against France. "Millions for defense, but not one cent for tribute" became the slogan of the hour. One faction of the Federalist Party, led by Alexander Hamilton, hoped that by going to war the United States could gain French and Spanish lands in North America.

President Adams, on the other hand, resisted the popular sentiment for war. Recognizing that the U.S. Army and Navy were not yet strong enough to fight a major power, the president avoided war and sent new ministers to Paris.

The Alien and Sedition Acts Anger against France strengthened the Federalists in the congressional elections of 1798 enough to win a majority in both houses. The Federalists took advantage of their victory by enacting laws to restrict their political opponents, the Democratic-Republicans. For example, since most immigrants voted Democratic-Republican, the Federalists passed the Naturalization Act, which increased from 5 to 14 the years required for immigrants to qualify for U.S. citizenship. They also passed the Alien Acts, which authorized the president to deport aliens considered dangerous and to detain enemy aliens in time of war. Most seriously, they passed the Sedition Act, which made it illegal for newspaper editors to criticize either the president or Congress and imposed fines or imprisonment for editors who violated the law.

The Kentucky and Virginia Resolutions Democratic-Republicans argued that the Alien and Sedition Acts violated rights guaranteed by the 1st Amendment of the Constitution. In 1799, however, the Supreme Court had not yet established the principle of judicial review, the idea that the court could overturn a law that it found in conflict with the Constitution (see Topic 4.2). Democratic-Republican leaders challenged the legislation of the Federalist Congress by enacting nullifying laws of their own in the state legislatures. The Kentucky legislature adopted a resolution that had been written by Thomas Jefferson, and the Virginia legislature adopted a resolution introduced by James Madison. Both resolutions declared that the states had entered into a "compact" in forming the national government. Therefore, if any act of the federal government broke the compact, a state could nullify the federal law. Although only Kentucky and Virginia adopted nullifying resolutions in 1799, they set forth an argument and rationale that would be widely used in the nullification controversy of the 1830s (see Topic 4.8).

The immediate crisis over the Alien and Sedition Acts faded when the Federalists lost control of Congress after the election of 1800, and the Democratic-Republican majority allowed the acts to expire or repealed them. Further, in 1803, the Supreme Court under Chief Justice John Marshall asserted its power in deciding whether federal laws were constitutional.

REFLECT ON THE LEARNING OBJECTIVE

1. Explain how and why disagreements deepened struggles among peoples and nations from 1754 to 1800.

MULTIPLE-CHOICE QUESTIONS

Questions 1-3 refer to the following excerpt.

"Friends and Fellow Citizens: I should now apprise you of the resolution I have formed to decline being considered among the number of those out of whom a choice is to be made. . . .

I have already intimated to you the danger of parties . . . with particular reference to . . . geographical discriminations. . . .

Let it simply be asked—where is the security for property, for reputation, for life, if the sense of religious obligation desert the oaths. . . .

As a very important source of strength and security, cherish public credit . . . avoiding likewise the accumulation of debt . . . which unavoidable wars may have occasioned . . . in mind that toward the payment of debt there must be . . . taxes. . . .

By interweaving our destiny with that of any part of Europe, [we] entangle our peace and prosperity in the toils of European ambition, rivalship, interest, humor, or caprice. . . . It is our true policy to steer clear of permanent alliances with any portion of the foreign world."

George Washington, Farewell Address, 1796

1. One of the primary reasons Washington and others warned against political parties was concern about
   (A) damage to the national reputation
   (B) divisive sectionalism
   (C) rights of property owners
   (D) unavoidable wars

2. One of the outcomes of the Farewell Address was
   (A) the two-party system
   (B) the precedent of a two-term limit
   (C) the first presidential library
   (D) the beginning of greater U.S. involvement overseas

3. Which of the following developments during Washington's presidency most likely had a direct impact on the views he expressed in the excerpt?
   (A) The status of American Indians
   (B) The creation of a federal court system
   (C) The Proclamation of Neutrality
   (D) The National Bank

SHORT-ANSWER QUESTION

Use complete sentences; an outline or bulleted list alone is not acceptable.

1. Answer (a), (b), and (c).
   (a) Briefly explain ONE historical event or development in the period 1789 to 1800 that is an example of the American foreign policy of avoiding war.
   (b) Briefly explain ONE positive or negative result in the period 1789 to 1800 of the American foreign policy of avoiding war.
   (c) Briefly explain how ONE person or group in the U.S. in the period 1789 to 1800 challenged the United States government's foreign policy.

Developing an American Identity

The American is a new man, who acts upon new principles; he must therefore entertain new ideas, and form new opinions.

J. Hector St. John Crèvecoeur, *Letters from an American Farmer,* 1782

Learning Objective: Explain the continuities and changes in American culture from 1754 to 1800.

A truly unique American identity would take at least a generation, if not more, to became clearly established and recognized. Admiration of the influence of the "founding fathers," the leaders who declared independence, fought a war to achieve it, and created a new system of government, became the core of an American identity which continues today. A clear example of this influence is demonstrated by the actions of George Washington. His Farewell Address (Topic 3.10) and two-term tradition as president retain their relevancy in varying degrees today. That people still debate the meaning of the founding fathers' words and ideas reflects their importance in understanding the United States and its people, then and now. In the process of forging an identity, Americans retained much of their ancestors' culture and traditions. The evolving identity would be built on the foundation of the people and culture of the 13 colonies (Topic 2.7), formed by the thought and experience of the Revolution (Topics 3.4 and 3.6), and enlarged by regional differences (Topic 2.3) and the ongoing additions of immigrants.

Social Change

In addition to revolutionizing the politics of the 13 states, the War for Independence also profoundly changed American society. Some changes occurred immediately before the war ended, while others evolved gradually as the ideas of the Revolution began to filter into the attitudes of the common people. Together, these changes fostered growing awareness of how the United States was different from Great Britain and the rest of Europe.

Abolition of Aristocratic Titles State constitutions and laws abolished old institutions that had originated in medieval Europe. No legislature could grant titles of nobility, nor could any court recognize the feudal practice of primogeniture (the first-born son's right to inherit his family's property). Whatever aristocracy existed in colonial America was further weakened by the confiscation of large estates owned by Loyalists. Many such estates were subdivided and sold to raise money for the war.

Separation of Church and State Most states adopted the principle of separation of church and state. In other words, they refused to give financial support to any religious group. The Anglican Church (which became known as the Episcopal Church in the United States) formerly had been closely tied to the king's government. However, it was disestablished (lost state support) in the south. Only in three New England states—New Hampshire, Connecticut, and Massachusetts—did the Congregational Church continue to receive state support in the form of a religious tax. This practice was finally discontinued in New England early in the 1830s.

Regional Variations As the example of church-state separation shows, all of the states did not change at the same time. The regional differences that emerged in the colonial period continued to shape how the states evolved. The term "southerner" had entered common usage in the 1780s. The biggest difference was in slavery. While slavery continued to decline in northern states, it became stronger than ever in southern states.

Visitors also noticed differences in how people acted. In 1785, Jefferson wrote to a friend in France that an observant visitor could determine the line of latitude simply by paying attention to the character of the people in the area. In general, said Jefferson, northerners were more serious and persevering in their work, while southerners were more generous and forthright in their speech.

Political Change

The development of political parties (Topic 3.10) both added to and reflected the American identity. The distinctions between the two initial parties, the Federalist and Democratic-Republican, had their origins in the debate between Federalists and Anti-Federalists over the ratification of the Constitution. These distinctions matured largely based on regional differences and distinct views of the roles, functions, and powers of the federal government. The evolution of political parties continues today, as does the distinctiveness of an American identity.

The Great Seal includes symbols that represent the United States. For example, the stars represent the 13 original states, the olive branch represents a desire for peace, and the arrows represent a readiness to go to war. The white stripes represent purity, the red stripes represent courage, and the blue field represents vigilance.
Source: U.S. Government. Wikipedia.org.

Cultural Change

While much of the nation's culture reflected its British origins, gradually a distinctive national identity evolved. This change was facilitated by the expansion of newspapers in the late 1700s as a means of communication and a source for political discussion. Writer Charles Brockden Brown explored the meaning of an American identity through novels. In Philadelphia, **Charles Wilson Peale** opened what is recognized as the first art gallery. In the 1790s, **Pierre-Charles L'Enfant** developed the design for Washington, D.C., **Gilbert Stuart** painted the nation's leaders, and the American Academy of Fine Arts held its first exhibition. Later, developments such as the first dictionary for American English and a book on American geography would continue the process of creating a distinctive culture.

REFLECT ON THE LEARNING OBJECTIVE

1. Explain what stayed the same and what was altered in American culture in the period from 1754 to 1800.

KEY TERMS BY THEME

Culture (ARC)
Charles Wilson Peale
Pierre-Charles L'Enfant
Gilbert Stuart

MULTIPLE-CHOICE QUESTIONS

Questions 1-2 refer to the following excerpt.

"Friends, what then is the American, this new man? He is either a European, or the descendant of a European, hence that strange mixture of blood, which you will find in no other country. I could point out to you a family whose grandfather was an Englishman, whose wife was Dutch, whose son married a Frenchwoman, and whose present four sons have now four wives of different nations.

He is an American, who leaving behind him all his ancient prejudices and manners, receives new ones from the new mode of life he has embraced, the new government he obeys, and the new rank he holds. He becomes an American by being received in the broad lap of our great alma mater. Here individuals of all nations are melted into a new race of men, whose labors and posterity will one day cause great changes in the world. . . .

The American is a new man, who acts upon new principles; he must therefore entertain new ideas and form new opinions. From involuntary idleness, servile dependence, penury [poverty], and useless labor he has passed to toils of a very different nature, rewarded by ample subsistence—this is an American."

J. Hector St. John Crèvecoeur, *Letters from
an American Farmer,* 1782

1. The clearest way to modify or refute the answer given in the excerpt to the question, "What then is the American, this new man?" would be to point out the important role of

   (A) the enslaved African Americans who worked on plantations

   (B) the leaders who wrote the Constitution

   (C) the development of political parties

   (D) the ideas in Washington's Farewell Address

2. Which of the following groups best represents the change described in the last sentence of the excerpt?

   (A) American Indians who lived in the region before Europeans arrived

   (B) Puritans who settled in Massachusetts Bay in the 17th century

   (C) Indentured servants who became free after working for a master for several years

   (D) Elected leaders who served in legislative bodies during the colonial period

SHORT-ANSWER QUESTION

Use complete sentences; an outline or bulleted list alone is not acceptable.

1. Answer (a), (b), and (c).

   (a) Briefly explain ONE specific historical difference between the cultural life in the American colonies under British rule and life in the newly independent United States.

   (b) Briefly explain ONE specific historical similarity between the cultural life in the American colonies under British rule and life in the newly independent United States.

   (c) Briefly explain how ONE legal change impacted the cultural life of the colonies and the United States in the period 1754 to 1800.

Movement in the Early Republic

I have long since given up the expectation of any early provision for getting in the extinguishment of slavery among us.

Thomas Jefferson letter to William Burwell, 1805

Learning Objective 1: Explain how and why migration and immigration to and within North America caused competition and conflict over time.

Learning Objective 2: Explain the continuities and changes in regional attitudes about slavery as it expanded from 1754 to 1800.

The founding of the Republic increased the movement of people, mainly westward. The uncertainties of rebellion and war had ended. With peace and the removal of British control came a re-ordering of government and life. At the same time, however, hostile forces remained on the borders of the new nation. The British to the north and west, and the Spanish to the south and west, both threatened the young country's existence. In addition, both within and on the borders lived Native Americans who resented the expansion of European settlers onto their lands.

Migration and Settlement

The people who moved west, whether they were born in America or came as free immigrants or indentured servants or enslaved Africans, faced a range of forces, both friendly and hostile. This movement was recognized and accepted from the very beginning of the nation. The **Northwest Ordinance** (Topic 3.7), enacted under the Articles of Confederation, provided a mechanism for migration and settlement. It planned for the sale of government land, an orderly adoption of western territory into new states, public education, and outlawed slavery in the territory. While the government had foreseen migration, it still could not eliminate the disputes and conflicts that developed.

American Indians

By the end of the 18th century, Native Americans found themselves losing conflicts with settlers. As a result, they were increasingly either living on reservations or forced to migrate west.

Laws In 1790, the **Indian Intercourse Act** was one of the first laws passed by the new nation. The act placed the federal government in control of all legal actions with Native Americans. Only the federal government, not the states, could purchase their land and regulate any trade and traveling over their lands. These laws were largely ignored by the traders and settlers migrating westward.

Resistance While the settlers ignored laws and treaties intended to maintain peace with the American Indians, the government usually supported the settlers when disputes turned violent. For example, in the Northwest Territory in the 1790s, a confederation of Shawnee and other American Indians twice successfully defeated government troops. In response, a larger government force defeated the confederation at the **Battle of Fallen Timbers** in what is today northwestern Ohio (Topic 3.10). The American Indian position was further weakened in this area as the British, who had supported them, gradually closed the trading forts that they had maintained there in the years immediately following the Revolution.

West of the Mississippi Migration was a survivable option for many tribes. They faced overwhelming force, fatal foreign diseases, and the destruction of their hunting grounds depriving them of food and furs to trade. Some did remain where their ancestors had settled. They were unwilling to leave their traditional lands despite being surrounded by hostile settlers. The Iroquois stayed on reservations or moved north to Canada. Many, including the Shawnee in the north and Cherokees further south (Topic 4.8), moved across the Mississippi River. These journeys were perilous as those tribes native to the west resisted these incursions into their traditional lands.

The Southern Frontier Further south, near New Orleans and in Florida, the Spanish were primarily concerned with stopping the incursion of settlers from the United States. As a result, they allowed Native Americans more freedom.

NEW STATES IN THE UNION, 1796 to 1803

Population Change

The population increased for several reasons.

- Europeans continued to immigrate to the United States, but in small numbers. The flow increased or decreased in reaction to political and economic upheavals in Europe.

- Enslaved Africans continued to be brought into the country. Slaveowners recognized that the Constitution allowed this trade to end after 1808.

- The largest population gain was natural, as births exceeded deaths. The high birth rate was tied to a plentiful food supply and the desire of families to have children who could help on the farms.

The westward movement was aided by scouts and early settlers who blazed trails through the wilderness for others to follow. Men such as the legendary **Daniel Boone** led the way across the Appalachian Mountains and established the early White settlements in the old northwest.

Slavery

By the late 18th century, some people openly opposed slavery. Many of these were Quakers, Mennonites, or other people motivated by their Christian faith. Some were influenced by the Enlightenment ideals about equality and liberty. They saw no place for slavery in a democratic republic. In addition, many people, including slaveowners such as James Madison, disliked slavery, hoping it would fade away as it had in Europe and was beginning to do in parts of Latin America. They believed that increasing immigration would provide low-cost free labor to replace enslaved workers.

Cotton Slavery, though, grew rather than declined beginning in 1793. In that year, **Eli Whitney** invented the **cotton gin**, a device for separating cotton fiber from the seeds. This turned a slow, costly process into a quick, inexpensive one. The change transformed the agriculture of the south. Suddenly, growing cotton became immensely profitable and the demand for enslaved African Americans increased dramatically.

Mechanization of the textile industry also increased the value of cotton. The British were the first to mechanize. To protect their advantage, they passed laws against taking knowledge of their factory designs outside the country. However, a young apprentice named Samuel Slater broke the British law. He memorized a factory design, moved to the United States, and built his own factory. This launched the a new, more efficient textile industry in the United States.

The combination of the cotton gin and mechanization of the textile industry made cotton cloth less expensive and more plentiful than ever before. The production of cotton goods became a potent global industry.

Conflict Over Expansion of Slavery Within the United States, plantation owners eager to increase cotton production based on enslave labor looked westward for more land. After 1800, they quickly settled in Alabama and Mississippi, which each had excellent climate and geography for growing cotton. However, their desire for lands farther west and north would soon face resistance. The growing number of northerners who opposed slavery or who hoped to settle these land themselves without competition from enslaved workers reflected an increasing regional conflict over slavery.

The Movements of Enslaved African Americans Some enslaved people were able to escape bondage. They might find liberty by reaching a free state in the north, although the Constitution included a clause that required states to return fugitives to their owners. Some went to Canada. More settled in land controlled by Indians or in Florida, which belonged to Spain until 1821.

Most enslaved people who moved did so because of their owners' search for greater profits. By the 1790s, the Chesapeake area planters had more enslaved people than they wanted. A decline in the uncertain tobacco market combined with a growing enslaved population through natural increases and expanded importation created a surplus of enslaved people. Efforts to train enslaved people in skilled trades or lease them as servants in the growing cities did not meet the owners' financial desires. In addition, moving enslaved people from the fields to towns, where they could more easily board boats and carriages, added to the risk of people escaping to freedom in the north.

The growing demand for workers in cotton fields provided Chesapeake planters a new opportunity. They could sell their enslaved African Americans to cotton planters in newly settled lands farther south and west, such as Alabama and Mississippi. This interregional slave trade became very large, with between 500,000 and 1 million people transported before the Civil War began in 1861. This trade was particularly cruel because it often broke families apart. Many of the enslaved people who were sold never saw their parents, children, or other relatives again.

STATES WITH AT LEAST 20 PERCENT OF PEOPLE ENSLAVED, 1790				
State	**White**	**Free Nonwhite**	**Enslaved**	**Percent Enslaved**
Maryland	208,649	8,043	103,036	32
Virginia	442,117	12,866	292,627	39
North Carolina	140,178	4,975	100,572	25
South Carolina	140,178	1,801	107,094	43
Georgia	52,886	398	29,264	35

Source: U.S. Census, 1790

REFLECT ON THE LEARNING OBJECTIVE

1. Explain the reasons and ways the movement to and within North America caused rivalries and clashes during this period.

Expansion (MIG, POL)	Battle of Fallen Timbers	**Slave industry (MIG, WXT)**
Northwest Ordinance	Daniel Boone	
Indian Intercourse Act		Eli Whitney
		cotton gin

MULTIPLE-CHOICE QUESTIONS

Questions 1–3 refer to the following excerpt.

"ARTICLE I. *No person* demeaning himself in a peaceable and orderly manner shall ever be molested on account of his mode of worship or religious sentiments…

ARTICLE II. *The inhabitants* of said territory shall always be entitled to the benefits of the writs of habeas corpus and the trial by jury…

ARTICLE III. *Religion, morality, and knowledge* being necessary to good government and the happiness of mankind, schools and the means of education shall forever be encouraged. The utmost good faith shall always be observed toward the Indians; their lands and property shall never be taken from them without their consent…

ARTICLE IV. *The said Territory,* and the states which may be formed therein, shall forever remain a part of this Confederacy of the United States of America…

ARTICLE VI. *There shall be* neither slavery nor involuntary servitude in the said territory.

Northwest Ordinance, July 13, 1787

1. Which of the following processes provided the best model for how the principles expressed in Article III could work?
   (A) The treatment of the Aztecs by the Spanish in the 16th century
   (B) The negotiations between American Indians and colonists in Pennsylvania in the 17th century
   (C) The relationship between American Indians and settlers in New England in the 17th century
   (D) The reaction by colonists to the line created by the British in the Proclamation of 1763

2. Articles I and II most closely reflected ideas expressed in which of the following documents?
   (A) Declaration of Independence
   (B) Articles of Confederation
   (C) Constitution as ratified
   (D) Bill of Rights

3. The Northwest Ordinance established both an immediate and long-lasting process for which of the following?
   (A) Methods for reaching agreements among states
   (B) Policies toward American Indians
   (C) Formation of new states
   (D) Procedures to end slavery

SHORT-ANSWER QUESTION

Use complete sentences; an outline or bulleted list alone is not acceptable.

1. "Sir, suffer me to recall to your mind that time, in which the arms and tyranny of the British crown were exerted. . . .

   This, Sir, was a time when you clearly saw into the injustice of a State of slavery . . . that you publicly held forth this true and invaluable doctrine. . . . 'We hold these truths to be self-evident, that all men are created equal; that they are endowed by their Creator with certain inalienable rights. . . .'

   But, Sir, how pitiable is it to reflect, that although you were so fully convinced of the benevolence of the Father of Mankind, and of his equal and impartial distribution of these rights and privileges, which he hath conferred upon them, that you should at the same time counteract his mercies, in detaining by fraud and violence so numerous a part of my brethren, under groaning captivity, and cruel oppression."

   Benjamin Banneker, African American scientist and surveyor,
letter to Secretary of State Thomas Jefferson, 1792

   Using the excerpt, answer (a), (b), and (c).
   (a) Briefly explain ONE specific reason for Banneker's letter to Jefferson.
   (b) Briefly explain ONE critic's response to Banneker's position.
   (c) Briefly explain ONE specific way Thomas Jefferson might have responded to Banneker's questions about slavery.

Continuity and Change in Period 3

Learning Objective: Explain how the American independence movement affected society from 1754 to 1800.

The reasoning skill of "Continuity and Change" is the suggested focus for evaluating this period. As explained in the contextualization for Period 3, there are many factors to consider in the topic of the American independence movement's effects on society and the national identity. A reasonable argument to explain the effects of independence on society requires one to examine the *relevant historical evidence*.

On the AP exam, a question may be focused on any one factor such as the impact of the ideas that stimulated independence on new values dealing with politics, religion, and society. In response, one would have to present specific historical evidence of a *change* in values, such as the expansion of rights to include recognition of a new role for women including *Republican Motherhood*. At the same time, evidence also supports a *continuity* of values in that a woman's status was still considered inferior to men.

This period includes many examples of continuity and change in religion, commerce, foreign policy, politics, civil liberties, and relations between White Americans and Native Americans. After the United States won independence, state support for churches declined but religious fervor remained strong. One could also cite historical evidence to argue that the independence movement did not always bring change. The generally hostile attitudes of the settlers toward Native Americans continued and government legal efforts to maintain peace failed, just as they had under British rule.

QUESTIONS ABOUT CONTINUITY AND CHANGE

Use the questions below to make a historically defensible claim.

1. Explain the extent to which the ideas that inspired the revolution changed society while maintaining much of British culture. For example, people examined women's role in society more closely while they continued to follow traditional British religious practices.

2. Explain how the independence efforts supported efforts to protect individual freedoms while still continuing to limit some rights. For example, view how the Bill of Rights protected individuals while at the same time the government continued to limit the right to vote.

To analyze historical evidence, you must be able to identify historical ideas and then explain them. Identifying a historical idea is fairly simple. You just say what it is.

The idea you identify may fall into one of three categories.

- **Historical concept:** This is the broadest category. A concept can be an idea or a general understanding of something. Colonization, religious toleration, and salutary neglect are examples of concepts.

- **Historical development:** A development is a change or occurrence. For instance, you have learned about the development of an economic and cultural system within each colony. Also, you have learned about the development of the slave trade and the development of a U.S. national identity.

- **Historical process:** A process is a series of actions or events that lead to an end. You have already learned about the political process. You have also learned about the processes of adding new states to the Union and the process of harvesting cotton.

Historians do much more than identify concepts, developments, and processes. They also explain them. This means describing what it is and how it works, and perhaps providing one or more examples.

An AP® exam might include multiple-choice questions that require you to identify the best example of a historical concept, development, or processes. The short-answer and long-answer questions will also require explanations of historical ideas. Improving your skills at identifying and explaining will help you on the AP® exams, as well as in other courses. Beyond school, they are two of the most basic, commonly used skills in work and everyday life.

For each text section below, identify a concept, development, or process in that section. Then explain it.

1. "Conflicting Views of Government," pages 84–85: development

2. "The First Three Wars," pages 86–87: development

3. "British Actions and Colonial Reactions," page 92: concept

4. "New Revenues and Regulations," pages 93–94: process

5. "Enlightenment Ideas," pages 100–101: concept

6. "Political Demands," page 112: concept

7. "The Path to Ratification," page 127: process

UNIT 3 — Period 3 Review: 1754–1800

As you have read, the first stage in writing a long essay is to carefully read and analyze the question so you know exactly what the framework is for your response. (See pages xli–xlii.) In addition to surface-level analysis of the terms of the question, you also apply the thinking skill of analyzing historical developments and processes for a deeper understanding of the question.

Suppose, for example, you choose to answer the following long essay question: "Evaluate the extent to which economic factors in the period from 1763–1776 were the primary cause of the American Revolution."

For a surface level analysis, you could complete a chart like the one below.

Key Terms and Framework	
Key Terms	Evaluate, extent, economic factors, cause, American Revolution
Framework	*Geographic Areas:* the 13 colonies *Time Period:* 1763–1776
Reasoning Process	Causation

For a deeper analysis of the question, use the thinking skill of analyzing historical developments and processes. Ask questions such as the following to arrive at a deeper understanding of the question.

Questions for Deeper Analysis
• What were the elements of the economy in the 13 colonies? • How did regions of colonies develop different economic patterns? • What was the economic role of the colonies in the British Empire? • How British economic policies change after 1763? • Why did colonists and British leaders view the Seven Years' War differently? • What non-economic factors contributed to the American Revolution?

In the next stage of writing, these questions will help you focus the evidence you gather to answer the question.

Application: Suppose you choose to answer the following long essay question: "Evaluate the extent to which economic factors in the period from 1763–1787 were the primary cause of the writing of the U.S. Constitution." Complete a Key Terms and Framework chart for the question to understand the basic requirements of the task. Then create a Questions for Deeper Analysis chart to help you develop a more complex understanding of the question.

For current free-response question samples, visit: https://apcentral.collegeboard.org/courses/ap-united-states-history/exam

Directions: The suggested writing time for each question is 40 minutes. In your response you should do the following:

- Respond to the prompt with a historically defensible thesis or claim that establishes a line of reasoning.
- Describe a broader historical context relevant to the prompt.
- Support an argument in response to the prompt using specific and relevant examples of evidence.
- Use historical reasoning (e.g., comparison, causation, continuity or change) to frame or structure an argument that addresses the prompt.
- Use evidence to corroborate, qualify, or modify an argument that addresses the prompt.

1. Evaluate the extent to which economic factors in the period from 1763–1776 were the primary cause of the American Revolution.

2. Evaluate the extent to which economic factors in the period from 1763–1787 were the primary cause of the writing of the U.S. Constitution.

3. Evaluate the extent to which the leadership provided by the founding fathers during the period from 1763–1776 was the key to winning the Revolutionary War.

4. Evaluate the extent to which the leadership provided by the founding fathers during the period from 1763–1787 was the key to the successful ratification of the Constitution.

5. Evaluate the extent to which African Americans influenced the course of independence in the period from 1763–1781.

6. Evaluate the extent to which African Americans influenced the writing of the Constitution in the period from 1763–1787.

DOCUMENT-BASED QUESTION

Directions: Question 1 is based on the accompanying documents. The documents have been edited for the purpose of this exercise. You are advised to spend 15 minutes planning and 45 minutes writing your answer. In your response you should do the following:

- Respond to the prompt with a historically defensible thesis or claim that establishes a line of reasoning.
- Describe a broader historical context relevant to the prompt.
- Support an argument in response to the prompt using at least six documents.
- Use at least one additional piece of specific historical evidence (beyond that found in the documents) relevant to an argument about the prompt.
- For at least three documents, explain how or why the document's point of view, purpose, historical situation, and/or audience is relevant to an argument.
- Use evidence to corroborate, qualify, or modify an argument that addresses the prompt.

1. Evaluate the extent to which the opposition to taxation without representation was the primary force motivating the American revolutionary movement during the period 1763–1776.

Document 1

Source: Resolution of the Virginia House of Burgesses, 1764

Resolved, That a most humble and dutiful Address be presented to his Majesty, imploring his Royal Protection of his faithful Subjects, the People of this Colony, in the Enjoyment of all their natural and civil Rights, as Men, and as Descendants of Britons; which rights must be violated, if Laws respecting the internal Government, and Taxation of themselves, are imposed upon them by any other Power than that derived from their own Consent, by and with the Approbation of their Sovereign, or his Substitute.

Document 2

Source: Resolutions of the Stamp Act Congress, 1765

Section 4. That the people of these colonies are not, and from their local circumstances cannot be, represented in the House of Commons in Great-Britain.
Section 5. That the only representatives of the people of these colonies, are persons chosen therein by themselves, and that no taxes ever have been, or can be constitutionally imposed on them, but by their respective legislatures.

Document 3

Source: Daniel Dulany, Maryland lawyer, "Considerations on the Propriety of Imposing Taxes in the British Colonies," 1765

A right to impose an internal tax on the colonies, without their consent for the single purpose of revenue, is denied, a right to regulate their trade without their consent is admitted.

Document 4

Source: The Bostonians Paying the Excise (tax) Man, 1774

THE BOSTONIANS PAYING THE EXCISE-MAN OR TARRING & FEATHERING

Document 5

Document 6

Document 7

Topic 4.1

Contextualizing Period 4

Learning Objective: Explain the context in which the republic developed from 1800 to 1848.

In the first half of the 19th century, the young nation expanded economically, politically, and culturally. Economically this meant taking advantage of new lands, new forms of transportation, and new industries. Politically it meant allowing more people to participate directly in their democracy. Culturally it meant developing distinctively American expressions of literature and art. In 1826, in the midst of the years covered in this period, the young nation of the United States celebrated its 50th birthday with great optimism. The founders of the country were passing on, and a new generation was taking over leadership. In this period, the leaders dealt with the challenges that accompanied the development of the young nation.

Independence had been declared, a Revolutionary War won, a Constitution written and ratified, and a new government established. Between 1800 and 1848, the United States went through rapid demographic, economic, and territorial growth as the new republic worked to define itself. In 1800, the country extended from the Atlantic Ocean to the Mississippi River. By 1848, it controlled territory all the way to the Pacific Ocean.

Reforms, Revivals, and Identity In response to this growth, the country reformed several institutions and practices. It expanded participation in political parties. By dropping property ownership as a requirement to vote, nearly all adult White males could cast ballots. By using nominating conventions, more people could help choose party candidates. More public school laws were enacted to educate the children. Reforms were made to prisons and asylums to make them more humane. A religious revival, an awakening, spread across the country. Much of this development of rights and reforms still excluded American Indians, African Americans, and all women.

The country developed its own art, literature, and philosophy to reflect a sense of itself as independent from Europe. In this sense, the country developed a national culture. However, different sections of the country also continued to grow more distinctive. Slavery shaped a distinctively southern way of life, while the northeastern states became more focused on commerce and the Midwest region on agriculture.

Markets, Farming, and Manufacturing These changes took place as a market economy emerged. People became less dependent on what they raised or made for themselves and more involved in buying and selling goods. The country benefited from the addition of fertile land farther west and advances in industry and transportation everywhere. Agriculture and manufacturing grew together, with the help of local, state, and federal governments to build roads, canals, and harbors. New technology made both farming and manufacturing more productive. The greater reliance on markets meant that more men worked away from home and women had greater control over homelife.

National Strength and Signs of Division In this period, the country grew stronger and larger. Politically, President Andrew Jackson, elected in 1828 and 1832, led efforts to solidify the power of the federal government over states. In general, the United States promoted foreign trade (particularly the export of cotton) but avoided entanglement in European diplomatic affairs and wars. Efforts to improve life succeeded for many but not those enslaved. Landmarks in the institution of slavery came earlier, with the development of the cotton gin in 1793 and the end of the importation of enslaved Africans in 1808. With the territorial and economic growth, conflict with American Indians continued while rising concerns over slavery focused on whether it should be allowed in the newly acquired lands.

As this period ended, most people had a positive view of a prosperous country. However, some recognized that the growing regional differences and the question of whether to allow slavery to expand into new states and territories needed to be resolved.

ANALYZE THE CONTEXT

1. Explain a historical context for the development of a reform movement during this period.

2. Explain a historical context for the forces that brought about the market revolution that affected all of the people of the young nation.

LANDMARK EVENTS: 1800-1848

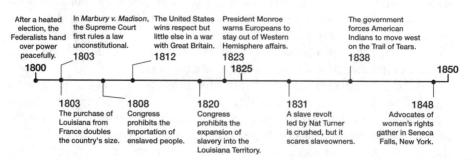

After a heated election, the Federalists hand over power peacefully.
1800

In *Marbury v. Madison*, the Supreme Court first rules a law unconstitutional.
1803

The United States wins respect but little else in a war with Great Britain.
1812

President Monroe warns Europeans to stay out of Western Hemisphere affairs.
1823

1825

The government forces American Indians to move west on the Trail of Tears.
1838

1850

1803
The purchase of Louisiana from France doubles the country's size.

1808
Congress prohibits the importation of enslaved people.

1820
Congress prohibits the expansion of slavery into the Louisiana Territory.

1831
A slave revolt led by Nat Turner is crushed, but it scares slaveowners.

1848
Advocates of women's rights gather in Seneca Falls, New York.

The Rise of Political Parties and the Era of Jefferson

But every difference of opinion is not a difference of principle. We have called by different names brethren of the same principle. We are all Republicans, we are all Federalists.

Thomas Jefferson, First Inaugural Address, 1801

Learning Objective: Explain the causes and effects of policy debates in the early republic.

Despite President Washington's warning against forming political parties, two groups quickly emerged in the new republic. The Federalists, following the visions of Alexander Hamilton, and the Democratic-Republicans, espousing Thomas Jefferson's views, competed for public approval and control of the government.

The Election of 1800

During Adams's presidency, the Federalists rapidly lost popularity. People disliked the Alien and Sedition Acts. Further, they complained about the new taxes imposed to pay for a possible war against France. Though Adams avoided war, he had persuaded Congress that building up the U.S. Navy was necessary for the nation's defense.

Establishment of Political Parties The presidential election of 1800 provided the first election with a clear choice between political parties. The Federalist Party stood for a stronger national government and leaned toward Great Britain in European affairs. The Democratic-Republican Party emphasized the powers reserved to states and leaned toward the French.

Both parties supported tariffs on imports as a way to raise revenue. Throughout the 19th century, tariffs would be the largest single source of revenue for the federal government. The debate on tariffs broke down on regional lines. Northern industrialists wanted higher tariffs to protect their companies from foreign competition. Southerners relied on exports of cotton and other crops. They pushed for lower tariffs in order to encourage trade.

Election Results Determining the winner of the 1800 presidential election was complicated. According to the original Constitution, each member of the Electoral College cast two votes for president. The winner became president, and the second-place finisher became vice president. In 1800, a majority of the presidential electors cast their ballots for two Democratic-Republicans: one for Thomas Jefferson and one for Aaron Burr. The two tied for the presidency. As the Constitution required, the House of Representatives voted to choose the winner, with each state allowed one vote. They debated and voted for days before they finally gave a majority to Jefferson. (Alexander Hamilton had urged his followers to support Jefferson, whom he considered less dangerous and of higher character than Burr.)

Democratic-Republican lawmakers elected in 1800 also took control of both the House and the Senate in the elections. So the Federalists had been swept from power in both the executive and legislative branches of the U.S. government.

A Peaceful Revolution The passing of power in 1801 from one political party to another was accomplished without violence. This was a rare event for the times and a major indication that the U.S. constitutional system would endure the various strains that were placed upon it. The Federalists quietly accepted their defeat in the election of 1800 and peacefully relinquished control of the federal government to Jefferson's party, the Democratic-Republicans. The change from Federalist to Democratic-Republican control is known as the Revolution of 1800.

Jefferson's Presidency

During his first term, Jefferson attempted to win the allegiance and trust of Federalist opponents by maintaining the national bank and debt-repayment plan of Hamilton. In foreign policy, he carried on the neutrality policies of Washington and Adams. At the same time, Jefferson retained the loyalty of Democratic-Republican supporters by adhering to his party's guiding principle of limited central government. He reduced the size of the military, eliminated a number of federal jobs, repealed the excise taxes—including those on whiskey—and lowered the national debt. However, hoping to avoid internal divisions that distracted Washington, he appointed only Democratic-Republicans to his cabinet. Compared to Adams's troubled administration, Jefferson's first four years in office were relatively free of discord.

The Louisiana Purchase

The single most important achievement of Jefferson's first administration was the acquisition by purchase of vast western lands known as the Louisiana Territory. This region encompassed a large tract of western land through which the Mississippi and Missouri rivers flowed, land little explored by Europeans. At the mouth of the Mississippi lay the territory's most valuable property in terms of commerce—the port of New Orleans.

The Louisiana Territory had once been claimed by France, which then lost its claim to Spain. But in 1800, the French military and political leader Napoleon Bonaparte secretly forced Spain to give the Louisiana Territory back to France. Napoleon hoped to restore the French empire in the Americas. By 1803, however, Napoleon had lost interest in this plan for two reasons:

- He wanted to concentrate French resources on fighting Great Britain
- A rebellion led by Toussaint Louverture against French rule on the island of Santo Domingo had resulted in heavy French losses.

U.S. Interest in the Mississippi River During Jefferson's presidency, the western frontier extended beyond Ohio and Kentucky into the Indiana Territory. Settlers in this region depended for their economic existence on transporting goods on rivers that flowed westward into the Mississippi and southward as far as New Orleans. They were greatly alarmed therefore when, in 1802, Spanish officials, who were still in charge of New Orleans, closed the port to Americans. They revoked the *right of deposit* granted in the Pinckney Treaty of 1795, which had allowed American farmers tax-free use of the port. People on the frontier clamored for government action. In addition to being concerned about the economic impact of the closing of New Orleans, President Jefferson was troubled by its consequences on foreign policy. He feared that so long as a foreign power controlled the river at New Orleans, the United States risked entanglement in European affairs.

Negotiations Jefferson sent ministers to France with instructions to offer up to $10 million for both New Orleans and a strip of land extending from that port eastward to Florida. If the American ministers failed in their negotiations with the French, they were instructed to begin discussions with Britain for a U.S.-Britain alliance. Napoleon's ministers, seeking funds for a war against Britain, offered to sell not only New Orleans but also the entire Louisiana Territory for $15 million. The opportunity to purchase so much land surprised American ministers. They quickly went beyond their instructions and accepted the French offer.

Constitutional Predicament Jefferson and most Americans strongly approved of the Louisiana Purchase. Nevertheless, a constitutional problem troubled the president. Jefferson was committed to a **strict interpretation** of the Constitution and rejected Hamilton's argument that certain powers were implied. No clause in the Constitution explicitly stated that a president could purchase foreign land.

In this case, Jefferson determined to set aside his idealism for the country's good. He submitted the purchase agreement to the Senate, arguing that lands could be added to the United States as an application of the president's power to make treaties. Federalist senators criticized the treaty. However, casting aside the Federalist attacks, the Democratic-Republican majority in the Senate quickly ratified the purchase.

THE LOUISIANA PURCHASE, 1803

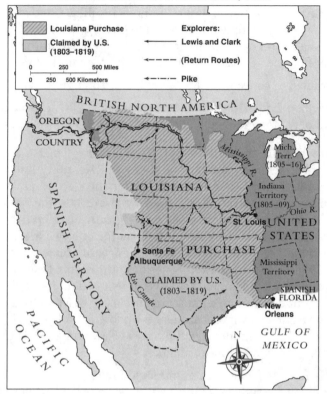

Consequences The Louisiana Purchase more than doubled the size of the United States, removed a European presence from the nation's borders, and extended the western frontier to lands beyond the Mississippi. Furthermore, the acquisition of millions of acres of land strengthened Jefferson's hopes that his country's future would be based on an agrarian society of independent farmers rather than Hamilton's vision of an urban and industrial society. In political terms, the Louisiana Purchase increased Jefferson's popularity and showed the Federalists to be a weak, sectionalist (New England-based) party that could do little more than complain about Democratic-Republican policies.

Lewis and Clark Expedition Even before Louisiana was purchased, Jefferson had persuaded Congress to fund a scientific exploration of the trans-Mississippi West to be led by Captain Meriwether Lewis and Lieutenant William Clark. The Louisiana Purchase greatly increased the importance of the expedition. Lewis and Clark set out from St. Louis in 1804, crossed the Rockies, reached the Oregon coast on the Pacific Ocean, and then turned back and completed the return journey in 1806. The benefits of the expedition were many: greater geographic and scientific knowledge of the region, stronger U.S.

claims to the Oregon Territory, better relations with American Indians, and more accurate maps and land routes for fur trappers and future settlers.

Judicial Impeachments

Jefferson tried various methods for overturning past Federalist measures and appointments. Soon after entering office, he suspended the Alien and Sedition Acts and released those jailed under them. The Federalist appointments to the courts previously made by Washington and Adams were not subject to recall or removal except by impeachment. Federalist judges therefore continued in office, much to the annoyance of the Democratic-Republican president, Jefferson. Hoping to remove partisan Federalist judges, Jefferson supported a campaign of impeachment. The judge of one federal district was found to be mentally unbalanced. The House voted for his impeachment, and the Senate then voted to remove him. The House also impeached a Supreme Court justice, Samuel Chase, but the Senate acquitted him after finding no evidence of "high crimes."

Except for these two cases, the impeachment campaign was largely a failure, as almost all the Federalist judges remained in office. Even so, the threat of impeachment caused the judges to be more cautious and less partisan in their decisions.

Jefferson's Reelection

In 1804, Jefferson won reelection by an overwhelming margin, receiving all but 14 of the 176 electoral votes. His second term was marked by growing difficulties. He faced a plot by his former vice president, Aaron Burr. The Democratic-Republican Party split, with a faction (the "Quids") accusing him of abandoning the party's principles. Foreign troubles came from the Napoleonic wars in Europe.

Aaron Burr

A Democratic-Republican caucus (a closed meeting) in 1804 decided not to nominate Aaron Burr for a second term as vice president. Burr then embarked on a series of ventures, one of which threatened to break up the Union and another of which resulted in the death of Alexander Hamilton.

Federalist Conspiracy Secretly forming a political pact with some radical New England Federalists, Burr planned to win the governorship of New York in 1804, unite that state with the New England states, and then lead this group of states to secede from the nation. Most Federalists followed Alexander Hamilton in opposing Burr, who was defeated in the New York election. The conspiracy then disintegrated.

Duel with Hamilton Angered by an insulting remark attributed to Hamilton, Burr challenged the Federalist leader to a duel and fatally shot him. Hamilton's death in 1804 deprived the Federalists of their last great leader and earned Burr the enmity of many.

Trial for Treason By 1806, Burr's intrigues had turned westward with a plan to take Mexico from Spain and possibly unite it with Louisiana under his rule. Learning of the conspiracy, Jefferson ordered Burr's arrest and trial for treason. Presiding at the trial was Chief Justice of the Supreme Court John Marshall, a long-time adversary of Jefferson. A jury acquitted Burr, basing its decision on Marshall's narrow definition of treason and the lack of witnesses to any "overt act" by Burr.

John Marshall's Supreme Court and Federal Power

One Federalist official continued to have major influence throughout the years of Democratic-Republican ascendancy: John Marshall. His decisions consistently favored the central government and the rights of property against the advocates of states' rights.

John Marshall

Ironically, the Federalist judge who caused Jefferson the most grief was one of his own cousins from Virginia, John Marshall. Marshall had been appointed chief justice of the Supreme Court during the final months of the presidency of John Adams. He held his post for 34 years, during which time he exerted as strong an influence on the Supreme Court as Washington had exerted on the presidency. Even when justices appointed by Democratic-Republican presidents formed a majority on the Court, they often sided with Marshall because they were persuaded that the U.S. Constitution had created a federal government with strong and flexible powers.

Source: Getty Images

In 1955, John Marshall became one of the first Supreme Court justices to appear on a postage stamp. It came at a time when the Supreme Court was asserting the power of the federal courts to protect individual liberties, particularly against racial discrimination and unconstitutional criminal proceedings (see Topics 8.6 and 8.11).

Influential Cases

Several of Marshall's decisions became landmarks that defined the relationship between the central government and the states. First and foremost of these was *Marbury v. Madison* (1803), which established the principle of **judicial review**.

Marbury v. Madison **(1803)** The first major case decided by Marshall put him in direct conflict with President Jefferson. Just before leaving office, President John Adams made several "midnight appointments" of Federalists as judges. However, their commissions were not formally delivered before Jefferson took office. Jefferson wanted to block these appointments, so he ordered the new secretary of state, James Madison, not to deliver the commissions. One of the Adams appointees, William Marbury, sued for his commission. The case of *Marbury v. Madison* went to the Supreme Court in 1803. Marshall ruled that Marbury had a right to his commission according to the Judiciary Act passed by Congress in 1789. However, Marshall said the Judiciary Act of 1789 had given to the Court greater power than the Constitution allowed. Therefore, the law was unconstitutional and Marbury would not receive his commission.

In effect, Marshall sacrificed what would have been a small Federalist gain (the appointment of Marbury) for a much larger, long-term judicial victory. By ruling a law of Congress to be unconstitutional, Marshall established the doctrine of *judicial review*. From this point on, the Supreme Court would exercise the power to decide whether an act of Congress or of the president was allowed by the Constitution. The Supreme Court could now overrule actions of the other two branches of the federal government.

Fletcher v. Peck **(1810)** In a case involving land fraud in Georgia, Marshall concluded that a state could not pass legislation invalidating a contract. This was the first time that the Supreme Court declared a state law to be unconstitutional and invalid. (In *Marbury v. Madison,* the Court ruled a federal law unconstitutional.)

Martin v. Hunter's Lease **(1816)** The Supreme Court established that it had jurisdiction over state courts in cases involving constitutional rights.

Dartmouth College v. Woodward **(1819)** This case involved a law of New Hampshire that changed Dartmouth College from a privately chartered college into a public institution. The Marshall Court struck down the state law as unconstitutional, arguing that a contract for a private corporation could not be altered by the state.

McCulloch v. Maryland **(1819)** Maryland attempted to tax the Second Bank of the United States, which was located in Maryland. Marshall ruled that a state could not tax a federal institution because "the power to tax is the power to destroy" and federal laws are supreme over state laws. In addition, Marshall settled the long-running debate over constitutionality of the national bank. Using a loose interpretation of the Constitution, Marshall ruled that, even though no clause in the Constitution specifically mentions a national bank, the Constitution gave the federal government the **implied power** to create one.

Cohens v. Virginia (1821) A pair of brothers named Cohen were convicted in Virginia of illegally selling tickets for a lottery authorized by Congress for Washington, D.C. While Marshall and the Court upheld the conviction, they established the principle that the Supreme Court could review a state court's decision involving any of the powers of the federal government.

Gibbons v. Ogden (1821) Could the state of New York grant a monopoly to a steamboat company if that action conflicted with a charter authorized by Congress? In ruling that the New York monopoly was unconstitutional, Marshall established the federal government's broad control of interstate commerce.

Madison's Presidency

Jefferson believed strongly in the precedent set by Washington of voluntarily retiring from the presidency after a second term. For his party's nomination for president, he supported his close friend, Secretary of State James Madison.

The Election of 1808

Ever since leading the effort to write and ratify the Constitution, Madison was widely viewed as a brilliant thinker. He had worked tirelessly with Jefferson in developing the Democratic-Republican Party. On the other hand, he was a weak public speaker, possessed a stubborn temperament, and lacked Jefferson's political skills. With Jefferson's backing, Madison was nominated for president by a caucus of congressional Democratic-Republicans. Other factions of the Democratic-Republican Party nominated two other candidates. Even so, Madison was able to win a majority of electoral votes and to defeat both his Democratic-Republican opponents and the Federalist candidate, Charles Pinckney.

REFLECT ON THE LEARNING OBJECTIVE

1. Explain what caused the major political disputes and the consequences of them during the early years of the new nation.

KEY TERMS BY THEME		
Decisions (NAT, POL)	**Supreme Court (PCE)**	*McCulloch v. Maryland*
Thomas Jefferson	strict interpretation	*Dartmouth College v.*
Louisiana Purchase	John Marshall	*Woodward*
Aaron Burr	judicial review	*Gibbons v. Ogden*
Exploration (GEO)	*Marbury v. Madison*	implied powers
Lewis and Clark	*Fletcher v. Peck*	

MULTIPLE-CHOICE QUESTIONS

Questions 1–3 refer to the following excerpt.

"All, too, will bear in mind this sacred principle, that though the will of the majority is in all cases to prevail, that will to be rightful must be reasonable; that the minority possess their equal rights, which equal law must protect, and to violate would be oppression. . . . We have called by different names brethren of the same principle. We are all Republicans, we are all Federalists. If there be any among us who would wish to dissolve this Union or to change its republican form, let them stand undisturbed as monuments of the safety with which error of opinion may be tolerated where reason is left free to combat it. . . .

Equal and exact justice to all men, of whatever state or persuasion, religious or political; peace, commerce, and honest friendship with all nations, entangling alliances with none."

Thomas Jefferson, First Inaugural Address, 1801

1. Which of the following describes a policy of Jefferson's that reflects the attitude toward Federalists expressed in this speech?
   (A) He adopted a Federalist plan for increasing the size of the military.
   (B) He appealed to Federalists by increasing taxes to pay for new roads.
   (C) He attempted to gain the trust of Federalists by continuing the national bank.
   (D) He showed that party was unimportant by appointing some Federalists to his cabinet.

2. Jefferson's statement that "we are all Republicans, we are all Federalists" is most directly refuted by his actions to
   (A) continue the neutrality policies of Adams
   (B) keep economic institutions established by Hamilton
   (C) attempt to impeach federal judges
   (D) purchase the Louisiana Territory

3. Jefferson's call to avoid entangling alliances is similar to advice found in
   (A) the Declaration of Independence
   (B) *The Federalist Papers*
   (C) the Kentucky Resolutions
   (D) Washington's Farewell Address

Use complete sentences; an outline or bulleted list alone is not acceptable.

1. "The issue, then, is not whether Jefferson's policies toward Louisiana were right or wrong but rather how he managed to implement decisions that defied in so many ways his long-standing commitment to limitations on executive power and the near-sacred character of republican principles. . . . Jefferson was not simply seized by power-hungry impulses once he assumed the presidency, since in a broad range of other policy areas he exhibited considerable discipline over the executive branch and habitual deference to the Congress; . . . he did not suddenly discover a pragmatic streak in his political philosophy, . . . he clung tenaciously to Jeffersonian principles despite massive evidence that they were at odds with reality. . . . The answer would seem to be the special, indeed almost mystical place the West had in his thinking. . . . For Jefferson more than any other major figure in the revolutionary generation, the West was America's future."

    Joseph J. Ellis, historian, *American Sphinx*, 1997

    "The story of the Louisiana Purchase is one of strength, of Jefferson's adaptability and, most important, his determination to secure the territory from France, . . . A slower or less courageous politician might have bungled the acquisition; an overly idealistic one might have lost it by insisting on strict constitutional scruples. . . . The philosophical Jefferson had believed an amendment necessary. The political Jefferson, however, was not going to allow theory to get in the way of reality. . . . [He] expanded the powers of the executive in ways that would have likely driven Jefferson to distraction had another man been president. Much of his political life, though, had been devoted to the study and the wise exercise of power. He did what had to be done to preserve the possibility of republicanism and progress. Things were neat only in theory. And despite his love of ideas and image of himself, Thomas Jefferson was as much a man of action as he was of theory."

    Jon Meacham, historian, *Thomas Jefferson: The Art of Power*, 2012

    Using the excerpts, answer (a), (b), and (c).

    (a) Briefly explain ONE major difference between Ellis's and Meacham's historical interpretations of how Thomas Jefferson came to approve the Louisiana Purchase.

    (b) Briefly explain how ONE historical event or development in the period 1787 to 1803 that is not explicitly mentioned in the excerpts could be used to support Ellis's interpretation.

    (c) Briefly explain how ONE historical event or development in the period 1787 to 1803 that is not explicitly mentioned in the excerpts could be used to support Meacham's interpretation.

Topic 4.3

Politics and Regional Interests

But this momentous question [the Missouri Compromise],
like a firebell in the night awakened and filled me with terror.
I considered it the knell of the Union.

Thomas Jefferson, April 1820

Learning Objective: Explain how different regional interests affected debates about the role of the federal government in the early republic.

The election of James Monroe as president in 1816 (less than two years after the last battle of the War of 1812) inaugurated what one newspaper editorial characterized as an "Era of Good Feelings." The term gained wide currency and was later adopted by historians to describe Monroe's two terms in office. A closer examination of this period shows a more complicated picture.

The Era of Good Feelings

The period's nickname suggests the Monroe years were marked by a spirit of nationalism, optimism, and goodwill. In some ways, they were. One party, the Federalists, faded into oblivion, and Monroe's party, the Democratic-Republicans, adopted some of their policies and dominated politics.

This perception of unity and harmony, however, can be misleading and oversimplified. Throughout the era, people had heated debates over tariffs, the national bank, internal improvements, and public land sales. Sectionalist tensions over slavery were increasing. Moreover, even a sense of party unity was illusory since antagonistic factions among Democratic-Republicans would soon split it in two. The actual period of "good feelings" may have lasted only from the election of 1816 to the Panic of 1819.

James Monroe

As a young man, James Monroe had fought in the Revolutionary War and suffered through the Valley Forge winter. He had become prominent in Virginia politics and had served as Jefferson's minister to Great Britain and as Madison's secretary of state. He continued the Virginia dynasty: of the first five presidents, four were from Virginia. The other, John Adams, was from Massachusetts.

In the election of 1816, Monroe defeated the Federalist, Rufus King, overwhelmingly—183 electoral votes to 34. By 1820, the Federalist Party had practically vanished, and Monroe received every electoral vote except one. With no organized political opposition, Monroe represented the growing nationalism of the American people. Under Monroe, the country acquired Florida, agreed on the Missouri Compromise, and adopted the Monroe Doctrine.

Economic Nationalism

One outgrowth of the War of 1812 was a political movement to support the growth of the nation's economy. Subsidizing internal improvements (the building of roads and canals) was one aspect of the movement. Protecting budding U.S. industries from European competition was a second aspect. Often opinions on these economic issues were based on what appeared best for one's section or region.

Tariff of 1816 Before the War of 1812, Congress had levied low tariffs on imports as a method for raising government revenue. Then, during the war, manufacturers erected many factories to supply goods that previously had been imported from Britain. Now in peacetime, these American manufacturers feared that British goods would be dumped on American markets and take away much of their business. Congress raised tariffs for the express purpose of protecting U.S. manufacturers from competition rather than to simply raise revenue. This was the first **protective tariff** in U.S. history—the first of many to come.

New England, which had little manufacturing at the time, was the only section to oppose the higher tariffs. Even the South and West, which had opposed tariffs in the past and would oppose them in the future, generally supported the 1816 tariff, believing that it was needed for national prosperity.

Henry Clay's American System Henry Clay of Kentucky, a leader in the House of Representatives, proposed a comprehensive method for advancing the nation's economic growth. His plan, which he called the American System, consisted of three parts: (1) protective tariffs, (2) a national bank, and (3) internal improvements. Clay argued that protective tariffs would promote American manufacturing and also raise revenue with which to build a national transportation system of federally constructed roads and canals. A national bank would keep the system running smoothly by providing a national currency. The tariffs would chiefly benefit the East, internal improvements would promote growth in the West and the South, and the bank would aid the economies of all sections.

Two parts of Clay's system were already in place in 1816, the last year of James Madison's presidency. Congress in that year adopted a protective tariff and also chartered the **Second Bank of the United States**. (The charter of the First Bank—Hamilton's brainchild—had been allowed to expire in 1811.)

On the matter of internal improvements, however, both Madison and Monroe objected that the Constitution did not explicitly provide for the spending of federal money on roads and canals. Throughout his presidency, Monroe consistently vetoed acts of Congress providing funds for road-building and canal-building projects. Thus, the individual states were left to make internal improvements on their own.

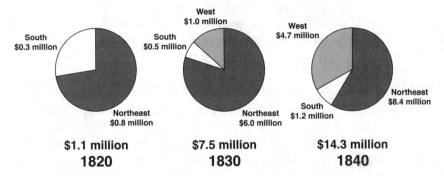

CANAL BUILDING, 1820 to 1840

West
$1.0 million

South
$0.3 million

South
$0.5 million

West
$4.7 million

Northeast
$0.8 million

Northeast
$6.0 million

Northeast
$8.4 million

South
$1.2 million

$1.1 million
1820

$7.5 million
1830

$14.3 million
1840

Source: Bureau of the Census, *Historical Statistics of the United States, Colonial Times to 1970*

The Panic of 1819

The first major financial panic since the Constitution had been ratified shook the nation in 1819. The economic disaster occurred after the Second Bank of the United States tightened credit in an effort to control inflation. Many state banks closed, and unemployment, bankruptcies, and imprisonment for debt increased sharply. The depression hit the West hardest, where many people were in debt because they had speculated on land during the euphoria after the War of 1812. In 1819, the Bank of the United States foreclosed on large amounts of western farmland. As a result of the bank panic and depression, nationalistic beliefs were shaken. In the West, the economic crisis changed many voters' political outlook. Westerners began calling for land reform and expressing strong opposition to both the national bank and debtors' prisons.

Political Changes

The Federalist Party declined rapidly because it failed to adapt as the nation grew. After opposing the War of 1812 (see Topic 4.4) and leading a secessionist convention at Hartford, the party seemed out of step with the nationalistic temper of the times. After its crushing defeat in the election of 1816, it ceased to be a national party and failed to nominate a presidential candidate in 1820.

Changes in the Democratic-Republican Party Meanwhile, the Democratic-Republican Party, the only remaining national party, faced serious internal strains as it adjusted to changing times. Members such as John Randolph clung to the old party ideals of limited government and a strict interpretation of the Constitution. Most members, however, adopted what had once been Federalist ideas, such as maintaining a large army and navy and supporting a national bank. Some members reversed their views from one decade to the next. For example, Daniel Webster of Massachusetts strongly opposed both the tariffs of 1816 and 1824, but then supported even higher tariff rates in 1828. John C. Calhoun of South Carolina was another Democratic-Republican leader who reversed positions. An outspoken war hawk and nationalist in 1812, Calhoun championed states' rights after 1828.

Political factions and sectional differences became more intense during Monroe's second term. When Monroe, honoring the two-term tradition, declined to be a candidate again, four other Democratic-Republicans sought election as president in 1824. How this election split the party and led to the emergence of two rival parties is explained in Topic 4.8.

Western Settlement and the Missouri Compromise

In the ten years after the start of the War of 1812, the population of settlers west of the Appalachian Mountains had doubled. Most went to the region between the Appalachians and the Mississippi River. Some, though, were beginning to settle in the Louisiana Territory purchased in 1803. Much of the nationalistic and economic interest in the country was centered on the West, which presented both opportunities and new questions.

Reasons for Westward Movement

Several factors combined to stimulate rapid growth along the western frontier during the presidencies of Madison and Monroe.

Acquisition of Lands Military victories under Generals William Henry Harrison in the Indiana Territory and Andrew Jackson in Florida and the South over American Indians opened vast new territories for White settlers.

Economic Pressures The economic difficulties in the Northeast from the embargo and the war caused people from this region to seek a new future across the Appalachians. In the South, tobacco planters needed new land to replace the soil exhausted by years of poor farming methods. They found good land for planting cotton in Alabama, Mississippi, and Arkansas.

Improved Transportation Pioneers had an easier time reaching the frontier as a result of the building of roads and canals, steamboats, and railroads.

Immigrants More Europeans were being attracted to America by speculators offering cheap land in the Great Lakes region and in the valleys of the Ohio, Cumberland, and Mississippi rivers.

New Questions and Issues

Despite their rapid growth, the new states of the West were small relative to those of the other two sections. To enhance their limited political influence in Congress, western representatives bargained with politicians from other sections. The primary concerns of the western states were as follows: (1) "cheap money" (easy credit) from state banks rather than from the Bank of the United States, (2) low prices for land sold by the federal government, and (3) improved transportation.

However, on the critical issue of slavery, westerners disagreed over permitting it. Those settling territory to the south wanted slavery for economic reasons (labor for the cotton fields), while those settling to the north had no use for slavery. In 1819, when the Missouri Territory applied to Congress for statehood, the slavery issue became a subject of angry debate.

The Missouri Compromise

Ever since 1791–1792, when Vermont entered the Union as a free state and Kentucky entered as a slave state, politicians in Congress had attempted to preserve a sectional balance between the North and the South. Keeping a balance in the House of Representatives was difficult because the population in the North was growing more rapidly than in the South. By 1818, the northern states held a majority of 105 to 81 in the House. However, in the Senate, the votes remained divided evenly: 11 slave states and 11 free states. As long as this balance was preserved, southern senators could block legislation that they believed threatened the interests of their section.

Missouri's bid for statehood alarmed the North because slavery was well established there. If Missouri came in as a slave state, it would tip the political balance in the South's favor. Furthermore, Missouri was the first part of the Louisiana Purchase to apply for statehood. Southerners and northerners alike worried about the future status of other new territories applying for statehood from the rest of the vast Louisiana Purchase.

Tallmadge Amendment Representative James Tallmadge from New York ignited the debate about the Missouri question by proposing an amendment to the bill for Missouri's admission. The amendment called for (1) prohibiting the further introduction of slaves into Missouri and (2) requiring the children of Missouri slaves to be emancipated at the age of 25. If adopted, the Tallmadge Amendment would have led to the gradual elimination of slavery in Missouri. The amendment was defeated in the Senate as enraged southerners saw it as the first step in a northern effort to abolish slavery in all states.

THE MISSOURI COMPROMISE

Clay's Proposals After months of heated debate in Congress and throughout the nation, Henry Clay won majority support for three bills that, taken together, represented a compromise:

1. admit Missouri as a slave-holding state

2. admit Maine as a free state

3. prohibit slavery in the rest of the Louisiana Territory north of latitude 36° 30′

Both houses passed the bills, and President Monroe added his signature in March 1820 to what became known as the **Missouri Compromise**.

Aftermath Sectional feelings on the slavery issue subsided after 1820. The Missouri Compromise preserved sectional balance for more than 30 years and provided time for the nation to mature. Nevertheless, if an era of good feelings existed, it was badly damaged by the storm of sectional controversy over Missouri. After this political crisis, Americans were torn between feelings of nationalism (loyalty to the Union) on the one hand and feelings of **sectionalism** (loyalty to one's own region) on the other.

REFLECT ON THE LEARNING OBJECTIVE

1. Explain how the viewpoints from the different sections of the new republic impacted the discussion of the role of the Federal government.

KEY TERMS BY THEME

Public Confidence (NAT)	Industry (WXT)	
Era of Good Feelings	Tariff of 1816	Second Bank of the United States
James Monroe	protective tariff	Panic of 1819
economic nationalism	Henry Clay	**Making the Law (POL)**
sectionalism	American System	Tallmadge Amendment
		Missouri Compromise (1820)

MULTIPLE-CHOICE QUESTIONS

Questions 1–3 refer to the following excerpt.

"It is hushed indeed for the moment. but this [Missouri Compromise] is a reprieve only, not a final sentence. a geographical line, coinciding with a marked principle, moral and political, once conceived and held up to the angry passions of men, will never be obliterated; and every new irritation will mark it deeper and deeper. I can say with conscious truth that there is not a man on earth who would sacrifice more than I would, to relieve us from this heavy reproach, in any *practicable* way. . . . to regulate the condition of the different descriptions of men composing a state. This certainly is the exclusive right of every state, which nothing in the constitution has taken from them and given to the general government."

Thomas Jefferson, letter to John Holmes, April 22, 1820

1. Which of the following provided a precedent on the issue described by Jefferson that was reflected in the Missouri Compromise?
    (A) The Declaration of Independence, which declared all men equal
    (B) The Articles of Confederation, which did not allow the national government to tax individuals
    (C) The Northwest Ordinance, which limited the expansion of slavery
    (D) The Louisiana Purchase, which showed how the federal government could expand its power

2. Which of the following was most necessary for the passage of the Missouri Compromise?
    (A) Admission of Maine as a free state
    (B) Support from John Quincy Adams
    (C) Adding the Tallmadge Amendment
    (D) A unified Democratic-Republican Party

3. Which of the following groups would most strongly agree with Jefferson's views about the future impact of the Missouri Compromise?
    (A) Federalists calling for a stronger national government
    (B) Abolitionists demanding an immediate end to slavery
    (C) Democratic-Republicans recognizing the need for more compromises
    (D) Settlers in the Louisiana Territory seeking more land

SHORT-ANSWER QUESTION

Use complete sentences; an outline or bulleted list alone is not acceptable.

1. Answer (a), (b), and (c).
    (a) Briefly explain ONE specific part of Henry Clay's proposed American System.
    (b) Briefly explain why ONE region favored the American System during the period from 1800 to 1848.
    (c) Briefly explain why ONE region opposed the American System during the period from 1800 to 1848.

America on the World Stage

The war has renewed and reinstated the national feelings and character which the Revolution had given, and which were daily lessened. . . . I hope the permanency of the Union is thereby better secured.

Secretary of the Treasury Albert Gallatin, 1816

Learning Objective: Explain how and why American foreign policy developed over time.

From their founding as colonies to their fight for independence, the United States was strongly influenced by the actions of other nations. Even President Washington had to deal with foreign "entanglements" (see Topic 3.10) likely leading to his warning against "permanent alliances" in foreign affairs.

Jefferson's Foreign Policy

President Jefferson brought considerable experience in dealing with foreign affairs. He had served as a foreign minister in Europe and secretary of state prior to his election in 1800. This experience led to success with the Louisiana Purchase but would be challenged by numerous other foreign affairs questions.

Difficulties Abroad

As a matter of policy and principle, Jefferson tried to avoid war. Rejecting permanent alliances, he sought to maintain U.S. neutrality despite increasing provocations from both France and Britain during the Napoleonic wars.

Barbary Pirates The first major challenge to Jefferson's foreign policy came not from a major European power but from the piracy practiced by the Barbary states on the North African coast. To protect U.S. merchant ships from being seized by Barbary pirates, Presidents Washington and Adams had reluctantly agreed to pay tribute to the Barbary governments. The ruler of Tripoli demanded a higher sum in tribute from Jefferson. Refusing to pay, Jefferson sent a small fleet of the U.S. Navy to the Mediterranean. Sporadic fighting with Tripoli lasted for four years (1801–1805). Although the American navy did not achieve a decisive victory, it did gain some respect and offered a measure of protection to U.S. vessels trading in Mediterranean waters.

Challenges to U.S. Neutrality Meanwhile, the Napoleonic wars continued to dominate the politics of Europe—and to shape the commercial economy of the United States. The two principal belligerents, France and Britain, attempted naval blockades of enemy ports. They regularly seized the ships of neutral nations and confiscated their cargoes. The chief offender from the U.S. point of view was Britain, since its navy dominated the Atlantic. Most infuriating was the British practice of capturing U.S. sailors who it claimed were British citizens and impressing (forcing) them to serve in the British navy.

Chesapeake-Leopard **Affair** One incident at sea especially aroused American anger and almost led to war. In 1807, only a few miles off the coast of Virginia, the British warship *Leopard* fired on the U.S. warship *Chesapeake*. Three Americans were killed, and four others were taken captive and impressed into the British navy. Anti-British feeling ran high, and many Americans demanded war. Jefferson, however, resorted to diplomacy and economic pressure as his response to the crisis.

Embargo Act (1807) As an alternative to war, Jefferson persuaded the Democratic-Republican majority in Congress to pass the Embargo Act in 1807. This measure prohibited American merchant ships from sailing to any foreign port. Since the United States was Britain's largest trading partner, Jefferson hoped that the British would stop violating the rights of neutral nations rather than lose U.S. trade. The embargo, however, backfired and brought greater economic hardship to the United States than to Britain. The British were determined to control the seas at all costs, and they had little difficulty substituting supplies from South America for U.S. goods.

The embargo's effect on the U.S. economy, however, was devastating, especially for the merchant marine and shipbuilders of New England. So bad was the depression that a movement developed in the New England states to secede from the Union.

Recognizing that the Embargo Act had failed, Jefferson called for its repeal in 1809 during the final days of his presidency. Even after repeal, however, U.S. ships could trade legally with all nations except Britain and France.

President Madison's Foreign Policy

Madison's presidency was dominated by the same European problems that had plagued Jefferson's second term.

Commercial Warfare

Like Jefferson, Madison attempted a combination of diplomacy and economic pressure to deal with the Napoleonic wars. Unlike Jefferson, he finally consented to take the United States to war.

Nonintercourse Act of 1809 After the repeal of Jefferson's disastrous embargo act, Madison hoped to end economic hardship while maintaining his country's rights as a neutral nation. The Nonintercourse Act of 1809 provided that Americans could now trade with all nations except Britain and France.

FOREIGN TRADE, 1805 to 1817

Source: U.S. Bureau of the Census, *Historical Statistics of the United States, Colonial Times to 1970*

Macon's Bill No. 2 (1810) Economic hardships continued into 1810. Nathaniel Macon, a member of Congress, introduced a bill that restored U.S. trade with Britain and France. Macon's Bill No. 2 provided, however, that if either Britain or France formally agreed to respect U.S. neutral rights at sea, then the United States would prohibit trade with that nation's foe.

Napoleon's Deception Upon hearing of Congress's action, Napoleon announced his intention of revoking the decrees that had violated U.S. neutral rights. Taking Napoleon at his word, Madison carried out the terms of Macon's Bill No. 2 by embargoing U.S. trade with Britain in 1811. However, he soon realized that Napoleon had no intention of fulfilling his promise. The French continued to seize American merchant ships.

The War of 1812

Neither Britain nor the United States wanted their dispute to end in war. And yet war between them did break out in 1812.

Causes of the War

From the U.S. point of view, the pressures leading to war came from two directions: the continued violation of U.S. neutral rights at sea and troubles with the British on the western frontier.

Free Seas and Trade As a trading nation, the United States depended upon the free flow of shipping across the Atlantic. Yet the chief belligerents in Europe, Britain, and France had no interest in respecting neutral rights so long as they were locked in a life-and-death struggle with one another. They well remembered that Britain had seemed a cruel enemy during the American Revolution and the French had supported the colonists. In addition, Jeffersonian Democratic-Republicans applauded the French for having overthrown their monarchy in their own revolution. Moreover, even though both the French and the British violated U.S. neutral rights, the British violations were worse because of the British navy's practice of impressing American sailors.

Frontier Pressures Added to long-standing grievances over British actions at sea were the ambitions of western Americans for more land. Americans on the frontier longed for the lands of British Canada and Spanish Florida. Standing in the way were the British and their Indian and Spanish allies.

Conflict with the American Indians was a perennial problem for the restless westerners. For decades, settlers had been gradually pushing the American Indians farther and farther westward. In an effort to defend their lands from further encroachment, Shawnee brothers—a warrior named Tecumseh and a religious leader known as the Prophet—attempted to unite all of the tribes east of the Mississippi River. White settlers became suspicious of Tecumseh and persuaded the governor of the Indiana Territory, General William Henry Harrison, to take aggressive action. In the Battle of Tippecanoe, in 1811, Harrison destroyed the Shawnee headquarters, which ended Tecumseh's efforts to form an Indian confederacy. The British had provided only a little aid to Tecumseh. Nevertheless, Americans on the frontier blamed the British for instigating the rebellion.

War Hawks A congressional election in 1810 had brought a group of new, young Democratic-Republicans to Congress, many of them from frontier states (Kentucky, Tennessee, and Ohio). Known as war hawks because of their eagerness for war with Britain, they quickly gained significant influence in the House of Representatives. Led by Henry Clay of Kentucky and John C. Calhoun of South Carolina, the war hawk members of Congress argued that war with Britain would be the only way to defend American honor, gain Canada, and destroy American Indian resistance on the frontier.

Declaration of War British delays in meeting U.S. demands over neutral rights combined with political pressures from the war hawks finally persuaded Madison to seek a declaration of war against Britain. Ironically, the British government had by this time (June 1812) agreed to suspend its naval blockade. News of its decision reached the White House after Congress had declared war.

A Divided Nation

Neither Congress nor the American people were united in support of the war. In Congress, Pennsylvania and Vermont joined the southern and western states to provide a slight majority for the war declaration. Voting against the war were most representatives from New York, New Jersey, and New England.

Election of 1812 A similar division of opinion was seen in the presidential election of 1812, in which Democratic-Republican strength in the South and West overcame Federalist and antiwar Democratic-Republican opposition to war in the North. Madison won reelection, defeating De Witt Clinton of New York, the candidate of the Federalists and antiwar Democratic-Republicans.

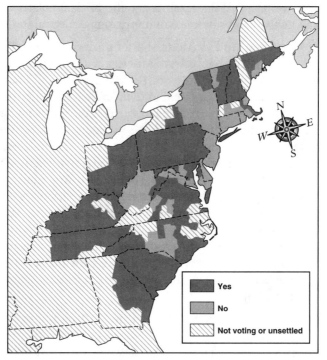

VOTE ON DECLARING WAR IN 1812

Legend:
- Yes
- No
- Not voting or unsettled

Opposition to the War Americans who opposed the war viewed it as "Mr. Madison's War" and the work of the war hawks in Congress. Most outspoken in their criticism of the war were New England merchants, Federalist politicians, and "**Quids**," or "Old" Democratic-Republicans. New England merchants were opposed because, after the repeal of the Embargo Act, they were making sizable profits from the European war and viewed **impressment** as merely a minor inconvenience. Both commercial interests and religious ties to Protestantism made them more sympathetic to the Protestant British than to the Catholic French. Federalist politicians viewed the war as a Democratic-Republican scheme to conquer Canada and Florida, with the ultimate aim of increasing Democratic-Republican voting strength. For their part, the "Quids" criticized the war because it violated the classic Democratic-Republican commitment to limited federal power and to the maintenance of peace.

Military Defeats and Naval Victories

Facing Britain's overwhelming naval power, Madison's military strategists based their hope for victory on (1) Napoleon's continued success in Europe and (2) a U.S. land campaign against Canada.

Invasion of Canada A poorly equipped American army initiated military action in 1812 by launching a three-part invasion of Canada, one force starting out from Detroit, another from Niagara, and a third from Lake Champlain.

These and later forays into Canada were easily repulsed by the British defenders. An American raid and burning of government buildings in York (Toronto) in 1813 only served to encourage retaliation by the British.

Naval Battles The U.S. navy achieved some notable victories due largely to superior shipbuilding and the valorous deeds of American sailors, including many free African Americans. In late 1812, the U.S. warship *Constitution* (nicknamed "**Old Ironsides**") raised American morale by defeating and sinking a British ship off the coast of Nova Scotia. American privateers, motivated by both patriotism and profit, captured numerous British merchant ships. Offsetting these gains was the success of the British navy in establishing a blockade of the U.S. coast, which crippled trading and fishing.

Probably the most important naval battle of the war was in 1813 on **Lake Erie** with American Captain **Oliver Hazard Perry**, declaring victory with, "We have met the enemy and they are ours." This led the way for General William Henry Harrison's victory at the **Battle of the Thames** (near Detroit), in which Tecumseh was killed. The next year, 1814, ships commanded by **Thomas Macdonough** defeated a British fleet on **Lake Champlain**. As a result, the British had to retreat and abandon their plan to invade New York and New England.

Chesapeake Campaign By the spring of 1814, the defeat of Napoleon in Europe enabled the British to increase their forces in North America. In the summer of that year, a British army marched through the nation's capital, Washington, D.C., and set fire to the White House, the Capitol, and other government buildings. The British also attempted to take Baltimore, but Fort McHenry held out after a night's bombardment—an event immortalized by **Francis Scott Key** in the words of "**The Star-Spangled Banner**."

Southern Campaign Meanwhile, U.S. troops in the South were ably commanded by General **Andrew Jackson**. In March 1814, at the **Battle of Horseshoe Bend** in present-day Alabama, Jackson ended the power of an important British ally, the **Creek nation**. The victory eliminated the Indians and opened new lands to White settlers. A British effort to control the Mississippi River was halted at New Orleans by Jackson leading a force of frontier soldiers, free African Americans, and Creoles. The victory was impressive—but also meaningless. The **Battle of New Orleans** was fought on January 8, 1815, two weeks after a treaty ending the war had been signed in Ghent, Belgium, but before news of the treaty had reached the military forces.

The Treaty of Ghent

By 1814, the British were weary of war. Having fought Napoleon for more than a decade, they now faced the prospect of maintaining the peace in Europe. At the same time, Madison's government recognized that the Americans would be unable to win a decisive victory. American peace commissioners traveled to Ghent, Belgium, to discuss terms of peace with British diplomats. On Christmas Eve 1814, an agreement was reached. The terms halted fighting, returned all conquered territory to the prewar claimant, and recognized the prewar boundary between Canada and the United States.

The Treaty of Ghent, promptly ratified by the Senate in 1815, said nothing at all about the grievances that led to war. Britain made no concessions concerning impressment, blockades, or other maritime differences. Thus, the war ended in stalemate with no gain for either side.

The Hartford Convention

Just before the war ended, the New England states threatened to secede from the Union. Bitterly opposed to both the war and the Democratic-Republican government in Washington, radical Federalists in New England urged that the Constitution be amended and that, as a last resort, secession be voted upon. To consider these matters, a special convention was held at Hartford, Connecticut, in December 1814. Delegates from the New England states rejected the radical calls for secession. But to limit the growing power of the Democratic-Republicans in the South and West, they adopted a number of proposals. One of them called for a two-thirds vote of both houses for any future declaration of war.

Shortly after the convention dissolved, news came of both Jackson's victory at New Orleans and the Treaty of Ghent. These events ended criticism of the war and further weakened the Federalists by stamping them as unpatriotic.

The War's Legacy

From Madison's point of view, the war achieved none of its original aims. Nevertheless, it had a number of important consequences for the future development of the American republic, including the following:

1. Having survived two wars with Britain, the United States gained the respect of other nations.

2. The United States accepted Canada as a part of the British Empire.

3. Denounced for its talk of secession, the Federalist Party came to an end as a national force and declined even in New England.

4. Talk of nullification and secession in New England set a precedent that would later be used by the South.

5. Abandoned by the British, American Indians were forced to surrender land to White settlement.

6. With the British naval blockade limiting European goods, U.S. factories were built and Americans moved toward industrial self-sufficiency.

7. War heroes such as Andrew Jackson and William Henry Harrison would soon be in the forefront of a new generation of political leaders.

8. The feeling of nationalism grew stronger as did a belief that the future for the United States lay in the West and away from Europe.

Monroe and Foreign Affairs

Following the War of 1812, the United States adopted a more aggressive, nationalistic approach in its relations with other nations. During Madison's presidency, when problems with the Barbary pirates again developed, a fleet under **Stephen Decatur** was sent in 1815 to force the rulers of North Africa to allow American shipping the free use of the Mediterranean. President Monroe and Secretary of State John Quincy Adams continued to follow a nationalistic policy that actively advanced American interests while maintaining peace.

Canada

Although the Treaty of Ghent of 1814 had ended the war between Britain and the United States, it left unresolved most of their diplomatic differences, including many involving Canada.

Rush-Bagot Agreement (1817) During Monroe's first year as president, British and American negotiators agreed to a major disarmament pact. The Rush-Bagot Agreement strictly limited naval armament on the Great Lakes. In time, the agreement was extended to place limits on border fortifications as well. Ultimately, the border between the United States and Canada was to become the longest unfortified border in the world.

Treaty of 1818 Improved relations between the United States and Britain continued in a treaty that provided for (1) shared fishing rights off the coast of Newfoundland; (2) joint occupation of the Oregon Territory for ten years; and (3) the setting of the northern limits of the Louisiana Territory at the 49th parallel, thus establishing the western U.S.-Canada boundary line.

Florida

During the War of 1812, U.S. troops had occupied western Florida, a strip of land on the Gulf of Mexico extending all the way to the Mississippi Delta. Previously, this land had been held by Spain, Britain's ally. After the war, Spain had difficulty governing the rest of Florida (the peninsula itself) because its troops had been removed from Florida to battle revolts in the South American colonies. The chaotic conditions permitted groups of Seminoles, runaway slaves, and White outlaws to conduct raids into U.S. territory and retreat to safety across the Florida border. These disorders gave Monroe and General Andrew Jackson an opportunity to take military action in Spanish Florida, a territory long coveted by American expansionists.

Jackson's Military Campaign In late 1817, the president commissioned General Jackson to stop the raiders and, if necessary, pursue them across the border into Spanish west Florida. Jackson carried out his orders with a vengeance and probably went beyond his instructions. In 1818, he led a force of militia into Florida, destroyed Seminole villages, and hanged two Seminole chiefs. Capturing Pensacola, Jackson drove out the Spanish governor and hanged two British traders accused of aiding the Seminoles.

Many members of Congress feared that Jackson's overzealousness would precipitate a war with both Spain and Britain. However, Secretary of State John Quincy Adams persuaded Monroe to support Jackson, and the British decided not to intervene.

Florida Purchase Treaty (1819) Spain, worried that the United States would seize Florida and preoccupied with troubles in Latin America, decided to get the best possible terms for Florida. By treaty in 1819, Spain turned over all of its possessions in Florida and its own claims in the Oregon Territory to the United States. In exchange, the United States agreed to assume $5 million in claims against Spain and give up any U.S. territorial claims to the Spanish province of Texas. The agreement is also called the Adams-Onís Treaty.

The Monroe Doctrine

Although focused on its own growth, the United States did not ignore the ambitions of Europe in the Western Hemisphere. The restoration of a number of monarchies in Europe after the fall of Napoleon in 1815 produced a backlash against republican movements. Restored monarchies in France, Austria, and Prussia, together with Russia, worked together to suppress liberal elements in Italy and Spain. They also considered helping Spain to return to power in South America, where a number of republics had recently declared their independence.

In addition, Russia's presence in Alaska worried both Britain and the United States. Using their trading posts in Alaska as a base, Russian seal hunters had spread southward and established a trading post at San Francisco Bay. British and U.S. leaders decided they had a common interest in protecting North and South America from possible aggression by a European power.

British Initiative British naval power deterred the Spanish from attempting a comeback in Latin America. But to maintain British trade with the Latin American republics required diplomacy. British Foreign Secretary George Canning proposed to Richard Rush, the U.S. minister in London, a joint Anglo-American warning to the European powers not to intervene in South America.

American Response Monroe and most of his advisers thought Canning's idea of a joint declaration made sense. However, Secretary of State John Quincy Adams disagreed. He believed that joint action with Britain would restrict U.S. opportunities for further expansion in the hemisphere. Adams reasoned as follows: (1) If the United States acted alone, Britain could be counted upon to stand behind the U.S. policy; (2) No European power would risk going to war in South America, and if it did, the British navy would surely defeat the aggressor. President Monroe decided to act as Adams advised—to issue a statement to the world that did not have Britain as a coauthor.

The Doctrine On December 2, 1823, President Monroe inserted into his annual message to Congress a declaration of U.S. policy toward Europe and Latin America. The Monroe Doctrine, as it came to be called, asserted "as a principle in which the rights and interests of the United States are involved, that the American continents, by the free and independent condition which they have assumed and maintain, are henceforth not to be considered as subjects for future colonization by any European powers."

Monroe declared further that the United States opposed attempts by a European power to interfere in the affairs of any republic in the Western Hemisphere.

Impact Monroe's bold words of nationalistic purpose were applauded by the American public but were soon forgotten, as most citizens were more concerned with domestic issues. In Britain, Canning was annoyed by the doctrine because he recognized that it applied not just to the other European powers but to his country as well. The British, too, were warned not to intervene and not to seek new territory in the Western Hemisphere. The European monarchs reacted angrily to Monroe's message. Still, they recognized that their purposes were thwarted not by his words but by the might of the British navy.

The Monroe Doctrine had less significance at the time than in later decades, when it would be hailed by politicians and citizens alike as the cornerstone of U.S. foreign policy toward Latin America. In the 1840s, President James Polk was the first of many presidents to justify his foreign policy by referring to Monroe's warning words.

REFLECT ON THE LEARNING OBJECTIVE

1. Explain the reasons and ways that American foreign policy changed during this period.

KEY TERMS BY THEME

Support (NAT, POL)
war hawks
Henry Clay
John C. Calhoun

Opposition (POL)
"Quids"
Hartford Convention (1814)

The West (MIG, ARC)
Tecumseh
Prophet
William Henry Harrison
Battle of Tippecanoe

War (WOR)
Napoleon Bonaparte
Barbary pirates

neutrality
impressment
Chesapeake-Leopard affair
Embargo Act (1807)
James Madison
Nonintercourse Act (1809)
Macon's Bill No. 2 (1810)
War of 1812
"Old Ironsides"
Battle of Lake Erie
Oliver Hazard Perry
Battle of the Thames
Thomas Macdonough
Battle of Lake Champlain
Andrew Jackson
Battle of Horseshoe Bend

Creek nation
Battle of New Orleans
Treaty of Ghent (1814)

Foreign Affairs (WOR)
Stephen Decatur
Rush-Bagot Agreement (1817)
Treaty of 1818
Andrew Jackson
Florida Purchase Treaty (1819)
Monroe Doctrine (1823)

The Anthem (SOC)
Francis Scott Key
"The Star-Spangled Banner"

MULTIPLE-CHOICE QUESTIONS

Questions 1–3 refer to the following excerpt.

> "I am ready to allow, Mr. President, that both Great Britain and France have given us abundant cause for war . . . . My plan would be, and my first wish is, to prepare for it—to put the country in complete armor—in the attitude imperiously demanded in a crisis of war, and to which it must be brought before any war can be effective . . . . I must call on every member of this Senate to pause before he leaps into or crosses the Rubicon [Roman leader Julius Caesar touched off a war in 49 BCE when he and his troops crossed the Rubicon River]—declaring war is passing the Rubicon in reality."

> Senator Obadiah German of New York, speech in the Senate, June 1812

1. Support for the War of 1812 was the strongest among
   (A) frontier settlers who wanted more land from American Indians
   (B) New England merchants who feared impressment
   (C) Protestants who had religious sympathies with Great Britain
   (D) the Democratic-Republicans who most emphasized states' rights

2. Who would be most likely to agree with German's Rubicon reference?
   (A) John Calhoun and other politicians from the South
   (B) Henry Clay and other politicians from the West
   (C) Officials from the executive branch
   (D) Merchants from New England

3. Which of the following is the best support for German's claim that the United States had "abundant cause for war"?
   (A) The impressment of U.S. sailors
   (B) The controversy over the Louisiana Purchase
   (C) The actions by the Barbary pirates
   (D) The findings of the Lewis and Clark expedition

SHORT-ANSWER QUESTION

1. Answer (a), (b), and (c).
   (a) Briefly explain how ONE specific event or historical development was used by supporters of going to war against Britain in 1812.
   (b) Briefly explain how ONE specific event or historical development was used by opponents of going to war against Britain in 1812.
   (c) Briefly explain how ONE reason for or against the War of 1812 played a major role in U.S. politics and policies after the war.

Market Revolution

I never thought my cotton gin would change history.

Eli Whitney (1765–1825)

Learning Objective: Explain the causes and effects of the innovations in technology, agriculture, and commerce over time.

In the early 1800s, the Jeffersonian dream of a nation of independent farmers remained strong in rural areas. Innovations and new technology in the 19th century would steadily decrease the demand for people working in agriculture and increase the demand for people working in commerce. Ironically, Jefferson, a father of a political revolution, would see his ideal nation of small farmers overwhelmed by an economic revolution based on new knowledge.

As the 19th century progressed, an increasing percentage of the American people were swept up in the dynamic economic changes of the Industrial Revolution. Political conflicts over tariffs, internal improvements, and the Bank of the United States (see Topics 4.3 and 4.8) reflected the importance to people's lives of a national economy that was rapidly growing.

Development of the Northwest

The **Old Northwest** consisted of six states that joined the Union before 1860: Ohio (1803), Indiana (1816), Illinois (1818), Michigan (1837), Wisconsin (1848), and Minnesota (1858). These states came from territories formed out of land ceded to the national government in the 1780s by one of the original 13 states. The procedure for turning these territories into states was part of the Northwest Ordinance passed by Congress in 1787 (see Topics 3.7 and 3.12).

In the early years of the 19th century, much of the Old Northwest was unsettled frontier and the part of it that was settled relied upon the Mississippi to transport grain to southern markets and the port of New Orleans. By mid-century, however, this region became closely tied to the other northern states by two factors: (1) military campaigns by federal troops that drove American Indians from the land and (2) the building of canals and railroads that established common markets between the Great Lakes and the East Coast.

Agriculture In the Old Northwest, corn and wheat were very profitable and fed people in growing urban areas. Using the newly invented steel plow (by **John Deere**) and mechanical reaper (by **Cyrus McCormick**), a farm family was more efficient and could plant more acres, needing to supplement its labor only with a few hired workers at harvest time. Part of the crop was used to feed cattle and hogs and also to supply distillers and brewers with grain for making whiskey and beer. Farmers shipped grain quickly to cities to avoid spoilage.

Transportation

Vital to the development of both a national and an industrial economy was an efficient network of interconnecting roads and canals for moving people, raw materials, and manufactured goods.

Roads Pennsylvania's **Lancaster Turnpike**, built in the 1790s, connected Philadelphia with the rich farmlands around Lancaster. Its success stimulated the construction of other privately built and relatively short toll roads that, by the mid-1820s, connected most of the country's major cities.

Despite the need for interstate roads, states' rights advocates blocked the spending of federal funds on internal improvements. Construction of highways that crossed state lines was therefore unusual. One notable exception was the **National, or Cumberland Road**, a paved highway and major route to the west extending more than a thousand miles from Maryland to Illinois. It was begun in 1811 and completed in the 1850s, using both federal and state money, with the different states receiving ownership of segments of the highway.

Canals The completion of the **Erie Canal** in New York State in 1825 was a major event in linking the economies of western farms and eastern cities. The success of this canal in stimulating economic growth touched off a frenzy of canal building in other states. In little more than a decade, canals joined together all of the major lakes and rivers east of the Mississippi. Improved transportation meant lower food prices in the East, more immigrants settling in the West, and stronger economic ties between the two sections.

Steam Engines and Steamboats The development of steam-powered engines in the 18th century revolutionized the location of factories. When factories ran on the power of moving water, they had to be located on a stream. However, a steam engine could be set up anywhere—in mills, mines, and factories. They first became widely used in Great Britain, but they spread to the United States in the 19th century.

The age of mechanized, steam-powered travel began in 1807 with the successful voyage up the Hudson River of the *Clermont,* a steamboat developed by **Robert Fulton**. Early steamboats could travel upriver at speeds of almost five miles per hour. Commercially operated steamboat lines soon made round-trip shipping on the nation's great rivers both faster and cheaper. Hauling freight from Cincinnati to New York took more than seven weeks before the days of steamboats and canals. After, it took less than three weeks.

Railroads Even more rapid and reliable links between cities became possible with the building of the first U.S. railroad lines in the late 1820s. The early railroads were hampered at first by safety problems, but by the 1830s, they were competing directly with canals as an alternative method for carrying passengers and freight. The combination of railroads with the other major improvements in transportation rapidly changed small western towns such as Cleveland, Cincinnati, Detroit, and Chicago into booming commercial centers of the expanding national economy. These improvements in transportation linked the regions of the North and the Midwest, as people in growing cities in Massachusetts and New York purchased much-needed wheat and corn raised in Ohio, Illinois, and states farther west. However, railroads were less common in the South, which continued to rely on rivers more than rails.

Communication

Changes in transportation brought the country closer together. But it could travel only as fast as ships could sail and horses could run. In 1844, inventor Samuel F. B. Morse demonstrated a successful **telegraph**, which transmitted messages along wires almost instantaneously. As wires were strung around the country, often along railroad tracks and later under oceans, for the first time in human history, people were able to communicate as fast as electricity could travel. Suddenly, managers in New York City, government officials in Washington, D.C., and military leaders in headquarters could direct people dozens, hundreds, or thousands of miles away more easily than ever before.

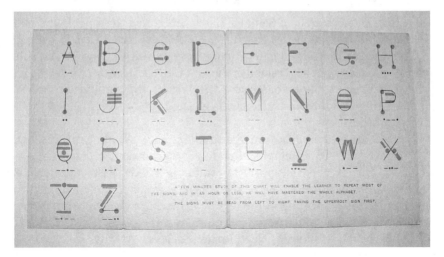

Source: Getty Images

Telegraphs used a system of short and long signals (dots and dashes) to send messages. The chart above provided a visual way to learn the code for each letter, asserting that people who studied it could learn the code in one hour or less.

Growth of Industry

At the start of the 19th century, a manufacturing economy had barely begun in the United States. By mid-century, however, U.S. manufacturing surpassed agriculture in value, and by century's end, it was the world's leader. This rapid industrial growth was the result of a unique combination of factors.

Mechanical Inventions Protected by patent laws, inventors looked forward to handsome rewards if their ideas for new tools or machines proved practical. **Eli Whitney**, who had developed the cotton gin in 1793 (see Topic 3.12), was only the most famous of hundreds of Americans whose long hours of tinkering in their workshops resulted in improved technology. During the War of 1812, he developed a system for making rifles using **interchangeable parts**, identical components that can be assembled to make a final product. Before this, the parts of a rifle were not standardized enough that one could be replaced for another. Under Eli's system, each part could be mass produced and then the parts could be put together to make a gun. This vastly increased the efficiency of making guns and other items. Interchangeable parts then became the basis for mass production methods in the new northern factories.

Corporations for Raising Capital In 1811, New York passed a law that made it easier for a business to incorporate and raise capital (money) by selling shares of stock. Other states soon followed New York's lead. Owners of a corporation risked only the amount of money that they invested in a venture. They were not personally responsible for losses incurred by the corporation. Changes in state corporation laws facilitated the raising of the large sums of capital necessary for building factories, canals, and railroads.

Factory System When Samuel Slater emigrated from Britain, taking information about factory designs out of the country was illegal. However, he had memorized the system and technology used in British cotton mills, and he applied these secrets to help establish the first U.S. textile factory in 1791. Early in the next century, the embargo and the War of 1812 stimulated domestic manufacturing and the protective tariffs enacted by Congress helped the new factories prosper.

In the 1820s, New England emerged as the country's leading manufacturing center as a result of the region's abundant waterpower for driving the new machinery and excellent seaports for shipping goods. Also, the decline of New England's maritime industry made capital available for manufacturing, while the decline of farming in the region yielded a ready labor supply. Other northern states with similar resources and problems—New York, New Jersey, and Pennsylvania—followed New England's lead. As the factory system expanded, it encouraged the growth of financial businesses such as banking and insurance.

Labor At first, factory owners had difficulty finding workers for their mills. Factory life could not compete with the lure of cheap land in the West. In response to this difficulty, **textile mills** in Lowell, Massachusetts, recruited young farm women and housed them in company dormitories. In the 1830s, other factories imitated the **Lowell System**. Many factories also made extensive use of child labor. Children as young as seven left home to work in the new factories. Toward the middle of the century, northern manufacturers began to employ immigrants in large numbers.

Unions Trade (or craft) unions were organized in major cities as early as the 1790s and increased in number as the factory system took hold. Many skilled workers (shoemakers and weavers, for example) had to seek employment in factories because their own small shops (the crafts system) produced items that could no longer compete with lower-priced, mass-produced goods. Long hours, low pay, and poor working conditions led to widespread discontent among factory workers. A prime goal of the early unions was to reduce the workday to ten hours. The obstacles to union success, however, were many: (1) immigrant replacement workers, (2) state laws outlawing unions, and (3) frequent economic depressions with high unemployment.

Commercial Agriculture

In the early 1800s, farming became more of a commercial enterprise and less of a means of providing subsistence for the family. Several factors promoted this switch to cash crops:

- Large areas of western land were made available at low prices by the federal government.

- State banks made acquiring land easier by providing farmers with loans at low interest rates.

- Initially, western farmers were limited to sending their products down the Ohio and Mississippi rivers to southern markets. The development of canals and railroads opened new markets in the growing factory cities in the East.

Cotton and the South

Throughout the 19th century, the principal cash crop in the South was cotton. Eli Whitney's invention of the **cotton gin** in 1793 (see Topic 3.12) transformed the agriculture of an entire region. Now that they could easily separate the cotton fiber from the seeds, southern planters found cotton more profitable than tobacco and indigo, the leading crops of the colonial period. They invested their capital in the purchase of enslaved African Americans and new land in Alabama and Mississippi (see Topic 4.13).

The cotton industry connected the South with a global economy. Mills in New England and Europe depended on cotton grown by enslaved workers in the South. Shipping firms, banks, and insurance companies based in the North, particularly New York City, prospered through their roles in the transport of cotton. Further, in order to devote all of their land to growing cotton, many plantation owners purchased pork, corn, and other food from states in the Midwest.

REFLECT ON THE LEARNING OBJECTIVE

1. Explain the motivation and results from the new developments in technology, farming, and business during this period.

Industry (WXT)
Lancaster Turnpike
National (Cumberland)
   Road
John Deere
Cyrus McCormick
Erie Canal

Robert Fulton; steamboats
railroads
telegraph
Eli Whitney;
   interchangeable parts
corporations
Samuel Slater

factory system
Lowell System; textile mills
unions
cotton gin
market revolution

Identities (ARC)
Old Northwest

MULTIPLE-CHOICE QUESTIONS

Questions 1–3 refer to the following excerpt.

"At home the people are the sovereign power. . . .

The industrial classes are the true sovereigns. Idleness is a condition so unrecognized and unrespected with us, that the few professing it find themselves immediately thrown out of the great machine of active life which constitutes American society.

"The CULTIVATORS OF THE SOIL constitute the great industrial class in this country. . . for, at this moment they do not only feed all other classes but also no insignificant portion of needy Europe, furnish the raw material for manufactures, and raise the great staples which figure so largely in the accounts of the merchant, the ship owner and manufacturer, in every village, town, and seaport in the Union. . . .

"The system of railroads and cheap transportation already begins to supply the seaboard cities with some fair and beautiful fruits of the fertile West."

A. J. Downing, editor, The Horticulturalist, 1848

1. The crop that best fits Downing's description as one of the "great staples which figure so largely in the accounts of the merchant, the ship owner and manufacturer" was

    (A) corn, because it was the most important food crop in the Ohio River Valley

    (B) tobacco, because it was the crop that first fostered the growth of slavery in Virginia

    (C) sugar, because it was the most profitable crop in the British and French colonies in the Americas

    (D) cotton, because it was the dominant export crop in the United States

2. The development of commercial farming in the Old Northwest contributed to increases in

(A) the develoment of interchangeable parts

(B) the number of enslaved people becoming fugitives

(C) the territory where slavery was allowed

(D) the number and size of towns and cities

3. The description in the third paragraph of the excerpt most clearly expresses which of the following visions of the United States?

(A) Alexander Hamilton's plan for a new nation

(B) Crèvecoeur's description of the American "New Man"

(C) Henry Clay's plan for economic growth

(D) Andrew Jackson's "politics of the Common Man"

SHORT-ANSWER QUESTION

Use complete sentences; an outline or bulleted list alone is not acceptable.

1. Answer (a), (b), and (c).

(a) Briefly explain ONE historical event or development in the period 1820 to 1860 that influenced the westward movement from the states along the Atlantic coast.

(b) Briefly explain ONE specific factor in the period 1820 to 1860 that resulted in the rapid population growth of cities on the Atlantic coast.

(c) Briefly explain how ONE specific group in the period 1820 to 1860 did not benefit from the westward movement.

Topic 4.6

Effects of the Market Revolution on Society and Culture

A high and honorable feeling generally prevails, and the people begin to assume, more and more, a national character . . . .

Hezekiah Niles, *Niles' Weekly Register*, 1815

Learning Objective: Explain how and why innovation in technology, agriculture, and commerce affected various segments of American society over time.

The wide impact of the market revolution that resulted from the innovations in technology, agriculture, and commerce affected all groups of people in the growing nation. They resulted in the development of a distinctively American culture, an increase in religious fervor, and support for various reform movements.

Specialization on the farm, the growth of cities, industrialization, and the development of modern capitalism meant the end of self-sufficient households and a growing interdependence among people. These changes combined to bring about a revolution in the marketplace. Farmers provided food to feed workers in cities, who in turn provided an array of mass-produced goods to farm families. For most Americans, the standard of living increased. At the same time, however, adapting to an impersonal, fast-changing economy presented challenges and problems.

Women

As American society became more urban and industrialized, the nature of work and family life changed for women, many of whom no longer worked next to their husbands on family farms. Women seeking employment in a city were usually limited to two choices: domestic service or teaching. Factory jobs, as in the Lowell System, were not common. The overwhelming majority of working women were single. If they married, they left their jobs and took up duties in the home.

In both urban and rural settings, women were gaining relatively more control over their lives. As more men worked away from home, women took on new responsibilities as moral leaders within the home, a development known as the cult of domesticity (see Topic 4.11). Marriages arranged by one's parents became less common, and some women elected to have fewer children. Nevertheless, legal restrictions on women remained. For example, they could not vote.

Economic and Social Mobility

Real wages improved for most urban workers in the early 1800s, but the gap between the very wealthy and the very poor increased. Social mobility (moving upward in income level and social status) did occur from one generation to the next, and economic opportunities in the United States were greater than in Europe. Extreme examples of poor, hard-working people becoming millionaires, however, were rare.

Population Growth and Change

Population growth provided both the laborers and the consumers required for industrial development. Between 1800 and 1825, the U.S. population doubled; in the following 25 years, it doubled again. A high birthrate accounted for most of this growth, but it was strongly supplemented after 1830 by immigrants arriving from Europe, particularly from Great Britain and Germany. The nonwhite population—African Americans and American Indians—also grew in total number. However, as a percentage of the total population, nonwhites declined from almost 20 percent in 1790 to 15 percent in the 1850s. The enslaved population increased steadily despite the ban on the importation of enslaved Africans after 1808. In no other country in the Americas did the enslaved population generally increase after the slave trade ended.

By the 1830s, almost one-third of the population lived west of the Alleghenies. At the same time, both old and new urban areas were growing rapidly.

Immigration In 1820, about 8,000 immigrants arrived from Europe, but beginning in 1832, there was a sudden increase. After 1832, the number of new arrivals never fell below 50,000 a year and in one year, 1854, climbed as high as 428,000. From the 1830s through the 1850s, nearly 4 million people from northern Europe crossed the Atlantic to seek a new life in the United States.

The surge in immigration between 1830 and 1860 was chiefly the result of the following: (1) the development of inexpensive and relatively rapid ocean transportation, (2) famines and revolutions in Europe that drove people from their homelands, and (3) the growing reputation of the United States as a country offering economic opportunities and political freedom.

Arriving by ship in the northern seacoast cities of Boston, New York, and Philadelphia, many immigrants remained where they landed while others traveled to farms and cities of the Old Northwest. Few journeyed to the South, where the plantation economy and slavery limited the opportunities for free labor. The immigrants strengthened the U.S. economy by providing both a steady stream of inexpensive labor and an increased demand for mass-produced consumer goods.

Urban Life The North's urban population grew from approximately 5 percent of the population in 1800 to 15 percent by 1850. As a result of such rapid growth in cities from Boston to Baltimore, slums also expanded. Crowded housing, poor sanitation, infectious diseases, and high rates of crime soon became characteristic of large working-class neighborhoods. Nevertheless, the new opportunities in cities offered by the **Industrial Revolution** continued to attract people from farming communities, including both native-born Americans and immigrants from Europe.

New Cities At key transportation points, small towns grew into thriving cities after 1820: Buffalo, Cleveland, Detroit, and Chicago on the Great Lakes, Cincinnati on the Ohio River, and St. Louis on the Mississippi River. The cities served as transfer points, processing farm products for shipment to the East and distributing manufactured goods from the East to their region.

U.S. MANUFACTURING BY REGION, 1860			
Region	Number of Establishments	Number of Employees	Value of Product
North Atlantic	69,831	900,107	$1,213,897,518
Old Northwest	33,335	188,651	$346,675,290
South	27,779	166,803	$248,090,580
West	8,777	50,204	$71,229,989

Source: U.S. Bureau of the Census. *Manufactures of the United States in 1860*

Organized Labor

As manufacturing became increasingly important in the economy, goods became less expensive. For those who could afford them, the standard of living improved. The shift in the economy also created a small class of people, including some factory owners and bankers, who were very wealthy and a growing middle class of people.

Industrial development meant that a large number of people who had once earned their living as independent farmers and artisans became dependent on wages earned in a factory. With the common problems of low pay, long hours, and unsafe working conditions, urban workers in different cities organized both unions and local political parties to protect their interests. The first U.S. labor party, founded in Philadelphia in 1828, succeeded in electing a few members of the city council. For a brief period in the 1830s, an increasing number of urban workers joined unions and participated in strikes.

Organized labor achieved one notable victory in 1842 when the Massachusetts Supreme Court ruled in *Commonwealth v. Hunt* that "peaceful unions" had the right to negotiate labor contracts with employers. During the 1840s, some state legislatures in the North passed laws establishing a **ten-hour workday** for industrial workers. Improvement for workers, however, continued to be limited by (1) periodic depressions, (2) employers and courts that were hostile to unions, and (3) an abundant supply of low-wage immigrant labor.

REFLECT ON THE LEARNING OBJECTIVE

1. Explain the reasons and ways advances in technology, agriculture, and commerce influenced different groups in American society during this period.

KEY TERMS BY THEME

Urban Growth (MIG) urban life new cities	**Industry & Problems (WXT)** Industrial Revolution unions	*Commonwealth v. Hunt* ten-hour workday

---

MULTIPLE-CHOICE QUESTIONS

Questions 1–3 refer to the following excerpt.

"We, the Journeyman Mechanics of the City and County of Philadelphia . . . are desirous of forming an association which shall avert as much as possible those evils which poverty and incessant toil have already inflicted . . . .

"If the mass of the people were enabled by their labor to procure for themselves and families a full and abundant supply of the comforts and conveniences of life, the consumption . . . would amount to at least twice the quantity it does at present, and of course the demand, by which alone employers are enabled either to subsist or accumulate, would likewise be increased in an equal proportion.

"The real object, therefore, of this association is to avert, if possible, the desolating evils which must inevitably arise from a depreciation of the intrinsic value of human labor; to raise the mechanical and productive classes to that condition of true independence and equality."

Philadelphia Mechanics' Union of Trade Associations, 1828

1. This excerpt supports the argument that the primary reason to form a union during the 1820s was to
   (A) improve working conditions so people would have better lives
   (B) lengthen the typical workday so people would earn more
   (C) stop immigration so workers would have less competition for jobs
   (D) form an alliance between White and Black laborers so workers would have more strength

2. Craftworkers and artisans in the 1820s were most negatively affected by

    (A) transportation improvements

    (B) ethnic rivalries

    (C) federal laws

    (D) technological changes

3. Urban workers attempted to improve their conditions through organizing labor unions and

    (A) joining religious institutions

    (B) forming political parties

    (C) creating ethnic societies

    (D) moving to working-class neighborhoods

SHORT-ANSWER QUESTIONS

Use complete sentences; an outline or bulleted list alone is not acceptable.

1. Answer (a), (b), and (c).

    (a) Briefly describe ONE historical event or development in the period 1830 to 1860 that resulted in the rapid increase in immigration.

    (b) Briefly describe how ONE specific effect that the immigrants who settled in the United States in the period 1830 to 1860 had on the development of the country.

    (c) Briefly explain ONE reason immigrants had for settling in ONE specific region of the country in the period 1830 to 1860.

2. Answer (a), (b), and (c).

    (a) Briefly explain ONE specific way the market revolution caused women's role in society to change.

    (b) Briefly explain ONE specific way the market revolution caused the population to increase.

    (c) Briefly explain ONE specific way the market revolution caused changes in the urban areas.

Expanding Democracy

"The political activity which pervades the United States must be seen in order to be understood. No sooner do you set foot upon American soil than you are stunned by a kind of tumult.

Alexis de Tocqueville, *Democracy in America*, 1835

Learning Objective: Explain the causes and effects of the expansion of participatory democracy from 1800 to 1848.

The changing politics of the period from 1800 to 1848 paralleled complex social and economic changes.

Greater Equality

Visitors to the United States in the 1830s such as Alexis de Tocqueville, a young French aristocrat, were amazed by the informal manners and democratic attitudes of Americans. In hotels, men and women from all classes ate together at common tables. On stagecoaches, steamboats, and later in railroad cars, there was also only one class for passengers, so rich and poor alike sat together in the same compartments. European visitors could not distinguish between classes in the United States. Men of all backgrounds wore simple dark trousers and jackets, while less well-to-do women emulated the fanciful and confining styles illustrated in wide-circulation women's magazines like *Godey's Lady's Book*. Equality was becoming the governing principle of American society.

The Rise of a Democratic Society

Among the White majority in American society, people shared a belief in the principle of equality—more precisely, equality of opportunity for White males. These beliefs ignored the enslavement of most African Americans and discrimination against everyone who was not White. Equality of opportunity would, at least in theory, allow a young man of humble origins to rise as far as his natural talent and industry would take him. The hero of the age was the "self-made man."

There was no equivalent belief in the "self-made woman." Restrictions, both legal and cultural, limited what women could do. But by the end of the 1840s, feminists would take up the theme of equal rights and insist that it should be applied to both women and men (see Topic 4.11).

Politics of the Common Man

Between 1824 and 1840, politics moved out of the fine homes of rich southern planters and northern merchants who had dominated government in past eras and into middle- and lower-class homes. Several factors contributed to the spread of democracy, including new suffrage laws, changes in political parties and campaigns, improved education, and increases in newspaper circulation.

Universal White Male Suffrage Western states newly admitted to the Union—Indiana (1816), Illinois (1818), and Missouri (1821)—adopted state constitutions that allowed all White males to vote and hold office. These newer constitutions omitted any religious or property qualifications for voting. Most eastern states soon followed suit, eliminating such restrictions. As a result, throughout the country, all White males could vote regardless of their social class or religion. Voting for president rose from about 350,000 in 1824 to more than 2.4 million in 1840, a nearly sevenfold increase in just 16 years, mostly as a result of changes in voting laws. In addition, political offices could be held by people in the lower and middle ranks of society.

Changes to Parties and Campaigns

Though not mentioned in the Constitution, political parties quickly became important. They channeled the energies of people into choosing leaders.

Party Nominating Conventions In the past, candidates for office had commonly been nominated either by state legislatures or by "**King Caucus**"—a closed-door meeting of a political party's leaders in Congress. Common citizens had no opportunity to participate. In the 1830s, however, caucuses were replaced by nominating conventions. Party politicians and voters would gather in a large meeting hall to nominate the party's candidates. The **Anti-Masonic Party** was the first to hold such a nominating convention. This method was more open to popular participation, hence more democratic.

Popular Election of the Electors In the presidential election of 1832, only South Carolina used the old system in which the state legislature chose the electors for president. All other states had adopted the more democratic method of allowing the voters to choose a state's slate of presidential electors.

Two-Party System The popular election of presidential electors—and, indirectly, the president—had important consequences for the two-party system. Campaigns for president now had to be conducted on a national scale. To organize these campaigns, candidates needed large political parties.

Rise of Third Parties While only the large national parties (the Democrats and the Whigs in the 1830s) could hope to win the presidency, other political parties also emerged. The Anti-Masonic Party and the **Workingmen's Party**, for example, reached out to groups of people who previously had shown little interest in politics. The Anti-Masons attacked the secret societies of Masons and accused them of belonging to an antidemocratic elite. The Workingmen's Party tried to unite artisans and skilled laborers into a political organization.

More Elected Offices During the Jacksonian era, a larger proportion of state and local officials were elected to office instead of being appointed as they had been in the past. This change gave the voters more voice in their government and also tended to increase their interest in participating in elections.

Popular Campaigning Candidates for office directed their campaigns to the interests and prejudices of the common people. Politics also became a form of local entertainment. Campaigns of the 1830s and 1840s featured parades of floats and marching bands and large rallies in which voters were treated to free food and drink. The negative side to the new campaign techniques was that in appealing to the masses, candidates would often resort to personal attacks and ignore the issues. A politician, for example, might attack an opponent's "aristocratic airs" and make him seem unfriendly to "the common man."

Spoils System and Rotation of Officeholders Winning government jobs became the lifeblood of party organizations. At the national level, President Jackson believed in appointing people to federal jobs (as postmasters, for example) strictly according to whether they had actively campaigned for the Democratic Party. Any previous holder of the office who was not a Democrat was fired and replaced with a loyal Democrat. This practice of dispensing government jobs in return for party loyalty was called the *spoils system* because of a comment that, in a war, victors seize the spoils, or wealth, of the defeated.

In addition, Jackson believed in a system of **rotation in office**. By limiting a person to one term in office, he could then appoint some other deserving Democrat in his place. Jackson defended the replacement and rotation of officeholders as a democratic reform. "No man," he said, "has any more intrinsic claim to office than another." Both the spoils system and the rotation of officeholders affirmed the democratic ideal that one man was as good as another and that ordinary Americans were capable of holding any government office. These beliefs also helped build a strong two-party system.

HISTORICAL PERSPECTIVES: *THE JACKSONIANS AND EXPANDING DEMOCRACY*

Historians debate whether the election of Jackson in 1828 marked a revolutionary and democratic turn in American politics. The traditional view is that Jackson's election began the era of the common man, when the masses of newly enfranchised voters drove out the entrenched ruling class and elected one of their own. The Revolution of 1828 was a victory of the democratic West against the aristocratic East. On the other hand, 19th-century Whig historians viewed Jackson as a despot whose appeal to the uneducated masses and "corrupt" spoils system threatened the republic.

Urban Workers In the 1940s, the historian Arthur M. Schlesinger Jr. argued that Jacksonian democracy relied as much on the support of eastern urban workers as on western farmers. Jackson's coalition of farmers and workers foreshadowed a similar coalition that elected another Democratic president, Franklin D. Roosevelt, in the 1930s.

Cultural Influence Contemporary historians have used quantitative analysis of voting returns to show that increased voter participation was evident in local elections years before 1828 and did not reach a peak until the election of 1840, an election that the Whig Party won. Some historians argue that religion and ethnicity were more important than economic class in shaping votes. For example, Catholic immigrants objected to the imposition of the Puritan moral code (e.g., temperance) by the native-born Protestants.

Economic Clash Recent historians see Jackson's popularity in the 1830s as a reaction of subsistence farmers and urban workers against threatening forces of economic change. A capitalist, or market, economy was taking shape in the early years of the 19th century. This market revolution divided the electorate. Some, including many Whigs, wanted a greater role for business owners. Jackson's veto of the bank captured popular fears about the rise of capitalism.

Support an Argument *Explain two perspectives on the factors that caused the expansion of democracy in the early 19th century.*

REFLECT ON THE LEARNING OBJECTIVE

1. Explain what brought about changes in democracy during this period, and identify the changes.

KEY TERMS BY THEME

Common Man (NAT, POL)	Politics (POL)
common man	Anti-Masonic Party
universal White male suffrage	Workingmen's Party
party nominating convention	popular campaigning
"King Caucus"	spoils system
popular election of president	rotation in office

MULTIPLE-CHOICE QUESTIONS

Questions 1–3 refer to the following excerpt.

"Our citizens who have not yet voted, have one more day in which they may exercise the privilege of determining whom they will have for their rulers. The old party lines are nearly obliterated, but there has sprung up a new interest which is formidable, both for the number of its adherents, and the disorganizing purposes by which they are actuated. By throwing open the polls to every man that walks, we have placed the power in the hands of those who have neither property, talents, nor influence in other circumstances; and who require in their public offices no higher qualifications than they possess themselves."

New York Journal of Commerce, November 7, 1829

1. The remarks in the excerpt were most likely made in response to which of the following?
   (A) Popular campaigning
   (B) Universal White male suffrage
   (C) Expanding caucus system
   (D) Return of a two-party system

2. Which of the following developments most directly supports the claim in the excerpt that "the old party lines are nearly obliterated"?
   (A) The rise of the Federalist Party, particularly in New England
   (B) The increased use of the spoils system to fill government jobs
   (C) The idea of rotation in office as advocated by Andrew Jackson
   (D) The rise of new parties such as the Workingmen's Party

3. Which of the following statements about the period 1824 to 1840 could be used to modify or refute the claim in the last sentence of the excerpt?
   (A) More states used popular elections to choose members of the Electoral College.
   (B) Political parties began to use conventions to nominate candidates.
   (C) The number of votes in presidential elections increased sevenfold.
   (D) The opportunities for women and African Americans to participate in politics remained unchanged.

SHORT-ANSWER QUESTION

Use complete sentences; an outline or bulleted list alone is not acceptable.

1. Answer (a), (b), and (c).
   (a) Briefly explain ONE historical event or development in the period 1824 to 1840 that demonstrated the spread of democracy and the "politics of the common man."
   (b) Briefly explain how ONE specific group in the period 1824 to 1840 did not share in the spread of democracy and the "politics of the common man."
   (c) Briefly explain ONE historical event or development in the period 1824 to 1840 that demonstrated the growth of political parties.

Jackson and Federal Power

It is to be regretted that the rich and powerful too often bend the acts of government to their own selfish purposes.

Andrew Jackson, on his veto of the national bank bill, July 10, 1832

Learning Objective: Explain the causes and effects of continuing policy debates about the role of the federal government from 1800 to 1848.

The era marked by the emergence of popular politics in the 1820s and the presidency of **Andrew Jackson** (1829–1837) is often called the Age of the Common Man or the Era of Jacksonian Democracy. Historians debate whether Jackson was a major molder of events, a political opportunist exploiting the democratic ferment of the times, or merely a symbol of the era. Nevertheless, the era and Jackson's name are strongly linked.

Jackson Versus Adams

Political change in the Jacksonian era began several years before Jackson moved into the White House as president. In the controversial election in 1824, Jackson won more popular and electoral votes than any other candidate but he ended up losing the election.

The Election of 1824

Recall the brief Era of Good Feelings that characterized U.S. politics during the two-term presidency of James Monroe. The era ended in political bad feelings in 1824, the year of a bitterly contested and divisive presidential election. By then, the old congressional caucus system for choosing presidential candidates had broken down. As a result, four candidates from the Democratic-Republican Party of Jefferson campaigned for the presidency: **John Quincy Adams, Henry Clay**, William Crawford, and Andrew Jackson.

Among voters in states that counted popular votes (six did not), Jackson won. But because the vote was split four ways, he lacked a majority in the Electoral College as required by the Constitution. Therefore, the House of Representatives had to choose a president from among the top three candidates. Henry Clay used his influence in the House to provide John Quincy Adams of Massachusetts with enough votes to win the election. When President Adams appointed Clay his secretary of state, Jackson and his followers charged that the decision of the voters had been foiled by secret political maneuvers. Angry Jackson supporters accused Adams and Clay of making a "**corrupt bargain**."

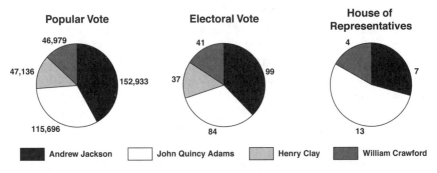

THE ELECTION OF 1824

Popular Vote

46,979
47,136
152,933
115,696

Electoral Vote

41
37
99
84

House of Representatives

4
7
13

■ Andrew Jackson   □ John Quincy Adams   ▨ Henry Clay   ▨ William Crawford

Source: Jeffrey B. Morris and Richard B. Morris, editors. *Encyclopedia of American History*

President John Quincy Adams

Adams further alienated the followers of Jackson when he asked Congress for money for internal improvements, aid to manufacturing, and even a national university and an astronomical observatory. Jacksonians viewed all these measures as a waste of money and a violation of the Constitution. Most significantly, in 1828, Congress patched together a new tariff law, which generally satisfied northern manufacturers but alienated southern planters. Southerners denounced it as a "tariff of abominations."

The Revolution of 1828

Adams sought reelection in 1828. But the Jacksonians were now ready to use the discontent of southerners and westerners and the new campaign tactics of party organization to sweep "Old Hickory" (Jackson) into office. Going beyond parades and barbecues, Jackson's party resorted to smearing the president and accusing Adams's wife of being born out of wedlock. Supporters of Adams retaliated in kind, accusing Jackson's wife of adultery. The mudslinging campaign attracted a lot of interest, and voter turnout soared.

Jackson won handily, carrying every state west of the Appalachians. His reputation as a war hero and man of the western frontier accounted for his victory more than the positions he took on issues of the day.

The Presidency of Andrew Jackson

Jackson was a different kind of president from any of his predecessors. A strong leader, he not only dominated politics for eight years but also became a symbol of the emerging working class and middle class (the so-called common man). Born in a frontier cabin, Jackson gained fame as an Indian fighter and as hero of the Battle of New Orleans and came to live in a fine mansion in Tennessee as a wealthy planter and slaveowner. But he never lost the rough manners of **the frontier**. He chewed tobacco, fought several duels, and displayed a violent temper. Jackson was the first president since Washington to be without a college education. In a phrase, he could be described as an extraordinary ordinary man. This self-made man and living legend drew support from every social group and every section of the country.

Presidential Power Jackson presented himself as the representative of all the people and the protector of the common man against abuses of power by the rich and the privileged. He was a frugal Jeffersonian, who opposed increasing federal spending and the national debt. Jackson interpreted the powers of Congress narrowly and, therefore, vetoed more bills—12—than all six preceding presidents combined. For example, he vetoed the use of federal money to construct the Maysville Road because it was wholly within one state, Kentucky, the home state of Jackson's rival, Henry Clay.

Jackson's closest advisers were a group known as his "kitchen cabinet" who did not belong to his official cabinet. Because of them, the appointed cabinet had less influence on policy than under earlier presidents.

Peggy Eaton Affair The champion of the common man also went to the aid of the common woman, at least in the case of Peggy O'Neale Eaton. The wife of Jackson's secretary of war, she was the target of malicious gossip by other cabinet wives, much as Jackson's recently deceased wife had been in the 1828 campaign. When Jackson tried to force the cabinet wives to accept Peggy Eaton socially, most of the cabinet resigned. This controversy contributed to the resignation of Jackson's vice president, **John C. Calhoun**, a year later. For remaining loyal during this crisis, **Martin Van Buren** of New York was chosen as vice president for Jackson's second term.

Indian Removal Act (1830) Jackson's concept of democracy did not extend to American Indians. Jackson sympathized with land-hungry citizens who were impatient to take over lands held by American Indians. Jackson thought the most humane solution was to compel the American Indians to leave their traditional homelands and resettle west of the Mississippi. In 1830, he signed into law the Indian Removal Act, which forced the resettlement of many thousands of American Indians.

By 1835, most eastern tribes had reluctantly complied and moved west. The Bureau of Indian Affairs was created in 1836 to assist the resettled tribes.

Most politicians supported a policy of Indian removal. Georgia and other states passed laws requiring the Cherokees to migrate to **the West**. When the Cherokees challenged Georgia in the courts, the Supreme Court ruled in *Cherokee Nation v. Georgia* (1831) that Cherokees were not a foreign nation with the right to sue in a federal court. But in a second case, *Worcester v. Georgia* (1832), the high court ruled that the laws of Georgia had no force within Cherokee territory. In this clash between a state's laws and the federal courts, Jackson sided with the states. The Court was powerless to enforce its decision without the President's support.

Trail of Tears Most Cherokees repudiated the settlement of 1835, which provided land in the Indian territory. In 1838, after Jackson had left office, the U.S. Army forced 15,000 Cherokees to leave Georgia. The hardships on the **Trail of Tears** westward caused the deaths of 4,000 Cherokees.

INDIAN REMOVAL IN THE 1830s

Nullification Crisis Jackson favored **states' rights**—but not disunion. In 1828, the South Carolina legislature declared the increased tariff of 1828, the so-called **Tariff of Abominations**, to be unconstitutional. In doing so, it affirmed a theory advanced by Jackson's first vice president, John C. Calhoun. According to this *nullification theory*, each state had the right to decide whether to obey a federal law or to declare it null and void (of no effect).

In 1830, the conflicting views of the nature of the federal Union under the Constitution led to a dramatic exchange of speeches between Senators Daniel Webster of Massachusetts and Robert Hayne of South Carolina. Hayne argued for the rights of states. In response, Webster attacked the idea that any state could defy or leave the Union.

Following this famous **Webster-Hayne debate**, President Jackson declared his own position in a toast he presented at a political dinner. "Our federal Union," he declared, "it must be preserved." Calhoun responded immediately with another toast: "The Union, next to our liberties, most dear!"

In 1832, Calhoun's South Carolina increased tensions by holding a special convention to nullify both the hated 1828 tariff and a new tariff of 1832. The convention passed a resolution forbidding collection of tariffs within the state. Jackson reacted decisively. He told the secretary of war to prepare the military. He persuaded Congress to pass the Force Bill, which gave him authority to act against South Carolina. Jackson also issued a **Proclamation to the People of South Carolina**, stating that nullification and disunion were treason.

But federal troops did not march in this crisis. Jackson opened the door for compromise by suggesting that Congress lower the tariff. South Carolina postponed nullification and later formally rescinded it after Congress enacted a new tariff along the lines suggested by the president, along with some adjustments that appealed to Northern industrialists.

Opposition to Antislavery Efforts Jackson's strong defense of federal authority forced the militant advocates of states' rights to retreat. On another issue, however, militant southerners had Jackson's support. The president shared southerners' alarm about the growing antislavery movement in the North. He used his executive power to stop antislavery literature from being sent through the U.S. mail. Southern Jacksonians trusted that Jackson would not extend democracy to African Americans.

Bank Veto Another major issue of Jackson's presidency concerned the rechartering of the **Bank of the United States**. This bank and its branches, although privately owned, received federal deposits and attempted to serve a public purpose by cushioning the ups and downs of the national economy. The bank's president, **Nicholas Biddle**, managed it effectively. Biddle's arrogance, however, contributed to popular suspicion that the bank abused its powers and served the interests of only the wealthy. Jackson shared this suspicion. In addition, Jackson believed that the Bank of the United States was unconstitutional.

Henry Clay, Jackson's chief political opponent, favored the bank. In 1832, an election year, Clay challenged Jackson by persuading a majority in Congress to pass a bank recharter bill. Jackson promptly vetoed it, denouncing the bank as a private monopoly that enriched the wealthy and foreigners at the expense of the common people and a "hydra of corruption." The voters backed Jackson, who won reelection with more than three-fourths of the electoral vote.

The Two-Party System

The brief one-party system that had characterized Monroe's presidency (the Era of Good Feelings) had given way to a two-party system under Jackson. Supporters of Jackson were now known as **Democrats**, while supporters of his leading rival, Henry Clay, were called **Whigs**. The Democratic Party harked back to the old Democratic-Republican Party of Jefferson, and the Whig Party resembled the defunct Federalist Party of Hamilton. Just as the Federalists had supported a national bank and a national road in order to promote economic growth, the Whigs supported spending federal money for internal improvements, such as roads, canals, and harbors.

At the same time, the new parties reflected the changed conditions of the Jacksonian era. Democrats and Whigs alike were challenged to respond to the relentless westward expansion of the nation and the emergence of an industrial economy.

Jackson's Second Term

After winning reelection in 1832, Jackson moved to destroy the Bank of the United States.

Pet Banks Jackson attacked the bank by withdrawing all federal funds. Aided by Secretary of the Treasury **Roger Taney**, he transferred the funds to various state banks, which Jackson's critics called "pet banks."

Specie Circular As a result of both Jackson's financial policies and the feverish purchase of western lands by many speculators, prices for land and various goods became greatly inflated. Jackson hoped to check the inflationary trend by issuing a presidential order known as the Specie Circular. It required that all future purchases of federal lands be made in specie (gold and silver) rather than in paper banknotes. Soon afterward, banknotes lost their value and land sales plummeted. Right after Jackson left office, a financial crisis—the **Panic of 1837**—plunged the nation's economy into a depression.

The Election of 1836

Following the two-term tradition set by his predecessors, Jackson did not seek a third term. To make sure his policies were carried out even in his retirement, Jackson persuaded the Democratic Party to nominate his loyal vice president, Martin Van Buren, who was a master of practical politics.

Fearing defeat, the Whig Party adopted the unusual strategy of nominating three candidates from three different regions. In doing so, the Whigs hoped to throw the election into the House of Representatives, where each state had one vote in the selection of the president. The Whig strategy failed, however, as Van Buren took 58 percent of the electoral vote.

DEMOCRATS AND WHIGS IN THE AGE OF JACKSON		
	Democrats	**Whigs**
Issues	• Opposed a national bank • Opposed protective tariffs • Opposed federal spending for internal improvements • Concerned about high land prices in the West • Concerned about business monopolies	• Supported a national bank • Supported protective tariffs • Support federal spending for internal improvements • Concerned about crime associated with immigrants
Base of Voter Support	• The South and West • Urban workers	• New England and the Mid-Atlantic states • Urban professionals

President Van Buren and the Panic of 1837

Just as Van Buren took office, the country suffered a financial panic as one bank after another closed its doors. Jackson's opposition to the rechartering of the Bank of the United States was only one of many causes of the panic and resulting economic depression. But the Whigs were quick to blame the

Democrats for their laissez-faire economics, which advocated for little federal involvement in the economy.

The "Log Cabin and Hard Cider" Campaign of 1840

In the election of 1840, the Whigs were in a strong position to defeat Van Buren and the Jacksonian Democrats. Voters were unhappy with the bad state of the economy. In addition, the Whigs were better organized than the Democrats and had a popular war hero, William Henry "Tippecanoe" Harrison, as their presidential candidate. The Whigs took campaign hoopla to new heights. To symbolize Harrison's humble origins, they put log cabins on wheels and paraded them down the streets of cities and towns. They also passed out hard cider for voters to drink and buttons and hats to wear. Name-calling as a propaganda device also marked the 1840 campaign. The Whigs attacked "Martin Van Ruin" as an aristocrat with a taste for foreign wines.

A remarkable 78 percent of eligible voters (White males) cast their ballots. Old "Tippecanoe" and John Tyler of Virginia, a former states' rights Democrat who joined the Whigs, took 53 percent of the popular vote and most of the electoral votes in all three sections: North, South, and West. This election established the Whigs as a national party.

However, Harrison died of pneumonia less than a month after taking office, and "His Accidency," John Tyler, became the first vice president to succeed to the presidency. President Tyler was not much of a Whig. He vetoed the Whigs' national bank bills and other legislation and favored southern and expansionist Democrats during the balance of his term (1841–1845).

The Western Frontier

Jackson's view of Native Americans and the Trail of Tears both reflect a common opinion and approach in the 19th century. If as the United States expanded westward, the definition of the "West" kept changing, attitudes towards the land and the American Indians remained constant. In the 1600s, the West referred to all the lands not along the Atlantic coast. In the 1700s, the West meant lands on the other side of the Appalachian Mountains. By the mid-1800s, the West lay beyond the Mississippi River and reached to California and the Oregon Territory on the Pacific coast.

American Indians

The original settlers of the West—and the entire North American continent—were various groups of American Indians. However, from the time of Columbus, American Indians were cajoled, pushed, or driven westward as White settlers encroached on their original homelands.

Exodus By 1850, the vast majority of American Indians were living west of the Mississippi River. Those to the east had either been killed by disease, died in battles, emigrated reluctantly, or had been forced to leave their land by treaty or military action. The **Great Plains**, however, would provide only a temporary respite from conflict with White settlers.

Life on the Plains Horses brought to America by the Spanish in the 1500s revolutionized life for American Indians on the Great Plains. Some tribes continued to live in villages and farm, but the horse allowed tribes such as the Cheyenne and the Sioux to become nomadic hunters following the buffalo. Those living a nomadic way of life could more easily move away from advancing settlers or oppose their encroachments by force.

The Frontier

Although the location of the western frontier constantly shifted, the *concept* of the frontier remained the same from generation to generation. The same forces that had brought the original colonists to the Americas motivated their descendants and new immigrants to move westward. In the public imagination, the West represented the possibility of a fresh start for those willing to venture there. If not in fact, at least in theory and myth, the West beckoned as a place promising greater freedom for all ethnic groups: American Indians, African Americans, European Americans, and eventually Asian Americans as well.

Mountain Men From the point of view of White Americans, the Rocky Mountains in the 1820s were a far-distant frontier—a total wilderness except for American Indian villages. The earliest White people in the area had followed Lewis and Clark and explored American Indian trails as they trapped for furs. These mountain men, as they were called, served as the guides and pathfinders for settlers crossing the mountains into California and Oregon in the 1840s.

White Settlers on the Western Frontier

Whether the frontier lay in Minnesota or Oregon or California in the 1830s and 1840s, daily life for White settlers was similar to that of the early colonists. They worked hard from sunrise to sunset and lived in log cabins, sod huts, or other shelters built from locally available resources. Disease and malnutrition were far greater dangers than attacks by American Indians.

Women Often living many miles from the nearest neighbor, pioneer women performed myriad daily tasks, including those of doctor, teacher, seamstress, and cook—as well as chief assistant in the fields to their farmer husbands. The isolation, endless work, and rigors of childbirth resulted in a short lifespan for frontier women.

Environmental Damage Settlers had little understanding of the fragile nature of land and wildlife. As settlers moved into an area, they would clear entire forests and after only two generations, exhaust the soil with poor farming methods. At the same time, trappers and hunters brought the beaver and the buffalo to the brink of **extinction**.

IMPACT OF EUROPEAN SETTLEMENT ON FORESTED LAND		
State	Forested Land before European Settlement	Forested Land after Extensive European Settlement
Pennsylvania	90% to 95%	35%
Illinois	40%	12%
Wisconsin	63% to 86%	50%
Iowa	19%	8%

Sources: Pennsylvania Bureau of Forestry, University of Illinois Extension, University of Wisconsin—Stevens Point, Iowa State Forest Resource Assessment

REFLECT ON THE LEARNING OBJECTIVE

1. Explain the reasons for and results from the ongoing arguments over the powers of the federal government.

KEY TERMS BY THEME

Migration (NAT, MIG)
Indian Removal Act (1830)
Cherokee Nation v. Georgia
Worcester v. Georgia
Trail of Tears
Great Plains
White settlers

Economics (WXT)
Bank of the United States
Nicholas Biddle
Roger Taney
"pet banks"
Specie Circular
Panic of 1837
Martin Van Buren

Jacksonian Politics (POL)
John Quincy Adams
Henry Clay
"corrupt bargain"
Tariff of 1828; Tariff of Abominations

Revolution of 1828
Andrew Jackson
role of the president
Peggy Eaton affair
states' rights
nullification crisis
Webster-Hayne debate
John C. Calhoun
Proclamation to the People of South Carolina
two-party system
Democrats
Whigs
"log cabin and hard cider" campaign

Identities & Conflict (ARC)
the West
the frontier

Ignorance (GEO)
environmental damage
extinction

Questions 1–3 refer to the following excerpt.

"It is to be regretted that the rich and powerful too often bend the acts of government to their selfish purposes. Distinctions in society will always exist under every just government. . . . In the full enjoyment of the gifts of Heaven and the fruits of superior industry, economy, and virtue, every man is equally entitled to protection by law; but when the laws undertake to add to these natural and just advantages artificial distinctions . . . to make the rich richer . . . the humble members of society—the farmers, mechanics, and laborers . . . have a right to complain of the injustices of their government. There are no necessary evils in government. . . . If it would confine itself to equal protection . . . the rich and the poor, it would be an unqualified blessing. In the act before me there seems to be a wide and unnecessary departure from these just principles."

> President Andrew Jackson, message vetoing the Bank of
> the United States, July 10, 1832

1. As expressed in this excerpt, President Jackson's guiding principle to check "the injustices of government" was
   (A) limited government
   (B) the two-party system
   (C) the principle of nullification
   (D) the civil service system

2. Jackson's action on the bank bill supported his views in this excerpt because he saw the bank as a symbol of
   (A) the natural distinctions that exist in a society
   (B) the results of the superior industry by some people
   (C) the role of the government to provide equal protection
   (D) the government helping the rich more than the poor

3. President Jackson's veto of the bank bill contributed most significantly to
   (A) lower interest rates
   (B) a financial panic
   (C) increased land sales
   (D) more political support for Henry Clay

SHORT-ANSWER QUESTIONS

Use complete sentences; an outline or bulleted list alone is not acceptable.

1. "He [Jackson] believed that removal was the Indians' only salvation against certain extinction. . . .

   Not that the President was motivated by concerns for the Indians . . . . Andrew Jackson was motivated principally by two considerations: first . . . military safety . . . that Indians must not occupy areas that might jeopardize the defense of this nation; and second, . . . the principle that all persons residing within states are subject to the jurisdiction and laws of those states. . . .

   Would it have been worse had the Indians remained in the East? Jackson thought so. He said that they would 'disappear and be forgotten.' One thing does seem certain: the Indians would have been forced to yield to state laws and white society. Indian Nations per se would have been obliterated."

   Robert V. Remini, historian, Andrew Jackson: The Course of
American Freedom, 1822–1832, 1998

   "The Georgia legislature passed a law extending the state's jurisdiction . . . over the Cherokees living within the state.

   Georgia's action forced the President's hand. He must see to it that a removal policy long covertly pursued by the White House would now be enacted into law by Congress. . . .

   Jackson as usual spoke publicly in a tone of friendship and concern for Indian welfare. . . . He, as President, could be their friend only if they removed beyond the Mississippi, where they should have a 'land of their own, which they shall possess as long as Grass grows or water runs . . . .'

   A harsh policy was nevertheless quickly put in place.

   It is abundantly clear that Jackson and his administration were determined to permit the extension of state sovereignty because it would result in the harassment of Indians, powerless to resist, by speculators and intruders hungry for Indian land."

   Anthony F. C. Wallace, historian, The Long, Bitter Trail:
Andrew Jackson and the Indians, 1993

Using the excerpts, answer (a), (b), and (c).

(a) Briefly describe ONE major difference between Remini's and Wallace's historical interpretations of Jackson's Indian removal policies.

(b) Briefly explain how ONE specific historical event or development in the period 1824 to 1844 that is not explicitly mentioned in the excerpts could be used to support Remini's interpretation.

(c) Briefly explain how ONE specific historical event or development in the period 1824 to 1844 that is not explicitly mentioned in the excerpts could be used to support Wallace's interpretation.

2. Answer (a), (b), and (c).

(a) Briefly explain ONE historical event or development in the period 1824 to 1840 that demonstrated the efforts of President Andrew Jackson to increase the powers of the federal government.

(b) Briefly explain ONE historical event or development in the period 1824 to 1840 that challenged the efforts of President Andrew Jackson to increase the powers of the federal government?

(c) Briefly explain ONE historical event or development in the period 1824 to 1840 that demonstrated President Andrew Jackson's view of the role of nonwhite people in America.

Topic 4.9

The Development of an American Culture

He is the true artist whose life is his material; every stroke of the chisel must enter his own flesh and bone and not grate dully on marble.

Henry David Thoreau, *Journal*, June 1840

Learning Objective: Explain how and why a new national culture developed from 1800 to 1848.

Much of America's early culture reflected that of Britain and the other European countries from which settlers had come. With their independence assured by the early 19th century, Americans increasingly developed a culture of their own, often one with a strong nationalistic tone. However, Americans continued to be influenced by their European heritage and to look to Europe for new ideas. Furthermore, the growing national culture emerged at the same time regional variations of it became increasingly evident.

Cultural Nationalism

The generation of Americans that became adults in the first decades of the 19th century had concerns that differed from those of the nation's founders. The young were excited about the prospects of the new nation expanding westward and had little interest in European politics now that the Napoleonic wars (as well as the War of 1812) were in the past. As fervent nationalists, they believed their young country was entering an era of unlimited prosperity. Patriotic themes infused every aspect of American society, from art to schoolbooks. Heroes of the Revolution were enshrined in the paintings by Gilbert Stuart, Charles Willson Peale, and John Trumbull. A fictionalized biography extolling the virtues of George Washington, written by Parson Mason Weems, was widely read. The expanding public schools embraced Noah Webster's blue-backed speller, which promoted patriotism long before his famous dictionary was published. The basic ideas and ideals of nationalism and patriotism would dominate most of the 19th century.

A Changing Culture: Ideas, the Arts, and Literature

In Europe, during the early years of the 19th century, artists and writers shifted away from the Enlightenment emphasis on reason, order, and balance and toward intuition, feelings, individual acts of heroism, and the study of nature. This new movement, known as **romanticism**, was most clearly expressed in the United States by the **transcendentalists**, a small group of New England thinkers.

The Transcendentalists

Writers such as **Ralph Waldo Emerson** and **Henry David Thoreau** questioned the doctrines of established churches and the business practices of the merchant class. They argued for a mystical and intuitive way of thinking as a means for discovering one's inner self and looking for the essence of God in nature. Their views challenged the materialism of American society by suggesting that artistic expression was more important than the pursuit of wealth. Although the transcendentalists valued individualism highly and downplayed the importance of organized institutions, they supported a variety of reforms, especially the antislavery movement.

Ralph Waldo Emerson (1803–1882) The best-known transcendentalist, Ralph Waldo Emerson, was a very popular American writer and speaker. His essays and lectures expressed the individualistic and nationalistic spirit of Americans by urging them not to imitate European culture but to create a distinctive *American* culture. He argued for self-reliance, independent thinking, and the primacy of spiritual matters over material ones. A northerner who lived in Concord, Massachusetts, Emerson became a leading critic of slavery in the 1850s and then an ardent supporter of the Union during the Civil War.

Henry David Thoreau (1817–1862) Also living in Concord and a close friend of Emerson was Henry David Thoreau. To test his transcendentalist philosophy, Thoreau conducted a two-year experiment of living simply in a cabin in the woods outside town. He used observations of nature to help him search for essential truths about life and the universe. Thoreau's writings from these years were published in the book for which he is best known, *Walden* (1854). Because of this book, Thoreau is remembered today as a pioneer ecologist and conservationist.

Though often detached from politics, Thoreau felt strongly that the U.S. war against Mexico (1846–1848) was immoral. To express his opposition, he refused to pay a tax that would support the war. For breaking the tax law, Thoreau was arrested and jailed. He stayed only one night—an unknown person paid his tax for him. Thoreau's reflections on the necessity for disobeying unjust laws and accepting the penalty in his essay known as "**On Civil Disobedience**" added to his lasting fame. In the 20th century, Thoreau's ideas and actions would inspire the nonviolent movements of both Mohandas Gandhi in India and Martin Luther King Jr. in the United States.

Brook Farm Could a community of people live out the transcendentalist ideal? In 1841, **George Ripley**, a Protestant minister, launched a communal experiment at Brook Farm in Massachusetts. His goal was to achieve "a more natural union between intellectual and manual labor." Living at Brook Farm at times were some of the leading intellectuals of the period. Emerson went, as did **Margaret Fuller**, a **feminist** (advocate of women's rights) writer and editor; **Theodore Parker**, a theologian and radical reformer; and **Nathaniel Hawthorne**, a novelist. A bad fire and heavy debts forced the end of the experiment in 1849. But Brook Farm was remembered for its atmosphere of artistic creativity, its innovative school, and its appeal to New England's intellectual elite and their children.

Other Communal Experiments

Brook Farm was just one attempt to set up an intentionally organized society. The idea of withdrawing from conventional society to create an ideal community, or **utopia**, in a fresh setting was not a new idea. But never before were social experiments so numerous as during the **antebellum** years. The open lands of the United States proved fertile ground for more than a hundred experimental communities. The early members of the Church of Jesus Christ of Latter-day Saints undertook one type of a religious communal effort (see Topic 4.10). Brook Farm was an example of a humanistic, or secular, experiment. Although many of the communities were short-lived, these "backwoods utopias" reflect the diversity of the reform ideas of the time.

Shakers One of the earliest religious communal movements, the Shakers had about 6,000 members in various communities by the 1840s. Shakers held property in common and kept women and men strictly separate (forbidding marriage and sexual relations). For lack of new recruits, the Shaker communities virtually died out by the mid-1900s.

The Amana Colonies The settlers of the Amana Colonies in Iowa were Germans who belonged to the religious reform movement known as Pietism. Like the Shakers, they emphasized simple, communal living. However, they allowed for marriage. Their communities continue to prosper, although they no longer practice their communal ways of living.

New Harmony The secular (nonreligious) experiment in New Harmony, Indiana, was the work of the Welsh industrialist and reformer **Robert Owen**. Owen hoped his utopian socialist community would provide an answer to the problems of inequity and alienation caused by the Industrial Revolution. The experiment failed, however, as a result of both financial problems and disagreements among members of the community.

Oneida Community After undergoing a religious conversion, John Humphrey Noyes started a cooperative community in Oneida, New York, in 1848. Dedicated to an ideal of perfect social and economic equality, community members shared property and, later, marriage partners. Critics attacked the Oneida system of planned reproduction and communal child-rearing as a sinful experiment in "free love." Despite the controversy, the community managed to prosper economically by producing and selling silverware of excellent quality.

Fourier Phalanxes In the 1840s, the theories of the French socialist **Charles Fourier** attracted the interest of many Americans. In response to the problems of a fiercely competitive society, Fourier advocated that people share work and housing in communities known as Fourier Phalanxes. This movement died out quickly as Americans proved too individualistic to live communally.

Arts and Literature

The democratic and reforming impulses of the Age of Jackson expressed themselves in painting, architecture, and literature.

Painting Genre painting—portraying the everyday life of ordinary people doing ordinary things such as riding riverboats and voting on election day—became popular among artists in the 1830s. For example, George Caleb Bingham depicted common people in various settings and carrying out domestic chores. William S. Mount won popularity for his lively rural compositions. Thomas Cole and Frederick Church emphasized the heroic beauty of American landscapes, especially in dramatic scenes along the Hudson River in New York state and the western frontier wilderness. The Hudson River School, as it was called, expressed the Romantic Age's fascination with the natural world.

Architecture Inspired by the democracy of classical Athens, American architects adapted Greek styles to glorify the democratic spirit of the republic. Columned facades like those of ancient Greek temples graced the entryways to public buildings, banks, hotels, and even some private homes.

Literature In addition to the transcendentalist authors (notably Emerson and Thoreau), other writers helped to create a literature that was both Romantic and yet distinctively American. Partly as a result of the War of 1812, the American people became more nationalistic and eager to read works about American themes by American writers. Most prominent writers came from New England or the Mid-Atlantic states:

- **Washington Irving** wrote fiction, such as "Rip Van Winkle" and "The Legend of Sleepy Hollow," using American settings.

- **James Fenimore Cooper**'s *Leatherstocking Tales* were a series of novels written from 1824 to 1841 that glorified the nobility of scouts and settlers on the American frontier.

- **Nathaniel Hawthorne** questioned the intolerance and conformity in American life in short stories and novels, including *The Scarlet Letter* (1850).

- **Herman Melville**'s innovative novel *Moby-Dick* (1855) reflected the theological and cultural conflicts of the era as it told the story of Captain Ahab's pursuit of a white whale.

- **Edgar Allan Poe,** like many Romantic writers, focused on irrational aspects of human behavior. His poems such as "The Raven" and short stories such as "The Tell-Tale Heart" portrayed mysterious or even horrifying events.

Source: *Fur Traders Descending the Missouri* by George Caleb Bingham, 1845. Wikimedia Commons/The Yorck Project/Metropolitan Museum of Art, New York City

REFLECT ON THE LEARNING OBJECTIVE

1. Explain why a new American culture developed during the period from 1800 to 1848 and what characterized it.

KEY TERMS BY THEME

Public Confidence (NAT)
cultural nationalism

Alternative Groups (NAT)
utopia
Shakers
Amana Colonies
Robert Owen
New Harmony
John Henry Noyes
Oneida Community
Charles Fourier
Fourier Phalanxes

New Ideas (SOC)
antebellum
romanticism

transcendentalists
Ralph Waldo Emerson
Henry David Thoreau; *Walden;* "On Civil Disobedience"
Brook Farm
George Ripley
feminists
Margaret Fuller
Theodore Parker
George Caleb Bingham
William S. Mount
Thomas Cole
Frederick Church
Hudson River School
Washington Irving
James Fenimore Cooper
Nathaniel Hawthorne

Questions 1–3 refer to the following excerpt.

"Unlike those who call themselves no-government men, I ask for, not . . . no government, but . . . a better government. . . .

It is not desirable to cultivate a respect for the law, so much as for the right. The only obligation which I have a right to assume is to do at any time what I think right. . . .

There are thousands who are in opinion opposed to slavery and to the war [with Mexico], who yet in effect do nothing to put an end to them . . . .

Under a government which imprisons any unjustly, the true place for a just man is also a prison. . . . If the alternative is to keep all just men in prison, or give up war and slavery, the State will not hesitate which to choose. If a thousand men were not to pay their tax-bills this year, that would not be a violent and bloody measure . . . . This is . . . the definition of a peaceable revolution."

Henry David Thoreau, author, "Resistance to Civil
Government," (also known as "Civil Disobedience"), 1849

1. Thoreau's ideology about the individual and society was most similar to
   (A) Anne Hutchinson's beliefs about her duty to follow Puritan religious leaders
   (B) Sam Adams's ideas about the tactics colonists should use to win independence
   (C) John Calhoun's conclusions about the role of enslaved people in South Carolina
   (D) Andrew Jackson's treatment of American Indians who dissented from federal land policies

2. Which of the following best explains why Thoreau stated that "under a government which imprisons any unjustly, the true place for a just man is also a prison"?
   (A) Thinkers such as Ralph Waldo Emerson were questioning business practices of the merchant class.
   (B) Communal experiments were providing places where people could live in what they hoped would be an ideal community.
   (C) People were expressing democratic impulses in painting, architecture, and literature.
   (D) The United States was at war with Mexico, which some people supported as an effort to extend slavery.

3. Which of the following groups held views about how an individual should act that were most similar to those expressed in this excerpt?

(A) People who attended revivals because they were influenced by participating in large meetings

(B) People known as transcendentalists because they emphasized acting on what they felt was right more than on what the law said

(C) People who joined phalanxes because their actions were shaped by one type of socialist ideas

(D) People who followed millennialism and made decisions based on their belief that the world would end soon

SHORT-ANSWER QUESTION

Use complete sentences; an outline or bulleted list alone is not acceptable.

1. "America is beginning to assert herself to the senses and to the imagination of her children, and Europe is receding in the same degree. . . .

Prudent men have begun to see that every American should be educated with a view to the values of land. . . .

The land is the appointed remedy for whatever is false . . . in our culture. . . .

Gentlemen, the development of our American internal resources, the extension to the utmost of the commercial system, and the appearance of new moral causes which are to modify the State, are giving an aspect of greatness to the Future, which the imagination fears to open."

Ralph Waldo Emerson, writer, "The Young American," 1844

Using the excerpt, answer (a), (b), and (c).

(a) Briefly explain ONE perspective expressed by Emerson on the reform movements in the mid-19th century.

(b) Briefly explain ONE specific way in which developments in the mid-19th century supported Emerson's point of view.

(c) Briefly explain ONE specific way in which developments in the mid-19th century challenged Emerson's point of view.

The Second Great Awakening

A revival is nothing else than a new beginning of obedience to God.

Reverend Charles Grandison Finney, "What a Revival of Religion Is," 1835

Learning Objective: Explain the causes of the Second Great Awakening.

Religious **revivals** swept through the United States starting in the late 18th century and through the first half of the 19th century. Some of these, known as the **Second Great Awakening**, marked a reassertion of the traditional Calvinist (Puritan) teachings of original sin and predestination. Others represented new developments in Christianity in the United States.

Causes of Religious Reform

Several factors fostered the conditions for the religious reforms of the late 18th and first half of the 19th century known as the Second Great Awakening:

- The growing emphasis on democracy and the individual that influenced politics and the arts also affected how people viewed religion. Worshippers were attracted to services that were more participatory and less formal.

- The rational approach to religion favored by the Deists and Unitarians prompted a reaction toward more emotional expressions of beliefs in worship services.

- The market revolution caused people to fear that growing industrialization and commercialization were leading to increased greed and sin.

- The disruptions caused by the market revolution and the mobility of people led them to look for worship settings that were outside formal churches based in urban areas.

Revivals

The Second Great Awakening began among highly educated people such as Reverend **Timothy Dwight**, president of Yale College in Connecticut. Dwight and others saw themselves as traditional Calvinists leading a counterattack against the liberal views that emerged in the 1790s. His campus revivals motivated a generation of young men to become evangelical preachers. In the revivals of the early 1800s, successful preachers were audience-centered and easily understood by the uneducated. They spoke about the opportunity for salvation for all, a message attuned to the democratization of American society. They attracted thousands to existing churches and led the establishment of new religious organizations.

Revivalism on the Frontier In 1823, Presbyterian minister **Charles Grandison Finney** started a series of revivals in upstate New York, where many New Englanders had settled. Instead of delivering sermons based on rational argument, Finney appealed to people's emotions and fear of damnation. He prompted thousands to publicly declare their revived faith. He preached that every individual could be saved through faith and hard work—ideas that strongly appealed to the rising middle class. Because of Finney's influence, western New York became known as the "burned-over district" for its frequent "hell-and-brimstone" revivals.

Baptists and Methodists In the South and on the western frontier, Baptist and Methodist circuit preachers, such as Peter Cartwright, would travel from one location to another and attract thousands to hear their dramatic preaching at outdoor revivals, or **camp meetings**. These preachers activated the faith of many who had never belonged to a church. By 1850, the Baptists and the Methodists were the largest Protestant denominations in the country.

METHODIST CAMP MEETING

Source: Getty Images

Camp meetings featured a preacher speaking to a crowd of people who often traveled from miles around to attend. The tents in the background provided places for people to stay if they could not return home at night.

New Denominations

Besides energizing existing denominations, the religious fervor of the time fostered the growth of new ones. Two were particularly influential.

Millennialism Much of the religious enthusiasm of the time was based on the widespread belief that the world was about to end with the second coming of Jesus. One preacher, William Miller, gained tens of thousands of followers by predicting a specific date (October 21, 1844) for the second coming. Nothing happened on the appointed day, but the Millerites continued as a new Christian denomination, the Seventh-Day Adventists.

Church of Jesus Christ of Latter-day Saints The Church of Jesus Christ of Latter-day Saints, formerly called the Mormon Church, was founded by **Joseph Smith** in 1830 in New York. Smith based his beliefs on a book of Scripture—*The Book of Mormon*—that traced a connection between American Indians and the lost tribes of Israel. Smith and his followers, facing persecution, moved to Ohio, then Missouri, and then Illinois. There, Smith was murdered by a local mob.

To survive, Church members, led by **Brigham Young**, migrated to the western frontier. They settled on the banks of the Great Salt Lake in Utah and named their community **New Zion**. Their cooperative social organization helped them prosper in the wilderness.

However, the Church faced strong opposition because Smith had approved the practice of polygamy, allowing a man to have more than one wife. The Church of Jesus Christ of Latter-day Saints officially prohibited polygamy in 1890. It is no longer affiliated with any group that allows it.

Reforms Backed by Religion

The Second Great Awakening, like the first in the 18th century, caused divisions between the newer evangelical sects and the older Protestant churches throughout the country. But it also touched off several social reform movements, including efforts to reduce drinking, end slavery, and provide better treatment for people with mental illness. Activist religious groups provided both the leadership and the well-organized voluntary societies that drove many reform movements during the antebellum era.

REFLECT ON THE LEARNING OBJECTIVE

1. What caused the Second Great Awakening?

Thoughts on Religion (SOC)
Second Great Awakening
Timothy Dwight
revivalism; revivals; camp meetings
Charles Grandison Finney

millennialism
Church of Jesus Christ of Latter-day Saints
  (Mormons)
Joseph Smith
Brigham Young
New Zion

MULTIPLE-CHOICE QUESTIONS

Questions 1–2 refer to the following excerpt.

"In a revival of religion, there are involved both the glory of God, so far as it respects the government of this world, and the salvation of men . . . .

The Church must take right ground in regard to politics. Do not suppose that I am going to preach a political sermon, or that I wish to have you join in getting up a Christian party in politics. . . .

Christians have been exceedingly guilty in this matter. But the time has come when they must act differently. As on the subjects of Slavery and Temperance, so on this subject the Church must act rightly or the country will be ruined. . . .

The Churches must take right ground on the subject of Slavery. . . .

Christians can no more take neutral ground on this subject, since it has come up for discussion, than they can take neutral ground on the subject of the sanctification of the Sabbath. It [slavery] is a great national sin."

Charles Grandison Finney, *Revival Lectures, XV,* 1825–1835

1. Finney's views in the excerpt on slavery would find the greatest support from whom among the following?
   (A) Thomas Jefferson and others who owned enslaved people
   (B) Andrew Jackson and others who did not focus on the slavery issue
   (C) John C. Calhoun and others who advocated for slavery
   (D) John Quincy Adams and others who supported steps to end slavery

2. Finney's assertions were most closely related to those of
   (A) supporters of a spiritual awakening during the 18th century
   (B) Enlightenment thinkers from the late 18th century
   (C) revolutionaries during the fight for colonial independence
   (D) warhawks during the War of 1812

SHORT-ANSWER QUESTION

Use complete sentences; an outline or bulleted list alone is not acceptable.

1. "The transformation of American theology in the first quarter of the nineteenth century released the very forces of romantic perfectionism that conservatives most feared. . . . As it spread, perfectionism swept across denominational barriers and penetrated even secular thought. . . .

   As the sum of individual sins, social wrong would disappear when enough people had been converted and rededicated to right conduct. Deep and lasting reform, therefore, meant an educational crusade based on the assumption that when a sufficient number of individual Americans had seen the light, they would automatically solve the country's social problems. Thus formulated, perfectionist reform offered a program of mass conversion achieved through educational rather than political means. In the opinion of the romantic reformers the regeneration of American society began, not in legislative enactments or political manipulation, but in [an] . . . appeal to the American urge for individual self-improvement."

   John L. Thomas, historian, Romantic Reform in America, 1815–1865, 1965

   "In the United States, the public sphere formed itself in a void, growing lush from the fertilization of religious and political controversies as its signature forms spread rapidly from city to town and town to village. In the ensuing decades, the public realm became an arena of initiatives and experiments, religiously-inspired reform movements and heated political contests. . . .

   In creating vast pools of proselytizers . . . and designating the entire society a missionary field, the evangelical Protestants, particularly in the North, encouraged social activism. . . .

   The society as a whole had to be redeemed . . . . Once converted, men and women found ways to express their new-found spiritual awakening by getting government policy, public morals, and private lives to conform to biblical prescriptions."

   Joyce Appleby, historian, Inheriting the Revolution, 2000

   Using the excerpts, answer (a), (b), and (c).

   (a) Briefly explain ONE major difference between Thomas's and Appleby's historical interpretations of influences on the Constitution.

   (b) Briefly explain how ONE historical event or development in the period 1820 to 1860 that is not explicitly mentioned in the excerpts could be used to support Thomas's interpretation.

   (c) Briefly explain how ONE historical event or development in the period 1820 to 1860 that is not explicitly mentioned in the excerpts could be used to support Appleby's interpretation.

An Age of Reform

We would have every path laid open to Woman as freely as to Man . . . .
As the friend of the Negro assumes that one man cannot by right
hold another in bondage, so should the friend of Woman assume that
Man cannot by right lay even well-meant restrictions on Woman.

Margaret Fuller, reformer and activist, 1845

Learning Objective: Explain how and why various reform movements developed and expanded from 1800 to 1848.

Several historic reform movements began during the Jacksonian era and in the following decades. This period before the Civil War started in 1861 is known as the **antebellum period**. During it, a diverse mix of reformers dedicated themselves to such causes as establishing free (tax-supported) public schools, improving the treatment of the mentally ill, controlling or ending the sale of alcohol, winning equal rights for women, and abolishing slavery. The enthusiasm for reform had many historic sources: the Puritan sense of mission; the Enlightenment belief in human goodness; the Jacksonian emphasis on democracy; and the changes in relationships among men and women, social classes, and ethnic groups. Religious beliefs were an important source.

Improving Society

Reform movements evolved during the antebellum era. At first, the leaders of reform hoped to improve people's behavior through moral persuasion, appealing to individuals' sense of right and wrong. However, after they tried sermons and pamphlets, reformers often moved on to political action and to ideas for creating new institutions to replace the old.

Temperance

The high rate of alcohol consumption (five gallons of hard liquor per person in 1820) prompted reformers to target alcohol as a cause of crime, poverty, abuse of women, and other social ills. Temperance became the most popular of the reform movements.

The temperance movement began by using moral exhortation. In 1826, Protestant ministers and others concerned with drinking and its effects founded the **American Temperance Society**. The society tried to persuade drinkers to take a pledge of total abstinence. In 1840, a group of recovering alcoholics formed the **Washingtonians** and argued that alcoholism was a disease that needed practical, helpful treatment. By the 1840s, various temperance societies together had more than a million members.

German and Irish immigrants were largely opposed to the temperance campaign. But they lacked the political power to prevent state and city governments from passing reforms. Factory owners and politicians joined with the reformers when it became clear that temperance measures could increase workers' output on the job. In 1851, the state of Maine went beyond simply placing taxes on the sale of liquor and became the first state to prohibit the manufacture and sale of intoxicating liquors. Twelve states followed within a decade. However, in the 1850s, the issue of slavery came to overshadow the temperance movement. The movement would gain strength again in the late 1870s, with strong support from the **Woman's Christian Temperance Union**. It would achieve national success with the passage of the 18th Amendment in 1919, which banned the sale of intoxicating liquors.

Movement for Public Asylums

Humanitarian reformers of the 1820s and 1830s called attention to the increasing numbers of criminals, emotionally disturbed persons, and paupers. Often these people were forced to live in wretched conditions and were regularly either abused or neglected by their caretakers. To alleviate the suffering of these individuals, reformers proposed setting up new public institutions— state-supported prisons, mental hospitals, and poorhouses. Reformers hoped that inmates would be cured as a result of being withdrawn from squalid surroundings and treated to a disciplined pattern of life in some rural setting.

Mental Hospitals Dorothea Dix, a former schoolteacher from Massachusetts, was horrified to find mentally ill persons locked up with convicted criminals in unsanitary cells. She launched a cross-country crusade, publicizing the awful treatment she had witnessed. In the 1840s, one state legislature after another built new mental hospitals or improved existing institutions and mental patients began receiving professional treatment.

Schools for Blind and Deaf Persons Two other reformers founded special institutions to help people with physical disabilities. **Thomas Gallaudet** opened a school for the deaf, and **Dr. Samuel Gridley Howe** started a school for the blind. By the 1850s, special schools modeled after the work of these reformers had been established in many states of the Union.

Prisons Pennsylvania took the lead in prison reform, building new prisons called **penitentiaries** to take the place of crude jails. Reformers placed prisoners in solitary confinement to force them to reflect on their sins and repent. The experiment was dropped because of the high rate of prisoner suicides. These prison reforms reflected a major doctrine of the **asylum movement**: structure and discipline would bring about moral reform. A similar penal experiment, the **Auburn system** in New York, enforced rigid rules of discipline while also providing moral instruction and work programs.

Public Education

Another reform movement started in the Jacksonian era focused on the need for establishing free public schools for children of all classes. Middle-class reformers were motivated in part by their fears for the future of the republic posed by growing numbers of the uneducated poor—both immigrant and native-born. Workers' groups in the cities generally supported the reformers' campaign for free (tax-supported) schools.

Free Common Schools Horace Mann was the leading advocate of the **common (public) school movement**. As secretary of the newly founded Massachusetts Board of Education, Mann worked for compulsory attendance for all children, a longer school year, and increased teacher preparation. In the 1840s, the movement for public schools spread rapidly to other states.

Moral Education Mann and other educational reformers wanted children to learn not only basic literacy, but also moral principles. Toward this end, William Holmes McGuffey, a Pennsylvania teacher, created a series of elementary textbooks that became widely used to teach reading and morality. The **McGuffey readers** extolled the virtues of hard work, punctuality, and sobriety—the kind of behaviors needed in an emerging industrial society.

Many public schools reflected the Protestant beliefs of the majority of community residents. In response, Roman Catholics founded private schools for the instruction of Catholic children.

Higher Education The religious enthusiasm of the Second Great Awakening helped fuel the growth of private colleges. Beginning in the 1830s, various Protestant denominations founded small denominational colleges, especially in the newer western states (Ohio, Indiana, Illinois, and Iowa). Several new colleges, including Mount Holyoke College in Massachusetts (founded by Mary Lyon in 1837) and Oberlin College in Ohio, began to admit women. Adult education was furthered by lyceum lecture societies, which brought speakers such as Ralph Waldo Emerson to small-town audiences.

Changes in Families and Roles for Women

American society was still overwhelmingly rural in the mid-19th century. But in the growing cities, the impact of the Industrial Revolution was redefining the family. Industrialization reduced the economic value of children. In middle-class families, birth control was used to reduce average family size, which declined from 7.04 family members in 1800 to 5.42 in 1830. Affluent women now had the leisure time to devote to organizations based on religion or moral uplift. The New York Female Moral Reform Society, for example, helped impoverished young women avoid being forced into lives of prostitution.

Cult of Domesticity Industrialization also changed roles within families. In traditional farm families, men were the moral leaders. However, when men took jobs outside the home to work for salaries or wages in an office or a factory, they were absent most of the time. As a result, the women in these households who remained at home took charge of the household and children.

The idealized view of women as moral leaders in the home is called the *cult of domesticity*.

Women's Rights Women reformers, especially those involved in the antislavery movement, resented the way men relegated them to secondary roles in the movement. For example, men prevented women from taking part fully in policy discussions. Among the women who spoke out against discrimination was **Sarah Grimké** in *Letters on the Equality of the Sexes, and the Condition of Women* (1838). Sarah and her sister, **Angelina Grimké,** were among the leaders opposing slavery. Another pair of reformers, **Lucretia Mott** and **Elizabeth Cady Stanton**, began campaigning for women's rights after they had been barred from speaking at an antislavery convention.

Seneca Falls Convention (1848) The leading feminists met at Seneca Falls, New York, in 1848. At the conclusion of their convention—the first women's rights convention in American history—they issued a document closely modeled after the Declaration of Independence. Their "Declaration of Sentiments" declared that "all men and women are created equal" and listed women's grievances against laws and customs that discriminated against them.

Following the Seneca Falls Convention, Elizabeth Cady Stanton and Susan B. Anthony led the campaign for equal voting, legal, and property rights for women. In the 1850s, however, the issue of women's rights was overshadowed by the crisis over slavery.

Antislavery Movement

Opponents of slavery ranged from moderates who proposed gradual abolition to radicals who demanded immediate abolition without compensating their owners. The Second Great Awakening led many Christians to view slavery as a sin. This moral view made compromise with defenders of slavery difficult.

American Colonization Society The idea of transporting those people freed from slavery to an African colony was first tried in 1817 with the founding of the **American Colonization Society**. This appealed to some opponents of slavery. It also appealed to many White Americans who wanted to remove all free Black Americans from U.S. society. In 1822, the American Colonization Society established an African American settlement in Monrovia, Liberia. Colonization never proved practical. For the most part, free African Americans did not want to leave the land where they and their ancestors had been born. Between 1820 and 1860, only about 12,000 African Americans moved to Africa, while the enslaved population grew by 2.5 million.

American Antislavery Society In 1831, **William Lloyd Garrison** began publication of an abolitionist newspaper, *The Liberator*, an event that marks the beginning of the radical abolitionist movement. The uncompromising Garrison advocated immediate abolition of slavery in every state and territory without compensating the slaveowners. In 1833, Garrison and other abolitionists founded the American Antislavery Society. Garrison stepped up his attacks by condemning and burning the Constitution as a proslavery document. He argued for "no Union with slaveholders" until they repented for their sins by freeing their slaves.

Liberty Party Garrison's radicalism soon led to a split in the abolitionist movement. Believing that political action was a more practical route to reform than Garrison's moral crusade, a group of northerners formed the **Liberty Party** in 1840. They ran James Birney as their candidate for president in 1840 and 1844. The party's one campaign pledge was to bring about the end of slavery by political and legal means.

Black Abolitionists Individuals who had escaped enslavement and free African Americans were among the most outspoken and convincing critics of slavery. One who was formerly enslaved, such as **Frederick Douglass**, could speak about the brutality and degradation of slavery from firsthand experience. An early follower of Garrison, Douglass later advocated both political and direct action to end slavery and racial prejudice. In 1847, he started the antislavery journal *The North Star*. Other African American leaders, such as **Harriet Tubman, David Ruggles, Sojourner Truth**, and **William Still**, helped organize the effort to assist fugitive slaves escape to free territory in the North or to Canada, where slavery was prohibited.

Violent Abolitionism **David Walker** and **Henry Highland Garnet** were two northern African Americans who advocated the most radical solution to the slavery question. They argued that those enslaved should take action themselves by rising up in revolt against their owners. In 1831, an enslaved Virginian, **Nat Turner**, led a revolt in which 55 Whites were killed. In retaliation, Whites killed hundreds of African Americans in brutal fashion and put down the revolt. Before this event, there had been some antislavery sentiment and discussion in the South. After the revolt, fear of future uprisings as well as Garrison's inflamed rhetoric put an end to antislavery talk in the South.

Other Reforms

Efforts to reform individuals and society during the antebellum era also included several smaller movements besides those calling for temperance and abolition:

- The **American Peace Society**, founded in 1828, had the objective of abolishing war. It actively protested the war with Mexico in 1846.
- Some reformers fought for laws to protect sailors from being flogged.
- Advocates of dietary reforms, such as eating whole wheat bread or Sylvester Graham's crackers, wanted to promote good digestion.
- Several women called for dress reform for women so they could move about more easily. For example, Amelia Bloomer called for women to wear pantalettes instead of long skirts.
- One unusual reform was phrenology, a pseudoscience that studied the bumps on a person's skull to assess the person's character and ability.

1. Explain reasons different reform efforts started and how the efforts developed differently from 1800 to 1848.

KEY TERMS BY THEME

Reforming Society (POL)
temperance
American Temperance
  Society
Washingtonians
Woman's Christian
  Temperance Union
asylum movement
Dorothea Dix
Thomas Gallaudet
Dr. Samuel Gridley Howe
penitentiaries
Auburn system
Horace Mann
common (public) school
  movement
McGuffey readers

Seneca Falls Convention
  (1848)
Susan B. Anthony
American Peace Society
Abolition Efforts (POL)
American Colonization
  Society
American Antislavery
  Society
abolition
William Lloyd Garrison; *The
  Liberator*
Liberty Party
Frederick Douglass; *The
  North Star*
Harriet Tubman
David Ruggles

Sojourner Truth
William Still
David Walker
Henry Highland Garnet
Nat Turner
Women's Rights (SOC)
antebellum period
women's rights
cult of domesticity
Sarah Grimké
Angelina Grimké
*Letters on the Equality
  of the Sexes, and the
  Condition of Woman*
Lucretia Mott
Elizabeth Cady Stanton
Susan B. Anthony

MULTIPLE-CHOICE QUESTIONS

Questions 1–3 refer to the following excerpt.

"If, then education be of admitted importance to the people, under all forms of Governments, and of unquestioned *necessity* when they govern themselves, it follows of course that its cultivation and diffusion is a matter of *public* concern and a duty which every government owes to its people. . . .

"Many complain of this tax, not so much on account of its amount, as because it is for the benefit of others and not themselves. This is a mistake; it is for *their own* benefit, inasmuch as it perpetuates the Government . . . .

He who would oppose it, either through inability to comprehend the advantages of general education, or from unwillingness to bestow them on all his fellow citizens, even to the lowest and the poorest, or from dread of popular vengeance, seems to me to want [lack] either the head of the philosopher, the heart of the philanthropist, or the nerve of the hero."

> Representative Thaddeus Stevens, speech to
> the Pennsylvania Legislature, 1835

1. Which of the following statements best describes the issues causing the sentiments expressed in the excerpt?
   (A) People inspired by Henry David Thoreau were refusing to pay taxes.
   (B) Reformers in many states were advocating for publicly funded education.
   (C) Pennsylvania was slower than most states in passing social reforms.
   (D) Debates on most issues were based on the growing division over slavery.

2. The views of Stevens on education were most similar to those of which of the following groups during the colonial era?
   (A) Small farmers in rural regions
   (B) Merchants based in large cities
   (C) Puritans in New England
   (D) Plantation owners in southern colonies

3. Stevens said, "Many complain of this tax, not so much on account of its amount, as because it is for the benefit of others and not themselves. This is a mistake." This statement supported which of the following positions?
   (A) Free public education would help everyone in a society.
   (B) High taxes benefit only the poorest people in a society.
   (C) Society works best when people act in what they see as their self-interest.
   (D) Society suffers when citizens allow government to expand its role.

SHORT-ANSWER QUESTION

Use complete sentences; an outline or bulleted list alone is not acceptable.

1. Answer (a), (b), and (c).
   (a) Briefly explain ONE specific development in the opposition to slavery in the period 1820 to 1860.
   (b) Briefly explain ONE historical event or development related to women's rights in the period 1820 to 1860.
   (c) Briefly explain ONE specific government response to the reform movements in the period 1820 to 1860.

Topic 4.12

African Americans in the Early Republic

*Now I've been free, I know what a dreadful condition slavery is.
I have seen hundreds of escaped slaves, but I never saw
one who was willing to go back and be a slave.*

Harriet Tubman, 1856

Learning Objective: Explain the continuities and changes in the experience of African Americans from 1800 to 1848.

At the outset of the 19th century, many people throughout the nation believed and hoped that slavery would gradually disappear. They thought that the exhaustion of soil in the coastal lands of Virginia and the Carolinas and the constitutional ban on the importation and enslaving of Africans after 1808 would make slavery economically unfeasible. However, the rapid growth of the cotton industry and the expansion of slavery into new states such as Alabama and Mississippi ended hopes for a quiet end to slavery. As the arguments over the Missouri Compromise suggested, the slavery issue defied easy answers.

UNITED STATES LABOR FORCE, 1800–1860 (IN MILLIONS)			
Year	Free	Enslaved	Total
1800	1.4	0.5	1.9
1810	1.6	0.7	2.3
1820	2.1	1.0	3.1
1830	3.0	1.2	4.2
1840	4.2	1.5	5.7
1850	6.3	2.0	8.3
1860	8.8	2.3	11.1

Source: U.S. Bureau of the Census. *Historical Statistics of the United States, Colonial Times to 1970*

Free African Americans

By 1860, there were approximately 500,000 free African Americans living throughout the United States.

In the North The 250,000 African Americans who lived in the North in 1860 constituted only 1 percent of northerners. However, they represented 50 percent of all free African Americans in the country. Freedom enabled them to maintain a family and, in some instances, own land. In response to discrimination in White-dominated churches, many free African Americans formed their own Christian congregations. Some of these congregations joined together as the African Methodist Episcopal Church.

However, freedom did not mean economic or political equality for African Americans, since strong racial prejudices kept them from voting and holding jobs in most skilled professions and crafts. In the mid-1800s, immigrants displaced them from occupations and jobs that they had held since the time of the Revolution. Denied membership in unions, African Americans were often hired as strikebreakers—and often dismissed after the strike ended.

In the South As many as 250,000 African Americans in the South were not enslaved. They were free citizens (even though, as in the North, racial prejudice restricted their liberties). A number of those enslaved had been emancipated during the American Revolution. Some were mulatto children whose White fathers had decided to liberate them. Others achieved freedom on their own, when permitted, through self-purchase—if they were fortunate enough to have been paid wages for extra work, usually as skilled craftspeople.

Most free southern Blacks lived in cities where they could own property. By state law, they were not equal with Whites, were not permitted to vote, and were barred from entering certain occupations. Constantly in danger of being kidnapped by slave traders, they had to show legal papers proving their free status. They remained in the South for various reasons. Some wanted to be near family members who were still in bondage. Others thought of the South as their home and believed the North offered no greater opportunities.

Resistance by the Enslaved

Conditions of slavery varied from one plantation to the next, but all suffered from being deprived of their freedom. Families could be separated at any time by an owner's decision to sell a wife, a husband, or a child. Women were vulnerable to sexual exploitation. Despite the hard, nearly hopeless circumstances of their lives, enslaved African Americans maintained a strong sense of family and of religious faith.

Those enslaved contested their status through a range of actions, including restrained resistance, running away, or open rebellion. The search for freedom was continuous and took many forms.

Restrained Actions On a daily basis, an untold number of those enslaved engaged in work slowdowns and equipment sabotage. What Whites called "laziness" in those enslaved was in reality a subtle defiance against their situation.

Runaways For an individual, escape from enslavement was a challenging goal. It was even more difficult for women who were caring for their children or pregnant. All escaping faced organized militia patrols and hunters who were paid a bounty for those they captured. Those returned to their owners were normally severely physically mistreated. The growth of the "Underground Railroad" and increasing demands of Southerners for stricter fugitive slave laws (see Topics 4.11, 5.4, 5.5) demonstrate the increasing number of slaves willing to attempt running away despite the risks.

DESPERATE CONFLICT IN A BARN.

Source: Library of Congress

When Robert Jackson and two other enslaved men from Virginia attempted to escape, they were caught in a barn in Maryland. After a violent struggle, they were captured and returned to slavery.

Rebellions While there were few large uprisings instigated by those enslaved, their impact on both other enslaved people and on White Southerners was considerable. In particularly, the successful slave revolt and the establishment of an independent nation in Haiti in the early 1800s caused consternation among slaveholders in the South. For years Southerners resisted political recognition or any diplomatic interaction with Haiti.

One of the earliest reported organized efforts to rebel was on a plantation near Richmond, Virginia, in 1800. Gabriel Prosser is reputed to have engaged approximately a thousand others enslaved to rise up against their oppressors. Betrayed before they could take action, Gabriel and a number of his followers were executed.

Another notable conspiracy for freedom was organized by **Denmark Vesey**, a free African American, in 1822, near Charleston, South Carolina. Vesey and other fellow congregants of a large African Methodist Church that included many slaves were reputedly inspired by their readings from the Bible and possibly discussions of the recent Missouri Compromise limiting the spread of slavery. They forged a plan to seize ships in the harbor and sail away to freedom, possibly to Haiti. These efforts were ended by informers before Vesey could act, and he along with over thirty conspirators were hanged.

There is one instance of an uprising by those enslaved that was well known. **Nat Turner**, enslaved in Southampton County, Virginia, in 1831, and considered a religious zealot by some, organized an attack on his surrounding community. In a single day, over 50 White men, women, and children were killed. Reaction was swift, and the militia killed not only Turner and his followers but also many innocent African Americans in reprisal for the rebellion.

While any efforts at organized rebellions were quickly and violently suppressed, they had a lasting influence. They gave hope to enslaved African Americans, drove southern states to tighten already strict **slave codes** with growing fear, and demonstrated to many the evils of slavery. Revolts polarized the country by making slaveholders more defensive about slavery and nonslaveholders more critical of the institution.

POPULATION OF ENSLAVED AFRICAN AMERICANS			
	1800	1830	1860
New York	20,613	75	0
Maryland	106,635	102,994	87,189
Virginia	346,671	469,767	490,865
Georgia	59,699	217,531	462,198
Alabama	—	117,549	435,080
Mississippi	—	65,659	436,631
Arkansas	—	4,576	111,115
All States	893,605	2,009,043	3,953,760

Source: State-level data from Historical Census Browser from the University of Virginia, Geospatial and Statistical Data Center. Data drawn from the U.S. Census.

REFLECT ON THE LEARNING OBJECTIVE

1. Explain what stayed the same and what became different for African Americans during the period from 1800 to 1848.

Identities & Conflict (ARC)
free African Americans

The Slave Industry (MIG, WXT)
Denmark Vesey
Nat Turner
slave codes

MULTIPLE-CHOICE QUESTIONS

Questions 1–2 refer to the following excerpt.

> "I think that 'twixt the negroes of the South and the women at the North, all talking about rights, the white men will be in a fix pretty soon. But what's all this here talk about?
>
> That man over there says that women need to be helped . . . . Nobody ever helps me. . .! And ain't I a woman?
>
> Then they talk about this thing in the head . . . [audience member whispers "intellect"] . . . What's that got to do with women's rights or negro's rights? If my cup won't hold but a pint, and yours holds a quart, wouldn't you be mean not to let me have my little half measure full?
>
> Then that little man in black there, he says women can't have as much rights as men, 'cause Christ wasn't a woman! Where did your Christ come from? . . . From God and a woman! Man had nothing to do with Him."

> Sojourner Truth, abolitionist and former slave, speech to a
> Women's Convention in Ohio, 1851

1. Sojourner Truth most clearly rejects criticisms of women that are based on which of the following?

(A) The ideas of transcendentalism

(B) The principles of the Enlightenment

(C) The teachings of religion

(D) The working status of women

2. Sojourner Truth saw connections between the women's rights movement and

(A) the Second Great Awakening

(B) the antislavery movement

(C) the cult of domesticity

(D) the Constitution

1. "Slaves apparently thought of the South's peculiar institution chiefly as a system of labor extortion. Of course they felt its impact in other ways—in their social status, their legal status, and their private lives—but they felt it most acutely in their lack of control of their own time and labor. . . .

   In Africa the Negroes had been accustomed to a strictly regulated family life and a rigidly enforced moral code. But in America the disintegration of their social organization removed the traditional sanctions which had encouraged them to respect their old customs. . . . Here, as at so many other points, the slaves had lost their native culture without being able to find a workable substitute and therefore lived in a kind of cultural chaos. . . . Marriage, insisted Frederick Douglass, had no existence among slaves. . . . His consolation was that at least some slaves 'maintained their honor, where all around was corrupt.'"

   Kenneth M. Stampp, historian, The Peculiar Institution, 1956

   "We have made a great error in the way in which we have viewed slave life, and this error has been perpetuated by both whites and blacks, racists and antiracists. . . .

   What the sources show . . . is that the average plantation slave lived in a family setting, developed strong family ties, and held the nuclear family as the proper social norm. . . . We do not know just how many slaves lived as a family or were willing and able to maintain a stable family life during slavery. But the number was certainly great, whatever the percentage, and as a result, the social norm that black people carried from slavery to freedom was that of the nuclear family. . . . There are moments in the history of every people—in which they cannot do more than succeed in keeping themselves together and maintaining themselves as human beings with a sense of individual dignity and collective identity. Slavery was such a moment for black people in America."

   Eugene Genovese, historian, American Slaves and Their History, 1971

   Using the excerpts, answer (a), (b), and (c).

   (a) Briefly explain ONE major difference between Stampp's and Genovese's historical interpretations of the nature of slavery.

   (b) Briefly explain how ONE historical event or development in the period 1820 to 1860 that is not explicitly mentioned in the excerpts could be used to support Stampp's interpretation.

   (c) Briefly explain how ONE historical event or development in the period 1820 to 1860 that is not explicitly mentioned in the excerpts could be used to support Genovese's interpretation.

Southern Society in the Early Republic

I never use the word "nation" in speaking of the United States.
I always use the word "Union" or "Confederacy." We are not a nation
but a union, a confederacy of equal and sovereign States.

Senator John C. Calhoun, South Carolina, 1849

Learning Objective: Explain how geographic and environmental factors shaped the development of the South from 1800 to 1848.

Initially the English colonies had developed as parts of distinct regions: New England, Middle, and Southern. A combination of geography and cultural differences among immigrants, compounded by limited contact because of poor transportation, shaped the differences among the regions. As the colonies became states and as transportation improved in the 19th century, the regional distinctions remained, based on a combination of geography and economics.

The states where slavery was widely practiced formed a distinctive region, the South. By 1861, the region included 15 states, all but four of which (Delaware, Maryland, Kentucky, and Missouri) seceded and joined the Confederacy.

Agriculture and King Cotton

Agriculture was the foundation of the South's economy, even though by the 1850s, small factories in the region were producing approximately 15 percent of the nation's manufactured goods. Tobacco, rice, and sugarcane were important cash crops, but these were far exceeded by the South's chief economic activity: the production and sale of cotton.

The development of mechanized textile mills in England, coupled with **Eli Whitney**'s cotton gin, made cotton cloth affordable, not just in Europe and the United States, but throughout the world. Before 1860, the world depended chiefly on Britain's mills for its supply of cloth, and Britain, in turn, depended chiefly on the American South for its supply of cotton fiber. Originally, the cotton was grown almost entirely in two states, South Carolina and Georgia, but as demand and profits increased, **planters** moved westward into Alabama, Mississippi, Louisiana, and Texas. New land was constantly in demand because the high cotton yields desired for profits quickly depleted the soil. By the 1850s, cotton provided two-thirds of all U.S. exports and linked the South and Great Britain. "Cotton is king," said one southerner of his region's greatest asset.

AGRICULTURE, MINING, AND
MANUFACTURING BEFORE THE CIVIL WAR

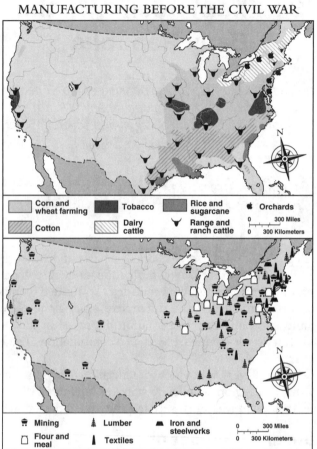

Slavery, the "Peculiar Institution"

Wealth in the South was measured in terms of land and enslaved people. The latter were treated as a form of property, subject to being bought and sold. However, some Whites were sensitive about how they treated the other humans, so they referred to slavery as "that peculiar institution." In colonial times, people justified slavery as an economic necessity, but in the 19th century, apologists for slavery mustered historical and religious arguments to support their claim that it was good for both the enslaved and the master.

Population The cotton boom was largely responsible for a fourfold increase in the number of people held in slavery, from 1 million in 1800 to nearly 4 million in 1860. Most of the increase came from natural growth, although thousands of Africans were also smuggled into the South in violation of the 1808 law against importing enslaved people. In parts of the **Deep**

South, enslaved African Americans made up as much as 75 percent of the total population. Fearing slave revolts, southern legislatures added increased restrictions on movement and education to their **slave codes**.

Economics Enslaved workers were employed doing whatever their owners demanded of them. Most labored in the fields, but many learned skilled crafts or worked as house servants, in factories, or on construction gangs. Because of the greater profits to be made on the new cotton plantations in the West, many owners in the Upper South sold their enslaved workers to owners in the cotton-rich Deep South of the lower Mississippi Valley. By 1860, the value of an enslaved field hand had risen to almost $2,000 at a time when a typical wage for a laborer was $1 a day. One result of the heavy capital investment in slavery was that the South had much less capital than the North to undertake industrialization.

White Society

Southern Whites observed a rigid hierarchy among themselves. Aristocratic planters lived comfortably at the top of society, while poor farmers and mountain people struggled at the bottom.

Aristocracy Members of the South's small elite of wealthy planters owned at least 100 enslaved people and at least 1,000 acres. The planter aristocracy maintained its power by dominating the state legislatures of the South and enacting laws that favored the large landholders' economic interests.

Farmers The vast majority of slaveholders held fewer than 20 people in bondage and worked only several hundred acres. Southern White farmers produced the bulk of the cotton crop, worked in the fields alongside enslaved African Americans, and lived as modestly as farmers of the North.

Poor Whites Three-fourths of the White households in the South owned no enslaved people. They could not afford the rich river-bottom farmland controlled by the planters, and many lived in the hills as subsistence farmers. These **"hillbillies"** or "poor White trash," as planters derisively called them, defended the system, hoping that some day they, too, could own enslaved people. Further, the slave system meant that White farmers, no matter how poor, still felt superior on the social scale to Black people.

Mountain People A number of small farmers lived in frontier conditions along the slopes and valleys of the Appalachian and Ozark mountains. They were somewhat isolated from the rest of the South. The mountain people disliked the planters and slavery. During the Civil War, many (including a future president, Andrew Johnson of Tennessee) remained loyal to the Union.

Cities The South was an agricultural region with few large commercial cities. The largest city in the region was New Orleans, with a population of about 170,000. It was the fifth-largest city in the country, after New York, Philadelphia, Baltimore, and Boston. Only three other southern cities—St. Louis, Louisville, and Charleston—had populations greater than 40,000 people.

The South developed a unique culture and outlook on life. As cotton became the basis of its economy, slavery became the focus of its political thought. White southerners felt increasingly isolated and defensive about slavery as northerners grew hostile toward it, and as Great Britain, France, Mexico, and other European and Latin America states outlawed it altogether.

Code of Chivalry Dominated by the aristocratic planter class, the agricultural South was in some ways a feudal society. Southern gentlemen ascribed to a code of chivalrous conduct, which included a strong sense of personal honor, the defense of womanhood, and paternalistic attitudes toward all who were deemed inferior, especially slaves.

Education The upper class valued a college education for their children. Acceptable professions for gentlemen were limited to farming, law, the ministry, and the military. For the lower classes, schooling beyond the early elementary grades was generally not available. To reduce the risk of slave revolts, the law strictly prohibited teaching enslaved people to read or write.

Religion The slavery question affected churches. Partly because they preached biblical support for slavery, both Methodist and Baptist denominations gained members in the South. However, both groups split into northern and southern branches in the 1840s. The Unitarians, who challenged slavery, faced declining membership and hostility. Even Catholics and Episcopalians, who took a neutral stand on slavery, saw their numbers decline in the South.

Social Reform The antebellum reform movement of the first half of the 19th century was largely found in the northern and western states, with little impact in the South. While "modernizers" worked to perfect society in the North, southerners were more committed to tradition and slower to support public education and humanitarian reforms. They were alarmed to see northern reformers join forces to support the antislavery movement. Increasingly, they viewed social reform as a northern threat against the southern way of life.

REFLECT ON THE LEARNING OBJECTIVE

1. Explain the influences of geography and the environment on the growth of the South in the period from 1800 to 1848.

HISTORICAL PERSPECTIVES: *WHAT WAS THE NATURE OF SLAVERY?*

During the two decades following the end of World War II, Black Americans led a vigorous fight against racial discrimination. In the context of this civil rights movement, historians began to revaluate slavery.

Features of Slavery Before 1945, scholarship on slavery followed Ulrich B. Phillips's *American Negro Slavery* (1918). He portrayed slavery as failing economically but maintained by paternalistic White owners who gave civilization to enslaved but contented Black Americans. Most of his views have been entirely discredited. For example, historians demonstrated that owners and enslaved people were in continual conflict. Kenneth Stampp summarized this view in *The Peculiar Institution: Slavery in the Ante-Bellum South* (1956). Two years later, Alfred Conrad and John Meyers published an influential article that provided evidence that slavery was profitable, adding to the argument that the institution would not fade away as it had in most of Latin America.

Slavery's Impact on Black Culture Historians have bitterly disagreed over the legacy of slavery on the culture of African Americans. Stanley Elkins, in *Slavery: A Problem in American Institutional Life* (1959), argued that slavery was so oppressive that no distinctive Black culture could develop. In contrast, Eugene Genovese's *Roll, Jordan, Roll: The World the Slaves Made* (1974) argued that enslaved African Americans did develop and maintain a culture based on family life, tradition, and religion.

Recent scholars have expanded on how enslaved people not only created their own culture but found creative ways to resist their condition. Tera W. Hunter's *Bound in Wedlock: Slave and Free Black Marriage in the Nineteenth Century* (2017) highlighted how enslaved people developed long-term relationships, despite obstacles to traditional marriage created by their owners.

Support an Argument *Explain two perspectives on the nature of slavery.*

KEY TERMS BY THEME

Identities & Conflict (ARC)	Migration (NAT, MIG)	The Slave Industry (MIG, WXT)
planters	Deep South	King Cotton
code of chivalry		Eli Whitney
poor Whites		peculiar institution
hillbillies		slave codes
mountain people		

MULTIPLE-CHOICE QUESTIONS

Questions 1–2 refer to the following excerpt.

> "That we have cultivated cotton, cotton, cotton and bought everything else, has long enough been our opprobrium [disgrace]. It is time we should be roused by some means or other to see, that such a course of conduct will inevitably terminate in our ultimate poverty and ruin. Let us manufacture, because it is our best policy. Let us go more on provision crops and less on cotton, because we have had every thing about us poor and impoverished long enough— . . . If we have followed a ruinous policy and bought all the articles of subsistence instead of raising them, who is to blame? . . . Let us change our policy . . . . We have good land, unlimited water-powers, capital in plenty, and a patriotism which is running over in some places."
>
> *Georgia Courier,* June 21, 1827

1. The remarks in the excerpt were directed most clearly toward which of the following groups?

   (A) Bankers who did not want to invest money outside their own region

   (B) Manufacturers who failed to market their products effectively

   (C) Farmers who grew crops and raised livestock mostly for their own consumption

   (D) Plantation owners who profited from producing crops they could sell overseas

2. At the time this excerpt was written, in which of the following was the largest amount of Southern capital invested?

   (A) Railroads and other transportation systems to connect urban areas

   (B) Enslaved people who mostly performed agricultural labor

   (C) Land that was purchased for use or sale at a later time

   (D) Small factories that produced a variety of goods for export

SHORT-ANSWER QUESTION

1. "That a country should become eminently prosperous in agriculture, without a high state of perfection in the mechanic arts, is a thing next to impossible ... that we shall follow the footsteps of our forefathers, and still further exhaust our soil by the exclusive cultivation of cotton?

   Unless we betake ourselves to some more profitable employment than the planting of cotton, what is to prevent our most enterprising planters from moving, with their negro capital, to the Southwest?

   Cotton ... has produced us such an abundant supply of all the luxuries and elegancies of life, with so little exertion on our part, that we have become ... unfitted for other more laborious pursuits, and unprepared to meet the state of things, which sooner or later must come about."

   William Gregg, manufacturer in South Carolina,
   "Essays on Domestic Industry," 1845

   Using the excerpt, answer (a), (b), and (c).

   (a) Briefly explain ONE specific factor that contributed to the lack of manufacturing in the South during the first half of the 19th century.

   (b) Briefly explain ONE specific advantage, if any, the North had over the South in developing manufacturing during the first half of the 19th century.

   (c) Briefly explain ONE specific long-term effect on the Southern economy as a result of its lack of a large manufacturing base.

Topic 4.14

Causation in Period 4

Learning Objective: Explain the extent to which politics, economics, and foreign policy promoted the development of American identity from 1800 to 1848.

You can use the reasoning skill "causation" with the content of Period 4 to consider the extent to which politics, economics, and foreign policy influenced the development of American identity between 1800 and 1848. By examining the *relationships among the pieces of historical evidence*, one can develop an argument to explain how the rise of one political party, Democratic-Republicans, was connected to the fall of another, the Federalists. These developments caused people to use political parties to express their American identity.

In economics, the development of new means of transportation led to the market revolution. The shift toward a market economy caused people to change how they thought of themselves. They identified as producers of goods to sell others and as workers for others, and they took pride in being industrious. The market revolution also influenced foreign policy. People looked to territorial expansion such as the Louisiana Purchase to provide new opportunities. They focused on the west and away from foreign involvements.

While the historical evidence relates to the coalescence of a stronger American identity, this same evidence shows a people with growing differences resulting from new religious and cultural ideas. These differences were particularly sharp over the place of slavery in the growing nation.

QUESTIONS ABOUT CAUSATION

Use the questions below to make a historically defensible claim.

1. Explain the factors that caused the expansion of participation in politics, including the right to vote. For example, as new states were formed on the western frontier, they embraced the ideal of equality for all White males and adopted universal male suffrage as well as nominating conventions to limit the power of any elite group.

2. Explain the developments in technology, agriculture, and commerce that caused the market revolution during the period from 1800 to 1848. For example, technological innovations that produced a canal system, steamboats, and railroads tied together the cities and farms and thus enabled the development of the market system.

When analyzing sources, you need to identify the author's argument. Then you need to weigh the evidence used to support it. To a historian, an effective argument is a historically defensible claim backed up with reasons and evidence that are logical and relevant. Breaking the tasks down into steps makes it easier:

- **Identify the argument.** What claim is the source making? What position is the source taking about a person, event, or issue?

- **Identify the evidence.** What information does the source use to support the argument? Are there facts, statistics, quotations, details, or images? Consider whether this information directly relates to the argument.

- **Compare arguments.** Historians and witnesses to history often have conflicting opinions about any individual, event, or issue. Which arguments have more evidence? Which arguments have higher-quality evidence?

The AP® exam includes long essay questions and a document-based question that ask you to develop an argument. Some short-answer items and some multiple-choice items also relate to claims and evidence in sources.

Read the two sources about the Missouri Compromise. Then answer the questions.

Source 1

"This momentous question, like a fire bell in the night, awakened and filled me with terror. I considered it at once as the knell [approaching end] of the Union. It is hushed, indeed, for the moment. But this is a reprieve only, not a final sentence. A geographical line, coinciding with a marked principle, moral and political, once conceived and held up to the angry passions of men, will never be obliterated; and every new irritation will mark it deeper and deeper."

Thomas Jefferson, personal letter, April 22, 1820

Source 2

"The discussion on the Missouri question has undoubtedly contributed to weaken in some degree the attachment of our southern and western people to the Union; but the agitators of that question have, in my opinion, not only completely failed; but have destroyed to a great extent their capacity for future mischief. Should Missouri be admitted at the next session, as I think she will without difficulty, the evil effects of the discussion must gradually subside."

Secretary of War John C. Calhoun, letter to Andrew Jackson, June 1, 1820

1. Describe the argument Jefferson makes in Source 1.
2. Describe the argument Calhoun makes in Source 2.
3. Describe evidence that would support Jefferson's argument.
4. Describe evidence that would support Calhoun's argument.
5. Based on the sources and what you know about the historical period, explain which argument you think is more defensible.

WRITE AS A HISTORIAN: *GATHER AND ORGANIZE THE EVIDENCE*

After analyzing the task and developing questions you need to answer to complete it (see page 157), the next step in writing a long essay is to gather and organize your evidence. *Gathering evidence* relies on recall—how much you remember from your reading and other studies. *Organizing evidence* requires the skills of seeing patterns and connections and using historical reasoning.

Suppose you are answering this long essay question: "Evaluate the extent to which the American Revolution was primarily an effort to maintain basic British rights. Make a list of questions for deeper analysis (see page 157), and answer them. In doing so, you should list the information you will use in your essay to answer the question. Your essay might include the following:

- British rights included beliefs about taxation, such as the difference between direct and indirect taxation.

- Colonists believed that as British citizens, they had certain individual liberty and restraints on government.

- Colonists felt that the British had ignored or violated these rights.

- Colonists often traded goods with non-British colonies and countries in violation of British laws. The right to smuggle was not a basic British right, but it was a custom that colonists wanted to defend.

- Colonists had gone further than the British in recognizing press freedom (the Zenger case) and religious toleration.

After writing everything you can remember, organize your evidence. Review your notes, looking for patterns related to the task. Which pieces of evidence represent a continuity, a way to preserve British rights? Which represent a change from how British rights were traditionally interpreted? Make a simple chart to place the evidence in the correct category. Then evaluate the extent to which change outweighed continuity or vice versa.

Application: On a separate sheet of paper, expand on the evidence you recall about colonial attitudes regarding basic British rights by adding notes to the above list. Then make a chart like the one below. Place each piece of evidence in the appropriate column.

Continuities	Changes

For current free-response question samples, visit: https://apcentral.collegeboard.org/ courses/ap-united-states-history/exam.

LONG ESSAY QUESTIONS

Directions: The suggested writing time for each question is 40 minutes. In your response, you should do the following:

- Respond to the prompt with a historically defensible thesis or claim that establishes a line of reasoning.
- Describe a broader historical context relevant to the prompt.
- Support an argument in response to the prompt using specific and relevant examples of evidence.
- Use historical reasoning (e.g., comparison, causation, continuity, or change) to frame or structure an argument that addresses the prompt.
- Use evidence to corroborate, qualify, or modify an argument that addresses the prompt.

1. Evaluate the extent to which economic factors contributed to the development of regional rivalries during the period of 1800–1848.

2. Evaluate the extent of the influence of the Monroe Doctrine on the formation of United States foreign policy in the early 19th century.

3. Evaluate the extent of the similarities between the policies of President George Washington and those of President Thomas Jefferson.

4. Evaluate the extent to which the decisions of the Supreme Court under Chief Justice John Marshall defined the relationship between the central government and the states.

5. Evaluate the extent to which Andrew Jackson's economic views affected the economy during the 1830s.

6. Evaluate the extent to which the election of Andrew Jackson fostered a change in politics during the period of 1800–1848.

7. Evaluate the extent to which the United States developed its own culture distinct from Europe during the period of 1800–1848.

8. Evaluate the extent of the similarities among the reform movements during the period of 1800–1848.

DOCUMENT-BASED QUESTION

Directions: Question 1 is based on the accompanying documents. The documents have been edited for the purpose of this exercise. You are advised to spend 15 minutes planning and 45 minutes writing your answer. In your response you should do the following:

- Respond to the prompt with a historically defensible thesis or claim that establishes a line of reasoning.
- Describe a broader historical context relevant to the prompt.
- Support an argument in response to the prompt using at least six documents.
- Use at least one additional piece of specific historical evidence (beyond that found in the documents) relevant to an argument about the prompt.
- For at least three documents, explain how or why the document's point of view, purpose, historical situation, and/or audience is relevant to an argument.
- Use evidence to corroborate, qualify, or modify an argument that addresses the prompt.

1. Evaluate the extent to which sectionalism overcame nationalism in U.S. politics during the years from 1800 to 1848.

Document 1

Source: Stephen Decatur, naval officer, toast given at Norfolk, Virginia, 1816

Our Country! In her intercourse with foreign nations may she always be in the right; but our country, right or wrong!

Document 2

Source: Joseph Rodman Drake, poet, "The American Flag," 1819

> Flag of the free heart's hope and home,
> By angel hands to valor given,
> Thy stars have lit the welkin dome,
> And all thy hues were born in heaven!
> Forever float that standard sheet
> Where breathes the foe but falls before us,
> With Freedom's soil beneath our feet,
> And Freedom's banner streaming o'er us!

Document 3

Source: Emma Hart Willard, educator and feminist, address to the New York Legislature, 1819

But where is that wise and heroic country which has considered that our rights [as women] are sacred . . . ? History shows not that country. . . . Yet though history lifts not her finger to such a one, anticipation does. She points to a nation which, having thrown off the shackles of authority and precedent, shrinks not from schemes of improvement because other nations have never attempted them; but which, in its pride of independence, would rather lead than follow in the march of human improvement: a nation, wise and magnanimous to plan, enterprising to undertake, and rich in resources to execute. Does not every American exult that this country is his own?

Document 4

Source: Henry Clay, Speech in Congress, March 31, 1824

Are we doomed to behold our industry languish and decay yet more and more? But there is a remedy, and that remedy consists in modifying our foreign policy, and in adopting a genuine American System. We must naturalize the arts in our country; and we must naturalize them by the only means which the wisdom of nations has yet discovered to be effectual—by adequate protection against the otherwise overwhelming influence of foreigners. This is only to be accomplished by the establishment of a tariff, to the consideration of which I am now brought. . . . The sole object of the tariff is to tax the produce of foreign industry with the view of promoting American industry . . . . The tax is exclusively leveled at foreign industry.

Document 5

Source: John Quincy Adams, *Diary*, March 3, 1820

I have favored this Missouri Compromise, believing it to be all that could be effected under the present Constitution, and from extreme unwillingness to put the Union at hazard. But perhaps it would have been a wiser as well as a bolder course to have persisted in the restriction upon Missouri, till it should have terminated in a convention of the States to revise and amend the Constitution. This would have produced a new Union of thirteen or fourteen States, unpolluted with slavery, with a great and glorious object to effect, namely, that of rallying to their standard the other States by the universal emancipation of their slaves. If the Union must be dissolved, slavery is precisely the question upon which it ought to break. For the present, however, this contest is laid asleep.

Document 6

Source: Thomas Jefferson, Letter to Congressman John Holmes of Massachusetts, April 22, 1820

I thank you, dear sir, for the copy you have been so kind to send me of the letter to your constituents on the Missouri question. It is perfect justification to them. I had for a long time ceased to read newspapers, or pay any attention to public affairs, confident they were in good hands . . . . But this momentous question, like a firebell in the night, awakened and filled me with terror. I considered it at once as the knell of the union. It is hushed, indeed, for the moment. But this is a reprieve only, not a final sentence. A geographical line, coinciding with a marked principle, moral and political, once conceived and held up to the angry passions of men, will never be obliterated; and every new irritation will mark it deeper and deeper.

Document 7

Source: *Congressional Record*, 1816

VOTE ON THE TARIFF OF 1816 IN THE U.S. HOUSE OF REPRESENTATIVES		
Region	**For**	**Against**
New England	17	10
Middle States	44	10
South	23	34
Total	88	54

Topic 5.1

Contextualizing Period 5

Learning Objective: Explain the context in which sectional conflict emerged from 1844 to 1877.

Between 1844 and 1877, the United States expanded its territory to the Pacific Ocean and suffered from rising sectionalism over the issue of expanding slavery into this new territory. In 1861, tensions exploded into the Civil War that permanently expanded the power of the federal government. After four years of fighting and the death of 750,000 people, the country emerged with a "new birth of freedom" as a result of the end of slavery. But racism remained.

The first half of the 19th century included many advances in the young nation. Political, demographic, economic, and territorial development changed the country. The right to vote expanded political participation. New technology and transportation combined to support a market revolution that altered the relationships between peoples in the different regions. Reforms in education and other areas improved life. New expressions in art and literature signified an emergent American culture. Yet these advancements were not shared by all, and challenges, particularly over foreign affairs and slavery, remained.

Growth in Land and Population Between 1844 and 1877, the United States expanded westward, with many citizens believing it had a destiny to control all the land to the Pacific Ocean. The country added land through negotiations, purchase, and war. The largest acquisition came from the Mexican War, through which the United States established its southern border and claimed ports on the Pacific.

This rapid expansion attracted new immigrants, who left Europe because of famine, poverty, and political turmoil. In response to immigration, particularly of people from Ireland and China, some native-born Americans argued against citizenship for new residents. This resulted in the forming of political organizations to restrict immigration and citizenship.

Political Conflicts over Slavery Expansion and sectionalism also intensified differences over politics, economics, and, most seriously, slavery. Slaveowners became more insistent on their right to own enslaved people and argued for strong federal laws to return enslaved people who escaped bondage. Abolitionists became more insistent on ending slavery. Free-Soilers argued that the institution should not be allowed into the territories. Opponents of slavery organized an "underground railroad" to help fugitives escape from slavery. Congress passed a series of compromises attempting to settle the issue of whether slavery could expand into new territories.

The Civil War and Reconstruction Then, in 1860, the Republicans nominated Abraham Lincoln for president. Though opposed to slavery, he also opposed immediate abolition. Still, his election frightened slaveholders. They feared that, despite his pledge to allow slavery to continue where it existed, his opposition to the expansion of slavery would lead to its eventual end. Eleven states left the Union, and a four-year civil war ravaged the country.

The Union victory ended slavery and shifted power to the federal government from the states. The 12 years after the war, known as Reconstruction, were marked by conflict. It was a period of fierce confrontations between the executive and legislative branches and between the federal and state governments. These confrontations reshaped how people thought about federalism and the separation of powers among the branches of government.

Racism and Discrimination Further, the country suffered from tremendous racial conflict. As the freed African Americans worked to established new lives, White-dominated legislatures passed Black Codes that restricted the basic rights of Black citizens. In place of slavery, a new labor system known as sharecropping emerged that kept Black farmers in conditions almost as subservient to White landowners as slavery had. Finally, White Americans attempting to maintain racial supremacy killed thousands of Black citizens.

While the Civil War preserved the Union, historians vigorously debate the successes and failures of Reconstruction. In the future, the nation that survived a civil war would continue to grow, expand, and industrialize. Further, it would continue to struggle over achieving equal treatment for all of its people.

ANALYZE THE CONTEXT

1. Explain the historical context for the debate over slavery in the 1850s.

2. Explain the historical context for the varied results of Reconstruction.

LANDMARK EVENTS: 1844–1877

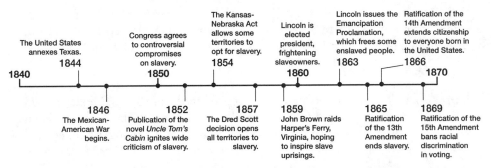

The Idea of Manifest Destiny

Away, away with all these cobweb issues of the rights of discovery, exploration, settlement, contiguity [nearness], etc. . . . [The American] claim is by the right of our manifest destiny to overspread and to possess the whole of the continent which Providence has given us for the development of the great experiment of liberty.

John L. O'Sullivan, **"The True Title,"** *New York Morning News*, 1845

Learning Objective: Explain the causes and effects of westward expansion from 1844 to 1877.

While European settlers began assuming a right to territorial conquest during the colonial era, writers such as John O'Sullivan promoted that idea across the land in the 1840s and 1850s. Expansionists wanted the United States to extend westward to the Pacific and southward into Mexico, Cuba, and Central America. By the 1890s, expansionists fixed their sights on acquiring islands in the Pacific and the Caribbean.

The phrase **Manifest Destiny** expressed the popular belief that the United States had a divine mission to extend its power and civilization across the breadth of North America. (For a map showing the territorial expansion of the United States, see the multiple-choice questions in Topic 5.3.) Enthusiasm for expansion reached a fever pitch in the 1840s. It was driven by a number of forces: nationalism, population increase, rapid economic development, technological advances, and reform ideals. But not all Americans united behind expansionism. Critics argued vehemently that at the root of the expansionist drive was the ambition to spread slavery into western lands.

Conflicts Over Texas, Maine, and Oregon

U.S. interest in pushing its borders south into **Texas** (a Mexican province) and west into the **Oregon Territory** (claimed by Britain) largely resulted from American pioneers migrating into these lands during the 1820s and 1830s.

Texas

In 1823, after having won its national independence from Spain, Mexico hoped to attract settlers—including Anglo settlers—to farm its sparsely populated northern frontier province of Texas. Moses Austin, a Missouri banker, had obtained a large land grant in Texas but died before he could recruit American settlers for the land. His son, **Stephen Austin**, succeeded in bringing 300 families into Texas and thereby beginning a steady migration of American settlers into the vast frontier territory. By 1830, Americans (both White farmers and enslaved Black people) outnumbered Mexicans in Texas by three to one.

Friction between the Americans and the Mexicans worsened in 1829 when Mexico outlawed slavery and required all immigrants to convert to Roman Catholicism. Many settlers refused to obey these laws. In reaction, Mexico closed Texas to additional American immigrants. Land-hungry Americans from the Southern states ignored the Mexican prohibition and streamed into Texas by the thousands.

Revolt and Independence A change in Mexico's government intensified the conflict. In 1834, General **Antonio López de Santa Anna** made himself dictator of Mexico and abolished that nation's federal system of government. When Santa Anna attempted to enforce Mexico's laws in Texas, a group of American settlers led by **Sam Houston** revolted and declared Texas an independent republic in March 1836. In its new constitution, Texas made slavery legal again.

A Mexican army led by Santa Anna captured the town of Goliad and attacked the **Alamo** in San Antonio, killing every one of its American defenders. Shortly afterward, however, at the Battle of the San Jacinto River, an army under Sam Houston caught the Mexicans by surprise and captured their general, Santa Anna. Under the threat of death, the Mexican leader was forced to sign a treaty that recognized independence for Texas and granted the new republic all territory north of the Rio Grande. However, when the news of San Jacinto reached Mexico City, the Mexican legislature rejected the treaty and insisted that Texas was still part of Mexico.

Annexation Denied As the first president of the Republic of Texas (or Lone Star Republic), Houston applied to the U.S. government for his country to be annexed, or added to, the United States as a new state. However, presidents Jackson and Van Buren both put off the request for annexation primarily because of political opposition among Northerners to the expansion of slavery. If annexed, Texas might be divided into five new states, which could mean ten additional proslavery members of the U.S. Senate. The threat of a costly war with Mexico also dampened expansionist zeal. The next president, William Henry Harrison, died after a month in office. His successor, **John Tyler** (1841–1845), was a Southern Whig who was worried about the growing influence of the British in Texas. He worked to annex Texas, but the U.S. Senate rejected his treaty of annexation in 1844.

Boundary Dispute in Maine

Another diplomatic issue arose in the 1840s over the ill-defined boundary between Maine and the Canadian province of New Brunswick. At this time, Canada was still under British rule and many Americans regarded Britain as their country's most significant enemy—an attitude carried over from the

Revolution and the War of 1812. A conflict between rival groups of lumber workers on the Maine-Canadian border erupted into open fighting. Known as the Aroostook War, or "battle of the maps," the conflict was soon resolved in a treaty negotiated by U.S. Secretary of State Daniel Webster and the British ambassador, Lord Alexander Ashburton. In the **Webster-Ashburton Treaty** of 1842, the disputed territory was split between Maine and British Canada. The treaty also settled the boundary of the Minnesota territory, leaving what proved to be the iron-rich Mesabi Range on the U.S. side of the border.

Boundary Dispute in Oregon

A far more serious British-American dispute involved Oregon, a vast territory on the Pacific Coast that originally stretched as far north as the Alaskan border. At one time, this territory was claimed by four different nations: Spain, Russia, Great Britain, and the United States. Spain gave up its claim to Oregon in a treaty with the United States (the Adams-Onís Treaty of 1819).

Britain based its claim to Oregon on the Hudson's Bay Company's profitable fur trade with the American Indians of the Pacific Northwest. However, by 1846, fewer than a thousand British settlers lived north of the Columbia River.

The United States based its claim on (1) the exploration of the Columbia River by Captain Robert Gray in 1792; (2) the overland expedition to the Pacific Coast by Meriwether Lewis and William Clark in 1805; and (3) the fur trading post and fort in Astoria, Oregon, established by John Jacob Astor in 1811. Protestant missionaries and farmers from the United States settled in the Willamette Valley in the 1840s. Their success in farming this fertile valley caused 5,000 Americans to catch "Oregon fever" and travel 2,000 miles over the Oregon Trail to settle in the area south of the Columbia River.

By the 1844 election, many Americans believed that taking undisputed possession of all of Oregon and annexing the Republic of Texas was their country's Manifest Destiny. In addition, expansionists hoped to persuade Mexico to give up its province on the West Coast—the huge land of California. By 1845, Mexican California had a small Spanish-Mexican population of some 7,000 along with a much larger number of American Indians, but American emigrants were arriving in sufficient numbers "to play the Texas game."

The Election of 1844

The possibility of annexing Texas and allowing the expansion of slavery split the Democratic Party in 1844. The party's Northern wing opposed immediate annexation and wanted to nominate former president Martin Van Buren to run again. Southern Whigs who were proslavery and proannexation rallied behind former vice president John C. Calhoun of South Carolina as a candidate.

The Van Buren-Calhoun dispute deadlocked the Democratic convention. After hours of wrangling, the Democrats finally nominated a *dark horse* (lesser-known candidate). They chose **James K. Polk** of Tennessee, a protegé of Andrew Jackson, who was firmly committed to Manifest Destiny. Polk favored the annexation of Texas, the acquisition of California, and the "reoccupation" of Oregon Territory all the way to the border with Russian Alaska at latitude 54° 40′. The Democratic slogan of **"Fifty-Four Forty or Fight!"** appealed strongly to American Westerners and Southerners who were in an expansionist mood.

Henry Clay of Kentucky, the Whig nominee, attempted to straddle the controversial issue of Texas annexation, opposing it and then supporting it. This strategy alienated a group of voters in New York State, who abandoned the Whig Party to support the antislavery Liberty Party (see Topic 4. 11). In a close election, the Whigs' loss of New York's electoral votes proved decisive and Polk, the Democratic dark horse, was the victor. The Democrats interpreted the election as a mandate to add Texas to the Union.

Annexing Texas and Dividing Oregon

Outgoing president John Tyler took the election of Polk as a signal to push the annexation of Texas through Congress. Instead of seeking Senate approval of a treaty that would have required a two-thirds vote, Tyler persuaded both houses of Congress to pass a joint resolution for annexation. This procedure required only a simple majority of each house. Tyler left Polk with the problem of dealing with Mexico's reaction to annexation.

On the Oregon question, Polk decided to back down from his party's bellicose campaign slogan. Instead of fighting for 54° 40′, he signed an agreement with the British to divide the Oregon territory at the 49th parallel (the parallel that had been established as the northern border in 1818 for the Louisiana Territory). Final settlement of the issue was delayed until the United States agreed to grant Vancouver Island and the right to navigate the Columbia River to Britain. In June 1846, the treaty was submitted to the Senate for ratification. Some Northerners viewed the treaty as a sellout to Southern interests because it removed British Columbia as a source of potential free states. Nevertheless, by this time war had broken out between the United States and Mexico. Not wanting to fight both Britain and Mexico, Senate opponents of the treaty reluctantly voted for the compromise settlement.

Settlement of the Western Territories

Following the peaceful acquisition of Oregon and the more violent acquisition of California (see Topic 5.3), the migration of Americans into these lands increased. The arid region between the Mississippi Valley and the Pacific Coast was popularly known in the 1850s and 1860s as the **Great American Desert**. Emigrants passed quickly over this vast area to reach the more inviting lands on the West Coast. Therefore, California and Oregon were settled several decades before people attempted to farm the Great Plains.

Fur Traders' Frontier

Fur traders known as mountain men were the earliest nonnative individuals to open the **Far West**. In the 1820s, they held yearly rendezvous in the Rockies with

American Indians to trade for animal skins. James Beckwourth, Jim Bridger, Kit Carson, and Jedediah Smith were among the hardy band of explorers and trappers who provided much of the early information about trails and frontier conditions to later settlers.

Overland Trails

After the mountain men, a much larger group of pioneers made the hazardous journey west in hopes of clearing the forests and farming the fertile valleys of California and Oregon. By 1860, hundreds of thousands had reached their westward goal by following the Oregon, California, Santa Fe, and Mormon trails. The long and arduous trek usually began in St. Joseph or Independence, Missouri, or in Council Bluffs, Iowa, and followed the river valleys through the Great Plains. Inching along at only 15 miles a day, a wagon train needed months to finally reach the foothills of the Rockies or face the hardships of the southwestern deserts. The final life-or-death challenge was to get through the mountain passes of the Sierras and Cascades before the first heavy snow. While pioneers feared attacks by American Indians, the most common and serious dangers were disease and depression from the harsh everyday conditions on the trail.

WESTWARD EXPANSION AND PIONEER TRAILS, 1840s

Mining Frontier

The discovery of gold in California in 1848 set off the first of many migrations to mineral-rich mountains of the West in the 1800s. Gold or silver rushes occurred in Colorado, Nevada, the Black Hills of the Dakotas, and other western territories. The mining boom brought tens of thousands of men and some women into the western mountains. Mining camps and towns—many of them short-lived—sprang up wherever a strike (discovery) was reported. Largely as a result of the gold rush, California's population soared from a mere 14,000 in 1848 to 380,000 by 1860. Booms attracted miners from around the world. By the 1860s, almost one-third of the miners in the West were Chinese.

Farming Frontier

Most pioneer families moved west to start homesteads and begin farming. Congress's Preemption Acts of the 1830s and 1840s gave squatters the right to settle public lands and purchase them for low prices once the government put them up for sale. In addition, the government made it easier for settlers by offering parcels of land as small as 40 acres for sale.

However, moving west was not for the poor. At a time when a typical laborer made about $1.00 per day, a family needed at least $200 to $300 to make the overland trip. The trek to California and Oregon was largely a middle-class movement.

The isolation of the frontier made life for pioneers especially difficult during the first years, but rural communities soon developed. The institutions that the people established (schools, churches, clubs, and political parties) were modeled after those that they had known in the East or, for immigrants from abroad, in their native lands.

Urban Frontier

Western cities that arose as a result of railroads, mineral wealth, and farming attracted a number of professionals and business owners. For example, San Francisco and Denver became instant cities created by the gold and silver rushes. Salt Lake City grew because it offered fresh supplies to travelers on overland trails for the balance of their westward journey.

Foreign Commerce

The growth in manufactured goods as well as in agricultural products (both Western grains and Southern cotton) caused a large growth of **exports and imports**. Other factors also played a role in the expansion of U.S. trade in the mid-1800s:

1. Shipping firms encouraged trade and travel across the Atlantic by establishing a regular schedule for departures instead of the 18th-century policy of waiting to sail until a ship was full.

2. The demand for whale oil to light the homes of middle-class Americans caused a whaling boom between 1830 and 1860. New England merchants took the lead in this industry.

3. Improvements in ship design came just in time to speed gold seekers on their journey to the California gold fields. The development of the American clipper ship cut the six-month trip from New York around the Horn of South America to San Francisco to as little as 89 days.

4. Steamships took the place of clipper ships in the mid-1850s because they had greater storage capacity, could be maintained at lower cost, and followed a schedule more reliably.

5. The United States expanded trade to Asia. New England merchants conducted profitable trade with China for tea, silk, and porcelain. The government sent Commodore **Matthew C. Perry** and a small fleet of naval ships to Japan, which had been closed to most foreigners for over two centuries. In 1854, Perry pressured Japan's government to sign the **Kanagawa Treaty**, which allowed U.S. vessels to enter two Japanese ports to take on coal. This treaty soon led to a trade agreement.

Expansion After the Civil War

From 1855 until 1870, the issues of union, slavery, civil war, and postwar reconstruction would overshadow the drive to acquire new territory. Even so, Manifest Destiny continued to be an important force for shaping U.S. policy. In 1867, for example, Secretary of State William Seward succeeded in purchasing Alaska at a time when the nation was just recovering from the Civil War.

REFLECT ON THE LEARNING OBJECTIVE

1. Explain the reasons for and results of westward expansion from 1844 to 1877.

KEY TERMS BY THEME

Belief (NAT)
Manifest Destiny

Westward (MIG, GEO, ARC)
Great American Desert
mountain men
Far West
overland trails
mining frontier
gold rush
silver rush

farming frontier
urban frontier

Expansion Politics (POL)
John Tyler
Oregon Territory
"Fifty-Four Forty or Fight!"
James K. Polk

Military & Diplomatic Expansion (WOR)
Texas
Stephen Austin

Antonio López de Santa Anna
Sam Houston
Alamo
Webster-Ashburton Treaty
foreign commerce
exports and imports
Matthew C. Perry
Kanagawa Treaty

Questions 1–2 refer to the following excerpt.

"Where, where was the heroic determination of the Executive to vindicate our title to *the whole of Oregon*—yes, sir, 'THE WHOLE OR NONE'. . . .

It has been openly avowed . . . that Oregon and Texas were born and cradled together in the Baltimore convention; that they were the twin offspring of that political conclave [meeting]; and in that avowal may be found the whole explanation of the difficulties and dangers with which the question is now attended. . . .

I maintain—

1. That this question . . . is . . . one for negotiations, compromise, and amicable adjustment.

2. That satisfactory evidence has not yet been afforded that no compromise which the United States ought to accept can be effected.

3. That, if no other mode of amicable settlement remains, arbitration ought to be resorted to."

Representative Robert C. Winthrop (Whig), speech to the
House of Representatives, January 3, 1846

1. Winthrop's position about territory in Oregon was based primarily on his desire to

(A) end all British power in North America

(B) obtain more land for settlers

(C) show his readiness to use military force

(D) oppose Southern desires to expand slavery

2. Which historical development illustrates the fulfillment of Winthrop's argument?

(A) Polk negotiated a compromise with the British over Oregon.

(B) Polk went to war to obtain the whole of Oregon from Great Britain.

(C) Polk called a meeting in Baltimore to discuss annexation of Oregon.

(D) Polk asked foreign countries to arbitrate the Oregon dispute.

Use complete sentences; an outline or bulleted list alone is not acceptable.

1. "The Manifest Destiny impulse fed off a mixture of crassness, truculence [hostility], and high idealism. Without question, there were those who proclaimed America's providential mission to expand as a eulogistic [honorary] cover for speculation in land and paper. But those were hardly the motives of John L. O'Sullivan, the writer who coined the term . . . . For O'Sullivan and his allies, the expansionist imperative was essentially democratic . . . in a supercharged moral sense, stressing America's duties to spread democratic values and institutions to a world still dominated by monarchs and deformed superstitions.'"

    Sean Wilentz, *The Rise of American Democracy*, 2005

    "O'Sullivan and Young America provided a . . . set of aspirations that could be embraced by expansionists with less lofty ambitions . . . . The 'young American' who would transport 'democracy' into new territories was recognizably white, male, probably Protestant, and of martial [confrontational] demeanor— . . . facing, as he saw it, a world beset by economic backwardness, political lethargy, ignorance, superstition, Catholicism, effeminacy, and racial mixing. Expansionism would defeat the institutions that bred these maladies [illnesses] and offer the benefits of 'civilization' for those who wished to seize them."

    Steven Hahn, *A Nation Without Borders*, 2016

    Using the excerpts, answer (a), (b), and (c).

    (a) Briefly explain ONE major difference between Wilentz's and Hahn's historical interpretations of Manifest Destiny.

    (b) Briefly explain how ONE historical event or development in the period 1830 to 1860 that is not explicitly mentioned in the excerpts could be used to support Wilentz's interpretation.

    (c) Briefly explain how ONE historical event or development in the period 1830 to 1860 that is not explicitly mentioned in the excerpts could be used to support Hahn's interpretation.

Topic 5.3

Manifest Destiny and the Mexican-American War

The Southern rebellion was largely the outgrowth of the Mexican war.

Ulysses S. Grant, *Personal Memoirs of General U.S. Grant*, 1885

Learning Objective: Explain the causes and effects of the Mexican–American War.

The U.S. annexation of Texas quickly led to diplomatic trouble with Mexico. The Mexicans' anger over the annexation and the newly elected President Polk's desire to expand the nation to the Pacific Ocean combined to bring both sides to the edge of war.

Conflict with Mexico

Upon taking office in 1845, President Polk dispatched John Slidell as his special envoy to the government in Mexico City. Polk wanted Slidell to (1) persuade Mexico to sell the **California** and New Mexico territories to the United States and (2) settle the disputed Mexico-Texas border. Slidell's mission failed on both counts. The Mexican government refused to sell California and insisted that Texas's southern border was on the **Nueces River**. Polk and Slidell asserted that the border lay farther to the south, along the **Rio Grande**.

Immediate Causes of the War

While Slidell waited for Mexico's response to the U.S. offer, Polk ordered General **Zachary Taylor** to move his army toward the Rio Grande, across territory claimed by Mexico. On April 24, 1846, a Mexican army crossed the Rio Grande and captured an American army patrol, killing 11. Polk used the incident to justify sending his prepared war message to Congress. Northern Whigs opposed going to war over the incident and doubted Polk's claim that American blood had been shed on American soil. Whig protests were in vain. A large majority in both houses approved the war resolution.

Military Campaigns

Most of the war was fought in Mexican territory by small armies of Americans. Leading a force that never exceeded 1,500, General **Stephen Kearney** succeeded in taking the New Mexico territory and southern California. Backed by only several dozen soldiers, a few navy officers, and American civilians who had recently settled in northern California, **John C. Frémont** quickly overthrew Mexican rule in the region in June 1846. He proclaimed California to be an independent republic. Because the new republic's flag included a California grizzly bear, it became known as the **Bear Flag Republic**.

Meanwhile, Zachary Taylor's force of 6,000 men drove the Mexican army from Texas, crossed the Rio Grande into northern Mexico, and won a major victory at Buena Vista (February 1847). President Polk then selected General **Winfield Scott** to invade central Mexico. The army of 14,000 under Scott's command succeeded in taking the coastal city of Vera Cruz and then captured Mexico City in September 1847.

Consequences of the War

For Mexico, the war was a military disaster from the start, but the Mexican government was unwilling to sue for peace and concede the loss of its northern lands. Finally, after the fall of Mexico City, the government had little choice but to agree to U.S. terms.

Treaty of Guadalupe Hidalgo (1848) The treaty negotiated by diplomat Nicholas Trist with Mexico consisted of terms favorable to the United States:

- Mexico recognized the Rio Grande as the southern border of Texas.

- The United States took possession of the former Mexican provinces of California and New Mexico—the **Mexican Cession**. For these territories, the United States paid $15 million and assumed responsibility for any claims of American citizens against Mexico.

In the Senate, some Whigs opposed the treaty because they saw the war as an immoral effort to expand slavery. A few Southern Democrats disliked the treaty for opposite reasons. As expansionists, they wanted the United States to take all of Mexico. Since this land was south of the line established in the Missouri Compromise dividing slave and free territory, it was a region where slavery could expand into. Nevertheless, the treaty was finally ratified in the Senate.

Wilmot Proviso The issue of slavery made the U.S. entry into a war with Mexico controversial from start to finish. In 1846, Pennsylvania Congressman David Wilmot proposed that an appropriations bill be amended to forbid slavery in any territory acquired from Mexico. This prohibition appealed to many voters and lawmakers who wanted to preserve the land for White settlers and protect them from having to compete with enslaved labor. The Wilmot Proviso, as it was called, passed the House, where the populous Northern states had greater power, twice. Both times, it was defeated in the Senate, where Southern states had greater influence.

Prelude to Civil War? By increasing tensions between the North and the South, did the war to acquire territories from Mexico lead inevitably to the American Civil War? Without question, the acquisition of vast western lands did renew the sectional debate over the extension of slavery. Many Northerners viewed the war with Mexico as part of a Southern plot to extend the "slave power." Southerners realized they could not count on Northerners to accept the expansion of slavery. The Wilmot Proviso was the first round in an escalating political conflict that led ultimately, though not inevitably, to civil war.

HISTORICAL PERSPECTIVES: *WHY WAS MANIFEST DESTINY SIGNIFICANT?*

Traditional historians stressed the accomplishments of westward expansion in bringing civilization and democratic institutions to a wilderness area. The heroic efforts of **mountain men** and pioneering families to overcome a hostile environment have long been celebrated by historians and the popular media.

Attitudes about Race As a result of the civil rights movement of the 1950s and 1960s and the continuing diversification of American society, historians became more sensitive than their predecessors to racist language and beliefs. They recognized the racial undercurrents in the political speeches of the 1840s that argued for expansion into American Indian, Mexican, and Central American territories.

Some historians argue that racist motives prompted the decision to withdraw U.S. troops from Mexico instead of occupying it. They point out that Americans who opposed the idea of keeping Mexico had asserted that it was undesirable to incorporate large non-Anglo populations into the republic.

Diverse Contributions Recent historians have broadened their research into westward movement. Rather than concentrating on the achievements of Anglo pioneers, they have focused more on these topics: (1) the impact on American Indians whose lands were taken, (2) the influence of Mexican culture on U.S. culture, (3) the contributions of African American and Asian American pioneers, and (4) the role of women in the development of western family and community life.

The Impact on Mexico Some Mexican historians point out that the Treaty of Guadalupe Hidalgo took half of Mexico's territory. They argue that the war of 1846 gave rise to a number of long-standing economic and political problems that have impeded Mexico's development as a modern nation.

Economics over Race Some historians argue that the war with Mexico, especially the taking of California, was motivated by imperialism rather than by racism. They argue that the United States had commercial ambitions in the Pacific and wanted California as a base for trade with China and Japan. U.S. policy makers were afraid that California would fall into the hands of Great Britain or another European power if the United States did not move in first.

Support an Argument *Explain two perspectives on either causes or effects of the belief in Manifest Destiny important during the 19th century.*

REFLECT ON THE LEARNING OBJECTIVE

1. Explain the reasons for and results of the Mexican War.

<table>
<tr><td colspan="3">KEY TERMS BY THEME</td></tr>
<tr><td>Military & Diplomatic
Expansion (WOR)
Mexican-American War
California
Nueces River</td><td>Rio Grande
Zachary Taylor
Stephen Kearney
John C. Frémont
Bear Flag Republic</td><td>Winfield Scott
Treaty of Guadalupe Hidalgo
Mexican Cession
Wilmot Proviso
mountain men</td></tr>
</table>

MULTIPLE-CHOICE QUESTIONS

Questions 1–3 refer to the map below.

LAND ACQUISITIONS BY THE UNITED STATES, 1776–1853

1. Why was the period of expansion between 1842 and 1853 so significant to the development of the United States?

   (A) The United States established borders that still exist today.

   (B) The United States purchased its largest single territory in one act.

   (C) The United States obtained territory along the Gulf of Mexico.

   (D) The United States expanded westward for the first time.

2. The acquisitions of land in the West before 1845 were similar to land acquisitions after 1845 because they both were motivated by the controversial desire to

(A) expand the institution of slavery

(B) build factories near mineral resources

(C) keep foreign influences out of the country

(D) take advantage of wars among European countries

3. Which territory did the United States gain most directly by going to war?

(A) Louisiana Purchase

(B) Texas Annexation

(C) Oregon Country

(D) Mexican Cession

SHORT-ANSWER QUESTIONS

Use complete sentences; an outline or bulleted list alone is not acceptable.

1. Answer (a), (b), and (c).

(a) Briefly explain ONE specific reason for American expansionism between 1840 and 1855.

(b) Briefly explain ONE specific criticism of American expansionism between 1840 and 1855.

(c) Briefly describe how ONE group of people were profoundly impacted by America's expansionism between 1800 and 1860.

2. Answer (a), (b), and (c).

(a) Briefly explain ONE historical event or development in the 1840s that contributed to causing the Mexican War.

(b) Briefly explain ONE historical event or development in the 1840s that contributed to the United States victory in the Mexican War.

(c) Briefly explain ONE specific consequence of the Mexican War for the United States.

The Compromise of 1850

*I owe a paramount allegiance to the whole Union—
a subordinate one to my own State.*

Senator Henry Clay, Kentucky, July 22, 1850

Learning Objective: Explain the similarities and differences in how regional attitudes affected federal policy in the period after the Mexican–American War.

Manifest Destiny and expansion intensified the debate about the spread of slavery. Abolitionists and White people eager to settle Western lands without the competition of slave labor opposed expansion. Slaveowners and people who felt they benefited from slavery wanted the continued growth of slavery. At the same time, most Americans still hoped for compromise that could keep the Union together.

Southern Expansion

Many Southerners resented the Missouri Compromise because it barred slavery from the Louisiana Purchase lands. They were also dissatisfied with the territorial gains from the Mexican War because they were not large enough. In general, they were eager to find new land for cultivation using enslaved labor.

Manifest Destiny to the South

In the early 1850s, many slaveowners hoped to acquire new territories, especially in areas of Latin America where they thought plantations worked by enslaved people were economically feasible. The most tempting, eagerly sought possibility in the eyes of Southern expansionists was the acquisition of Cuba.

Ostend Manifesto President Polk offered to purchase Cuba from Spain for $100 million, but Spain refused to sell the last major remnant of its once glorious empire in the Americas. Several Southern adventurers led small expeditions to Cuba in an effort to take the island by force. These forays, however, were easily defeated, and those who participated were executed by Spanish firing squads.

Elected to the presidency in 1852, Franklin Pierce adopted pro-Southern policies and dispatched three American diplomats to Ostend, Belgium, where they secretly negotiated to buy Cuba from Spain. The agreement that the diplomats drew up, called the **Ostend Manifesto**, was leaked to the press in the United States. Antislavery members of Congress reacted angrily and forced President Pierce to drop the scheme.

Walker Expedition Expansionists continued to seek new empires with or without the federal government's support. Southern adventurer William Walker had tried unsuccessfully to take Baja California, the long peninsula stretching south of San Diego, from Mexico in 1853. Then, leading a force mostly of Southerners, he seized power in Nicaragua in 1855. Walker's regime even gained temporary recognition from the United States in 1856. However, his grandiose scheme to develop a proslavery Central American empire collapsed when a coalition of Central American countries invaded his country and defeated him. Walker was executed by Honduran authorities in 1860.

Clayton-Bulwer Treaty (1850) Another American ambition was to build a canal through Central America. A canal would provide a shortcut to allow ships traveling from the Northern Atlantic to the Northern Pacific to avoid sailing around South America. Great Britain had the same ambition. To prevent each other from seizing this opportunity on its own, Great Britain and the United States agreed to the **Clayton-Bulwer Treaty** of 1850. It provided that neither nation would attempt to take exclusive control of any future canal route in Central America. This treaty continued in force until the end of the century. A new treaty signed in 1901 (the Hay-Pauncefote Treaty) gave the United States a free hand to build a canal without British participation.

Gadsden Purchase Although he failed to acquire Cuba, President Pierce succeeded in purchasing a small strip of land from Mexico in 1853 for $10 million (see map in Topic 5.2). Though the land was semidesert, it lay on the best route for a railroad through the region. Known as the **Gadsden Purchase**, it forms the southern sections of present-day New Mexico and Arizona.

Conflict Over Status of Territories

The issue of slavery in the territories gained in the Mexican War became the focus of sectional differences in the late 1840s. The Wilmot Proviso, which excluded slavery from the new territories, would have upset the Compromise of 1820 and the delicate balance of 15 free and 15 slave states. However, the proviso's defeat only increased sectional feelings.

Three Conflicting Positions on Slavery Expansion

Most people held one of three positions on whether to allow slavery in the Western territories. No single policy would appeal to them all, but many people hoped for a compromise that would allow each group to get something of what it wanted.

Free-Soil Movement Northern Democrats and Whigs supported the Wilmot Proviso and the position that all African Americans—slave and free—should be excluded from the Mexican Cession (territory ceded to the U.S. by Mexico in 1848). While abolitionists advocated eliminating slavery everywhere, many Northerners who opposed the westward expansion of slavery did not oppose slavery in the South. They sought to keep the West a land of opportunity for Whites only. This meant keeping out both enslaved and free African Americans. In 1848, Northerners who opposed allowing slavery in the territories organized the **Free-Soil Party**, which adopted the slogan "free soil, free labor, and free men." In addition to its chief objective—preventing the extension of slavery—the new party advocated free homesteads (public land grants to small farmers) and internal improvements such as roads and harbors.

Southern Positions Southern plantation owners, whose wealth and social status made them politically powerful, viewed attempts to restrict the expansion of slavery as violations of their constitutional right to take their property wherever they wished. They saw the Free-Soilers—and the abolitionists—as intent on the destruction of slavery. Some Southerners held more moderate views. They would agree to extend the Missouri Compromise line westward to the Pacific Ocean and permit territories north of that line to be free of slavery.

Popular Sovereignty A Democratic senator from Michigan, **Lewis Cass**, proposed a compromise solution that soon won considerable support from moderates across the country. Instead of Congress determining whether to allow slavery in a new western territory or state, Cass suggested that the matter be determined by a vote of the people who settled a territory. Cass's approach to the problem was known as squatter sovereignty, or **popular sovereignty**.

The Election of 1848

The expansion of slavery into the territories was a vital issue in the presidential race of 1848. Three parties represented different positions on the issue:

- The Democrats nominated Senator Cass and adopted a platform pledged to popular sovereignty.

- The Whigs nominated Mexican War hero General **Zachary Taylor**, who had never been involved in politics and took no position on slavery in the territories.

- A third party, the Free-Soil Party, opposed expansion. It nominated former president Martin Van Buren. The party consisted of Conscience Whigs (who opposed slavery) and antislavery Democrats. Members of this latter group were ridiculed as **"barnburners"** because their defection threatened to destroy the Democratic Party.

Taylor narrowly defeated Cass, in part because of the vote given the Free-Soil Party in key Northern states such as New York and Pennsylvania.

Compromises to Preserve the Union

The Gold Rush of 1849 and the influx of about 100,000 settlers into California created the need for law and order in the West. In 1849, Californians drafted a constitution for their new state—a constitution that banned slavery. Even though President Taylor was a Southern slaveholder himself, he supported the immediate admission of both California and New Mexico as free states. (At this time, however, the Mexican population of the New Mexico territory had little interest in applying for statehood.)

Taylor's plan sparked talk of secession among the "fire-eaters" (radicals) in the South. Some Southern extremists even met in Nashville in 1850 to discuss secession. By this time, however, the astute Kentucky senator **Henry Clay** had proposed yet another compromise for solving the political crisis:

- Admit California to the Union as a free state.
- Divide the remainder of the Mexican Cession into two territories— Utah and New Mexico—and allow the settlers in these territories to decide the slavery issue by majority vote, or popular sovereignty.
- Give the land in dispute between Texas and the New Mexico territory to the new territories in return for the federal government assuming Texas's public debt of $10 million.
- Ban the slave trade in the District of Columbia but permit Whites to own enslaved people there as before.
- Adopt a new Fugitive Slave Law and enforce it rigorously.

In the ensuing Senate debate over the compromise proposal, the three congressional giants of the age—Henry Clay of Kentucky, Daniel Webster of Massachusetts, and John C. Calhoun of South Carolina—delivered their last great speeches. (Webster and Calhoun, who were both born in 1782, died in 1850; Clay died two years later.) Webster argued for compromise in order to save the Union, and in so doing alienated the Massachusetts abolitionists who formed the base of his support. Calhoun argued against compromise and insisted that the South be given equal rights in the acquired territory.

Northern opposition to compromise came from younger antislavery lawmakers, such as Senator William H. Seward of New York, who argued that a higher law than the Constitution existed. Opponents managed to prevail until the sudden death in 1850 of President Taylor, who had also opposed Clay's plan. Succeeding him was a strong supporter of compromise, Vice President Millard Fillmore. Stephen A. Douglas, a young Democratic senator from Illinois, engineered different coalitions to pass each part of the compromise separately. President Fillmore readily signed the bills into law.

Passage The passage of the **Compromise of 1850** bought time for the Union. Because California was admitted as a free state, the compromise added to the North's political power. The political debate deepened the commitment of many Northerners to saving the Union from secession. Parts of the compromise became sources of controversy, especially the new Fugitive Slave Law and the provision for popular sovereignty.

REFLECT ON THE LEARNING OBJECTIVE

1. Explain how the different views of the individual regions influenced the federal government in the years after the Mexican-American War.

Expansion Politics (POL)
Ostend Manifesto (1852)
Military & Diplomatic
  Expansion (WOR)
Walker Expedition
Clayton-Bulwer Treaty

Gadsden Purchase
Battle for the Territories
  (MIG, POL)
free-soil movement
Free-Soil Party
"barnburners"

Compromising (POL)
Lewis Cass
popular sovereignty
Zachary Taylor
Henry Clay
Compromise of 1850

MULTIPLE-CHOICE QUESTIONS

Questions 1–3 refer to the following excerpts.

"It being desirable for the peace, concord, and harmony of the Union of these States, to settle and adjust amicably all existing questions of controversy between them arising out of the institution of slavery upon a fair, equitable, and just basis."

Henry Clay, Resolution on the Compromise of 1850

"We are told now . . . that the Union is threatened with subversion and destruction. . . . If the Union is to be dissolved for any existing causes, it will be dissolved because slavery is interdicted [interfered with] or not allowed to be introduced into the ceded Territories; because slavery is threatened to be abolished in the District of Columbia, and because fugitive slaves are not returned . . . to their masters. . . .

I am for staying within the Union and fighting for my rights."

Henry Clay, Speech on the Compromise Resolution, 1850

1. To which politician or politicians was Clay directing the last line of the second excerpt?
   (A) Southerners who were threatening to secede
   (B) Senators such as Daniel Webster who rejected any compromise
   (C) Advocates of popular sovereignty
   (D) The president, Zachary Taylor

2. The provision of the Compromise of 1850 that appealed most to advocates for slavery was the one regarding
   (A) the conditions under which California would become a state
   (B) the assumption of Texas's public debt by the federal government
   (C) the status of slave trade in Washington, D.C.
   (D) the features of a new Fugitive Slave Law

3. Clay's position on slavery in "ceded territories" was opposed by people who were mostly concerned that they could take enslaved people into

(A) islands in the Caribbean that might be acquired, such as Cuba

(B) the lands acquired in the Louisiana Purchase and from Mexico

(C) Texas, where slavery had been banned under Mexico

(D) Maine, which had been part of Massachussets

SHORT-ANSWER QUESTION

Use complete sentences; an outline or bulleted list alone is not acceptable.

1.

Source: Nathaniel Currier, 1848. Library of Congress

Using the cartoon, answer (a), (b), and (c). The figure on the right side of the cartoon is saying, "That's you Dad! more 'Free Soil.' We'll rat 'em out yet. Long life to Davy Wilmot."

(a) Briefly explain ONE historical perspective expressed by the artist concerning slavery in the territories in the period 1840 to 1854.

(b) Briefly explain ONE development in the period 1840 to 1854 that supported the perspective expressed by the artist.

(c) Briefly explain ONE development in the period 1840 to 1854 that challenged the perspective expressed by the artist.

Topic 5.5

Sectional Conflict: Regional Differences

I did not write it. God wrote it. I merely did his dictation.

Harriet Beecher Stowe, describing her book *Uncle Tom's Cabin*, 1879

Learning Objective 1: Explain the effects of immigration from various parts of the world on American culture from 1844 to 1877.

Learning Objective 2: Explain how regional differences related to slavery caused tension in the years leading up to the Civil War.

Among the issues that divided people politically in the mid-1800s were immigration, particularly by Roman Catholics, and how to promote and respond to industrial growth. However, the dominant issue increasingly became the possible expansion of slavery into the territories.

Immigration Controversy

As immigration increased, especially from Ireland and Germany, opposition arose on many fronts. Some Americans disliked the ethnicity or religious faiths of the immigrants, while others feared them as low-wage workers who might take their jobs.

Irish

During this period, half of all the immigrants—almost 2 million—came from Ireland. These **Irish** immigrants were mostly tenant farmers driven from their homeland by crop failures and a devastating famine in the 1840s. They came with limited interest in farming, few skills, and little money. They faced discrimination because of their **Roman Catholic** religion. The Irish worked hard, often competing with African Americans for domestic work and low-skill jobs that required physical strength and endurance. Most stayed where they landed, so strong Irish communities developed in Northern cities such as Boston, New York, and Philadelphia. In Irish neighborhoods, people continued the customs they brought with them. For example, perhaps one-third spoke Irish. Several newspapers included an Irish-language section and churches held services for Irish speakers.

The Irish did bring two valuable skills. Since their country was dominated by the British, most Irish spoke English well and understood electoral politics. Using these skills, many entered local politics. They often organized their fellow immigrants and joined the Democratic Party, which was traditionally anti-British and pro-worker. Initially excluded from New York City's Democratic organization, **Tammany Hall**, the Irish had secured jobs and influence by the 1850s. By the 1880s they controlled Tammany Hall.

Germans

Both economic hardships and the failure of democratic revolutions in 1848 caused more than 1 million **Germans** to seek refuge in the United States in the late 1840s and the 1850s. Most German immigrants had some modest means as well as considerable skills as farmers and artisans. Moving westward in search of cheap, fertile farmland, they established homesteads throughout the Old Northwest and generally prospered. At first their political influence was limited. As they became more active in public life, many strongly supported public education and staunchly opposed slavery.

Like the Irish, they often formed close-knit communities in cities where the German language was commonly spoken. Germans in rural areas often formed their own Roman Catholic or Lutheran churches.

Nativist Opposition to Immigration

Many native-born Americans were alarmed by the influx of immigrants, fearing that the newcomers would take their jobs and dilute the culture of the Anglo majority. These ethnic tensions were closely tied to religion. Most of the native-born opponents of immigration were Protestants and most of the Irish and many of the German immigrants were Roman Catholics. In the 1840s, hostility to these immigrants, known as **nativism**, led to sporadic rioting in the big cities.

Nativists formed a secretive antiforeign society, the Supreme Order of the Star-Spangled Banner, which evolved into a political organization, the American Party. Because party members often responded "I know nothing" to political questions, the American Party was commonly called the Know-Nothing Party. The policies they supported included increasing the time required for immigrants to attain citizenship from five years to twenty-one years and allowing only native-born citizens to hold public office.

For a short period in the early 1850s, as the Whig Party disintegrated, the Know-Nothing Party gained strength, particularly in the New England and the Mid-Atlantic states. In the 1856 presidential election the party unsuccessfully ran former president Millard Fillmore.

By the late 1850s, antiforeign feeling faded in importance as the North and the South grew increasingly divided over slavery. However, nativism would periodically return when enough native-born citizens felt threatened by a sudden increase in immigration.

Ethnic Conflict in the Southwest

Though not immigrants, American Indians and Mexican Americans who had become part of the United States because of the Mexican-American War also faced religious discrimination. Many were Roman Catholics or practiced traditional American Indian beliefs.

POPULATION BY REGION, 1820 TO 1860			
Region	1820	1840	1860
Northeast	4,360,000	6,761,000	10,594,000
North Central	859,000	3,352,000	9,097,000
South	4,419,000	6,951,000	11,133,000
West	—	—	619,000
All States	9,618,000	17,120,000	31,513,000

Source: U.S. Bureau of the Census. *Historical Statistics of the United States, Colonial Times to 1970.*

The Expanding Economy

The era of territorial expansion coincided with a period of remarkable economic growth from the 1840s to 1857.

Industrial Technology

Before 1840, factory production had been concentrated mainly in the textile mills of New England. After 1840, industrialization spread rapidly to the other states of the Northeast. New factories produced shoes, sewing machines, ready-to-wear clothing, firearms, precision tools, and iron products for **railroads** and other new technologies. The invention of the sewing machine by **Elias Howe** took much of the production of clothing out of homes and into factories. An electric telegraph demonstrated in 1844 by its inventor, **Samuel F. B. Morse**, went hand in hand with the growth of railroads in enormously speeding up communication and transportation across the country.

Railroads

The canal-building era of the 1820s and 1830s was replaced in the next two decades with the expansion of rail lines, especially across the Northeast and Midwest. The railroads soon emerged as America's largest industry. As such, they required immense amounts of capital and labor and gave rise to complex business organizations. Local merchants and farmers would often buy stocks in the new railroad companies in order to connect their area to the outside world. Local and state governments also helped the railroads grow by granting special loans and tax breaks. Then, in 1850, the U.S. government made its first land grant to railroads. It gave 2.6 million acres of federal land to build the Illinois Central Railroad from Lake Michigan to the Gulf of Mexico.

Cheap and rapid transportation particularly promoted Western agriculture. Farmers in Illinois and Iowa were now more closely linked by rail to the

Northeast than by the rivers to the South. The railroads united the commercial interests of the Northeast and Midwest and would also give the North strategic advantages in the Civil War.

Panic of 1857

In 1857 a financial panic caused a sharp decrease in prices for Midwestern agricultural products and a sharp increase in unemployment in Northern cities. However, cotton prices remained high and the South was less affected. As a result, some Southerners believed that their plantation economy was superior to the Northern economy and that continued union with the Northern economy was not needed.

Agitation Over Slavery

For a brief period—between the Compromise of 1850 and the passage of the Kansas-Nebraska Act in 1854—political tensions relaxed slightly. However, the enforcement of the Fugitive Slave Act and the publication of a best-selling antislavery novel kept the slavery question before the public.

Fugitive Slave Law

The passage of a strict **Fugitive Slave Law** in 1850 persuaded many Southerners to accept that California would be a free state. However, many Northerners bitterly resented the law. As a result, it drove a wedge between North and South.

Enforcement The law's purpose was to help owners track down runaway (fugitive) enslaved people who had escaped to a Northern state, capture them, and return them to their Southern owners. The law removed fugitive slave cases from state courts and made them the exclusive jurisdiction of the federal government. It also authorized special U.S. commissioners to issue warrants to arrest fugitives. A captured person who claimed to be free and not someone who had just escaped slavery was denied the right of trial by jury. State and local law enforcement officials were required to help enforce the federal law.

Opposition Anyone who attempted to hide a runaway or obstruct enforcement of the law was subject to heavy penalties. However, Black and White activists in the North bitterly resisted the law. Through court cases, protests, and sometimes force, they tried to protect African Americans from being returned—or taken for the first time—into slavery.

Underground Railroad

The **Underground Railroad** was a loose network of activists who helped enslaved people escape to freedom in the North or Canada. Most of the "conductors" and those operating the "stations" were free African Americans and people who had escaped slavery themselves with the assistance of White abolitionists. The most famous conductor was **Harriet Tubman**, a woman who had escaped slavery. She made at least 19 trips into the South to help some 300 people escape.

Free Black citizens in the North and abolitionists also organized vigilance committees to protect fugitive slaves from the slave catchers. During the Civil War, African American leaders such as Frederick Douglass, Harriet Tubman, and Sojourner Truth worked for emancipation and supported Black soldiers.

Books on Slavery—Pro and Con

Popular books as well as unpopular laws stirred the people of all regions.

Uncle Tom's Cabin The most influential book of its day was a novel about the conflict between an enslaved man, Tom, and the brutal White slave owner, Simon Legree. The publication of **Uncle Tom's Cabin** in 1852 by the Northern writer **Harriet Beecher Stowe** moved a generation of Northerners and many Europeans to regard all slave owners as cruel and inhuman. Southerners condemned the "untruths" in the novel and looked upon it as one more proof of the North's incurable prejudice against the Southern way of life. Later, when President Lincoln met Stowe, he is reported to have said, "So you're the little woman who wrote the book that made this great war."

In response to Stowe's book, Mary Eastman wrote the pro-slavery novel *Aunt Phillis's Cabin*. She portrayed a world of kind slaveowners and happily enslaved people.

Impending Crisis of the South Appearing in 1857, **Hinton R. Helper**'s nonfiction book, **Impending Crisis of the South**, attacked slavery from another angle. The author, a native of North Carolina, used statistics to demonstrate to fellow Southerners that slavery weakened the South's economy. Southern states quickly banned the book, but it was widely distributed in the North by antislavery and Free-Soil leaders.

COMPARING THE FREE AND SLAVE STATES IN THE 1850s			
Category	Free States	Slave States	Slave States as Percentage of Free States
Population	18,484,922	9,612,979	52%
Patents for New Inventions	1,929	268	14%
Value of Church Buildings	$67,778,477	$21,674,581	32%
Newspapers and Periodicals	1,790	740	41%
Capital	$230,100,840	$109,078,940	47%
Value of Exports	$167,520,098	$107,480,688	64%

Source: Hinton R. Helper, *Impending Crisis of the South*, 1857. Data from various years between 1850 and 1856.

Southern Reaction Responding to the Northern literature that condemned slavery, proslavery Southern Whites counterattacked, arguing that slavery was good for both the master and the enslaved. They pointed out that slavery was sanctioned by the Bible and grounded in philosophy and history. Slavery was also permitted by the U.S. Constitution. Southern authors contrasted the conditions of Northern wage workers—"wage slaves" forced to work long hours in factories and mines—with the familial bonds that developed on plantations between slaves and masters. **George Fitzhugh**, the best-known proslavery author, questioned the principle of equal rights for "unequal men" and attacked the wage system as worse than slavery. Among his works were *Sociology for the South* (1854) and *Cannibals All!* (1857).

Effect of Law and Literature

The Fugitive Slave Law and the books on slavery increasingly polarized the nation. Many Northerners who had opposed the expansion of slavery only for economic reasons and had scorned abolition became more concerned about slavery as a moral issue. At the same time, a growing number of Southerners, particularly wealthy ones, became more convinced that Northerners would abolish slavery and the way of life based upon it as soon as they could.

REFLECT ON THE LEARNING OBJECTIVE

1. Explain how sectional variations related to slavery increased hostilities in the years leading up to the Civil War.

KEY TERMS BY THEME

Expanding Economy (WXT)	**Urban Growth (MIG)**	Harriet Tubman
industrial technology	Irish	**Literature (ARC)**
Elias Howe	Roman Catholic	*Uncle Tom's Cabin*
Samuel F. B. Morse	Germans	Harriet Beecher Stowe
railroads	**Changing Politics (PCE)**	Hinton R. Helper
Panic of 1857	Tammany Hall	*Impending Crisis of the South*
Conflict (NAT)	**Slavery (POL, ARC)**	George Fitzhugh
nativism	Fugitive Slave Law	*Sociology for the South*
	Underground Railroad	

MULTIPLE-CHOICE QUESTIONS

Questions 1–2 refer to the following excerpt.

> "The gentleman . . . has been anxious to proclaim the death of native Americanism. Sir, it is a principle that can never die. . . .
>
> Native Americanism seeks to defend every institution that exists under that glorious Constitution . . . .
>
> But we have been told that we belong to a party of 'one idea.' . . . Our great object is to attain to unity of national character; and, as necessary to that end, we embrace every measure and policy decidedly American . . . . We go for every thing American in contradistinction to every thing foreign. That . . . may be called 'one idea'; but it is a glorious idea. . . .

No alien has a right to naturalization . . . . To prevent this universal admission to citizenship, we frame naturalization laws, and prescribe forms that operate as a check upon the interference of foreigners in our institutions. . . .

We are now struggling for national character and national identity . . . . We stand now on the very verge of overthrow by the impetuous force of invading foreigners."

Rep. Lewis C. Levin, Speech in Congress, December 18, 1845

1. Which of the following groups would have most likely supported Levin's concern "to attain unity of national character"?

   (A) Reformers who opposed the mistreatment of Native Americans

   (B) Southerners who viewed abolition as a threat to a long-standing institution

   (C) Protestants who viewed Roman Catholicism as a foreign faith

   (D) Men who opposed giving women the rights of citizenship, such as suffrage

2. How successful were Levin and his supporters in the mid-19th century?

   (A) They slowed down the growth of sectional division over slavery.

   (B) They helped pass a Fugitive Slave Law that appealed to Southerners.

   (C) They supported government funding of railroads to unite the country.

   (D) They formed a secretive society that evolved into a political party.

SHORT-ANSWER QUESTION

Use complete sentences; an outline or bulleted list alone is not acceptable.

1. Answer (a), (b), and (c).

   (a) Briefly explain ONE specific social or political response to immigration in the 1850s.

   (b) Briefly explain ONE specific social or political response to the conflict over slavery in the 1850s.

   (c) Briefly explain ONE specific example of how a piece of literature influenced social or political change in the 1850s.

Topic 5.6

Failure of Compromise

The real issue in this controversy—the one pressing upon every mind—is the sentiment on the part of one class that looks upon the institution of slavery as a wrong, and of another class that does not look upon it as a wrong.

Abraham Lincoln, during a debate with Stephen Douglas in Alton, Illinois, 1858

Learning Objective: Explain the political causes of the Civil War.

By 1861, politicians attempted many compromises to prevent war. Historians agree on the sequence of major events from 1848 to 1861 that led to the outbreak of the Civil War between the Union and the Confederacy. Facts alone, however, do not automatically assemble themselves into a convincing interpretation of *why* war occurred when it did. Three large issues, all related to slavery, divided the North and the South: (1) attitudes about the morality of slavery, (2) views about the constitutional rights of states, particularly the right to protect slavery, and (3) differences over economic policies between the free-labor industrial North and the slave-labor agricultural South. Some historians argue that solving these issues was possible but blundering politicians and extremism resulted in an unnecessary war. Others argue that the war was inevitable.

National Parties in Crisis

The potency of the slavery controversy increased political instability. The two major parties—the Democrats and the Whigs—grew weak and divided over how to resolve the sectional differences over slavery. One effort to settle the issue, the application of popular sovereignty in the territory of Kansas, resulted in disaster.

The Election of 1852

Signs of trouble for the Whig Party appeared in the 1852 election for president. The Whigs nominated another military hero of the Mexican War, General Winfield Scott. Attempting to ignore the slavery issue, the Whigs concentrated on the party's traditional platform: improving roads and harbors. But Scott quickly discovered that sectional issues could not be held in check. The antislavery and Southern factions of the party fell to quarreling, and the party was on the verge of splitting apart.

The Democrats nominated a compromise candidate, **Franklin Pierce** of New Hampshire, who they hoped would be a safe choice, one acceptable to people in all regions. A Northerner, Pierce was acceptable to Southern Democrats because he supported the Fugitive Slave Law. In the Electoral College, Pierce and the Democrats won all but four states, suggesting the days of the Whig Party were numbered.

The Kansas-Nebraska Act (1854)

The Democrats, firmly in control of both the White House and Congress, found they could not avoid the issue of slavery in the territories. Senator **Stephen A. Douglas** of Illinois proposed building a transcontinental railroad through the center of the country, with a major terminus in Chicago, to promote Western settlement (and increase the value of his own real estate in Chicago).

Southerners preferred a more southerly route. To win their support, Douglas introduced a bill to divide the Nebraska Territory into two parts, the Kansas and Nebraska territories, and allow settlers in each territory to decide whether to allow slavery. Since these territories were located *north* of the 36°30′ line, Douglas's bill gave Southerners an opportunity to expand slavery into lands that had been closed to it by the Missouri Compromise of 1820. Many Northern Democrats condemned the bill as a surrender to "slave power." Still, after three months of bitter debate, both houses of Congress passed Douglas's bill as the **Kansas-Nebraska Act** of 1854, and President Pierce signed it into law.

Extremists and Violence

The Kansas-Nebraska Act, in effect, repealed the Missouri Compromise that had lessened regional tensions for more than three decades. After 1854, the conflicts between antislavery and proslavery forces exploded, both in Kansas and on the floor of the United States Senate.

"Bleeding Kansas"

Stephen Douglas, the Kansas-Nebraska Act sponsor, expected the slavery issue in the territory to be settled peacefully by the antislavery farmers from the Midwest who migrated to Kansas and constituted a majority. Slaveholders from neighboring Missouri also set up homesteads in Kansas as a means of winning control for the South. Northern abolitionists and Free-Soilers responded by organizing the **New England Emigrant Aid Company** (1855), which paid for the transportation of antislavery settlers to Kansas. Fighting broke out between the proslavery and the antislavery groups, and the territory became known as **"bleeding Kansas."**

Proslavery Missourians, called "border ruffians" by their enemies, crossed the border to create a proslavery legislature in Lecompton, Kansas. Antislavery settlers refused to recognize this government and created their own legislature in Topeka. In 1856, proslavery forces attacked the free-soil town of Lawrence, killing two and destroying homes and businesses. Two days later, John Brown, a stern abolitionist, retaliated. He and his sons attacked a proslavery farm settlement at **Pottawatomie Creek**, killing five.

THE UNITED STATES AFTER
THE KANSAS–NEBRASKA ACT OF 1854

In Washington, the Pierce administration did nothing to keep order in the Kansas territory and failed to support honest elections there. As Kansas became bloodier, the Democratic Party became more divided between its Northern and Southern factions. The plan to let territories decide on slavery for themselves had resulted in chaos and bloodshed.

Caning of Senator Sumner The violence in Kansas spilled over into the halls of the U.S. Congress. In 1856, Massachusetts senator Charles Sumner attacked the Democratic administration in a vitriolic speech, "The Crime Against Kansas." His remarks included personal charges against South Carolina senator Andrew Butler. Butler's nephew, Congressman Preston Brooks, defended his uncle's honor by walking into the Senate chamber and beating Sumner over the head repeatedly with a cane. Sumner never fully recovered from the attack. The action by Brooks outraged the North, and the House voted to censure him while Southerners applauded the deed. The **Sumner-Brooks incident** was another sign of growing passions on both sides.

Birth of the Republican Party

The increasing tensions over slavery divided Northern and Southern Democrats, and completely broke apart the Whig Party. Ex-Whigs scattered. Those who were frightened about immigration joined the **Know-Nothing Party**. With the support of new members, the Know-Nothings won a few local and state elections in the mid-1850s. However, as the expansion of slavery became the paramount political issue, the significance of immigration declined, and along with it, the Know-Nothing Party.

Ex-Whigs who supported the expansion of slavery usually joined the Democratic Party. The South became the core of the party, although Democrats were still strong in the North.

Former Whigs who opposed slavery expansion formed the core of a new party. The **Republican Party** was founded in Wisconsin in 1854 as a reaction to the passage of the Kansas-Nebraska Act. Composed of Free-Soilers and antislavery Whigs and Democrats, its purpose was to oppose the spread of slavery in the territories—not to end slavery itself. Its first platform called for the repeal of both the Kansas-Nebraska Act and the Fugitive Slave Law. As violence increased in Kansas, more and more people, including some abolitionists, joined the Republican Party, and it became the second largest party in the country. But it was strictly a Northern, or sectional, party. Its success alienated and threatened the South.

The Election of 1856

The Republicans' first test of strength came in the presidential election of 1856. Their nominee was a California senator, the explorer and "Pathfinder," **John C. Frémont**. The Republican platform called for no expansion of slavery, free homesteads, and a probusiness protective tariff. The Know-Nothings also competed strongly in this election, with their candidate, former President **Millard Fillmore**, winning 20 percent of the popular vote.

As the one major national party, the Democrats expected to win. They nominated **James Buchanan** of Pennsylvania, rejecting President Pierce and Stephen Douglas because they were too closely identified with the controversial Kansas-Nebraska Act. As expected, the Democrats won a majority of the popular and electoral vote. The Republicans made a strong showing for a sectional party. In the Electoral College, Frémont carried 11 of the 16 free states. Some predicted that the antislavery Republicans could win the White House without a single vote from the South.

The election of 1856 foreshadowed the emergence of a powerful political party that would win all but four presidential elections between 1860 and 1932.

Constitutional Issues

Both the Democrats' position of popular sovereignty and the Republicans' stand against the expansion of slavery received serious blows during the Buchanan administration (1857–1861). Republicans attacked Buchanan as a weak president.

Lecompton Constitution

One of Buchanan's first challenges as president in 1857 was to decide whether to accept or reject a proslavery state constitution for Kansas submitted by the Southern legislature at Lecompton. Buchanan knew that the **Lecompton Constitution**, as it was called, did not have majority support. Even so, he asked Congress to accept the document and admit Kansas as a slave state. Congress did not do so because many Democrats, including Stephen Douglas, joined with the Republicans in rejecting the constitution. The next year, 1858, the proslavery document was overwhelmingly rejected by Kansas settlers, most of whom were antislavery Republicans.

Dred Scott v. Sandford (1857)

Congressional folly and presidential ineptitude contributed to the sectional crisis of the 1850s. Then the Supreme Court worsened the crisis when it infuriated many Northerners with a controversial proslavery decision in the case of an enslaved man named Dred Scott. Scott had been held in slavery in Missouri and then taken to the free territory of Wisconsin, where he lived for two years before returning to Missouri. Arguing that his residence on free soil made him a free citizen, Scott sued for his freedom in Missouri in 1846. The case worked its way through the court system. It finally reached the Supreme Court, which rendered its decision in March 1857, only two days after Buchanan was sworn in as president.

Presiding over the Court was Chief Justice **Roger Taney**, a Southern Democrat. A majority of the Court decided against Scott and gave these reasons:

- Dred Scott had no right to sue in a federal court because the Framers of the Constitution did not intend African Americans to be U.S. citizens.

- Congress did not have the power to deprive any person of property without due process of law. If slaves were a form of property, then Congress could not exclude slavery from any federal territory.

- The Missouri Compromise was unconstitutional because it excluded slavery from Wisconsin and other Northern territories.

The Court's ruling delighted Southern Democrats and infuriated Northern Republicans. In effect, the Court declared all parts of the Western territories open to slavery. Republicans denounced the decision as "the greatest crime in the annals of the republic." The timing of the decision, after Buchanan's inauguration, led Northerners to suspect the Democratic president and majority on the Supreme Court, including Taney, had planned the decision so that it would settle the slavery question. This increased Northern suspicions of a conspiracy and induced thousands of Democrats to vote Republican. Northern Democrats such as Senator Douglas were left with the impossible task of supporting popular sovereignty without rejecting the Dred Scott decision. Douglas's hopes for compromise and the presidency were in jeopardy.

Lincoln-Douglas Debates

In 1858, the focus of the nation was on Stephen Douglas's campaign for reelection as senator from Illinois. Challenging him was a successful trial lawyer and former member of the Illinois legislature, **Abraham Lincoln**, as the Republican candidate. Lincoln had served one term in Congress in the 1840s as a Whig. Nationally, he was an unknown compared to Douglas (the Little Giant), who was the champion of popular sovereignty and possibly the best hope for holding the nation together if elected president in 1860.

Lincoln was not an abolitionist. As a moderate who was against the expansion of slavery, he spoke effectively of slavery as a moral issue. ("If slavery is not wrong, nothing is wrong.") Accepting the Illinois Republicans' nomination, he delivered his celebrated **"house-divided" speech** that won him fame. "I believe this government," said Lincoln, "cannot endure, permanently half *slave* and half *free*," a statement that made Southerners view Lincoln as a radical. In seven campaign debates in different Illinois towns, Lincoln shared the platform with his famous opponent, Douglas. The Republican challenger attacked Douglas's indifference to slavery as a moral issue.

In a debate in Freeport, Illinois, Lincoln challenged Douglas to reconcile popular sovereignty with the Dred Scott decision. In what became known as the **Freeport Doctrine**, Douglas responded that slavery could not exist in a community if the local citizens did not pass laws (slave codes) maintaining it. His views angered Southern Democrats because, from their point of view, Douglas did not go far enough in supporting the implications of the Dred Scott decision.

Douglas won his campaign for reelection to the U.S. Senate. In the long run, however, he lost ground in his own party by alienating Southern Democrats. Lincoln, on the other hand, emerged from the debates as a national figure and a leading contender for the Republican nomination for president in 1860.

REFLECT ON THE LEARNING OBJECTIVE

1. Explain the political causes for the Civil War.

KEY TERMS BY THEME

Battle for the Territories (MIG, POL)
New England Emigrant Aid Company
"bleeding Kansas"
Pottawatomie Creek
Lecompton Constitution

Compromising (POL)
Stephen A. Douglas

Kansas-Nebraska Act

Politics in Crisis (POL)
Franklin Pierce
Know-Nothing Party
Republican Party
John C. Frémont
Millard Fillmore
James Buchanan

Slavery (POL, ARC)
Dred Scott v. Sandford
Roger Taney
Lincoln-Douglas debates
Abraham Lincoln
house-divided speech
Freeport Doctrine

Violent Responses (POL)
Sumner-Brooks incident

Questions 1–2 refer to the following excerpt.

"Mr. President . . . I proposed on Tuesday last, that the Senate should proceed to the consideration of the bill to organize the Territories of Nebraska and Kansas . . . .

Now I ask the friends and the opponents of this measure to look at it as it is. Is not the question involved the simple one, whether the people of the Territories shall be allowed to do as they please upon the question of slavery, subject only to the limitations of the Constitution? . . .

If the principle is right, let it be avowed and maintained. If it is wrong, let it be repudiated. Let all this quibbling about the Missouri Compromise, about the territory acquired from France, about the act of 1820, be cast behind you; for the simple question is, will you allow the people to legislate for themselves upon the subject of slavery? Why should you not?"

Stephen A. Douglas, Defense of the Kansas-Nebraska Bill, 1854

1. Which of the following ideas best describes what Douglas is proposing in this excerpt?

    (A) The theme of *The Impending Crisis of the South*

    (B) The concept of popular sovereignty

    (C) The right of a state to secede

    (D) The distinction between a territory and a state

2. Opponents of Douglas's views in this excerpt were mainly concerned that

    (A) the Supreme Court had ruled popular sovereignty unconstitutional

    (B) Congress was repealing a law that had held the Union together for more than 30 years

    (C) the president would not fully support implementation of a new law

    (D) European powers would object to the possibility of slavery's expansion

Use complete sentences; an outline or bulleted list alone is not acceptable.

Question 1 is based on the following excerpts.

1. "The country had been founded in compromise, and to compromise it was dedicated. . . . But this conception of compromise was in trouble, and the word would . . . become an epithet. . . .

   The underlying issue was the North's increasing power. And that power endangered slavery. Secessionists worried if slavery did not expand into the territories, the black population would stay where it was, bottled up and likely to explode. Fear motivated them. That is to say, racial anxiety was as pervasive as economic anxiety when it came to secession, though it was hard to separate the two, for they were threaded together with the rope that bound secessionists and many Southerners to their land, their way of life, their mint juleps, and their pride of race.

   Lincoln's election was thus not so much the *cause* of secession as its excuse: institutional restraints (read: the federal government) had insulted Southerners, imperiled their way of life, and held them in thrall to Northern financiers who had forced planters to buy goods in a protected market."

   Brenda Wineapple, Ecstatic Nation, 2013

   "During the 1850s, however, the forces that had worked to hold the nation together in the past fell victim to new and much more divisive pressures that were working to split the nation apart. Driving the sectional tensions of the 1850s was a battle over national policy toward the western territories which were clamoring to become states of the Union—and over the place of slavery within them. Should slavery be permitted in the new states? And who should decide whether to permit it or not? . . . Positions on slavery continued to harden in both the North and South until ultimately each region came to consider the other its enemy."

   Alan Brinkley, American History, 2003

   Using the excerpts, answer (a), (b), and (c).

   (a) Briefly explain ONE major difference between Wineapple's and Brinkley's historical interpretations of Manifest Destiny.

   (b) Briefly explain how ONE historical event or development in the period 1848 to 1861 that is not explicitly mentioned in the excerpts could be used to support Wineapple's interpretation.

   (c) Briefly explain how ONE historical event or development in the period 1848 to 1861 that is not explicitly mentioned in the excerpts could be used to support Brinkley's interpretation.

Topic 5.7

Election of 1860 and Secession

I, John Brown, am now quite certain that the crimes of this guilty land will never be purged away but with blood.

John Brown, December 1859

Learning Objective: Describe the effects of Lincoln's election.

In Northern states outside of Illinois where Douglas and the Democrats defeated Lincoln, the Republicans did well in the congressional elections of 1858. This greatly alarmed many Southerners. They worried not only about the antislavery plank in the Republicans' program but also about that party's economic program, which favored Northern industrialists at the expense of the South. The higher tariffs pledged by the Republicans would help Northern businesses but hurt the South, which depended on exporting cotton. The events leading up to Lincoln's election and the **secession** of eleven Southern states from the Union set the stage for war.

The Road to Secession

Southern fears grew that a Republican victory in 1860 would spell disaster for their economy and threaten their "constitutional right," as affirmed by the Supreme Court, to own enslaved people as property. Adding to their fears were Northern radicals supporting John Brown, the man who had massacred five farmers in Kansas in 1856.

John Brown's Raid at Harpers Ferry

John Brown confirmed the South's worst fears of radical abolitionism when he tried to start an uprising of enslaved people in Virginia. In October 1859, he led a small band of followers, including his four sons and some formerly enslaved people, to attack the federal arsenal at **Harpers Ferry**. His impractical plan was to use guns from the arsenal to arm Virginia's enslaved African Americans, whom he expected to rise up in revolt. Federal troops under the command of Robert E. Lee captured Brown and his band after a two-day siege. Brown and six of his followers were tried for treason by the state of Virginia. At the trial, Brown spoke with simple eloquence of his humanitarian motives in wanting to free enslaved people. However, he was convicted and hanged.

Brown's raid divided Northerners. Moderates condemned his use of violence, while abolitionists hailed him as a martyr. Southern whites saw the raid, and Northern support for it, as final proof of the North's true intentions—to use slave revolts to destroy the South.

The Election of 1860

After John Brown's raid, more and more Americans feared that their country was moving to disintegration. The presidential election of 1860 would test the Union.

Breakup of the Democratic Party As 1860 began, the Democratic Party represented the last hope for compromise. The Democrats held their national convention in Charleston, South Carolina. Stephen Douglas was the party's leading candidate and the most capable of winning the presidency. Blocking his nomination were angry Southerners and supporters of President Buchanan.

After deadlocking at Charleston, the Democrats held a second convention in Baltimore. Many delegates from the slave states walked out, enabling the remaining delegates to nominate Douglas on a platform of popular sovereignty and enforcement of the Fugitive Slave Law. Southern Democrats then held their own convention in Baltimore and nominated Vice President **John C. Breckinridge** of Kentucky as their candidate. The Southern Democratic platform called for the unrestricted extension of slavery in the territories and annexation of Cuba, a Spanish colony that still practiced slavery.

Republican Nomination of Lincoln When the Republicans met in Chicago, they enjoyed hopes of an easy win over the divided Democrats. They drafted a platform that appealed to the economic self-interest of Northerners and Westerners. They called for the exclusion of slavery from the territories, a protective tariff for industry, free land for homesteaders, and internal improvements to encourage Western settlement, including a railroad to the Pacific. To win moderates on slavery, they rejected the well-known New York Senator William Seward, a strong opponent of slavery. They turned to a little-known Illinois lawyer Abraham Lincoln, a strong debater. They believed that Lincoln could carry the Midwestern states of Illinois, Indiana, and Ohio. One cloud darkened the Republicans' otherwise bright future. In the South, radicals warned that if the country elected Lincoln, their states would leave the Union.

A Fourth Political Party Fearing a Republican victory, a group of former Whigs, Know-Nothings, and moderate Democrats formed a new party: the **Constitutional Union Party**. For president, they nominated **John Bell** of Tennessee and pledged enforcement of the laws and the Constitution and, above all, preservation of the Union.

Election Results While Douglas campaigned across the country, Lincoln remained at home in Springfield, Illinois, meeting with Republican leaders and giving statements to the press. The election results were predictable. Lincoln carried every free state of the North, which represented a solid majority of 59 percent of the electoral votes. Breckinridge, the Southern Democrat, carried the Deep South, leaving Douglas and Bell with just a few electoral votes in the **border states**.

However, Lincoln won only 39.8 percent of the *popular* vote, so he would be a minority president. The new political reality was that the populous free states had enough electoral votes to elect a president without any electoral votes from the South. Southern fears that the North would dominate the federal government—and could soon threaten slavery—appeared to be coming true.

Secession of the Deep South

In 1860, Republicans controlled neither the Senate nor the Supreme Court. Even so, the election of Lincoln was all that Southern secessionists needed to call for immediate disunion. In December 1860, a special convention in South Carolina voted unanimously to secede, saying they needed to protect slavery. Within six weeks, state conventions in Georgia, Florida, Alabama, Mississippi, Louisiana, and Texas did the same. In several states, particularly Georgia and Alabama, many people were uncertain about or opposed to secession. However, large slaveowners, arguing that states had a right to defend slavery, prevailed.

In February 1861, representatives of the seven states of the Deep South met in Montgomery, Alabama, and created the Confederate States of America. The constitution of this Southern country was like the U.S. Constitution, except that the Confederacy placed limits on the government's power to impose tariffs and restrict slavery. Elected president and vice president were Jefferson Davis of Mississippi and Alexander Stephens of Georgia.

THE ELECTION OF 1860

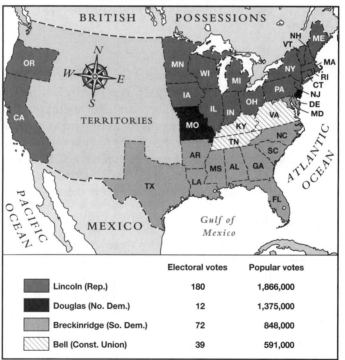

	Electoral votes	Popular votes
Lincoln (Rep.)	180	1,866,000
Douglas (No. Dem.)	12	1,375,000
Breckinridge (So. Dem.)	72	848,000
Bell (Const. Union)	39	591,000

Crittenden Compromise A lame-duck president (a leader completing a term after someone else has been elected to his or her office), Buchanan had five months in office before Lincoln succeeded him. Buchanan was a conservative who did nothing to prevent the secession. Congress was more active. In a last-ditch effort to appease the South, Senator John Crittenden of Kentucky proposed a constitutional amendment that would guarantee the right to hold slaves in all territories south of the old Missouri Compromise line, 36°30′. Lincoln, however, said that he could not accept this compromise because it violated the Republican position against extension of slavery into the territories.

Southern Whites who voted for secession believed they were acting in the tradition of the Revolution of 1776. They argued that they had a right to national independence and to dissolve a constitutional compact that no longer protected them from the "tyranny" of Northern rule. Many also thought that Lincoln, like Buchanan, might permit secession without a fight. Those who thought this had badly miscalculated.

A Nation Divided

When Lincoln took office as the president in March 1861, people wondered if he would challenge the secession militarily. In his inaugural address, Lincoln assured Southerners that he would not interfere with slavery where it existed. At the same time, he warned, no state had the right to break up the Union. He appealed for restraint: "In *your* hands, my dissatisfied fellow-countrymen, and not in *mine,* is the momentous issue of civil war. The government will not assail *you.* You can have no conflict without being yourselves the aggressors."

Fort Sumter

Despite the president's message of conciliation, the danger of a war was acute. Critical was the status of federal forts in states that had seceded. **Fort Sumter**, in the harbor of Charleston, South Carolina, was cut off by Southern control of the harbor. Rather than either giving up Fort Sumter or attempting to defend it, Lincoln announced that he was sending provisions of food to the small federal garrison. He thus gave South Carolina the choice of either permitting the fort to hold out or opening fire. Carolina's guns thundered and thus, on April 12, 1861, the war began. The attack on Fort Sumter and its capture after two days of pounding united most Northerners behind a patriotic fight to save the Union.

Secession of the Upper South

Before South Carolina attacked Fort Sumter, only seven states of the Deep South had seceded. After it was clear that Lincoln would use troops to defend the Union, four states of the Upper South—Virginia, North Carolina, Tennessee, and Arkansas—seceded and joined the Confederacy. As in the earlier states, the decision to secede was controversial. The Confederates then moved their capital to Richmond, Virginia. The people of western Virginia remained loyal to the Union, becoming a separate state in 1863.

Keeping the Border States in the Union

Four other slaveholding states remained in the Union. The decisions of Delaware, Maryland, Missouri, and Kentucky *not* to join the Confederacy were partly a result of pro-Union sentiment in those states and partly the result of shrewd federal policies. In Maryland, pro-secessionists attacked Union troops and threatened the railroad to Washington. The Union army resorted to martial law to keep the state under federal control. In Missouri, U.S. troops prevented the pro-South elements from gaining control, although guerrilla forces for the Confederacy were active during the war. In Kentucky, the state legislature voted to remain neutral. Lincoln initially respected its neutrality and waited for the South to violate it before moving in federal troops.

Keeping the border states in the Union was a military and political goal for Lincoln. Their loss would increase the Confederate population by 50 percent and weaken the North's strategic position. Partly to avoid alienating Unionists in the border states, Lincoln rejected initial calls for the emancipation of slaves.

HISTORICAL PERSPECTIVES: *WHAT CAUSED THE CIVIL WAR?*

Was slavery the primary cause of the Civil War? In the decades after the war, Northern historians argued emphatically that the South's attachment to slavery was the principal, if not the only, cause. They blamed the war on a conspiracy of slave owners—a small minority of Southerners—who wanted only to expand slavery at the expense of White and Black Americans alike.

Southern historians, on the other hand, viewed the conflict between the two sections, North and South, as a dispute over the nature of the Constitution. They argued that Northern politicians violated the original compact of the states by attacking their property rights (the ownership of enslaved people). Therefore, the Southern states had to secede to defend their constitutional rights and escape tyranny of the Northern majority.

By the early 20th century, passions had cooled on both sides, and scholars of the Progressive era (1900–1917) thought economic interests were the foundation of all political conflict. The Civil War, then, was a clash between two opposing economic systems: the industrial North versus the agricultural South. They downplayed the divisive issue of slavery.

American disillusionment with World War I led historians to question whether the Civil War was necessary or inevitable. Previously, people had assumed that the Civil War was an "irrepressible conflict." In the 1920s and 1930s, historians challenged that assumption, arguing that blundering politicians and fanaticism on both sides, such as radical abolitionists in the North and secessionists in the South, were chiefly responsible for the war. The leaders admired from this perspective were politicians of the 1850s who worked for compromise, such as Henry Clay and Stephen Douglas. They criticized Lincoln for his passionate "house-divided" speech.

In the 1950s and 1960s, the civil rights movement provided the backdrop for rethinking the causes of the Civil War. Historians who were affected by African Americans' struggles for civil rights returned to the view that slavery was the chief cause of disunion after all. Arthur Schlesinger, Jr., a leading historian of the 1950s, argued: "A society closed in the defense of evil institutions thus creates moral differences far too profound to be solved by compromise." In this view, slavery was an inherently evil institution and the root of a conflict that was indeed "irrepressible."

REFLECT ON THE LEARNING OBJECTIVE

1. Explain the consequences of Lincoln's election.

KEY TERMS BY THEME

Violent Responses (POL)
John Brown
Harpers Ferry

Politics in Crisis (POL)
John C. Breckenridge

Constitutional Union Party
John Bell
secession

Compromising (POL)
Crittenden Compromise

The Break (NAT, POL)
border states

The Fighting (POL, GEO, CUL)
Fort Sumter

MULTIPLE-CHOICE QUESTIONS

Questions 1–2 refer to the following excerpt.

> "Apprehension seems to exist among the people of the Southern States that by the accession of a Republican administration their property and their peace and personal security are endangered. There has never been any reasonable cause for such apprehension. . . .
>
> In *your* hands, my dissatisfied fellow countrymen, and not in *mine*, is the momentous issue of civil war. The Government will not assail *you*. You can have no conflict without being yourself the aggressors. *You* have no oath registered in heaven to destroy the Government, while *I* shall have the most solemn one to 'preserve, protect, and defend it.'"

Abraham Lincoln, First Inaugural Address, March 4, 1861

1. Which of the following actions by the Confederates was the first sign of their rejection of Lincoln's words in the excerpt above?

(A) The secession of seven states in the Deep South

(B) The decision to locate the Confederate capital in Virginia

(C) The adoption of a new constitution by the Confederacy

(D) The attack on Fort Sumter by South Carolina

2. The position of Lincoln and the Republicans on which of the following issues caused the greatest fear among Southern defenders of slavery?

(A) The extension of slavery into the territories

(B) The Fugitive Slave Act

(C) The slave trade in Washington, D.C.

(D) The Dred Scott decision

Use complete sentences; an outline or bulleted list alone is not acceptable.

1. "[In the Civil War,] great issues were at stake, issues about which Americans were willing to fight and die, issues whose resolution profoundly transformed and redefined the United States. The Civil War was a total war in three senses: It mobilized the total human and material resources of both sides; it ended not in a negotiated peace but in total victory by one side and unconditional surrender by the other; it destroyed the economy and social system of the loser and established those of the winner as the norm for the future. . . .

   The North went to war to preserve the Union; it ended by creating a nation."

   James M. McPherson, historian, "A War That Never Goes
Away," American Heritage, March 1990

   "Should we consecrate a war that killed and maimed over a million Americans? Or should we question . . . whether this was really a war of necessity that justified its appalling costs? . . .

   Very few Northerners went to war seeking or anticipating the destruction of slavery. They fought for the Union, and the Emancipation Proclamation was a means to that end: a desperate measure to undermine the South and save a democratic nation that Lincoln called 'the last, best hope of earth.' . . .

   From the distance of 150 years, Lincoln's transcendent vision at Gettysburg of a 'new birth of freedom' seems premature. . . . Rather than simply consecrate the dead with words, he said, it is for 'us the living' to rededicate ourselves to the unfinished work of the Civil War."

   Tony Horwitz, journalist and writer, "150 Years of
Misunderstanding the Civil War," The Atlantic, June 2013

   Using the excerpts, answer (a), (b), and (c).

   (a) Briefly explain ONE major difference between McPherson's and Horwitz's historical interpretations of the Civil War.

   (b) Briefly explain how ONE historical event or development from the period 1861 to 1865 not directly mentioned in the excerpts supports McPherson's interpretation.

   (c) Briefly explain how ONE historical event or development from the period 1861 to 1865 not directly mentioned in the excerpts supports Horwitz's interpretation.

Topic 5.8

Military Conflict in the Civil War

It is enough to make the whole world start to see the awful amount of death and destruction that now stalks abroad. I see no signs of a remission till one or both the armies are destroyed.

General William T. Sherman, June 1864

Learning Objective: Explain the various factors that contributed to the Union victory in the Civil War.

The Civil War between the Union and the Confederacy (1861–1865) was the costliest American war in terms of the loss of human life, resulting in the deaths of 750,000 people. Most important, the Civil War freed 4 million enslaved African Americans, giving the nation what President Lincoln called a "new birth of freedom." The war also transformed American society by accelerating industrialization and modernization in the North and destroying much of the South. These changes were so fundamental and profound that some historians refer to the Civil War as the **Second American Revolution**.

War

Less than 100 years after fighting a war to establish their republic, the Union and the Confederacy each entered the Civil War with strengths and weaknesses.

Military Differences The Confederacy started with the advantage of having to fight only a defensive war to win, while the Union had to conquer an area as large as Western Europe. The Confederacy had to move troops and supplies shorter distances than the Union. It had a long, indented coastline that was difficult to blockade, experienced military leaders, and high troop morale.

The Union's population of 22 million against the Confederate's of 5.5 million free Whites would work to its favor in a war of attrition. Its population advantage was aided by 800,000 immigrants, and emancipation brought 180,000 African Americans into the Union army. The Union could also count on a loyal U.S. Navy, which ultimately gave it command of the rivers and territorial waters.

Economic Differences The Union dominated the nation's economy, controlling most of the banking and capital of the country, 85 percent of the factories, 70 percent of the railroads, and 65 percent of the farmland. The skills of Northern clerks and bookkeepers proved valuable in the logistical support of military operations. Confederates hoped that European demand for its cotton would bring recognition and financial aid. Like other rebel movements in history, the Confederates counted on outside help to be successful.

Political Differences The two sides had distinct goals. The Confederates were struggling for independence, while the Union was fighting to preserve the Union. But states' rights proved a liability for the Confederate government; to win the war, they needed a strong central government with strong public support. They had neither, while the Union had an established central government. The ultimate hope of the Confederates was that the people of the Union would turn against Lincoln and the Republicans and quit the war because it was too costly.

The Confederate States of America The Confederate constitution was modeled after the U.S. Constitution, but it denied the Confederate congress the powers to levy a protective tariff and to appropriate funds for internal improvements. However, it did prohibit the foreign slave trade. President **Jefferson Davis** tried to increase his executive powers during the war, but Southern governors resisted his attempts, some holding back troops and resources to protect their own states. At one point, Vice President **Alexander H. Stephens**, in defense of states' rights, even urged the secession of Georgia in response to the "despotic" actions of the Confederate government.

The Confederacy was chronically short of money. It tried loans, income taxes, and even impressment of private property, but these revenues paid only a part of war costs. The government issued more than $1 billion in paper money, causing severe inflation. By war's end, a Confederate dollar was worth less than two cents. The Confederate congress nationalized railroads to promote industrial growth, but it was not enough. In a war of attrition, the Confederacy faced the challenge of making its resources last until the Union stopped fighting.

First Years of a Long War: 1861–1862

People at first expected the war to last no more than weeks. Lincoln called the first volunteers for a period of only 90 days. "On to Richmond!" was the cry, but it would take four years of fighting before Union troops marched into the Confederate capital.

Union Strategy General-in-Chief **Winfield Scott**, veteran of the 1812 and Mexican wars, devised a three-part strategy for winning a long war:

- Use the U.S. Navy to blockade Southern ports (called the **Anaconda Plan**), cutting off essential supplies from reaching the Confederacy

- Take control of the Mississippi River, dividing the Confederacy in two

- Raise and train an army 500,000 strong to conquer Richmond

The first two parts of the strategy proved easier to achieve than the third, but ultimately all three were important in achieving Northern victory.

After the Union's defeat at **Bull Run**, federal armies experienced a succession of crushing defeats as they attempted various campaigns in Virginia.

First Battle of Bull Run In the first major battle of the war (July 1861), 30,000 federal troops marched from Washington, D.C., to attack Confederate forces near Bull Run Creek at Manassas Junction, Virginia. As the Union forces seemed close to victory, Confederate reinforcements under General **Thomas (Stonewall) Jackson** counterattacked and sent the inexperienced Union troops in disorderly flight back to Washington. The battle ended the illusion of a short war and also promoted the myth that the rebels were invincible in battle.

Peninsula Campaign General **George B. McClellan**, the new commander of the Union army in the East, insisted that his troops be given a long period of training before going into battle. Finally, after many delays that tested Lincoln's patience, McClellan's army invaded Virginia in March 1862. The Union army was stopped by brilliant tactical moves by Confederate general **Robert E. Lee**, the commander of the South's eastern forces. After five months, McClellan was forced to retreat and was ordered back to the Potomac, where he was replaced by General John Pope.

THE CIVIL WAR: THE UNION VS. THE CONFEDERACY

Second Battle of Bull Run Lee struck quickly against Pope's army in Northern Virginia. He drew Pope into a trap, struck the enemy's flank, and sent the Union army back to Bull Run. Pope withdrew to defend Washington.

Antietam Following his victory at Bull Run, Lee led his army across the Potomac into Maryland. He hoped that a Confederate victory in a Union state would convince Britain to give recognition and support to the Confederacy. By this time (September 1862), Lincoln had restored McClellan to command. McClellan had the advantage of knowing Lee's plan because a copy of it had been dropped accidentally by a Confederate officer. The Union army intercepted the Confederates at **Antietam** Creek in the Maryland town of Sharpsburg. Here the bloodiest single day of combat in the entire war took place, with more than 22,000 soldiers killed or wounded.

Unable to break through Union lines, Lee's army retreated to Virginia. Disappointed with McClellan for failing to pursue Lee's army, Lincoln removed him for the final time as the Union commander.

While essentially a draw on the battlefield, Antietam was among the most significant battles of the war. Because the Confederates did not win, they failed to get what they so urgently needed—recognition and aid from Great Britain and France. Because the Union did not lose, Lincoln found enough encouragement in a Union victory. As explained in Topic 5.9, Lincoln used the partial triumph to announce a direct assault on the institution of slavery.

Fredericksburg Replacing McClellan with the aggressive General Ambrose Burnside, Lincoln discovered that a strategy of reckless attack could have even worse consequences than McClellan's strategy of caution. In December 1862, a Union army under Burnside attacked Lee's army at **Fredericksburg**, Virginia, and suffered immense losses: 12,000 dead or wounded compared to 5,000 Confederate casualties. Both Union and Confederate generals were slow to learn that improved weaponry took the romance out of heroic charges against entrenched positions. By the end of 1862, the awful magnitude of the war was all too clear—with no prospect of victory for either side.

The second year of war, 1862, was a disastrous one for the Union except for two engagements, one at sea and the other on the rivers of the West.

Monitor* vs. *Merrimac The Union's hopes for winning the war depended upon its ability to maximize its economic advantages by an effective blockade of Confederate ports (the Anaconda Plan). During McClellan's Peninsula campaign, the Union's blockade strategy was jeopardized by an unusual Confederate ship, the *Merrimac*, that attacked and sank several Union ships near Hampton Roads, Virginia. Unlike the standard wooden ships of the day, the *Merrimac* was covered with metal plates. The "ironclad" seemed unstoppable. However, on March 9, 1862, the Union's own ironclad, the *Monitor,* engaged the *Merrimac* in a five-hour duel. The battle ended in a draw, but the *Monitor* prevented the Confederates' new weapon from breaking the U.S. naval blockade. The two ships marked a turning point in naval warfare, as ironclad ships replaced wooden ones.

Grant in the West The battle of the ironclads occurred at about the same time as a bloodier encounter was taking place in western Tennessee. The Union's campaign for control of the Mississippi River was partly under the command of a West Point graduate, **Ulysses S. Grant**, who had joined up for the war after an unsuccessful civilian career. Striking south from Illinois in early 1862, Grant used a combination of gunboats and army maneuvers to capture Fort Henry and Fort Donelson on the Cumberland River (a branch of the Mississippi). These stunning victories, in which 14,000 Confederate soldiers were taken prisoner, opened up the state of Mississippi to Union attack.

A few weeks later, a Confederate army under Albert Johnston surprised Grant at **Shiloh**, Tennessee, but the Union army forced the Confederates to retreat after terrible losses on both sides (more than 23,000 dead and wounded). Grant's drive down the Mississippi was complemented in April 1862 by the capture of New Orleans by the Union navy under **David Farragut**.

Foreign Affairs and Diplomacy

The Confederacy's hopes for independence hinged as much on its diplomats as on soldiers. Confederate leaders expected that cotton would prove to be "king" and induce Britain or France, or both, to give aid to their war effort. Besides cotton for their textile mills, wealthy British industrialists and aristocrats looked forward to ending the American democratic experiment. From the Union's point of view, it was critically important to prevent the Confederacy from gaining the foreign support and recognition that it desperately needed.

***Trent* Affair** Britain came close to siding with the Confederacy in late 1861 over an incident at sea. Confederate diplomats James Mason and John Slidell were traveling to England on a British steamer, the *Trent*, on a mission to gain recognition for their government. A Union warship stopped the British ship, removed Mason and Slidell, and brought them to the United States as prisoners of war. Britain threatened war over the incident unless the diplomats were released. Despite intense criticism, Lincoln gave in to British demands. Mason and Slidell were set free, but they failed to obtain full recognition of the Confederacy from either Britain or France.

Confederate Raiders The British did allow the Confederates to purchase warships from British shipyards. These commerce-raiders did serious harm to U.S. merchant ships. One of them, the *Alabama*, captured more than 60 vessels before being sunk off the coast of France by a Union warship. After the war, Great Britain eventually agreed to pay the United States $15.5 million for damages caused by Confederate attacks in ships built in Britain.

Failure of Cotton Diplomacy In the end, the Confederacy's hopes for European intervention were disappointed. "King Cotton" did not have the power, as Europe quickly found ways of obtaining cotton from other sources. Shipments of cotton began arriving from Egypt and India for the British textile industry. Also, other materials could be used for textiles, and the woolen and linen industries took advantage of this opportunity.

Two other factors went into Britain's decision not to recognize the Confederacy. First, General Lee's setback at Antietam played a role. Without a decisive Confederate victory, the British government would not risk recognition. Second, Lincoln's Emancipation Proclamation (January 1863) made the end of slavery an objective of the Union, which appealed strongly to Britain's working class. While conservative leaders of Britain were sympathetic to the Confederacy, they could not defy the pro-Northern, antislavery feelings of the British majority.

The Union Triumphs, 1863–1865

By early 1863, the fortunes of war were turning against the Confederacy. Although General Lee started the year with a victory at Chancellorsville, Virginia, the Confederate economy was in bad shape as planters lost control of their slave labor, and an increasing number of starving soldiers were deserting the Confederate army.

Turning Point

The decisive turning point in the war came in the first week of July when the Confederacy suffered two crushing defeats in the West and the East.

Vicksburg In the West, by the spring of 1863, Union forces controlled New Orleans as well as most of the Mississippi River and surrounding valley. The Union objective of securing complete control of the Mississippi River was close when General Grant began his siege of the heavily fortified city of **Vicksburg**, Mississippi. Union artillery bombarded Vicksburg for seven weeks before the Confederates finally surrendered the city (and nearly 29,000 soldiers) on July 4. Federal warships now controlled the full length of the Mississippi, which cut off Texas, Louisiana, and Arkansas from the rest of the Confederacy.

Gettysburg Meanwhile, in the East, Lee again took the offensive by leading an army into Maryland and Pennsylvania. If he could either destroy the Union army or capture a major Northern city, Lee hoped to force the Union to call for peace—or to gain foreign intervention for the Confederacy. On July 1, 1863, the Confederate army surprised Union units at **Gettysburg** in southern Pennsylvania. What followed was the most crucial battle of the war and the bloodiest, with more than 50,000 casualties. Lee's assault on Union lines on the second and third days, including a famous but unsuccessful charge led by George Pickett, proved futile and destroyed part of the Confederate army. Lee's forces retreated to Virginia, never to regain the offensive.

Grant in Command

In Grant, Lincoln finally found a general who would fight and could win. In early 1864, he brought Grant east to Virginia and made him commander of all Union armies. Grant settled on a strategy of war by attrition. He aimed to wear down the Confederacy's armies and destroy their lines of supply. Fighting for months, Grant's Army of the Potomac suffered heavier casualties than Lee's forces in the battles of the Wilderness, Spotsylvania, and Cold Harbor. But Grant succeeded in reducing Lee's army in each battle and forcing it into a defensive line around Richmond. Rather than a small-scale war "between gentlemen" over control of territory, the war had become more like a modern "total" war in which victory depended on undercutting civilian support for the opponent's military.

Sherman's March The chief instrument of Grant's aggressive tactics for subduing the South was the veteran general **William Tecumseh Sherman**. Leading a force of 100,000 men, Sherman set out from Chattanooga, Tennessee, on a campaign of deliberate destruction that went across the state of Georgia and then swept north into South Carolina. Sherman was a pioneer of the tactics of total war. Marching through Georgia, his troops destroyed everything, burning cotton fields, barns, and houses—everything the enemy might use to survive. Sherman took Atlanta in September 1864 in time to help Lincoln's reelection. He marched into Savannah in December and completed his campaign in February 1865 by setting fire to Columbia, the capital of South Carolina and cradle of secession. Sherman's march had its intended effect: to break the spirit of the Confederacy and destroy its will to fight.

The End of the War

The effects of the Union blockade, combined with Sherman's march of destruction, spread hunger through much of the South in the winter of 1864–1865. In Virginia, Grant continued to outflank Lee's lines until they collapsed around Petersburg, resulting in the fall of Richmond on April 3, 1865. Everyone knew the end was near.

Surrender at Appomattox The Confederate government tried to negotiate for peace. However, Lincoln would accept nothing short of restoration of the Union, and Jefferson Davis still demanded nothing less than independence. Lee retreated from Richmond with an army of fewer than 30,000 men. He tried to escape to the mountains, only to be cut off and forced to surrender to Grant at Appomattox Court House, Virginia, on April 9, 1865. The Union general treated his longtime enemy with respect and allowed Lee's men to return to their homes with their horses.

Still to be seen were the long-term effects of the war. What would be the impact of the many changes led by Lincoln and his government on the policies, laws, and society of the United States? What would the nearly 4 million African Americans freed from slavery do as free people? What would happen to American democracy?

REFLECT ON THE LEARNING OBJECTIVE

1. Explain several reasons for the Union victory in the Civil War.

MULTIPLE-CHOICE QUESTIONS

Questions 1–3 refer to the following excerpt.

"We drift fast toward war with England, but I think we shall not reach that point. The shopkeepers who own England want to do us all harm they can and to give all possible aid and comfort to our slave-breeding and woman-flogging adversary, for England has degenerated into a trader, manufacturer, and banker, and has lost all the instincts and sympathies that her name still suggests . . . .

She cannot ally herself with slavery, as she inclines to do, without closing a profitable market, exposing her commerce to [Yankee] privateers, and diminishing the supply of [Northern] breadstuffs on which her operatives depend for life. On the other side, however, is the consideration that by allowing piratical *Alabamas* to be built, armed, and manned in her ports to prey on our commerce, she is making a great deal of money."

George Templeton Strong, New York lawyer, *Diary,* 1863

1. A major part of the Confederate strategy for winning independence was based on
   (A) building a modern navy to break the Union blockade
   (B) developing factories to manufacture weapons
   (C) encircling the Union capital, Washington, D.C.
   (D) winning recognition and support from Great Britain

2. Which of the following describes a reason not mentioned by Strong in this excerpt that discouraged Britain from recognizing the Confederacy?

(A) Concern about retaliation by British leaders in Canada

(B) Desire for closer ties with Mexico by British investors

(C) Respect for the Monroe Doctrine by the British public

(D) Opposition to slavery among the British working class

3. The Union was most disturbed because they believed that Britain was supporting the Confederates by doing which of the following?

(A) Allowing British shipyards to build warships for the Confederacy

(B) Transporting Confederate diplomats on British ships

(C) Lending money to Confederate states

(D) Supplying food to the Confederate army

SHORT-ANSWER QUESTION

Question 1 is based on the following cartoon.

 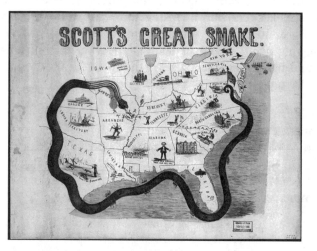

SCOTT'S GREAT SNAKE.

Source: J. B. Elliot, 1861. Library of Congress

Using the cartoon, answer (a), (b), and (c).

(a) Briefly explain ONE perspective expressed by the author of this political cartoon.

(b) Briefly explain ONE historical event or development in the period 1861 to 1865 that resulted from the Union strategy to win the war.

(c) Briefly explain ONE specific part of the Confederate strategy to counteract the Union strategy illustrated here.

Government Policies During the Civil War

The dogmas of the quiet past are inadequate to the stormy present. The occasion is piled high with difficulty, and we must rise—with the occasion.

Abraham Lincoln, Annual Message to Congress, December 1, 1862

Learning Objective: Explain how Lincoln's leadership during the Civil War impacted American ideals over the course of the war.

More than any previous president, Lincoln acted in unprecedented ways, drawing upon his powers as both chief executive and commander in chief, often without the authorization or approval of Congress. For example, right after the Fort Sumter crisis he (1) called for 75,000 volunteers to put down the "insurrection" in the Confederacy, (2) authorized spending for a war, and (3) suspended the privilege of the writ of **habeas corpus**. Since Congress was not in session, the president acted completely on his own authority, explaining that it was "indispensable to the public safety."

The End of Slavery

Though Lincoln in the 1850s spoke out against slavery as "an unqualified evil," as president he hesitated to take action against slavery. Lincoln's concerns included (1) a wish to keep the support of the border states, (2) the constitutional protections of slavery, (3) the racial prejudice of many Northerners, and (4) the fear that premature action could be overturned in the next election. All these concerns made the timing and method of ending slavery difficult. Enslaved individuals were freed during the war as a result of military events, governmental policy, and their own actions.

Confiscation Acts

Early in the war (May 1861), several enslaved people escaped to the Union lines. General Benjamin Butler refused to return them to their Confederate owners, arguing that their labor could be used to help the Confederates. Therefore, they were "contraband," and he was not required to return them. Building on this example, Congress passed two laws known as the **Confiscation Acts**:

- The law passed in August 1861 gave the Union army the power to seize enemy property, including enslaved people, used to wage war against the United States. The law also empowered the president to use those freed in the Union army in any capacity, including battle.

- The law passed in July 1862 freed persons enslaved by any individual in rebellion against the United States.

Because of these laws, thousands of "contrabands" were using their feet to escape slavery by going into Union camps. As they did, they added pressure on the Union to abolish slavery. At the same time, they deprived the Confederacy of badly needed laborers to grow food to avoid starvation.

Emancipation Proclamation

By July 1862, Lincoln had decided to use his powers as commander in chief to free all enslaved persons in the states then at war. He justified his policy as a "military necessity." However, he worried that such a move would alienate conservative Northerners who were pro-Union and pro-slavery. Furthermore, the action might look desperate if it came when the army was losing battles, so he delayed announcement of the policy. At the same time, he encouraged the border states to plan for emancipation that provided compensation to the owners. No one proposed providing compensation to the freedpeople.

After the Confederates retreated at the Battle of Antietam on September 22, 1862, Lincoln issued a warning that slaves in states still in rebellion on January 1, 1863, would be "then, thenceforward, and forever free." On the first day of the new year, 1863, he issued his **Emancipation Proclamation**, which stated:

> I do order and declare that all persons held as slaves within said designated States and parts of States are, and henceforward shall be, free; and that the Executive Government of the United States, including the military and naval authorities thereof, shall recognize and maintain the freedom of said persons.

Consequences Since the president's proclamation applied only to the Confederate states *outside* Union control, it freed only about 1 percent of enslaved people. Slavery in the border states also continued. Still, the proclamation was important because it enlarged the purpose of the war by adding weight to the Confiscation Acts. Now Union armies were openly fighting against slavery, not merely against secession. By the end of the war, hundreds of thousands of enslaved people had become free by escaping to Union lines.

African Americans in the War

An even greater blow to the Confederacy was that the Union army soon had thousands of dedicated new recruits. Almost 200,000 African Americans, most of whom had recently escaped slavery, served in the Union army and navy. Segregated into all-Black units, such as the **Massachusetts 54th Regiment**, they won the respect of White Union soldiers for their bravery under fire. More than 37,000 African American soldiers died in this "Army of Freedom."

Effects of the War on Civilian Life

Both during the war and in the years that followed, American society underwent deep and sometimes wrenching changes.

Political Change

The electoral process continued during the war with surprisingly few restrictions. Secession of the Southern states left Republican majorities in both houses of Congress. Northerners were split into several factions:

- Radical Republicans demanded immediate abolition of slavery.
- Free-Soil Republicans focused on economic opportunities for Whites.
- Most Democrats supported the war but criticized Lincoln's conduct of it.
- Some Democrats, called Peace Democrats or **Copperheads**, opposed the war and wanted a negotiated peace.

Civil Liberties Like many wartime leaders, Lincoln focused more on prosecuting the war than on protecting constitutional rights. Early in the war, he suspended the writ of habeas corpus in states with strong pro-Confederate sentiment. Suspension of this constitutional right meant that persons could be arrested without being informed of the charges against them. During the war, an estimated 13,000 people were arrested on suspicion of aiding the enemy. Without a right to habeas corpus, many of them were held without trial.

Democrats accused Lincoln of tyranny, but most historians have been less critical. In the border states, people had difficulty distinguishing between combatants and noncombatants. Furthermore, the Constitution allows only Congress, not the president, to suspend the writ of habeas corpus "when in cases of rebellion or invasion the public safety may require it." After the war, the Supreme Court ruled in *Ex Parte Milligan* (1866) that the government had improperly subjected civilians to military trials. The Court declared that such procedures could be used only when regular civilian courts were unavailable.

The Draft When the war began in 1861, those who fought were volunteers. As the need for replacements increased, both the Union and the Confederacy resorted to laws for conscripting, or drafting, men into service. The Union's March 1863 Conscription Act made all men aged 20 to 45 liable for military service. However, a draftee could avoid service by finding a substitute to serve or paying a $300 exemption fee. The law provoked fierce opposition among poorer laborers, most of whom were Irish or German immigrants. They feared that when they returned to civilian life their jobs would be taken by freed African Americans. In July 1863, protests against the draft in New York City quickly turned into a riot against the city's Black residents. About 117 people were killed before federal troops and a temporary suspension of the draft restored order.

The Election of 1864 The Democrats' nominee for president was the popular General George McClellan, whose platform calling for peace had wide appeal among millions of war-weary voters. The Republicans renamed their party the Unionist Party as a way of attracting the votes of "War Democrats" (those who disagreed with the Democratic platform). A brief "ditch Lincoln" movement fizzled out, and the Republican (Unionist) convention again chose Lincoln as its presidential candidate and a loyal War Democrat from Tennessee, Senator Andrew Johnson, as his running mate. The Lincoln-Johnson ticket won 212 electoral votes to the Democrats' 21. The popular vote was much closer as McClellan took 45 percent of the total votes cast.

Political Dominance of the North The suspension of habeas corpus and the operation of the draft were only temporary. More important were the long-term effects of the power of the federal government and the balance of power between the North and the South. With the military triumph of the Union came a clearer definition of the nature of the federal union. Old arguments for nullification and secession receded. After the Civil War, few people doubted the supremacy of the federal government.

The abolition of slavery—in addition to its importance to freed African Americans—gave new meaning to the concept of American democracy. In his famous **Gettysburg Address**, November 19, 1863, Lincoln rallied Americans to the idea that their nation was "dedicated to the proposition that all men are created equal." Lincoln was probably alluding to the Emancipation Proclamation when he spoke of the war bringing "a new birth of freedom." His words— and even more, the abolition of slavery—advanced the cause of democratic government in the United States and inspired democracy around the world.

Economic Change

The costs of the war in both money and men were staggering and called for extraordinary measures by the government.

Financing the War The Union financed the war by borrowing $2.6 billion through the sale of government bonds. To gain added funds, Congress raised tariffs, added excise taxes, and instituted the first income tax. The U.S. Treasury also issued $430 million in a paper currency, **greenbacks**, not backed by gold, which contributed to creeping inflation. Prices in the North rose by about 80 percent during the war. To manage the added revenue Congress created a national banking system in 1863, the first since Andrew Jackson vetoed the recharter of the Bank of the United States in the 1830s.

CIVILIANS EMPLOYED BY THE FEDERAL GOVERNMENT				
Year	Post Office	Defense	Other	Total
1841	14,290	598	3,150	18,038
1851	21,391	403	4,480	26,274
1861	30,269	946	5,457	36,672
1871	36,696	1,183	13,741	51,020
1881	56,421	16,297	27,302	100,020

Source: U.S. Bureau of the Census. *Historical Statistics of the United States, Colonial Times to 1970*

Modernizing Northern Society Economic historians differ on the question of whether, in the short run, the war promoted or retarded the growth of the Northern economy. Workers' wages did not keep pace with inflation, but the war accelerated many aspects of a modern industrial economy. By placing a premium on mass production and complex organization, the war sped up the consolidation of the North's manufacturing businesses. War profiteers took advantage of the need for military supplies to sell shoddy goods at high prices—a problem that decreased after the federal government took control of the contract process away from the states. Fortunes made during the war produced a concentration of capital in the hands of a new class of millionaires who would finance the North's industrialization in the postwar years.

Republican politics also stimulated the economic growth of the North and the West. With a wartime majority in Congress, the Republicans passed the probusiness Whig program that was designed to stimulate the industrial and commercial growth of the United States:

- The *Morrill Tariff Act* (1861) raised tariff rates to increase revenue and protect American manufacturers. Its passage initiated a Republican program of high protective tariffs to help industrialists.

- The *Homestead Act* (1862) promoted settlement of the Great Plains by offering parcels of 160 acres of public land free to any person or family that farmed that land for at least five years. Like the headright system in colonial Virginia and the sale of land in the Northwest Territory, this act helped many White settlers, but very few African Americans.

- The *Morrill Land Grant Act* (1862) encouraged states to use the sale of **federal land grants** to found and maintain agricultural and technical colleges. These schools not only educated farmers, engineers, and scientists, but they also became centers of research and innovation.

- The *Pacific Railway Act* (1862) authorized the building of a transcontinental railroad over a northern route in order to link the economies of California and the Western territories with the Eastern states.

While four years of nearly total war, the tragic human loss of 750,000 lives and an estimated $15 billion in war costs and property losses had enormous effects on the nation, far greater changes were set in motion. The Civil War destroyed slavery and devastated the Southern economy. It also acted as a catalyst to transform America into a complex modern industrial society of capital, technology, national organizations, and large corporations.

Assassination of Lincoln

Only a month before Lee's surrender, Lincoln delivered one of his greatest speeches, the second inaugural address. He urged that the defeated South be treated benevolently, "with malice toward none; with charity for all."

On April 14, John Wilkes Booth, an embittered actor and Confederate sympathizer, shot and killed the president while he was attending a performance at Ford's Theater in Washington. On the same night, a co-conspirator attacked and wounded Secretary of State William Seward. These shocking events aroused the fury of Northerners when the Confederates most needed a sympathetic hearing. The loss of Lincoln's leadership was widely mourned, but the extent of the loss was not fully appreciated until the two sections of a reunited country had to cope with the problems of Reconstruction.

REFLECT ON THE LEARNING OBJECTIVE

1. Explain how Lincoln's governance during the Civil War influenced American principles during the war.

KEY TERMS BY THEME

Economic Growth (WXT)
greenbacks
Morrill Tariff Act
Morrill Land Grant Act
federal land grants
Pacific Railway Act

Free Land (MIG)
Homestead Act (1862)

War and the Law (POL)
habeas corpus
Confiscation Acts
Emancipation Proclamation
Ex Parte Milligan

Wartime Politics (POL)
Copperheads

Social Impact (NAT, SOC)
Gettysburg Address
Massachusetts 54th
  Regiment

MULTIPLE-CHOICE QUESTIONS

Questions 1–3 refer to the map below.

UNITED STATES, JULY 1861

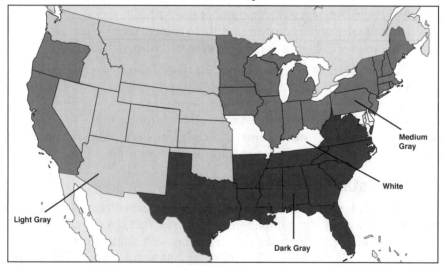

1. In July of 1861, President Lincoln was particularly concerned about how his policies on slavery would affect which areas?
   (A) The states in white because they were slave states that remained in the Union
   (B) The states in medium gray because they were home to most of his political supporters
   (C) The states in dark gray because he thought he could persuade them to rejoin the Union
   (D) The region in light gray because it consisted of territories that had not yet become states

2. Which of the following statements best describes the states in medium gray?
   (A) Most people lived in large cities.
   (B) Most people advocated abolition of slavery.
   (C) They lacked good river transportation.
   (D) They included most of the country's population.

3. Which of the following statements best describes the states in dark gray?
   (A) They were economically self-sufficient.
   (B) They were well connected by railroads.
   (C) They were fighting a defensive war.
   (D) They had a strong navy.

SHORT-ANSWER QUESTION

Use complete sentences; an outline or bulleted list alone is not acceptable.

1. Answer (a), (b), and (c).
   (a) Briefly explain ONE specific action of President Abraham Lincoln during the Civil War that supports the view that he was one of the most democratic presidents.
   (b) Briefly explain ONE specific action of President Abraham Lincoln during the Civil War that supports the view that he was one of the most autocratic presidents.
   (c) Briefly explain how ONE president who came before Lincoln was both democratic and autocratic.

Reconstruction

"The whole fabric of Southern society must be changed, and never can it be done if this opportunity is lost. Without this, this government can never be, as it never has been, a true republic."

Thaddeus Stevens, September 6, 1865

Learning Objective: Explain the effects of government policy during Reconstruction on society from 1865 to 1877.

The silencing of the cannons of war left the victorious United States with immense challenges. How would the South rebuild its shattered society and economy after four years of war? What would be the place in that society of 4 million freed Black Americans? How responsible was the federal government for helping former slaves adjust to freedom? Should the states of the Confederacy be treated as though they had never left the Union—Lincoln's position—or as conquered territory under military occupation? Under what conditions would those states be fully accepted as equal partners in the Union? Finally, who had the authority to decide these questions, the president or Congress?

Postwar Conditions

Slavery gradually crumbled as African Americans escaped to Union-controlled territory. The last people to hear they were free lived in Texas. The date they heard the news, June 19th, became a day for celebration known as Juneteenth.

Most freedpeople began their free lives with no money, no land, and no formal education. Near the end of the war, some freedpeople in South Carolina and Georgia received "40 acres and a mule" under an order from Union General William Sherman. However, this order was soon cancelled by President Andrew Johnson. The land they had was taken away from them.

The South was devastated by the war. It had lost about one-third of its horses, cattle, and hogs. Roads, bridges, railroad tracks, and fencing had been destroyed. Though people had not died from mass starvation as often happens in war, chronic food shortages, particularly for African Americans, left many in poor health and susceptible to epidemic diseases.

The regional, political, and economic conflicts that existed before and during the Civil War continued after the war. Northern Republicans wanted to continue the economic progress begun during the war. Southern aristocrats still wanted low-cost labor to work their plantations. The freedmen and freedwomen hoped for independence and equal rights. However, traditional beliefs limited the actions of the federal government. Concepts of limited government and states' rights discouraged national leaders from taking bold action. Little economic help was given to White or Black Southerners, as most Americans believed that people had an opportunity and a responsibility to care for themselves. The physical rebuilding of the South was left up to the states and individuals, while the federal government concentrated on political issues.

Reconstruction Plans of Lincoln and Johnson

Throughout his presidency, Abraham Lincoln held firmly to the belief that the Southern states could not constitutionally leave the Union and therefore never did leave. He viewed the Confederates as only a disloyal minority. After Lincoln's assassination, **Andrew Johnson** attempted to carry out Lincoln's plan for the political **Reconstruction** of the 11 former states of the Confederacy.

Lincoln's Policies

Lincoln believed the Southern states could regain their full place in the Union by meeting a minimum test of political loyalty.

Proclamation of Amnesty and Reconstruction (1863) As early as December 1863, Lincoln set up a process for political reconstruction of the state governments in the South so that Unionists were in charge rather than secessionists. The president's **Proclamation of Amnesty and Reconstruction** was simple:

- Full presidential pardons would be granted to most Confederates who (1) took an oath of allegiance to the Union and the U.S. Constitution, and (2) accepted the emancipation of slaves.

- A state government could be reestablished and accepted as legitimate by the U.S. president as soon as at least 10 percent of the voters in that state took the loyalty oath.

In practice, Lincoln meant that each Southern state would be required to rewrite its state constitution to abolish slavery. Lincoln's seemingly lenient policy was designed both to shorten the war and to give added weight to his Emancipation Proclamation.

Wade-Davis Bill (1864) Many Republicans in Congress objected to Lincoln's 10-percent plan, arguing that it would allow supposedly reconstructed state governments to be dominated by disloyal secessionists. In 1864, Congress passed the **Wade-Davis Bill**, which required 50 percent of the voters of a state to take a loyalty oath and permitted only non-Confederates to vote for a new state constitution. Lincoln pocket-vetoed the bill after Congress adjourned. Congress was ready to reassert its powers, as Congresses usually do after a war.

Freedmen's Bureau In March 1865, Congress created an important new agency: the Bureau of Refugees, Freedmen, and Abandoned Lands, or **Freedmen's Bureau**. The bureau acted as a welfare agency, providing food, shelter, and medical aid for both Black and White Americans left destitute by the war. At first, the Freedmen's Bureau had authority to resettle freedpeople on confiscated farmlands in the South. Its efforts at resettlement, however, were later frustrated when President Johnson pardoned Confederate owners of the confiscated lands, and courts restored most of the lands to their original owners.

The bureau's greatest success was in education. Under the able leadership of General Oliver O. Howard, it established nearly 3,000 schools for freedpeople, including several colleges. Before federal funding was stopped in 1870, the bureau's schools taught an estimated 200,000 African Americans how to read.

Johnson and Reconstruction

Andrew Johnson's origins were as humble as Lincoln's. A self-taught tailor, he rose in Tennessee politics by championing poor Whites in conflict with rich planters. Johnson was the only senator from a Confederate state who remained loyal to the Union. He was appointed Tennessee's governor when it was occupied by Union troops. Johnson was a Southern Democrat, but Republicans picked him to encourage pro-Union Democrats to vote for Lincoln. Johnson ended up being the wrong man for the job. As a White supremacist, he was bound to clash with Republicans in Congress who believed that the war was fought not just to preserve the Union but also to liberate African Americans from slavery.

Johnson's Reconstruction Policy At first, many Republicans in Congress welcomed Johnson's presidency because of his animosity toward the Southern aristocrats who had led the Confederacy. In May 1865, Johnson issued his own Reconstruction plan. In addition to Lincoln's terms, it provided for the disenfranchisement (loss of the right to vote and hold office) of (1) all former leaders and officeholders of the Confederacy and (2) Confederates with more than $20,000 in taxable property. However, the president could grant individual pardons to "disloyal" Southerners. This was an escape clause for the wealthy planters, and Johnson made use of it. As a result of his pardons, many former Confederate leaders were back in office by the fall of 1865.

Johnson's Vetoes One sign of the battle between Congress and the presidents was his use of the veto. The three presidents before Johnson vetoed a total of 23 bills. In his one term, he vetoed 29 bills. Johnson alienated even moderate Republicans in early 1866 with vetoes of two bills. One increased the services and protection of the Freedmen's Bureau. The other was a civil rights bill that nullified the Black Codes and guaranteed full citizenship and equal rights to African Americans. The vetoes marked the end of the first round of Reconstruction. During this round, Presidents Lincoln and Johnson had restored the 11 former Confederate states to the Union, ex-Confederates had returned to high offices, and Southern states began passing Black Codes to restrict the rights of former slaves.

Congressional Reconstruction

By the spring of 1866, the angry response of many members of Congress to Johnson's policies led to the second round of Reconstruction. This one was dominated by Congress and featured policies that were harsher on Southern Whites and more protective of freed African Americans.

Radical Republicans

Republicans had long been divided between (1) moderates, who were chiefly concerned with economic gains for the White middle class, and (2) radicals, who championed civil rights for Black citizens. Although most Republicans were moderates, several became more radical in 1866, partly out of fear that a reunified Democratic Party might again become dominant. After all, now that the federal census counted all people equally (no longer applying the old three-fifths rule for enslaved persons), the South would have more representatives in Congress than before the war and more strength in the Electoral College.

The leading Radical Republican in the Senate was **Charles Sumner** of Massachusetts. In the House, Thaddeus Stevens of Pennsylvania hoped to revolutionize Southern society through a period of military rule in which African Americans could exercise their civil rights, attend schools operated by the federal government, and take ownership of lands confiscated from the planters. Many Radical Republicans endorsed several liberal causes: women's suffrage, rights for labor unions, and civil rights for Northern African Americans. Although their program was never fully implemented, the Radical Republicans struggled to extend equal rights to all Americans.

Thirteenth Amendment Laws, but not the U.S. Constitution, banned slavery. To free all enslaved people in the border states, the country needed to ratify an amendment. Even the abolitionists gave Lincoln credit for playing an active role in the political struggle to secure enough votes in Congress to pass the **13th Amendment**. By December 1865 (months after Lincoln's death), this amendment abolishing slavery was ratified by the required number of states. Its language was clear: "Neither slavery nor involuntary servitude, except as a punishment for crime whereof the party shall have been duly convicted, shall exist within the United States, or any place subject to their jurisdiction."

After the adoption of the 13th Amendment in 1865, 4 million people (3.5 million in the Confederate states and 500,000 in the border states) were "freedmen" and "freedwomen." For these people and their descendants, economic hardship and political oppression would continue for generations. Even so, the end of slavery represented a momentous step. Suddenly, formerly enslaved people who had no rights could claim protection by the U.S. Constitution and had open-ended possibilities of freedom.

Civil Rights Act of 1866 Among the first actions in Congressional Reconstruction were votes to override, with some modifications, Johnson's vetoes of both the Freedmen's Bureau Act and the first Civil Rights Act. The Civil Rights Act pronounced that all African Americans were U.S. citizens (thereby nullifying the decision in the Dred Scott case) and attempted to provide a legal shield against the operation of the Southern states' Black Codes. Fearing that the law could be repealed if the Democrats ever won control of

Congress, Republicans looked for a more permanent solution in the form of a constitutional amendment.

Fourteenth Amendment In June 1866, Congress passed and sent to the states an amendment, ratified in 1868, that had immediate and even greater long-term significance:

- It declared that all persons born or naturalized in the United States were citizens.
- It obligated the states to respect the rights of U.S. citizens and provide them with "**equal protection of the laws**" and "**due process of law.**"

For the first time, the Constitution required *states* as well as the federal government to uphold the rights of citizens. The amendment's key clauses about citizenship and rights produced mixed results in 19th-century courtrooms. However, in the 1950s and later, the Supreme Court used the power of the federal government to protect individuals from encroachment of their constitutional rights by state and local governments, making "equal protection of the laws" and the "due process" clause the keystone of civil rights for minorities, women, children, disabled persons, and those accused of crimes.

Other parts of the **14th Amendment** applied specifically to Congress's plan of Reconstruction. These clauses:

- disqualified former Confederate political leaders from holding either state or federal offices
- repudiated the debts of the defeated governments of the Confederacy
- penalized a state if it kept any eligible person from voting by reducing that state's proportional representation in Congress and the Electoral College

Report of the Joint Committee In June 1866, a joint committee of the House and the Senate issued a report declaring that the reorganized Confederate states were not entitled to representation in Congress. Therefore, those elected from the South as senators and representatives should not be permitted to take their seats. The report further asserted that Congress, not the president, had the authority to determine the conditions for allowing reconstructed states to rejoin the Union. By this report, Congress officially rejected the presidential plan of Reconstruction and promised to substitute its own plan, part of which was embodied in the 14th Amendment.

The Election of 1866 Unable to work with Congress, Johnson took to the road in the fall of 1866 to attack his opponents. His speeches appealed to the racial prejudices of White citizens by arguing that equal rights for Black Americans would result in an "Africanized" society. Republicans counterattacked by accusing Johnson of being a drunkard and a traitor. They appealed to anti-Southern prejudices by "waving the bloody shirt"—inflaming the anger of Northern voters by reminding them of the hardships of war.

Republican propaganda emphasized that Southerners were Democrats and, by a jump in logic, branded the Democrats a party of rebellion and treason.

Election results gave the Republicans an overwhelming victory. After 1866, Johnson's political adversaries—both moderate and Radical Republicans—had more than a two-thirds majority in both the House and the Senate.

Reconstruction Acts of 1867 Over Johnson's vetoes, Congress passed three Reconstruction Acts in 1867 that placed the South under military occupation. The acts divided the former Confederate states into five military districts, each under the control of the Union army. In addition, the acts increased the requirements for gaining readmission to the Union: an ex-Confederate state had to ratify the 14th Amendment and place guarantees in its constitution to grant the franchise (right to vote) to all adult males, regardless of race.

Impeachment of Andrew Johnson

Also in 1867, Congress passed the **Tenure of Office Act** over Johnson's veto. This law prohibited the president from removing a federal official or military commander without Senate approval. The purpose of the law was strictly political. Congress wanted to protect the Radical Republicans in Johnson's cabinet, such as Secretary of War **Edwin Stanton**, who was in charge of the military governments in the South.

Johnson challenged the constitutionality of the new law by dismissing Stanton. The House responded by impeaching Johnson. He was charged with 11 "high crimes and misdemeanors," thus becoming the first president to be impeached. In 1868, after a three-month Senate trial, Johnson's foes fell one vote short of the two-thirds vote needed to remove him from office.

Reforms After Grant's Election

The impeachment and trial of Andrew Johnson occurred in 1868, a presidential election year. At their convention, the Democrats nominated another candidate, Horatio Seymour, so that Johnson's presidency would have ended soon in any case, with or without a conviction in Congress.

The Election of 1868 At their presidential convention, the Republicans turned to a war hero, General Ulysses S. Grant, even though he had no political experience. Despite Grant's popularity in the North, he managed to win only 300,000 more popular votes than his Democratic opponent. The votes of 500,000 Black men gave the Republican ticket its margin of victory. Even the most moderate Republicans began to realize that the voting rights of the freedmen needed federal protection if their party hoped to keep control of the White House in future elections.

Fifteenth Amendment Republican majorities in Congress acted quickly in 1869 to secure the vote for African Americans. Adding one more Reconstruction amendment to those already adopted (the 13th Amendment in 1865 and the 14th Amendment in 1868), Congress passed the **15th Amendment**, which prohibited any state from denying or abridging a citizen's right to vote "on account of race, color, or previous condition of servitude." It was ratified in 1870. While it banned open racial discrimination in voting laws, it did not prevent states from passing other restrictions on voting rights that disproportionately affected African Americans.

Civil Rights Act of 1875 The last civil rights reform passed by Congress during Reconstruction was the Civil Rights Act of 1875. This guaranteed equal accommodations in public places (hotels, railroads, and theaters) and prohibited courts from excluding African Americans from juries. The law was poorly enforced, as moderate and conservative Republicans tired of trying to reform an unwilling South and feared losing White votes in the North. By 1877, Reconstruction was abandoned by Congress.

Reconstruction in the South

During the second round of Reconstruction by Congress, the Republican Party in the South dominated the governments of the former Confederate states. Beginning in 1867, each Republican-controlled government was under the military protection of the Army until Congress was satisfied that a state had met its Reconstruction requirements. Then the troops were withdrawn. The period of Republican rule in a Southern state lasted from as little as one year (Tennessee) to as much as nine years (Florida), depending on how long it took conservative Democrats to regain control.

CONGRESSIONAL RECONSTRUCTION 1865–1877

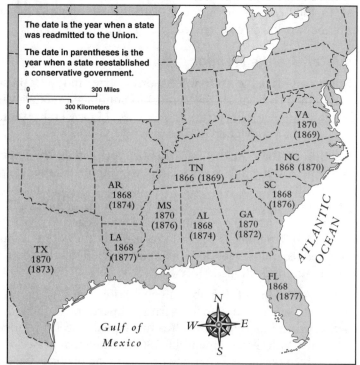

Composition of the Reconstruction Governments

In every Republican state government in the South except South Carolina, Whites were in the majority in both houses of the legislature. In South Carolina, freedmen controlled the lower house in 1873. Republican legislators included native-born White Southerners, freedmen, and recently arrived Northerners.

"Scalawags" and "Carpetbaggers" Democratic opponents derisively called Southern Republicans "**scalawags**" and Northern newcomers "**carpetbaggers**" (after cheap luggage made from carpet fabric). Southern Whites who supported the Republican governments were usually former Whigs who were interested in economic development for their states and peace between the sections. Northerners went south after the war for various reasons. Some were investors interested in setting up new businesses, while others were ministers and teachers with humanitarian goals. Some went simply to plunder.

African American Legislators Most African Americans who held elective office in the reconstructed state governments were educated property holders who took moderate positions on most issues. During the Reconstruction era, Republicans in the South sent two African Americans, **Blanche K. Bruce** and **Hiram Revels**, to the Senate and more than a dozen African Americans to the House of Representatives. Revels was elected in 1870 to take the Mississippi Senate seat once held by Jefferson Davis. Seeing African Americans and former slaves in positions of power caused bitter resentment among ex-Confederates.

African Americans Adjusting to Freedom

Undoubtedly, the Southerners who had the greatest adjustment to make during the Reconstruction era were the freedmen and freedwomen. Having been so recently emancipated from slavery, they were faced with the challenges of securing their economic survival as well as their political rights as citizens.

Building Black Communities Freedom meant many things to African Americans: reuniting families, learning to read and write, or migrating to cities where "freedom was freer." Most of all, formerly enslaved people viewed emancipation as an opportunity for achieving independence from White control. This drive for autonomy was most evident in the founding of hundreds of independent African American churches after the war. By the hundreds of thousands, Black members left White-dominated churches for the Negro Baptist and African Methodist Episcopal churches. During Reconstruction, Black ministers emerged as leaders in the African American community.

The desire for education induced large numbers of African Americans to use their scarce resources to establish independent schools for their children and to pay educated African Americans to become their teachers. Black colleges such as Howard, Atlanta, Fisk, and Morehouse were established during Reconstruction to prepare African American ministers and teachers.

Another aspect of African Americans' search for independence and self-sufficiency was the decision of many freedpeople to migrate away from the South and establish new Black communities in frontier states such as Kansas.

PERCENTAGE OF SCHOOL-AGE CHILDREN ENROLLED, 1850 TO 1880		
Year	White	African American
1850	56	2
1860	60	2
1870	54	10
1880	62	34

Source: U.S. Bureau of the Census. *Historical Statistics of the United States, Colonial Times to 1970*

The North During Reconstruction

The North's economy in the postwar years continued to be driven by the Industrial Revolution and the probusiness policies of the Republicans. As the South struggled to reorganize its labor system, Northerners focused on railroads, steel, labor problems, and money.

Greed and Corruption

During the Grant administration, as the material interests of the age took center stage, the idealism of Lincoln's generation and the Radical Republicans' crusade for civil rights were pushed aside.

Rise of the Spoilsmen In the early 1870s, Republican Party leadership passed from reformers (**Thaddeus Stevens**, Charles Sumner, and **Benjamin Wade**) to political manipulators such as senators Roscoe Conkling of New York and James Blaine of Maine. These politicians were masters of the game of **patronage**—giving jobs and government favors (spoils) to their supporters.

Corruption in Business and Government The postwar years were notorious for the corrupt schemes devised by business bosses and political bosses to enrich themselves at the public's expense. For example, in 1869, Wall Street financiers **Jay Gould** and James Fisk obtained the help of President Grant's brother-in-law in a scheme to corner the gold market. The Treasury Department broke the scheme, but not before Gould had made a huge profit.

In the **Crédit Mobilier** affair, insiders gave stock to influential members of Congress to avoid investigation of the profits they were making—as high as 348 percent—from government subsidies for building the transcontinental railroad. In the case of the Whiskey Ring, federal revenue agents conspired with the liquor industry to defraud the government of millions in taxes. While Grant himself did not personally profit from the corruption, his loyalty to dishonest men around him badly tarnished his presidency.

Local politics in the Grant years were equally scandalous. In New York City, **William Tweed**, the boss of the local Democratic Party, masterminded dozens of schemes for helping himself and his cronies steal $200 million from New York's taxpayers before *The New York Times* and the cartoonist **Thomas Nast** exposed "Boss" Tweed and brought about his arrest and imprisonment in 1871.

The Election of 1872

The scandals of the Grant administration drove reform-minded Republicans to break with the party in 1872 and select **Horace Greeley**, editor of the *New York Tribune,* as their presidential candidate. The **Liberal Republicans** advocated civil-service reform, an end to railroad subsidies, withdrawal of troops from the South, reduced tariffs, and freer trade. Surprisingly, the Democrats also nominated Greeley. The regular Republicans countered by merely "waving the bloody shirt" again—and it worked. Grant was reelected in a landslide.

The Panic of 1873

Grant's second term began with an economic disaster that rendered thousands of Northern laborers both jobless and homeless. Overspeculation by financiers and overbuilding by industry and railroads led to widespread business failures and depression. Debtors on the farms and in the cities argued about what should be done. Grant finally adopted the ideas of Eastern bankers and creditors, setting a new trend for the Republican Party. Black Southerners were the biggest losers, as preoccupation with the financial crisis diverted the North's attention away from what was happening in the South.

Women's Changing Roles

Every part of American society away from the battlefield was touched by the war. The impact of the war on the roles and opportunities of women was significant.

The absence of millions of men from the fields and factories added to the responsibilities of women in all regions. They stepped into the vacuum created by the war, operating farms and plantations and taking factory jobs customarily held by men. In addition, women played a critical role as military nurses and as volunteers in soldiers' aid societies. When the war ended and the war veterans returned home, most urban women vacated their jobs in government and industry, while rural women gladly accepted male assistance on the farm.

Women's Suffrage

The responsibilities undertaken by women during the war also boosted demands for equal voting rights for women. Some members of the women's suffrage movement who had worked tirelessly for the abolition of slavery opposed the passage of the 14th and 15th Amendments. While they supported extending the franchise to African Americans, they objected to the fact that these amendments specifically limited it to men. Ironically, this was the first time sex was mentioned in the Constitution, in an amendment meant to extend rights but that ended up discriminating against half the nation's citizens.

In 1869, Wyoming Territory became the first territory or state to grant women full suffrage rights. The suffragists' goal would not be achieved until women's efforts in another war—World War I— finally convinced enough male conservatives to adopt the 19th Amendment, with wording that echoed that of the 15th Amendment.

1. Explain the consequences of government policy during Reconstruction on society from 1865 to 1877.

KEY TERMS BY THEME

Equality (NAT, POL)
13th Amendment
Civil Rights Act of 1866
14th Amendment
equal protection of the
   laws
due process of law
15th Amendment
Civil Rights Act of 1875

Corruption (WXT, POL)
Jay Gould
Crédit Mobilier
William Tweed

Politics (POL)
spoilsmen

patronage
Thomas Nast
Horace Greeley
Liberal Republicans
Panic of 1873

**Reconstruction
   (POL, SOC, ARC)**
Reconstruction
Proclamation of Amnesty
   and Reconstruction
Wade-Davis Bill
Andrew Johnson
Freedmen's Bureau
congressional
   Reconstruction

Radical Republicans
Charles Sumner
Thaddeus Stephens
Benjamin Wade
Reconstruction Acts
Tenure of Office Act
Edwin Stanton
impeachment
scalawags
carpetbaggers
Blanche K. Bruce
Hiram Revels

Social Impact (NAT, SOC)
women's suffrage

MULTIPLE-CHOICE QUESTIONS

Questions 1–2 refer to the following excerpt.

"All persons born or naturalized in the United States . . . are citizens. . . . No State shall make or enforce any law which shall abridge the privileges or immunities of citizens . . . nor shall any State deprive any person of life, liberty, or property, without due process; nor deny . . . equal protection of the laws.

Representatives shall be apportioned among the several States . . . counting the whole number of persons in each State, excluding Indians not taxed. But when the right to vote at any election . . . thereof, is denied to any of the male inhabitants . . . being twenty-one years of age, and citizens . . . or in any way abridged, except for . . . crime, . . . the basis of representation therein shall be reduced. . . .

No person shall . . . hold any office . . . who, having previously taken an oath . . . shall have engaged in insurrection or rebellion against the same . . . But Congress may by a vote of two-thirds of each House, remove such disability."

14th Amendment, Constitution of the United States, July 9, 1868

1. In proclaiming that all persons born in the United States were citizens, the 14th Amendment directly repudiated which of the following?

    (A) Compromise of 1850

    (B) Dred Scott decision

    (C) Johnson's Reconstruction plan

    (D) Wade-Davis Bill

2. Which of the following provisions would be the basis of one of the most contentious judicial issues of the late 19th and early 20th centuries?

    (A) "nor deny . . . equal protection of the laws"

    (B) "Representatives shall be apportioned"

    (C) "the basis of representation therein shall be reduced"

    (D) "shall have engaged in insurrection or rebellion"

SHORT-ANSWER QUESTIONS

Use complete sentences; an outline or bulleted list alone is not acceptable.

1. Answer (a), (b), and (c).

    (a) Briefly explain how federal government actions taken during Reconstruction were similar to federal government actions taken during the Civil War.

    (b) Briefly explain how federal government actions taken during Reconstruction were different from federal government actions taken during the Civil War.

    (c) Briefly explain ONE factor that accounts for the difference in federal government actions during the two periods.

2. Answer (a), (b), and (c).

    (a) Briefly explain ONE specific part or aspect of President Lincoln's plan for Reconstruction.

    (b) Briefly explain ONE specific part or aspect of President Johnson's approach to Reconstruction.

    (c) Briefly explain ONE specific example of the efforts of formerly enslaved African Americans to use their freedom during the period of Reconstruction.

Topic 5.11

Failure of Reconstruction

Though slavery was abolished, the wrongs of my people were not ended. Though they were not slaves, they were not yet quite free.

Frederick Douglass, 1882

Learning Objective: Explain how and why Reconstruction resulted in continuity and change in regional and national understandings of what it meant to be American.

Views of Reconstruction have varied greatly. Many historians have seen it as a missed opportunity to promote racial equality. However, some have pointed out that the institutions and amendments from the Reconstruction era provided the foundation for the civil rights movement that emerged nearly a century after the Civil War ended.

Lincoln's Last Speech

In his last public address (April 11, 1865), Lincoln encouraged Northerners to accept Louisiana as a reconstructed state. (Louisiana had already drawn up a new constitution that abolished slavery in the state and provided for African Americans' education.) The president also addressed the question—highly controversial at the time—of whether freedmen should be granted the right to vote. Lincoln said: "I myself prefer that it were *now* conferred on the very intelligent, and on those who serve our cause as soldiers." Three days later, Lincoln's evolving plans for Reconstruction were ended with his assassination. His last speech suggested that, had he lived, he probably would have moved closer to the position taken by the progressive, or Radical, Republicans. In any event, hope for lasting reform was dealt a devastating blow by the sudden removal of Lincoln's skillful leadership.

Evaluating the Republican Record

As mentioned in Topic 5.10, Congress and presidents fought over specific amendments, laws, and actions. In evaluating Reconstruction, it is particularly useful to look at the controversial record of the Republicans during their brief control of Southern state politics. Did they abuse their power for selfish ends (corruption and plunder), or did they govern responsibly in the public interest? They did some of each.

Accomplishments On the positive side, Republican legislators liberalized state constitutions in the South by providing for universal male suffrage, property rights for women, debt relief, and modern penal codes. They promoted the building of railroads, roads, bridges, and other internal improvements. They established such institutions as hospitals, asylums, and homes for the disabled. The reformers provided for state-supported public-school systems, which benefited Whites and African Americans alike. They paid for all of this by overhauling the tax system and selling bonds.

Failures Long after Reconstruction ended, many Southerners and some Northern historians continued to depict Republican rule as utterly wasteful and corrupt. Some instances of graft and wasteful spending did occur, as Republican politicians took advantage of their power to take kickbacks and bribes from contractors who did business with the state. However, corruption occurred throughout the country, in Northern states and cities as well. No geographic section, political party, or ethnic group was immune to the decline in ethics in government during the postwar era.

The End of Reconstruction

The way Reconstruction ended shows how it failed to fulfill the nation's needs. During Grant's second term, it was apparent that Reconstruction had entered a third phase, which would be its final one. With Radical Republicanism on the wane, Southern conservatives—known as **redeemers**—took control of one state government after another. This process was completed by 1877. The redeemers had different backgrounds, but they agreed on their political program: states' rights, reduced taxes and spending on social programs, and White supremacy.

White Supremacy and the Ku Klux Klan

During the period that Republicans controlled state governments in the South, some Whites organized secret societies to intimidate African Americans and White reformers. The most prominent of these was the **Ku Klux Klan**, founded in 1867 by a former Confederate general, Nathaniel Bedford Forrest. The "invisible empire" burned Black-owned buildings and flogged and murdered several thousand freedmen to keep them from exercising their voting rights. To give federal authorities the power to stop Ku Klux Klan violence and to protect the civil rights of citizens, Congress passed the **Force Acts** of 1870 and 1871.

Southern Governments Just eight months after Johnson took office in 1865, all 11 of the ex-Confederate states qualified under the president's Reconstruction plan to become part of the Union. The Southern states drew up constitutions that repudiated secession, negated the debts of the Confederate government, and ratified the 13th Amendment abolishing slavery. On the other hand, none of the new constitutions extended voting rights to Blacks citizens. Furthermore, to the dismay of Republicans, former leaders of the Confederacy won seats in Congress. For example, Alexander Stephens, the former Confederate vice president, was elected U.S. senator from Georgia.

Black Codes The Republicans became further disillusioned with Johnson as Southern state legislatures adopted **Black Codes** that restricted the rights and movements of African Americans:

- They could not rent land or nor borrow money to buy land.
- They could not testity against Whites in court.
- They had to sign work agreements or they could be arrested for vagrancy. Under this contract-labor system, African Americans worked cotton fields under White supervision for deferred wages.

The costs of being convicted of any crime could be disastrous for an African American. The 13th Amendment had abolished slavery "except as a punishment for crime." Hence, a person convicted of a minor or even made-up offense could be rented from the government by a landowner or business and used as essentially slave labor.

Sharecropping The South's agricultural economy was in turmoil after the war, in part because landowners had lost their compulsory labor force. At first, White landowners attempted to force freed African Americans into signing contracts to work the fields. These contracts set terms that bound the signer to almost permanent and unrestricted labor. African Americans' insistence on autonomy, however, combined with changes in the postwar economy, led White landowners to adopt a system based on tenancy and sharecropping. Under **sharecropping**, the landlord provided the seed and needed farm supplies in return for a share (usually half) of the harvest.

While sharecropping gave poor people of all races in the rural South the opportunity to work a piece of land for themselves, sharecroppers usually remained dependent on the landowners or in debt to local merchants. By 1880, no more than 5 percent of Southern African Americans owned their own land. Sharecropping had evolved into a new form of servitude.

The Amnesty Act of 1872

Seven years after Lee's surrender at Appomattox, many Northerners were ready to put the war behind them. In 1872 Congress passed a general Amnesty Act that removed the last restrictions on ex-Confederates, except for the top leaders. The chief political consequence of the act was to allow Southern conservatives to vote for Democrats and thus to retake control of state governments.

The Election of 1876

By 1876, federal troops had been withdrawn from all Southern states except— South Carolina, Florida, and Louisiana. The Democrats had returned to power in all of the other former Confederate states. This was important in the presidential election.

At their convention, the Republicans looked for someone untouched by the corruption of the Grant administration. They nominated the governor of Ohio, **Rutherford B. Hayes**. The Democrats chose New York's reform governor,

Samuel J. Tilden, who had fought the corrupt Tweed Ring. In the popular votes, the Democrats won a clear majority and expected to put Tilden in the White House. However, in three Southern states, the returns were contested. To win the election, Tilden needed only one *electoral* vote from the contested returns of South Carolina, Florida, and Louisiana.

A special electoral commission was created to determine who was entitled to the disputed votes of the three states. In a straight party vote of 8–7, the commission gave all the votes to Hayes, the Republican. Outraged Democrats threatened to filibuster the results and send the election to the House of Representatives, which they controlled.

The Compromise of 1877

Leaders of the two parties worked out an informal deal. The Democrats would allow Hayes to become president. In return, he would (1) immediately end federal support for the Republicans in the South, and (2) support the building of a Southern transcontinental railroad. Shortly after his inauguration, President Hayes fulfilled his part in the Compromise of 1877 and promptly withdrew the last of the federal troops protecting African Americans and other Republicans.

The end of a federal military presence in the South was not the only thing that brought Reconstruction to an end. In a series of decisions in the 1880s and 1890s, the Supreme Court struck down a number of Reconstruction laws that protected Black citizens from discrimination. Even though some Southern leaders called for a "New South" based on industrial development, most Southerners, regardless of race, remained poor farmers. The region fell further behind the rest of the nation in prosperity.

By 1877 the nation was more interested in its recent Centennial celebration and was again looking westward and for industrial growth. Tired of Reconstruction, the majority left it to the historians to decide the success or failure of Reconstruction.

HISTORICAL PERSPECTIVES: *DID RECONSTRUCTION FAIL?*

Historical opinions on Reconstruction have changed dramatically over the past century. Scholars have disagreed over how well it worked and who deserves praise or blame for what happened.

Blame for Too Much Equality Generations of both Northern and Southern historians, starting with William Dunning in the early 1900s, portrayed Reconstruction as a failure. Dunning and others charged that illiterate African Americans and corrupt Northern carpetbaggers abused the rights of Southern Whites and stole vast sums from the state governments. These historians blamed the Radical Republicans for bringing on these conditions by their desire to punish the South and to give formerly enslaved people too many rights. The Dunning school of historical thought provided a rationale for the racial segregation in the early 20th century. It was given popular expression in a 1915 movie, D. W. Griffith's *The Birth of a Nation,* which pictured the Ku

Klux Klansmen as heroes coming to the rescue of Southern Whites oppressed by vindictive Northern radicals and African Americans.

Praise for Accomplishments African American historians such as W. E. B. Du Bois and John Hope Franklin countered Dunning by highlighting the positive achievements of the Reconstruction governments and Black leaders. Their view was supported and expanded upon in 1965 with the publication of Kenneth Stampp's *Era of Reconstruction.* Other historians of the 1960s and 1970s also stressed the significance of the civil rights legislation passed by the Radical Republicans and pointed out the humanitarian work of Northern reformers.

Blame for Too Little Equality By the 1980s, some historians criticized Congress's approach to Reconstruction, not for being too radical, but for being not radical enough. They argued that Congress failed to provide land for African Americans, which would have enabled them to achieve economic independence. Furthermore, these historians argued, the military occupation of the South should have lasted longer to protect the freedmen's political rights. Eric Foner's comprehensive *Reconstruction: America's Unfinished Revolution* (1988) acknowledged the limitations of Reconstruction in achieving lasting reforms but also pointed out that, in the post-Civil War years, the freedmen and freedwomen established many of the institutions in the African American community upon which later progress depended: churches, schools, universities, and businesses. According to Foner, it took a "second Reconstruction" after World War II (the civil rights movement of the 1950s and 1960s) to achieve the promise of the "first Reconstruction."

Support an Argument *Explain two perspectives on the failures of Reconstruction.*

REFLECT ON THE LEARNING OBJECTIVE

1. Explain how Reconstruction caused both continuity and change in the regional and national views of what it meant to be American.

KEY TERMS BY THEME

Politics (POL)	Reconstruction (POL, SOC, ARC)
redeemers	Ku Klux Klan
Rutherford B. Hayes	Force Acts
Samuel J. Tilden	Black Codes
Election of 1876	sharecropping
Compromise of 1877	Amnesty Act of 1872

Questions 1–3 refer to the map below.

PRESIDENTIAL ELECTION RESULTS, 1876

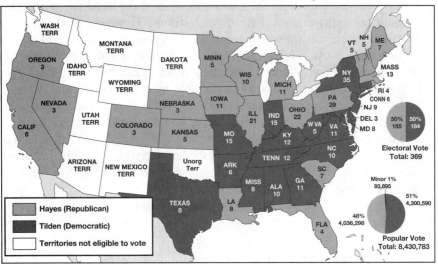

1. Which of the following was most important in enabling the Democratic Party to regain political power in the South?

   (A) The limits on education for the freedpeople

   (B) The restrictions on the voting rights of the freedmen

   (C) The effects of the Panic of 1873

   (D) The impact of the development of sharecropping

2. The victor in the 1876 presidential election was decided based on the recommendation of

   (A) a special electoral commission

   (B) a meeting of state governors

   (C) the Senate

   (D) the Supreme Court

3. Democrats agreed to accept Rutherford B. Hayes as president in 1876 because he agreed to

   (A) support a nationwide Black Code

   (B) remove federal troops from the South

   (C) promote Southern industrial development

   (D) support civil service reform

Use complete sentences; an outline or bulleted list alone is not acceptable.

1. "Alone among the societies that abolished slavery in the nineteenth century, the United States, for a moment, offered the freedmen a measure of political control over their own destinies. However brief its sway, Reconstruction allowed scope for a remarkable political and social mobilization of the black community. It opened doors of opportunity that could never be completely closed. Reconstruction transformed the lives of Southern blacks in ways unmeasurable by statistics and unreachable by law. It raised their expectations and aspirations, redefined their status in relation to the larger society, and allowed space for the creation of institutions that enabled them to survive the repression that followed. And it established constitutional principles of civil and political equality that, while flagrantly violated after Redemption, planted the seeds of future struggle."

> Eric Foner, "The New View of Reconstruction,"
> *American Heritage,* 1983

"Reconstruction, which was far from radical, constituted the most democratic decades of the nineteenth century, South or North, so much so that it amounted to the first progressive era in the nation's history. Just ten years after Supreme Court Chief Justice Roger B. Taney endorsed the expansion of slavery into the western territories and announced that black Americans, even if free born, could not be citizens of the republic, blacks were fighting for the franchise in northern states; battling to integrate streetcars in Charleston, New Orleans, and San Francisco; funding integrated public schools; and voting and standing for office in the erstwhile Confederacy. . . . Black veterans, activists, ministers, assemblymen, registrars, poll workers, editors, and a handful of dedicated white allies risked their lives in this cause, nearly brought down a racist president, but ultimately lost their fight because of white violence."

> Douglas R. Egerton, *The Wars of Reconstruction,* 2014

Using the excerpts, answer (a), (b), and (c).

(a) Briefly explain ONE major difference between Foner's and Egerton's historical interpretations of the success or failure of Reconstruction.

(b) Briefly explain how ONE historical event or development in the period 1863 to 1877 that is not explicitly mentioned in the excerpts could be used to support Foner's interpretation.

(c) Briefly explain how ONE historical event or development in the period 1863 to 1877 that is not explicitly mentioned in the excerpts could be used to support Egerton's interpretation.

Comparison in Period 5

Learning Objective: Compare the relative significance of the effects of the Civil War on American values.

The reasoning process of *comparison* is based on describing similarities and differences between specific historical developments. It helps highlight the many factors that show the effects of the Civil War on American values.

For example, consider the role of Manifest Destiny in influencing Americans and how they viewed slavery. Use *historical reasoning* to understand how expansion affected those who wanted new land and the expansion of slavery as opposed to those who wanted to abolish slavery or to reserve western lands for White settlers as the nation extended its borders. For some on each side, this was a question supported by *historical evidence* from many areas including economic, cultural (religious), and regional interests.

The development of distinct views on slavery and the Civil War continued through Reconstruction. Presidents Lincoln and Johnson proposed quick reunification and forgiveness of the former Confederates. In contrast, Radical Republicans wanted to control the rebels and protect the rights of those formerly enslaved. What was the general reaction of the majority of Americans? Overall, the country supported equal rights as reflected in the 13th, 14th, and 15th Amendments, yet many people supported or at least accepted Black Codes and the idea of White supremacy. Reasoned comparison of the evidence is needed to understand American values during this period.

QUESTIONS ABOUT COMPARISON

Use the questions below to make a historically defensible claim.

1. Explain the extent to which people in the North and South held different views on Manifest Destiny. For example, compare how Northerners viewed expansion as new lands for immigrants and the market revolution while Southerners saw it as a way to spread slavery.

2. Explain the extent of the impact on the country of parallel efforts by Northerners and Southerners to compromise over the issue of slavery in the 1840s and 1850s. For example, compare the acceptance by Northerners and Southerners of banning slave trading in Washington, D.C., but allowing ownership of enslaved people to continue.

An important part of the skill of argumentation is being able to respond to a claim or argument that a source makes. You can usually respond in three ways:

- **Support a claim:** This means you provide reasons, quotations, facts, statistics, visuals, or other evidence to back up the claim. This evidence should be logical, relevant, and from a reliable source.

- **Modify a claim:** When you modify a claim, you provide evidence that part of it is true and part of it is false. Or perhaps part is relevant and part is not relevant, or part is accurate and part is exaggerated.

- **Refute a claim:** This means you provide evidence that the claim is not true. For instance, you might provide different statistics from a more reliable source, or an eyewitness account that contradicts the claim.

Consider how one argument might be supported, modified, or refuted.

Argument: Abraham Lincoln's performance in the Lincoln-Douglas debates made it a certainty that he would become president.

- **Statement 1:** After the debates, Lincoln lost the election to Douglas.

- **Statement 2:** Lincoln's ideas and performance made him well-known.

- **Statement 3:** Although Lincoln won the Republican nomination in 1860, he had to run against candidates from three other parties.

Which statement supports the argument, which modifies it, and which refutes it? Take a few moments to decide before reading further.

Statement 1 refutes the argument by pointing out that Lincoln lost the election. Statement 2 supports the argument. If the debates had interested local voters only, then Lincoln would not have become well known nationally. Statement 3 qualifies the argument. People often assume that there have always been two parties in U.S. politics, but there have at times been more than that.

Read the argument and statements. Then answer the questions.

Argument: Lincoln's handling of the crisis at Fort Sumter showed his willingness to plunge the country into civil war.

- **Statement 1:** Lincoln said, "The government will not assail you. You can have no conflict without being yourselves the aggressors."

- **Statement 2:** Lincoln chose to resupply the fort even though it was unfinished and already obsolete.

- **Statement 3:** Lincoln did not abandon the fort, but he did not send troops to it either. He merely sent supplies to the soldiers already there.

1. Which statement supports the claim? Explain your answer.

2. Which statement modifies the claim? Explain your answer.

3. Which statement refutes the claim? Explain your answer.

WRITE AS A HISTORIAN: *DEVELOP A THESIS*

The thesis statement must 1) assert a historically defensible claim, 2) lay out a line of reasoning, and 3) directly address the topic and focus of the task.

Historically Defensible Claim A thesis, or claim, is a nonfactual statement asserted to be true. It is a statement about which people can disagree because it requires an explanation or evaluation. A historically defensible claim is one that can be supported with sound historical evidence. For example, a writer could claim that building railroads contributed to the Civil War. This is a defensible claim because it could point to how railroads connected the Northeast and Midwest more than they did the South. Others could disagree, noting that the South needed fewer railroads because it was linked to the Northeast through the cotton industry and the Midwest through trade on the Mississippi River.

Line of Reasoning A thesis or claim also conveys a line of reasoning for the argument that will be used to explain the relationships among pieces of evidence. In the thesis on railroads, for example, the line of reasoning uses *comparison*: the similarities and differences in regional ties. Other lines of reasoning include causation and continuity/change. Each line of reasoning needs to be embedded in a strong thesis statement.

Topic and Focus of Task A strong thesis or claim directly addresses the topic and focus of the task. It must be limited to the time and geography stated in the long essay question. Questions often ask the writer to "evaluate the extent" to which something happened. Which historical events or trends were the most important, significant, influential, long-lasting, or in other ways largest in scope? What evidence supports your evaluation?

Application: Read the following long essay question and a thesis statement developed to address it. Evaluate the thesis statement on how well it 1) expresses a historically defensible claim, 2) embeds a line of reasoning, and 3) addresses the topic and task, including evaluating extent, and stays within the limitations of the question. Revise the thesis statement as appropriate so that it meets all three standards.

Long Essay Question: Evaluate the extent of the importance of the efforts of the Confederate states in gaining international support during the Civil War.

Thesis Statement: Between 1861 and 1865, Confederate failure to gain international support was a primary reason the Union won the Civil War.

For current free-response question samples, visit: https://apcentral.collegeboard.org/courses/ap-united-states-history/exam

LONG ESSAY QUESTIONS

Directions: The suggested writing time for each question is 40 minutes. In your response you should do the following:

- Respond to the prompt with a historically defensible thesis or claim that establishes a line of reasoning.
- Describe a broader historical context relevant to the prompt.
- Support an argument in response to the prompt using specific and relevant examples of evidence.
- Use historical reasoning (e.g., comparison, causation, continuity or change) to frame or structure an argument that addresses the prompt.
- Use evidence to corroborate, qualify, or modify an argument that addresses the prompt.

1. Evaluate the extent to which the idea of Manifest Destiny fostered the territorial expansion in the period from 1844 to 1877.

2. Evaluate the extent to which the United States changed how it handled its border disputes in the period from 1844 to 1877.

3. Evaluate the extent to which the reaction to immigration changed in the period from 1844 to 1877.

4. Evaluate the extent to which the arguments about slavery presented by Abraham Lincoln in his debates with Stephen A. Douglas had an effect on national politics in the period from 1858 to 1861.

5. Evaluate the extent to which the actions of Abraham Lincoln had an effect on the decision of states to secede in the period 1860 to 1865.

6. Evaluate the extent to which the efforts of the Confederate states to gain international support during the Civil War had an effect on the conduct of the war.

7. Evaluate the extent to which the Reconstruction plans of President Andrew Johnson and the Radical Republicans differed.

8. Evaluate the extent to which efforts to protect equal rights for all citizens had an effect during the period of Reconstruction.

Directions: Question 1 is based on the accompanying documents. The documents have been edited for the purpose of this exercise. You are advised to spend 15 minutes planning and 45 minutes writing your answer. In your response you should do the following:

- Respond to the prompt with a historically defensible thesis or claim that establishes a line of reasoning.
- Describe a broader historical context relevant to the prompt.
- Support an argument in response to the prompt using at least six documents.
- Use at least one additional piece of specific historical evidence (beyond that found in the documents) relevant to an argument about the prompt.
- For at least three documents, explain how or why the document's point of view, purpose, historical situation, and/or audience is relevant to an argument.
- Use evidence to corroborate, qualify, or modify an argument that addresses the prompt.

1. Evaluate the extent to which the territorial expansion of Manifest Destiny caused the United States to become more unified in the period of the 1830s and 1840s.

Document 1

Source: William Ellery Channing, abolitionist and pacifist, statement opposing the annexation of Texas, 1837

Texas is the first step to Mexico. The moment we plant authority on Texas, the boundaries of these two countries will become nominal, will be little more than lines on the sand. . . .

A country has no right to adopt a policy, however gainful, which, as it may foresee, will determine it to a career of war. A nation, like an individual, is bound to seek, even by sacrifices, a position which will favor peace, justice, and the exercise of beneficent influence on the world. A nation provoking war by cupidity, by encroachment, and above all, by efforts to propagate the curse of slavery, is alike false to itself, to God, and to the human race.

Document 2

Source: President James Polk, Inaugural Address, 1845

None can fail to see the danger to our safety and future peace if Texas remains an independent state, or becomes an ally or dependency of some foreign nation more powerful than herself. Is there one among our citizens who would not prefer perpetual peace with Texas to occasional wars, which often occur between bordering independent nations? Is there one who would not prefer free intercourse with her, to high duties on all our products and manufactures which enter her ports or cross her frontiers? Is there one who would not prefer an unrestricted communication with her citizens, to the frontier obstructions which must occur if she remains out of the Union?

Document 3

Source: Anonymous, "California and the National Interest," *American Review* (a Whig journal), 1846

The natural progress of events will undoubtedly give us that province [California] just as it gave us Texas. Already American emigrants thither are to be numbered by thousands, and we may, at almost any moment, look for a declaration, which shall dissolve the slight bonds that now link the province to Mexico, and prepare the way for its ultimate annexation to the United States. . . .

Here, then, lies the Pacific coast, adjoining our western border . . . which embrace the southern sections of the United States and stretching northward to the southern boundary of Oregon. . . .

California, to become the seat of wealth and power for which nature has marked it, must pass into the hands of another race. And who can conjecture what would now have been its condition, had its first colonists been of the stock which peopled the Atlantic coast?

Document 4

Source: John L. O'Sullivan, editor, *Democratic Review,* 1846

California will, probably, next fall away from [Mexico]. . . . The Anglo-Saxon foot is already on its borders. Already the advance guard of the irresistible army of Anglo-Saxon emigration has begun to pour down upon it, armed with the plough and the rifle, and marking its trail with schools and colleges, courts and representative halls, mills and meeting-houses. A population will soon be in actual occupation of California, over which it be idle for Mexico to dream of dominion. They will necessarily become independent. All this without . . . responsibility of our people—in the natural flow of events.

Document 5

Source: Editorial, "New Territory versus No Territory," *United States Magazine and Democratic Review*, October 1847

This occupation of territory by the people is the great movement of the age, and until every acre of the North American continent is occupied by citizens of the United States, the foundation of the future empire will not have been laid. . . .

When these new states come into the Union, they are controlled by the Constitution only; and as that instrument permits slavery in all the states that are parties to it, how can Congress prevent it? . . .

When through the results of war, territory comes into the possession of the Union, it is equally a violation of the Constitution for Congress to undertake to say that there shall be no slavery then. The people of the United States were nearly unanimous for the admission of Texas into the Union; but probably not an insignificant fraction require its annexation "for the purpose" of extending slavery.

Document 6

Source: Senator Thomas Corwin, Speech, 1847

What is the territory, Mr. President, which you propose to wrest from Mexico? . . .

Sir, look at this pretense of want of room.

There is one topic connected with this subject which I tremble when I approach, and yet I cannot forbear to notice it. It meets you in every step you take; it threatens you which way soever you go in prosecution of this war. I allude to the question of slavery . . . the North and the South are brought together into a collision on a point where neither will yield. Who can foresee or foretell the result . . . why should we participate this fearful struggle, by continuing a war the result of which must be to force us at once upon a civil conflict? . . . Let us wash Mexican blood from our hands, and . . . swear to preserve honorable peace with all the world.

Document 7

Source: Senator Charles Sumner, Massachusetts Legislature, 1847

Resolved, That the present war with Mexico has its primary origin in the unconstitutional annexation to the United States of the foreign state of Texas while the same was still at war with Mexico; that it was unconstitutionally commenced by the order of the President . . . —by a powerful nation against a weak neighbor— unnecessarily and without just cause, at immense cost of a portion of her territory, from which slavery has already been excluded, with the triple object of extending slavery, of strengthening "Slave Power," and of obtaining the control of the Free States, under the Constitution of the United States.

Resolved, That our attention is directed anew to the wrong and "enormity" of slavery, and to the tyranny and usurpation of the "Slave Power," as displayed in the history of our country, particularly in the annexation of Texas and the present war with Mexico.

Topic 6.1

Contextualizing Period 6

Learning Objective 1: Explain the historical context for the rise of industrial capitalism in the United States during the period from 1865 to 1898.

Learning Objective 2: Explain a historical context for the increased international and internal migration in the United States during the period from 1865 to 1898.

Between the end of the Civil War in 1865 and the start of the Spanish-American War in 1898, the United States emerged as the world's largest economy. Railroads expanded more than 45,000 miles a decade, faster than in others countries. During this "Gilded Age," the "captains of industry" controlled large corporations, created great fortunes, and lived in European-style palaces. The context for the rise of large-scale industries and capitalism involved a variety of economic, political, social, and cultural developments.

Economic Changes Large-scale industries, such as railroads, steel mills, and mining, were *capital* intensive. Europeans with surplus wealth joined well-to-do Americans to fund stock and bond sales needed for expanding industries. Many businesses were based in New York City, which was home to large banks, stock exchanges, and leaders of industry, such as the Astors and Vanderbilts.

The dynamic advances in *technology* increased productivity of large-scale industries, such as the steel industry, which made steel cheaper and stronger. The 440,000 new patents from 1860 to 1890 sparked a "second" industrial revolution based on new electric- and oil-related technologies.

Industries depended on expanding *markets* connected by railroads, steamships, and networks of telegraphs, cables, and later telephones. For example, the meatpacking houses of Chicago and the steel mills of Pittsburgh reached their customers in days instead of weeks. American industries also began to look for international markets in Europe, Latin America, and Asia.

Political Change American businesses also benefited from pro-growth *government policies* that protected property rights, refrained from regulating business operations, sheltered domestic manufacturers with high tariffs, and subsidized railroads with land grants and loans. However, federal, state, and local governments largely ignored the problems of workers, farmers, consumers, and growing cities. The lack of action in these areas generated debates over the proper role of government in the economy. During this period, the economy suffered panics and depressions, and large inequities in wealth distribution.

Migration and Urbanization Opportunities in growing industrial cities and westward expansion pulled many *migrants* from rural areas within the country as well as from abroad. During the late 1800s, large waves of "new" immigrants from southern and eastern Europe and Asia entered the United States. Migration benefited economic growth and cultural diversity, but it also produced conflicts and threatened the very existence of Native Americans.

Industrialization also accelerated *urban development.* Unplanned and unregulated growth produced cities that lacked sanitary systems, degraded the environment, and had weak law enforcement. Low wages, lack of housing, and overcrowding resulted in squalid conditions for many migrant families. However, an expanding *middle class* enjoyed more leisure time and developed an urban culture featuring new forms of sports, music, and theater.

The successes and failures of the period inspired new *intellectual movements* that both supported and challenged laissez-faire capitalism and the social order of the Gilded Age. Industrialization and urbanization stimulated new ideas about government, religion, education, architecture, literature, and the arts.

Reform Efforts In response to these economic and cultural changes, *reform movements* arose. Workers, farmers, and the growing middle class began to demand changes in economic, political, and cultural institutions. Farm organizations protested against unfair railroad rates and banking practices, while industrial workers fought for higher wages and the right to organize. Women organized to gain voting rights and led the campaign for temperance. Many reform movements did not succeed at first, but they did provide the 20th century with the reform ideas and political organizations to implement them.

ANALYZE THE CONTEXT

1. Explain a historical context for the rise of industrial capitalism in the United States during the period from 1865 to 1898.

2. Explain a historical context for the increased international and internal migration in the United States during the period from 1865 to 1898.

LANDMARK EVENTS: 1850–1900

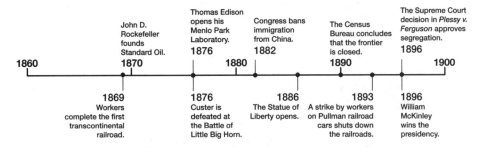

John D. Rockefeller founds Standard Oil.

Thomas Edison opens his Menlo Park Laboratory. 1876

Congress bans immigration from China. 1882

The Census Bureau concludes that the frontier is closed.

The Supreme Court decision in *Plessy v. Ferguson* approves segregation. 1896

1860 — 1870 — 1880 — 1890 — 1900

1869 Workers complete the first transcontinental railroad.

1876 Custer is defeated at the Battle of Little Big Horn.

1886 The Statue of Liberty opens.

1893 A strike by workers on Pullman railroad cars shuts down the railroads.

1896 William McKinley wins the presidency.

Westward Expansion: Economic Development

Pioneers! O pioneers!
We primeval forests felling,
We the rivers stemming, vexing we and piecing deep the mines within,
We the surface broad surveying, we the virgin soil upheaving . . . .

Walt Whitman, 1865

Learning Objective: Explain the causes and effects of the settlement of the West from 1877 to 1898.

The development of the western United States after 1865 differed from the settlement patterns of the colonial and early national frontiers because of industrialization. The most apparent difference was the building of transcontinental railroads across the Far West.

Transcontinental Railroads

The great age of railroad building coincided with the settlement of the last western frontiers. Railroads not only promoted settlement on the **Great Plains**, but they also linked the West with the East to create one great national market.

The First Route During the Civil War, Congress authorized land grants and loans for the building of the first transcontinental railroad to tie California to the rest of the Union. Two newly incorporated railroad companies divided the task. The Union Pacific (UP) started from Omaha, Nebraska, and built westward across the Great Plains. The UP employed thousands of war veterans and Irish immigrants under the direction of General Grenville Dodge. The Central Pacific started from Sacramento, California, and built eastward. Led by Charles Crocker, the workers, including as many as 20,000 Chinese immigrants, took on the great risks of laying track and blasting tunnels through the Sierra Nevada Mountains.

The two railroads came together on May 10, 1869, at Promontory Point, Utah, where a golden spike was ceremoniously driven into the rail tie to mark the linking of the Atlantic and the Pacific states.

Four Additional Routes In 1883, three other transcontinental railroads were completed. The Southern Pacific tied New Orleans to Los Angeles. The Atchison, Topeka, and Santa Fe linked Kansas City and Los Angeles. The Northern Pacific connected Duluth, Minnesota, with Seattle, Washington. In

1893, the Great Northern finished the fifth transcontinental railroad, which ran from St. Paul, Minnesota, to Seattle. Companies built many other shortline and narrow-gauge railroads to open up the western interior to settlement by miners, ranchers, farmers, and business owners, leading to more towns and cities.

Negative Effects Progress came with significant costs. The railroads helped to transform the West during this period, but many proved failures as businesses. They were built in areas with few customers and with little promise of returning a profit in the near term. The frenzied rush for the West's natural resources seriously damaged the environment and nearly exterminated the buffalo. Most significantly, the American Indians who lived in the region paid a high human and cultural price.

Settlement of the Last West

At first, the settlement and economic development of the **Great Plains**, the Rocky Mountains, and the Western Plateau did not seem promising. Before 1860, these lands between the Mississippi River and the Pacific Coast were known as "the **Great American Desert**" by pioneers passing through on the way to the green valleys of Oregon and the goldfields of California. The plains west of the **100th meridian** had few trees and usually received less than 15 inches of rainfall a year, which was not considered enough moisture to support farming. Winter blizzards and hot dry summers discouraged settlement.

STATES ADMITTED TO THE UNION 1864–1896

However, after 1865 the Great Plains changed so dramatically that the former "frontier" largely vanished. By 1900, the great **buffalo herds** had been wiped out. The open western lands were fenced in by homesteads and ranches, crisscrossed by steel rails, and modernized by new towns. Ten new western states had been carved out of the last frontier. Only Arizona, New Mexico, and Oklahoma remained as territories awaiting statehood at the end of the century.

The Mining Frontier

California's great gold rush of 1849 set the pattern for other gold rushes. Individual prospectors poured into the region and used a method called placer mining to search for traces of gold in mountain streams. They needed only simple tools such as shovels and washing pans. Following these individuals came mining companies that could employ deep-shaft mining that required expensive equipment and the resources of wealthy investors. As the mines developed, companies employed experienced miners from Europe, Latin America, and China.

The California Gold Rush was only the first of a series of gold strikes and silver strikes in what became the states of South Dakota, Colorado, Montana, Idaho, Nevada, and Arizona. These strikes kept a steady flow of hopeful prospectors pushing into the western mountains into the 1890s that helped settle the West. The discovery of gold near Pike's Peak, Colorado, in 1859 brought nearly 100,000 miners to the area. In the same year, the discovery of the fabulous Comstock Lode (which produced more than $340 million in gold and silver by 1890) led to Nevada entering the Union in 1864. Idaho and Montana also received early statehood, largely because of mining booms.

Rich strikes created boomtowns, overnight towns that became infamous for saloons, dance-hall girls, and vigilante justice. Many of these, however, became lonely ghost towns within a few years after the gold or silver ran out. The mining towns that endured and grew evolved more like industrial cities than the frontier towns depicted in western films. For example, Nevada's Virginia City (created by the Comstock Lode), added theaters, churches, newspapers, schools, libraries, railroads, and police. Mark Twain started his career as a writer working on a Virginia City newspaper in the early 1860s. A few towns that served the mines, such as San Francisco, Sacramento, and Denver, expanded into prosperous cities.

The Cattle Frontier

The economic potential of the vast open grasslands that reached from Texas to Canada was realized by ranchers in the decades after the Civil War. Earlier, cattle had been raised and rounded up in Texas on a small scale by Mexican cowboys, or *vaqueros*. The traditions of the cattle business in the late 1800s, like the hardy "Texas" **longhorn cattle**, were borrowed from the Mexicans. By the 1860s, wild herds of about 5 million head of cattle roamed freely over the Texas grasslands. The Texas cattle business was easy to get into because both the cattle and the grass were free.

Railroads and Cattle The construction of railroads into Kansas after the war opened up eastern markets for the Texas cattle. Joseph G. McCoy built the first stockyards in the region, at Abilene, Kansas. Those stockyards held cattle that could be sold in Chicago for the high price of $30 to $50 per head. Dodge City and other cow towns sprang up along the railroads to handle the millions of cattle driven up the Chisholm, Goodnight-Loving, and other trails out of Texas during the 1860s and 1870s. The cowboys, many of whom were African Americans or Mexicans, received about a dollar a day for their dangerous work.

Decline of the Cattle Drives The long **cattle drives** began to end in the 1880s. Overgrazing destroyed the grass, and a winter blizzard and drought of 1885–1886 killed off 90 percent of the cattle. Another factor that closed down the cattle frontier was the arrival of homesteaders, who used **barbed wire** fencing to cut off access to the formerly open range. Wealthy cattle owners turned to developing huge ranches and using scientific ranching techniques. They raised new breeds of cattle that produced more tender beef by feeding the cattle hay and grains.

The Wild West was largely tamed by the 1890s. However, in these few decades, Americans' eating habits changed from pork to beef, and people created the enduring legend of the rugged, self-reliant American cowboy.

The Farming Frontier

The **Homestead Act** of 1862 encouraged farming on the Great Plains by offering 160 acres of public land free to any family that settled on it for a period of five years. The promise of free land combined with the promotions of railroads and land speculators induced hundreds of thousands of native-born and immigrant families to attempt to farm the Great Plains between 1870 and 1900. About 500,000 families took advantage of the Homestead Act. However, five times that number had to purchase their land, because the best public lands often ended up in the possession of railroad companies and speculators.

Problems and Solutions The first "sodbusters" on the dry and treeless plains often built their homes of sod bricks. Extremes of hot and cold weather, plagues of grasshoppers, and the lonesome life on the plains challenged even the most resourceful of the pioneer families. Water was scarce, and wood for fences was almost nonexistent. The invention of barbed wire by **Joseph Glidden** in 1874 helped farmers to fence in their lands on the lumber-scarce plains. Using mail-order windmills to drill deep wells provided some water.

Even so, many homesteaders discovered too late that 160 acres was not adequate for farming the Great Plains. Long spells of severe weather, together with falling prices for their crops and the cost of new machinery, caused the failure of two-thirds of the homesteaders' farms on the Great Plains by 1900. Western Kansas alone lost half of its population between 1888 and 1892.

Success on the Great Plains Those who managed to survive adopted **"dry farming"** and deep-plowing techniques to make the most of the moisture available. They also learned to plant hardy strains of Russian wheat that withstood the extreme weather. Ultimately, government programs to build dams and irrigation systems saved many western farmers, as humans reshaped the rivers and physical environment of the West to provide water for agriculture.

Farmers Organize

By the end of the 1800s, farmers had become a minority within American society. While the number of U.S. farms more than doubled between 1865 and 1900, people working as farmers declined from 60 percent of the working population in 1860 to less than 37 percent in 1900. At the same time, farmers faced growing economic threats from railroads, banks, and global markets.

Changes in Agriculture

With every passing decade in the late 1800s, farming became increasingly commercialized—and also more specialized. Northern and western farmers of the late 19th century concentrated on raising single **cash crops**, such as corn or wheat, for both national and international **markets**. As consumers, farmers began to procure their food from the stores in town and their manufactured goods from the mail-order catalogs sent to them by Montgomery Ward and Sears Roebuck. As producers, farmers became more dependent on large and expensive machines, such as steam engines, seeders, and reaper-thresher combines. Larger farms were run like factories. Unable to afford the new equipment, small, marginal farms could not compete and, in many cases, were driven out of business.

Falling Prices Increased production of crops such as wheat and corn in the United States as well as in Argentina, Russia, and Canada drove prices down for farmers around the world. In the United States, since the money supply was not growing as fast as the economy, each dollar became worth more. This put more downward pressure on prices, resulting in **deflation**. The data in the chart tell the depressing story for farmers.

WHEAT AND CORN PRICES PER BUSHEL, 1867 AND 1889		
Year	Wheat	Corn
1867	$2.01	$0.78
1889	$0.70	$0.28

Source: U.S. Bureau of the Census. *Historical Statistics of the United States, Colonial Times to 1970*

As prices fell, farmers with mortgages faced both high interest rates and the need to grow more and more to pay off old debts. Of course, increased production only lowered prices. The predictable results of this vicious circle were more debts, foreclosures by banks, and more independent farmers forced to become tenants and sharecroppers.

Rising Costs Farmers felt victimized by impersonal forces of the larger national economy. Industrial corporations were able to keep prices high on manufactured goods by forming monopolistic trusts. Wholesalers and retailers (known as "the **middlemen**") took their cut before selling to farmers. Railroads, warehouses, and elevators took what little profit remained by charging high or discriminatory rates for the shipment and storage of grain. Railroads would often charge more for short hauls on lines with no competition than for long hauls on lines with competition.

Taxes also seemed unfair to farmers. Local and state governments taxed property and land heavily but did not tax income from stocks and bonds. The tariffs protecting various American industries were viewed as just another unfair tax paid by farmers and consumers for the benefit of the industrialists.

Fighting Back

A long tradition of independence and individualism restrained farmers from taking collective action. Finally, however, they began to organize for their common interests and protection.

National Grange Movement The National Grange of Patrons of Husbandry was organized in 1868 by Oliver H. Kelley primarily as a social and educational organization for farmers and their families. Within five years, chapters of the Grange existed in almost every state, with the most in the Midwest. As the **National Grange Movement** expanded, it became active in economics and politics to defend members against middlemen, trusts, and railroads. For example, Grangers established **cooperatives**—businesses owned and run by the farmers to save the costs charged by middlemen. In Illinois, Iowa, Minnesota, and Wisconsin, the Grangers, with help from local businesses, successfully lobbied their state legislatures to pass laws regulating the rates charged by railroads and elevators. Other **Granger laws** made it illegal for railroads to fix prices by means of pools and to give rebates to privileged customers. In the landmark case of *Munn v. Illinois* (1877), the Supreme Court upheld the right of a state to regulate businesses of a public nature, such as railroads.

Farmers' Alliances Farmers also expressed their discontent by forming state and regional groups known as farmers' alliances. Like the Grange, the alliances taught about scientific farming methods. Unlike the Grange, alliances always had the goal of economic and political action. Hence, the alliance movement had serious potential for creating an independent national political party. By 1890, about 1 million farmers had joined farmers' alliances. In the South, both poor White and Black farmers joined the movement.

Ocala Platform That potential nearly became reality in 1890 when a national organization of farmers—the National Alliance—met in Ocala, Florida, to address the problems of rural America. The Alliance attacked both major parties as subversive to Wall Street bankers and big business. Ocala delegates created the **Ocala Platform** that called for significant reforms:

- Direct election of U.S. senators (in the original U.S. Constitution, senators were selected by state legislatures)
- Lower tariff rates
- A graduated income tax (people with higher incomes would pay higher rates of tax)
- A new banking system regulated by the federal government

In addition, the Alliance platform demanded that Treasury notes and silver be used to increase the amount of money in circulation. Farmers wanted to increase the supply of money in order to create inflation, thereby raising crop prices. The platform also proposed federal storage for farmers' crops and federal loans, freeing farmers from dependency on middlemen and creditors.

The alliances stopped short of forming a political party. However, local and state candidates who supported alliance goals received decisive electoral support from farmers. Many of the reform ideas of the Grange and the farmers' alliances would become part of the Populist movement, which would shake the foundations of the two-party system in the elections of 1892 and 1896.

REFLECT ON THE LEARNING OBJECTIVE

1. Explain three causes of the economic development of the West from 1865 to 1898.

KEY TERMS BY THEME

Western Settlement (MIG)
transcontinental railroads
Great Plains
Great American Desert
100th meridian
buffalo herds

Western Development (MIG)
vaqueros
longhorn cattle
cattle drives
barbed wire
Homestead Act

Joseph Glidden
"dry farming"

Farm Protest Movements (PCE)
cash crops
markets
deflation
middlemen
National Grange Movement
cooperatives
Granger laws
Munn v. Illinois
Ocala Platform

Questions 1–3 refer to the following excerpt.

1. We demand the abolition of national banks.

2. We demand that the government shall establish sub-treasuries or depositories in the several states, which shall loan money direct to the people at a low rate of interest, not to exceed two per cent per annum, on non-perishable farm products, and also upon real estate. . . .

3. We demand that the amount of the circulating medium be speedily increased to not less than $50 per capita.

4. We condemn the silver bill recently passed by Congress, and demand in lieu thereof the free and unlimited coinage of silver.

5. We further demand a removal of the existing heavy tariff tax from the necessities of life, that the poor of our land must have.

6. We further demand a just and equitable system of graduated tax on incomes.

7. We demand that the Congress of the United States submit an amendment to the Constitution providing for the election of United States Senators by direct vote of the people of each state.

Ocala Platform, December 1890

1. Which statement best explains the reason for the demand for "election of United States Senators by direct vote"?
   (A) Labor unions resented how the Senate often supported efforts to break strikes.
   (B) Reformers hoped that reforming the U.S. Senate would lead to similar reforms by states.
   (C) Residents of states with large populations argued that the Senate did not represent all people equally.
   (D) Many voters felt that the Senate had become dominated by powerful business interests.

2. The Ocala Platform was primarily based on the belief that
   (A) federal income taxes fell mainly on average working Americans
   (B) large banks had worked together to reduce interest rates on loans
   (C) higher tariffs would help farmers prosper
   (D) increasing the money supply would help farmers who were in debt

3. The Ocala Platform proved an important link between the alliance movement and which of the following later groups?

(A) Urban reformers

(B) The Populists

(C) The United Mine Workers

(D) Factory workers

SHORT-ANSWER QUESTIONS

Use complete sentences; an outline or bulleted list alone is not acceptable.

1.

Source: Getty Images

Using the image above, answer (a), (b), and (c).

(a) Briefly describe ONE perspective about railroads expressed through the image.

(b) Briefly explain ONE specific historical development that led to the perspective expressed in the image.

(c) Briefly explain ONE specific example of how farmer movements challenged railroads in the period from 1865 to 1898.

2. Answer (a), (b), and (c).

(a) Briefly describe ONE way the mining frontier changed in the period from 1865 to 1898.

(b) Briefly describe ONE way the cattle frontier changed in the period from 1865 to 1898.

(c) Briefly describe ONE way the economics of western farming changed in the period from 1865 to 1898.

Topic 6.3

Westward Expansion: Social and Cultural Development

American social development has been continually beginning over again on the frontier. . . . The true point of view in the history of this nation is not the Atlantic coast, it is the Great West.

Frederick Jackson Turner, 1893

Learning Objective: Explain the causes and effects of the settlement of the West from 1877 to 1898.

The historical perspective on the social and cultural development of the West has changed since the 1890s. At first, the settlement of the Great Plains and Far West was recorded as another frontier to be conquered and settled by Europeans. However, Native Americans, Mexican Americans, Asian immigrants, and other migrants were also there to shape the culture and diversity of the region.

The Closing of the Frontier

The Oklahoma Territory, once set aside for the use of American Indians, was opened for settlement in 1889, and hundreds of homesteaders took part in the last great land rush in the West. In 1890 the U.S. Census Bureau declared that the entire frontier—except for a few pockets—had been settled.

Turner's Frontier Thesis Three years after the Census Bureau declaration, historian **Frederick Jackson Turner** published a provocative, influential essay, **"The Significance of the Frontier in American History."** He presented the settling of the frontier as an evolutionary process of building civilization. Into an untamed wilderness came wave after wave of people. The first were hunters. Following them came cattle ranchers, miners, and farmers. Finally, people arrived who founded towns and cities. Turner argued that 300 years of frontier experience had shaped American culture, promoting independence, individualism, inventiveness, practical-mindedness, and democracy. But people also became wasteful of natural resources.

Role of Towns and Cities Historians have challenged Turner's evolutionary view by arguing that frontier cities were not a late addition. Rather, they played an early and primary role in development of the frontier, For example, 19th century developers or "boosters" tried to create settlements on the frontier overnight in the middle of nowhere. After laying out town plots on paper, boosters strove to establish their own town as a territory's central hub of development by competing to capture the county seat or state capital, a state asylum, a railroad depot, or a college.

Urban markets also made frontier development possible. The cattle ranchers' frontier developed because it was linked by the railroads to Chicago and eastern markets. By integrating the history of the city and the settlement of the frontier, it becomes clear that the development of the frontier especially after 1865 was interdependence with the growth of towns and cities.

American Without a Frontier The closing of the frontier troubled Turner. He saw the frontier as a safety valve for releasing discontent in American society. The frontier had always held the promise of a fresh start. Once the frontier was gone, Turner wondered, would the United States be condemned to follow the patterns of class division and social conflict that troubled Europe?

While many debate the Turner thesis, historians acknowledge that by the 1890s the largest movement of Americans was not from east to west, it was from rural communities to the cities. Migrants saw more opportunity in industry than in agriculture. Not only was the era of the western frontier coming to a close, but the dominance of rural America was also on a decline.

American Indians in the West

The American Indians who occupied the West in 1865 belonged to dozens of different cultural and tribal groups. In New Mexico and Arizona, Pueblo groups such as the Hopi and Zuni lived in permanent settlements raising corn and livestock. The Navajo and Apache peoples of the Southwest were nomadic hunter-gatherers who adopted a more settled way of life, not only raising crops and livestock but also producing arts and crafts. In the Pacific Northwest (Washington and Oregon), the Chinook, Shasta, and other tribes developed complex communities based on abundant fish and game.

About two-thirds of the western tribal groups lived on the Great Plains. These nomadic tribes, such as the Sioux, Blackfoot, Cheyenne, Crow, and Comanche, had given up farming in colonial times after the introduction of the horse by the Spanish. By the 1700s, they had become skillful horse riders and developed a way of life centered on the hunting of buffalo. Although they belonged to tribes of several thousand, they lived in smaller bands of 300 to 500 members. In the late 19th century, their conflicts with the U.S. government were partly the result of White Americans having little understanding of the Plains peoples' loose tribal organization and nomadic lifestyle.

Reservation Policy In the 1830s, President Andrew Jackson's policy of moving eastern American Indians to the West was based on the belief that lands west of the Mississippi would permanently remain "Indian country." This expectation soon proved false, as wagon trains rolled westward on the Oregon Trail, and plans were made for building a transcontinental railroad. In 1851, in councils (negotiations) at Fort Laramie (Wyoming) and Fort Atkinson

(Wisconsin), the federal government began to assign the Plains tribes large tracts of land—or reservations—with definite boundaries. Most Plains tribes, however, refused to restrict their movements to the reservations and continued to follow the migrating buffalo wherever they roamed.

Indian Wars In the late 1800s, the settlement by miners, ranchers, and homesteaders on American Indian lands led to violence. Fighting between U.S. troops and Plains Indians was often brutal, with the U.S. Army responsible for several massacres. In 1866, during the Sioux War, the tables were turned when Sioux fighters wiped out an an army column under Captain William Fetterman.

Following these wars, another round of treaties attempted to isolate the Plains Indians on smaller reservations with federal agents promising government support. However, gold miners refused to stay off American Indians' lands if gold was found on them, as it was in the Dakotas' Black Hills. Soon, minor chiefs not involved in the treaty-making and younger warriors denounced the treaties and tried to return to ancestral lands.

AMERICAN INDIANS IN THE WEST

A new round of conflicts in the West began in the 1870s. The Indian Appropriation Act of 1871 ended recognition of tribes as independent nations by the federal government and ended negotiation of treaties to be approved by Congress. Conflicts included the Red River War against the Comanche in the southern plains and a second Sioux War led by Sitting Bull and Crazy Horse in the northern plains. Before the Sioux were defeated, they ambushed and destroyed Colonel George Custer's command at **Little Big Horn** in 1876. Chief Joseph's courageous effort to lead a band of the Nez Percé into Canada ended in defeat and surrender in 1877.

The constant pressure of the U.S. Army forced tribe after tribe to comply with Washington's terms, even after the government violated treaties. In addition, the slaughter of most of the buffalo by the early 1880s doomed the way of life of the Plains peoples. As they lost the buffalo, Plains Indians had to change their traditions as a nomadic hunting culture.

Ghost Dancers and Wounded Knee The last effort of American Indians to resist U.S. government controls was the religiously inspired **Ghost Dance movement**. Leaders believed it could return prosperity to American Indians. In the government's campaign to suppress the movement, the famous Sioux medicine man Sitting Bull was killed during his arrest. Then in December 1890, the U.S. Army gunned down more than 200 American Indian men, women, and children in the "battle" (massacre) of Wounded Knee in the Dakotas. This final tragedy marked the end of the Indian Wars on the blood-crimsoned prairie.

Assimilationists The injustices done to American Indians were chronicled in a best-selling book by **Helen Hunt Jackson**, *A Century of Dishonor* (1881). Although this book created sympathy for American Indians, especially in the eastern United States, it also generated support for ending Indian culture through **assimilation**. Reformers advocated formal education, job training, and conversion to Christianity. They set up boarding schools such as the Carlisle School in Pennsylvania to segregate American Indian children from their people and teach them White culture and farming and industrial skills.

Dawes Severalty Act (1887) A new phase in the relationship between the U.S. government and American Indians was incorporated in the **Dawes Act of 1887**. The Act was designed to break up tribal organizations, which many felt kept American Indians from becoming "civilized" and law-abiding citizens. The Dawes Act divided the tribal lands into plots of up to 160 acres, depending on family size. U.S. citizenship was granted to those who stayed on the land for 25 years and "adopted the habits of civilized life."

Under the Dawes Act, as intended, the federal government distributed 47 million acres of land to American Indians. However, 90 million acres of former reservation land—often the best land—was sold over the years to White settlers by the government, speculators, or American Indians themselves. The new policy proved a failure. By the turn of the century, disease and poverty had reduced the American Indian population to just 200,000 persons, most of whom lived as wards of the federal government.

Changes in the 20th and 21st Centuries In 1924, in partial recognition that forced assimilation had failed, the federal government granted U.S. citizenship to all American Indians, whether or not they had complied with the Dawes Act. As part of President Franklin Roosevelt's New Deal in the 1930s, Congress adopted the **Indian Reorganization Act** (1934), which promoted the reestablishment of tribal organization and culture. Since then, the number of people identifying as American Indians has increased. Today, more than 3 million American Indians, belonging to 500 tribes, live in the United States.

Mexican Americans in the Southwest

Mexico's independence from Spain in 1821 increased trade and cultural exchange with the United States. The **Santa Fe Trail**, a nearly 1,000-mile overland route between Santa Fe, New Mexico, and western Missouri linked the regions. This trail opened up the Spanish-speaking southwest to economic development and settlement. It was a vital link until a railroad was completed in 1880.

Mexican landowners in the Southwest and California were guaranteed their property rights and granted citizenship after the Mexican War. However, drawn-out legal proceedings often resulted in the sale or loss of lands to new Anglo arrivals. Hispanic culture was preserved in dominant Spanish-speaking areas, such as the New Mexico territories, the border towns, and the barrios of California.

During this period, Mexican Americans moved throughout the West to find work. Many found employment in the sugar beet fields and the mines of Colorado, and in building railroads throughout the region. Before 1917, the border with Mexico was open, and few records were kept for either seasonal workers or permanent settlers. Mexicans, like their European counterparts, were drawn by the explosive economic development of the region. Mexican Americans, Native Americans, and White settlers competed for land and resources during this period.

The Conservation Movement

The concerns over **deforestation** sparked the conservation movement. The breathtaking paintings and photographs of western landscapes helped to push Congress to preserve such western icons as **Yosemite** Valley as a California state park in 1864 (it became a national park in 1890) and to dedicate the **Yellowstone** area as the first national park in 1872. In the 1800s, Secretary of the Interior Carl Schurz advocated creation of forest reserves and a federal forest service to protect federal lands from exploitation. Presidents Benjamin Harrison and Grover Cleveland reserved 33 million acres of national timber. (For more on the conservation movement, see Topic 7.4.)

With the closing of the frontier era, Americans grew increasingly concerned about the loss of public lands and the natural treasures they contained. The **Forest Reserve Act of 1891** and the **Forest Management Act of 1897** withdrew federal timberlands from development and regulated their use. While most **"conservationists"** believed in scientific management and regulated use of natural resources, "**preservationists**," such as **John Muir**, a leading founder of the **Sierra Club** in 1892, went a step further and aimed to preserve natural areas from human interference. The establishment of Arbor Day in 1872, a day dedicated to planting trees, and the educational efforts of the Audubon Society and the Sierra Club reflected a growing environmental awareness by 1900.

Source: Logging in California, 1909. Library of Congress

REFLECT ON THE LEARNING OBJECTIVE

1. Explain three effects of the settlement of the West on its social and cultural development from 1865 to 1898.

KEY TERMS BY THEME

Frontier Closing (MIG)
Frederick Jackson Turner
"The Significance of the Frontier in American History" (1893)

American Indians (MIG)
Little Big Horn
Ghost Dance movement
assimilationists
Helen Hunt Jackson
Dawes Act of 1887
Indian Reorganization Act

Mexican Americans (MIG)
Santa Fe Trail

Conservation (GEO)
deforestation
Yosemite
Yellowstone
Forest Reserve Act of 1891
Forest Management Act of 1897
conservationists
preservationists
John Muir
Sierra Club

Questions 1–2 refer to the following excerpt.

"When you first came we were many, and you were few; now you are many, and we are getting very few. . . . We are driven into very little land. . . . I came to Washington to see the Great Father [President] in order to have peace and in order to have peace continue. . . . In 1868 men came out and brought papers. . . . We wanted them to take away their forts, leave our country, not make war. The interpreters deceived us. . . . We do not want riches. . . . We want our children properly trained and brought up. . . . We would like to know why commissioners are sent out there to do nothing but rob [us] and get the riches of this world away from us. . . . I want to tell the people that we cannot trust [President Grant's] agents."

Chief Red Cloud, speech at Cooper Union in New York, July 16, 1870

1. The excerpt best illustrates which of the following issues of that time?
   (A) President Grant had instituted policies that protected tribal lands.
   (B) Migrants and Native Americans were clashing over tribal lands.
   (C) Tribal leaders believed that their growing population would give them more power to negotiate favorable treaties.
   (D) Tribal leaders wanted to end the conflicts with White Americans through assimilation.

2. Which of the following best explains the relationship of the United States government and Native American tribes before 1871?
   (A) Native tribes were recognized as "nations" within the United States.
   (B) Individual Native Americans enjoyed the same equal rights as White U.S. citizens.
   (C) Native Americans had no legal status and were treated as foreigners.
   (D) The federal government left agreements and treaties up to the states.

Use complete sentences; an outline or bulleted list alone is not acceptable.

1. "About the Indian wars that plagued the American West . . . it is commonly believed that they might have been avoided but for the avarice [greed] and aggression of the white man. The root of the trouble lay in the Plains Indian's rootlessness. It was freedom of movement, the privilege of ranging far and wide seasonally that gave his life meaning and dignity. . . . [T]hat given time and patience the Plains tribes could be persuaded to abandon their nomadic ways . . . was wishful thinking. . . . Civilization may have had a clear duty to save these people from themselves."

> S. L. A. Marshall, historian, *Crimsoned Prairie,* 1972

"The grand irony of the Great Plains is that none of the tribes with which the army would clash were native to the lands they claimed. All had been caught up in a vast migration, precipitated by the white settlements in the East. As the dislocated Indians spilled onto the Plains, they jockeyed with native tribes for the choicest hunting grounds. In a real sense, then—and this cannot be over emphasized—the wars that were to come between the Indians and the government for the Great Plains would represent a clash of emigrant peoples."

> Peter Cozzens, historian, *The Earth Is Weeping,* 2016

Using the excerpts above, answer (a), (b), and (c).

(a) Briefly describe ONE major difference between Marshall's and Cozzens's interpretations of the Indian Wars from 1865 to 1898.

(b) Briefly explain how ONE specific historical event or development that is not explicitly mentioned in the excerpts could be used to support Marshall's interpretation.

(c) Briefly explain how ONE specific historical event or development that is not explicitly mentioned in the excerpts could be used to support Cozzens's interpretation.

2. Answer (a), (b), and (c).

(a) Briefly describe ONE specific effect on American culture or character that historian Frederick Jackson Turner attributed to the frontier experience.

(b) Briefly explain ONE specific effect of the closing of the frontier on American society or economy.

(c) Briefly explain how ONE additional factor shaped American culture or character between 1865 and 1898.

Topic 6.4

The "New South"

Legislation is powerless to eradicate racial instincts.

Supreme Court majority opinion in *Plessy v. Ferguson*, 1896

Learning Objective: Explain how various factors contributed to continuity and change in the "New South" from 1877 to 1898.

While the West was being developed, the South was recovering from the devastation of the Civil War. Some Southerners promoted a vision for a **"New South"** with a self-sufficient economy, built on modern capitalist values, industrial growth, modernized transportation, and improved race relations. However, its agricultural past and racial divisions provided more continuity than change.

Growth of Industry

Henry Grady, the editor of the *Atlanta Constitution,* spread the gospel of the "New South" with editorials that argued for economic diversity and laissez-faire capitalism. To attract businesses, local governments offered tax exemptions to investors and the promise of low-wage labor. The growth of cities, the textile industry, and improved railroads symbolized efforts to create a "New South" in the late 19th century:

- **Birmingham**, Alabama, developed into one of the nation's leading **steel** producers.

- **Memphis**, Tennessee, prospered as a center for the South's growing **lumber** industry.

- **Richmond**, Virginia, the former capital of the Confederacy, became the capital of the nation's **tobacco** industry.

Georgia, North Carolina, and South Carolina overtook the New England states as the chief producers of textiles. By 1900, the South had 400 cotton mills employing almost 100,000 White workers. Southern railroad companies rapidly converted to the standard gauge rails used in the North and West, so the South was integrated into the **national rail network.** The South's rate of postwar growth from 1865 to 1900 equaled or surpassed that of the rest of the country in population, industry, and railroads.

However, two factors slowed industrial growth. To a greater extent than before the Civil War, Northern financing dominated much of the Southern economy. Northern investors controlled three-quarters of the Southern railroads and by 1900 had control of the South's steel industry as well. A large share of the profits from the new industries went to Northern banks and financiers instead of recirculating and expanding the Southern economy.

In addition, economic growth in the South was hampered by the failure of state and local governments to expand public education. They did not invest in technical and engineering schools for White or Black residents as the North had done. As a result, few Southerners had the skills needed to foster industrial development. Without adequate education, the Southern workforce faced limited economic opportunities in the fast-changing world of the late 19th century. Southern industrial workers (94 percent of whom were White) earned half the national average and worked longer hours than did workers elsewhere.

Agriculture and Poverty

While industry did grow in the South, the region remained largely agricultural—and also the poorest part of the country. By 1900, more than half the region's White farmers and three-quarters of the Black farmers were either **tenant farmers** who rented land or **sharecroppers** who paid for the use of land with a share of the crop. Since people were poor and profits from industry flowed to the North, Southern banks had little money to lend to farmers. This shortage of credit forced farmers to borrow supplies from local merchants in the spring with a lien, or mortgage, on their crops to be paid at harvest. The combination of sharecropping and crop liens kept farmers as virtual serfs tied to the land by debt. These farmers barely got by from year to year.

Cotton and Other Crops The South's postwar economy remained tied mainly to growing cotton. Between 1870 and 1900, the number of acres planted in cotton more than doubled. Increased output, however, only added to the cotton farmer's problems. The resulting glut of cotton on world markets caused cotton prices to decline by more than 50 percent by the 1890s. Per capita income in the South actually declined, and many farmers lost their farms.

Some Southern farmers sought to diversify their farming to escape the trap of depending entirely on cotton. **George Washington Carver**, an African American scientist at **Tuskegee Institute** in Alabama, promoted the growing of such crops as peanuts, sweet potatoes, and soybeans. His work played an important role in shifting southern agriculture toward a more diversified base.

Attempts to Organize Despite some diversification, most small farmers in the South remained in a cycle of debt and poverty. As in the North and the West, hard times produced a harvest of discontent. By 1890, the Farmers' Southern Alliance claimed more than 1 million members. A separate organization for African Americans, the Colored Farmers' National Alliance, had about 250,000 members. Both organizations rallied behind political reforms to solve the farmers' economic problems. If poor Black and poor White farmers in the South could have united, they would have been a potent political force, but the economic interests of the upper class and the powerful racial attitudes of Whites stood in their way.

Segregation

When Reconstruction ended in 1877, the North withdrew protection of African Americans and left Southerners to solve their social and economic problems. Democratic politicians who came to power in the southern states after Reconstruction, known as redeemers, won support from the business community and **White supremacists**. The latter group favored treating African Americans as social inferiors by separating, or segregating, public facilities by race. The redeemers often used race as a rallying cry to deflect attention from the real concerns of tenant farmers and the working poor. They discovered that they could exert political power by playing on the racial fears of Whites.

Discrimination and the Supreme Court During Reconstruction, federal laws protected African Americans from discrimination by local and state governments. Starting in the late 1870s, however, the U.S. Supreme Court struck down these laws. In the **Civil Rights Cases of 1883**, the Court ruled that Congress could not ban racial discrimination practiced by private citizens and businesses, including railroads and hotels, used by the public.

Then, in 1896, in the landmark case *Plessy v. Ferguson*, the Supreme Court upheld a Louisiana law requiring "separate but equal accommodations" for White and Black railroad passengers. The Court ruled that Louisiana's law did not violate the 14th Amendment's guarantee of "equal protection of the laws."

These federal court decisions supported a wave of segregation laws, commonly known as **Jim Crow laws**, that southern states adopted beginning in the 1870s. These laws required segregated washrooms, drinking fountains, park benches, and other facilities in virtually all public places. Only the use of streets and most stores was not restricted according to a person's race.

Loss of Civil Rights Other discriminatory laws resulted in the wholesale disenfranchisement of Black voters by 1900. In Louisiana, for example, 130,334 Black voters were registered in 1896 but only 1,342 in 1904—a 99 percent decline. Southern states invented various political and legal devices were to prevent African Americans from voting. Among the most common obstacles were **literacy tests**, **poll taxes**, and political party primaries for Whites only. Many Southern states adopted so-called **grandfather clauses**, which allowed a man to vote if his grandfather had voted in elections before Reconstruction. The Supreme Court again approved such laws in an 1898 case that upheld a state's right to use literacy tests to determine citizens' qualifications for voting.

Discrimination took many forms. In southern courts, African Americans could not serve on juries. If convicted of crimes, they often received stiffer penalties than Whites. In some cases, African Americans accused of crimes did not receive the formality of a court-ordered sentence. **Lynch mobs** killed more than 1,400 Black men during the 1890s. **Economic discrimination** was also widespread, keeping most southern African Americans out of skilled trades and even factory jobs. Thus, while poor Whites and immigrants learned the industrial skills that would help them rise into the middle class, African Americans remained engaged in farming and low-paying domestic work.

Responding to Segregation

Segregation, disenfranchisement, and lynching left African Americans in the South oppressed but not powerless. Some responded with confrontation. **Ida B. Wells**, editor of the *Memphis Free Speech,* a Black newspaper, campaigned against lynching and the Jim Crow laws. Death threats and the destruction of her printing press forced Wells to carry on her work from the North. Other Black leaders advocated leaving the South. Bishop Henry Turner formed the **International Migration Society** in 1894 to help Blacks emigrate to Africa. Many African Americans moved to Kansas and Oklahoma.

Booker T. Washington A third response to oppression, advocated by **Booker T. Washington**, was to accommodate it. Washington, who was born enslaved, had graduated from Hampton Institute in Virginia. In 1881, he established an industrial and agricultural school for African Americans in Tuskegee, Alabama. There, African Americans learned skilled trades while Washington preached the virtues of hard work, moderation, and economic self-help. Earning money, he said, was like having "a little green ballot" that would empower African Americans more effectively than a political ballot.

Speaking at an exposition in Atlanta in 1895, Washington argued that "the agitation of the questions of social equality is the extremist folly." He supported what became known as the **Atlanta Compromise**, a belief that Black and White Southerners shared a responsibility for making their region prosper. He thought African Americans should focus on working hard at their jobs and not challenge segregation and discrimination. In return, Whites should support education and even some legal rights for African Americans. "In all things that are purely social," Washington said, "we can be as separate as the fingers, yet one as the hand in all things essential to mutual progress."

In 1900, Washington organized the National Negro Business League, which established 320 chapters across the country to support businesses owned and operated by African Americans. Washington's emphasis on racial harmony and **economic cooperation** won praise from many Whites, including industrialist Andrew Carnegie and President Theodore Roosevelt.

Responses to Washington Later civil rights leaders had mixed reactions to Washington's approach, especially his Atlanta speech. Some criticized him as too willing to accept discrimination. For example, after 1900, the younger African American leader **W. E. B. Du Bois** would demand an end to segregation and the granting of equal civil rights to all Americans. In contrast, other writers praised Washington for paving the way for Black self-reliance because of his emphasis on starting and supporting Black-owned businesses.

Change came slowly to a region that clung to its past. White supremacy and segregation would continue to dominate race relations in the South until the civil rights movement of the 1950s and 1960s. The Southern economy would finally achieve the vision of the "New South" after World War II, as it shared in the prosperity of the postwar era.

REFLECT ON THE LEARNING OBJECTIVE

1. Explain three factors that contributed to continuity or change in the "New South" from 1877 to 1898.

KEY TERMS BY THEME

Southern Development (WXT)
"New South"
Henry Grady
Birmingham (steel)
Memphis (lumber)
Richmond (tobacco)
national rail network
tenant farmers
sharecroppers

George Washington Carver
Tuskegee Institute
Racial Discrimination (MIG, POL)
White supremacists
Civil Rights Cases of 1883
Plessy v. Ferguson
Jim Crow laws
literacy tests
poll taxes

grandfather clauses
lynch mobs
economic discrimination
Ida B. Wells
International Migration Society
Booker T. Washington
W. E. B. Du Bois
Atlanta Compromise
economic cooperation

MULTIPLE-CHOICE QUESTIONS

Questions 1–3 refer to the following excerpt.

"I attended a funeral once in Pickens County in my State. . . . They buried him in the heart of a pine forest, and yet the pine coffin was imported from Cincinnati. They buried him within touch of an iron mine, and yet the nails in his coffin and the iron in the shovel that dug his grave were imported from Pittsburgh. . . . The South didn't furnish a thing on earth for that funeral but the corpse and the hole in the ground. There they put him away and the clods rattled down on his coffin, and they buried him in a New York coat and a Boston pair of shoes and a pair of breeches from Chicago and a shirt from Cincinnati, leaving him nothing to carry into the next world with him to remind him of the country in which he lived, and for which he fought for four years, but the chill of blood in his veins and the marrow in his bones."

Henry Grady, editor of the *Atlanta Constitution,* 1889

1. The key idea in the excerpt is that Grady believes
   (A) the Civil War damaged the Southern economy
   (B) former Confederate soldiers deserved better treatment
   (C) the secession of the Confederacy was justified
   (D) the South needed to industrialize

2. Which of the following best demonstrates a change or condition that reflected Grady's hopes for the South?

(A) Railroads, textile mills, and steel factories developed.

(B) Formerly enslaved people often became tenant farmers.

(C) Northern investors controlled three-quarters of Southern railroads.

(D) The Southern economy remained mainly tied to agriculture.

3. Grady's comments best express the viewpoint of which group of people?

(A) Southerners who advocated developing a "New South"

(B) Populists who wanted a coalition between White and Black Southerners

(C) Redeemers who wanted to restore pre-Civil War Southern culture

(D) Political leaders who agreed with the decision in *Plessy v. Ferguson*

SHORT-ANSWER QUESTION

Use complete sentences; an outline or bulleted list alone is not acceptable.

1. "The wisest among my race understand that the agitation of questions of social equality is the extremist folly, and that progress in the enjoyment of all privileges that will come to us must be the result of severe and constant struggle rather than of artificial forcing. No race that has anything to contribute to the markets of the world is long in any degree ostracized. It is important and right that all privileges of the law be ours, but it is vastly more important that we be prepared for the exercises of these privileges. The opportunity to earn a dollar in a factory just now is worth infinitely more than the opportunity to spend a dollar in an opera house."

Booker T. Washington, speech at Cotton States and
International Exposition, Atlanta, September 18, 1895

Using the excerpt above, answer (a), (b), and (c).

(a) Briefly describe ONE specific way that Washington's policies were similar to the goals of the "New South" movement.

(b) Briefly explain ONE historical development that resulted from the perspectives presented by Washington.

(c) Briefly explain ONE historical development that contributed to the perspective presented by Washington.

Technological Innovation

*Only an inventor knows how to borrow, and every man
is or should be an inventor.*

Ralph Waldo Emerson, *Letter and Social Aims*, 1876

Learning Objective: Explain the effects of technological advances in the development of the United States over time.

Vital to industrial development of the United States were new inventions. Communications, transportation, basic industries, electric power, and urban growth were all improved by technological innovations.

Inventions

The first radical change in the speed of communications was the invention of a workable telegraph by Samuel F. B. Morse, initially demonstrated in 1844. By the time of the Civil War, electronic communication by telegraph and rapid transportation by railroad were already becoming standard parts of modern living, especially in the Northern states.

After the war, Cyrus W. Field's invention of an improved **transatlantic cable** in 1866 suddenly made it possible to send messages across the seas in minutes. By 1900, cables linked all inhabited continents of the world in an electronic network of nearly instantaneous, global communication. This communication revolution soon internationalized markets and prices for basic commodities, such as grains, coal, and steel, often placing local and smaller producers at the mercy of international forces.

Among the hundreds of noteworthy inventions of the late 19th century were the typewriter (1867), the **telephone** developed by **Alexander Graham Bell** (1876), the cash register (1879), the calculating machine (1887), and the adding machine (1888). These new products became essential tools for business. Products for the consumer that were in widespread use by the end of the century were George **Eastman's Kodak camera** (1888), Lewis E. Waterman's fountain pen (1884), and King Gillette's safety razor and blade (1895).

The Steel Industry

The technological breakthrough that launched the rise of heavy industry was the discovery of a new process for making large quantities of steel, a more durable metal than iron. In the 1850s, both **Henry Bessemer** in England

and William Kelly in the United States discovered that blasting air through molten iron produced high-quality steel. Because the Great Lakes region from Pennsylvania to Illinois had abundant coal reserves and access to the iron ore of Minnesota's Mesabi Range, it emerged as the center of steel production.

Edison and Westinghouse

Possibly the greatest inventor of the 19th century, **Thomas Edison** worked as a telegraph operator as a young man. In 1869, at age 22, he patented his first invention, a machine for recording votes. Income from his early inventions enabled Edison to establish a research laboratory in **Menlo Park**, New Jersey, in 1876. This was the world's first modern research laboratory, which was Edison's "invention factory." He declared that it would turn out "a minor invention every ten days and a big thing every six months or so." It ranks among Edison's most important contributions to science and industry because it introduced the concept of mechanics and engineers working on a project as a team rather than independently.

Out of Edison's lab came more than a thousand patented inventions, including the phonograph, the dynamo for generating **electric power**, the mimeograph machine, and the motion picture camera. Of all the inventions of the era, Edison's improvements to the incandescent lamp in 1879 (the first practical electric lightbulb), was arguably the most significant. **Electric light** revolutionized life, especially in the cities, from the way people worked to the way they shopped. During his lifetime, Edison became a mythic figure, even though others inventors improved on his work.

Another remarkable inventor, **George Westinghouse**, held more than 400 patents and was responsible for developing an air brake for railroads (1869) and a transformer for producing high-voltage alternating current (AC). The latter invention made possible the **lighting** of cities and the operation of electric streetcars, subways, and electrically powered machinery and appliances. Westinghouse and General Electric came to dominate electric technology with their AC power supply systems, which came to replace Edison's direct current technology. By 1900, various electric trades employed nearly a million people, making electric light and power one of the nation's largest and fastest growing industries.

Technology and Growth of Cities

Developments in how people moved from place to place and the kind of buildings they lived and worked in remade the urban landscape. Cities grew both outward and upward.

Changes in Transportation Improvements in urban transportation made the growth of cities possible. In the walking cities of the pre-Civil War era, people had little choice but to live within walking distance of their shops or jobs. Such cities gave way to streetcar cities, in which people lived in residences many miles from their jobs and commuted to work on horse-drawn streetcars. By the 1890s, both horse-drawn cars and cable cars were being replaced by electric trolleys, elevated railroads, and **subways**, which could transport people to urban residences even farther from the city's commercial center. The building of massive steel suspension bridges such as New York's **Brooklyn Bridge** (1883) also made possible longer commutes between residential areas and city centers.

Skyscrapers As cities expanded outward, they also soared upward, since increasing land values in the central business district made the construction of taller and taller buildings profitable. In 1885, Chicago became the home of the first true **skyscraper** with a steel skeleton, a ten-story building designed by William Le Baron Jenny. Structures of this size were made possible by such innovations as the **Otis elevator** and the central steam-heating system with radiators in every room. By 1900, steel-framed skyscrapers for offices of industry had replaced church spires as the dominant feature of American urban skylines.

Marketing Consumer Goods

The increased output of U.S. factories and the invention of new consumer products enabled businesses to sell merchandise to a large public. **R. H. Macy** in New York and Marshall Field in Chicago made the **large department store** popular in urban centers. Frank Woolworth's five-and-dime stores brought nationwide chain stores to towns and urban neighborhoods. Two large **mail-order companies**, Sears, Roebuck and Co., and Montgomery Ward, used the improved rail system to ship to rural customers everything from hats to houses that people ordered from each company's thick catalog. The Sears catalog became famous as the "wish book."

Packaged foods under such brand names as Kellogg and Post became common items in American homes. Refrigerated railroad cars and **canning** enabled **Gustavus Swift** and other packers to change the eating habits of Americans with mass-produced meat and vegetable products. **Advertising** and new marketing techniques not only promoted a **consumer economy** but also created a consumer culture in which shopping became a favorite pastime.

REFLECT ON THE LEARNING OBJECTIVE

1. Explain three technological innovations and their effects during the period from 1865 to 1898.

KEY TERMS BY THEME

Technology (WXT)	electric light	large department store
transatlantic cable	George Westinghouse	mail-order companies
telephone	subways	Sears, Roebuck & Co.
Alexander Graham Bell	Brooklyn Bridge	packaged foods
Eastman's Kodak camera	skyscraper	canning
Henry Bessemer	Otis elevator	Gustavus Swift
Thomas Edison	**Marketing Innovations**	advertising
Menlo Park	**(WXT)**	consumer economy
electric power	R. H. Macy	

Questions 1–2 refer to the following excerpt.

> My laboratory will soon be completed. . . . I will have the best equipped and largest Laboratory extant, and the facilities incomparably superior to any other for rapid and cheap development of an invention and working it up into Commercial shape with models, patterns and special machinery. . . . In fact there is no similar institution in Existence. We do our own castings and forging. Can build anything from a lady's watch to a Locomotive.
>
> Thomas Alva Edison, letter, November 14, 1887

1. What did Edison mean with the claim that "there is no similar institution in Existence"?

   (A) He had created the first factory to mass-produce commercial products.

   (B) He had created the first laboratory dedicated to producing inventions.

   (C) He had developed the designs for electric-powered streetcars and locomotives.

   (D) He had developed marketing practices that promoted a consumer economy.

2. How did the development described in the excerpt cause a lasting change in how science and industry operated?

   (A) It showed that large corporations would need to invent new products in order to survive.

   (B) It marked the first time an inventor became famous for developing something new.

   (C) It started the tradition of individual inventors working on their own.

   (D) It promoted the idea that teams of people working together could invent new products profitably.

SHORT-ANSWER QUESTION

1. Answer (a), (b), and (c).

   (a) Briefly explain how ONE innovation caused changes in communications during the period from 1865 to 1898.

   (b) Briefly explain how ONE innovation caused changes in the marketing of consumer goods during the period from 1865 to 1898.

   (c) Briefly explain how ONE innovation caused changes in the development of cities during the period from 1865 to 1898.

The Rise of Industrial Capitalism

Then, again, the ability to organize and conduct industrial, commercial, or financial enterprises is rare; the great captains of industry are as rare as great generals.

William Graham Sumner, "What Social Classes Owe to Each Other," 1903

Learning Objective: Explain the socioeconomic continuities and changes associated with the growth of industrial capitalism from 1865 to 1898.

While new technologies played a key role in the economic growth after 1865, in many ways the more important "inventions" were the management and financial structures that helped to create the large-scale industries that came to dominate the era. The continued quest for increased profits inspired a variety of approaches to the consolidation of businesses and wealth.

The Business of Railroads

The dynamic combination of business leadership, capital, technology, markets, labor, and government support was especially evident in the development of the **nation's first big business**—railroads. After the Civil War, railroad mileage increased more than fivefold in a 35-year period (from 35,000 miles in 1865 to 193,000 miles in 1900). The federal government subsidized this growth by providing companies low-interest loans and millions of acres of public lands. Railroads created a market for goods that was national in scale and by so doing encouraged mass production, mass consumption, and economic specialization. The resources used in railroad building promoted the growth of other industries, especially coal and steel.

Railroads also affected the routines of daily life. Prior to 1883, each community or region could determine when noon was for itself based on when the sun was directly overhead. In effect, the country had 144 different time zones. In 1883 that ended. The **American Railroad Association** divided the country into four **time zones**. Railroad time became standard time for all Americans.

Maybe the most important innovation of the railroads was the creation of the modern stockholder corporation. Railroads required so much investment that they needed to develop complex structures in finance, business management, and the regulation of competition.

Competition and Consolidation

In the early decades of railroading (1830–1860), the building of dozens of separate local lines had resulted in different gauges (distance between tracks) and incompatible equipment. These inefficiencies were reduced after the Civil War through the **consolidation** of competing railroads into integrated trunk lines. A trunk line was the major route between large cities; smaller branch lines connected the trunk line with outlying towns. "Commodore" **Cornelius Vanderbilt** used his millions earned from a steamboat business to merge local railroads into the New York Central Railroad (1867), which ran from New York City to Chicago. It operated more than 4,500 miles of track. Other trunk lines, such as the Baltimore and Ohio Railroad and the Pennsylvania Railroad, connected eastern seaports with Chicago and other Midwestern cities and set standards of excellence and efficiency for the rest of the industry.

Problems and Corruption However, railroads were not always efficient. As has been the case with other forms of new technology throught history, investors overbuilt in the 1870s and 1880s. Some companies suffered from mismanagement and outright fraud. Speculators such as **Jay Gould** entered the railroad business for quick profits and made their millions by selling off assets and **watering stock** (inflating the value of a corporation's assets and profits before selling its stock to the public). In a ruthless scramble to survive, railroads competed by offering **rebates** (discounts) and kickbacks to favored shippers while charging exorbitant freight rates to smaller customers such as farmers. Railroads also attempted to increase profits by forming **pools**, in which competing companies agreed secretly to fix rates and share traffic.

Concentration of Railroad Ownership A financial panic in 1893 forced one-quarter of all railroads into **bankruptcy**. Bankers led by **J. Pierpont Morgan** quickly moved in to take control of the bankrupt railroads and consolidate them. With competition eliminated, they could stabilize rates and reduce debts. By 1900, seven giant systems controlled nearly two-thirds of the nation's railroads. The consolidation made the rail system more efficient. However, the system was controlled by a few powerful men such as Morgan, who dominated the boards of competing railroad corporations through **interlocking directorates** (the same directors ran competing companies). In effect, they created regional railroad monopolies.

Railroad Power Railroads captured the imagination of late-19th century America, as the public, local communities, states, and federal government invested in their development. At the same time, however, customers and small investors often felt that they were the victims of slick financial schemes and ruthless practices. Early attempts to regulate the railroads by law did little good. Granger laws passed by Midwestern states in the 1870s were overturned by the Supreme Court, and the federal Interstate Commerce Act of 1887 was at first ineffective (see Topic 6.12). Not until the Progressive era in the early 20th century did Congress expand the powers of the Interstate Commerce Commission to protect the public interest.

TRANSCONTINENTAL RAILROADS, 1865–1900

0   500   1000 Miles
0   500   1000 Kilometers

CANADA

Great Northern R.R.

Northern Pacific R.R.

Southern Pacific R.R.

N.Y. Central R.R.

Promontory Peak

Union Pacific R.R.

Central Pacific R.R.

Pennsylvania R.R.

Atchison, Topeka & Santa Fe R.R.

Southern Railway

Southern Pacific R.R.

Southern Pacific R.R.

PACIFIC OCEAN

ATLANTIC OCEAN

MEXICO

Gulf of Mexico

Industrial Empires

The late 19th century witnessed a major shift in the nature of industrial production. Early factories had concentrated on producing textiles, clothing, and leather products. After the Civil War, a "second Industrial Revolution" resulted in the growth of large-scale industry and the production of steel, petroleum, electric power, and the industrial machinery to produce other goods.

Andrew Carnegie and the Steel Industry Leadership of the fast-growing steel industry passed to a shrewd business genius, **Andrew Carnegie**. Born in 1835 in Scotland, Carnegie immigrated to the United States and worked his way up from poverty to become the superintendent of a Pennsylvania railroad. In the 1870s, he started manufacturing steel in Pittsburgh and soon outdistanced his competitors by a combination of salesmanship and the use of the latest technology. Carnegie employed a business strategy known as *vertical integration*, in which a company would control every stage of the industrial process, from mining the raw materials to transporting the finished product. By 1900, Carnegie Steel employed 20,000 workers and produced more steel than all the mills in Britain.

Deciding to retire from business to devote himself to philanthropy, Carnegie sold his company in 1900 for more than $400 million to a new steel combination headed by Morgan. The new corporation, **United States Steel,** was the first billion-dollar company. It was also the largest enterprise in the world, employing 168,000 people and controlling more than three-fifths of the nation's steel business.

Rockefeller and the Oil Industry The first U.S. oil well was drilled by Edwin Drake in 1859 in Pennsylvania. Only four years later, in 1863, a young **John D. Rockefeller** founded a company that would quickly eliminate its competition and take control of most of the nation's oil refineries. By 1881, his company—by then known as the **Standard Oil** Trust—controlled 90 percent of the oil refinery business. It had become a **monopoly**, a company that dominates a market so much that it faces little or no competition from other companies. By controlling the supply and prices of oil, Standard Oil's profits soared and so did Rockefeller's fortune. When he retired, his fortune was worth about $900 million.

In part, Standard Oil grew because Rockefeller applied new technology and efficient management practices. Sometimes this kept prices low for consumers. However, as the company grew, it became very powerful. Rockefeller was able to extort rebates from railroad companies and temporarily cut prices in order to force rival companies to sell out.

Controversy over Corporate Power Emulating the success of Rockefeller, Carnegie, and Morgan, leaders in the meat, sugar, tobacco, and other industries also formed dominant companies to gain control of the markets. These companies were organized in various ways:

- A **trust** is an organization or board that manages the assets of other companies. Under Rockefeller, Standard Oil became a trust in which one board of trustees managed a combination of once-competing oil companies. ("Trust" added other meanings in later years.)

- **Horizontal integration** is a process through which one company takes control of all its former competitors in a specific industry, such as oil refining or coal mining.

- **Vertical integration** is a process through which one company takes control of all stages of making a product. For example, Carnegie Steel controlled coal mines, the ore ships, steel mills, and distribution systems for the steel company to reduce costs, improve efficiency, and increase profits.

- A **holding company** is one created to own and control diverse companies. Banker J. Pierpont Morgan managed a holding company that orchestrated the management of the companies it had acquired in various industries, such as banking, rail transportation, and steel.

Critics of these giant corporations charged that they were bad for the economy. By creating monopolies, they subverted competition in open and free markets. According to the critics, monopolies slowed innovation, overcharged consumers, and developed excessive political influence. The word "monopoly" came to stand for a company that was so large and powerful that it threatened the public interest.

Laissez-Faire Capitalism

Federal, state, and local government all supported businesses and economic growth with actions such as passing high tariffs, building infrastructure, and operating public schools and universities. However, the prevailing economic, scientific, and religious beliefs of the late 19th century led people to reject government regulation of business. The economic expression of these beliefs was summed up in the phrase "**laissez-faire**."

Conservative Economics

In 1776, economist **Adam Smith** had argued in *The Wealth of Nations* that mercantilism, which included extensive regulation of trade by government, was less efficient than allowing businesses to be guided by the "invisible hand" (impersonal economic forces) of the law of supply and demand. While Smith supported some government regulations, he believed that in general, unregulated businesses would be motivated by their own self-interest to offer improved goods and services at low prices.

In the 19th century, American industrialists appealed to laissez-faire theory to justify their methods of doing business. The rise of monopolistic trusts in the 1880s seemed to undercut the very competition needed for natural regulation. Even so, among conservatives and business leaders, laissez-faire theory was constantly invoked in legislative halls and lobbies to ward off any threat of government regulation.

Social Darwinism Charles Darwin's theory of natural selection in biology offended the beliefs of many religious conservatives, but it bolstered the views of economic conservatives. Led by English social philosopher Herbert Spencer, some people argued for **Social Darwinism**, the belief that Darwin's ideas of natural selection and **survival of the fittest** should be applied to the marketplace. Spencer believed that concentrating wealth in the hands of the "fit" benefited everyone.

A student of Spencer's beliefs, Professor **William Graham Sumner** of Yale University, introduced the principles of Social Darwinism to the study of sociology in the United States. He argued that helping the poor was misguided because it interfered with the laws of nature and would only weaken the evolution of the species by preserving the unfit. The teachings of respected scholars such as Sumner provided a "scientific" sanction for racial intolerance. Race theories about the superiority of one group over others would continue into the 20th century.

Protestant Work Ethic A number of Americans found religion more convincing than Social Darwinism in justifying the wealth of successful industrialists and bankers. John D. Rockefeller diligently applied the **Protestant**

work ethic (that material success was a sign of God's favor and a just reward for hard work) to both his business and personal life. Because of this, he concluded that "God gave me my riches." In a popular lecture, "Acres of Diamonds," the Reverend Russell Conwell preached that everyone had a duty to become rich.

The Concentration of Wealth

By the 1890s, the richest 10 percent of the U.S. population controlled 90 percent of the nation's wealth. Industrialization created a new class of millionaires, some of whom flaunted their wealth by living in ostentatious mansions, sailing enormous yachts, and throwing lavish parties. The Vanderbilts graced the waterfront of Newport, Rhode Island, with summer homes that rivaled the villas of European royalty. Guests at one of their dinner parties were invited to hunt for their party favors by using small silver shovels to seek out the precious gems hidden in sand on long silver trays.

Many Americans ignored the widening gap between the rich and the poor. They found hope in the examples of **"self-made men"** in business such as Andrew Carnegie and Thomas Edison and novels by **Horatio Alger** Jr. Every Alger novel portrayed a young man of modest means who becomes wealthy through honesty, hard work, and a little luck. In reality, opportunities for upward mobility (movement into a higher economic bracket) did exist, but the rags-to-riches career of an Andrew Carnegie was unusual. Statistical studies demonstrate that the typical wealthy businessperson of the day was a White, Anglo-Saxon, Protestant male who came from an upper- or middle-class background and whose father was in business or banking.

Business Influence Outside the United States

Corporations in the late 19th century increasingly desired to do business in Latin America and Asia. Industries wanted the raw materials they could process into finished goods. Around 1900, imports from Cuba, Brazil, and Asia of products such as sugar and rubber accounted for about 30 percent of U.S. imports. Businesses also wanted to sell manufactured goods and agricultural products abroad. Around 1900, the United States included about 5 percent of the world population but accounted for about 15 percent of world exports. The growth of business interests around the world was one reason the United States became more involved in international affairs in the late 1800s and early 1900s (see Topics 7.1 and 7.2).

REFLECT ON THE LEARNING OBJECTIVE

1. Explain three socioeconomic changes associated with the growth of industrial capitalism from 1865 to 1898.

KEY TERMS BY THEME

Business of Railroads (WXT)
nation's first big business
American Railroad
  Association
time zones
consolidation
Cornelius Vanderbilt
Jay Gould
watering stock
rebates
pools
bankruptcy
J. Pierpont Morgan

Large Scale Industry (WXT)
interlocking directorates
Andrew Carnegie
United States Steel
John D. Rockefeller
monopoly
Standard Oil
trust
horizontal integration
vertical integration
holding company

Capitalism (CUL)
laissez-faire
Adam Smith
Social Darwinism
survival of the fittest
William Graham Sumner
Protestant work ethic
concentration of wealth
"self-made men"
Horatio Alger

MULTIPLE-CHOICE QUESTIONS

Questions 1–3 refer to the following excerpt.

"Competition therefore is the law of nature. Nature is entirely neutral; she submits to him who most energetically and resolutely assails her. She grants her rewards to the fittest; therefore, without regard to other considerations of any kind. . . . Such is the system of nature. If we do not like it and if we try to amend it, there is one way in which we can do it. We take from the better and give to the worse. . . . Let it be understood that we cannot go outside this alternative: liberty, inequality, survival of the fittest; not-liberty, equality, survival of the unfittest. The former carries society forward and favors all its best members; the latter carries society downward and favors all its worst members."

William Graham Sumner, sociologist, *The Challenge of Facts,* 1882

1. Sumner most clearly expresses ideas associated in the 19th century with

(A) John Locke's description of the social contract in the *Second Treatise of Government*

(B) Thomas Jefferson's belief about human equality in the Declaration of Independence

(C) Charles Darwin's explanation on why some species survive and others do not in *On the Origins of Species*

(D) J. Pierpont Morgan's use of interlocking directorates to consolidate ownership among railroads

2. Supporters of the position expressed by Sumner would likely defend

(A) monopolies because they reduced destructive economic competition

(B) laissez-faire capitalism because it reduced business regulations

(C) socialism because it emphasized equality among people

(D) populism because it helped farmers who were poor

3. Which of the following developments would be most consistent with the beliefs expressed in the excerpt?

(A) Consolidation of wealth by an elite

(B) Expansion of rights for women

(C) Passage of antitrust legislation

(D) Spread of organized labor

SHORT-ANSWER QUESTIONS

Use complete sentences; an outline or bulleted list alone is not acceptable.

1. "We accept and welcome . . . the law of competition between these, as being not only beneficial, but essential for the progress of the race."

Andrew Carnegie, "Gospel of Wealth," 1889

"The struggle for the survival of the fittest . . . as well as the law of supply and demand, were observed in all ages past until Standard Oil company preached cooperation, and it did cooperate so successfully."

John D. Rockefeller, interview given around 1917

Using the excerpts above, answer (a), (b), and (c).

(a) Briefly explain ONE significant difference between Carnegie's perspective and Rockefeller's perspective on the role of competition in industrial development.

(b) Briefly explain ONE historical event or development from Carnegie's career that supports his view on competition.

(c) Briefly explain ONE historical event or development from Rockefeller's career that supports his view on competition.

2. Answer (a), (b), and (c).

(a) Briefly explain ONE specific example of how government promoted the growth of railroads in the United States before 1900.

(b) Briefly explain ONE specific example of how the rise of large corporations influenced the U.S. economy from 1865 to 1900.

(c) Briefly explain ONE specific text or belief that influenced the United States to follow laissez-faire policies.

Labor in the Gilded Age

We have been brought to the ragged edge of anarchy.

Richard Olney, U.S. Attorney General on the
Pullman Strike, July 4, 1894

Learning Objective: Explain the socioeconomic continuities and changes associated with the growth of industrial capitalism from 1865 to 1898.

The expression *Gilded Age*, first used by Mark Twain in 1873 as the title of a book, referred to the superficial glitter of the new wealth so prominently displayed in the late 19th century. The characterization of the period from 1865 to 1898 as the Gilded Age has proved a useful label for an era in which the "captains of industry" controlled large corporations, created great fortunes, and dominated politics. At the same time, the problems faced by workers, farmers, and burgeoning cities festered under the surface of the new wealth.

Challenges for Wage Earners

The growth of industry was based on hard physical labor in mines and factories. However, for the people doing these jobs, life was hard.

Wages By 1900, two-thirds of all employed Americans worked for wages, usually at jobs that required them to labor ten hours a day, six days a week. Wages were determined by the laws of supply and demand. Because there was usually a large supply of immigrants competing for factory jobs, wages were barely above the level needed for bare subsistence. Low wages were justified by David Ricardo (1772–1823), whose famous **"iron law of wages"** argued that raising wages would only increase the working population, and the availability of more workers would in turn cause wages to fall, thus creating a cycle of misery and starvation.

Real wages (income adjusted for inflation or deflation) rose steadily in the late 19th century, but even so most **wage earners** could not support a family decently on one income. Therefore, working-class families depended on the income of women and children. In 1870, about 12 percent of children were employed outside the home. By 1900, that number had increased to about 20 percent. In 1890, 11 million of the 12.5 million families in the United States averaged less than $380 a year in income.

Labor Discontent Before the Industrial Revolution, workers labored in small workplaces that valued an artisan's skills. People often felt a sense of accomplishment in creating a product from start to finish. Factory work was radically different. Industrial workers were often assigned just one step in the manufacturing of a product, performing semiskilled tasks monotonously. Both immigrants from abroad and migrants from rural America had to learn to work under the tyranny of the clock. In many industries, such as railroads and mining, working conditions were dangerous. Many workers were exposed to chemicals and pollutants that only later were discovered to cause chronic illness and early death.

Industrial workers rebelled against intolerable working conditions by missing work or quitting. They changed jobs on the average of every three years. About 20 percent of those who worked in factories eventually dropped out of the industrial workplace rather than continuing. This was a far higher percentage than those who protested by joining labor unions.

The Struggles of Organized Labor

The late 19th century witnessed the most deadly—and frequent—labor conflicts in the nation's history. Many feared the country was heading toward open warfare between capital and labor.

Industrial Warfare

With a surplus of low-cost labor, management held most of the power in its struggles with organized labor. Strikers could easily be replaced by bringing in strikebreakers, or scabs—unemployed persons desperate for jobs. Employers used several tactics for defeating unions:

- *Lockout:* the act of closing a factory to break a labor movement before it could get organized
- *Blacklist:* a roster of the names of pro-union workers that employers circulated so that these people could not find work
- *Yellow-dog contract:* a contract that included as a condition of employment that workers could not join a union
- *Private guards* and *state militia:* forces used by employers to put down strikes
- *Court injunction:* judicial action used by an employer to prevent or end a strike

Moreover, management fostered public fear of unions as anarchistic and un-American. Before 1900, management won most of its battles with organized labor because, if violence developed, employers could almost always count on the support of the federal and state governments.

Tactics by Labor Workers were divided on the best methods for defending themselves against management. Some union leaders advocated political action. Others favored direct confrontation: strikes, picketing, boycotts, and slowdowns to achieve union recognition and **collective bargaining,** the ability of workers to negotiate as a group with an employer over wages and working conditions.

Great Railroad Strike of 1877 One of the worst outbreaks of labor violence in the century erupted in 1877. During an economic depression, the railroad companies cut wages in order to reduce costs. A strike on the Baltimore and Ohio Railroad quickly spread across 11 states and shut down two-thirds of the country's rail lines. Railroad workers were joined by 500,000 workers from other industries in an escalating strike that quickly became national in scale. For the first time since the 1830s, a president (Rutherford B. Hayes) used federal troops to end a labor dispute. The strike and the violence finally ended, but not before more than 100 people had been killed. After the strike, some employers addressed the workers' grievances by improving wages and working conditions, while others took a harder line by busting workers' organizations.

Attempts to Organize National Unions

Before the 1860s, unions had been organized as local associations in one city or region. They were usually **craft unions,** ones focused on one type of work.

National Labor Union The first attempt to organize all workers in all states—skilled and unskilled, agricultural and industrial—was the **National Labor Union**. Founded in 1866, it had some 640,000 members by 1868. Besides championing the goals of higher wages and the eight-hour day, it also had a broad social program: equal rights for women and African Americans, monetary reform, and worker cooperatives. Its chief victory was winning the eight-hour day for federal government workers. It lost support, however, after a depression began in 1873 and after the unsuccessful strikes of 1877.

Knights of Labor A second national labor union, the **Knights of Labor**, began in 1869 as a secret society in order to avoid detection by employers. Under the leadership of Terence V. Powderly, the union went public in 1881, opening its membership to all workers, including African Americans and women. Powderly advocated a variety of reforms: (1) forming worker cooperatives "to make each man his own employer," (2) abolishing child labor, (3) abolishing trusts and monopolies, and (4) settling labor disputes by arbitration rather than strikes. Because the Knights were loosely organized, however, Powderly could not control local units that decided to strike.

The Knights of Labor grew rapidly, attaining a peak membership of 730,000 workers in 1886. However, it also declined rapidly after the violence of the Haymarket riot in Chicago in 1886 turned public opinion against the union.

Haymarket Bombing Chicago, with about 80,000 Knights in 1886, was the site of the first May Day labor movement. Also living in Chicago were about 200 anarchists who advocated the violent overthrow of all government. In response to the May Day movement calling for a general strike to achieve an eight-hour day, labor violence broke out at Chicago's McCormick Harvester plant. On May 4, workers held a public meeting in Haymarket Square, and as police attempted to break up the meeting, someone threw a bomb, which killed seven police officers. The bomb thrower was never found. Even so, eight anarchist leaders were tried for the crime, and seven were sentenced to death. Horrified by the bomb incident, many Americans concluded that the union movement was radical and violent. The Knights of Labor, as the most visible union at the time, lost popularity and membership.

American Federation of Labor Unlike the reform-minded Knights of Labor, the **American Federation of Labor** (AFL) concentrated on "bread-and-butter unonism," attaining narrower economic goals. Founded in 1886 as an association of 25 craft unions of skilled workers, and led by **Samuel Gompers** until 1924, the AF of L focused on just higher wages and improved working conditions. Gompers directed his local unions to walk out until the employer agreed to negotiate a new contract through collective bargaining. By 1901, the AF of L was by far the nation's largest labor organization, with 1 million members. Even this union, however, would not achieve major successes until the early decades of the 20th century.

Strikes and Strikebreaking in the 1890s

Two massive strikes in the last decade of the 19th century demonstrated both the growing discontent of labor and the continued power of management to prevail in industrial disputes.

Homestead Strike Henry Clay Frick, the manager of Andrew Carnegie's Homestead Steel plant near Pittsburgh, precipitated a strike in 1892 by cutting wages by nearly 20 percent. Frick used the weapons of the lockout, private guards, and strikebreakers to defeat the steelworkers' walkout after five months. Sixteen people, mostly steelworkers, died in the conflict. The failure of the **Homestead strike** set back the union movement in the steel industry until the New Deal in the 1930s.

Pullman Strike Even more alarming to conservatives was a strike started by workers living in George Pullman's company town near Chicago. The Pullman Palace Car Company manufactured widely used railroad sleeping cars. In 1894, Pullman announced a general cut in wages and fired the leaders of the workers' delegation who came to bargain with him. The workers at Pullman laid down their tools and appealed for help from the American Railroad Union. The ARU's leader, **Eugene V. Debs**, directed railroad workers not to handle any trains with Pullman cars. The union's boycott tied up rail transportation across the country.

Railroad owners supported Pullman by linking Pullman cars to mail trains. They then appealed to President Grover Cleveland, persuading him to use the army to keep the mail trains running. A federal court issued an injunction forbidding interference with the operation of the mail and ordering railroad workers to abandon the boycott and the strike. For failing to respond to this injunction, Debs and other union leaders were arrested and jailed. The jailing of Debs and others effectively ended the strike. In the case of *In re Debs* (1895), the Supreme Court approved the use of court injunctions against strikes, which gave employers a very powerful legal weapon to break unions.

After serving a six-month jail sentence, Debs concluded that more radical solutions were needed to cure labor's problems. He turned to socialism and the American Socialist Party, which he helped to found in 1900.

Conditions in 1900

By 1900, only 3 percent of American workers belonged to unions. Management held the upper hand in labor disputes, with government generally taking its side. However, people were beginning to recognize the need for a better balance between the demands of employers and employees to avoid the numerous strikes and violence that characterized the late 19th century.

During the Gilded Age, industrial growth was concentrated in the Northeast and Midwest regions, the parts of the country with the largest populations, the most capital, and the best transportation. As industries grew, these regions developed more cities and attracted more immigrants from overseas and migrants from rural areas.

REFLECT ON THE LEARNING OBJECTIVE

1. Explain three changes for workers during the period associated with the growth of industrial capitalism from 1865 to 1898.

KEY TERMS BY THEME

Organized Labor (WXT)	craft unions	Samuel Gompers
"iron law of wages"	National Labor Union	Homestead strike
wage earners	Knights of Labor	Pullman strike
collective bargaining	Haymarket bombing	Eugene V. Debs
railroad strike of 1877	American Federation of Labor (AFL)	

MULTIPLE-CHOICE QUESTIONS

Questions 1–3 refer to the following excerpt.

"You evidently have observed the growth of corporate wealth and influence. You recognize that wealth, in order to become more highly productive, is concentrated into fewer hands, and controlled by representatives and directors, and yet you sing the old siren song that the workingman should depend entirely upon his own 'individual effort.'

The school of laissez-faire, of which you seem to be a pronounced advocate, has produced great men in advocating the theory of each for himself and his Satanic majesty taking the hindermost, but the most pronounced advocates of your school of thought in economics have, when practically put to the test, been compelled to admit that combination and organizations of the toiling masses are essential both to prevent the deterioration and to secure an improvement in the condition of the wage earners."

Samuel Gompers, Letter to Judge Peter Grosscup,
"Labor in Industrial Society," 1894

1. This excerpt was written to most directly support which of the following?

   (A) Formation of trusts

   (B) The right to organize and bargain collectively

   (C) The antitrust movement

   (D) Employee ownership of business

2. Which of the following best explains why Gompers thought that "organizations of the toiling masses are essential both to prevent the deterioration and to secure an improvement in the condition of the wage earners"?

   (A) The school of laissez-faire economics

   (B) The rise of the captains of industry

   (C) The concentration of corporate wealth and power

   (D) The belief in individualism and self-reliance

3. The ideas expressed in this excerpt are most closely allied with

   (A) the theory of wages by David Ricardo

   (B) the practice of horizontal integration

   (C) the establishment of Pullman's company town for workers

   (D) the rise of the American Federation of Labor

SHORT-ANSWER QUESTION

Use complete sentences; an outline or bulleted list alone is not acceptable.

1. Answer (a), (b), and (c).

   (a) Briefly explain ONE specific example of the impact of a labor organization during the period from 1865 to 1900.

   (b) Briefly explain ONE specific example of a tactic used by employers to defeat the organization of labor unions.

   (c) Briefly explain ONE specific example of the role of government in a labor conflict during the period from 1865 to 1900.

Immigration and Migration in the Gilded Age

Give me your tired, your poor,
Your huddled masses yearning to breathe free,
The wretched refuse of your teeming shore,
Send these, the homeless, tempest-tossed, to me:
I lift my lamp beside the golden door.

Emma Lazarus, "The New Colossus," 1883, later inscribed
on the Statue of Liberty

Learning Objective: Explain how cultural and economic factors affected migration patterns over time.

In 1893, more than 12 million people attended a world's fair in Chicago known as the World's Columbian Exposition. In just six decades, Chicago's population had grown from a small town of fewer than 4,000 people to the country's second largest city with more than a million residents, the fastest growing city in the nation, if not the world. However, visitors complained of the confusion of tongues, "worse than the tower of Babel," for in 1893 Chicago was a city of immigrants. More than three-fourths of its population were either foreign-born or the children of the foreign-born.

Growth of Immigration

The growing connections between the United States and the world are evident during this period, especially in the area of immigration. In the last half of the 19th century, the U.S. population more than tripled, from about 23.2 million in 1850 to 76.2 million in 1900. The arrival of 16.2 million immigrants fueled the growth. An additional 8.8 million more arrived during the peak years of immigration, 1901–1910.

Push and Pull Factors An increased combination of **"pushes"** (negative factors from which people are fleeing) and **"pulls"** (positive attractions of the adopted country) increased migrations around the world. Several negative forces drove Europeans to emigrate:

- The poverty of displaced farmworkers driven from the land by political turmoil and the mechanization of farm work

- Overcrowding and joblessness in European cities as a result of population growth
- Religious persecution, particularly against Jews in eastern Europe

Positive reasons for moving to the United States included the country's reputation for political and religious freedom and the economic opportunities afforded by the settling of the West and the abundance of industrial jobs in U.S. cities. Economic opportunity fluctuated with the economy. The years of prosperity attracted more immigrants than did the years of depression. Furthermore, the introduction of large steamships and the relatively inexpensive one-way passage in the ships' steerage" made it possible for millions of poor people to emigrate.

"Old" Immigrants from Europe Through the 1880s, the vast majority of immigrants came from northern and western Europe: the British Isles, Germany, and Scandinavia. Most of these **"old" immigrants** were Protestants. Their language (mostly English-speaking) and high level of literacy and occupational skills made it relatively easy for these immigrants to blend into a mostly rural American society in the early decades of the 19th century. However, Irish and German Roman Catholics faced significant discrimination.

"New" Immigrants from Europe Beginning in the 1890s and continuing to the outbreak of World War I in 1914, the national origins of most immigrants changed. The **"new" immigrant**s came from southern and eastern Europe. They were Italians, Greeks, Croats, Slovaks, Poles, and Russians. Many were poor and illiterate peasants who had left autocratic countries and therefore were unaccustomed to democratic traditions. Unlike the earlier groups of Protestant immigrants, the newcomers were largely Roman Catholic, Greek Orthodox, Russian Orthodox, or Jewish. On arrival, most new immigrants crowded into poor ethnic neighborhoods in New York, Chicago, and other major U.S. cities. An estimated 25 percent of them were "birds of passage," young men contracted for unskilled factory, mining, and construction jobs, who would return to their native lands once they had saved a fair sum of money to bring back to their families.

Immigrants from Asia The first large migration of Asians to the United States came from China after gold was discovered in California in 1848. Passage of the **Chinese Exclusion Act** in 1882 ended the immigration of people from China (see Topic 6.9). However, Japanese, Korean, and Filipino immigrants found work in Hawaii, and some settled in California and other states. The first immigrants from South Asia arrived in the early 1900s. However, in response to anti-Asia feelings, Congress passed immigration restrictions in 1917 and 1924 that almost completely stopped immigration from the entire continent. Only Filipinos, because the United States took possession of the Philippines in 1898, could immigrate (see Topic 7.3).

Immigration and Growth of Cities

Urbanization and industrialization developed together. Cities provided both laborers for factories and a market for factory-made goods. The shift in population from rural to urban became more obvious with each passing decade. By 1900, almost 40 percent of Americans lived in towns or cities. By 1920, for the first time, more Americans lived in urban areas—then defined as places with 2,500 people or more—than in rural areas.

People moving into the cities included both immigrants and internal migrants born in the rural United States. In the late 19th century, millions of young Americans from rural areas decided to seek new economic opportunities in the cities. They left the farms for industrial and commercial jobs, and few of them returned. Among those who joined the movement from farms to cities were African Americans from the South. Between 1897 and 1930, nearly 1 million Black Southerners resettled in northern and western cities.

Patterns of Urban Development Cities of the late 19th century underwent significant developments. Not only did they grow in size, but also their internal structure and design changed.

Mass transportation had the effect of segregating urban workers by income. The upper and middle classes moved to **streetcar suburbs** (communities the grew along transit routes leading to an urban center) to escape the pollution, **poverty**, and crime of the city. The exodus of higher-income residents left older sections of the city to the working poor, many of whom were immigrants. The residential areas of the cities and suburbs both reflected and contributed to the class, race, ethnic, and cultural divisions in American society.

Ethnic Neighborhoods As affluent citizens moved out of residences near the business districts, the poor moved into them. To increase their profits, landlords divided up inner-city housing into small, windowless rooms. The resulting slums and **tenement apartments** could cram more than 4,000 people into one city block. In an attempt to correct unlivable conditions, New York City passed a law in 1879 that required each bedroom to have a window. The cheapest way for landlords to respond to the law was to build the so-called **dumbbell tenements**, buildings constructed with open ventilation shafts in the center to provide windows for each room. However, overcrowding and filth in new tenements continued to promote the spread of deadly diseases, such as cholera, typhoid, and tuberculosis.

In their crowded tenement quarters, immigrant groups created distinct **ethnic neighborhoods** where each group could maintain its own language, culture, church or temple, and social club. Many groups even supported their own newspapers and schools. While often crowded, unhealthy, and crime-ridden, these neighborhoods (sometimes called "ghettos") often served as springboards for ambitious and hardworking immigrants and their children to achieve their version of the American Dream.

This explosive growth of immigrants to the United States after 1865 renewed populist protests to keep down the number of immigrants, especially ones who differed by ethnicity, languages, and religions from the "old" immigrants. The efforts to discourage or restrict "new" immigrants drew upon earlier opposition to Irish, Italian, and Chinese immigration.

REFLECT ON THE LEARNING OBJECTIVE

1. Explain how three cultural and economic factors affected migration patterns during the Gilded Age.

KEY TERMS BY THEME

Immigration (MIG)
"pushes"
"pulls"
"old" immigrants
"new" immigrants

Chinese Exclusion Act
streetcar suburbs
tenement apartments
dumbbell tenements
ethnic neighborhoods

MULTIPLE-CHOICE QUESTIONS

Questions 1–2 refer to the following graph.

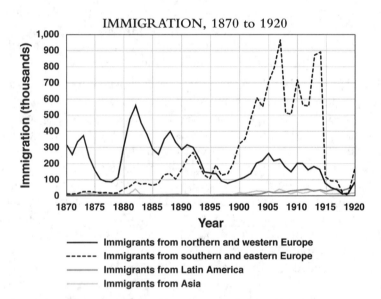

IMMIGRATION, 1870 to 1920

— Immigrants from northern and western Europe
----- Immigrants from southern and eastern Europe
— Immigrants from Latin America
— Immigrants from Asia

Source: U.S. Bureau of the Census. *Historical Statistics of the United States, Colonial Times to 1970*

1. In the graph above, the group of immigrants who would be considered "new" immigrants were those from
   (A) northern and western Europe
   (B) southern and eastern Europe
   (C) Latin America
   (D) Asia

2. Which of the following best explains why immigration declined in some years between 1870 and 1900?

(A) Increased religious persecution in Europe

(B) Military conflicts in Europe

(C) Economic depressions in the United States

(D) Restrictions on Europeans entering the United States

SHORT-ANSWER QUESTION

Use complete sentences; an outline or bulleted list alone is not acceptable.

1. "Between 1820 and 1930, over 62 million people uprooted themselves from their native countries to seek a better life in newer lands around the globe. Almost two-thirds of these enterprising souls came to the United States. . . . Other new countries like Australia and Argentine, it is true, are as much the product of immigration as the United States, but all these such countries were peopled by a very narrow range of nationalities. . . . Only in America were many nationalities mixed together."

Carl N. Degler, historian, *Out of Our Past,* 1970

"Relatively few outsiders entered the [Southern] region. The borders of the old Confederacy might as well have been a dam, so effectively did they turn aside immigrants and hold Southerners within the confines of Dixie. The percentage of foreign born in the South actually fell from 1860 to 1900. By 1910 only 2 percent of the Southern population had been born outside the United States, compared with 14.7 percent for the country as a whole. Immigrants avoided the South because of low wages, sharecropping."

Richard White, historian, *The Republic for Which It Stands,* 2017

Using the excerpts above, answer (a), (b), and (c).

(a) Briefly describe ONE major difference between Degler's and White's historical interpretations of immigration to the United States.

(b) Briefly explain how ONE specific historical event or development in the period 1865 to 1900 that is not explicitly mentioned in the excerpts could be used to support Degler's interpretation.

(c) Briefly explain how ONE specific historical event or development in the period 1865 to 1900 that is not explicitly mentioned in the excerpts could be used to support White's interpretation.

Responses to Immigration in the Gilded Age

Wide open and unguarded stand our gates,
And through them presses a wild, motley throng . . .
O liberty, white Goddess: Is it well
To leave the gates unguarded?

Thomas Bailey Aldrich, "The Unguarded Gates?," 1892

Learning Objective: Explain the various responses to immigration in the period over time.

In the 1870s, when the French sculptor Frédéric-Auguste Bartholdi began work on the **Statue of Liberty**, few laws restricted immigration to the United States. The only large restriction banned Chinese immigrants. By 1886, however—the year that the great welcoming statue was placed on its pedestal in New York Harbor—Congress had passed a number of new laws restricting immigration.

Opposition to Immigration

Several groups supported efforts to restrict immigration in the period from 1865 to 1898. Each focused on its own reasons, though often these reasons overlapped.

- Labor union members were motivated by economic concerns. They resented that employers used immigrants to depress wages and break strikes.

- Employers benefitted from competition among workers for jobs, but they feared that immigrants would advocate radical reforms. Business owners often blamed strikes and the labor movement on foreign agitators.

- Nativists felt alarmed that immigrants would not only take their jobs but would also weaken the culture of the Anglo majority. Often, nativists were Protestants who were openly prejudiced against Roman Catholics. The largest anti-Catholic organization of the 1890s was the **American Protective Association**.

- Social Darwinists believed that southern and eastern Europeans and all non-Europeans were biologically inferior to people of English and Germanic heritage. This idea was supported by many of the leading biologists of the 19th century before it was completely discredited.

Restrictions on Chinese and Other Immigrants The first major laws limiting immigration based on race and nationality targeted the Chinese. This hostility toward the Chinese mainly came from the western states. In many mining towns, half the population was foreign-born, and often most of these were Chinese immigrants. In response to pressure from native-born miners, California passed a Miner's Tax of $20 a month on all foreign-born miners. Then, in 1882, Congress passed the **Chinese Exclusion Act**, which banned all new immigration from China. The restrictions were not fully lifted until 1965.

Restrictions also came in 1882 on the immigration of "undesirable" persons, such as paupers, criminals, convicts, and those diagnosed as mentally incompetent. The **Contract Labor Law of 1885** restricted temporary workers, an effort to protect American workers from competition. A literacy test for immigrants was vetoed by President Cleveland but passed in 1917. Soon after the opening of **Ellis Island** in New York harbor as an immigration center in 1892, new arrivals had to pass more rigorous medical examinations and pay a tax before entering the United States. During a severe depression in the 1890s, nativist sentiment increased, as some jobless workers and employers used foreign-born residents as a convenient scapegoat for economic problems.

The Impact of Restrictions However, anti-immigrant feelings and early restrictions did not stop the flow of newcomers. Between 1860 and 1920, the foreign-born population numbered consistently between 13 and 15 percent of the population. The Statue of Liberty remained a beacon of hope for the poor and the oppressed of southern and eastern Europe until the Quota Acts of the 1920s almost closed Liberty's golden door (see Topic 7.8).

Boss and Machine Politics

In many cities, politicians welcomed newly arrived immigrants to gain their loyalty in future elections. These tightly organized groups of politicians became known as **political machines**. Each machine had its **"boss,"** the top politician who gave orders to the rank and file and doled out government jobs to loyal supporters. Several political machines, such as **Tammany Hall** in New York City, started as social clubs and later developed into power centers to coordinate the needs of businesses, immigrants, and the underprivileged. In return, machines asked for people's votes on election day.

Successful party bosses knew how to manage the competing social, ethnic, and economic groups in the city. Political machines often brought modern services to the city, including a crude form of welfare for urban newcomers. The political organization would find jobs and apartments for recently arrived immigrants and show up at a poor family's door with baskets of food during hard times.

But the political machines could be greedy as well as generous and often stole millions from the taxpayers in the form of graft and fraud. In New York City in the 1860s, for example, an estimated 65 percent of public building funds ended up in the pockets of Tammany Hall's "Boss" Tweed and his cronies.

Settlement Houses

Concerned about the lives of the poor and new immigrants, a number of young, well-educated, middle-class women and men settled into immigrant neighborhoods to learn about the problems of immigrant families firsthand. Living and working in places called **settlement houses**, the young reformers hoped to relieve the effects of poverty by providing social services for people in the neighborhood. The most famous such experiment was Hull House in Chicago, which was started by **Jane Addams** and a college classmate in 1889. Settlement houses taught English to immigrants, pioneered early-childhood education, taught industrial arts, and established neighborhood theaters and music schools. By 1910, there were more than 400 settlement houses in America's largest cities.

Although many immigrants remained in low paying jobs and lived in relative poverty in tenements, their children who took advantage of public education and the many opportunities of the industrial economy did join the growing middle class of this period.

HISTORICAL PERSPECTIVES: *WAS THE UNITED STATES A MELTING POT?*

Politicians in the United States often claim that the country is a land of immigrants. To what extent did immigrants give up their heritage to become Americanized, or fully assimilated, into the existing culture?

The Melting Pot Idea The prevailing view in the 19th and early 20th centuries was that the United States was a **melting pot**, in which immigrant groups quickly shed old-world characteristics in order to become successful citizens of their adopted country. This view was expressed as early as 1782 by a naturalized Frenchman, J. Hector St. John Crèvecoeur. In his *Letters From an American Farmer*, Crèvecoeur described how the American experience "melted" European immigrants "into a new race of men." The term "melting pot" became firmly associated with immigration in a popular play by that name: Israel Zangwill's *The Melting Pot* (1908). One line of this drama described "how the great Alchemist melts and fuses them [immigrants] with purging flames!"

The Salad Bowl Comparison In recent decades, the melting pot concept has come under intense scrutiny and has been challenged by modern historians. Carl N. Degler, for example, has argued that a more accurate metaphor would be the salad bowl, in which each ingredient (ethnic culture) remains intact. To support this view, Degler points to the diversity of religions in the United States. Neither immigrants nor their descendants gave up their religions for the Protestantism of the American majority.

Alienation In his groundbreaking study of immigration, *The Uprooted* (1952), Oscar Handlin observed that newcomers to a strange land often became alienated from both their native culture and the culture of their new country. According to Handlin, first-generation immigrants remained alienated and did not lose their cultural identity in the melting pot. Only the immigrants' children and children's children became fully assimilated into mainstream culture. Many historians agree with Handlin that, after two or three generations, the melting pot, or assimilation, process reduced the cultural differences among most ethnic groups.

African Americans However, certain groups have had a different experience. Historian Richard C. Wade has observed that African Americans who migrated to northern cities faced the special problem of racism, which has created seemingly permanent ghettos with "a growingly alienated and embittered group."

Ongoing Debate Historians remain divided in their analyses of the melting pot. Those who accept the concept see people of diverse ethnic backgrounds coming together to build a common culture. Others see American urban history characterized by intergroup hostility, alienation, crime, and corruption. The questions about past immigration shape current views of ethnic tensions in contemporary society. Is there a process, common to all groups, in which initial prejudice against the most recent immigrants fades after two or three generations?

Support an Argument *Explain two perspectives on the assimilation of immigrants.*

REFLECT ON THE LEARNING OBJECTIVE

1. Explain three responses to immigration during the period from 1865 to 1898.

KEY TERMS BY THEME

Responses to Immigration (MIG)	"boss"
Statue of Liberty	Tammany Hall
American Protective Association	Jane Addams
Chinese Exclusion Act	settlement houses
Ellis Island	melting pot
political machines	cultural diversity

MULTIPLE-CHOICE QUESTIONS

Questions 1–3 refer to the excerpt.

"Today three-fourths of its [New York's] people live in tenements. . . .

If it shall appear that the sufferings and the sins of the 'other half,' and the evil they breed, are but as a just punishment upon the community that gave it no other choice, it will be because that is the truth. . . . In the tenements all the influences make for evil; because they are the hotbeds of the epidemics that carry death to rich and poor alike; the nurseries of pauperism and crime that fill our jails and police courts; that throw off a scum of forty thousand human wrecks to the island asylums and workhouses year by year; that turned out in the last eight years around half million beggars to prey upon our charities; that maintain a standing army of ten thousand tramps with all that that implies; because above all, they touch the family life with deadly moral contagion."

Jacob A. Riis, journalist, *How the Other Half Lives*, 1890

1. Which phrase best summarizes what Riis considers the cause of the problems he sees?
   (A) "are but as a just punishment upon the community"
   (B) "In the tenements all the influences make for evil"
   (C) "throw off a scum of forty thousand human wrecks"
   (D) "touch the family life with deadly moral contagion"

2. During the late 19th century, which of the following groups used the conditions described by Riis to become powerful?
   (A) Religious organizations such as churches and synagogues
   (B) Political machines that operated in big cities
   (C) Social Darwinists who were influenced by Herbert Spencer
   (D) Residents who lived in tenements

3. Which group would be most likely to support government intervention to change the housing conditions described by Riis?
   (A) Opponents of raising taxes
   (B) Advocates of laissez-faire policies
   (C) Members of nativist organizations
   (D) Workers in the settlement house movement

1.

FRANK LESLIE'S ILLUSTRATED NEWSPAPER.

GOLDEN
GATE OF LIBERTY

NOTICE –
COMMUNIST
NIHILIST –
SOCIALIST
FENIAN
& HOODLUM
WELCOME
BUT NO
ADMITTANCE
TO
CHINAMEN

PEACE

INDUSTRY

ORDER

THE ONLY ONE BARRED OUT.
Enlightened American Statesman.—" We must draw the line *somewhere*, you know."

Source: *Frank Leslie's Illustrated Newspaper*, 1882. Library of Congress

Using the cartoon above, answer (a), (b), and (c).

(a) Briefly describe ONE specific event or historical development in the period from 1865 to 1900 that caused the creation of this cartoon.

(b) Briefly describe ONE specific event or historical development in the period from 1865 to 1900 that caused some people to disagree with this cartoon's perspective.

(c) Briefly explain ONE specific event or historical development in the period from 1865 to 1900 that showed this cartoon's effectiveness.

2. Answer (a), (b), and (c).

(a) Briefly explain ONE specific result of the influx of immigrants into American cities during the period from 1865 to 1900.

(b) Briefly explain ONE reason that American cities were slow to address issues or problems such as the one identified above.

(c) Briefly explain ONE specific reform movement that developed in the period from 1865 to 1900 to address urban problems.

Development of the Middle Class

*It is the tendency of all social burdens to crush out the middle class,
and to force the society into an organization of only two classes,
one at each social extreme.*

William Graham Sumner, "What Makes the
Rich Richer and the Poor Poorer?" 1887

Learning Objective: Explain the causes of increased economic
opportunity and its effects on society.

The inequality and widening gap between the nation's wealthy and the
working class during the Gilded Age should not obscure the development
of the American middle class. The industrialization also created many better
paying jobs. Cities needed more professionals and specialists, and changes
in American education also created more opportunities for both men and
women. The growing middle class had more leisure time, which contributed to
the development of the popular culture.

The Expanding Middle Class

Since colonial times, self-employed doctors, lawyers, merchants, and artisans
had formed a middle class between the small wealthy elite and the numerous
small farmers and farm laborers. The growth of large industries and corporations
created new jobs for millions of **white-collar workers** (salaried employees
whose jobs generally do not involve manual labor). **Middle management**
was needed to coordinate the operations between the chief executives and
the factories. Advanced technologies needed scientists and engineers. Sales
and marketing departments required salespersons, accountants, and clerical
workers. In turn, these middle-class employees increased the demand for
services from other middle-class workers: professionals (doctors and lawyers),
public employees, and storekeepers. The number of white-collar and salaried
jobs increased to more than a fourth of all nonagricultural employees by 1910.

The Gospel of Wealth

The role wealthy and upper-income Americans played in the late 19th century
went beyond starting businesses and creating jobs. Many business leaders
joined civic organizations and charitable institutions to address problems
related to rapid urbanization. Andrew Carnegie's **"Gospel of Wealth"** argued

that the wealthy had a moral responsibility to carry out projects of civic **philanthropy** to help other members of society to better themselves and in turn improve society. Carnegie defended unregulated capitalism, arguing that though it might be "hard for the individual" it was "best for the race."

However, he also believed that the wealthy had a duty to use their wealth wisely to improve the community. Practicing what he preached, Carnegie distributed more than $350 million of his fortune to fund libraries, universities, concert halls, and other public institutions. Critics attack his philosophy as paternalistic and based on the bogus racial science of his times.

Working Women

One adult woman out of every five in 1900 was in the labor force working for wages. Most were young and single—only 5 percent of married women worked outside the home. In 1900, men and women alike believed that, if a family could afford it, a woman's proper role was in the home raising children. However, some women with access to higher education broke into **professions** as doctors, lawyers, and college professors. As the demand for clerical workers increased, women moved into formerly male occupations as secretaries, bookkeepers, typists, and telephone operators. Occupations or professions, such as nursing and teaching, that became feminized (women becoming the majority) usually lost status and received lower wages and salaries. Factory work for women was usually in industries that people perceived as an extension of the home, such as the textile, garment, and food-processing businesses.

Impact of Income on Urban Development

Cities of the late 19th century underwent significant changes not only in their size but also in their internal structure and design. The residential pattern in the United States contrasted with that in Europe, where higher-income people remained near the business districts of modern cities and lower-income people lived in the outlying areas. In the United States the wealthy and middle class migrated to the "healthier" suburbs to escape the problems of the cities.

Growth of Suburbs Middle-class families moved out of large cities to create suburbs for several reasons:

- Low-cost, abundant land reduced the price of buying a home.
- The inexpensive transportation by rail made commuting to work easy.
- The spread of new construction methods such as the building of wooden, balloon-frame houses reduced the cost of building homes.
- Some people wanted to live in an all-White community because of their ethnic and racial prejudice.
- Many people enjoyed having grass, privacy, and detached individual houses.

Landscape architect Frederick Law Olmsted, who designed New York's Central Park in the 1860s, went on to design suburban communities with graceful curved roads and open spaces—"a village in the park." By 1900, suburbs had grown up around every major U.S. city. Owning a single-family home surrounded by an ornamental lawn soon became the American ideal of comfortable living and a hallmark of middle-class status. Thus began the world's first suburban nation.

Private City Versus Public City At first, city residents tried to carry on life in large cities much as they had in small villages. Private enterprise shaped the development of American cities and provided services such as streetcars and utilities for a profit. Over time, increasing disease, crime, waste, water pollution, and air pollution slowly convinced reform-minded citizens and city governments of the need for municipal water purification, sewerage systems, waste disposal, street lighting, police departments, and zoning laws to regulate urban development. In the 1890s, the **"City Beautiful" movement** advanced grand plans to remake American cities with tree-lined boulevards, public parks, and public cultural attractions. The debate between the private good and the public good in urban growth and development has continued as an open issue.

Changes in Education

The growth of the middle class, industry, and knowledge in the physical and social sciences raised challenging questions about what schools should teach.

Public Schools Elementary schools after 1865 continued to emphasize the "3 Rs" (reading, writing, arithmetic). They taught traditional moral values through texts such as McGuffey's readers that had been used in schools since the 1840s. New compulsory education laws that required children to attend school dramatically increased the number of students enrolled. As a result, the literacy rate rose to 90 percent of the population by 1900. The practice of sending children to **kindergarten** (a concept borrowed from Germany) became popular and reflected the growing interest in early-childhood education.

Perhaps even more significant than lower-grade schools was the growing support for tax-supported **public high schools**. At first these schools followed the college preparatory curriculum of private academies, but soon the public high schools became more comprehensive. They began to provide vocational and citizenship education for a changing urban society.

Higher Education The growing demand for white-collar workers prompted a sharp increase in number and size of U.S. colleges in the late 1800s. Funding for these schools came from several sources:

- The federal Morrill Acts of 1862 and 1890 provided land grants to states to establish colleges. While earlier schools prepared students to be clergy or lawyers, land-grant schools focused on careers in agriculture, mining, engineering, science, and industry. These state-run colleges were also more affordable for the middle class, and they became valuable research centers that created new products and techniques.

- Wealthy philanthropists founded new colleges or helped existing ones grow. For example, John D. Rockefeller provided the money to start the University of Chicago.

- Advocates of education for females founded new colleges for women, such as Smith, Bryn Mawr, and Mount Holyoke. By 1900, 71 percent of colleges admitted women, and they made up more than one-third of all students.

- Supporters of education for African Americans founded more than 50 private and public colleges and universities, including Fisk, Howard, Morehouse, and Meharry Medical College.

The availability of an affordable college education encouraged a boost in enrollment, from 50,000 students nationwide in 1870 to more than 600,000 students by 1920.

The college curriculum also changed greatly in the late 19th century. Soon after becoming president of Harvard in 1869, Charles W. Eliot reduced the number of required courses and introduced **electives** (courses chosen by students) to accommodate the teaching of modern languages and the sciences: physics, chemistry, biology, and geology. **Johns Hopkins University** was founded in Baltimore in 1876 as the first American institution to specialize in advanced graduate studies. Following the model of German universities, Johns Hopkins emphasized research and free inquiry. As a result of such innovations in curriculum, the United States produced its first generation of scholars who could compete with the intellectual achievements of Europeans. As the curriculum was changing, colleges added social activities, fraternities, and intercollegiate sports, additions that soon dominated the college experience for many students.

Social Sciences The application of the scientific method and the theory of evolution to the study of human affairs revolutionized how scholars analyzed human society in the late 19th century. New fields, known as the **social sciences**, emerged, such as psychology, sociology, anthropology, and political science, which focused on using data to address social issues. For example, **Richard T. Ely** of Johns Hopkins studied labor unions, trusts, and other existing economic institutions not only to understand them but also to suggest remedies for economic problems of the day. Based on his research, he attacked laissez-faire economic thought as dogmatic and outdated. Evolutionary theory influenced leading sociologists (Lester F. Ward), political scientists (Woodrow Wilson), and historians (Frederick Jackson Turner) to study the dynamic process of actual human behavior instead of logical, unchanging abstractions.

One social scientist who used new statistical methods to study crime in urban neighborhoods was **W. E. B. Du Bois**. The first African American to receive a doctorate from Harvard, Du Bois was the leading Black intellectual of the era. He advocated for racial equality, integrated schools, and equal access to higher education for the "talented tenth" of African Americans.

The Professions Scientific theory and methodology also influenced the work of doctors, educators, social workers, and lawyers. **Oliver Wendell Holmes Jr.** argued that the law should evolve with the times in response to changing needs and not remain restricted by legal precedents and judicial decisions of the past. **Clarence Darrow**, a famous lawyer, argued that criminal behavior could be caused by a person's environment of poverty, neglect, and abuse. Darrow's view challenged the traditional belief that people were born as criminals or consciously chose to become lawbreakers. These changes in the professions, along with changes in the universities, would provide a boost to progressive legislation and liberal reform in the 20th century.

Growth of Popular Culture

The **growth of leisure time**, especially for the expanding middle class, became a big business in the late 19th century. In addition to higher incomes, other factors also promoted the growth of leisure-time activities: (1) a gradual reduction in the hours people worked, (2) improved transportation, (3) promotional billboards and advertising, and (4) the decline of restrictive Puritan and Victorian values that discouraged "wasting" time on play.

Popular Press Mass-circulation newspapers had been around since the 1830s, but the first newspaper to exceed a million in circulation was **Joseph Pulitzer**'s *New York World*, around 1890. Pulitzer filled his daily paper with both sensational stories of crimes and disasters and crusading feature stories about political and economic corruption. Another New York publisher, **William Randolph Hearst**, pushed scandal and sensationalism to new heights (or lows).

Mass-circulation magazines also became common in the 1880s. Advertising revenues and new printing technologies made it possible for the *Ladies' Home Journal* and similar magazines to sell for as little as 10 cents a copy.

Amusements Theaters that presented comedies and dramas flourished in most large cities, but vaudeville, with its variety of acts, drew the largest audiences. Traveling **circuses** such as ones operated by the Ringling Brothers and by **Barnum and Bailey** (**"The Greatest Show on Earth"**) used the new railroad network to move a huge number of acts and animals from town to town. Also immensely popular was the **Wild West show** brought to urban audiences by William F. Cody (**"Buffalo Bill"**) and headlining such personalities as Sitting Bull and the markswoman Annie Oakley.

Commuter streetcar and railroad companies also promoted weekend recreation in order to keep their cars running on Sundays and holidays. They created parks in the countryside near the end of the line so that urban families could enjoy picnics and outdoor recreation.

Music With the growth of cities came increasing demand for musical performances appealing to a variety of tastes. By 1900, most large cities had an orchestra, an opera house, or both. In smaller towns, outdoor bandstands were the setting for the playing of popular marches by **John Philip Sousa**.

Among the greatest innovators of the era were African Americans in New Orleans. **Jelly Roll Morton** and Buddy Bolden expanded the audience for **jazz**, a musical form that combined African rhythms with European instruments, and mixed improvisation with a structured format. The remarkable Black composer and performer **Scott Joplin** sold nearly a million copies of sheet music of his "Maple Leaf Rag" (1899). Also from the South came **blues** music that expressed the pain of the Black experience. **Jazz, ragtime, and blues** music gained popularity during the early 20th century as New Orleans performers headed north into the urban centers of Memphis, St. Louis, Kansas City, and Chicago.

Spectator Sports Professional **spectator sports** originated in the late 19th century. **Baseball**, while it recalled a rural past of green fields and fences, was very much an urban game that demanded the teamwork needed for an industrial age. Owners organized teams into leagues, much as trusts of the day were organized. In 1909, when President William Howard Taft started the tradition of the president throwing out the first ball of the season, baseball was the national pastime. However, Jim Crow laws and customs prevented Black players from joining all-White big-league baseball teams between the 1890s and 1947.

Football developed out of earlier games, primarily as a college activity. The first game was played in 1869 beween two New Jersey colleges, Rutgers and Princeton. In the 1920s professional football teams and leagues were organized. Basketball was invented in 1891 at Springfield College, in Massachusetts. Within a few years, high schools and colleges across the nation had teams. The first professional basketball league was organized in 1898. It took years for some spectator sports, such as football, to gain middle-class respectability.

Amateur Sports The value of sports as healthy exercise for the body gained acceptance by the middle and upper classes in the late 19th century. Women were considered unfit for most competitive sports, but they engaged in such recreational activities as croquet and **bicycling**. Sports such as **golf** and **tennis** grew, but mostly among the prosperous members of **athletic clubs**. The very rich pursued the expensive sports of **polo** and **yachting**. Private clubs generally discriminated against Jews, Catholics, and African Americans.

During the Gilded Age of industrialization, urban development and immigration created both problems and opportunities for the nation. The next topic will explore how the expanding middle class, along with intellectuals, religious leaders, artists, and others promoted a wide spectrum of reforms of American economic, political, social, and cultural institutions.

REFLECT ON THE LEARNING OBJECTIVE

1. Explain two causes of increased economic opportunity and two effects on society during the late 19th century and early 20th century.

MULTIPLE-CHOICE QUESTIONS

Questions 1–2 refer to the following excerpt.

"The problem of our age is the proper administration of wealth, so that the ties of brotherhood may still bind together the rich and poor in harmonious relationship. . . . By taxing estates heavily at death the state marks its condemnation of the selfish millionaire's unworthy life. . . .This policy would work powerfully to induce the rich man to attend to the administration of wealth during his life. . . . Thus is the problem of Rich and Poor to be solved. The laws of accumulation will be left free; the laws of distribution free. Individualism will continue, but the millionaire will be but a trustee for the poor; [entrusted] for a season with a great part of the increased wealth of the community, but administering it for the community far better than it could or would have done for itself. . . . 'The man who dies thus rich dies disgraced.' Such, in my opinion, is the true Gospel concerning Wealth."

"Wealth," Andrew Carnegie, 1889

1. Carnegie's remarks in the excerpt were most likely in response to
   (A) the development of the social sciences
   (B) the spread of racial theories about the survival of the fittest
   (C) the rise of monopolies in major industries, such as oil and steel
   (D) the discontent in society over the increase in economic inequality

2. Carnegie was most likely hoping his comments would promote
   (A) the passage of a graduated income tax by the government
   (B) the religious values that could reform greedy behavior
   (C) an increase in large-scale philanthropy to fund civic institutions
   (D) an increase in contributions by working people to religious institutions

SHORT-ANSWER QUESTIONS

Use complete sentences; an outline or bulleted list alone is not acceptable.

1. "The continuing process of sorting out classes at the workplace and in metropolitan space made the denial of class more difficult in the post-Civil War America.... In nineteenth century America, 'middle class' represented a specific set of experiences, a specific style of living, and a specific social identity."

   Stuart M. Blumin, The Emergence of the Middle Class, 1989

   Using the excerpt above, answer (a), (b), and (c).
   (a) Briefly explain ONE specific cause of the process of "sorting out classes at the workplace" that Blumin referred to during the period from 1865 to 1900.
   (b) Briefly explain ONE specific cause of the development of what Blumin called a "specific social identity" during the period from 1865 to 1900.
   (c) Briefly explain ONE specific example of how the changes described by Blumin affected working women during the period from 1865 to 1900.

2. Answer (a), (b), and (c).
   (a) Briefly explain ONE historical development in education that was influenced by the economic or cultural changes from 1865 to 1898.
   (b) Briefly explain ONE way in which urban development was affected by the growth of the middle class during the period from 1865 to 1898.
   (c) Briefly explain ONE way in which popular culture was affected by the growth of the middle class during the period from 1865 to 1898.

Reform in the Gilded Age

For every wrong there must be a remedy. But the remedy can be nothing less than the abolition of the wrong.

Henry George, *Social Problems*, 1884

Learning Objective: Explain how different reform movements responded to the rise of industrial capitalism in the Gilded Age.

Early efforts by farmers to regulate railroads (see Topic 6.2) and by workers to establish labor unions (see Topic 6.6) largely failed during the Gilded Age. However, many reform ideas and movements gained strength with the development of an educated middle class who also had the time to create and join organizations to bring about change. Literature, the arts, and architecture also responded in new ways to the challenge of industrialization and urbanization.

Awakening of Reform

Urban problems, including the desperate poverty of working-class families, inspired a new social consciousness among the middle class. Reform movements begun in earlier decades increased strength in the 1880s and 1890s.

Books of Social Criticism A San Francisco journalist, **Henry George**, published a provocative book in 1879 that became an instant bestseller and jolted readers to look more critically at the effects of laissez-faire economics. George called attention to the alarming inequalities in wealth caused by industrialization. In his book *Progress and Poverty*, George proposed an innovative solution to poverty: replacing all taxes with a single tax on land.

Another popular book of social criticism, *Looking Backward, 2000–1887*, was written by **Edward Bellamy** in 1888. It envisioned life in the year 2000, when a cooperative society had eliminated poverty, greed, and crime.

George and Bellamy shared some similarities. Both were criticized as utopians. Both inspired enthusiastic followers who supported other reform movements. Both encouraged a shift in American public opinion away from laissez-faire and toward greater government regulation. Because of their criticisms of the economic system of their time, George and Bellamy were sometime categorized as socialists.

Religion and Society All religions adapted to the stresses and challenges of modern urban living. Roman Catholicism grew rapidly in the United States from the influx of new immigrants from Ireland, Italy, and eastern Europe. Catholic leaders such as **Cardinal James Gibbons** of Baltimore inspired the devoted support of old and new immigrants by defending the Knights of Labor and the cause of organized labor.

Among Protestants, **Dwight Moody**, who founded the Moody Bible Institute in Chicago in 1889, would help generations of urban evangelists to adapt traditional Christianity to city life. The **Salvation Army**, imported from England in 1879, provided basic necessities to the homeless and the poor while preaching the Christian gospel.

The Social Gospel Movement In the 1880s and 1890s, a number of Protestant clergy espoused the cause of social justice for the poor—especially the urban poor. They preached what they called the **Social Gospel**, or the importance of applying Christian principles to social problems by improving housing, raising wages, and supporting public health measures. They believed that addressing issues of poverty would enable people to find individual salvation. This was a contrast with the beliefs of many traditional Christians, who argued that focusing on individual salvation would lead to a society with fewer problems.

Leading the Social Gospel movement in the late 19th and early 20th centuries was a Baptist minister from New York, **Walter Rauschenbusch**. He worked in the poverty-stricken neighborhood of New York City called Hell's Kitchen and wrote several books urging organized religions to take up the cause of social justice. His Social Gospel preaching linked Christianity with the Progressive reform movement and encouraged many middle-class Protestants to attack urban problems (see Topic 7.4).

Social Workers Settlement workers, such as **Jane Addams** of Hull House in Chicago, were civic-minded volunteers who created the foundation for the later job of social worker. Many were also political activists who crusaded for child-labor laws, housing reform, and women's rights. Two settlement workers, Frances Perkins and Harry Hopkins, went on to leadership roles in President Franklin Roosevelt's reform program, the New Deal, in the 1930s.

Families in Urban Society Urban life placed severe strains on parents and their children by isolating them from the extended family (relatives beyond the family nucleus of parents and children) and village support. **Divorce** rates increased to 1 in 12 marriages by 1900, partly because a number of state legislatures had expanded the grounds for divorce to include cruelty and desertion. Another consequence of the shift from rural to urban living was a reduction in **family size**. Children were an economic asset on the farm, where their labor was needed at an early age. In the city, however, they were more of an economic liability. Therefore, in the last decades of the 19th century, the national average for birthrates and family size continued to drop.

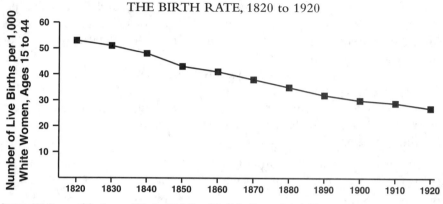

THE BIRTH RATE, 1820 to 1920

Number of Live Births per 1,000 White Women, Ages 15 to 44

Source: U.S. Bureau of the Census. *Historical Statistics of the United States, Colonial Times to 1970*

Voting Rights for Women The cause of women's suffrage, launched at Seneca Falls in 1848, was vigorously carried forward by a number of middle-class women. In 1890, two of the pioneer feminists of the 1840s, Elizabeth Cady Stanton and **Susan B. Anthony** of New York, helped found the National American Woman Suffrage Association (**NAWSA**) to secure the vote for women. A western state, Wyoming, was the first to grant full suffrage to women, in 1869. By 1900, some states allowed women to vote in local elections, and most allowed women to own and control property after marriage.

Temperance Movement Another cause that attracted the attention of urban reformers was temperance. Excessive drinking of alcohol by male factory workers was one cause of poverty for immigrant and working-class families. The Woman's Christian Temperance Union (**WCTU**) was formed in 1874. Advocating total abstinence from alcohol, the WCTU, under the leadership of **Frances E. Willard** of Evanston, Illinois, had 500,000 members by 1898. The **Anti-Saloon League**, founded in 1893, became a powerful political force and by 1916 had persuaded 21 states to close down all saloons and bars. Unwilling to wait for the laws to change, **Carry A. Nation** of Kansas created a sensation by raiding saloons and smashing barrels of beer with a hatchet.

Urban Reforms Across the country, grassroots efforts arose to combat corruption in city governments. In New York, a reformer named Theodore Roosevelt tried to clean up the New York City Police Department. As a result of his efforts, he became a vice-presidential nominee in 1896 and later the president (see Topic 7.4). However, many of the reformers of the Gilded Age would not see their efforts reach fruition or have a national impact until the early 20th century.

Literature and the Arts

American writers and artists responded in diverse ways to industrialization and urban problems. In general, the work of the best-known innovators of the era reflected a new **realism** and an attempt to express an authentic American style.

Realism and Naturalism Many of the popular works of literature of the post-Civil War years were romantic novels that depicted ideal heroes and heroines. Breaking with this genteel literary tradition were regionalist writers such as Bret Harte, who depicted life in the rough mining camps of the West. **Mark Twain** (the pen name for Samuel L. Clemens) became the first great realist author. His classic work, *The Adventures of Huckleberry Finn* (1884), revealed the greed, violence, and racism in American society.

A younger generation of authors who emerged in the 1890s became known for their **naturalism**, which focused on how emotions and experience shaped human experience. In his naturalistic novel *Maggie: A Girl of the Streets* (1893), **Stephen Crane** told how a brutal urban environment could destroy the lives of young people. Crane also wrote the popular *The Red Badge of Courage* about fear and human nature on the Civil War battlefield before dying himself of tuberculosis at only 29. **Jack London**, a young California writer and adventurer, portrayed the conflict between nature and civilization in novels such as *The Call of the Wild* (1903). A naturalistic book that caused a sensation and shocked the moral sensibilities of the time was **Theodore Dreiser**'s novel about a poor working girl in Chicago, *Sister Carrie* (1900).

Painting Some American painters continued to cater to the popular taste for romantic subjects, but others responded to the new emphasis on realism. **Winslow Homer**, the foremost American painter of seascapes and watercolors, often rendered scenes of nature in a matter-of-fact way. **Thomas Eakins**'s realism included paintings of surgical scenes and the everyday lives of working-class men and women. He also used the new technology of serial-action photographs to study human anatomy and paint it more realistically.

James McNeill Whistler was born in Massachusetts but spent most of his life in Paris and London. His most famous painting, *Arrangement in Grey and Black, No. 1* (popularly known as "Whistler's Mother"), hangs in the Louvre. This study of color, rather than subject matter, influenced the development of modern art. A distinguished portrait painter, **Mary Cassatt**, also spent much of her life in France, where she learned the techniques of **impressionism**, especially in her use of pastel colors. As the 19th century ended, a group of social realists, such as George Bellows of the **Ashcan School**, painted scenes of everyday life in poor urban neighborhoods.

Upsetting to romanticists and realists alike were abstract, nonrepresentational paintings that some artists were experimenting with. A large exhibit of these works, the **Armory Show** in New York City in 1913, sent shocks through the artistic community. Art of this kind would be rejected by most Americans until the 1950s, when it finally achieved respect among collectors of fine art.

Architecture In the 1870s, **Henry Hobson Richardson** changed the direction of American architecture. While earlier architects found inspiration in classical Greek and Roman styles, his designs were often based on the medieval **Romanesque style** of massive stone walls and rounded arches. Richardson gave a gravity and stateliness to functional commercial buildings. **Louis Sullivan** of Chicago went a step further by rejecting historical styles in his quest for a suitable style for the tall, steel-framed office buildings of the 1880s and 1890s. Sullivan's buildings achieved a much-admired aesthetic unity, in which the form of a building flowed from its function—a hallmark of the Chicago School of architecture.

Source: Frank Lloyd Wright, Robie House, Chicago, 1909. Library of Congress

Frank Lloyd Wright, an employee of Sullivan's in the 1890s, developed an "organic" style of architecture that was in harmony with its natural surroundings. Wright's vision is exemplified in the long, horizontal lines of his prairie-style houses. Wright became the most famous American architect of the 20th century. Some architects, such as Daniel H. Burnham, who revived classical Greek and Roman architecture in his designs for the World's Columbian Exposition of 1893, continued to explore historical styles.

One of the most influential urbanists, **Frederick Law Olmsted** specialized in the planning of city parks and scenic boulevards, including Central Park in New York City and the grounds of the U.S. Capitol in Washington. As the originator of **landscape architecture**, Olmsted not only designed parks, parkways, campuses, and suburbs but also established the basis for later urban landscaping.

Preparation for Change While laissez-faire policies still dominated business and politics in the Gilded Age, the foundations for cultural change and reforms that would come about in the early 20th century had been established during the 1880s and 1890s. Critics and artists informed the expanding middle class on alternative visions for the economy and society.

REFLECT ON THE LEARNING OBJECTIVE

1. Explain how three reform movements responded to the rise of industrial capitalism in the Gilded Age.

MULTIPLE-CHOICE QUESTIONS

Questions 1–3 refer to the following excerpt.

"I stand before you tonight under indictment for the alleged crime of having voted at the last presidential election, without having a lawful right to vote. It shall be my work this evening to prove to you that in thus voting, I not only committed no crime, but, instead, simply exercised my citizen's rights, guaranteed to me and all United States citizens by the National Constitution, beyond the power of any state to deny. . . . Are women persons? And I hardly believe any of our opponents will have the hardihood to say they are not. Being persons, then, women are citizens; and no state has a right to make any law, or to enforce any old law, that shall abridge their privileges or immunities. Hence, every discrimination against women in the constitutions and laws of the several states is today null and void, precisely as is every one against Negroes."

Susan B. Anthony, "Is It a Crime for a Citizen of the United States to Vote?" 1873

1. Susan B. Anthony was arrested and fined $100 for casting an illegal vote in the presidential election of 1872. She refused to pay the fine. Her protest was most similar to which of the following?

   (A) The dumping of chests of British tea into the Boston Harbor by colonists disguised as American Indians

   (B) The jailing of Henry David Thoreau for not paying taxes for what he considered an immoral war

   (C) The federal suit to free the enslaved Dred Scott after he resided in a free state

   (D) The raid of abolitionists led by John Brown on the federal arsenal at Harpers Ferry

2. Anthony's arguments expressed in the excerpt above can best be understood in the context of

(A) the Supreme Court decision in *Marbury v. Madison*

(B) the proclamation of the Monroe Doctrine

(C) the ratification of the three Reconstruction-era amendments

(D) the strength of the American Protective Association

3. Which of the following best describes why Anthony targeted states in this excerpt?

(A) The United States Constitution generally left the power to states to determine who could vote.

(B) The states kept women in an inferior legal position to men through marriage laws.

(C) The president had vowed to veto any laws passed by Congress designed to protect suffrage for women.

(D) Congress was already shown strong support for a suffrage amendment that included women.

SHORT-ANSWER QUESTIONS

Use complete sentences; an outline or bulleted list alone is not acceptable.

1. Answer (a), (b), and (c).

(a) Briefly explain ONE specific response of religious institutions to the urban problems of the Gilded Age.

(b) Briefly explain ONE impact that the urban experience had on family life during the Gilded Age.

(c) Briefly explain ONE reason why temperance gained such strength as a reform movement during the Gilded Age.

2. Answer (a), (b), and (c).

(a) Briefly explain ONE effect that social and cultural changes had on American literature in the period from 1865 to 1898.

(b) Briefly explain ONE effect that social and cultural changes had on the visual arts in the period from 1865 to 1898.

(c) Briefly explain ONE effect that economic and urban developments had on architecture in the period from 1865 to 1898.

Role of Government in the Gilded Age

To explain the causes which keep much of the finest intellect of the country away from national business is one thing; to deny the unfortunate results would be quite another.

James Bryce, *The American Commonwealth*, 1891

Learning Objective: Explain the continuities and changes in the role of the government in the U.S. economy.

The "do-little" governments of this period were in tune with two popular ideas of the time: laissez-faire economics and Social Darwinism (see Topic 6.6). The laissez-faire views of the business leaders and their political supporters opposed most government actions to regulate businesses, levy taxes, or take steps to counter serious economic downturn or depressions. Supporters argued that the economy would grow most quickly if allowed to work without government intervention, even during economic downturns. The federal courts generally supported these views. Decisions narrowly interpreted the government's powers to regulate business, which limited the impact of the few regulatory laws that Congress did pass.

However, the federal government was involved in the economy to promote business growth. It provided land grants to railroads at the expense of taxpayers, passed high tariffs to protect industries but cost consumers, and followed hard money policies that aided banks but hurt farmers.

Government Actions

Government was less active in the economy than it would be in later periods. However, it did take some steps to promote growth and competition.

Federal Land Grants Even though governments were reluctant to regulate businesses, they were willing to subsidize them. The federal government provided railroad companies with huge subsidies in the form of loans and land grants to promote progress. The government gave 80 railroad companies more than 170 million acres of public land, a total area larger than the state of Texas. The land was given in alternate mile-square sections in a checkerboard pattern along the proposed route of the railroad. The government expected that the railroad would sell the land to new settlers to finance construction. Furthermore, the completed railroad might both increase the value of government lands and provide preferred rates for carrying the mail and transporting troops.

The subsidies carried some negative consequences. The land grants and cash loans promoted hasty and poor construction and led to **corruption** in all levels of government. Insiders used construction companies, like the notorious **Crédit Mobilier**, to bribe government officials and pocket huge profits. Protests against the land grants mounted in the 1880s when citizens discovered that the railroads controlled half of the land in some western states.

Interstate Commerce Act (1887) State laws passed earlier to regulate **railroad rates** (see Topic 6.2) ran into numerous legal problems. The Supreme Court ruled in the case of *Wabash v. Illinois* (1886) that individual states could not regulate interstate commerce. In effect, the Court's decision nullified many of the state regulations achieved by the Grangers. Congress responded to the outcry of farmers and shippers by passing the first federal effort to regulate the railroads. The **Interstate Commerce Act of 1887** required railroad rates to be "reasonable and just." It also set up the first federal regulatory agency, the Interstate Commerce Commission (ICC), which had the power to investigate pools, rebates, and other discriminatory practices and prosecute companies participating in them.

Ironically, the first U.S. regulatory commission helped the railroads more than the farmers. The new commission lost most of its cases in the federal courts in the 1890s. On the other hand, the ICC helped railroads by stabilizing rates and curtailing destructive competition, providing little help to farmers and other shippers until the law was strengthened in the 20th century.

Antitrust Movement The corporate trusts, such as the Standard Oil Trust, came under widespread scrutiny and attack in the 1880s. Middle-class citizens feared the trusts' unchecked concentration of power, and urban elites (old wealth) resented the increasing influence of the new rich. After failing to curb trusts on the state level, reformers finally moved Congress to pass the **Sherman Antitrust Act** of 1890, which prohibited any "contract, combination, in the form of trust or otherwise, or conspiracy in restraint of trade or commerce."

Although a federal law against monopolies was now on the books, it was too vaguely worded to stop the development of trusts in the 1890s. Furthermore, the Supreme Court in **United States v. E. C. Knight Co.** (1895) ruled that the Sherman Antitrust Act could be applied only to commerce, not to manufacturing. As a result, the U.S. Department of Justice secured few convictions until the law was strengthened during the Progressive Era.

Foreign Policy and the Economy The government also used its foreign policy to shape economic changes. For example, the United States purchased Alaska from Russia and annexed the Hawaii Islands to promote trade with Asia and became more involved in Latin American affairs (see Topic 7.2).

Political Issues: Civil Service, Currency, and Tariffs

During the 1870s and 1880s, the Congresses in Washington were chiefly concerned with such issues as patronage, the money supply, and the tariff issue.

They left the states and local governments to deal with the growing problems related to urbanization and industrialization.

Civil Service Reform Public outrage over the **assassination of President Garfield** in 1881 by a deranged office seeker pushed Congress to remove certain government jobs from the control of party patronage. The **Pendleton Act of 1881** set up the **Civil Service Commission** and created a system by which applicants for classified federal jobs would be selected on the basis of their scores on a competitive examination. The law also prohibited civil servants from making political contributions. At first, the law applied to only 10 percent of federal employees, but in later decades, the system was expanded until most federal jobs were classified (that is, taken out of the hands of politicians).

Politicians adapted to the reform by depending less on their armies of party workers and more on the rich to fund their campaigns. People still debate which approach is more harmful to democratic government.

Money Question The most hotly debated issue of the Gilded Age was how much to expand the money supply. For the economy to grow soundly, it needed more money in circulation. However, the money question reflected the growing tension in the era between the "haves" and the "have-nots."

Debtors, farmers, and start-up businesses wanted more "easy" or **"soft" money** in circulation, since this would enable them to (1) borrow money at lower interest rates and (2) pay off their loans more easily with inflated dollars. After the **Panic of 1873**, many Americans blamed the gold standard for restricting the money supply and causing the depression. To expand the supply of U.S. currency, easy-money advocates campaigned first for more paper money (greenbacks) and then for the unlimited minting of silver coins.

On the opposite side of the question, bankers, **creditors**, investors, and established businesses stood firm for "sound" or **"hard" money**—meaning currency backed by gold stored in government vaults. Supporters of hard money argued that dollars backed by gold would hold their value against inflation. Holders of money understood that as the U.S. economy and population grew faster than the number of gold-backed dollars, each dollar would gain in value. As predicted, the dollar did increase in value by as much as 300 percent between 1865 and 1895.

Greenback Party Paper money not backed by specie (gold or silver) had been issued by the federal government in the 1860s as an emergency measure for financing the Civil War. Northern farmers, who received high prices during the war, prospered from the use of "greenbacks." On the other hand, creditors and investors attacked the use of unbacked paper money as a violation of natural law. In 1875, Congress sided with the creditors and passed the Specie Resumption Act, which withdrew all greenbacks from circulation.

Supporters of paper money formed a new political party, the Greenback Party. In the congressional election of 1878, Greenback candidates received nearly 1 million votes, and 14 members were elected to Congress, including James B. Weaver of Iowa (a future leader of the Populist Party). When the hard times of the 1870s ended, the Greenback Party died out, but the goal of increasing the amount of money in circulation did not.

Demands for Silver Money In addition to removing greenbacks, Congress in the 1870s also stopped the coining of silver. Critics call this action the **"Crime of 1873."** Then silver discoveries in Nevada revived demands for the use of silver to expand the money supply. A compromise law, the **Bland-Allison Act**, was passed. It allowed only a limited coinage of between $2 million and $4 million in silver each month at the standard silver-to-gold ratio of 16 to 1. Not satisfied, farmers, debtors, and western miners continued to press for the unlimited coinage of silver.

Tariff Issue During the Civil War, the Republican Congress had raised tariffs to protect U.S. industry and also fund the Union government. After the war, southern Democrats and some northern Democrats objected to **high tariffs** because these taxes raised prices for **consumers**. Protective tariffs also caused other nations to retaliate by placing taxes of their own on U.S. farm products. American farmers lost some overseas sales, contributing to surpluses of corn and wheat and resulting in lower farm prices and profits. From a farmer's point of view, industry seemed to be growing rich at the expense of rural America.

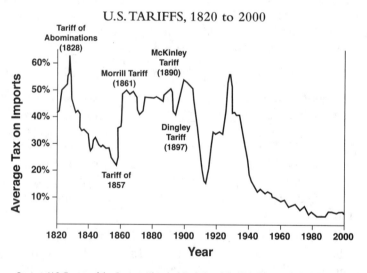

U.S. TARIFFS, 1820 to 2000

Source: U.S. Bureau of the Census. *Historical Statistics of the United States, Colonial Times to 1970*

The politics of stalemate and complacency would begin to lose their hold on the voters by the late 1880s. Protests over government corruption, the money issue, tariffs, railroads, and monopolistic trusts were growing. In response, politicians began to take small steps to respond to public concerns, but it would take a third party (the Populists) and a major depression in 1893 to shake the Democrats and the Republicans from their lethargy.

1. Explain three examples of changes in the role of the government in the U.S. economy from 1865 to 1898.

KEY TERMS BY THEME

Role of Government (PCE)	Sherman Antitrust Act of 1890	"soft" money
federal land grants	*United States v. E. C. Knight Co.*	Panic of 1873
corruption	assassination of President Garfield	creditors
Crédit Mobilier		"hard" money
railroad rates	Pendleton Act of 1881	"Crime of 73"
Interstate Commerce Act of 1887	Civil Service Commission	high tariffs
antitrust movement	debtors	Bland-Allison Act
		consumers

MULTIPLE-CHOICE QUESTIONS

Questions 1–3 refer to the following chart.

MONEY IN CIRCULATION IN THE UNITED STATES, 1865-1895		
Year	**Total currency (in billions of dollars)**	**Population (in thousands)**
1865	1.2	35,701
1870	0.9	39,905
1875	0.9	45,073
1880	1.2	50,262
1885	1.5	56,658
1890	1.7	63,056
1895	1.8	69,580

Source: U.S. Bureau of the Census. *Historical Statistics of the United States, Colonial Times to 1970*

1. Which of the following most likely explains the change in the amount of currency in circulation between 1865 and 1870?

 (A) The decline of gold mining in the United States

 (B) The withdrawal of "greenbacks" from circulation

 (C) The refusal of Congress to purchase silver for coinage

 (D) The increasing poverty of most Americans

2. Which group supported the change in the total money supply between 1875 and 1895 but wanted the change to be larger than it was?

 (A) Many farmers who were in debt

 (B) Many bankers who had loaned money to individuals

 (C) Many merchants who had sold goods on credit

 (D) Many state governments that were trying to reduce taxes

3. The change in the amount of money in circulation in the 1890s would most likely have made

   (A) wages for most workers decrease slightly

   (B) prices for most goods decrease slightly

   (C) loans slightly easier to repay

   (D) tariffs slightly harder to pay

SHORT-ANSWER QUESTIONS

Use complete sentences; an outline or bulleted list alone is not acceptable.

1.

Source: 1896, The Granger Collection, NYC

Using the cartoon above, answer (a), (b), and (c).

(a) Briefly explain ONE historical perspective expressed by the artist about the changes in the economy from 1865 to 1900.

(b) Briefly explain ONE development in the period from 1865 to 1900 that supported the perspective expressed by the artist.

(c) Briefly explain ONE development in the period from 1865 to 1900 that challenged the perspective expressed by the artist.

2. Answer (a), (b), and (c).

(a) Briefly explain ONE example of a federal government action to promote economic development from 1865 to 1900.

(b) Briefly explain ONE example of a federal government action to regulate business practices from 1865 to 1900.

(c) Briefly explain ONE reason that caused tariff policies to become an important political issue during the period from 1877 to 1900.

Politics in the Gilded Age

*My country, 'tis of thee, Once land of liberty, Of thee I sing.
Land of the millionaire; Farmers with pockets bare;
Caused by the cursed snare—The Money Ring.*

Alliance Songster, 1890

Learning Objective: Explain the similarities and differences between the political parties during the Gilded Age.

Congress had enacted an ambitious reform program during the 1860s and 1870s—the era of Civil War and Reconstruction. After the Compromise of 1877, the national government settled into an era of stalemate and comparative inactivity. It was an era of "forgettable" presidents, none of whom served two consecutive terms, and of politicians who largely ignored problems arising from the growth of industry and cities. Both major parties avoided taking stands on controversial issues. They rarely debated political ideology.

Political Stalemate

Several factors accounted for the complacency and conservatism of the era: (1) the way parties conducted campaigns, (2) the importance of party patronage, and (3) the beliefs about political strategy.

Popular Politics Election campaigns of the time were characterized by brass bands, flags, campaign buttons, picnics, free beer, and crowd-pleasing oratory. Both parties had strong organizations, the Republicans more on the state level and the Democrats more in the cities. Nearly 80 percent of the eligible voters voted in presidential elections, much higher than elections in later periods. The high turnout was a function of strong party identification and loyalty, often connected with the regional, religious, and ethnic ties of voters.

Party Patronage Since neither party had an active legislative agenda, politics in this era was chiefly a game of winning elections, holding office, and providing government jobs to the party faithful. Who got the patronage jobs within the party became a more important issue than any policy. Reform-minded politicians who did not play the patronage game were ridiculed as "Mugwumps" for sitting on the fence—their "mugs" on one side of the fence and "wumps" on the other. Because politicians failed to address pressing policy issues, historians generally consider this era a low point in American politics.

Republicans In the North, Republican politicians kept memories of the Civil War alive during the Gilded Age by figuratively waving the **"bloody shirt."** This meant reminding the millions of **veterans of the Union army** that their wounds had been caused by (southern) Democrats and that Abraham Lincoln had been murdered by a Democrat. The party of Lincoln, because of its antislavery past, kept the votes of **reformers** and **African Americans**. The core of Republican strength came from men in business and from middle-class, **Anglo-Saxon Protestants**, many of whom supported **temperance** or prohibition. Republicans followed the **Hamiltonian tradition** and **Whig past**, supporting a **pro-business** economic program of high protective tariffs.

Democrats After 1877, Democrats could count upon winning every election in the **"solid South,"** the **former states of the Confederacy**, until the mid-20th century. In the North, Democratic strength came from **big-city political machines** and **immigrant voters**. Democrats were often **Catholics, Lutherans, and Jews** who objected to temperance and prohibition crusades conducted by Protestant (and largely Republican) groups. Gilded Age Democrats, following in the **Jeffersonian tradition** argued for **states' rights** and **limited federal power**.

Campaign Strategy The closeness of elections between 1876 and 1892 was one reason that Republicans and Democrats alike avoided taking strong positions on the issues. The Democrats won only two presidential contests in the Electoral College (but four in the popular vote). They nevertheless controlled the House of Representatives after eight of the ten general elections. The result was divided government in Washington. With elections so evenly matched, the main objective for many politicians was to hold on to office by offering patronage jobs and government contracts to help their supporters.

Rise of the Populists

Politics as usual was disrupted in the 1890s by growing agrarian discontent in the West and the South. Members of the **Farmers' Alliances** elected U.S. senators and representatives, the governors of several states, and majorities in four state legislatures in the West.

Omaha Platform The Alliance movement provided the foundation of a new political party—the People's, or Populist, Party. Delegates from different states met in Omaha, Nebraska, in 1892 to draft a political platform and nominate candidates for president and vice president for the new party. Populists were determined to do something about the concentration of economic power held by trusts and bankers, and they saw the government as the tool they needed.

Their **Omaha Platform** called for both political and economic reforms. Politically, it demanded an increase in the power of common voters through (1) direct popular election of U.S. senators (instead of indirect election by state legislatures) and (2) the use of initiatives and referendums, procedures that allowed citizens to vote directly on proposed laws. Economically, the Populist platform was even more ambitious. Populists advocated (1) unlimited coinage of silver to increase the money supply; (2) a graduated income tax—the greater a person's income, the higher the percentage of the tax on his or her income; (3) **government ownership** of railroads, telegraph lines, and the telephone systems; (4) loans and federal warehouses for farmers to enable them to stabilize prices for their crops; and (5) an eight-hour day for industrial workers.

The Populist movement seemed revolutionary both for its attack on laissez-faire capitalism and its attempt to unite White and Black poor people politically. In the South, **Thomas Watson** of Georgia appealed to poor farmers of both races who shared economic grievances to join the People's Party.

The Election of 1892 In 1892, James Weaver of Iowa, the Populist candidate for president, won more than 1 million votes and 22 electoral votes, making him one of the few third-party candidates to win votes in the Electoral College. Nevertheless, the Populist demand that government regulate the economic system more strongly did not overcome other concerns. The ticket failed to attract urban workers in the North. It lost badly in the South, where the fear of Populists uniting all poor people drove conservative Democrats to use every technique to disfranchise African Americans (see Topic 6.4).

The two major parties provided a rematch between President Harrison and former president **Grover Cleveland**. This time, Cleveland won a solid victory in both the popular and electoral vote. He won in part because of the unpopularity of the high-tax McKinley Tariff. Cleveland became the first and only former president thus far to return to the White House after having left it.

Depression Politics

Cleveland took office in March 1893. Almost immediately, the country entered into one of the worst and longest depressions in its history.

Panic of 1893 In the spring and summer of 1893, the stock market crashed as a result of overspeculation, and dozens of railroads went into bankruptcy as a result of overbuilding. The depression continued for almost four years. Farm foreclosures reached new highs, and the unemployed reached 20 percent of the workforce. Many people ended up relying on soup kitchens and riding the rails as hoboes. President Cleveland, more conservative than he had been in the 1880s, dealt with the crisis by championing the gold standard and otherwise adopting a hands-off policy toward the economy.

Gold Reserve and the Pullman Strike A decline in silver prices encouraged investors to trade their silver dollars for gold dollars. The gold reserve (bars of gold bullion stored by the U.S. Treasury) fell to a dangerously low level, and Cleveland decided to repeal the Sherman Silver Purchase Act of 1890. This action, however, failed to stop the gold drain. The president then turned to the Wall Street banker J. Pierpont Morgan to borrow $65 million in gold to support the dollar and the gold standard. This deal convinced many Americans that the government in Washington was only a tool of rich eastern bankers. Workers became further disenchanted with Cleveland when he used court injunctions and federal troops to crush the Pullman strike in 1894 (see Topic 6.7).

Tariff Reform and an Income Tax The Democrats did enact one measure that was somewhat more popular. Congress passed the Wilson-Gorman Tariff in 1894, which (1) provided a moderate reduction in tariff rates and (2) included a 2 percent income tax on incomes of more than $2,000. Since the average American income at this time was less than $500, only those with higher incomes would be subject to the income tax. Within a year after the passage of the law, however, the conservative Supreme Court declared an income tax unconstitutional. (Ratification of the 16th Amendment in 1913 made an income tax constitutional.)

Jobless on the March As the depression worsened and the numbers of jobless people grew, conservatives feared class war between capital and labor. They were especially alarmed by the spread of the Pullman strike across the nation (see Topic 6.7) and the **march to Washington** in 1894 by thousands of the unemployed led by Populist Jacob S. Coxey of Ohio. **"Coxey's Army"** demanded that the federal government spend $500 million on public works programs to create jobs. Coxey and other protest leaders were arrested for trespassing, and the dejected marchers returned home.

Also in 1894, a little book by William H. Harvey presenting lessons in economics seemed to offer easy answers for ending the depression. Illustrated with cartoons, *Coin's Financial School* taught millions of discontented Americans that their troubles were caused by a conspiracy of rich bankers and that prosperity would return if the government coined silver in unlimited quantities.

Turning Point in American Politics: 1896

National politics was in transition. The repeal of the Silver Purchase Act and Cleveland's handling of the depression thoroughly discredited the conservative leadership of the Democratic Party. The Democrats were buried in the congressional elections of 1894 by the Republicans. At the same time, the Populists continued to gain both votes and legislative seats. The stage was set for a major reshaping of party politics in 1896.

The 1896 Presidential Race

The election of 1896 was one of the most emotional in U.S. history. The party alignments still reflected the Civil War, with Republicans strong in the North and Midwest and the Democrats strong in the South. The issues remained similar to those of the previous 20 years. Republicans advocated for high tariffs and against silver coinage, with Democrats calling for lower tariffs and divided on currency issues. Both parties claimed to oppose corruption. Democrats attacked the Republicans for their ties to trusts and big-money interests. Republicans attacked Democrats for representing urban party bosses (see Topic 6.9). However, 1896 also marked the beginning of a new era in American politics.

Bryan, Democrats, and Populists Democrats were divided in 1896 between "gold" Democrats loyal to Cleveland and pro-silver Democrats looking for a leader. Their national convention in Chicago in the summer of 1896 was dominated by the pro-silver forces. Addressing the convention, **William Jennings Bryan** of Nebraska captured the hearts of the delegates with a speech that ended with the words "We will answer their demands for a gold standard by saying to them: 'You shall not press down upon the brow of labor this crown of thorns, you shall not crucify mankind upon a cross of gold.'" So powerful was Bryan's **"Cross of Gold" speech** that it made him instantly the Democratic nominee for president. Bryan was only 36 years old.

The Democratic platform favored the **unlimited coinage of silver** at the traditional, but inflationary, ratio of 16 ounces of silver to one ounce of gold. (The market price then was about 32 to 1.) Thus, the Democrats had taken over the leading issue of the Populist platform. Given little choice, the Populist convention in 1896 also nominated Bryan and conducted

Source: Library of Congress

Caption: Bryan's "Cross of Gold" speech was so famous that he reprinted it on a campaign poster.

a "fused" campaign for "free silver." Unhappy with Bryan and free silver, the conservative faction of **"Gold Bug" Democrats**, including Cleveland, either formed the separate National Democratic Party or voted Republican.

McKinley, Hanna, and Republicans For their presidential nominee, the Republicans nominated **William McKinley** of Ohio, best known for his support of a **high protective tariff** but also considered a friend of labor. **Marcus (Mark) Hanna**, who had made a fortune in business, was the financial power behind McKinley's nomination as well as the subsequent campaign for president. After blaming the Democrats for the Panic of 1893, the Republicans offered the American people the promise of a strong and prosperous industrial nation. The Republican platform proposed a high tariff to protect industry and upheld the **gold standard** against unlimited coinage of silver.

The Campaign The defection of Gold Bug Democrats over the silver issue gave the Republicans an early advantage. Bryan countered by turning the Democratic-Populist campaign into a nationwide crusade. Traveling by train from one end of the country to the other, the young candidate covered 18,000 miles and gave more than 600 speeches. His energy, positive attitude, and rousing oratory convinced millions of farmers and debtors that the unlimited coinage of silver was their salvation.

Mark Hanna meanwhile did most of the work of campaigning for McKinley. He raised millions of dollars for the Republican ticket from business leaders who feared that "silver lunacy" would lead to runaway inflation. Hanna used the money to sell McKinley through the **mass media** (newspapers, magazines), while the Republican candidate stayed home and conducted a safe, front-porch campaign, greeting delegations of supporters.

In the campaign's last weeks, Bryan was hurt by a rise in wheat prices, which made farmers less desperate, and threats by employers telling their workers that factories would shut down if Bryan won. In a decisive victory, McKinley carried all of the Northeast and the upper Midwest, winning both the popular vote (7.1 million to 6.5 million) and the electoral vote (271 to 176).

McKinley's Presidency

McKinley was lucky to take office just as the economy began to revive. Gold discoveries in Alaska in 1897 increased the money supply under the gold standard, which resulted in the inflation that the silverites had wanted. Farm prices rose, factory production increased, and the stock market climbed. The Republicans honored their platform by enacting the Dingley Tariff of 1897 that increased the tariff to more than 46 percent and, in 1900, made gold the official standard of the U.S. currency. McKinley was a well-liked, well-traveled president who tried to bring conflicting interests together. As leader during the war with Spain in 1898, he helped to make the United States a world power.

Significance of the Election of 1896

The election of 1896 had significant short-term and long-term consequences on American politics. It marked the end of the stalemate and stagnation that had characterized politics in the Gilded Age.

Populist Demise The Populist Party declined after 1896 and soon ceased to be a national party. In the South, Thomas Watson and other Populist leaders gave up trying to unite White and Black people, having discovered the hard lesson that **racism** was stronger than common economic interests. Ironically, in defeat, much of the Populist reform agenda, such as the graduated income tax and popular election of senators, was adopted by both the Democrats and reform-minded Republicans during the Progressive Era (1900–1917).

Beginning of Modern Politics The defeat of Bryan and the Populist free-silver movement initiated an **era of Republican dominance** of the presidency, electing six of the next seven presidents, and controlling both houses of Congress for 17 of the next 20 sessions. Once the party of "free soil, free labor, and free men," the Republicans had become the party of business and industry, though it continued to advocate for a strong national government. Mark Hanna, the master of high-finance politics, created a model for organizing and financing a successful campaign. Campaigns focused on winning favorable publicity in the dominant mass media of the day: print newspapers.

Urban Dominance The election of 1896 was a clear victory for big business, urban centers, conservative economics, and moderate, middle-class values. It proved to be the last hope of rural America to reclaim its former dominance in American politics. Some historians see the election marking the triumph of the values of modern industrial and urban America over the rural ideals of the America of Jefferson and Jackson.

President McKinley emerged as the **first modern president**, an active leader who took the United States from being relatively isolated to becoming a major player in international affairs during the 20th century. During the Gilded Age, the United States had developed into a leading industrial nation, but its role on the world stage had been of secondary importance. That would soon change with the Spanish-American War (see Topic 7.3).

REFLECT ON THE LEARNING OBJECTIVE

1. Explain three differences between the political parties during the Gilded Age.

KEY TERMS BY THEME

Republican Party (PCE)
"bloody shirt"
veterans of the Union army
reformers
African Americans
Anglo-Saxon Protestants
temperance
Hamiltonian tradition
Whig past
pro-business

Democratic Party (PCE)
"solid South"
former states of the Confederacy
big-city political machines
immigrant voters
Catholics, Lutherans, and Jews
Jeffersonian tradition
states' rights
limited federal power

Rise of Discontent (PCE)
rise of the Populists
Farmers' Alliances

Omaha Platform
government ownership
Thomas Watson
election of 1892
Grover Cleveland
Panic of 1893
march to Washington
"Coxey's Army"
Coin's Financial School
racism

Election of 1896 (PCE)
William Jennings Bryan
"Cross of Gold" speech
unlimited coinage of silver
"Gold Bug" Democrats
William McKinley
high protective tariff
Marcus (Mark) Hanna
gold standard
mass media
era of Republican dominance
first modern president

MULTIPLE-CHOICE QUESTIONS

Questions 1–3 refer to the following excerpt.

"My Dear Nephew,

"Never allow yourself to lose sight of that fact that politics, and not poker, is our great American game. If this could be beaten into the heads of some presumably well-meaning but glaringly unpractical people, we should hear less idiotic talk about reform in connection with politics. Nobody ever dreams of organizing a reform movement in poker. . . .

Mr. Lincoln, a very estimable and justly popular, but in some respects an impracticable man, formulated another widely different error in regard to politics. He held that ours is a government of the people, by the people, for the people. I maintain, on the contrary, that it is government of politicians, by politicians, for politicians. If your political career is to be a success, you must understand and respect this distinction with a difference."

> William McElroy, journalist, "An Old War-Horse to a Young Politician," a satire published anonymously in *The Atlantic Monthly*, 1880

1. Which of the following statements best reflects McElroy's perspective about politics in his era?
   (A) Americans should support politicians that talk about reform.
   (B) Elections were so close that candidates saw them as gambling.
   (C) Lincoln should not be admired by the general public.
   (D) People held public office primarily for personal gain.

2. The best example that modifies or refutes McElroy's description of "idiotic talk about reform in connection with politics" were the changes made in government hiring procedures after
   (A) the compromise between parties to settle the election of 1876
   (B) the successes by the Greenback Party in the elections in 1878
   (C) the assassination of President James Garfield in 1881
   (D) the loss by Grover Cleveland in the election of 1888

3. What is McElroy's purpose in writing this article?
   (A) To criticize young politicians because they were not well-meaning
   (B) To explain to young politicans how to apply the ideas of Lincoln
   (C) To encourage young politicians to find other careers
   (D) To revel to his readers the cynicism and corruption in U.S. politics

SHORT-ANSWER QUESTIONS

Use complete sentences; an outline or bulleted list alone is not acceptable.

1. "The Populists looked backward with longing to the lost Eden, to the republican America of the early years of the nineteenth century in which there were few millionaires . . . when the laborer had excellent prospects and the farmers had abundance, when statesmen responded to the mood of the people and there was no such thing as the money power."

   Richard Hofstadter, *The Age of Reform*, 1955

   "Populists sought to rethink the meaning of freedom to meet the exigencies of the 1890s. . . . Like the labor movement Populists rejected the era's laissez-faire orthodoxy. . . . A generation would pass before a major party offered so sweeping a plan for government action on the behalf of economic freedom as the Omaha platform."

   Eric Foner, *The Story of American Freedom*, 1998

   Using the excerpts above, answer (a), (b), and (c).

   (a) Briefly explain ONE significant difference between Hofstadter's and Foner's interpretations of the Populists.

   (b) Briefly explain ONE historical event or development from 1865 to 1900 that could support Hofstadter's interpretation of the Populists.

   (c) Briefly explain ONE historical event or development from 1865 to 1900 that could support Foner's interpretation of the Populists.

2. Answer (a), (b), and (c).

   (a) Briefly explain ONE specific proposal of the Populist Party to change politics or elections in the United States.

   (b) Briefly explain ONE specific way the debate over the money supply changed the 1896 election.

   (c) Briefly explain ONE specific result of the election of 1896 to support the interpretation that it was an important change in American politics.

Continuity and Change Period 6

Learning Objective: Explain the extent to which industrialization brought changes from 1865 to 1898.

You can use the reasoning process of continuity and change to consider the many aspects of industrialization from 1865 to 1898. On the AP® exam, a question might focus on one factor such as markets, technological innovation, government policies, migration, or urban development. In an effort to "Explain the extent to which large-scale industries changed markets in the United States from 1865 to 1898," one could make the argument that larger, more efficient manufacturers such as Carnegie Steel demonstrated a continuation of long-term trends. This argument could be made more complex in multiple ways:

- One could *corroborate* the argument with examples from other industries. For example, Rockefeller's Standard Oil business improved efficiency and bought up competitors to dominate the oil industry.

- One could *qualify* the argument by pointing out changes introduced by industry. For example, Carnegie used vertical integration.

- One could *modify* the argument by explaining that some markets continued to be dominated by regional businesses such as local railroads and breweries.

The ability to corroborate, qualify, or modify an argument using diverse evidence is one way to develop a *complex* argument in an essay.

QUESTIONS ABOUT CONTINUITY AND CHANGE

1. Explain the extent to which industrialization led to continuity or change in migration patterns to and within the United States from 1865 to 1898. For example, the main argument might be that jobs created by industrialization greatly increased migration to Northeastern and Midwestern cities,

2. Explain the extent to which industrialization led to changes in American culture from 1865 to 1898. For example, the main argument might be that industrialization helped to expand the middle class in the United States, which influenced changes in reform movements, education, and literature.

In everyday language, context means the words or conditions around something. The context for this passage is that it is part of a book about U.S. history. The context in which are reading it is a class. To a historian, context includes a broader historical picture. Contextualization involves two skills:

- **Identify a context:** This means the test makers present you with a specific example of a person, event, object, or location. Then you identify or describe the context—the broader historical picture in which it took place.

- **Explain specifics:** This mean the test makers provide you with a historical context. Then you list or describe one or more people, events, objects, or locations that were affected by that context.

For example, an item on the AP® exam might name a specific invention, such as barbed wire. The test makers might ask you to identify a context related to that invention. In the case of barbed wire, you could identify the context of the rise of the cattle-ranching industry in some western states. Or you could identify the pushing of Native Americans off their lands, the closing of the American frontier, or the establishment of the cattle frontier.

What about explaining specifics related to a larger historical context? For instance, an item on the exam might mention the labor movement and ask you to name a specific example related to that context. In this case, you might mention the names of specific labor leaders or business owners. You might also name a specific strike or describe one aspect of industrial warfare (such as blacklists).

Items related to contextualization may appear anywhere on the AP® exam. The easiest way to understand this skill is to practice it.

Read each example below. For each one, write a sentence or two that identifies its context.

1. The Great Railroad Strike of 1877

2. The Chinese Exclusion Act of 1882

3. Hull House being established in Chicago in 1889

4. The opening of an immigrant processing facility on Ellis Island in 1892

5. W. E. B. Du Bois receiving a doctorate from Harvard in 1895

Read each context below. For each one, identify one specific example that was shaped by that context.

6. Growth of the popular press

7. The rise of spectator sports

8. Women's suffrage

9. The conservation movement

10. Technology in cities

UNIT 6 — Period 6 Review: 1865–1898

After you analyze the task, gather and organize evidence, and develop an effective thesis statement, much of the hard work in writing a long essay is behind you. The most challenging task still remaining is to write an introduction that 1) serves as a blueprint for the rest of the essay and 2) casts the topic in a broader historical perspective.

The Introduction as Blueprint A good introduction conveys the framework or limits of the topic as well as a clear debatable and defensible claim. The claim should be expressed in one or more sentences in the same location—ideally the introduction. The introduction also suggests the organizational pattern and reasoning process that will unfold in the rest of the essay. In other words, it conveys (without saying), "Here's what I'm going to argue. Here's the reasoning process I am going to use to convince you. Here's the order I will use to present my ideas." The reasoning process may be causation, continuity and change, or comparison.

Historical Perspective A good introduction also demonstrates contextualization by relating the topic of the prompt to broader historical events, developments, or processes that occur before or during or that continue after the time frame of the question. The introduction is a good place to state the historical perspective, but it will need further development.

Application: Find both the blueprint and historical perspective in the following introduction. How does the introduction answer these questions:

- What is the author's argument?
- What reasoning process will the author use?
- What order will the author likely use?
- How does the topic relate to broader historical events, developments, or processes?

The rise of industrial capitalism in the United States between 1865 and 1898 marked a dramatic break with the economic values that guided Americans before 1865. The beliefs of the Puritans toward work, the individualism represented by Benajmin Franklin, and the pragmatic use of government in Henry Clay's American Plan were left behind as the country developed new ways to think about the economy. This change was part of a larger shift in the culture away from individualism that was reflected in politics and the arts.

For current free-response question samples, visit: https://apcentral.collegeboard.org/courses/ap-united-states-history/exam

LONG ESSAY QUESTIONS

Directions: The suggested writing time for each question is 40 minutes. In your response you should do the following:

- Respond to the prompt with a historically defensible thesis or claim that establishes a line of reasoning.
- Describe a broader historical context relevant to the prompt.
- Support an argument in response to the prompt using specific and relevant examples of evidence.
- Use historical reasoning (e.g., comparison, causation, continuity or change) to frame or structure an argument that addresses the prompt.
- Use evidence to corroborate, qualify, or modify an argument that addresses the prompt.

1. Evaluate the extent to which economic issues fostered continuity in the "New South" in the period from 1865 to 1898.

2. Evaluate the extent to which industrial capitalism fostered change in society in the period from 1865 to 1898.

3. Evaluate the extent to which the federal government's role in the economy in the period from 1865 to 1898 differed from its role before 1865.

4. Evaluate the extent to which the major political parties were similar during the Gilded Age.

5. Evaluate the extent to which changes in how businesses were organized and reached consumers influenced the development of the United States between 1865 and 1898.

6. Evaluate the extent to which cultural factors influenced internal migration patterns during the period from 1865 to 1898.

7. Evaluate the extent to which reform movements responded to problems of industrialization in the period from 1865 to 1898.

8. Evaluate the extent to which Social Darwinism was used to defend the economic order in the period from 1865 to 1898.

DOCUMENT-BASED QUESTION

Directions: Question 1 is based on the accompanying documents. The documents have been edited for the purpose of this exercise. You are advised to spend 15 minutes planning and 45 minutes writing your answer. In your response you should do the following:

- Respond to the prompt with a historically defensible thesis or claim that establishes a line of reasoning.
- Describe a broader historical context relevant to the prompt.
- Support an argument in response to the prompt using at least six documents.
- Use at least one additional piece of specific historical evidence (beyond that found in the documents) relevant to an argument about the prompt.
- For at least three documents, explain how or why the document's point of view, purpose, historical situation, and/or audience is relevant to an argument.
- Use evidence to corroborate, qualify, or modify an argument that addresses the prompt.

1. Evaluate the impact of the business leaders on the American economy and society from 1865 to 1900.

Document 1

> **Source:** Interview with William H. Vanderbilt, *Chicago Daily News*, 1882
>
> Q: How is the freight and passenger pool working?
> W.V.: Very satisfactorily. I don't like that expression "pool," however, that's a common construction applied by the people to a combination which the leading roads have entered into to keep rates at a point where they will pay dividends to the stockholders. The railroads are not run for the benefit of the "dear public"—that cry is all nonsense—they are built by men who invest their money and expect to get a fair percentage on the same.
>
> Q: Does your limited express pay?
> W.V.: No; not a bit of it. We only run it because we are forced to do so by the action of the Pennsylvania road. It doesn't pay expenses. We would abandon it if it was not for our competitor keeping its train on.
>
> Q: But don't you run it for the public benefit?
> W.V.: The public be damned. What does the public care for the railroads except to get as much out of them for as small consideration as possible? I don't take any stock in this silly nonsense about working for anybody's good but our own.

Document 2

Source: Thomas Alva Edison, letter written November 14, 1887

My laboratory will soon be completed. . . . I will have the best equipped and largest Laboratory extant, and the facilities incomparably superior to any other for rapid & cheap development of an invention, & working it up into Commercial shape with models, patterns & special machinery. In fact there is no similar institution in Existence. We do our own castings and forgings. Can build anything from a lady's watch to a Locomotive.

The Machine shop is sufficiently large to employ 50 men & 30 men can be worked in other parts of the works. Invention that formerly took months & cost a large sum can now be done in 2 or 3 days with very small expense, as I shall carry a stock of almost every conceivable material of every size, and with the latest machinery a man will produce 10 times as much as in a laboratory which has but little material, not of a size, delays of days waiting for castings and machinery not universal or modern. . . .

You are aware from your long acquaintance with me that I do not fly any financial Kites, or speculate, and that the works I control are well-managed. In the early days of the shops it was necessary that I should largely manage them [alone], first because the art had to be created, 2nd, because I could get no men who were competent in such a new business. But as soon as it was possible I put other persons in charge. I am perfectly well aware of the fact that my place is in the Laboratory; but I think you will admit that I know how a shop should be managed & also know how to select men to manage them.

Document 3

Source: Andrew Carnegie, "Wealth," *North American Review,* 1889

The problem of our age is the proper administration of wealth so that the ties of brotherhood may still bind together the rich and poor in harmony. . . .

The price which society pays for the law of competition, like the price it pays for cheap comforts and luxuries, is also great; but the advantages of this law are also greater still. For it is to this law that we owe our wonderful material development which brings improved conditions. While the law may be sometimes hard for the individual, it is best for the race, because it insures the survival of the fittest in every department. We welcome, therefore, as conditions to which we must accommodate ourselves, great inequality of environment, the concentration of business, industrial and commercial, in the hands of a few; and the law of competition between these, as being not only beneficial, but essential for the future progress of the race.

Document 4

It is clear that trusts are contrary to public policy and hence in conflict with the common law. They are monopolies organized to destroy competition and restrain trade. . . .

It is contended by those interested in trusts that they tend to cheapen production and diminish the price of the article to the consumer. . . . Trusts are speculative in their purpose and formed to make money. Once they secure control of a given line of business, they are masters of the situation and can dictate to the two great classes with which they deal—the producer of the raw material and the consumer of the finished product. They limit the price of the raw material so as to impoverish the producer, drive him to a single market, reduce the price of every class of labor connected with the trade, throw out of employment large numbers of persons who had before been engaged in a meritorious calling and finally . . . they increase the price to the consumer. . . . The main weapons of the trust are threats, intimidation, bribery, fraud, wreck, and pillage.

Document 5

Document 6

Source: Statement of Pullman Strikers, June 1894

Pullman, both the man and the town, is an ulcer on the body politic. He owns the houses, the schoolhouses, and the churches of God in the town he gave his once humble name. The revenue he derives from these wages he pays out with one hand—the Pullman Palace Car Company—he takes back with the other—the Pullman Land Association. He is able by this to bid under any contract car shop in this country. His competitors in business, to meet this, must reduce the wages of their men. This gives him the excuse to reduce ours to conform to the market. His business rivals must in turn scale down, so must he. And thus the merry war—the dance of skeletons bathed in human tears—goes on; and it will go on, brothers, forever unless you, the American Railway Union, stop it.

Document 7

Source: Major gifts by John D. Rockefeller before his death (1937)

American Baptist Foreign Mission Society New York City	$6,845,688.52
American Baptist Home Mission Society, New York City	6,994,831.62
American Baptist Missionary Society, Dayton, Ohio	1,902,132.58
General Education Board	129,209,167.10
Laura Spelman Rockefeller Memorial, New York	73,985,313.77
Minister and Missionaries Benefit Board of Northern Baptist Convention	7,090,579.06
Rockefeller Foundation, New York	182,851,480.90
Rockefeller Institute for Medical Research	59,931,891.60
University of Chicago, Chicago, Illinois	34,708,375.28
Yale University, New Haven	1,001,000.00
Y.M.C.A. International Committee	2,295,580.73
TOTAL	**$506,816,041.18**

Topic 7.1

Contextualizing Period 7

Learning Objective: Explain the context in which America grew into the role as a world power.

In the 55 years from 1890 to 1945, Americans went from horses and buggies to automobiles and airplanes. Within these decades, the United States fought in two horrific world wars, experienced the worst depression in its history, and emerged a world leader. Altogether, this period brought dramatic changes to how Americans lived and the role of their government.

By 1890 the United States had surpassed Great Britain as the leading industrial power in the world, and it would increase that economic leadership through World War II. A strong economy also provided the foundation for America's expanding role in international affairs and its emergence in 1945 as the world's leading political and military power. Industrialization, urbanization, and immigration continued to shape events during these years.

Economic Growth U.S. *economic expansion* continued during this period as the nation continued the transition from a rural, agricultural economy to an urban, industrial one. This development included the growth of *large corporations* and the repetition of earlier cycles of economic booms and busts, culminating in severe hardship during the Great Depression of the 1930s.

Stability and Democracy Economic changes along with political and social issues resulted in two significant *reform periods*, the time of the *Progressives* and the New Deal. Progressives in the first two decades of the 20th century turned to *government action* to address *economic instability* through the creation of the Federal Reserve to regulate banking and the business cycle. Progressives also responded to *political corruption* by reforming election practices, such as instituting the direct elections of U.S. senators by voters. *Social reforms* included a constitutional amendment that gave women the right to vote, a landmark in the struggle for gender equality that would continue into the present.

Responding to an Economic Crisis The economic collapse and mass unemployment of the *Great Depression* challenged the *laissez-faire* economic policies of the 1920s. In response, the Democrats' *New Deal* created a *limited welfare state* to address mass unemployment, to reduce poverty among the elderly, and to help others experiencing economic hardships. Congress passed laws regulating banks and the stock market, guaranteeing a minimum wage, creating Social Security and protecting workers in labor unions. The increasing role and size of government to meet problems caused by industrialization fostered the emerging ideology of *American liberalism*.

Conflicts in Culture and Society *Popular culture* grew dramatically with the introduction of new *mass media*, such as radio and motion pictures. Changes in popular culture sparked *value conflicts* over morals, education, religion and science. Some churches objected to the science of evolution being taught in public schools. Reactions to the growth of immigration and internal migration resulted in debates over *national identity* and the passage of federal *restrictions on immigration* based on one's ethnicity or national origin. A resurgent Ku Klux Klan attacked, both politically and physically, African Americans, Roman Catholics, Jews, and immigrants.

Shifts in Foreign Relations The conflicts over imperialism and two world wars renewed debate over America's *role in the world*. The acquisition of new territories after the Spanish-American War caused some people to question its commitment to traditional *national values* of freedom, independence, and self-government. In World War I, Americans disagreed over the degree of *American interests* in the conflict and the best approach to insure *national security*. After the war, Congress and voters rejected membership in the League of Nations.

However, World War II thrust the United States, with its unrivaled economic, political, and military power, into a *leadership role* in the world. In 1945, the United States embraced the concept of *collective security* and played a leading role in creating the United Nations. Decisions made after the war, such as the nation's close alliance with western Europe and its commitment to anti-communism, shaped American foreign policy through the end of the century.

ANALYZE THE CONTEXT

1. Explain a historical context for the increased role of the federal government in the U.S. economy during the period from 1890 to 1945.

2. Explain a historical context for the increased role of the United States in world affairs during the period from 1890 to 1945.

LANDMARK EVENTS: 1890–1950

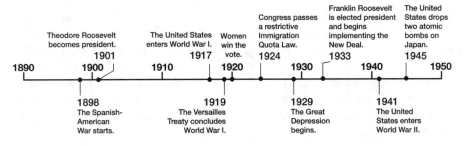

Imperialism: Debates

Our form of government, our traditions, our present interests, and our future welfare, all forbid our entering upon a career of conquest.

William Jennings Bryan, December 13, 1898

Learning Objective: Explain the similarities and differences in attitudes about the nation's proper role in the world.

After the 1790s, U.S. foreign policy had centered on expanding westward, protecting U.S. interests abroad, and limiting foreign influences in the Americas. After the Civil War, with a booming industrial economy, the United States showed increasing interest not only in overseas trade, but also in establishing bases and territories in the Caribbean Sea and across the Pacific Ocean. After 1890, the nation carried on a growing debate over whether it should join the competition for overseas territories with imperialist nations of the world or remain true to its anti-colonial traditions.

Expansion after the Civil War

William H. Seward of New York served as secretary of state (1861–1869) under both Abraham Lincoln and Andrew Johnson. Seward was the most influential secretary of state since John Quincy Adams (who formulated the **Monroe Doctrine** in 1823). During the Civil War, Seward helped prevent Great Britain and France from entering the war on the side of the Confederacy. He led the drive to annex Midway Island in the Pacific, gained rights to build a canal in Nicaragua, and purchased the vast territory of Alaska. Despite his powerful advocacy for expansionism, Seward failed to convince Congress to annex Hawaii and to purchase the Danish West Indies.

The Purchase of Alaska For decades, Russia and Great Britain both claimed the vast territory of Alaska. Russia finally assumed control and established a small colony for seal hunting, but the territory soon became an economic burden because of the threat of a British takeover. Seeking buyers, Russia found Seward to be an enthusiastic champion of the idea of the United States purchasing Alaska. As a result of Seward's lobbying, and also in appreciation of Russian support during the Civil War, Congress in 1867 agreed to buy Alaska for $7.2 million. However, for many years Americans saw no value in Alaska and referred to it derisively as "Seward's Folly" or "Seward's Icebox" and ignored its development.

Hawaiian Islands Since the mid-1800s, American missionaries and entrepreneurs had settled in the Pacific islands of **Hawaii**. Later, a U.S. commission explored the use of **Pearl Harbor** in Hawaii, or the Sandwich Islands, which lay astride the sea-lanes from California to China. In 1870, Ulysses S. Grant sought control of Pearl Harbor on Oahu and new trade treaties with the native kingdom. Hawaiians agreed to a treaty in 1875 giving the United States exclusive rights to Hawaiian sugar. In 1893, American settlers aided in the overthrow of the Hawaiian monarch, **Queen Liliuokalani** and then petitioned for annexation by the United States. If Hawaii became part of the United States, Hawaiian sugar would not be subject to the high U.S. tariffs on imports. However, President **Grover Cleveland** opposed imperialism and blocked Republican efforts to annex Hawaii.

The Era of "New Imperialism"

The conquest and division of many parts of Africa, Asia, and the Pacific Islands by more industrialized nations during the 19th century marked a renewed interest in imperialism. Britain, France, Germany, Russia, Japan, and other nations, some as small as Belgium, gained control by arms or by economic dominance. The United States also participated in this contest. Most U.S. advocates of expansionism hoped to succeed through economic and diplomatic means, without resorting to military action. Expansion into new territories continued a long pattern in U.S. history, but adding land overseas was a change from the past. People supported expansion for different combinations of reasons.

Economic Interests The country's growing industries were strong supporters of expanding U.S. economic interests around the world. Foreign countries offered both valuable raw materials, including minerals, oil, and rubber, and provided markets for products. Many in the Republican Party were closely allied with business leaders and therefore generally endorsed an imperialist foreign policy. Like industrialists, farmers were eager to sell overseas. They saw the growing populations of cities, both in the United States and internationally, as potential markets for wheat, corn, and livestock.

Political and Military Power Some people believed that the United States needed to compete with the imperialistic nations or it would be sidelined as a second-class power in world affairs. Chief among these was U.S. Navy Captain **Alfred Thayer Mahan**. He shaped the debate over the need for naval bases with his book *The Influence of Sea Power Upon History* (1890). He argued that a strong navy was crucial to a country's ambitions of securing foreign markets and becoming a world power. Mahan's book was widely read by prominent American citizens as well as by political leaders in Europe and Japan.

Using arguments in Mahan's book, U.S. naval strategists persuaded Congress to finance the construction of modern steel ships and encouraged the acquisition of overseas islands. Among these islands were Samoa and others in the Pacific Ocean that provided coaling and supply stations so that the new fleet could project power globally. By 1900, the U.S. Navy was the third largest in the world. Among politicians, Assistant Secretary of the Navy and later President Theodore Roosevelt and Senator Henry Cabot Lodge were the leading proponents of expanding U.S. naval power and influence in the world.

Social Fears The Panic of 1893, the violence of labor-management conflicts, and the perception that the country no longer had a frontier in the 1890s caused fear of increasing social turmoil. Overseas territories and adventures offered the country a possible safety valve for dissatisfied urban workers and farmers.

Darwinism and Religion Some saw expansion into the Caribbean, Central America, and the Pacific Ocean as an extension of the idea of Manifest Destiny that had long fostered westward expansion. In addition, they applied Darwin's concept of the survival of the fittest not only to competition in business but also to competition among countries. Therefore, to demonstrate strength in the international arena, **expansionists** wanted to acquire territories overseas. In his book *Our Country: Its Possible Future and Present Crisis* (1885), the Reverend **Josiah Strong** wrote that people of Anglo-Saxon stock were "the fittest to survive." He believed that Protestant Americans had a religious duty to colonize other lands in order to spread Christianity and the benefits of their "superior" civilization (medicine, science, and technology) to "less fortunate" peoples of the world. Many missionaries who traveled to Africa, Asia, and the Pacific Islands believed in the racial superiority of White people, although some went more for humanitarian reasons. To support these missionaries, many Americans called for active U.S. government involvement in foreign affairs.

Popular Press Newspaper and magazine editors found that they could increase circulation by printing adventure stories about distant places exotic to their readers. Stories in the popular press increased public interest and stimulated demands for a larger U.S. role in world affairs.

Opposition to Imperialism
Many people in the United States strongly opposed imperialism. They did so for a combination of reasons:

- They believed in self-determination. One of the founding principles of the United States was that people should govern themselves. They believed that this principle applied to people everywhere, not just in the United States. They felt that imperialism was morally wrong.

- They rejected imperialist racial theories. Some denied that Whites were biologically superior to people of Asia or Africa, and so Whites had no right to rule others. However, many Americans feared adding nonwhite people to the country.

- They supported isolationism. George Washington had advised the country to avoid involvement in foreign affairs. Anti-imperialists argued that this was still good advice.

- They opposed the expense of imperialism. Building a large navy and controlling foreign territories would cost more than they were worth.

Latin America

Beginning with the Monroe Doctrine in the 1820s, the United States had taken a special interest in problems of the Western Hemisphere and had assumed the role of protector of Latin America from European ambitions. Benjamin Harrison's Secretary of State **James G. Blaine** of Maine played a principal role in extending this tradition.

Pan-American Diplomacy Blaine's repeated efforts to establish closer ties between the United States and its southern neighbors bore fruit in 1889 with the meeting of the first **Pan-American Conference** in Washington. Representatives from various nations of the Western Hemisphere decided to create a permanent organization to promote cooperation on trade and other issues. Blaine had hoped to reduce tariff rates. Although this goal was not achieved, the foundation was established for the larger goal of hemispheric cooperation on both economic and political issues. The Pan-American Union continues today as part of the Organization of American States, which was established in 1948.

Cleveland, Olney, and the Monroe Doctrine One of the most important uses of the Monroe Doctrine in the late 19th century concerned a boundary dispute between Venezuela and its neighbor—the British colony of Guiana. In 1895 and 1896, President Cleveland and Secretary of State **Richard Olney** insisted that Great Britain agree to arbitrate the dispute. The British initially said the matter was not the business of the United States. However, the United States argued that the Monroe Doctrine applied to the situation. If the British did not arbitrate, the United States would back up its argument with military force.

Deciding that U.S. friendship was more important to its long-term interests than a boundary dispute in South America, the British agreed to U.S. demands. As it turned out, the arbitrators ruled mainly in favor of Britain, not Venezuela. Even so, Latin American nations appreciated U.S. efforts to protect them from European domination. The **Venezuela boundary dispute** marked a turning point in U.S.–British relations. From 1895 on, the two countries cultivated a friendship rather than continuing their former rivalry. The friendship would prove vital for both nations in the 20th century.

Growing Conflict over Imperialism The precedent of the Monroe Doctrine provided expansionists an open invitation to interfere in the other nations of the Americas. This was the beginning of a fierce political battle over the future of the country. One side represented the anti-colonial and self-government traditions of the nation rooted in the struggle for independence against Great Britain. The other side expressed the interests of those committed to economic and global power. The conflict between imperialists and anti-imperialists over controlling overseas territories intensified in the debate over the Spanish-American War and the colonization of the Philippines (see Topic 7.3).

REFLECT ON THE LEARNING OBJECTIVE

1. Explain two differences between American imperialists and anti-imperialists.

KEY TERMS BY THEME

Overseas Involvement (WOR)
William H. Seward
Monroe Doctrine
purchase of Alaska (1867)
Hawaii
Pearl Harbor
Queen Liliuokalani
Grover Cleveland
James G. Blaine

Pan-American Conference (1889)
Richard Olney
Venezuela boundary dispute
Causes of U.S. Imperialism (WOR)
"New Imperialism"
Alfred Thayer Mahan
Darwinism
expansionists
Josiah Strong

MULTIPLE-CHOICE QUESTIONS

Questions 1–2 refer to the following excerpt.

> "We hold that the policy known as imperialism is hostile to liberty and tends toward militarism, an evil from which it has been our glory to be free. We regret that it has become necessary in the land of Washington and Lincoln to reaffirm that all men, of whatever race or color, are entitled to life, liberty, and the pursuit of happiness. . . .
>
> "We earnestly condemn the policy of the present national administration in the Philippines. It seeks to extinguish the spirit of 1776 in those islands. . . . We denounce the slaughter of the Filipinos as a needless horror. We protest against the extension of American sovereignty by Spanish methods. We demand the immediate cessation of the war against liberty, begun by Spain and continued by us. We urge that Congress be promptly convened to announce to the Filipinos our purpose to concede to them the independence for which they have so long fought and which of right is theirs."
>
> Platform of the American Anti-Imperialist
> League, October 17, 1899

1. Supporters of this excerpt would most likely agree with which of the following beliefs?

   (A) The peoples of Asia had a right to govern themselves without outside interference.

   (B) The United States had a duty to bring the benefits of civilization and religion to others.

   (C) The people of underdeveloped countries were unprepared and unfit to govern themselves.

   (D) The United States should take over weak countries that might fall to other great powers.

2. Which of the following most directly contributed to the sentiments expressed in the excerpt?

   (A) The sensationalism of the popular press of the time

   (B) The values expressed in the Declaration of Independence

   (C) The views of Theodore Roosevelt and Henry Cabot Lodge

   (D) The changing interpretation of the Monroe Doctrine

SHORT-ANSWER QUESTION

Use complete sentences; an outline or bulleted list alone is not acceptable.

1. Answer (a), (b), and (c).

   (a) Briefly explain ONE difference between the position of imperialists and anti-imperialists on the acquisition of overseas territories in the period of the Spanish-American War.

   (b) Briefly describe ONE controversial territorial acquisition and why expansionists favored it in the period from 1865 to 1900.

   (c) Briefly describe ONE controversial territorial acquisition and why anti-imperialists opposed it in the period from 1865 to 1900.

The Spanish-American War and U.S. Foreign Policy to 1917

We are Anglo-Saxons, and must obey our blood and occupy new markets, and, if necessary, new lands.

Senator Albert Beveridge, April 27, 1898

Learning Objective: Explain the causes and effects of the Spanish-American War.

The first targets of American imperialism were nearby Caribbean islands. Expansionists from the South had coveted Cuba as early as the 1850s. Now, in the 1890s, large American investments in Cuban sugar, Spanish misrule of Cuba, and the Monroe Doctrine all provided reasons for U.S. intervention in the Caribbean's largest island. Connected to U.S. involvement on Cuba, an island only 90 miles south of mainland United States, came involvement in the Philippines, islands over 7,000 miles to the west.

Spanish-American War

In the 1890s, American public opinion was being swept by a growing wave of **jingoism**—an intense form of nationalism calling for an aggressive foreign policy. Expansionists demanded that the United States take its place with the imperialist nations of Europe as a world power. Not everyone favored such a policy. Presidents Cleveland and McKinley were among many who thought military action abroad was both morally wrong and economically unsound. Nevertheless, specific events combined with background pressures led to overwhelming popular demand for war against Spain.

Causes of the War

A combination of jingoism, economic interests, and moral concerns made the United States more willing to go to war than it had been. These factors came together in 1898.

Cuban Revolt Cuban nationalists fought but failed to overthrow Spanish colonial rule between 1868 and 1878. They renewed the struggle in 1895. Through sabotage and attacks on Cuban plantations, they hoped to either push Spain out or pull the United States in as an ally. In response, Spain sent autocratic General Valeriano Weyler and 100,000 troops to crush the revolt. Weyler forced civilians into camps, where tens of thousands died of starvation and disease. This action gained him the title of "the Butcher" in the U.S. press.

Yellow Press Actively promoting war fever in the United States was **"yellow journalism,"** sensationalistic reporting that featured bold and lurid headlines of crime, disaster, and scandal. Among the most sensationalistic newspapers were Joseph Pulitzer's *New York World* and William Randolph Hearst's *New York Journal*. These papers printed exaggerated and false accounts of Spanish atrocities in Cuba. Believing what they read daily in their newspapers, many Americans urged Congress and the president to intervene in Cuba for humanitarian reasons and put a stop to the atrocities and suffering.

De Lôme Letter (1898) One story that caused a storm of outrage was a Spanish diplomat's letter that was leaked to the press and printed on the front page of Hearst's *Journal*. Written by the Spanish minister to the United States, Dupuy de Lôme, the letter was highly critical of President McKinley. Many considered it an official Spanish insult against the U.S. national honor.

Sinking of the *Maine* Less than one week after the de Lôme letter made headlines, a far more shocking event occurred. On February 15, 1898, the U.S. battleship USS *Maine* was at anchor in the harbor of Havana, Cuba, when it suddenly exploded, killing 260 Americans on board. The yellow press accused Spain of deliberately blowing up the ship. However, experts later concluded that the explosion was probably an accident.

McKinley's War Message Following the sinking of the USS *Maine*, President McKinley issued an ultimatum to Spain demanding that it agree to a ceasefire in Cuba. Spain agreed to this demand, but U.S. newspapers and a majority in Congress kept clamoring for war. McKinley yielded to the public pressure in April by sending a war message to Congress. He offered four reasons why the United States should support the Cuban rebels:

1. "Put an end to the barbarities, bloodshed, starvation, and horrible miseries" in Cuba

2. Protect the lives and property of U.S. citizens living in Cuba

3. End "the very serious injury to the commerce, trade, and business of our people"

4. End "the constant menace to our peace" arising from disorder in Cuba

Teller Amendment Responding to the president's message, Congress passed a joint resolution on April 20, 1898, authorizing war. Part of the resolution, the **Teller Amendment**, declared that the United States had no intention of taking political control of Cuba and that, once peace was restored to the island, the Cuban people would control their own government.

Fighting the War

The first shots of the Spanish-American War were fired in Manila Bay in the Philippines, over 9,000 miles from Cuba. The last shots were fired only a few months later in August. So swift was the U.S. victory that Secretary of State John Hay called it **"a splendid little war."**

The Philippines Theodore Roosevelt, McKinley's assistant secretary of the navy, was an expansionist eager to show off the power of his country's new, all-steel navy. Anticipating war, and recognizing the strategic value of Spain's territories in the Pacific, Roosevelt had ordered a fleet commanded by Commodore **George Dewey** to go to the Philippines. This large group of islands had been under Spanish control ever since the 1500s.

On May 1, shortly after war was declared, Commodore Dewey's fleet fired on Spanish ships in Manila Bay. The Spanish fleet was soon pounded into submission by U.S. naval guns. The fight on land took longer. Allied with Filipino rebels, U.S. troops captured the city of Manila on August 13.

Invasion of Cuba More difficult than the Philippines was Cuba. An ill-prepared, largely volunteer U.S. force landed in Cuba in June. The most lethal foe proved to be not Spanish bullets but tropical diseases. Fewer than 500 U.S. soldiers died in battle, but at least 5,000 died of malaria, typhoid, and dysentery.

Attacks by both American and Cuban forces succeeded in defeating the much larger, but poorly led, Spanish army. Next to Dewey's victory in Manila Bay, the most celebrated event of the war was a cavalry charge up San Juan Hill in Cuba by the Rough Riders, a regiment of volunteers led by Theodore Roosevelt, who had resigned his navy post to take part in the war. Roosevelt's volunteers were aided in victory by veteran regiments of African Americans. Less dramatic but more important than the taking of San Juan Hill was the success of the U.S. Navy in destroying the Spanish fleet at Santiago Bay on July 3. Without a navy, Spain realized that it could not continue fighting, and in early August 1898 asked the U.S. for terms of peace.

Annexation of Hawaii

The outbreak of war in the Philippines gave Congress and President McKinley the pretext to complete the annexation of Hawaii in July 1898. The Hawaiian Islands became a U.S. territory in 1900 and the fiftieth state in the Union in August 1959 (Topic 7.2).

Controversy over the Treaty of Peace

More controversial than the war itself was the peace treaty signed in Paris on December 10, 1898. It provided for (1) recognition of Cuban independence, (2) U.S. acquisition of two Spanish islands—**Puerto Rico** in the Caribbean and **Guam** in the Pacific, and (3) U.S. control of the Philippines in return for a $20 million payment to Spain. Since the avowed purpose of the U.S. war effort was to liberate Cuba, Americans accepted this provision of the treaty. However, many opposed taking over the Philippines, a large island nation, as a colony.

The Philippine Question Controversy over the Philippine question took many months longer to resolve than the brief war with Spain. Opinion both in Congress and with the public at large became sharply divided between imperialists who favored annexing the Philippines and anti-imperialists who opposed it. In the Senate, where a two-thirds vote was required to ratify the **Treaty of Paris**, anti-imperialists were determined to defeat the treaty because of its provision for acquiring the Philippines. Anti-imperialists argued that the United States would be taking possession of a heavily populated territory whose people were of a different race and culture. Such action, they thought, violated the principles of the Declaration of Independence by depriving Filipinos of the right to "life, liberty, and the pursuit of happiness." Further, annexation would entangle the United States in the political conflicts of Asia.

On February 6, 1899, the Treaty of Paris (including Philippine annexation) came to a vote in Congress. The treaty was approved 57 to 27, just one vote more than the two-thirds majority required by the Constitution for ratification. The anti-imperialists fell just two votes short of defeating the treaty.

The people of the Philippines were outraged that their hopes for national independence from Spain were now being denied by the United States. Filipino nationalist leader **Emilio Aguinaldo** had fought alongside U.S. troops during the Spanish-American War. Now he led bands of guerrilla fighters in a war against U.S. control. It took U.S. troops three years to defeat the insurrection. The conflict resulted in the deaths of about 5,000 people from the United States and several hundred thousand Filipinos—mostly civilians who died from diseases.

Other Results of the War

Imperialism remained a major issue in the United States even after ratification of the Treaty of Paris. The American **Anti-Imperialist League** led by William Jennings Bryan rallied opposition to further acts of expansion in the Pacific.

Insular Cases One question concerned the constitutional rights of the Philippine people: Did the Constitution follow the flag? In other words, did the provisions of the U.S. Constitution apply to whatever territories fell under U.S. control, including the Philippines and Puerto Rico? Bryan and other anti-imperialists argued in the affirmative, while leading imperialists argued in the negative. The issue was resolved in favor of the imperialists in a series of Supreme Court cases (1901–1903) known as the Insular (island) Cases. The Court ruled that constitutional rights were not automatically extended to territorial possessions and that the power to decide whether or not to grant such rights belonged to Congress.

Cuba and the Platt Amendment (1901) Previously, the Teller Amendment to the war resolution of 1898 had guaranteed U.S. respect for Cuba's sovereignty as an independent nation. Nevertheless, U.S. troops remained in Cuba from 1898 until 1901. In the latter year, Congress made withdrawal of troops conditional upon Cuba's acceptance of terms included in an amendment to an army appropriations bill—the **Platt Amendment**. Bitterly resented by Cuban nationalists, the Platt Amendment required Cuba to agree (1) to never sign a treaty with a foreign power that impaired its independence, (2) to permit the United States to intervene in Cuba's affairs to preserve its independence and maintain law and order, and (3) to allow the U.S. to maintain naval bases in Cuba, including one permanent base at Guantanamo Bay.

A Cuban convention reluctantly accepted these terms, adding them to its country's new constitution. In effect, the Platt Amendment made Cuba a U.S. protectorate. As a result, Cuba's foreign policy would, for many years, be subject to U.S. oversight and control.

Election of 1900 The Republicans re-nominated President McKinley, along with war hero and New York Governor Theodore Roosevelt for vice president. The Democrats, as in 1896, nominated William Jennings Bryan. He again argued for free silver and vigorously attacked American imperialism. However, most voters accepted the recently enacted gold standard and the acquisition of new territory, including the Philippines, and felt the economy was recovering. McKinley won by a larger margin of victory than in 1896.

U.S. TERRITORIES AND PROTECTORATES, 1917

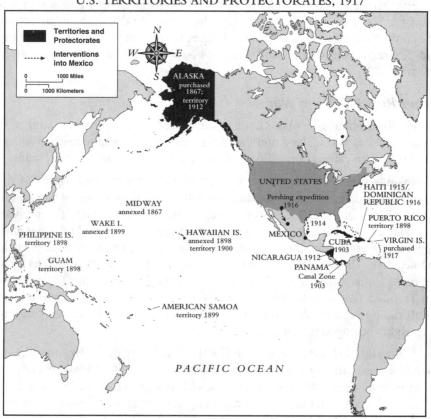

Recognition of U.S. Power One consequence of the Spanish-American War was its effect on how Americans and Europeans thought about U.S. power. The decisive U.S. victory in the war filled Americans with national pride. Southerners shared in this pride and became more attached to the Union after their bitter experience in the 1860s. At the same time, France, Great Britain, and other European nations recognized that the United States was a first-class power with a strong navy and a new willingness to act in international affairs.

Open Door Policy in China

Europeans were further impressed by U.S. involvement in global politics as a result of **John Hay**'s policies toward China. As McKinley's secretary of state, Hay was alarmed that the Chinese empire, weakened by political corruption and failure to modernize, was falling under the control of various outside powers. In the 1890s, Russia, Japan, Great Britain, France, and Germany had all established **spheres of influence** in China, meaning that they could dominate trade and investment within their sphere (a particular port or region of China) and shut out competitors.

To prevent the United States from losing access to the lucrative China trade, Hay dispatched a diplomatic note in 1899 to nations controlling spheres of influence. He asked them to accept the concept of an Open Door, by which all nations would have equal trading privileges in China. The replies to Hay's note were evasive. However, because no nation rejected the concept, Hay declared that all had accepted the **Open Door policy**. The press hailed Hay's initiative as a diplomatic triumph.

Boxer Rebellion (1900) As the 19th century ended, nationalism and *xenophobia* (hatred and fear of foreigners) were on the rise in China. In 1900, a secret society of Chinese nationalists—the Society of Harmonious Fists, or Boxers—attacked foreign settlements and murdered dozens of Christian missionaries. To protect American lives and property, U.S. troops participated in an international force that marched into Peking (Beijing) and quickly crushed the rebellion of the Boxers. The countries forced China to pay a huge indemnity, which further weakened the imperial regime.

Hay's Second Round of Notes Hay feared that the expeditionary force in China might attempt to occupy the country and destroy its independence. In 1900, therefore, he wrote a second note to the imperialistic powers stating U.S. commitment to (1) preserve China's territorial integrity as well as (2) safeguard "equal and impartial trade with all parts of the Chinese empire." Hay's first and second notes set U.S. policy on China not only for the administrations of McKinley and Theodore Roosevelt but also for future presidents. In the 1930s, this Open Door policy for China would strongly influence U.S. relations with Japan.

Hay's notes in themselves did not deter other nations from exploiting the situation in China. For the moment, European powers were kept from grabbing larger pieces of China by the political rivalries among themselves.

Theodore Roosevelt's "Big Stick" Policy

In 1901, only a few months after being inaugurated president for a second time, McKinley was fatally shot by an anarchist (a person who opposes all government). Succeeding him in office was the Republican vice president—the young expansionist and hero of the Spanish-American War, **Theodore Roosevelt**. Describing his foreign policy, the new president had once said that it was his motto to "speak softly and carry a big stick." The press therefore applied the label "big stick" to Roosevelt's aggressive foreign policy. By acting boldly and decisively in a number of situations, Roosevelt attempted to build the reputation of the United States as a world power. Imperialists applauded his every move, but critics disliked breaking the tradition of nonentanglement in global politics.

The Panama Canal

As a result of the Spanish-American War, the new American empire stretched from Puerto Rico in the Caribbean to the Philippines in the Pacific. As a strategic necessity for holding on to these far-flung islands, the United States desired a canal through Central America to connect the Atlantic and Pacific oceans. However, building a canal would be difficult. The French had already failed to complete a canal through the tropic jungles. And before the United States could even try, it needed to negotiate an agreement with the British to abrogate (cancel) the 1850 Clayton-Bulwer Treaty, which stated that any canal in Central America was to be under joint British-U.S. control. This new agreement, called the Hay-Pauncefote Treaty, was signed in 1901. With the British agreement to let the United States build a canal alone, the young and activist President Roosevelt took charge.

Revolution in Panama Roosevelt was eager to begin the construction of a canal through the narrow but rugged terrain of the isthmus of Panama. He was frustrated, however, by Colombia's control of this isthmus and its refusal to agree to U.S. terms for digging the canal through its territory. Losing patience with Colombia's demands of more money and sovereignty over the canal, Roosevelt orchestrated a revolt for Panama's independence in 1903. With the support of the U.S. Navy, the rebellion succeeded immediately and almost without bloodshed. However, the new government of an independent Panama had to sign the **Hay-Bunau-Varilla Treaty** of 1903 granting the United States all rights over the 51-mile-long and 10-mile-wide Canal Zone as "if it were sovereign . . . in perpetuity" to keep U.S. protection. Years later, Roosevelt boasted, "I took the Canal Zone and let Congress debate."

Building the Canal Started in 1904, the **Panama Canal** was completed in 1914. Hundreds of laborers lost their lives in the effort. The work was completed thanks in great measure to the skills of two Army colonels—George Goethals, the chief engineer of the canal, and Dr. William Gorgas, whose efforts eliminated the mosquitoes that spread deadly yellow fever.

Most Americans approved of Roosevelt's determination to build the canal, but many were unhappy with his high-handed tactics to secure the Canal Zone. Latin Americans were especially resentful. To compensate, Congress finally voted in 1921 to pay Colombia an indemnity of $25 million for its loss of Panama. In 1999, the United States returned the Canal Zone to the Republic of Panama to end the bitterness over the original treaty.

The Roosevelt Corollary to the Monroe Doctrine

Another application of Roosevelt's big stick diplomacy involved Latin American nations that were in deep financial trouble and could not pay their debts to European creditors. For example, in 1902, the British dispatched warships to Venezuela to force that country to pay its debts.

In 1904, it appeared that European powers stood ready to intervene in **Santo Domingo** (the Dominican Republic) for the same reason. Rather than let Europeans intervene in Latin America—a blatant violation of the Monroe Doctrine—Roosevelt declared in December 1904 that the United States would intervene instead, whenever necessary. This policy became known as the **Roosevelt Corollary** to the Monroe Doctrine. It meant, for example, that the United States would send gunboats to a Latin American country that was delinquent in paying its debts. U.S. sailors and marines would then occupy the country's major ports to manage the collection of customs taxes until European debts were satisfied.

Over the next 20 years, U.S. presidents used the Roosevelt Corollary to justify sending U.S. forces into Haiti, Honduras, the Dominican Republic, and Nicaragua. One long-term result of such interventions was poor U.S. relations with the entire region of Latin America.

Roosevelt and Asia

As the 20th century began, Japan and the United States were both relatively new imperialist powers in East Asia. Their relationship during Theodore Roosevelt's presidency, though at first friendly, grew increasingly competitive.

Russo-Japanese War Imperialist rivalry between Russia and Japan led to war in 1904, a war Japan was winning. To end the conflict, Roosevelt arranged a diplomatic conference between the two foes at Portsmouth, New Hampshire, in 1905. Although both Japan and Russia agreed to the **Treaty of Portsmouth**, Japanese nationalists blamed the United States for not giving their country all that they believed they deserved from Russia.

"Gentlemen's Agreement" A major cause of friction between Japan and the United States were laws in California that discriminated against Japanese Americans. San Francisco's practice of requiring Japanese American children to attend **segregated schools** was considered a national insult in Japan. In 1908, President Roosevelt arranged a compromise by means of an informal understanding, or **"gentlemen's agreement."** The Japanese government secretly agreed to restrict the emigration of Japanese workers to the United States in return for Roosevelt persuading California to repeal its discriminatory laws.

Great White Fleet To demonstrate U.S. naval power to Japan and other nations, Roosevelt sent a fleet of battleships on an around-the-world cruise (1907–1909). The great white ships made an impressive sight, and the Japanese government warmly welcomed their arrival in Tokyo Bay.

Root-Takahira Agreement (1908) The United States and Japan concluded an important executive agreement in 1908. Secretary of State Elihu Root and Japanese Ambassador Takahira pledged mutual respect for each nation's Pacific possessions and support for the Open Door policy in China.

Peace Efforts Roosevelt saw his big stick policies as a way to promote peaceful solutions to international disputes. For his work in settling the Russo-Japanese War, Roosevelt was awarded the **Nobel Peace Prize** in 1906. In the same year, he helped arrange the **Algeciras Conference** in Spain, which succeeded in settling a conflict between France and Germany over claims to Morocco. The president also directed U.S. participation at the Second **International Peace Conference** at The Hague in 1907, which discussed rules for limiting warfare. As an expansionist, an interventionist, and finally as an internationalist, Theodore Roosevelt embodied the vigor of a youthful nation arriving on the world stage.

William Howard Taft and Dollar Diplomacy

Roosevelt's successor, **William Howard Taft** (1909–1913), did not carry the same "big stick." He adopted a foreign policy that was mildly expansionist but depended more on investors' dollars than on the navy's battleships. His policy of promoting U.S. trade by supporting American enterprises abroad was known as **"dollar diplomacy."**

American Investors Taft believed that private American financial investment in China and Central America would lead to greater stability there, while at the same time promoting U.S. business interests. His policy, however, was thwarted by one major obstacle: growing **anti-imperialism** both in the United States and overseas.

Railroads in China Taft first tested his policy in China. Wanting U.S. bankers to be included in a British, French, and German plan to invest in railroads in China, Taft succeeded in securing American participation in an agreement signed in 1911. In China's northern province of **Manchuria**, however, the United States was excluded from an agreement between Russia and Japan to build railroads. In defiance of the U.S. Open Door policy, Russia and Japan agreed to treat Manchuria as a jointly held sphere of influence.

Intervention in Nicaragua To protect American investments, the United States intervened in Nicaragua's financial affairs in 1911 and sent in marines when a civil war broke out in 1912. The marines remained, except for a short period, until 1933.

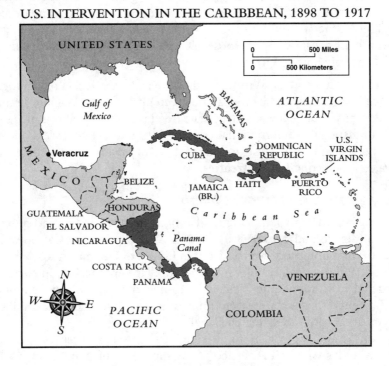

U.S. INTERVENTION IN THE CARIBBEAN, 1898 TO 1917

Woodrow Wilson and Foreign Affairs

In his campaign for president in 1912, the Democratic candidate **Woodrow Wilson** promised a *New Freedom* for the country, part of which was a moral approach to foreign affairs. Wilson said he opposed imperialism and the big stick and dollar diplomacy policies of his Republican predecessors.

Wilson's Moral Diplomacy

In his first term as president (1913–1917), Wilson had limited success applying a high moral standard to foreign relations. He and Secretary of State **William Jennings Bryan** attempted to show that the United States respected other nations' rights and supported the spread of democracy. Hoping to demonstrate that his presidency was opposed to self-interested imperialism, Wilson took steps to correct what he viewed as wrongful policies of the past.

The Philippines Wilson won passage of the **Jones Act** of 1916, which (1) granted full territorial status to the Philippines, (2) guaranteed a bill of rights and universal male suffrage to Filipino citizens, and (3) promised independence for the Philippines as soon as a stable government was established. Philippine independence was delayed by the events surrounding World War II until July 4, 1946.

Puerto Rico An act of Congress in 1917 granted U.S. citizenship to all Puerto Ricans and also provided for limited self-government.

The Panama Canal Wilson persuaded Congress in 1914 to repeal an act that had granted U.S. ships an exemption from paying the standard canal tolls charged other nations. Wilson's policy on Panama Canal tolls angered American nationalists such as Roosevelt and Lodge but pleased the British, who had strongly objected to the U.S. exemption.

Conciliation Treaties Wilson's commitment to the ideals of democracy and peace was fully shared by his famous secretary of state, William Jennings Bryan. Bryan's pet project was to negotiate treaties in which nations pledged to (1) submit disputes to international commissions and (2) observe a one-year cooling-off period before taking military action. Bryan arranged, with Wilson's approval, 30 such **conciliation treaties**.

Military Intervention Under Wilson

Wilson's commitment to democracy and anti-colonialism had a blind spot with respect to Mexico and countries of Central America and the Caribbean. He went far beyond both Roosevelt and Taft in his use of U.S. marines in response to financial and political troubles in the region. He kept marines in Nicaragua and ordered U.S. troops into Haiti in 1915 and the Dominican Republic in 1916. He argued that such intervention was necessary to maintain stability in the region and protect the Panama Canal.

Wilson's moral approach to foreign affairs was severely tested by a revolution and civil war in Mexico. As a supporter of democracy, Wilson refused to recognize the military dictatorship of General Victoriano Huerta, who had seized power in 1913 after having the democratically elected president killed.

Tampico Incident To aid revolutionaries fighting Huerta, Wilson called for an arms embargo against the Mexican government and sent a fleet to blockade the port of Vera Cruz. In 1914, several U.S. sailors went ashore at Tampico where they were arrested by Mexican authorities. They were soon released. However, Huerta refused to apologize as demanded by a U.S. naval officer. Wilson retaliated by ordering the U.S. Navy to occupy Veracruz. War seemed imminent. It was averted, however, when South America's ABC powers—Argentina, Brazil, and Chile—offered to mediate the dispute. This was the first dispute in the Americas to be settled through joint mediation.

Pancho Villa and the U.S. Expeditionary Force Huerta fell from power in late 1914. Replacing him was a more democratic regime led by Venustiano Carranza. Almost immediately, the new government was challenged by a band of rebels loyal to **Pancho Villa**. Hoping to destabilize his opponent's government, Villa led raids across the U.S.–Mexican border and murdered several people in Texas and New Mexico. In March 1916, President Wilson ordered General **John J. Pershing** and an "**expeditionary force**" to pursue Villa into northern Mexico. They failed to capture Villa. President Carranza protested the U.S. presence in Mexico. In January 1917, the growing possibility of U.S. entry into World War I caused Wilson to withdraw Pershing's troops.

Uncertain Rise to Power The Spanish-American War debuted the United States as a rising power in the international arena. However, most Americans were more concerned with domestic matters than foreign affairs during the Progressive era from 1900 to 1917 (Topic 7.4). American reluctance to get involved in World War I and to take a leadership role after the war reflected a long held and deep concern over the dangers of entanglement in overseas conflicts (Topic 7.5).

REFLECT ON THE LEARNING OBJECTIVE

1. Explain two effects of the Spanish-American War on American foreign policy.

KEY TERMS BY THEME

Spanish-American War (WOR, PCE)
"jingoism"
Cuban revolt
"yellow journalism"
de Lôme Letter
sinking of the *Maine*
Teller Amendment
"a splendid little war"
the Philippines
George Dewey
Rough Riders
Puerto Rico
Guam
Treaty of Paris
Emilio Aguinaldo
Anti-Imperialist League
Insular Cases
Platt Amendment (1901)

China Policy (WOR)
John Hay
spheres of influence
Open Door policy
Boxer Rebellion

TR Policies (WOR)
"big stick" policy
Theodore Roosevelt
Hay-Bunau-Varilla Treaty (1903)
Panama Canal

Santo Domingo
Roosevelt Corollary
Russo-Japanese War
Treaty of Portsmouth (1905)
segregated schools
"gentlemen's agreement"
Great White Fleet
Root-Takahira Agreement (1908)
Noble Peace Prize (1906)
Algeciras Conference (1906)
International Peace Conference (1907)

Dollar Diplomacy (WOR, WXT)
William Howard Taft
"dollar diplomacy"
railroads in China
Manchuria
intervention in Nicaragua

Moral Diplomacy (WOR)
anti-imperialism
Woodrow Wilson
William Jennings Bryan
Jones Act (1916)
conciliation treaties
military intervention
Pancho Villa
John J. Pershing
expeditionary force

Questions 1–3 refer to the newspaper below.

Source: *New York Journal*, February 17, 1898. The Granger Collection, NYC

1. Newspaper headlines such as those above most directly contributed to which of the following?

   (A) The capture of the terrorists by American authorities

   (B) The selection of Roosevelt as a vice presidential candidate

   (C) The declaration of war against Spain by the U.S. Congress

   (D) The attack by the U.S. Navy on Manila Bay

2. Which of the following groups would most strongly support the sentiments in these headlines?

(A) Members of Protestant missionary societies

(B) Midwestern and western Democrats

(C) Humanitarians opposed to Spanish rule

(D) Expansionists who were interested in overseas markets

3. The point of view of this newspaper most clearly reflects

(A) the theory of the safety valve

(B) the concept of jingoism

(C) the idea of isolationism

(D) the views of the Anti-Imperialist League

SHORT-ANSWER QUESTIONS

1. "Theodore Roosevelt, who was widely traveled, easily ranks as the most internationally minded President of his generation. He understood the role of the United States in the world of power politics more clearly than any of his predecessors and most of his successors. . . . He is far better known for his efforts at peacemaking than at warmaking. And, what is more, he deserved this acclaim."

> Thomas B. Bailey, *A Diplomatic History of the American People*, 1974

"[Theodore Roosevelt was] a person of his times. . . . He hailed the advance of Western and especially Anglo-Saxon civilization as a world movement, the key to peace and progress. . . . He viewed "barbaric" people as the major threat to civilization and had no difficulty rationalizing the use of force to keep them in line. . . . He was less clear how to keep peace among the so-called civilized nations."

> George C. Herring, *From Colony to Superpower*, 2008

Using the excerpts, answer (a), (b), and (c).

(a) Briefly describe ONE major difference between Bailey's and Herring's historical interpretation of Roosevelt's foreign policy.

(b) Briefly explain ONE specific historical event or development that is not explicitly mentioned in the excerpts that could be used to support Bailey's interpretation of Roosevelt's foreign policy.

(c) Briefly explain ONE specific historical event or development that is not explicitly mentioned in the excerpts that could be used to support Herring's interpretation of Roosevelt's foreign policy.

2.

WOODROW WILSON, THE SCHOOL TEACHER.

Source: 1914, The Granger Collection, NYC

Using the cartoon, answer (a), (b), and (c). The teacher represents Woodrow Wilson. The board says, "We can have no sympathy with those who seek to seize the power of government to advance their own personal interests or ambition." The hats say Venezuela, Nicaragua, and Mexico.

(a) Briefly explain ONE perspective expressed by the artist about Woodrow Wilson's foreign policy.

(b) Briefly explain ONE specific event or development that contributed to this perspective during the Woodrow Wilson administration.

(c) Briefly explain ONE difference or similarity between the policies of Wilson and either Theodore Roosevelt or William Howard Taft.

The Progressives

I am, therefore, a Progressive because we have not kept up with our own changes of conditions, either in the economic field or in the political field.

Woodrow Wilson, campaign speech, 1912

Learning Objective: Compare the goals and effects of the Progressive reform movement.

Like the Gilded Age reformers, those of the Progressive period in the early 20th century advocated for a larger role for government and greater democracy. Unlike the earlier reformers, though, the Progressives were more successful. The four constitutional amendments passed during this era illustrate its range and complexity: a graduated income tax that first affected the wealthy, direct election of senators to reform Congress, the right to vote for women, and an effort to improve society through the prohibition of alcohol. The Progressive movement's successes and failures remain controversial, but its lasting impact on American politics is undisputed.

Origins of Progressivism

As America entered the 20th century, the rapid and transforming changes of industrialization were unsettling for many. For decades, middle-class Americans had been alarmed by the power of big business, the uncertainties of business cycles, the increasing gap between rich and poor, the violent conflict between labor and capital, and the dominance of corrupt political machines in cities. Most disturbing to minorities were the racist Jim Crow laws in the South that relegated African Americans to the status of second-class citizens. Crusaders for women's suffrage added their voices to the call for greater democracy.

The Progressive movement built on the work of populist reformers and union activists of the Gilded Age. However, it acquired additional national momentum with the unexpected swearing into office of a young president, Theodore Roosevelt, in 1901. The Progressive era lasted through the presidencies of Republicans Theodore Roosevelt (1901–1909) and William Howard Taft (1909–1913) and the first term of the Democrat Woodrow Wilson (1913–1917). U.S. entry into World War I in 1917 diverted public attention away from domestic issues and brought the era to an end. By then, though, Congress and state legislatures had enacted major regulatory laws.

Who Were the Progressives?

A diverse group of reformers were loosely united in the Progressive movement. Protestant church leaders, African Americans, union leaders, and feminists each lobbied for different specific reforms. However, they shared some basic beliefs:

- Society badly needed changes to limit the power of big business, improve democracy, and strengthen social justice.

- Government, whether at the local, state, or federal level, was the proper agency for making these changes.

- Moderate reforms were usually better than radical ones.

Urban Middle Class Unlike the Populists of the 1890s, whose strength came from rural America, most Progressives were middle-class men and women who lived in cities. The urban middle class had steadily grown in the final decades of the 19th century. In addition to doctors, lawyers, ministers, and storekeepers (who were once the heart of the middle class), the economy now employed an increasing number of white-collar office workers and middle managers employed in banks, manufacturing firms, and other businesses.

Professional Class Members of this business and professional middle class took their civic responsibilities seriously. Some were versed in scientific and statistical methods and the findings of the new social sciences. They belonged to the hundreds of national business and **professional associations** that provided platforms to address corrupt business and government practices and urban social and economic problems.

Religion A missionary spirit inspired some middle-class reformers. Protestant churches preached against vice and taught a code of social responsibility, which emphasized caring for the less fortunate and promoting honesty in public life. The Social Gospel popularized by Walter Rauschenbusch (see Topic 6.11) was an important element in Protestant Christians' response to the problem of urban poverty. Most of these **Protestants** were native-born and **older stock** Americans, often from families of older elites who felt that their central role in society had been replaced by wealthy industrialists and urban political machines.

Leadership Without strong leadership, the diverse forces of reform could not have overcome conservatives' resistance to change. Fortunately for the Progressives, a number of dedicated and able leaders entered politics at the turn of the century to challenge the status quo. Theodore Roosevelt and Robert La Follette in the Republican Party and William Jennings Bryan and Woodrow Wilson in the Democratic Party demonstrated vigorous political leadership that had been lacking in national politics during the Gilded Age.

The Progressives' Philosophy The reform impulse was hardly new. In fact, many historians see progressivism as just one more phase in a reform tradition going back to the Jeffersonians in the early 1800s, the Jacksonians in the 1830s, and the Populists in the 1890s. The Progressives—like American reformers before them—were committed to democratic values and shared in the belief that honest government and just laws could improve peoples' lives.

Pragmatism A revolution in thinking occurred at the same time as the Industrial Revolution. Charles Darwin, in his *On the Origin of Species* (1859), presented the concept of evolution by natural selection. Though Darwin was writing about the natural world, others applied his concepts to human society to justify accumulating great wealth and laissez-faire capitalism (Topic 6.6).

Others challenged the prevailing philosophy of romantic transcendentalism with what became called **pragmatism**. In the early 20th century, **William James** and **John Dewey**, two leading American advocates of this new philosophy, argued that "truth" should be able to pass the public test of observable results in an open, democratic society. In a democracy, citizens and institutions should experiment with ideas and laws and test them in action until they found something that would produce a well-functioning democratic society.

Progressive thinkers adopted the new philosophy of pragmatism because it enabled them to challenge fixed ideas and beliefs that stood in the way of reform. For example, they rejected the laissez-faire theory as impractical. The old standard of rugged individualism no longer seemed viable in a modern society dominated by complex business organizations.

Scientific Management Another idea that gained widespread acceptance among Progressives came from the practical studies of **Frederick W. Taylor**. By using a stopwatch to time the tasks performed by factory workers, Taylor discovered ways of organizing people in the most efficient manner—the **scientific management** system, also known as Taylorism. Many Progressives believed that government too could be made more efficient if placed in the hands of experts and scientific managers. They objected to the corruption of political bosses partly because it was antidemocratic and partly because it was an inefficient way to run things.

The Muckrakers

Before the public could be roused to action, it first had to be well-informed about the scandalous realities of politics, factories, and slums. Publishers found that their middle-class readers were attracted to reports about corruption in business and politics. Investigative journalists created in-depth articles about child labor, corrupt political bosses and monopolistic business practices. President Theodore Roosevelt criticized writers who focused on negative stories as "muckrakers." The term caught on.

Origins One of the earliest muckrakers was Chicago reporter **Henry Demarest Lloyd**, who in 1881 wrote a series of articles for the *Atlantic Monthly* attacking the practices of the **Standard Oil Company** and the railroads. Published in book form in 1894, Lloyd's *Wealth Against Commonwealth* fully exposed the corruption and greed of the oil monopoly but failed to suggest how to control it.

Magazines An Irish immigrant, Samuel Sidney McClure, founded *McClure's Magazine* in 1893, which became a major success by running a series of muckraking articles by **Lincoln Steffens** (*Tweed Days in St. Louis,* 1902) and another series by **Ida Tarbell** (*The History of the Standard Oil Company,* also in 1902). Combining careful research with sensationalism, these articles set a standard for the deluge of muckraking that followed. Popular 10- and 15-cent magazines such as *McClure's, Collier's,* and *Cosmopolitan* competed fiercely to outdo their rivals with shocking exposés of political and economic corruption.

Books The most popular series of muckraking articles were usually collected and published as best-selling books. Articles on tenement life by **Jacob Riis**, one of the first photojournalists, were published as *How the Other Half Lives* (1890). Lincoln Steffens' *The Shame of the Cities* (1904) also caused a sensation by describing in detail the corrupt deals that characterized big-city politics from Philadelphia to Minneapolis.

Several muckraking books were novels. Two of **Theodore Dreiser**'s novels, *The Financier* and *The Titan,* portrayed the avarice and ruthlessness of an industrialist. Fictional accounts such as Frank Norris' *The Octopus* (about the tyrannical power of railroad companies) and *The Pit* (about the impact of grain speculation) stirrred up public demands for government regulations. One of the most powerful novels that portrayed the difficult life of immigrants

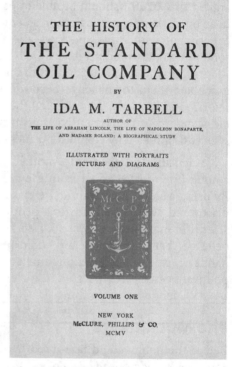

After Ida Tarbell published her account of the rise of the Standard Oil Company in magazine articles, she turned it into a best-selling book.

Source: Library of Congress.

and horrendous sanitary conditions of the meat packing industry was *The Jungle* by Upton Sinclair (see more later in this topic). These novels were more influential than many journalistic accounts.

Decline of Muckraking The popularity of muckraking books and magazine articles began to decline after 1910 for several reasons:

- Writers found it more and more difficult to top the sensationalism of the last story.
- Publishers were expanding and faced economic pressures from banks and advertisers to tone down their treatment of business.
- By 1910, corporations were becoming more aware of their public image and developing a new specialty: the field of public relations.

Nevertheless, muckraking had a lasting effect on the Progressive era. It exposed inequities, educated the public about corruption in high places, and prepared the way for corrective action.

Political Reforms in Cities and States

A cornerstone of Progressive ideology was faith in efficient government. However, Progressives expressed this ideology differently. Some looked to professional and technical experts for objective, pragmatic advice. Often, these Progressives distrusted the urban political machines that relied on immigrants for support, so they supported restrictions on immigration.

Other Progressives placed more trust in common people. They opposed immigration restrictions, in part because they believed that, given a chance, the majority of voters would elect honest officials. Progressives advocated a number of reforms for increasing the participation of the average citizen in political decision-making.

Australian, or Secret, Ballot Political parties could manipulate and intimidate voters by printing lists (or "tickets") of party candidates and watching voters drop them into the ballot box on election day. In 1888, Massachusetts was the first state to adopt a system successfully tried in Australia of issuing ballots printed by the state and requiring voters to mark their choices secretly within a private booth. By 1910, all states had adopted the **secret ballot**.

Direct Primaries In the late 19th century, Republicans and Democrats commonly nominated candidates for state and federal offices in state conventions controlled by party bosses. In 1903, the Progressive governor of Wisconsin, **Robert La Follette**, introduced a new system for bypassing politicians and placing the nominating process directly in the hands of the voters—the **direct primary**. By 1915, some form of the direct primary was used in every state. The system's effectiveness in overthrowing boss rule was limited, as politicians devised ways of confusing the voters and splitting the anti-political machine vote. Since primaries were run for the parties rather than for the general population, some Southern states used White-only primaries to exclude African Americans from voting.

Direct Election of U.S. Senators Under the original Constitution, U.S. senators had been chosen by the state legislatures rather than by direct vote of the people. Progressives believed this was a principal reason that the Senate had become a millionaires' club dominated by big business. Nevada in 1899 was the first state to give the voters the opportunity to elect U.S. senators directly. By

1912, a total of 30 states had adopted this reform, and in 1913, ratification of the **17th Amendment** required that all U.S. senators be elected by popular vote.

Initiative, Referendum, and Recall If politicians in the state legislatures balked at obeying the "will of the people," then Progressives proposed two methods for forcing them to act. Amendments to state constitutions offered voters (1) the *initiative*—a method by which voters could compel the legislature to consider a bill and (2) the *referendum*—a method that allowed citizens to vote on proposed laws printed on their ballots. A third Progressive measure, the *recall*, enabled voters to remove a corrupt or unsatisfactory politician from office by majority vote before that official's term had expired.

Municipal Reforms

City bosses and their corrupt alliances with local businesses (trolley lines and utility companies, for example) were among the first targets of Progressive leaders. In Toledo, Ohio, in 1897, a self-made millionaire with strong memories of his origins as a workingman became the Republican mayor. Adopting "golden rule" as both his policy and his middle name, Mayor Samuel M. "Golden Rule" Jones delighted Toledo's citizens by introducing a comprehensive program of **municipal reform**, including free kindergartens, night schools, and public playgrounds. Another Ohioan, Tom L. Johnson, devoted himself to tax reform and three-cent trolley fares for the people of Cleveland. As Cleveland's mayor from 1901 to 1909, Johnson fought hard—but without success—for public ownership and operation of the city's public utilities and services (water, electricity, and trolleys).

Controlling Public Utilities Reform leaders arose in other cities throughout the nation seeking to break the power of the city bosses and take utilities out of the hands of private companies. By 1915, fully two-thirds of the nation's cities owned their own water systems. As a result of the Progressives' efforts, many cities also came to own and operate gas lines, electric power plants, and urban transportation systems.

Commissions and City Managers New types of municipal government were another Progressive innovation. In 1900, Galveston, Texas, was the first city to adopt a **commission plan** of government, in which voters elected the heads of city departments (fire, police, and sanitation), not just the mayor. Ultimately proving itself more effective than the commission plan was a system first tried in Dayton, Ohio, in 1913. An elected city council there hired an expert manager to direct the work of the various departments of city government. By 1923, more than 300 cities had adopted the **manager-council plan** of municipal government.

State Reforms

At the state level, reform governors battled corporate interests and championed such measures as the initiative, the referendum, and the direct primary to give common people control of their own government. In New York, **Charles Evans**

Hughes battled fraudulent insurance companies. In California, **Hiram Johnson** successfully fought against the economic and political power of the Southern Pacific Railroad. In Wisconsin, Robert La Follette established a strong personal following as the governor (1900–1904) who won passage of the **"Wisconsin Idea"**—a series of Progressive measures that included a direct primary law, tax reform, and state **regulatory commissions** to monitor railroads, utilities, and businesses such as insurance.

Temperance and Prohibition Whether or not to shut down saloons and prohibit the drinking of alcohol sharply divided reformers. While urban Progressives recognized that saloons were often the neighborhood headquarters of political machines, they generally had little sympathy for the temperance movement. Rural reformers, on the other hand, thought they could clean up morals and politics in one stroke by abolishing liquor. The drys (prohibitionists) were determined and well-organized. Among their leaders was Carrie Nation, whose blunt language and attack on taverns with a hatchet made her famous. By 1915, the drys had persuaded the legislatures of two-thirds of the states to prohibit the sale of alcoholic beverages.

Social Welfare Urban life in the Progressive era was improved not only by political reformers but also by the efforts of settlement house workers and other civic-minded volunteers. Jane Addams, Florence Kelley, and other leaders of the social justice movement found that they needed political support in the state legislatures for meeting the needs of immigrants and the working class (see Topic 6.9). They lobbied vigorously and with considerable success for better schools, juvenile courts, liberalized divorce laws, and safety regulations for tenements and factories. Believing that criminals could learn to become effective citizens, reformers fought for such measures as a system of parole, separate reformatories for juveniles, and limits on the death penalty.

Child and Women Labor Progressives were most outraged by the treatment of children by industry. The **National Child Labor Committee** proposed model state child labor laws that were passed by two-thirds of the states by 1907. Ultimately, state **compulsory school attendance** laws proved most effective in keeping children out of the mines and factories.

Florence Kelley and the **National Consumers' League** organized to pass state laws to protect women from long working hours. In *Lochner v. New York* (1905) the Supreme Court ruled against a state law limiting workers to a ten-hour workday. However, in *Muller v. Oregon* (1908) the high court ruled that the health of women needed special protection from long hours. The **Triangle Shirtwaist fire** (1911) in a New York City high-rise garment factory took 146 lives, mostly women. The tragedy sparked greater women's activism and pushed states to pass laws to improve safety and working conditions in factories.

One consequence of efforts to protect women in the workplace was that the legislation kept women out of physically demanding but higher paying jobs in industry and mining. Later, many in the women's movement wanted these restrictions lifted so that women could compete as equals with men.

Political Reform in the Nation

While Progressive governors and mayors were battling conservative forces in the state houses and city halls, three presidents—Roosevelt, Taft, and Wilson—sought broad reforms and regulations at the national level.

Theodore Roosevelt's Square Deal

Following President McKinley's assassination in September 1901, Theodore Roosevelt became, at the age of 42, the youngest president in U.S. history. He was also one of the most athletic. He was unusual not simply because of his age and vigor but also because he believed that the president should do much more than lead the executive departments. He thought it was the president's job to set the legislative agenda for Congress as well. Thus, by the accident of McKinley's death, the Progressive movement suddenly shot into high gear under the dynamic leadership of a reform-minded president.

"Square Deal" for Labor Presidents in the 19th century had consistently taken the side of owners in conflicts with labor (most notably Hayes in the railroad strike of 1877 and Cleveland in the Pullman strike of 1894).

However, in the first economic crisis in his presidency, Roosevelt quickly demonstrated that he favored neither business nor labor but insisted on a **"Square Deal"** for both. Pennsylvania coal miners had been on strike through much of 1902. If the strike continued, many Americans feared that, without coal, they would freeze to death in winter. Roosevelt took the unusual step of trying to mediate the labor dispute by calling a union leader and mine owners to the White House. The owners' stubborn refusal to compromise angered the president. To ensure the delivery of coal to consumers, he threatened to take over the mines with federal troops. The owners finally agreed to accept the findings of a commission: a 10 percent wage increase and a nine-hour workday. However, the owners did not have to recognize the union.

Voters seemed to approve of Roosevelt and his Square Deal. They elected him by a landslide in 1904.

Trust-Busting Roosevelt further increased his popularity by being the first president since the passage of the Sherman Antitrust Act in 1890 to enforce that poorly written law. The trust that he most wanted to bust was a combination of railroads known as the Northern Securities Company. Reversing its position in earlier cases, the Supreme Court in 1904 upheld Roosevelt's action in breaking up the railroad monopoly. Roosevelt later directed his attorney general to take antitrust action against Standard Oil and more than 40 other large corporations. Roosevelt did make a distinction between breaking up **"bad trusts,"** which harmed the public and stifled competition, and regulating **"good trusts,"** which through efficiency and low prices dominated a market.

Railroad Regulation President Roosevelt also took the initiative in persuading a Republican majority in Congress to pass two laws that significantly strengthened the regulatory powers of the Interstate Commerce Commission (ICC). Under the **Elkins Act** (1903), the ICC had greater authority to stop railroads from granting rebates to favored customers. Under the **Hepburn Act** (1906), the commission could fix "just and reasonable" rates for railroads.

Consumer Protection *The Jungle*, a muckraking book by **Upton Sinclair**, described in horrifying detail the conditions in the Chicago stockyards and meatpacking industry. The public outcry following the publication of Sinclair's novel caused Congress to enact two regulatory laws in 1906: first, the **Pure Food and Drug Act** forbade the manufacture, sale, and transportation of adulterated or mislabeled foods and drugs, and then the **Meat Inspection Act** provided that federal inspectors visit meatpacking plants to ensure that they met minimum standards of sanitation.

Conservation As a lover of the wilderness and outdoor life, Roosevelt enthusiastically championed the cause of conservation. In fact, Roosevelt's most original and lasting contribution in domestic policy may have been his efforts to protect the nation's natural resources. Three actions were particularly important:

1. Roosevelt made repeated use of the Forest Reserve Act of 1891 to set aside 150 million acres of federal land as national reserves that could not be sold to private interests.

2. In 1902, Roosevelt won passage of the **Newlands Reclamation Act**, a law providing money from the sale of public land for irrigation projects in western states.

3. In 1908, the president publicized the need for conservation by hosting a **White House Conference** of Governors to promote coordinated conservation planning by federal and state governments. Following this conference, a National Conservation Commission was established under **Gifford Pinchot** of Pennsylvania, whom Roosevelt had earlier appointed to be the first director of the U.S. Forest Service.

Taft's Presidency

The good-natured William Howard Taft had served in Roosevelt's cabinet as secretary of war. Honoring the two-term tradition, Roosevelt refused to seek reelection and picked Taft to be his successor. The Republican Party readily endorsed Taft as its nominee for president in 1908 and, as expected, defeated for a third time the Democrats' campaigner, William Jennings Bryan.

Progressive Economic Policies Taft built on many of Roosevelt's accomplishments. As a trust-buster, Taft ordered the prosecution of almost twice the number of antitrust cases as his predecessor. However, among these cases was one against U.S. Steel, which included a merger approved by then-President Theodore Roosevelt. An angry Roosevelt viewed Taft's action as a personal attack on his integrity.

Two other Progressive measures were at least equal in importance to legislation enacted under Roosevelt. The **Mann-Elkins Act** of 1910 gave the Interstate Commerce Commission the power to suspend new railroad rates and to oversee telephone and telegraph companies. The **16th Amendment**, ratified by the states in 1913, authorized the U.S. government to collect an **income tax**. Progressives heartily approved the new tax, which applied only to the wealthy.

Controversy over Conservation Like Roosevelt, Taft sided more with the conservationists than the preservationists in the debate over using natural resources that began in the 1890s (see Topic 6.3). Taft established the Bureau of Mines, added large tracts in the Appalachians to the national forest reserves, and set aside federal oil lands (the first president to do so). However, when Roosevelt ally Gifford Pinchot criticized a Taft cabinet member for opening public lands in Alaska for development, Taft supported firing Pinchot.

Split in the Republican Party The **firing of Pinchot** was just one reason some Progressives accused Taft of betraying their cause and joining the conservative wing of the party. Taft had promised to lower the tariff. Instead, he signed the conservative **Payne-Aldrich Tariff** in 1909, which raised the tariff on most imports. In the mid-term elections of 1910, Taft openly supported conservative candidates for Congress. Progressive Republicans from the Midwest easily defeated the candidates endorsed by Taft. After this election, the Republican Party split wide open between a conservative faction loyal to Taft and a Progressive faction who hoped Theodore Roosevelt would run again in 1912.

Rise of the Socialist Party

A third party, the Socialists, emerged in the early 1900s to advocate for the working class. Unlike the Progressives, who called for moderate regulation, the Socialists called for public ownership of the railroads, utilities, and major industries such as oil and steel. One of the party's founders, **Eugene V. Debs**, a former railway union leader, became a socialist while in jail for supporting the Pullman strike. Debs was the party's candidate for president in five elections from 1900 to 1920 and gained up to a million votes in those campaigns. Eventually, some ideas championed by Debs and the Socialists were accepted: public ownership of utilities, worker's compensation insurance, minimum wage laws, the eight-hour workday, and pensions for employees.

The Election of 1912

President Taft was nominated by the Republicans after his supporters excluded Theodore Roosevelt's delegates from the party's convention. Progressive Republicans met and nominated Roosevelt. Their party became known as the **Bull Moose Party** after one of Roosevelt's nicknames. After lengthy balloting, Democrats united behind Woodrow Wilson, a political newcomer who had first been elected to office in 1910 as governor of New Jersey.

Campaign The election came down to a battle between Theodore Roosevelt and Woodrow Wilson. Roosevelt's plan, called **New Nationalism**, included more government regulation of business and unions, more social welfare programs, and women's suffrage. Wilson's plan, called **New Freedom**, would limit both big business and big government, bring about reform by ending corruption, and revive competition by supporting small business.

Wilson won less than a majority of the popular vote, but with the Republicans split, he won a landslide in the Electoral College, and the Democrats gained control of Congress. The overwhelming support for two Progressive presidential candidates proved that reformers had strong support. Roosevelt lost, but his New Nationalism had a lasting influence on later Democratic Party reforms such as the New Deal of the 1930s.

PRESIDENTIAL ELECTION, 1912

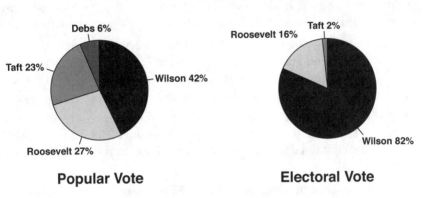

Popular Vote

Electoral Vote

Source: U.S. Bureau of the Census. *Historical Statistics of the United States, Colonial Times to 1970*

Woodrow Wilson's Progressive Program

Wilson, who grew up in Virginia during the Civil War, was only the second Democrat elected president since the war (Cleveland was the other). He was the first southerner to occupy the White House since Zachary Taylor (1849–1850). Wilson was idealistic, intellectual, righteous, and inflexible. Like Roosevelt, he believed that a president should actively lead Congress and, as necessary, appeal directly to the people to rally support for his legislative program.

In his inaugural address in 1913, the Democratic president pledged again his commitment to a New Freedom. To bring back conditions of free and fair competition in the economy, Wilson attacked "the triple wall of privilege": tariffs, banking, and trusts.

Tariff Reduction Wasting no time to fulfill a campaign pledge, Wilson on the first day of his presidency called a special session of Congress to lower the tariff. Past presidents had always sent written messages to Congress, but Wilson broke this longstanding tradition by addressing Congress in person about the need for lower tariff rates to bring consumer prices down. Passage of the **Underwood Tariff** in 1913 substantially lowered tariffs for the first time in over 50 years. To compensate for the reduced tariff revenues, the Underwood bill included a graduated income tax with rates from 1 to 6 percent.

Banking Reform Wilson then focused on the banking system and the money supply. He was persuaded that the gold standard was inflexible and that banks, rather than serving the public interest, were too much influenced by stock speculators on Wall Street. He proposed a national banking system with 12 district banks supervised by a **Federal Reserve Board** appointed by the president. Congress approved his idea and passed the **Federal Reserve Act** in 1914. The Federal Reserve was designed to provide stability and flexibility to the U.S. financial system by regulating interest rates and the capital reserves required of banks.

Additional Economic Reforms Wilson initially was opposed to any legislation that seemed to favor special interests, such as farmers or unions. However, he shifted his position to support a variety of laws and new agencies:

- The **Federal Trade Commission** was to protect consumers by investigating and taking action against any "unfair trade practice" in any industry except banking and transportation. (Those two industries were already regulated by other agencies.)

- The **Clayton Antitrust Act** strengthened the Sherman Antitrust Act's power to break up monopolies. Most important for organized labor, the new law contained a clause exempting unions from being prosecuted as trusts.

- The **Federal Farm Loan Act** created 12 regional federal farm loan banks established to provide farm loans at low interest rates.

- The **Child Labor Act,** long favored by settlement house workers and labor unions alike, was enacted in 1916. It prohibited the shipment in interstate commerce of products manufactured by children under 14 years old. However, a conservative Supreme Court found this act to be unconstitutional.

African Americans in the Progressive Era

Racial equality was, for the most part, ignored by Progressive leaders and politicians. Some Progressives actively supported the tradition of segregation in the South. Others simply ignored its existence. For example, President Wilson, with a strong southern heritage and many of the racist attitudes of the times, agreed with the segregation of federal workers and buildings.

The status of African Americans had declined steadily since Reconstruction. With the Supreme Court's "separate but equal" decision in *Plessy v. Ferguson* (1896), **racial segregation** had been the rule in the South and, unofficially, in much of the North. Ironically and tragically, the Progressive era coincided with years when thousands of Black men and women were lynched by racist mobs. Few White Progressives did anything about segregation, and **lynchings** continued at an average rate of almost two per week between 1900 and 1914. Activist Ida B. Wells led the battle to end lynching (see Topic 6.4).

Two Approaches: Washington and Du Bois

Though lacking widespread White support, African Americans took action to alleviate poverty and discrimination. Economic deprivation and exploitation were one problem; denial of civil rights was another. Which of these problems should take precedence became the focus of a debate between two African American leaders: **Booker T. Washington** and **W. E. B. Du Bois**.

Washington's Stress on Economics Washington, the leader of the Tuskegee Institute in Alabama, argued that Black youths' needs for education and economic progress were of foremost importance, and that they should concentrate on learning industrial skills for better wages. Only after establishing a secure economic base, said Washington, could African Americans hope to realize their other goals of political and social equality (Topic 6.4).

Du Bois's Stress on Civil Rights Unlike Washington, who had been born into an enslaved family on a southern plantation, W. E. B. Du Bois was a northerner from a free family. He was the first African American to earn a doctorate from Harvard University and became a distinguished scholar and writer. In his book *The Souls of Black Folk* (1903), Du Bois criticized Booker T. Washington's approach and demanded equal rights for African Americans. He argued that political and social rights were a prerequisite for economic independence.

In their public statements, Washington's focus on economic advancement and accommodation to White racism contrasted with Du Bois's more confrontational demands for equal civil rights. Their two approaches framed a debate in the African American community that continued throughout the 20th century. Behind the scenes, though, their differences were less dramatic. Washington quietly helped pay legal fees for court cases challenging segregation.

New Civil Rights Organizations

Racial discrimination prompted Black leaders to found three powerful civil rights organizations in just six years. In 1905, W. E. B. Du Bois met with a group of Black intellectuals in Niagara Falls, Canada, to discuss a program of protest and action aimed at securing equal rights for African Americans. They and others who later joined them became known as the *Niagara Movement*.

On Lincoln's birthday in 1908, Du Bois, other members of the Niagara Movement, and a group of White Progressives founded the **National Association for the Advancement of Colored People** (NAACP). Their mission was no less than to abolish all forms of segregation and to increase educational opportunities for African American children. By 1920, the NAACP was the nation's largest civil rights organization, with over 100,000 members.

Another organization, the **National Urban League**, was formed in 1911 to help people migrating from the South to adjust to northern cities. The league's motto, "Not Alms But Opportunity," reflected its emphasis on self-reliance and economic advancement.

Women and the Progressive Movement

The Progressive era was a time of increased activism and optimism for a new generation of feminists. By 1900, the older generation of suffrage crusaders led by Susan B. Anthony and Elizabeth Cady Stanton had passed the torch to younger women. The new leaders sought allies among male Progressives, but not always with success. For example, President Wilson refused to support the suffragists' call for a national amendment until late in his presidency.

The Campaign for Women's Suffrage

Carrie Chapman Catt, an energetic reformer from Iowa, became the new president of the **National American Woman Suffrage Association** (NAWSA) in 1900. Catt argued for the vote as a broadening of democracy that would empower women, thus enabling them to more actively care for their families in an industrial society. At first, Catt continued NAWSA's drive to win votes for women at the state level before changing strategies and seeking a suffrage amendment to the U.S. Constitution.

Militant Suffragists A more assertive approach to gaining the vote was adopted by some women, who took to the streets with mass pickets, parades, and hunger strikes. Their leader, **Alice Paul** of New Jersey, broke from NAWSA in 1916 to form the **National Woman's Party**. From the beginning, Paul focused on winning the support of Congress and the president for an amendment to the Constitution.

Nineteenth Amendment (1920) The dedicated efforts of women on the home front in World War I finally persuaded a two-thirds majority in Congress to support a women's suffrage amendment. Its ratification as the 19th Amendment in 1920 guaranteed women's right to vote in all elections at the local, state, and national levels. Following the victory of her cause, Carrie Chapman Catt organized the **League of Women Voters**, a civic organization dedicated to keeping voters informed about candidates and issues.

Other Issues In addition to winning the right to vote, Progressive women worked on other issues. **Margaret Sanger** advocated birth control education, especially among the poor. Over time, the movement developed into the Planned Parenthood organization. Women made progress in securing educational equality, liberalizing marriage and divorce laws, reducing discrimination in business and the professions, and recognizing women's rights to own property.

REFLECT ON THE LEARNING OBJECTIVE

1. Compare the goals and effects of two Progressive reforms.

KEY TERMS BY THEME

Progressive Movement (SOC, ARC)
urban middle class
professional associations
Protestants
older stock
pragmatism
William James
John Dewey
Frederick W. Taylor
scientific management

Muckrakers (SOC)
Henry Demarest Lloyd
Standard Oil Company
Lincoln Steffens
Ida Tarbell
Jacob Riis
Theodore Dreiser

Voting Rights (PCE)
secret ballot
Robert La Follette
direct primary
direct election of U.S. senators
17th Amendment
initiative, referendum, and recall

City and State Government (PCE)
municipal reform
commission plan
manager-council plan
Charles Evans Hughes
Hiram Johnson
"Wisconsin Idea"
regulatory commissions

Social and Labor Reform (PCE)
temperance and prohibition
National Child Labor Committee
compulsory school attendance
Florence Kelley
National Consumers' League
Lochner v. New York
Muller v. Oregon
Triangle Shirtwaist fire

Theodore Roosevelt Presidency (PCE, GEO)
"Square Deal"
trust-busting
"bad trusts" and "good trusts "

Elkins Act (1903)
Hepburn Act (1906)
The Jungle
Upton Sinclair
Pure Food and Drug Act (1906)
Meat Inspection Act (1906)
conservation
Newlands Reclamation Act (1902)
White House Conference
Gifford Pinchot

William Howard Taft Presidency (PCE)
Mann-Elkins Act (1910)
16th Amendment; income tax
firing of Pinchot
Payne-Aldrich Tariff (1909)

Election of 1912 (PCE)
Socialist Party
Eugene V. Debs
Bull Moose Party
New Nationalism
New Freedom

Woodrow Wilson Presidency (PCE)
Underwood Tariff (1913)
Federal Reserve Act (1914)
Federal Reserve Board
Clayton Antitrust Act (1914)
Federal Trade Commission
Federal Farm Loan Act (1916)
Child Labor Act (1916)

African Americans (NAT)
racial segregation
lynchings
Booker T. Washington
W. E. B. Du Bois
National Association for the Advancement
   of Colored People (NAACP)
National Urban League

Women's Movement (NAT, PCE)
Carrie Chapman Catt
National American Woman Suffrage
   Association
Alice Paul
National Woman's Party
19th Amendment
League of Women Voters
Margaret Sanger

MULTIPLE-CHOICE QUESTIONS

Questions 1–3 refer to the following excerpt.

> "Worst of any, however, were the fertilizer men, and those who served in the cooking rooms. These people could not be shown to the visitor— for the odor of a fertilizer man would scare any ordinary visitor at a hundred yards, and as for other men, who worked in tank rooms full of steam, their peculiar trouble was that they fell into the vats; and when they were fished out, there was never enough of them left to be worth exhibiting — sometimes they would be overlooked for days, till all but the bones of them has gone out to the world as Durham's Pure Leaf Lard!"
>
> Upton Sinclair, *The Jungle*, 1906

1. Which group of Progressives is most closely associated with the perspective promoted in the above excerpt?
   (A) Politicians who supported state regulatory commissions to curtail abuses in business
   (B) Reformers who fought to break up monopolies and trusts
   (C) Investigative journalists and authors known as "muckrakers"
   (D) The union movement associated with the American Federation of Labor

2. This excerpt is from a book that most directly contributed to
   (A) federal regulations to promote safety and health protection for industrial workers
   (B) a federal inspection system to ensure minimum standards for processed meats and food
   (C) the shutdown of Chicago meatpacking factories by the state of Illinois
   (D) pressure on publishers to reduce sensational articles and books attacking businesses

3. Which of the following most effectively provided a way to address Sinclair's view about working conditions for people in industrial jobs?
   (A) Legislation in some states that limited the hours and working conditions for children
   (B) President Theodore Roosevelt's promise for an impartial set of rules, or a "Square Deal," for labor
   (C) Legislation passed during the Wilson presidency to protect unions from being prosecuted unders laws designed to break up trusts
   (D) The election of William Howard Taft and Republicans in 1908

Question 1 is based on the excerpts below.

1. "According to the liberal view of the Progressive Era, the major political innovations of reform involved the equalization of political power through the primary, the direct election of public officials, and the initiative, referendum, and recall. . . . But they provided at best only an occasional and often incidental process of decision-making. Far more important in continuous, sustained, day-to-day processes of government were those innovations which centralized decision-making in the hands of fewer and fewer people."

> Samuel L. Hays, *The Politics of Reform in Municipal Government in the Progressive Era*, 1964

"Progressivism owed much of its success to a distinctive method of reform. . . . They typically began by organizing voluntary associations, investigating a problem, gathering relevant facts, and analyzing them. From such analysis a proposed solution would emerge, be popularized through campaigns of education and moral suasion, and . . . to be taken over by some level of government as a public function. . . . These tactics were pioneered in many cases by women. . . . It fell to women to invent their own means to improve the world."

> Richard L. McCormick, *Public Life in Industrial America, 1877–1917*, 1997

Using the excerpts, answer (a), (b), and (c).

(a) Briefly describe ONE major difference between Hays' and McCormick's historical interpretation of the Progressive Era.

(b) Briefly explain how ONE specific historical event or development that is not explicitly mentioned in the excerpts could be used to support Hays' interpretation of the Progressive Era.

(c) Briefly explain how ONE specific historical event or development that is not explicitly mentioned in the excerpts could be used to support McCormick's interpretation of the Progressive Era.

2. Answer (a), (b), and (c).

(a) Briefly explain ONE specific way the Wilson administration fulfilled the goals of reforming the United States banking system.

(b) Briefly explain ONE specific way the Wilson administration fulfilled the goals of reforming federal tariffs and taxation.

(c) Briefly explain how ONE reform identified above either reflected or violated Wilson's New Freedom policies.

World War I:
Military and Diplomacy

It breaks his heart that kings must murder still,
That all his hours of travail here for men
Seem yet in vain. And who will bring white peace
That he may sleep upon his hill again?

Vachel Lindsay, "Abraham Lincoln Walks at Midnight," 1914

Learning Objective: Explain the causes and consequences of U.S. involvement in World War I.

World War I broke out with stunning rapidity after a Serbian nationalist assassinated Austrian Archduke Francis Ferdinand, the heir to the throne of the Austro-Hungarian Empire, and his wife. Within a week, before calm minds could prevail, Austria-Hungary and Germany were in a full-scale war against Russia, France, and Great Britain. The assassination of the archduke sparked the war, but the underlying causes were (1) nationalism, (2) imperialism, (3) militarism, and (4) a combination of public and secret alliances. It was a tragedy that haunted generations of future leaders and that motivated President Woodrow Wilson to search for a lasting peace.

Neutrality

President Wilson's first response to the outbreak of the European war was a declaration of U.S. **neutrality**, in the tradition of noninvolvement started by Washington and Jefferson. He called upon the American people to support his policy by not taking sides. However, Wilson found it difficult—if not impossible—to both steer a neutral course that favored neither the **Allied powers** (Great Britain, France, and Russia) nor the **Central powers** (Germany, Austria-Hungary, and the Ottoman Empire of Turkey) and still protected U.S. trading rights. During a relatively short period (1914–1919), the United States and its people rapidly moved through a wide range of roles: first as a contented neutral country, next as a country waging a war for peace, then as a victorious world power, and finally as an alienated and isolationist nation.

Freedom of the Seas In World War I (as in the War of 1812), the trouble for the United States arose as belligerent powers tried to stop supplies from reaching a foe. Having the stronger navy, Great Britain was the first to declare a naval blockade against Germany. Britain mined the North Sea and seized ships—including U.S. ships—attempting to run the blockade. Wilson protested British seizure of U.S. ships as violating a neutral nation's right to freedom of the seas.

Submarine Warfare Germany's one hope for challenging British power at sea lay with a new naval weapon, the submarine. In February 1915, Germany answered the British blockade by announcing a blockade of its own and warned that ships attempting to enter the "war zone" (waters near the British Isles) risked being sunk on sight by German submarines.

Lusitania **Crisis** The first major crisis challenging U.S. neutrality occurred on May 7, 1915, when German torpedoes hit and sank a British passenger liner, the *Lusitania*. Most of the passengers drowned, including 128 Americans. In response, Wilson sent Germany a strongly worded diplomatic message warning that Germany would be held to "strict accountability" if it continued its policy of sinking unarmed ships. Secretary of State William Jennings Bryan objected to this message as too warlike and resigned from the president's cabinet.

Other Sinkings In August 1915, two more Americans lost their lives at sea as the result of a German submarine attack on another passenger ship, the *Arabic*. This time, Wilson's note of protest prevailed upon the German government to pledge that no unarmed passenger ships would be sunk without warning, which would allow time for passengers to get into lifeboats.

Germany kept its word until March 1916, when a German torpedo struck an unarmed merchant ship, the *Sussex*, injuring several American passengers. Wilson threatened to cut off U.S. diplomatic relations with Germany—a step preparatory to war. Once again, rather than risk U.S. entry into the war on the British side, Germany backed down. Its reply to the president, known as the **Sussex pledge**, promised not to sink merchant or passenger ships without giving due warning. For the remainder of 1916, Germany was true to its word.

Economic Links with Britain and France

Even though the United States was officially a neutral nation, its economy became closely tied to those of the Allied powers of Great Britain and France. In early 1914, before the war began, the United States had been in an economic recession. Soon after the outbreak of war, the economy rebounded in part because of orders for war supplies from the British and the French. By 1915, U.S. businesses had never been so prosperous.

In theory, U.S. manufacturers could have shipped supplies to Germany as well, but the British blockade effectively prevented such trade. Wilson's policy did not deliberately favor the Allied powers. Nevertheless, because the president more or less tolerated the British blockade while restricting Germany's submarine blockade, U.S. economic support was going to one side (Britain and France) and not the other. Between 1914 and 1917, U.S. trade with the Allies quadrupled while its trade with Germany dwindled to the vanishing point.

Loans When the Allies could not purchase everything they needed, the U.S. government permitted U.S. bankers (particularly the bank of J. Pierpont Morgan) to extend as much as $3 billion in credit to Britain and France. These loans promoted U.S. prosperity as they sustained the Allies' war effort.

OPPOSING SIDES IN WORLD WAR I

Public Opinion

If Wilson's policies favored Britain, so did the attitudes of most Americans. In August 1914, as Americans read in their newspapers about German armies marching ruthlessly through Belgium, they perceived Germany as a cruel bully whose armies were commanded by a mean-spirited autocrat, Kaiser Wilhelm. The sinking of the *Lusitania* reinforced this negative view of Germany.

Ethnic Influences In 1914, first- and second-generation citizens made up more than 30 percent of the U.S. population. They were glad to be out of the fighting and strongly supported neutrality. Even so, their sympathies reflected their ancestries. For example, German Americans strongly identified with the struggles of their "homeland." And many Irish Americans, who hated Britain because of its oppressive rule of Ireland, openly backed the Central powers. On the other hand, when Italy joined the Allies in 1915, Italian Americans began cheering on the Allies in their desperate struggle to fend off German assaults on the Western Front (entrenched positions in France).

Overall, though, most native-born Americans supported the Allies. Positive U.S. relations with France since the Revolutionary War bolstered public support for the French. Americans also tended to sympathize with Britain and France because of their democratic governments. President Wilson himself, a person of Scottish-English descent, had long admired the British political system.

British War Propaganda Not only did Britain command the seas, it also commanded the war news that was cabled daily to U.S. newspapers and magazines. Fully recognizing the importance of influencing U.S. public opinion, the British government made sure the American press was well supplied with stories of German soldiers committing atrocities in Belgium and the German-occupied part of eastern France.

The War Debate

After the *Lusitania* crisis, a small but vocal minority of influential Republicans from the East—including Theodore Roosevelt—argued for U.S. entry into the war against Germany. Foreign policy realists believed that a German victory would change the balance of power and that the United States needed a strong British navy to protect the status quo. However, the majority of Americans remained thankful for a booming economy and peace.

Preparedness Eastern Republicans such as Roosevelt were the first to recognize that the U.S. military was hopelessly unprepared for a major war. They clamored for "**preparedness**" (greater defense expenditures) soon after the European war broke out.

At first, President Wilson opposed the call for preparedness, but in late 1915 he changed his policy. Wilson urged Congress to approve an ambitious expansion of the armed forces. The president's proposal provoked a storm of controversy, especially among Democrats, who until then were largely opposed to military increases. After a nationwide speaking tour on behalf of preparedness, Wilson finally convinced Congress to pass the National Defense Act in June 1916, which increased the regular army to a force of nearly 175,000. A month later, Congress approved the construction of more than 50 warships (battleships, cruisers, destroyers, and submarines) in just one year.

Opposition to War Many Americans, especially in the Midwest and West, were adamantly opposed to preparedness, fearing that it would soon lead to U.S. involvement in the war. The antiwar activists included Populists, Progressives, and Socialists. Leaders among the peace-minded Progressives were William Jennings Bryan, Jane Addams, and **Jeannette Rankin**—the latter the first woman to be elected to Congress. Women suffragists actively campaigned against any military buildup (although after the U.S. declaration of war in 1917, they supported the war effort).

The Election of 1916

President Wilson was well aware that, as a Democrat, he had won election to the presidency in 1912 only because of the split in Republican ranks between Taft conservatives and Roosevelt Progressives. Despite his own Progressive record, Wilson's chances for reelection did not seem strong after Theodore Roosevelt declined the Progressive Party's nomination for president in 1916 and rejoined the Republicans. (Roosevelt's decision virtually destroyed any chance of the Progressive Party surviving.) Charles Evans Hughes, a Supreme Court justice and former governor of New York, became the presidential candidate of a reunited Republican Party.

"He Kept Us Out of War" The Democrats adopted as their campaign slogan "He kept us out of war." The peace sentiment in the country, Wilson's record of Progressive leadership, and Hughes' weakness as a candidate combined to give the president the victory in an extremely close election. Democratic strength in the South and West overcame Republican power in the East.

Peace Efforts

Wilson made repeated efforts to fulfill his party's campaign promise to keep out of the war. Before the election, in 1915, he had sent his chief foreign policy adviser, Colonel **Edward House** of Texas, to London, Paris, and Berlin to negotiate a peace settlement. This mission, however, had been unsuccessful. Other efforts at mediation also were turned aside by both the Allies and the Central powers. Finally, in January 1917, Wilson made a speech to the Senate declaring U.S. commitment to his idealistic hope for "peace without victory."

Decision for War

In April 1917, only one month after being sworn into office a second time, President Wilson went before Congress to ask for a declaration of war against Germany. What had happened to change his policy from neutrality to war?

Unrestricted Submarine Warfare

Most important in the U.S. decision for war was a sudden change in German military strategy. The German high command had decided in early January 1917 to resume unrestricted submarine warfare. Germany recognized the risk of the United States entering the war but believed that, by cutting off supplies to the Allies, they could win the war before Americans could react. Germany communicated its decision to the U.S. government on January 31. A few days later, Wilson broke off U.S. diplomatic relations with Germany.

Immediate Causes

Wilson still hesitated, but a series of events in March 1917, as well as the president's hopes for arranging a permanent peace in Europe, convinced him that U.S. participation in the war was now unavoidable.

Zimmermann Telegram On March 1, U.S. newspapers carried the shocking news of a secret offer made by Germany to Mexico. Intercepted by British intelligence, a telegram to Mexico from the German foreign minister, Arthur Zimmermann, proposed that Mexico ally itself with Germany in return for Germany's pledge to help Mexico recover lost territories: Texas, New Mexico, and Arizona. Mexico never considered accepting the offer. However, the Zimmermann Telegram aroused the nationalist anger of the American people and convinced Wilson that Germany fully expected a war with the United States.

Russian Revolution Applying the principle of moral diplomacy, Wilson wanted the war to be fought for a worthy purpose: the triumph of democracy. It bothered him that one of the Allies was Russia, a nation governed by an autocratic czar. This barrier to U.S. participation was suddenly removed on March 15, when Russian revolutionaries overthrew the czar's government and proclaimed a republic. (Only later, in November, would the revolutionary government be taken over by Communists.)

Renewed Submarine Attacks In the first weeks of March, German submarines sank five unarmed U.S. merchant ships. Wilson was ready for war.

Declaration of War

On April 2, 1917, President Wilson stood before a special session of senators and representatives and called upon them to defend humanitarian and democratic principles. Wilson solemnly asked Congress to recognize that a state of war existed between Germany and the United States. His speech condemned Germany's submarine policy as "warfare against mankind" and declared that "The world must be made safe for democracy." On April 6, an overwhelming majority in Congress voted for a declaration of war, although a few pacifists, including Robert La Follette and Jeanette Rankin, defiantly voted no.

Fighting the War

By the time the first U.S. troops shipped overseas in late 1917, millions of European soldiers on both sides had already died in three years of fighting. The Allies hoped that fresh troops would be enough to bring victory. The conflict's trench warfare was made more deadly in the industrial age by heavy artillery, machine guns, poison gas, tanks, and airplanes. A second revolution in Russia by **Bolsheviks** (or Communists) took that nation out of the war. With no Eastern Front to divide its forces, Germany concentrated on one all-out push to break through Allied lines in France.

Naval Operations

Germany's policy of unrestricted submarine warfare was having its intended effect. Merchant ships bound for Britain were being sunk at a staggering rate: 900,000 tons of shipping were lost in just one month (April 1917). U.S. response to this Allied emergency was to undertake a record-setting program of ship construction. The U.S. Navy also implemented a convoy system of armed escorts for groups of merchant ships. By the end of 1917, the system was working well enough to ensure that Britain and France would not be starved into submission.

American Expeditionary Force

Unable to imagine the grim realities of trench warfare, U.S. troops were eager for action. The idealism of both the troops and the public is reflected in the popular song of George M. Cohan that many were singing:

> Over there, over there,
> Send the word, send the word over there
> That the Yanks are coming,
> The Yanks are coming,
> The drums rum-tumming ev'ry where—

The **American Expeditionary Force** (AEF) was commanded by General **John J. Pershing**. The first U.S. troops to see action were used to plug weaknesses in the French and British lines. But by the summer of 1918, as American forces arrived by the hundreds of thousands, the AEF assumed independent responsibility for one segment of the **Western Front**.

Last German Offensive Enough U.S. troops were in place in spring 1918 to hold the line against the last ferocious assault by German forces. At Château-Thierry on the Marne River, Americans stopped the German advance (June 1918) and struck back with a successful counterattack at Belleau Wood.

Drive to Victory In August, September, and October, an Allied offensive along the Meuse River and through the Argonne Forest (the Meuse–Argonne offensive) succeeded in driving an exhausted German army backward toward the German border. U.S. troops participated in this drive at St. Mihiel—the southern sector of the Allied line. On **November 11, 1918**, the Germans signed an armistice in which they agreed to surrender their arms, give up much of their navy, and evacuate occupied territory.

U.S. Casualties After only a few months of fighting, U.S. combat deaths totaled nearly 49,000. Many more thousands died of disease, including a flu epidemic in the training camps, bringing total U.S. fatalities in World War I to 112,432. Total deaths in the war were around 20 million people, most of whom were civilians.

Making the Peace

During the war, Woodrow Wilson never lost sight of his ambition to shape the peace settlement when the war ended. In January 1917, he had said that the United States would insist on **"peace without victory."** A year later he presented to Congress a detailed list of war aims, known as the Fourteen Points, designed to address the causes of World War I and prevent another world war.

The Fourteen Points

Several of the president's **Fourteen Points** related to specific territorial questions. For example, Wilson called on Germany to return the regions of Alsace and Lorraine to France and to evacuate Belgium in the west and Romania and Serbia in the east. Of greater significance were the broad principles for securing a lasting peace:

- Recognition of freedom of the seas
- An end to the practice of making secret treaties
- Reduction of national armaments
- An "impartial adjustment of all colonial claims"
- Self-determination for the various nationalities
- Removal of trade barriers
- "A general association of nations . . . for the purpose of affording mutual guarantees of political independence and territorial integrity to great and small states alike"

The last point was the one that Wilson valued the most. The international peace association that he envisioned would soon be named the League of Nations.

The Treaty of Versailles

The peace conference following the armistice took place in the Palace of Versailles outside Paris, beginning in January 1919. Every nation that had fought on the Allied side in the war was represented. No U.S. president had ever traveled abroad to attend a diplomatic conference, but President Wilson decided that his personal participation at Versailles was vital to defending his Fourteen Points. Republicans criticized him for being accompanied to Paris by several Democrats but only one Republican, whose advice was never sought.

The Big Four Other heads of state at Versailles made it clear that their nations wanted both revenge against Germany and compensation in the form of indemnities and territory. They did not share Wilson's idealism, which called for peace without victory. David Lloyd George of Great Britain, Georges Clemenceau of France, and Vittorio Orlando of Italy met with Wilson almost daily as the **Big Four**. After months of argument, the president reluctantly agreed to compromise on most of his Fourteen Points. He insisted, however, that the other delegations accept his plan for a League of Nations.

Peace Terms When the peace conference adjourned in June 1919, the **Treaty of Versailles** included the following terms:

1. To punish Germany, Germany was disarmed and stripped of its colonies in Asia and Africa. It was also forced to admit guilt for the war, accept French occupation of the Rhineland for 15 years, and pay a huge sum of money in reparations to Great Britain and France.

2. To apply the principle of **self-determination**, territories once controlled by Germany, Austria-Hungary, and Russia were taken by the Allies; independence was granted to Estonia, Latvia, Lithuania, Finland, and Poland; and the new nations of Czechoslovakia and Yugoslavia were established.

3. To maintain peace, signers of the treaty joined an international peacekeeping organization, the **League of Nations**. **Article X** of the covenant (charter) of the League called on each member nation to stand ready to protect the independence and territorial integrity of other nations.

EUROPE AFTER WORLD WAR I (1919)

The Battle for Ratification

Returning to the United States, President Wilson had to win approval of two-thirds of the Senate for all parts of the Treaty of Versailles, including the League of Nations covenant. Republican senators raised objections to the League, especially to Article X. They argued that U.S. membership in such a body might interfere with U.S. sovereignty and might also cause European nations to interfere in the Western Hemisphere (a violation of the Monroe Doctrine).

Increased Partisanship After the War Wilson made winning Senate ratification difficult. In October 1918, he had asked voters to support Democrats in the midterm elections as an act of patriotism. This appeal had backfired badly. In the 1918 election, Republicans had won a solid majority in the House and a majority of two in the Senate. In 1919, Wilson needed Republican votes in the Senate to ratify the Treaty of Versailles. Instead, he faced the determined hostility of a leading Senate Republican, **Henry Cabot Lodge**.

Opponents: Irreconcilables and Reservationists Senators opposed to the Treaty of Versailles formed two groups. The **Irreconcilable** faction could not accept U.S. membership in the League, no matter how the covenant was worded. The **Reservationist** faction, a larger group led by Senator Lodge, said it could accept the League if certain reservations were added to the covenant. Wilson had the option of either accepting Lodge's reservations or fighting for the treaty as it stood. He chose to fight.

Wilson's Western Tour and Breakdown Wilson believed he could personally rally enough public support to prevail and push ratification of the League through Congress. With confidence, he undertook an arduous speaking tour by train of the West. On September 25, 1919, he collapsed after a speech in Colorado. He returned to Washington. A few days later he suffered a massive stroke from which he never fully recovered.

Rejection of the Treaty The Senate defeated the treaty without reservations. When it came up with reservations, the ailing Wilson directed his Senate allies to reject the compromise, and they joined with the Irreconcilables in defeating the treaty a second time. After Wilson left office in 1921, the United States officially made peace with Germany. However, it never ratified the Versailles Treaty nor joined the League of Nations.

REFLECT ON THE LEARNING OBJECTIVE

1. Explain two causes and two effects of U.S. involvement in World War I.

KEY TERMS BY THEME

Causes of WWI (WOR)
neutrality
Allied powers
Central powers
submarine warfare
Lusitania
Sussex pledge
propaganda
ethnic influences

Debate over War (WOR)
preparedness
election of 1916
Jeannette Rankin
Edward House
Zimmermann Telegram
Russian Revolution
declaration of war

Fighting in Europe (WOR)
Bolsheviks
American Expeditionary Force
John J. Pershing
Western Front
November 11, 1918

Peace Treaty (WOR)
"peace without victory"
Fourteen Points
Big Four
Treaty of Versailles
self-determination
League of Nations
Article X

Debate over Treaty (PCE)
Henry Cabot Lodge
Irreconcilables
Reservationists
rejection of the treaty

Questions 1–3 refer to the following excerpt.

"On the first of February, we intend to begin submarine warfare unrestricted. In spite of this it is our intention to keep neutral the United States of America.

"If this attempt is not successful we propose an alliance on the following basis with Mexico: that we shall make war together and together make peace. We shall give financial support, and it is understood that Mexico is to reconquer the lost territory in New Mexico, Texas and Arizona. The details are left for your settlement."

> Arthur Zimmermann, German Foreign Minister,
> January 19, 1917

1. Which of the following possible causes of U.S. entry into World War I could best be supported using the excerpt as evidence?
   (A) The U.S. reaction to Germany's policy of unrestricted submarine warfare
   (B) The opportunity to promote democracy, particularly after the overthrow of the czar in Russia
   (C) The ethnic ties between many Americans and the European country their ancestors had left
   (D) The economic links connecting U.S. businesses with Great Britain and France

2. When the Zimmermann message was made public, most people in the United States
   (A) viewed it as a threat by Germany against Mexico
   (B) feared that a German victory would split the United States
   (C) expressed nationalist anger against Germany
   (D) assumed it was the result of Allied propaganda

3. The issue of freedom of the seas in World War I most closely resembles the cause of which of the following conflicts?
   (A) War of 1812
   (B) Mexican War of 1846
   (C) The American Civil War
   (D) Spanish-American War of 1898

Use complete sentences; an outline or bulleted list alone is not acceptable.

1. "The League of Nations failed to take hold in America because the country was not yet ready for so global a role. Nevertheless, Wilson's intellectual victory proved more seminal than any political victory could have been. For, whenever America has faced the task of constructing a new world order, it has returned in one way or another to Woodrow Wilson's precepts."

   Henry Kissinger, former secretary of state, Diplomacy, 1994

   "The United States would never ratify the treaty and would never join the League of Nations. Many newspapers and commentators expressed regret at the outcome, and most laid the blame on Wilson—properly so. [Connecticut Senator] Brandegee's cruel remark about Wilson's strangling his own child was not far off the mark. Wilson had blocked every effort at compromise."

   John Milton Cooper Jr., historian, Woodrow Wilson, 2009

   Using the excerpts, answer (a), (b), and (c).

   (a) Briefly describe ONE major difference between Kissinger's and Cooper's interpretations about the Versailles Treaty and the League of Nations.

   (b) Briefly explain how ONE specific historical event that is not explicitly mentioned in the excerpts could be used to support Kissinger's interpretation.

   (c) Briefly explain how ONE specific historical event that is not explicitly mentioned in the excerpts could be used to support Cooper's interpretation.

2.

Source: Library of Congress.

Using the image, answer (a), (b), and (c).

(a) Briefly explain ONE perspective expressed in this image about United States foreign policy during World War I.

(b) Briefly explain ONE specific action taken by the Wilson administration in response to the issues raised by this image.

(c) Briefly explain ONE similarity between the event shown in this image and another specific historical event that involved the rights of the people in United States during wartime.

Topic 7.6

World War I: Home Front

When a nation is at war many things that might be said in time of peace are such a hindrance to its efforts that their utterance will not be endured as long as men fight.

Supreme Court, *Schenck v. United States*, 1919

Learning Objective: Explain the causes and effects of international and internal migration patterns over time.

Mobilization

U.S. mobilization for war in 1917 was a race against time. Germany was preparing to deliver a knockout blow to end the war on German terms. Could the United States mobilize its vast economic resources fast enough to make a difference? That was the question Wilson and his advisers confronted in the critical early months of U.S. involvement in the war.

Industry and Labor The Wilson administration, with Progressive efficiency, created hundreds of temporary wartime agencies and commissions staffed by experts from business and government. The legacy of this mobilization of the domestic economy under governmental leadership proved significant in the New Deal programs enacted during Great Depression in the 1930s. For example:

- Bernard Baruch, a Wall Street broker, volunteered to use his extensive contacts in industry to help win the war. Under his direction, the War Industries Board set production priorities and established centralized control over raw materials and prices.

- Herbert Hoover, a distinguished engineer, took charge of the **Food Administration**, which encouraged American households to eat less meat and bread so that more food could be shipped abroad for the French and British troops. The conservation drive paid off. In two years, U.S. shipment of food overseas tripled.

- Harry Garfield volunteered to head the Fuel Administration, which directed efforts to save coal. Nonessential factories were closed, and daylight saving time went into effect for the first time.

- Treasury Secretary William McAdoo headed the **Railroad Administration** which took public control of the railroads to coordinate traffic and promote standardized railroad equipment.

- Former President William Howard Taft helped arbitrate disputes between workers and employers as head of the **National War Labor Board**. Labor won concessions during the war that had earlier been denied. Wages rose, the eight-hour work day became more common, and union membership increased.

Finance Paying for the costly war presented a huge challenge. Wilson's war government managed to raise $33 billion in two years through a combination of loans and taxes. It conducted four massive drives to convince Americans to put their savings into federal government **Liberty Bonds**. Congress also increased personal income and corporate taxes, and placed a new tax on luxury goods.

Public Opinion

The U.S. government used techniques of both patriotic persuasion and legal intimidation to ensure public support for the war effort. Journalist **George Creel** took charge of a propaganda agency called the **Committee on Public Information**, which enlisted the voluntary services of artists, writers, vaudeville performers, and movie stars to depict the heroism of the "boys" (U.S. soldiers) and the villainy of the kaiser. They created films, posters, and pamphlets and organized volunteer speakers—all urging Americans to watch out for German spies and to "do your bit" for the war.

Source: Frederick Strothmann, 1918. Poster from the Third Liberty Loan Drive. Library of Congress

Civil Liberties

War hysteria and patriotic enthusiasm provided an excuse for nativist groups to express their prejudices by charging minorities with disloyalty. One such group, the American Protective League, mounted "Hate the Hun" campaigns and used vigilante actions to attack all things German—from performing Beethoven's music to cooking sauerkraut. Under the order of the U.S. Secretary of Labor, manufacturers of war materials could refuse to hire and could fire American citizens of German extraction.

Limits on Immigration More generally, the Barred Zone Act (the Immigration Act of 1917) prohibited anyone residing in a region from the Middle East to southeast Asia from entering the United States. It also included a literacy test designed to prevent immigration from southern and eastern Europe. This act set the stage for sharp restrictions on immigration in the 1920s.

Espionage and Sedition Acts A number of socialists and pacifists bravely criticized the government's war policy even as Congress passed laws restricting free speech. The **Espionage Act** (1917) provided for imprisonment of up to 20 years for persons who tried to incite rebellion in the armed forces or obstructed the draft. The **Sedition Act** (1918) went much further by prohibiting anyone from making "disloyal" or "abusive" remarks about the U.S. government. Approximately 2,000 people were prosecuted under these laws, half of whom were convicted and jailed. Among them was the Socialist leader **Eugene Debs**, who was sentenced to ten years in federal prison for speaking against the war.

Schenck v. United States (1919) The Supreme Court upheld the constitutionality of the Espionage Act in a case involving a man who had been imprisoned for distributing pamphlets against the draft. Justice Oliver Wendell Holmes concluded that the right to free speech could be limited when it represented a "clear and present danger" to public safety.

Armed Forces

As soon as war was declared, thousands of young men voluntarily enlisted for military service. Still, the military thought it needed more soldiers and sailors.

Selective Service Act (1917) To meet this need, Secretary of War Newton D. Baker devised a "selective service" system to conscript (draft) men into the military. He wanted a democratic method run by local boards for ensuring that all groups in the population would be called into service. The government required all men between 21 and 30 (and later between 18 and 45) to register for possible induction into the military. Under the **Selective Service Act**, about 2.8 million men were eventually called by lottery, in addition to the almost 2 million who volunteered to serve. About half of all those in uniform made it to the Western Front.

African Americans Racial segregation applied to the army as it did to civilian life. Almost 400,000 African Americans served in World War I in segregated units. Only a few were permitted to be officers, and all were barred from the Marine Corps. Nevertheless, W. E. B. Du Bois believed that the record of **service by African Americans**, fighting to "make the world safe for democracy," would earn them equal rights at home when the war ended. However, he would be bitterly disappointed.

Effects on American Society

All groups in American society—business and labor, women and men, immigrants and native-born—had to adjust to the realities of a wartime economy. As factories needed workers to replace those in the military and to increase production of war goods, people moved from rural areas across the country to urban areas to take jobs.

More Jobs for Women As men were drafted into the military, the jobs they vacated were often taken by women, thousands of whom entered the workforce for the first time. Women's contributions to the war effort, both as volunteers and wage earners, finally convinced Wilson and Congress to support the 19th Amendment, which protected the right of women to vote.

Migration of Mexicans Job opportunities in wartime America, together with the upheavals of a revolution in Mexico, caused thousands of Mexicans to cross the border to work in agriculture and mining. Most were employed in the Southwest, but a significant number also traveled to the Midwest for factory jobs.

The Great Migration The largest movement of people consisted of African Americans who migrated north in the **Great Migration** (a term also used for 17th century movement of Puritans). At the close of the 19th century, about 90 percent of African Americans lived in southern states. This internal migration began in earnest between 1910 and 1930 when about 1 million people traveled north to seek jobs in the cities. Motivating their decision to leave the south were (1) deteriorating race relations marked by segregation and racial violence, (2) destruction of their cotton crops by the boll weevil, and (3) limited economic opportunities. In the face of these problems, job in northern factories were a tremendous attraction.

Migration slowed down in the 1930s because of the economic collapse known as the Great Depression, but it resumed during World War II (1941–1945). Between 1940 and 1970, over 4 million African Americans moved north. Although many succeeded in improving their economic conditions, the newcomers to northern cities also faced racial tension and discrimination.

AFRICAN AMERICAN POPULATION, 1900 TO 1960			
Region	1900	1930	1960
South	7,923,000	9,362,000	11,312,000
Northeast	385,000	1,147,000	3,028,000
Midwest	496,000	1,262,000	3,446,000
West	30,000	120,000	1,086,000

Source: U.S. Bureau of the Census. *Historical Statistics of the United States, Colonial Times to 1970.* All numbers in the above table are rounded.

Postwar Problems

Americans had trouble adjusting from the patriotic fervor of wartime to the economic and social stresses of postwar uncertainties. America's postwar recovery was troubled by a series of social and economic upheavals.

1918 Pandemic The same year that World War I ended, the most severe influenza outbreak of the 20th century started. It infected an estimated 500 million people worldwide and claimed an estimated 50 million lives. In the United States, it was first discovered in crowded military camps in the spring of 1918. Surprisingly, the pandemic had some of the highest mortality rates among 20 to 40 year olds. At the time there were no effective drugs to treat the virus, which killed 500,000 to 675,000 Americans. The rapid spread of the pandemic was underreported by the limited media coverage and government efforts to keep up morale during wartime.

Demobilization During the war, 4 million American men had been taken from civilian life and the domestic economy. Not all the returning soldiers could find jobs right away, but many who did took employment from the women and African Americans who, for a short time, had thrived on war work. The business boom of wartime also went flat, as factory orders for military products fell off. With European farm products back on the market, farm prices fell, which hurt U.S. farmers. In the cities, consumers went on a buying spree, leading to inflation and a short boom in 1920. The spree did not last. In 1921, the economy plunged into a **recession**, and 10 percent of the American workforce was unemployed.

The Red Scare In 1919, the country suffered from a volatile combination of unhappiness with the peace process, fears of communism fueled by the Communist takeover in Russia, and worries about labor unrest at home. The **anti-German hysteria** of the war years turned quickly into **anti-Communist hysteria** known as the Red Scare. These anti-Communist fears also fueled **xenophobia** that resulted in restrictions on immigration in the 1920s.

Palmer Raids A series of unexplained bombings caused Attorney General A. Mitchell Palmer to establish a special office under J. Edgar Hoover to gather information on radicals. Palmer also ordered mass arrests of anarchists, socialists, and labor agitators. From November 1919 through January 1920, more than 6,000 people were arrested based on limited criminal evidence. Most of the suspects were foreign born, and 500 of them, including the outspoken radical Emma Goldman, were deported. The scare faded almost as quickly as it arose. Palmer warned of huge riots on May Day, 1920, but they never took place. His loss of credibility, coupled with rising concerns about civil liberties, caused the hysteria to recede.

Labor Conflict In a nation that valued free enterprise and rugged individualism, a large part of the American public regarded unions with distrust. Antiunion attitudes had softened during the Progressive Era. Factory workers and their unions were offered a "Square Deal" under Theodore Roosevelt and protection from lawsuits under the Clayton Antitrust Act of 1914. During the war, unions made important gains. Afterwards, however, a series of strikes in 1919 as well as fear of revolution turned public opinion against unions.

Strikes of 1919 The first major strike of 1919 was in Seattle in February. Some 60,000 unionists joined shipyard workers in a peaceful strike for higher pay. Troops were called out, but there was no violence. In September, Boston police went on strike to protest the firing of a few officers who tried to unionize. Massachusetts Governor Calvin Coolidge sent in the National Guard to break the strike. Also in September, workers for the U.S. Steel Corporation struck. State and federal troops were called out, and after considerable violence and the death of 18 workers, the strike was broken in January 1920.

Racial Violence The decades after 1900 saw acute racial tension over the Jim Crow oppression in the South, the rapid growth of the Ku Klux Klan, the continued lynching of African Americans, and the Great Migration to northern cities. Whites resented the increased competition for jobs and housing. During the war, **race riots** had erupted, the largest in East St. Louis, Illinois, in 1917. In 1919, racial tensions led to violence in many cities. In Chicago, 40 people were killed and 500 were injured in a riot that started over the use of a beach.

What has been called "the single worst incident of racial violence in American history" happened in Tulsa, Oklahoma in 1921. The Tulsa Race Massacre began after African Americans thwarted the lynching of a Black man. White mobs destroyed more than 1,000 Black-owned homes and businesses in the neighborhood known for its prosperity as the Black Wall Street and killed 50 to 300 people The man whose lynching was prevented was later exonerated.

Confederate Monuments Another part of the resurgence of Southern White pride and racial tensions was the spike in building public monuments between 1900 and the 1920s to honor Jefferson Davis and top Confederate generals throughout the South. Many African American and human rights reformers believe that, unlike earlier memorials in cemeteries to veterans, these were built to glorify the traditions of the "Lost Cause" interpretation of the Confederacy, which included defending White supremacy and slavery.

Decline of the Progressive Impulse America's sacrifices and causalities suffered during World War I drained the last of the Progressive idealism in the crusade "to make the world safe for democracy." Instead, the majority of the nation wanted to return to a less complicated period, or what the next, more conservative president called "normalcy." The 1920s provided prosperity, automobiles, radio, jazz, and movie and sport heroes along with reactionary efforts to stop change by restricting immigration, denying science, and retreating from international commitments.

REFLECT ON THE LEARNING OBJECTIVE

1. Explain two effects of World War I mobilization on international and internal migration over time.

KEY TERMS BY THEME

Mobilization (PCE)
Food Administration
Railroad Administration
National War Labor Board
Liberty Bonds
Selective Service Act
service by African Americans

Civil Liberties (PCE)
George Creel
Committee on Public Information
Espionage Act (1917)
Sedition Act (1918)
Eugene Debs
Schenck v. United States

anti-German hysteria

Social Impact of the War (MIG, WXT)
jobs for women
migration of Mexicans
Great Migration

Aftermath of War (WXT, PCE, MIG)
1918 pandemic
recession
Red Scare
anti-Communist hysteria
xenophobia
Palmer raids
strikes of 1919
race riots

MULTIPLE-CHOICE QUESTIONS

Questions 1–3 refer to the following excerpt.

"I think all men recognize that in time of war the citizen must surrender some rights for the common good which he is entitled to enjoy in time of peace. But sir, the right to control their own government, according to constitutional forms, is not one of the rights that the citizens of this country are called upon to surrender in time of war. . . .

"Mr. President, our Government, above all others, is founded on the right of the people freely to discuss all matters pertaining to their Government, in war not less than in peace. . . . How can the popular will express itself between elections except by meetings, by speeches, by publications, by petitions, and by addresses to the representatives of the people?

"Any man who seeks to set a limit upon these rights, whether in war or peace, aims a blow at the most vital part of our Government."

Robert M. La Follette, *Congressional Record*, October 6, 1917

1. What does the author imply by the phrase "not one of the rights that the citizens of this country are called upon to surrender in time of war"?
   (A) Citizens do not lose their freedom of speech during war.
   (B) Citizens should not have to pay taxes during war.
   (C) The Constitution protects the rights of people to disrupt the draft.
   (D) The Constitution allows people to fight for the opponent in a war.

2. Which of the following during World War I proved the most direct threat to the perspective on civil rights in this excerpt?

(A) Spread of the Bolshevik Revolution

(B) The Espionage and Sedition Acts

(C) The Committee for Public Information

(D) *Schenck v. United States*

3. Which of the following conflicts raised the most similar concerns about the violation of civil rights as did World War I?

(A) War of 1812

(B) Mexican War of 1846

(C) American Civil War

(D) Spanish-American War of 1898

SHORT-ANSWER QUESTIONS

Use complete sentences; an outline or bulleted list alone is not acceptable.

1. Answer (a), (b), and (c).

(a) Briefly explain ONE specific example of how the federal government mobilized industry or labor during World War I.

(b) Briefly explain ONE specific example of how the federal government restricted freedom of speech during World War I.

(c) Briefly explain ONE specific example of how World War I affected either women or African Americans during this period.

2. Answer (a), (b), and (c).

(a) Briefly explain ONE specific example of how the Red Scare was related to World War I.

(b) Briefly explain ONE specific example of how the postwar labor problems were related to World War I.

(c) Briefly explain ONE specific example of how the racial conflicts of 1917 to 1919 were related to World War I.

1920s: Innovations in Communication and Technology

*Why does this magnificent applied science which saves work
and makes life easier bring us so little happiness?*

Albert Einstein, address to California Institute of Technology, 1931

Learning Objective: Explain the causes and effects of the innovations in communications and technology in the United States over time.

Politics took a backseat in the 1920s as Americans adapted to economic growth and social change. The decade began with a brief postwar recession (1921), included a lengthy period of **economic prosperity** (1922–1928), and ended in economic disaster (October 1929) with the nation's worst stock market crash to that time. During the boom years, unemployment was usually below 4 percent. The **standard of living** for most Americans improved significantly. Indoor plumbing and central heating became commonplace. By 1930, two-thirds of all homes had electricity. Real income for both the middle class and the working class increased substantially.

The prosperity, however, was far from universal. In fact, during the 1920s, as many as 40 percent of U.S. families in both rural and urban areas had incomes in the poverty range—they struggled to live on less than $1,500 a year. Farmers in particular did not share in the booming economy.

Causes of Economic Prosperity

The economic boom—led by a spectacular rise of 64 percent in manufacturing output between 1919 and 1929—resulted from several factors.

Increased Productivity Companies made greater use of research, expanding their use of Frederick W. Taylor's time-and-motion studies and principles of **scientific management**. The manufacturing process was made more efficient by the adoption of improved methods of mass production. In 1914, **Henry Ford** had perfected a system for manufacturing automobiles by means of an **assembly line**. Instead of losing time moving around a factory as in the past, Ford's workers remained at one place all day and performed the same simple operation over and over again at rapid speed. In the 1920s, most major industries adopted the assembly line and realized major gains in worker productivity.

Energy Technologies Another cause of economic growth was the increased use of oil and electricity, although coal was still used for railroads and to heat homes. Increasingly, oil was used to power factories and to provide gasoline for the rapidly increasing numbers of automobiles. By 1930, oil would account for 23 percent of U.S. energy consumption (up from 3 percent in 1900). Electric motors in factories and new appliances at home increased electrical generation more than 300 percent during the decade.

Government Policy Government at all levels in the 1920s favored the growth of big business by offering corporate tax cuts and doing almost nothing to enforce the antitrust laws of the Progressive Era. Large tax cuts for higher-income Americans also contributed to the imbalance in incomes and increased speculation in markets. The Federal Reserve contributed to the overheated economic boom through low interest rates and relaxed regulation of banks. Then, it began tightening the money supply as the economy began to decline—precisely the wrong time, according to economists today.

Consumer Economy Adding electricity in their homes enabled millions of Americans to purchase the new **consumer appliances** of the decade— refrigerators, vacuum cleaners, and washing machines. Automobiles became more affordable and sold by the millions, making the horse-and-buggy era a thing of the past. Advertising expanded as businesses found that they could increase consumers' demand for new products by appealing to desires for status and popularity. Stores increased sales of the new appliances and automobiles by allowing customers to buy on credit. Later, as consumers faced more "easy monthly payments" than they could afford, they curtailed buying, contributing to the collapse of the economic boom. Chain stores, such as Woolworth's and A & P, proliferated. Their greater variety of products were attractively displayed and often priced lower than the neighborhood stores, which they threatened to displace.

Impact of the Automobile More than any other new technology, the automobile changed society. In 1913, Americans owned 1.2 million automobiles. In 1929, that number reached 26.5 million, an average of almost one per family. Auto production replaced the railroad industry as the key promoter of economic growth. Other industries—steel, glass, rubber, gasoline, and highway construction—depended on automobile sales.

In social terms, the automobile affected all that Americans did: commuting to work, traveling for pleasure, shopping, even dating. Some changes were negative, such as traffic jams in cities and injuries and deaths on roads. Many people disliked the independence cars gave young people. They blamed the automobile, "a bordello on wheels," for a breakdown of morals.

Farm Problems

Many farmers did not share in the prosperity of the 1920s. Their best years had been 1916–1918, when crop prices had been kept high by (1) wartime demand in Europe and (2) the U.S. government's wartime policy of guaranteeing a minimum price for wheat and corn. When the war ended, so did farm prosperity. Farmers who had borrowed heavily to expand during the war were left with a heavy burden of debt. New technologies (such as chemical fertilizers and gasoline tractors) helped farmers increase their production in the 1920s but did not solve their problems. Increased productivity only added to the financial problems of farmers, as the resulting surpluses produced falling prices.

Labor Unions Struggle

Wages rose during the 1920s, but membership in unions declined 20 percent, partly because most companies insisted on an **"open shop"** (keeping jobs open to nonunion workers). Some companies also began to practice **welfare capitalism**—voluntarily offering their employees improved benefits and higher wages in order to reduce their interest in organizing unions. In the South, companies used police, state militia, and local mobs to violently resist efforts to unionize the textile industry.

In an era that so strongly favored business, strikes usually failed. The United Mine Workers, led by John L. Lewis, suffered setbacks in a series of violent and ultimately unsuccessful strikes in Pennsylvania, West Virginia, and Kentucky. Conservative courts routinely issued injunctions against strikes and nullified labor laws aimed at protecting workers' welfare.

Technology and Culture

The Census of 1920 reported that, for the first time, more than half of the American population lived in urban areas, defined as communities of 2,500 people or more. Many city residents had tastes, morals, and habits of mass consumption that were increasingly at odds with the religious and moral codes of many rural Americans.

Architecture and Industrial Design The fusion of art and technology during the 1920s and 1930s created a new profession of industrial designers. Influenced by Art Deco and streamlining styles, they created functional products from toasters to locomotives that had aesthetic appeal. Many skyscrapers, such as the Chrysler and Empire State buildings in New York, were built in the **Art Deco** style, which captured modernist simplification of forms while using machine age materials.

The Chrysler Building, New York City
Source: Carol M. Highsmith / Library of Congress

Mass Media Newspapers had once been the only medium of mass communication and entertainment. In the 1920s, a new medium—the **radio**—suddenly appeared. The first commercial radio station went on the air in 1920 and broadcast music to just a few thousand listeners. By 1930, there were more than 800 stations broadcasting to 10 million radios—about a third of all U.S. homes. The organization of the National Broadcasting Company (NBC) in 1924 and the Columbia Broadcasting System (CBS) in 1927 provided **networks** of radio stations that enabled people from coast to coast to listen to the same programs: news broadcasts, sporting events, soap operas, quiz shows, and comedies. They also provided national exposure to regional cultures. For example, the National Barn Dance show, later renamed the Grand Ole Opry, featured music from the southeastern United States, a style that evolved into today's country music.

Movie Business The **movie industry** centered in **Hollywood**, California, became big business in the 1920s. Going to the movies became a national habit in cities, suburbs, and small towns. Glamorous movie stars such as Greta Garbo and Rudolf Valentino were idolized by millions. Elaborate movie theater "palaces" were built for the general public. With the introduction of talking (sound) pictures in 1927, the movie industry reached new heights. By 1929, more than 80 million tickets to Hollywood movies were sold weekly.

Popular Music High school and college youth rebelled against their elders' culture by dancing to jazz music. Brought north by African American musicians, jazz became a symbol of the "new" and "modern" culture of cities. Like radio, **phonographs** made this new style of music available to a huge (and youthful) public. Other forms of music that spread in popularity were blues, classical, and "American standards" by composers such as Irving Berlin.

Aviation The improving technology of airplanes in the 1920s created the opportunity for aviators to set and break speed and distance records. Crowds would greet pilots after epic flights, and communities would hold huge street parades to honor them. The most celebrated hero was **Charles Lindbergh**, a young aviator who thrilled the entire world by flying nonstop across the Atlantic from Long Island to Paris in 1927. Americans listened to the radio for news of his flight and welcomed his return to the United States with ticker tape parades larger than the welcome given to the returning soldiers of World War I.

Popular Heroes In an earlier era, people admired politicians such as William Jennings Bryan, Theodore Roosevelt, and Woodrow Wilson as heroic figures. In the new age of radio and movies, Americans radically shifted their viewpoint and adopted as role models the larger-than-life personalities celebrated on the sports page and the movie screen. Every sport had its superstars who were nationally known. In the 1920s, people followed the knockouts of heavyweight boxer Jack Dempsey, the swimming records of Gertrude Ederle, the touchdowns scored by Jim Thorpe, the home runs hit by Babe Ruth, and the golf tournaments won by Bobby Jones.

Increasing Tension The prosperity and technological developments of the 1920s accompanied growing conflicts over cultural and political issues, such as immigration, Prohibition, and the roles of science and religion, which is the next topic.

REFLECT ON THE LEARNING OBJECTIVE

1. Explain two effects of the innovations in communications and technology during the 1920s in the United States.

KEY TERMS BY THEME

1920s Economy (WXT)	"open shop"	networks
economic prosperity	welfare capitalism	movie industry
standard of living	**Technology and Culture**	Hollywood
scientific management	**(WXT, ARC)**	popular music
Henry Ford	industrial design	phonographs
assembly line	Art Deco	popular heroes
consumer appliances	mass media	aviation
impact of the automobile	radio	Charles Lindberg

MULTIPLE-CHOICE QUESTIONS

Questions 1–3 refer to the advertisement below.

Source: General Motors, 1925, The Granger Collection, NYC

1. Which of the following trends of the 1920s is most clearly portrayed in this advertisement?

    (A) The expansion of auto dealers throughout the country

    (B) The use of extended payment plans to purchase consumer goods

    (C) The emergence of General Motors as the largest company

    (D) The growth of middle-class incomes

2. Which of the following statements best supports the argument of historians who criticize the economy that developed during the 1920s?

    (A) Consumerism weakened the moral character of the nation.

    (B) The growth of the auto industry badly hurt the railroads.

    (C) Advertising was based on gaining status and popularity.

    (D) The boom was based on speculation and borrowed money.

SHORT-ANSWER QUESTIONS

1. Answer (a), (b), and (c).

    (a) Briefly explain ONE specific example of how the automobile influenced American culture and society during the 1920s.

    (b) Briefly explain ONE specific example of how innovation and technology affected mass media during the 1920s.

    (c) Briefly explain ONE specific example of how innovation and technology produced heroes who came to dominate the culture during the 1920s.

2. Answer (a), (b), and (c).

    (a) Briefly describe ONE difference between the technological innovations of the 1920s and of the period from 1865 to 1900.

    (b) Briefly describe ONE similarity between the technological innovations of the 1920s and of the period from 1865 to 1900.

    (c) Briefly explain ONE reason for the difference between the technological innovations of the 1920s and of the period from 1865 to 1900.

1920s: Cultural and Political Controversies

My candle burns at both ends;
It will not last the night;
But ah, my foes, and oh, my friends—
It gives a lovely light!

Edna St. Vincent Millay, "First Fig." First published in
First Figs from Thistles (Harper and Bros., 1922)

Learning Objective 1: Explain the causes and effects of international and internal migration patterns over time.

Learning Objective 2: Explain the causes and effects of the developments in popular culture in America.

The dominant social and political issues of the 1920s expressed sharp divisions in U.S. society between the young and the old, religious modernists and religious fundamentalists, prohibitionists and anti-prohibitionists, and nativists and the foreign born. Because of the steady flow in previous decades of people from rural to urban areas in search of jobs, by 1920 most people lived in urban areas, then defined as places with more than 2,500 residents.

Religion, Science, and Politics

Divisions among Protestants reflected the tensions in society between the traditional values of rural areas and the modernizing forces of the cities.

Modernism A range of influences, including the changing role of women, the Social Gospel movement, and scientific knowledge, caused large numbers of Protestants to define their faith in new ways. Modernists took a historical and critical view of certain passages in the Bible and believed they could accept Darwin's theory of evolution without abandoning their religious faith.

Fundamentalism Protestant preachers, mostly in rural areas, condemned the modernists and taught that every word in the Bible was true literally. A key fundamentalist doctrine was that creationism (the belief that God had created the universe in seven days, as stated in the Bible) explained the origin of all life. Fundamentalists blamed modernists for causing a decline in morals.

Revivalists on the Radio Ever since the Great Awakening of the early 1700s, religious revivals periodically swept through America. **Revivalists** of the 1920s preached a fundamentalist message but did so for the first time making full use of the new tool of mass communication, the radio. One leading radio evangelist was **Billy Sunday**, who drew large crowds as he attacked drinking, gambling, and dancing. Another was **Aimee Semple McPherson**, who condemned the twin evils of communism and jazz music from her pulpit in Los Angeles.

Fundamentalism and Science

More than any other single event, a much-publicized trial in Tennessee focused the debate between religious fundamentalists in the rural South and modernists of the northern cities. Tennessee, like several other southern states, outlawed the teaching of Darwin's theory of evolution in public schools. To challenge the constitutionality of these laws, the American Civil Liberties Union persuaded a Tennessee biology teacher, John Scopes, to teach the theory of evolution to his high school class. For doing so, Scopes was arrested and tried in 1925.

The Trial The entire nation followed the **Scopes trial** both in newspapers and by radio. Defending Scopes was a famous lawyer from Chicago, **Clarence Darrow**. Representing the fundamentalists was three-time Democratic candidate for president William Jennings Bryan, who testified as an expert on the Bible. The courtroom clash between Darrow and Bryan dramatized that the debate on evolution symbolized a battle between two opposing views of the world.

Aftermath As expected, Scopes was convicted, but the conviction was later overturned on a technicality. Laws banning the teaching of evolution remained on the books for years, although they were rarely enforced. The northern press asserted that Darrow and the modernists had thoroughly discredited fundamentalism. However, to this day, questions about the relationship between religion and public schools remain controversial and unresolved.

Prohibition

Another controversy that helped define the 1920s concerned people's conflicting attitudes toward the 18th Amendment. Wartime concerns to conserve grain and maintain a sober workforce moved Congress to pass this amendment, which strictly prohibited the manufacture and sale of alcoholic beverages, including liquors, wines, and beers. It was ratified in 1919. The adoption of the Prohibition amendment and a federal law enforcing it (the **Volstead Act**, 1919) were the culmination of many decades of crusading by temperance forces.

Defying the Law Prohibition did not stop people from drinking alcohol either in public places or at home. Especially in the cities, it became fashionable to defy the law by going to clubs or bars known as speakeasies, where bootleg (smuggled) liquor was sold. City police and judges were paid to look the other way. Even elected officials such as President Harding served alcoholic drinks to guests. Liquors, beers, and wines were readily available from bootleggers who smuggled them from Canada or made them in their garages or basements.

Rival groups of gangsters, including a Chicago gang headed by **Al Capone**, fought for control of the lucrative bootlegging trade. **Organized crime** became big business. The millions made from the sale of illegal booze allowed the gangs to expand other illegal activities: prostitution, gambling, and narcotics.

Political Discord and Repeal Most Republicans publicly supported the "noble experiment" of Prohibition (although in private, many politicians drank). Democrats were divided on the issue, with southerners supporting it and northern city politicians calling for repeal. Supporters of the 18th Amendment pointed to declines in alcoholism and alcohol-related deaths. However, support weakened in the face of growing public resentment and clear evidence of increased criminal activity. With the coming of the Great Depression, economic arguments for repeal were added to the others. In 1933, the **21st Amendment**, which repealed the 18th Amendment, was ratified, and millions celebrated the new year by toasting the end of Prohibition.

Opposition to Immigration

The world war had interrupted the flow of immigrants to the United States, but as soon as the war ended, immigration shot upward. More than a million foreigners entered the country between 1919 and 1921. Like the immigrants of the prewar period, the new arrivals were mainly Catholics and Jews from eastern and southern Europe. Once again, nativist prejudices of native-born Protestants were aroused. Workers feared competition for jobs. Isolationists wanted minimal contact with Europe and feared that immigrants might foment revolution. In response to public demands for restrictive legislation, Congress acted quickly.

Quota Laws Congress passed two laws that severely limited immigration by setting quotas based on nationality. The first quota act of 1921 limited immigration to 3 percent of the number of foreign-born persons from a given nation counted in the 1910 Census (a maximum of 357,000). To reduce the number of immigrants from southern and eastern Europe, Congress passed a second quota act in 1924 that set quotas of 2 percent based on the Census of 1890 (before the arrival of most of the "new" immigrants). Although there were quotas for all European and Asian nationalities, the law chiefly restricted those groups considered "undesirable" by the nativists. By 1927, the quotas for all Asians and eastern and southern Europeans had been limited to 150,000, with all Japanese immigrants barred. With these acts, the traditional United States policy of unlimited immigration ended.

Canadians and Latin Americans were exempt from restrictions. Almost 500,000 Mexicans migrated legally to the Southwest during the 1920s.

Case of Sacco and Vanzetti Although liberal American artists and intellectuals were few in number, they loudly protested against racist and nativist prejudices. They rallied to the support of two Italian immigrants,

Nicola Sacco and Bartolomeo Vanzetti, who in 1921 had been convicted in a Massachusetts court of committing robbery and murder. Liberals protested that the two men had not received a fair trial and that they had been accused, convicted, and sentenced to die simply because they were poor Italians and anarchists (who rejected all government). After six years of appeals and national and international debates over the conduct of their trial, Sacco and Vanzetti were executed in 1927.

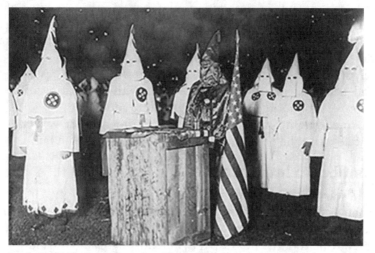

Nearly 30,000 Klan members gathered for a rally in Chicago around 1920.
Source: Library of Congress.

Ku Klux Klan

The most extreme expression of nativism in the 1920s was the resurgence of the **Ku Klux Klan**. Unlike the original Klan of the 1860s and 1870s, the new Klan founded in 1915 was as strong in the Midwest as in the South. The Klan attracted new members because of the popular silent film *Birth of a Nation*, which portrayed the KKK during Reconstruction as the heroes, and the White backlash to the race riots of 1919. The new Klan used modern advertising techniques to grow to 5 million members by 1925. It drew most of its support from lower-middle-class White Protestants in small cities and towns. This revival of the KKK directed hostility not only against African Americans but also against Catholics, Jews, foreigners, and suspected Communists.

Tactics The Klan employed various methods for terrorizing and intimidating anyone targeted as "un-American." Dressed in white hoods to disguise their identity, Klan members would burn crosses and apply vigilante justice, punishing their victims with whips, tar and feathers, and lynching. The overwhelming number of those killed were African American men. In its heyday in the early 1920s, the Klan developed strong political influence. In Indiana and Texas, its support became crucial for candidates hoping to win elections to state and local offices.

Decline At first, the majority of native-born White Americans appeared to tolerate the Klan because it vowed to uphold high standards of Christian morality and drive out bootleggers, gamblers, and adulterers. Beginning in 1923, however, investigative reports in the northern press revealed that fraud and corruption in the KKK were rife. In 1925, the leader of Indiana's Klan, Grand Dragon David Stephenson, was convicted of murder. After that, the Klan's influence and membership declined rapidly. Nevertheless, it and other White nationalist groups continued to exist and advocate for White supremacy into the 21st century.

Arts and Literature

Scorning religion as hypocritical and bitterly condemning the sacrifices of wartime as fraud perpetrated by money interests were two dominant themes of the leading writers of the postwar decade. This disillusionment caused the writer **Gertrude Stein** to call these writers a **"lost generation."** The novels of **F. Scott Fitzgerald**, **Ernest Hemingway**, and **Sinclair Lewis**; the poems of **Ezra Pound** and **T. S. Eliot**; and the plays of **Eugene O'Neill** expressed disillusionment with the ideals of an earlier time and with the materialism of a business-oriented culture. Fitzgerald and O'Neill took to a life of drinking, while Eliot and Hemingway expressed their unhappiness by moving into exile in Europe.

Painters such as **Edward Hopper** were inspired by the architecture of American cities to explore loneliness and isolation of urban life. **Regional artists** such as **Grant Wood** and **Thomas Hart Benton** celebrated the rural people and scenes of the heartland of America.

Musical theater changed in the 1920s with the Broadway premiere of *Show Boat*. It proved a radical departure in musical storytelling with a serious treatment of prejudice and race. Jewish immigrants played a major role in the development of the American musical theatre during this era. For example, composer **George Gershwin**, the son of Russian-Jewish immigrants, blended jazz and classical music in his symphonic *Rhapsody in Blue* and the folk opera *Porgy and Bess*.

Women, Family, and Education

Ratification of the 19th Amendment gave women the right to vote, but it did not change either women's lives or U.S. politics as much as reformers had hoped. Voting patterns in the election of 1920 showed that women did not vote as a bloc but usually shared the party preferences of their husbands or fathers.

Women at Home The traditional separation of labor between men and women continued into the 1920s. Most middle-class women expected to spend their lives as homemakers and mothers. The introduction into the home of such labor-saving devices as the washing machine and vacuum cleaner eased but did not substantially change the daily routines of the homemaker.

Women in the Labor Force Participation of women in the workforce remained about the same as before the war. Employed women usually lived in the cities; were limited to certain categories of jobs as clerks, nurses, teachers, and domestics; and received lower wages than men.

Revolution in Morals Probably the most significant change in the lives of young men and women of the 1920s was their revolt against sexual taboos. Some were influenced by the writings of the Austrian psychiatrist **Sigmund Freud**, who stressed the role of sexual repression in mental illness. Others, who perhaps had never heard of Freud, took to premarital sex as if it were—like radio and jazz music—one of the inventions of the modern age. Movies, novels, automobiles, and new dance steps (the foxtrot and the Charleston) also encouraged greater promiscuity. The use of contraceptives for birth control was still against the law in almost every state. Even so, because of the work of **Margaret Sanger** and other advocates of birth control, it achieved growing acceptance in the 1920s.

A special **fashion** that set young people apart from older generations was the flapper look. Influenced by movie actresses as well as their own desires for independence, young women shocked their elders by wearing dresses hemmed at the knee (instead of the ankle), "bobbing" (cutting short) their hair, smoking cigarettes, and driving cars. High school and college graduates also took office jobs until they married. Then, as married women, they were expected to abandon the flapper look, quit their jobs, and settle down as wives and mothers.

Divorce As a result of women's suffrage, state lawmakers were now forced to listen to feminists, who demanded changes in the divorce laws to permit women to escape abusive and incompatible husbands. Liberalized divorce laws were one reason that one in six marriages ended in divorce by 1930—a significant increase over the one-in-eight ratio of 1920.

Education Widespread belief in the value of education, together with economic prosperity, stimulated more state governments to enact compulsory school laws. Universal **high school education** became the new American goal. By the end of the 1920s, the proportion of high school graduates had doubled to over 25 percent of school-age young adults.

African American Cultural Renaissance

By 1930, almost 20 percent of African Americans lived in the North, as migration **from the South** continued. In the North, African Americans still faced discrimination in housing and jobs, but they found at least some improvement in their earnings and material standard of living. The largest African American community developed in the Harlem section of New York City. With a population of almost 200,000 by 1930, Harlem became famous in the 1920s for its concentration of talented actors, artists, musicians, and writers. Because of their artistic achievements, this period is known as the **"Harlem Renaissance."**

Poets and Musicians The leading Harlem poets included **Countee Cullen, Langston Hughes, James Weldon Johnson**, and **Claude McKay.** Commenting on African American heritage, their poems expressed a range of emotions, from bitterness and resentment to joy and hope.

African American jazz musicians such as **Duke Ellington** and **Louis Armstrong** were so popular among people of all races that the 1920s is often called the Jazz Age. Other great performers included blues singer **Bessie Smith** and the multitalented singer and actor **Paul Robeson**. While these artists sometimes performed before integrated audiences in Harlem, they often found themselves and their audiences segregated in much of the rest of the nation.

Marcus Garvey In 1916, the United Negro Improvement Association (UNIA) was brought to Harlem from Jamaica by a charismatic immigrant, **Marcus Garvey**. Garvey advocated individual and racial pride for African Americans and developed political ideas of Black nationalism. Building on W. E. B. Du Bois's pride in Black culture, Garvey established an organization for Black separatism, economic self-sufficiency, and a **back-to-Africa movement**. Garvey's sale of stock in the Black Star Steamship line led to federal charges of fraud. In 1925, he was tried, convicted, and jailed. Later, he was deported to Jamaica, and his movement collapsed.

W. E. B. Du Bois and other African American leaders disagreed with Garvey's back-to-Africa idea but endorsed his emphasis on racial pride and self-respect. In the 1960s, Garvey's thinking helped to inspire a later generation to embrace the cause of **Black pride** and nationalism.

Republican Majority

Through the 1920s, three Republican presidents would control the executive branch. Congress was also solidly Republican through a decade in which U.S. business boomed.

The great leader of the progressive wing of the Republican Party, Theodore Roosevelt, died in 1919. This loss, combined with public disillusionment over the war, allowed the return of the old-guard (conservative) Republicans. Unlike the Republicans of the Gilded Age, however, Republican leadership in the 1920s did not preach laissez-faire economics. Instead, Republicans accepted the idea of limited government regulation as an aid to stabilizing business. The regulatory commissions established in the Progressive Era were now administered by appointees who were more sympathetic to business than to the general public. The prevailing idea of the Republican Party was that the nation would benefit if business and the pursuit of profits took the lead in developing the economy.

The Presidency of Warren Harding

Warren Harding had been a newspaper publisher in Ohio before entering politics. He was handsome and well liked among the Republican political cronies with whom he regularly played poker. His abilities as a leader, however, were less than presidential. When the Republican National Convention of 1920 deadlocked, the party bosses decided "in a smoke-filled room" to deliver the nomination to Harding as a compromise choice.

A Few Good Choices Harding recognized his limitations and hoped to make up for them by appointing able men to his cabinet. He appointed the former presidential candidate and Supreme Court justice **Charles Evans Hughes** to be secretary of state, the greatly admired former mining engineer and Food Administration leader Herbert Hoover to be secretary of commerce, and the Pittsburgh industrialist and millionaire **Andrew Mellon** to be secretary of the treasury. When the Chief Justice's seat on the Supreme Court became vacant, Harding filled it by appointing former President William Howard Taft.

Domestic Policy Harding did little more than sign into law the measures adopted by the Republican Congress. He approved (1) a reduction in the income tax, (2) an increase in tariff rates under the **Fordney-McCumber Tariff Act** of 1922, and (3) the establishment of the **Bureau of the Budget**, with procedures for all government expenditures to be placed in a single budget for Congress to review and vote on.

Harding did surprise many people, particularly his conservative allies, by pardoning and releasing from federal prison Socialist leader Eugene Debs. Debs had been convicted of violating the Espionage Act during World War I. While imprisoned, Debs received 920,000 votes in the 1920 presidential election. Harding's decision to pardon Debs was prompted by the president's generous spirit.

Scandals and Death Harding's postwar presidency was marked by scandals and corruption similar to those that had occurred under an earlier postwar president, Ulysses S. Grant. Having appointed some excellent officials, Harding also selected a number of incompetent and dishonest men to fill important positions, including Secretary of the Interior **Albert B. Fall** and Attorney General **Harry M. Daugherty**. In 1924, Congress discovered that Fall had accepted bribes for granting oil leases near **Teapot Dome**, Wyoming. Daugherty also took bribes for agreeing not to prosecute certain criminal suspects.

However, in August 1923, shortly before these scandals were uncovered publicly, Harding died of a heart attack in California after traveling to Alaska. He was never implicated in any of the scandals.

The Presidency of Calvin Coolidge

Harding's vice president and successor, **Calvin Coolidge**, had won popularity in 1919 as the Massachusetts governor who broke the Boston police strike.

He was a man of few words who richly deserved the nickname "Silent Cal." Coolidge once explained why silence was good politics. "If you don't say anything," he said, "you won't be called on to repeat it." Also unanswerable was the president's sage comment "When more and more people are thrown out of work, unemployment results." Coolidge summarized both his presidency and his era in the phrase "The business of America is business."

The Election of 1924 After less than a year in office, Coolidge was the overwhelming choice of the Republican Party as their presidential nominee in 1924. The Democrats nominated a conservative lawyer from West Virginia, John W. Davis, and tried to make an issue of the Teapot Dome scandal. Unhappy with conservative dominance of both parties, liberals formed a new Progressive Party led by its presidential candidate, Robert La Follette of Wisconsin. Coolidge won the election easily, but the Progressive ticket did extremely well for a third party in a conservative era. La Follette received nearly 5 million votes, chiefly from discontented farmers and laborers.

Vetoes and Inaction Coolidge believed in limited government that stood aside while business conducted its own affairs. Little was accomplished in the White House except keeping a close watch on the budget. Cutting spending to the bone, Coolidge vetoed even the acts of the Republican majority in Congress. He would not allow bonuses for World War I veterans and vetoed a bill (the McNary-Haugen Bill of 1928) to help farmers as crop prices fell.

Hoover, Smith, and the Election of 1928

Coolidge declined to run for the presidency a second time. The Republicans therefore turned to an able leader with a spotless reputation, self-made millionaire and Secretary of Commerce **Herbert Hoover**. Hoover had served three presidents (Wilson, Harding, and Coolidge) in administrative roles but had never before campaigned for elective office. Nevertheless, in 1928, he was made the Republican nominee for president.

Hoover's Democratic opponent was the governor of New York, **Alfred E. Smith**. As a Roman Catholic and an opponent of Prohibition, Smith appealed to many immigrant voters in the cities. Many Protestants, however, were openly prejudiced against Smith.

Republicans boasted of "Coolidge prosperity," which Hoover promised to extend. He even suggested that poverty would soon be ended altogether. Hoover won in a landslide and even took a large number of the electoral votes in the South. In several southern states—including Texas, Florida, and Virginia—the taste of prosperity and general dislike for Smith's religion outweighed the voters' usual allegiance to the Democratic Party.

Hoover's dreams to end poverty quickly proved bitterly ironic. The prosperity of the 1920s turned into a deep economic depression starting in the fall of 1929. Topic 7.9 explores its causes and its chilling impact on the lives of all classes of Americans.

By the 1930s, the 1920s seemed to be a unique decade. It looked like a period of social fun and booming business wedged between the calamities of military conflict (World War I) and economic crisis (the Great Depression).

Conservative Ideas In his popular history **Only Yesterday** (1931), **Frederick Lewis Allen** gave support to the ideas of the leading social critics of the 1920s, H. L. Mencken and Sinclair Lewis. He portrayed the period as one of narrow-minded materialism in which the middle class abandoned Progressive reforms, embraced conservative Republican policies, and either supported or condoned nativism, racism, and fundamentalism. Historian Arthur Schlesinger Jr. generally accepted this view of the twenties, seeing it within the framework of his cyclical view of history. He argued that the politics of the decade represented a conservative reaction to the liberal reforms of the Progressive Era.

Dissenting Views Revisionist historians of the 1950s questioned whether the 1920s truly broke with the Progressive past. They argued that the period continued earlier protest movements such as Populism. Richard Hofstadter and other "consensus" writers distinguished between two middle classes: a new urban group with modern values and an older middle class with traditional values. William Leuchtenburg in *The Perils of Prosperity* (1958) portrayed the traditionalists as threatened by cultural pluralism and modern ideas.

Local Power A third assessment took a more positive view of the traditionalists. Some historians, including Alan Brinkley in the 1980s, argued that people in the "old" middle class, including fundamentalists and nativists, were understandably trying to protect their own economic and social self-interests. At the same time, they were seeking to preserve individual and community freedom in face of the modernist movement toward centralized bureaucratic and national control. This effort to maintain local control and independence from big government is seen as continuing from the 1920s to the present.

Importance of Materialism Given the extreme and deeply felt differences between the modernists and the traditionalists, some historians have wondered why there was not more conflict in the twenties. One explanation is the importance of the **consumer culture**. Some historians have shown how the influence of growing materialism and prosperity caused people to accept increased corporate and bureaucratic control of their lives. Others have placed varying emphasis on the ways in which material affluence, consumer goods, advertising, and a homogeneous mass culture redefined U.S. social and political values. In one way, by focusing on materialism and consumption, historians have returned to the views of Mencken, Lewis, and Allen.

Support an Argument *Explain two perspectives on the conservatism of the 1920s.*

REFLECT ON THE LEARNING OBJECTIVES

1. Explain two causes for the reduction of international migration to the United States during the 1920s.

2. Explain the effects of two developments in popular culture in America during the 1920s.

KEY TERMS BY THEME

Conflict over Religion (ARC)
modernism
fundamentalism
revivalists
Billy Sunday
Aimee Semple McPherson
Scopes trial
Clarence Darrow

Conflict over Prohibition (ARC)
Volstead Act (1919)
Al Capone
organized crime
21st Amendment

Conflict over Immigration (MIG)
quota laws
Sacco and Vanzetti
Ku Klux Klan
Birth of a Nation
African Americans
foreigners
suspected Communists

Literature and the Arts (ARC)
Gertrude Stein
"lost generation"
F. Scott Fitzgerald
Ernest Hemingway
Sinclair Lewis
Ezra Pound
T. S. Eliot
Eugene O'Neill
Edward Hopper
regional artists
Grant Wood
George Gershwin

Cultural Changes (ARC)
morals
Sigmund Freud
Margaret Sanger
fashion
high school education
consumer culture
Frederick Lewis Allen
Only Yesterday

African American Identity (SOC)
migration from the South
"Harlem Renaissance"
Countee Cullen
Langston Hughes
James Weldon Johnson
Claude McKay
Duke Ellington
Louis Armstrong
Bessie Smith
Paul Robeson
Back-to-Africa movement
Marcus Garvey
Black pride

1920s Politics (PCE)
Warren Harding
Charles Evans Hughes
Andrew Mellon
Fordney-McCumber Tariff Act
Bureau of the Budget
Harry M. Daugherty
Albert B. Fall
Teapot Dome
Calvin Coolidge
Herbert Hoover
Alfred E. Smith

MULTIPLE-CHOICE QUESTIONS

"A widely held view of the Republican administrations of the 1920s is that they represented a return to an older order that had existed before Theodore Roosevelt and Woodrow Wilson became the nation's chief executives. Harding and Coolidge especially are seen as latter-day McKinleys, political mediocrities who peopled their cabinets with routine, conservative party hacks of the kind almost universal in Washington from the end of the Civil War until the early 20th century. In this view, the 1920s politically were an effort to set back the clock."

David A. Shannon, historian, *Between the Wars: America, 1919–1941*, 1965

1. Which of the following groups from the 1920s would have been most likely to express the "widely held view" described in this excerpt?
   (A) Leaders of business and finance
   (B) Individuals who supported Progressive reforms
   (C) Supporters of reduced government spending and tax cuts
   (D) Native-born and older Americans with traditional values

2. Which of the following actions from the 1920s most clearly challenges the description of Harding and Coolidge given in the excerpt?
   (A) The disarmament agreement among the great powers to discourage military aggression
   (B) The passage of legislation to increase tariff rates and cut income taxes
   (C) The leasing of public lands to private oil companies
   (D) The reduction of federal regulations for businesses and the banking system

3. Which of the following groups of politicians from between 1865 and 1900 most closely resemble the corrupt politicians during the Harding administration?
   (A) Politicians who failed to protect the freedmen and freedwomen in the South
   (B) Politicians who accepted shares of railroad stock in return for government subsidies
   (C) Politicians who bribed election officials to help them win elections
   (D) Politicians who violated the temperance laws and their professed moral beliefs

Use complete sentences; an outline or bulleted list alone is not acceptable.

1. "Nor was this new material advance essentially gross and philistine [unsophisticated], as the popular historiography of the 1920s has it, 'a drunken fiesta.' . . . Intellectuals are a little too inclined to resent poorer people acquiring for the first time material possessions, and especially luxuries. . . . During the 1920s, in fact, America began suddenly to acquire a cultural density . . . which it had never before possessed."

   Paul Johnson, historian, *A History of the American People*, 1997

   "Never was a decade snuffed out so quickly as the 1920s. The stock market crash was taken as a judgment pronounced on the whole era, and, in the grim days of the depression, the 1920s were condemned as a time of irresponsibility and immaturity."

   William E. Leuchtenburg, historian,
   The Perils of Prosperity, 1959

   Using the excerpts, answer (a), (b), and (c).

   (a) Briefly describe ONE major difference between Leuchtenburg's and Johnson's historical interpretations of the 1920s in the United States.

   (b) Briefly explain how ONE specific historical event or development that is not explicitly mentioned in the excerpts could be used to support Leuchtenburg's interpretation.

   (c) Briefly explain how ONE specific historical event or development that is not explicitly mentioned in the excerpts could be used to support Johnson's interpretation.

2. Answer (a), (b), and (c).

   (a) Briefly explain ONE specific example of how religion and science were a source of conflict in American society during the 1920s.

   (b) Briefly explain ONE specific example of how Prohibition was a source of conflict in American society during the 1920s.

   (c) Briefly explain ONE specific difference in the immigrant legislation of the 1920s in comparison to the period from 1865 to 1914.

Topic 7.9

The Great Depression

Once I built a tower, to the sun.
Brick and rivet and lime,
Once I built a tower,
Now it's done,
Brother, can you spare a dime?

E. Y. Harburg and Jay Gorney, "Brother, Can You Spare a Dime?" 1932

Learning Objective: Explain the causes of the Great Depression and its effects on the economy.

The natural rhythm of the business cycle in a free market economy includes periods of growth, recession, and depression that typically last only a few years. However, the depressions beginning in 1837, 1873, and 1893 were unusual. Each included widespread bank failures and the collapse of investment and credit systems. The result was a depression that was severe and extended several years.

Causes of the 1929 Crash

This depression of the 1930s was even worse than the preceding ones. It lasted far longer, caused more **business failures** and **unemployment**, and affected more people—both middle class and working class—than any preceding period of hard times. This was in fact not just an ordinary depression, but the *Great Depression*. Before it was over, two presidents—**Herbert Hoover** and Franklin Roosevelt—would devote 12 years to seeking the elusive path toward recovery. What caused the spectacular business boom of the 1920s to collapse dramatically in October 1929?

Wall Street Crash The ever-rising stock prices had become both a symbol and a source of wealth during the prosperous 1920s. A "boom" was in full force both in the United States and in the world economy in the late 1920s. On the stock exchange on Wall Street in New York City, stock prices had kept going up and up for 18 months, from March 1928 to September 1929. On September 3, the Dow Jones Industrial Average of major stocks had reached an all-time high of 381. An average investor who bought $1,000 worth of such stocks at the time of Hoover's election (November 1928) would have doubled his or her money in less than a year. Millions of people did invest in the boom market of 1928—and millions lost their money in October 1929, when it collapsed.

Black Thursday and Black Tuesday Although stock prices had fluctuated greatly for several weeks preceding the crash, the true panic did not begin until a Thursday in late October. On this Black Thursday—October 24, 1929—there was an unprecedented volume of selling on Wall Street, and stock prices plunged. The next day, hoping to stave off disaster by stabilizing prices, a group of bankers bought millions of dollars of stocks. The strategy worked for only one business day, Friday. The selling frenzy resumed on Monday. On **Black Tuesday**, October 29, the bottom fell out, as millions of panicky investors ordered their brokers to sell —but almost no buyers could be found.

Prices on Wall Street steadily decreased. By late November, the **Dow Jones index** had fallen from its September high of 381 to 198. Three years later, stock prices would finally hit bottom at 41, less than one-ninth of their peak value.

Underlying Causes of the Great Depression

While the collapse of the stock market in 1929 may have triggered economic turmoil, it alone was not responsible for the Great Depression. The depression throughout the nation and the world was the result of a combination of factors.

Uneven Distribution of Income Wages had risen little compared to the large increases in productivity and corporate profits. Economic success was not shared by all, as the top 5 percent of the richest Americans received over 33 percent of all income. Once demand for their products declined, businesses laid off workers, contributing to a downward spiral in demand and more layoffs.

Stock Market Speculation Many people in all economic classes believed that they could get rich by "playing the market." Instead of investing money in order to share in the earnings of a company, people were speculating that the price of a stock would go up and that they could sell it for a quick profit. **Buying on margin** allowed people to borrow most of the cost of the stock, making down payments as low as 10 percent. Investors depended on the price of the stock increasing so that they could repay the loan. When stock prices dropped, the market collapsed, and many lost everything they had borrowed and invested.

Excessive Use of Credit Low interest rates and a belief of both consumers and business that the economic boom was permanent led to increased borrowing and installment buying. This over-indebtedness would result in defaults on loans and bank failures.

Overproduction of Consumer Goods Business growth, aided by increased productivity and use of credit, had produced a volume of goods that workers with stagnant wages could not continue to purchase.

Weak Farm Economy The prosperity of the 1920s never reached farmers, who had suffered from overproduction, high debt, and low prices since the end of World War I. As the depression continued through the 1930s, severe weather and a long drought added to farmers' difficulties.

Government Policies During the 1920s, the government had complete faith in business and did little to control or regulate it. Congress enacted **high tariffs** that protected U.S. industries but hurt farmers and international trade.

Some economists have concentrated blame on the **Federal Reserve** for its tight money policies, as hundreds of banks failed. Instead of trying to stabilize banks, the money supply, and prices, the Federal Reserve tried to preserve the gold standard. Without depositors' insurance, people panicked and sought to get their money out of the banks, which caused more **bank failures.**

Global Economic Problems Nations had become more interdependent because of international banking, manufacturing, and trade. Europe had never recovered from World War I, but the United States failed to recognize Europe's postwar problems. Instead, U.S. insistence on loan repayment in full and high tariff policies weakened Europe and contributed to the worldwide depression.

Effects of the Great Depression

The pervasive impact of the Great Depression is evident in several statistics:

- The U.S. **gross national product**—the value of all the goods and services produced by the nation in one year—dropped from $104 billion to $56 billion in just four years (1929 to 1932).

- The nation's income declined by over 50 percent.

- Approximately 20 percent of all banks closed, wiping out 10 million savings accounts.

- The money supply contracted by 30 percent.

- By 1933, the number of unemployed had reached 13 million people, or 25 percent of the workforce, not including farmers.

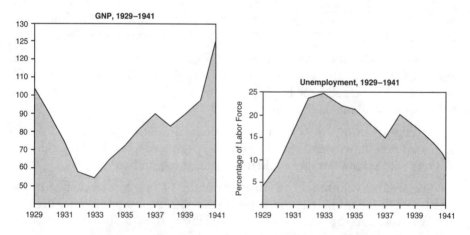

Source: U.S. Bureau of the Census. *Historical Statistics of the United States, Colonial Times to 1970*

Social Effects The social effects of the depression were felt by all classes. Those who had never fully shared in the prosperity of the 1920s, such as farmers and African Americans, had increased difficulties. **Poverty and homelessness** increased, as did the stress on families, as people searched for work. People continued to move from rural to urban areas, hoping that jobs would be more plentiful in cities. Mortgage foreclosures and evictions became commonplace. The homeless traveled in box cars and lived in shantytowns, named "Hoovervilles," in mock honor of their president.

President Hoover's Policies

At the time of the **stock market crash**, nobody could foresee how long the downward slide would last. President Hoover was wrong—but hardly alone—in thinking that prosperity would soon return. The president believed the nation could get through the difficult times if the people took his advice about exercising voluntary action and restraint. Hoover urged businesses not to cut wages, unions not to strike, and private charities to increase their efforts for the needy and the jobless. Until the summer of 1930, he hesitated to ask Congress for legislative action on the economy, afraid that government assistance to individuals would destroy their **self-reliance**.

Gradually, President Hoover came to recognize the need for more direct government action. However, he took the traditional view that public relief should come from state and local governments, not the federal government.

Responding to a Worldwide Depression

Repercussions from the crash on Wall Street were soon felt in the financial centers of Europe. Through trade and the Dawes Plan for the repayment of war debts, European prosperity was closely tied to that of the United States. Hoover's first major decision concerning the international situation was one of the worst mistakes of his presidency.

Hawley-Smoot Tariff (1930) In June 1930, the president signed into law a schedule of tariff rates that was the highest in history. The **Hawley-Smoot Tariff** (or Smoot-Hawley Tariff) passed by the Republican Congress set tax increases ranging from 31 percent to 49 percent on foreign imports. In retaliation for the U.S. tariff, European countries enacted higher tariffs of their own against U.S. goods. International trade was already declining because economic activity was slowing down in most countries, and the higher tariffs made the decline even sharper. Economies around the world sank further into depression.

Debt Moratorium By 1931, conditions became so bad both in Europe and the United States that the Dawes Plan for collecting war debts could no longer continue. Hoover therefore proposed a moratorium (suspension) on the payment of international debts. Britain and Germany readily accepted, but France balked. The international economy suffered from massive loan defaults, and banks on both sides of the Atlantic scrambled to meet the demands of the many depositors withdrawing their money.

Domestic Programs: Too Little, Too Late

By 1931, Hoover was convinced that some federal action was needed to pull the U.S. economy out of its doldrums. He therefore supported and signed into law programs that offered assistance to indebted farmers and struggling businesses.

Federal Farm Board The **Farm Board** was actually created in 1929, before the stock market crash, but its powers were later enlarged to meet the economic crisis. The board was authorized to help farmers stabilize prices by temporarily holding surplus grain and cotton in storage. The program, however, was far too modest to handle the continued overproduction of farm goods.

Reconstruction Finance Corporation (RFC) This federally funded, government-owned corporation was created by Congress early in 1932 as a measure for propping up faltering railroads, banks, life insurance companies, and other financial institutions. It marked an attempt by the federal government to become more active in financial markets. The president reasoned that emergency loans from the RFC would help to stabilize these key businesses. The benefits would then "trickle down" to smaller businesses and ultimately bring recovery. Democrats scoffed at this measure, saying it would help only the rich.

Despair and Protest

By 1932, millions of unemployed workers and impoverished farmers were bordering on desperation. Some decided to take direct action to battle the forces that seemed to be crushing them.

Unrest on the Farms In many communities, farmers banded together to stop banks from foreclosing on farms and evicting people from their homes. Farmers in the Midwest formed the Farm Holiday Association, which attempted to reverse the drop in prices by stopping the entire 1932 grain crop from reaching the market. The effort collapsed after some violence.

Bonus March Also in the desperate summer of 1932, a thousand unemployed World War I veterans marched to Washington, D.C., to demand immediate payment of the bonuses promised them at a later date (1945). They were eventually joined by thousands of other veterans who brought their wives and children and camped in improvised shacks near the Capitol. Congress failed to pass the bonus bill they sought. After two veterans were killed in a clash with police, General Douglas MacArthur, the army's chief of staff, used tanks and tear gas to destroy the shantytown and drive the veterans from Washington. The incident caused many Americans to regard Hoover as heartless and uncaring.

Changing Directions

In retrospect, the economic decline reached bottom in the winter of 1932–1933, although full recovery occurred only with the beginning of another world war, in 1939. The enduring crisis of the Great Depression had long-term influence on American thinking and policies. People accepted dramatic changes in policies and the expansion of the federal government. But in the short-term, it ended Republican domination of government. The growing discontent over the Depression and the Hoover administration resulted in a landslide victory for the Democrats in the presidential election of 1932. The confident and reassuring voice of the new president, Franklin D. Roosevelt, and the actions of the Democratic Congress helped to restore hope for the long march to recovery (Topic 7.10).

REFLECT ON THE LEARNING OBJECTIVE

1. Explain two causes of the Great Depression and two effects on the economy.

KEY TERMS BY THEME

Causes of the Depression (WXT)
Black Tuesday
Dow Jones index
buying on margin
uneven distribution of income
excessive use of credit
overproduction
high tariffs

Federal Reserve
stock market crash
Effects of the Depression (WXT)
business failures
unemployment
bank failures
gross national product
poverty and homelessness

Hoover Administration (PCE)
Herbert Hoover
self-reliance
Hawley-Smoot Tariff (1930)
debt moratorium
Farm Board
Reconstruction Finance Corporation
bonus march (1932)

MULTIPLE-CHOICE QUESTIONS

Questions 1–3 refer to the following excerpt.

"The farmers are being pauperized by the poverty of industrial populations and the industrial populations are being pauperized by the poverty of the farmers. Neither has the money to buy the product of the other, hence we have overproduction and under consumption at the same time and in the same country.

"I have not come here to stir you in a recital of the necessity for relief for our suffering fellow citizens. However, unless something is done for them and done soon, you will have a revolution on hand. . . .

"There is a feeling among the masses that something is radically wrong. . . . they say that this government is a conspiracy against the common people to enrich the already rich."

Oscar Ameringer, editor of the *Oklahoma Daily Leader,*
testimony to the House Committee on Labor, February, 1932

1. Which of the following statements most clearly supports the author's analysis?
   (A) The Dow Jones index fell from 381 in 1929 to 41 in 1932.
   (B) Bank assets fell from $72 billion in 1929 to $51 billion in 1932.
   (C) Farm income fell from $11.4 billion in 1929 to $6.3 billion in 1932.
   (D) Government spending rose from $3.2 billion in 1929 to $4.6 billion in 1932.

2. Which of the following was most directly related to the phrase in the testimony "the necessity for relief for our suffering fellow citizens"?
   (A) Twenty percent of the banks were closed.
   (B) The Dawes Plan was suspended.
   (C) The Federal Farm Board was created.
   (D) Twenty-five percent of the workforce was unemployed.

3. Which of the following actions would most clearly support the statement in the excerpt that "this government is a conspiracy against the common people to enrich the already rich"?
   (A) President Hoover's attempt to help workers by asking companies not to cut wages
   (B) The army's response to veterans living in shacks through its treatment of the Bonus Marchers
   (C) The Federal Farm Board's efforts to support farmers by stabilizing farm prices
   (D) The Dawes Plan to assist Germany in repaying its war debts

SHORT-ANSWER QUESTION

Use complete sentences; an outline or bulleted list alone is not acceptable.

1. Answer (a), (b), and (c).
   (a) Briefly explain ONE specific underlying cause of the Great Depression.
   (b) Briefly explain ONE specific effect of the Great Depression on U.S. banking.
   (c) Briefly explain ONE specific action or policy of the Hoover administration that contributed to the depth of the depression.

The New Deal

Let me assert my firm belief that the only thing we have to fear is fear itself—namely, unreasoning, unjustified terror which paralyses needed efforts to convert retreat into advance.

Franklin D. Roosevelt, First Inaugural Address, March 1933

Learning Objective: Explain how the Great Depression and the New Deal impacted American political, social, and economic life over time.

When the new Democratic president, Franklin D. Roosevelt, said in his 1933 inaugural address, "the only thing we have to fear is fear itself," he struck a note that the millions who listened to him on the radio could well understand. In 1933, after having experienced nearly four years of the worst economic depression in U.S. history, Americans were gripped by fear for their survival.

The Election of 1932

The depression's worst year, 1932, happened to be a presidential election year. The disheartened Republicans renominated Hoover, who warned that a Democratic victory would only result in worse economic problems.

Democrats At their convention, the Democrats nominated New York Governor **Franklin D. Roosevelt** for president and Speaker of the House John Nance Garner of Texas for vice president. As a candidate, Roosevelt pledged a "new deal" for the American people, the repeal of Prohibition, aid for the unemployed, and cuts in government spending.

Results In voters' minds, the only real issue was the depression, and whether Hoover or Roosevelt could do a better job of ending the hard times. Almost 60 percent of them concluded that it was time for a change. The Roosevelt-Garner ticket carried all but six states, Republican strongholds in the Northeast. Desperate for change, many Socialists deserted their candidate, Norman Thomas, to support Roosevelt. Not only was the new president a Democrat but both houses of Congress had large Democratic majorities.

Hoover as "Lame-Duck" President For the four months between Roosevelt's election and his inauguration in March 1933, Hoover was still president. However, he was a "lame duck," a person holding a position during the period when a successor had been elected but not yet taken office. Hoover was powerless to cope with the depression, which continued to get worse. He offered to work with the president-elect through the long period, but Roosevelt declined, not wanting to be tied to any of the Republican president's ideas. The 20th Amendment (known as the *lame-duck amendment*), passed in February 1933 and ratified by October 1933, shortened the period between presidential election and inauguration. The amendment set the start of each president's term for January 20.

Franklin D. Roosevelt as President

The new president was a distant cousin of President Theodore Roosevelt and was married to Theodore's niece, Eleanor. More than any other president, Franklin Delano Roosevelt—popularly known by his initials, FDR—expanded the size of the federal government, altered its scope of operations, and greatly enlarged presidential powers. He would dominate the nation and the government for an unprecedented stretch of time, 12 years and two months. FDR became one of the most influential world leaders of the 20th century.

FDR: The Man

Franklin Roosevelt was the only child of a wealthy New York family. He personally admired cousin Theodore and followed in his footsteps as a New York state legislator and then as U.S. assistant secretary of the navy. Unlike Republican Theodore, however, Franklin was a Democrat. In 1920, he was the Democratic nominee for vice president. He and James Cox, the presidential candidate, lost badly in Warren G. Harding's landslide victory.

Disability In the midst of a promising career, Roosevelt was paralyzed by polio in 1921. Although he was wealthy enough to retire, he labored instead to resume his career in politics and eventually regained the full power of his upper body, even though he could never again walk unaided and required the assistance of crutches, braces, and a wheelchair. Roosevelt's greatest strengths were his warm personality, his gifts as a speaker, and his ability to work with and inspire people. In 1928, campaigning from a car and in a wheelchair, FDR was elected governor of New York. In this office, he instituted a number of welfare and relief programs to help the jobless.

Eleanor Roosevelt Roosevelt's wife, Eleanor, emerged as a leader in her own right. She became the most active first lady in history, writing a newspaper column, giving speeches, and traveling the country. Though their personal relationship was strained, Eleanor and Franklin Roosevelt had a strong mutual respect. She served as the president's social conscience and influenced him to support minorities and the less fortunate.

The New Deal Philosophy

In his campaign for president in 1932, Roosevelt offered vague promises but no concrete programs. He did not have a detailed plan for ending the depression, but he was committed to action and willing to experiment with political solutions to economic problems.

The Three R's In his acceptance speech at the Democratic convention in 1932, Roosevelt had said: "I pledge you, I pledge myself, to a new deal for the American people." He had further promised in his campaign to help the "forgotten man at the bottom of the economic pyramid." During the early years of his presidency, it became clear that his **New Deal** programs were to serve **three R's**: *relief* for people out of work, *recovery* for business and the economy as a whole, and *reform* of American economic institutions.

Brain Trust and Other Advisers In giving shape to his New Deal, President Roosevelt relied on a group of advisers who had assisted him while he was governor of New York. Louis Howe was to be his chief political adviser. For advice on economic matters, Roosevelt turned to a group of university professors, known as the **Brain Trust**.

The people that Roosevelt appointed to high administrative positions were the most diverse in U.S. history to that time, with a record number of African Americans, Catholics, Jews, and women. For example, his secretary of labor was **Frances Perkins**, the first woman ever to serve in a president's cabinet.

The First Hundred Days

With the nation desperate and close to the brink of panic, the Democratic Congress looked to the new president for leadership, which Roosevelt was eager to provide. Immediately after being sworn into office on March 4, 1933, Roosevelt called Congress into a hundred-day-long special session. During this brief period, Congress passed into law every request of President Roosevelt, enacting more major legislation than any single Congress in history. Most of the new laws and agencies were commonly referred to by their initials: WPA, AAA, CCC, NRA.

Bank Holiday In early 1933, banks were failing at a frightening rate, as depositors flocked to withdraw funds. As many banks failed in 1933 (over 5,000) as had failed in all the previous years of the depression. To restore confidence in those banks that were still solvent, the president ordered the banks closed for a bank holiday on March 6, 1933. He went on the radio to explain that the banks would be reopened after allowing enough time for the government to reorganize them on a sound basis. Congress passed the Emergency Banking Act on March 9, and the banks reopened on March 13.

Repeal of Prohibition The new president kept a campaign promise to repeal Prohibition. He first had Congress pass the Beer-Wine Revenue Act, which legalized the sale of beer and wine, as a means of raising needed tax money. Later in 1933, the ratification of the 21st Amendment repealed the 18th Amendment, bringing Prohibition to an end.

Fireside Chats Roosevelt went on the radio on March 12, 1933, to present the first of many fireside chats to the American people. The president assured his listeners that the banks which reopened after the bank holiday were safe. The public responded as hoped, and the money deposited in the reopened banks exceeded the money withdrawn.

Relief for the Unemployed A number of programs created during the Hundred Days addressed the needs of the millions of unemployed workers. These plans created jobs with government stimulus dollars to provide both relief and to create more demand for goods and services. Roosevelt hoped that this would create more jobs in the private sector.

- The Federal Emergency Relief Administration (FERA) offered outright grants of federal money to states and local governments that were operating soup kitchens and other forms of relief for the jobless and homeless. The director of FERA was Harry Hopkins, one of the president's closest friends and advisers.

- The **Public Works Administration** (PWA), directed by Secretary of the Interior **Harold Ickes**, allotted money to state and local governments for building roads, bridges, dams, and other public works. Such construction projects were a source of thousands of jobs.

- The **Civilian Conservation Corps** (CCC) employed young men on projects on federal lands and paid their families small monthly sums.

- The **Tennessee Valley Authority** (TVA) was a huge experiment in regional development and public planning. As a government corporation, it hired thousands of people in one of the nation's poorest regions, the Tennessee Valley, to build dams, operate electric power plants, control flooding and erosion, and manufacture fertilizer. The TVA sold electricity to residents of the region at rates well below those previously charged by a private power company.

Financial Recovery and Reform Programs As the financial part of his New Deal, FDR persuaded Congress to enact the following measures:

- The **Emergency Banking Relief Act** authorized the government to examine the finances of banks closed during the bank holiday and reopen those judged to be sound.

- The **Glass-Steagall Act** increased regulation of the banks and limited how banks could invest customers' money.

- The **Federal Deposit Insurance Corporation** (FDIC) guaranteed individual bank deposits.

- The gold standard was restricted to international transactions, and Americans could no longer exchange their dollars for gold.

- The Home Owners Loan Corporation (HOLC) provided refinancing of small homes to prevent foreclosures.

- The Farm Credit Administration provided low-interest loans and mortgages to prevent foreclosures on the property of farmers.

Industrial Recovery Program The key measure in 1933 to combine immediate relief and long-term reform was the **National Recovery**

Administration (NRA). Directed by Hugh Johnson, the NRA was an attempt to guarantee reasonable profits for business and fair wages and hours for labor. With the antitrust laws temporarily suspended, the NRA could help each industry (such as steel, oil, and paper) set codes for wages, hours of work, levels of production, and prices of finished goods. The law creating the NRA also gave workers the right to organize and bargain collectively. The complex program operated with limited success for two years before the Supreme Court declared the NRA unconstitutional (*Schechter v. U.S.*) in 1935.

Farm Production Control Program Farmers were offered a program similar in concept to what the NRA did for industry. The Agricultural Adjustment Administration (AAA) encouraged farmers to reduce production (and thereby boost prices) by offering to pay government subsidies for every acre they plowed under. The AAA met the same fate as the NRA. It was declared unconstitutional in a 1935 Supreme Court decision.

Other Programs of the First New Deal

Congress adjourned briefly after its extraordinary legislative record in the first Hundred Days of the New Deal. Roosevelt, however, was not finished devising new remedies for the nation's ills. In late 1933 and through much of 1934, the Democratic Congress was easily persuaded to enact the following:

- The Civil Works Administration (CWA) was added to the PWA and other programs for creating jobs. This agency hired laborers for temporary construction projects sponsored by the federal government.

- The **Securities and Exchange Commission** (SEC) was created to regulate the stock market and to place strict limits on the kind of speculative practices that had led to the Wall Street crash in 1929. The SEC also required full audits of, and financial disclosure by, corporations to protect investors from fraud and insider trading.

- The **Federal Housing Administration** (FHA) gave both the building industry and homeowners a boost by insuring bank loans for building, repairing, and purchasing houses. It provided many families their first chance to buy a home and build wealth that they could pass on to their children. However, the FHA used "redlining" to define neighborhoods where African Americans lived, and did not make loans in those areas. Nearly all FHA loans made during the first thirty years of the program went to White applicants.

- A new law took the United States off the gold standard in an effort to halt deflation (falling prices). The value of the dollar was set at $35 per ounce of gold, but paper dollars were no longer redeemable in gold.

The Second New Deal

Roosevelt's first two years in office were largely focused on achieving one of the three R's: recovery. Democratic victories in the congressional elections of 1934 gave the president the popular mandate he needed to seek another round of laws and programs. In the summer of 1935, he launched the second New Deal, which concentrated on the other two R's: relief and reform. **Harry Hopkins** became even more prominent in Roosevelt's administration with the creation in 1935 of a new and larger relief agency.

Works Progress Administration (WPA) Much bigger than the relief agencies of the first New Deal, the WPA spent billions of dollars between 1935 and 1940 to provide people with jobs. After its first year of operation under Hopkins, it employed 3.4 million men and women who had formerly been on the relief rolls of state and local governments. It paid them double the relief rate but less than the going wage for regular workers. Most WPA workers were put to work constructing new bridges, roads, airports, and public buildings. Unemployed artists, writers, actors, and photographers were paid by the WPA to paint murals, write histories, and perform in plays.

One part of the WPA, the National Youth Administration (NYA), provided part-time jobs to help young people stay in high school and college or until they could get a job with a private employer.

Resettlement Administration (RA) Placed under the direction of one of the Brain Trust, Rexford Tugwell, the Resettlement Administration provided loans to sharecroppers, tenants, and small farmers. It also established federal camps where migrant workers could find decent housing.

Source: Carl Morris, Eugene, Oregon, Post Office, c. 1939, WPA Federal Arts Project. Oregon Scenic County Images

Reforms The reform legislation of the second New Deal reflected Roosevelt's belief that industrial workers and farmers needed to receive more government help than members of the business and privileged classes.

National Labor Relations (Wagner) Act (1935) This major labor law of 1935 replaced the labor provisions of the National Industrial Recovery Act, after that law was declared unconstitutional. The Wagner Act guaranteed a worker's right to join a union and a union's right to bargain collectively. It also outlawed business practices that were unfair to labor. A new agency, the National Labor Relations Board (NLRB), was empowered to enforce the law and make sure that workers' rights were protected.

Rural Electrification Administration (REA) This new agency provided loans for electrical cooperatives to supply power in rural areas.

Federal Taxes A revenue act of 1935 sharply increased the tax on incomes of the wealthy few. It also increased the tax on large gifts from parent to child and on capital gains (profits from the sale of stocks or other properties).

The Social Security Act

The reform that, for generations afterward, would affect the lives of nearly all Americans was the passage in 1935 of the **Social Security Act**. It created a federal insurance program based upon the automatic collection of payments from employees and employers throughout people's working careers. The Social Security trust fund would then be used to make monthly payments to retired persons over the age of 65. Also receiving benefits under this law were workers who lost their jobs (unemployment compensation), persons who were blind or otherwise disabled, and dependent children and their mothers.

Evaluating Roosevelt's First Term

In response to public demands for government action, the New Deal transformed the role of the federal government. Since the days of Alexander Hamilton, and under presidents as different as Abraham Lincoln and Woodrow Wilson, the federal government often intervened in the economy to promote growth. In addition, though, the government under Roosevelt created a **limited welfare state**, a government that regulated economic activity and aided the poor and unemployed in order to provide economic security for everyone. This view of government became the basis for **modern American liberalism.**

The Election of 1936

The economy was improving but was still weak and unstable in 1936 when the Democrats nominated Roosevelt for a second term. Because of his New Deal programs and active style of personal leadership, the president had become enormously popular among workers and small farmers. Business, however, generally disliked and even hated him because of his regulatory programs and pro-union measures such as the Wagner Act.

Alf Landon Challenging Roosevelt was the Republican nominee for president, Alfred (Alf) Landon, the progressive-minded governor of Kansas. Landon criticized the Democrats for spending too much money but in general accepted most of the New Deal legislation.

Political Realignment and the New Deal Coalition Roosevelt swamped Landon, winning every state except Maine and Vermont and more than 60 percent of the popular vote. Behind their president's New Deal, the Democratic Party could now count on the votes of a new coalition of popular support. Through the 1930s and into the 1960s, the Democratic or New Deal coalition would consist of the Solid South, White ethnic groups in the cities, Midwestern farmers, labor unions, and liberals. In addition, new support for the Democrats came from African Americans, mainly in northern cities, who left the Republican Party of Lincoln because of Roosevelt's New Deal.

Opponents of the New Deal

Opinion polls and election results showed that a large majority of Americans supported Roosevelt. Nevertheless, his New Deal programs were extremely controversial and became the target of vitriolic attacks by liberals, conservatives, and demagogues.

Critics from the Left Socialists, some unions, and more liberal members of the Democratic Party criticized the New Deal (especially the first New Deal of 1933–1934) for doing too much for business and too little for the unemployed and the working poor. They charged that the president failed to address the problems of ethnic minorities, women, and the elderly. The more radical of these critics charged that the New Deal was a way to save capitalism from a revolution. Roosevelt agreed with this view, although he did not consider it a criticism. He wanted to reform the system, not replace it.

Critics from the Right More numerous were conservatives in Congress and on the Supreme Court. Many Republicans and some Democrats attacked the New Deal for giving the federal government too much power. These critics charged that relief programs such as the WPA and labor laws such as the Wagner Act bordered on socialism or even communism. Business leaders were alarmed by (1) increased regulations, (2) the second New Deal's pro-union stance, and (3) the financing of government programs by means of borrowed money—a practice known as *deficit financing*.

Conservative Democrats, including former presidential candidates Alfred E. (Al) Smith and John W. Davis, joined with leading Republicans in 1934 to form an anti-New Deal organization called the American Liberty League. Its avowed purpose was to stop the New Deal from "subverting" the U.S. economic and political system.

Demagogues

Several critics played upon the American people's desperate need for immediate solutions to their problems. Using the radio to reach a mass audience, they proposed simplistic schemes for ending "evil conspiracies" (Father Coughlin), guaranteeing economic security for the elderly (Dr. Townsend), and redistributing wealth (Huey Long).

Father Charles E. Coughlin This Catholic priest attracted a huge popular following in the early 1930s through his weekly radio broadcasts. Father Coughlin founded the National Union for Social Justice, which called for issuing an inflated currency and nationalizing all banks. His attacks on the New Deal became increasingly anti-Semitic and fascist until his superiors in the Catholic Church ordered him to stop his broadcasts.

Dr. Francis E. Townsend Before the passage of the Social Security Act, a retired physician from Long Beach, California, became an instant hero to millions of senior citizens by proposing a simple plan for guaranteeing a secure income. Dr. Francis E. Townsend proposed that a 2 percent federal sales tax be used to create a special fund, from which every retired person over 60 years old would receive $200 a month. By spending their money promptly, Townsend argued, recipients would stimulate the economy and soon bring the depression to an end. The popularity of the Townsend Plan persuaded Roosevelt to substitute a more moderate plan of his own, which became the Social Security system.

Huey Long From Roosevelt's point of view, the most dangerous of the depression demagogues was the "Kingfish" from Louisiana, Senator Huey Long. Immensely popular in his own state, Long became a prominent national figure by proposing a "Share Our Wealth" program that promised a minimum annual income of $5,000 for every American family, to be paid for by taxing the wealthy. In 1935, Huey Long challenged Roosevelt's leadership of the Democratic Party by announcing his candidacy for president. Both his candidacy and his populist appeal were abruptly ended when he was assassinated by a local political rival.

The Supreme Court

Of all the challenges to Roosevelt's leadership in his first term in office, the conservative decisions of the U.S. **Supreme Court** proved the most frustrating. In two cases in 1935, the Supreme Court effectively killed both the NRA for business recovery and the AAA for agricultural recovery by deciding that the laws creating them were unconstitutional. Roosevelt interpreted his landslide reelection in 1936 as a mandate to end the obstacles posed by the Court.

Court Reorganization Plan President Roosevelt did not have an opportunity to appoint any justices to the Supreme Court during his first term. He hoped to remove the Court as an obstacle to the New Deal by proposing a judicial-reorganization bill in 1937. It proposed that the president be authorized to appoint to the Supreme Court an additional justice for each current justice who was older than a certain age (70 ½ years). In effect, the bill would have allowed Roosevelt to add up to six more justices to the Court—all of them presumably of liberal persuasion. Critics called it a "Court-packing" bill.

Reaction Republicans and many Democrats were outraged by what they saw as an attempt to tamper with the system of checks and balances. They accused the president of wanting to give himself the powers of a dictator. Roosevelt did not back down—and neither did the congressional opposition. For the first time in Roosevelt's presidency, a major bill that he proposed went down to decisive defeat by a defiant Congress. Even a majority of Democratic senators refused to support him on this controversial measure.

Aftermath Ironically, while Roosevelt was fighting to "pack" the Court, the justices were already backing off their former resistance to his program. In 1937, the Supreme Court upheld the constitutionality of several major New Deal laws, including the Wagner (Labor) Act and the Social Security Act. Also, as it happened, several justices retired during Roosevelt's second term, enabling him to appoint new justices who were more sympathetic to his reforms.

Labor Unions and Workers' Rights

Two New Deal measures—the National Industrial Recovery Act of 1933 and the Wagner Act of 1935—caused a lasting change in labor-management relations by legalizing labor unions. Union membership, which had slumped badly under the hostile policies of the 1920s, shot upward. It went from less than 3 million in the early 1930s to over 10 million (more than one out of four nonfarm workers) by 1941.

Formation of the CIO. As unions grew in size, so did tensions among them. The many different unions that made up the American Federation of Labor (AFL) were dominated by skilled White male workers and were organized according to crafts. A group of unions within the AFL wanted union membership to be extended to all workers in an industry regardless of their race and sex, including those who were unskilled. In 1935, the industrial unions, as they were called, joined together as the Committee of Industrial Organizations (CIO). Their leader was **John L. Lewis**, president of the United Mine Workers union. In 1936, the AFL suspended the CIO unions. Renamed the *Congress* **of Industrial Organizations**, the CIO. broke away from the AFL and became its chief rival. It concentrated on organizing unskilled workers in the automobile, steel, and southern textile industries.

Automobile Strikes Even though collective bargaining was now protected by federal law, many companies still resisted union demands. Strikes were therefore a frequent occurrence in the depression decade. At the huge General Motors plant in Flint, Michigan, in 1937, the workers insisted on their right to join a union by participating in a **sit-down strike** (literally sitting down at the assembly line and refusing to work or even leave the factory). Neither the president nor Michigan's governor agreed to the company's request to intervene with troops. Finally, the company yielded to striker demands by recognizing the United Auto Workers union (UAW). Union organizers at the Ford plant in Michigan, however, were beaten and driven away.

Steel Strikes In the steel industry, the giant U.S. Steel Corporation voluntarily recognized one of the CIO unions, but smaller companies resisted. On Memorial Day, 1937, a demonstration by union picketers at Republic Steel in Chicago ended in four deaths, as the police fired into the crowd. However, eventually almost all the smaller steel companies agreed to deal with the CIO by 1941.

During the sit-down strike in Flint, workers remained in the factory so they could not be replced by strike-breakers.
Source: Library of Congress.

Fair Labor Standards Act

A final political victory for organized labor in the 1930s was also the last major reform of the New Deal. In 1938, Congress enacted the **Fair Labor Standards Act**, which established several regulations on businesses in interstate commerce:

- A **minimum wage**, initially fixed at 40 cents an hour
- A maximum standard workweek of 40 hours, with extra pay ("time-and-a-half") for overtime
- Child labor restrictions on hiring people under 16 years old

Previously, the Supreme Court had declared unconstitutional a 1916 law prohibiting child labor. However, in the 1941 case of *United States v. Darby Lumber Co.*, the Supreme Court reversed its earlier ruling, upholding the child labor provisions of the Fair Labor Standards Act. Passage of this act was not only the last but also the only major reform of Roosevelt's second term. The New Deal lost momentum in the late 1930s for both economic and political reasons.

Recession, 1937–1938

From 1933 to 1937 (Roosevelt's first term), the economy showed signs of gradually pulling out of its nosedive. Banks were stabilizing, business earnings were increasing, and unemployment, though still high at 15 percent, had declined from the 25 percent figure in 1933. In the winter of 1937, however, the economy once again had a backward slide and entered into a recessionary period.

Causes Government policy was at least partly to blame. The new Social Security tax reduced consumer spending at the same time that Roosevelt was curtailing expenditures for relief and public works. In reducing spending for relief, the president hoped to balance the budget and reduce the national debt.

Keynesian Economics The writings of the British economist **John Maynard Keynes** taught Roosevelt that he had made a mistake in attempting to balance the budget. According to Keynesian theory, deficit spending was helpful in difficult times because the government needed to spend well above its tax revenues in order to initiate economic growth. Deficit spending "primed the pump" to increase investment and create jobs. Roosevelt's economic advisers adopted this theory in 1938 with positive results. As federal spending on public works and relief went up, so too did employment and industrial production.

Weakened New Deal Although the economy improved, there was no boom, and problems remained. After the Court-packing fight of 1937, the people and Congress no longer automatically followed FDR, and the 1938 elections brought a reduced Democratic majority in Congress. A **coalition** of Republicans and conservative Democrats blocked further New Deal reform legislation. Also, beginning in 1938, fears about the aggressive acts of Nazi Germany diverted attention from domestic concerns toward foreign affairs.

Life During the Depression

Millions of people who lived through the Great Depression and the hard times of the 1930s never got over it. They developed a **"depression mentality"**—an attitude of insecurity and economic concern that would always remain, even in times of prosperity.

Dust Bowl Farmers As if farmers did not already have enough problems, a severe **drought** in the early 1930s ruined crops in the Great Plains. This region became a **dust bowl**, as poor farming practices coupled with high winds blew away millions of tons of dried topsoil. With their farms turned to dust, and their health often compromised, thousands of **"Okies"** from Oklahoma and surrounding states migrated westward to California in search of farm or factory work that often could not be found. The novelist **John Steinbeck** wrote about their hardships in his classic study of economic heartbreak, *The Grapes of Wrath* (1939).

In response to one of the worst ecological disasters in American history, the federal government created the Soil Conservation Service in 1935. It taught the plains farmers who remained on their land to rotate crops, terrace fields, use contour plowing, and plant trees to stop soil erosion and conserve water. With the help of federal subsidies, the region recovered, but environmental issues remained.

Women The Great Depression increased pressures on many families in which an unemployed father searched for work while the mother struggled to feed and clothe the children on a reduced income. To supplement the family income, more women sought work, and their percentage of the total labor force increased. Critics accused women of taking jobs from men. However, women did not get factory jobs, and most men did not seek the types of jobs available to women. Even with Eleanor Roosevelt championing women's equality, many New Deal programs allowed women to receive lower pay than men.

African Americans Racial discrimination continued in the 1930s with devastating effects on African Americans, who were the last hired, first fired. Their unemployment rate was higher than the national average. Black sharecroppers were forced off the land in the South because of cutbacks in farm production. Often, despite their extreme poverty, jobless African Americans were excluded from state and local relief programs. Hard times increased racial tensions, particularly in the South where lynchings continued, though less frequently than in the 1890s. Civil rights leaders could get little support from President Roosevelt, who feared the loss of White southern Democratic votes.

Some New Deal programs, such as the WPA and the CCC did provide low-paying jobs for African Americans, though these jobs were often segregated. African Americans also received moral support from Eleanor Roosevelt and Secretary of the Interior Harold Ickes in a famous incident in 1939. The distinguished African American singer **Marian Anderson** had been refused the use of Constitution Hall in Washington, D.C., by the all-White Daughters of the American Revolution. Eleanor Roosevelt and Ickes promptly arranged for Anderson to give a special concert at the Lincoln Memorial.

Over one hundred African Americans were appointed to middle-level positions in federal departments by President Roosevelt. One of them, **Mary McLeod Bethune**, had been a longtime leader of efforts for improving education and economic opportunities for women. Invited to Washington to direct a division of the National Youth Administration, she established the Federal Council on Negro Affairs for the purpose of increasing African American involvement in the New Deal.

An executive order in 1941 set up a **Fair Employment Practices Committee** to assist minorities in gaining jobs in defense industries. President Roosevelt took this action only after **A. Philip Randolph**, head of the Railroad Porters Union, threatened a march on Washington to demand equal job opportunities for African Americans.

American Indians John Collier, a long-time advocate of American Indian rights, was appointed commissioner of the Bureau of Indian Affairs in 1933. He established conservation and CCC projects on reservations and gained American Indian involvement in the WPA and other New Deal programs.

In 1934, the **Indian Reorganization (Wheeler-Howard) Act** dramatically changed federal policies toward Native Americans. Congress first repealed the Dawes Act of 1887, which had encouraged American Indians to be independent farmers, and replaced it with a new act that returned former reservation lands to the control of tribes. The act also encouraged tribal organization and supported preservation of Native American cultures. Despite this major reform, critics later accused the New Deal of being paternalistic and withholding control from American Indians.

Mexican Americans In California and the Southwest, Mexican Americans had been an important source of agricultural labor in the 1920s. In response to difficult working conditions, many attempted to form unions to improve their situation. However, during the depression, high unemployment and drought in the Plains and the Midwest caused a dramatic growth in White migrant workers who pushed west in search of work. These White migrants made it easy for growers to replace their Mexican American workers.

In addition, President Hoover's administration, with the strong support of state and local governments, increased border patrols and began mass deportations of Mexican Americans. These repatriation efforts reflected the desire of many Americans for jobs to go to White workers, a sign of the long-standing prejudice against people of Mexican ancestry. The government forced at least 400,000 people, including many naturalized and native-born U.S. citizens, to move to Mexico in the 1930s

REFLECT ON THE LEARNING OBJECTIVE

1. Explain two effects that the New Deal had on each area of American life: politics, the economy, and society.

KEY TERMS BY THEME

Roosevelt Administration (PCE)
Franklin D. Roosevelt
Eleanor Roosevelt
New Deal
three R's (relief, recovery, reform)
Brain Trust
Frances Perkins
Hundred Days
bank holiday
repeal of Prohibition
fireside chats
Public Works Administration
Harold Ickes
Civilian Conservation Corps
Tennessee Valley Authority
Emergency Banking Relief Act
Glass-Steagall Act
Federal Deposit Insurance Corporation

National Recovery Administration
Schechter v. U.S.
Securities and Exchange Commission
Federal Housing Administration
Second New Deal (PCE)
Harry Hopkins
Works Progress Administration
National Labor Relations (Wagner) Act (1935)
Social Security Act (1935)
limited welfare state
modern American liberalism
election of 1936
New Deal coalition
recession, 1937–1938
John Maynard Keynes
New Deal Opponents (PCE)
Father Charles E. Coughlin
Francis E. Townsend

Huey Long
Supreme Court reorganization plan
Rise of Unions (WXT)
John L. Lewis
Congress of Industrial Organizations
sit-down strike
Fair Labor Standards Act
minimum wage
Impact on Americans (MIG)
"depression mentality"
drought
dust bowl
"Okies"
John Steinbeck, *The Grapes of Wrath*
Marian Anderson
Mary McLeod Bethune
Fair Employment Practices Committee
A. Philip Randolph
Indian Reorganization (Wheeler-Howard) Act

Questions 1–3 refer to the following excerpt.

"Illumined by the stern-lantern of history, the New Deal can be seen to have left in place a set of institutional arrangement that constituted a more coherent pattern than is dreamt of in many philosophies. That pattern can be summarized in a single word: security—security for vulnerable individuals, to be sure, as Roosevelt famously urged in his campaign for the Social Security Act of 1935, but security for capitalists and consumers, for workers and builders as well. Job-security, life-cycle security, financial security, market security—however it might be defined, achieving security was the leitmotif of virtually everything the New Deal attempted."

David M. Kennedy, historian, *Freedom From Fear,* 1999

1. Which of the following groups would most likely oppose the philosophy of the New Deal as explained in this excerpt?

    (A) Economists who wanted unregulated markets and balanced budgets

    (B) Social scientists who wanted to use data to support a public policy

    (C) Critics who wanted the New Deal to go farther to address poverty and inequality

    (D) Consumers who wanted greater confidence in the banking system and the stock markets

2. Which of the following New Deal policies most directly addressed "security for capitalists"?

    (A) Employment of young men in conservation jobs on federal lands

    (B) Allocation of federal funds for construction projects that pumped money into the economy

    (C) Regulation to curtail fraud in investment banking and the stock markets

    (D) Collection of funds to help people who were retired, unemployed, or hurt on the job

3. Which of the following New Deal policies most clearly addressed "job security" for workers?

    (A) Creation of an agency to insure loans for building, repairing, and purchasing houses

    (B) Passage of laws to guarantee worker rights to collective bargaining

    (C) Regulation of banks to limit how they could invest money

    (D) Declaration by Roosevelt of a "bank holiday" to allow for examination of banks' records

SHORT-ANSWER QUESTIONS

1. "When the New Deal was over, capitalism remained intact. The rich still controlled the nation's wealth, as well as its laws, courts, police, newspapers, churches, colleges. Enough help had been given to enough people to make Roosevelt a hero to millions, but the same system that had brought depression and crisis—the system of waste, of inequality, of concern for profit over human need—remained."

   Howard Zinn, *A People's History of the United States,* 1999

   "Most of Roosevelt's solutions did little. The public hoopla of 'job programs' barely dented unemployment numbers, which still stood at 12.5 percent in 1939, or ten times what they had been under Coolidge. . . . Did FDR do anything right? Yes. By taking the United States off the gold standard, he saved what was left of the banking system. But as they say, even a blind squirrel finds a nut once in a while."

   Larry Schweikart, *48 Liberal Lies about American History,* 2008

   Using the excerpts, answer (a), (b), and (c).

   (a) Briefly describe ONE major difference between Zinn's and Schweikart's historical interpretation about the effectiveness of Franklin Roosevelt and the New Deal.

   (b) Briefly explain how ONE specific historical event or development that is not explicitly mentioned in the excerpts could be used to support Zinn's interpretation.

   (c) Briefly explain how ONE specific historical event or development that is not explicitly mentioned in the excerpts could be used to support Schweikart's interpretation.

2. Answer (a), (b), and (c).

   (a) Briefly explain ONE specific program from the New Deal and its impact on working-class Americans.

   (b) Briefly explain ONE specific way the New Deal caused a long-term realignment in U.S. politics.

   (c) Briefly explain ONE specific political challenge to the New Deal or Franklin Roosevelt.

Topic 7.11

Interwar Foreign Policy

Only one thing holds this country from war today; that is the rising opposition of the American people. Our system of democracy . . . is on test today as it has been never before.

Charles Lindbergh, Des Moines, Iowa, September 1, 1941

Learning Objective: Explain the similarities and differences in attitudes about the nation's proper role in the world.

During the 1920s and 1930s, widespread disillusionment with World War I, Europe's postwar problems, and communism in the Soviet Union (as Russia was renamed) made Americans fearful of being pulled into another European conflict. Hence, Congress refused to join the League of Nations, marking a retreat into a type of isolationism. However, the country did not return to the policies of the Gilded Age. Instead, the United States followed a policy of unilateralism, in which the United States often acted on its own through military interventions, private investment overseas, and occasionally signing a treaty. Ultimately, though, the efforts to remain out of another world war failed.

Post-World War I Agreements

The Republican presidents of the 1920s tried to promote peace and also scale back expenditures on defense by arranging treaties of **disarmament**. The most successful disarmament conference—and the greatest achievement of Harding's presidency—was held in Washington, D.C., in 1921.

Washington Conference (1921) Secretary of State Charles Evans Hughes initiated talks on naval disarmament, hoping to stabilize the size of the U.S. Navy relative to that of other powers and to resolve conflicts in the Pacific. Representatives to the **Washington Conference** came from Belgium, China, France, Great Britain, Italy, Japan, the Netherlands, and Portugal. Three agreements to relieve tensions resulted from the discussions:

- **Five-Power Treaty** Nations with the five largest navies agreed to maintain the following ratio with respect to their largest warships, or battleships: the United States, 5; Great Britain, 5; Japan, 3; France, 1.67; Italy, 1.67. Britain and the United States also agreed not to fortify their possessions in the Pacific, while no limit was placed on the Japanese.

- **Four-Power Treaty** The United States, France, Great Britain, and Japan agreed to respect one another's territory in the Pacific.

- **Nine-Power Treaty** All nine nations represented at the conference agreed to respect the Open Door policy by guaranteeing the territorial integrity of China.

Kellogg-Briand Pact American women took the lead in a peace movement committed to outlawing future wars. (For her efforts on behalf of peace, Jane Addams won the Nobel Peace Prize in 1931.) The movement achieved its greatest success in 1928 with the signing of a treaty arranged by U.S. Secretary of State Frank Kellogg and French Foreign Minister Aristide Briand. Almost all the nations of the world signed the **Kellogg-Briand Pact**, which renounced the aggressive use of force to achieve national ends. This international agreement would prove ineffective, however, since it (1) permitted defensive wars and (2) failed to provide for taking action against violators of the agreement.

Business and Diplomacy

Republican presidents believed that pro-business policies brought prosperity at home and at the same time strengthened U.S. dealings with other nations. Thus, they found it natural to use diplomacy to advance American business interests in Latin America and other regions.

Latin America Mexico's constitution of 1917 mandated government ownership of all that nation's mineral and oil resources. U.S. investors in Mexico feared that the government might confiscate their properties. A peaceful resolution protecting their interests was negotiated by Coolidge's ambassador to Mexico, Dwight Morrow, in 1927.

Elsewhere in Latin America, Coolidge kept U.S. troops in Nicaragua and Haiti but withdrew them from the Dominican Republic in 1924. While American military influence declined, American economic impact increased. U.S. investments in Latin America doubled between 1919 and 1929.

Middle East The oil reserves in the Middle East were becoming recognized as a major source of potential wealth. British oil companies had a large head start in the region, but Secretary of State Hughes succeeded in winning oil-drilling rights for U.S. companies.

Tariffs Passed by Congress in 1922, the Fordney-McCumber Tariff increased the duties on foreign manufactured goods by 25 percent. It was protective of U.S. business interests in the short run but destructive in the long run. Because of it, European nations were slow to recover from the war and had difficulty repaying their **war debts** to the United States. They responded to the high U.S. tariffs by imposing tariffs of their own on American imports. Ultimately, these obstacles to international trade weakened the world economy and were one reason for the Great Depression of the 1930s.

War Debts and Reparations

Before World War I, the United States had been a debtor nation, importing more than it exported. It emerged from the war as a creditor nation, having lent more than $10 billion to the Allies. Harding and Coolidge insisted that Britain and France pay back every penny of their war debts. The British and French objected. They pointed out that they suffered much worse losses than the Americans during the war, that the borrowed money had been spent in the United States, and that high U.S. tariffs made it more difficult to pay the debts. To be sure, the Treaty of Versailles required Germany to pay $30 billion in **reparations** to the Allies. But how were Britain and France to collect this money? Germany was bankrupt, had soaring inflation, and was near anarchy.

Dawes Plan Charles Dawes, an American banker who would become Coolidge's vice president, negotiated a compromise that was accepted by all sides in 1924. The **Dawes Plan** established a cycle of payments flowing from the United States to Germany and from Germany to the Allies. U.S. banks would lend Germany huge sums to rebuild its economy and pay reparations to Britain and France. In turn, Britain and France would use the reparations money to pay their war debts to the United States. This cycle helped to ease financial problems on both sides of the Atlantic. After the stock market crash of 1929, however, U.S. bank loans stopped and the prosperity propped up by the Dawes Plan collapsed.

Legacy Ultimately, Finland was the only nation to repay its war debts in full. The unpaid debts of the other nations left bad feelings on all sides. Many Europeans resented what they saw as American greed, while Americans saw new reasons to follow an isolationist path in the 1930s.

Herbert Hoover's Foreign Policy

Hoover concurred with the prevailing opinion of the American people that the United States should not enter into firm commitments to preserve the security of other nations. Such an opinion, in the 1930s, would be labeled "isolationism."

Latin America Hoover actively pursued friendly relations with the countries of Latin America. In 1929, even before being inaugurated, the president-elect went on a goodwill tour of the region. As president, he ended the interventionist policies of Taft and Wilson by (1) arranging for U.S. troops to leave Nicaragua by 1933 and (2) negotiating a treaty with Haiti to remove all U.S. troops by 1934.

Japanese Aggression in Manchuria In the early 1930s, Japan posed the greatest threat to world peace. Defying both the Open Door policy and the covenant of the League of Nations, Japanese troops marched into Manchuria, a region of northeastern China, in September 1931. They renamed the territory Manchukuo and established a puppet government. This was part of a series of conflicts between Japan and China that began in the late 1800s.

Despite its commitment to resist blatant aggression, the League of Nations did nothing except to pass a resolution condemning Japan for invading Manchuria. The Japanese delegation then walked out of the League, never to return. In the Manchuria crisis, the League showed it was too weak to maintain peace. Its warnings would never be taken seriously by potential aggressors.

Stimson Doctrine U.S. response to Japan's violation of the Open Door policy was somewhat stronger than the League's response—but no more effective in deterring further aggression. Secretary of State Henry Stimson declared in 1932 that the United States would honor its treaty obligations under the Nine-Power Treaty (1922) by refusing to recognize the legitimacy of any regime like "Manchukuo" that had been established by force. The League of Nations readily endorsed the Stimson Doctrine and issued a similar declaration.

JAPANESE AGGRESSION IN ASIA IN THE 1930s

Franklin Roosevelt's Policies, 1933–1939

In his first term, Roosevelt concentrated on the economic crisis at home and gave little thought to foreign policy. He did, however, extend Hoover's efforts to improve U.S.-Latin America relations by initiating a good-neighbor policy.

Good-Neighbor Policy

In his first inaugural address in 1933, Roosevelt promised a "policy of the good neighbor" toward other nations of the Western Hemisphere. First, interventionism in support of dollar diplomacy no longer made economic sense, because U.S. businesses during the depression lacked the resources to invest in foreign operations. Second, the rise of militarist regimes in Germany and Italy prompted Roosevelt to seek Latin America's cooperation in defending the region from potential danger.

Pan-American Conferences At Roosevelt's direction, the U.S. delegation at the Seventh Pan-American Conference in Montevideo, Uruguay, in 1933, pledged never again to intervene in the internal affairs of a Latin American country. In effect, Franklin Roosevelt repudiated the policy of his older cousin, Theodore, who had justified intervention as a corollary to the Monroe Doctrine. Another Pan-American conference was held in Buenos Aires, Argentina, in 1936. Roosevelt himself attended the conference. He personally pledged to submit future disputes to arbitration and warned that if a European power such as Germany attempted "to commit acts of aggression against us," it would find "a hemisphere wholly prepared to consult together for our mutual safety and our mutual good."

Cuba Cubans had long resented the Platt Amendment, which had made their country's foreign policy subject to U.S. approval. In 1934, President Roosevelt persuaded Congress to nullify the Platt Amendment, retaining only the U.S. right to keep its naval base at Guantanamo Bay.

Mexico In 1938, Mexico tested U.S. patience and commitment to the good-neighbor policy when its president, Lázaro Cárdenas, seized oil properties owned by U.S. corporations. Roosevelt rejected corporate demands to intervene and encouraged American companies to negotiate a settlement.

Depression Diplomacy

Helping the U.S. economy was the chief motivation for Roosevelt's policies toward other foreign policy issues in his first term.

Recognition of the Soviet Union The Republican presidents of the 1920s had refused to grant diplomatic recognition to the Communist regime that ruled the Soviet Union. Roosevelt promptly changed this policy by granting recognition in 1933. His reason for doing so, he said, was to increase U.S. trade and thereby boost the economy.

Philippines Governing the Philippines cost money. As an economic measure, Roosevelt persuaded Congress to pass the Tydings-McDuffie Act in

1934, which provided for the **independence of the Philippines** by 1946 and the gradual removal of U.S. military presence from the islands.

Reciprocal Trade Agreements Acting in the tradition of Progressive Democrats such as William Jennings Bryan and Woodrow Wilson, President Roosevelt favored lower tariffs as a means of increasing international trade. In 1934, Congress enacted a plan suggested by Secretary of State Cordell Hull that gave the president power to reduce U.S. tariffs up to 50 percent for nations that reciprocated with comparable reductions for U.S. imports.

The Rise of Fascism and Militarism

The worldwide depression soon proved to have alarming repercussions for world politics. Combined with nationalist resentments after World War I, economic hardships gave rise to dictatorships in Italy in the 1920s and Japan and Germany in the 1930s. Eventually, in 1940, Japan, Italy, and Germany signed a treaty of alliance. Together, they became known as the **Axis powers**.

Italy A new regime seized power in Italy in 1922. **Benito Mussolini** led Italy's **Fascist Party**, which attracted dissatisfied war veterans, nationalists, and those afraid of rising communism. Dressed in black shirts, the Fascists marched on Rome and installed Mussolini in power as "Il Duce" (the Leader). **Fascism**—the idea that people should glorify their nation and their race through aggressive shows of force—became the dominant ideology in European dictatorships in the 1930s.

Germany The **Nazi Party** was the German equivalent of Italy's Fascist Party. It arose in the 1920s in reaction to deplorable economic conditions after the war and national resentments over the Treaty of Versailles. The Nazi leader, **Adolf Hitler,** used bullying tactics against Jews as well as Fascist ideology to increase his popularity with disgruntled, unemployed German workers. Hitler seized the opportunity presented by the depression to play upon anti-Semitic hatreds. With his personal army of "brown shirts," Hitler gained control of the German legislature in early 1933.

Japan Nationalists and militarists in Japan increased their power in the 1920s and 1930s. As economic conditions worsened, they persuaded Japan's nominal ruler, the emperor, that the country needed to invade China and Southeast Asia to seize raw materials (oil, tin, and iron). Doing so would give Japan control over what their leaders called the Greater East Asia Co-Prosperity Sphere. Full-scale war erupted when Japan invaded China on July 7, 1937. In this conflict, called the Second Sino-Japanese War, the Japanese committed atrocities included the Nanjing Massacre in 1937, in which they killed around 300,000 Chinese residents. The eight-year war resulted in millions of deaths.

American Isolationists

Public opinion in the United States was also nationalistic but expressed itself in an opposite way from fascism and militarism. Disillusioned with the results of World War I, American isolationists wanted to make sure that the United States would never again be drawn into a foreign war. Japanese aggression in Manchuria and the rise of fascism in Italy and Germany only increased the determination of isolationists to avoid war at all costs. Isolationist sentiment was strongest in the Midwest and among Republicans.

The Lesson of World War I In the early 1930s, Americans commonly felt that U.S. entry into World War I had been a terrible mistake. An investigating committee led by Senator **Gerald Nye** of North Dakota bolstered this view when it concluded in 1934 that the main reason for U.S. participation in the world war was to serve the greed of bankers and arms manufacturers. This committee's work influenced isolationist legislation in the following years.

Neutrality Acts Isolationist senators and representatives in both parties held a majority in Congress through 1938. To ensure that U.S. policy would be strictly neutral if war broke out in Europe, Congress adopted a series of neutrality acts, which Roosevelt signed with some reluctance. Each law applied to belligerent nations, ones that the president proclaimed to be at war.

- The *Neutrality Act of 1935* authorized the president to prohibit all arms shipments and to forbid U.S. citizens from travel on the ships of belligerents.
- The *Neutrality Act of 1936* forbade the extension of loans and credits to belligerents.
- The *Neutrality Act of 1937* forbade the shipment of arms to the opposing sides in the civil war in Spain.

Spanish Civil War The outbreak of civil war in Spain in 1936 was viewed in Europe and the United States as an ideological struggle between the forces of fascism, led by General **Francisco Franco**, and the forces of republicanism, called Loyalists. Roosevelt and most Americans sympathized with the Loyalists but, because of the Neutrality Acts, could not aid them. Ultimately, in 1939, Franco's Fascists prevailed and established a military dictatorship.

America First Committee In 1940, after World War II had begun in Asia and Europe, isolationists became alarmed by Roosevelt's pro-British policies. To mobilize American public opinion against war, they formed the **America First Committee** and engaged speakers such as **Charles Lindbergh** to travel the country warning against reengaging in Europe's troubles.

Prelude to Another War

In the years 1935 to 1938, a series of aggressive actions by the Fascist dictatorships made democratic governments in Britain and France extremely nervous. It was known that Hitler was creating an air force more powerful than anything they could match. Hoping to avoid open conflict with Germany, the democracies adopted a policy of appeasement—allowing Hitler to get away with relatively small acts of aggression and expansion. The United States went along with the British and French policy. Events in Africa, Europe, and Asia showed how unwilling western democracies were to challenge Fascist aggression.

- **Ethiopia, 1935** In a bid to prove fascism's military might, Mussolini ordered Italian troops to invade **Ethiopia**. The League of Nations and the United States objected but did nothing to stop the Italian aggressor, who succeeded in conquering the African country after a year of bitter fighting.

- **Rhineland, 1936** This region in western Germany was supposed to be permanently demilitarized, according to the Versailles Treaty. Hitler openly defied the treaty by ordering German troops to march into the **Rhineland**.

- **China, 1937** Full-scale war between Japan and China erupted in 1937 as Japan's troops invaded its weaker neighbor. A U.S. gunboat in China, the *Panay*, was bombed and sunk by Japanese planes. The U.S. government quickly accepted Japan's apology for the sinking.

- **Sudetenland, 1938** In Europe, Hitler insisted that Germany had a right to take over a strip of land in Czechoslovakia, the **Sudetenland**, where most people were German-speaking. To maintain peace, the British prime minister, Neville Chamberlain, and the French president, Édouard Daladier, with Roosevelt's support, met with Hitler and Mussolini in **Munich**. At this conference in September 1938, the British and French leaders agreed to allow Hitler to take the Sudetenland unopposed. The word *Munich* has since become synonymous with **appeasement**.

Quarantine Speech Roosevelt recognized the dangers of Fascist aggression but was limited by the isolationist feelings of the majority of Americans. When Japan invaded China in 1937, he tested public opinion by making a speech proposing that the democracies act together to "quarantine" the aggressor. Public reaction to the speech was overwhelmingly negative, and Roosevelt dropped the quarantine idea as politically unwise.

Preparedness Like Wilson in 1916, Roosevelt argued for neutrality and an arms buildup at the same time. Congress went along with his request in late 1938 by increasing the military and naval budgets by nearly two-thirds. Some isolationists accepted the increased defense spending, thinking it would be used only to protect against possible invasion of the Western Hemisphere.

Outbreak of World War II in Europe

In March 1939, Hitler broke the Munich agreement by sending troops to occupy all of Czechoslovakia. After this, it became clear that Hitler's ambitions had no limit and that war was probably unavoidable.

Recognizing the failure of appeasement, Britain and France pledged to fight if Poland was attacked. They had always assumed that they could count on the Soviet leader, Joseph Stalin, to oppose Hitler, since communism and fascism were ideological enemies. The democracies were therefore shocked in August 1939 when Stalin and Hitler signed a nonaggression pact. Secretly, the Soviet and German dictators agreed to divide Poland between them.

Invasion of Poland On September 1, 1939, German tanks and planes began a full-scale invasion of **Poland**. Keeping their pledge, Britain and France declared war against Germany—and soon afterward, they were also at war with its Axis allies, Italy and Japan. World War II in Europe had begun.

Poland was the first to fall to Germany's *blitzkrieg* (lightning war), an overwhelming use of air power and fast-moving tanks. After a relatively inactive winter, the war was resumed in the spring of 1940 with Germany attacking its Scandinavian neighbors to the north and its chief enemy, France, to the west. Denmark and Norway surrendered in a few days, France in only a week. By June 1940, the only ally that remained free of German troops was Great Britain.

AXIS AGGRESSION IN THE 1930s

Roosevelt Changes Policies

President Roosevelt countered **isolationism** in the United States by gradually giving aid to the Allies, especially Great Britain. Now that war had actually begun, most Americans were alarmed by news of Nazi tanks, planes, and troops conquering one country after another. They were strongly opposed to Hitler but still hoped to keep their country out of the war. President Roosevelt believed that British survival was crucial to U.S. security. The relationship that was built over the coming years between British Prime Minister Winston Churchill and FDR proved one of the keys to Allied success in the war. The president chipped away at the restrictive neutrality laws until practically nothing remained to prevent him from giving massive aid to Britain. After the surrender of France to the Germans in 1940, most Americans accepted the need to strengthen U.S. defenses, but giving direct aid to Britain was controversial.

"Cash and Carry" The British navy still controlled the seas. Therefore, if the United States ended its arms embargo, it would help only Britain, not Germany. Roosevelt persuaded Congress in 1939 to adopt a less restrictive Neutrality Act, which provided that a belligerent could buy U.S. arms if it used its own ships and paid cash. Technically, **"cash and carry"** was neutral, but in practice, it strongly favored Britain.

Selective Service Act (1940) Without actually naming Germany as the potential enemy, Roosevelt pushed neutrality back one more step by persuading Congress to enact a law for compulsory military service. The **Selective Training and Service Act** of September 1940 provided for the registration of all American men between the ages of 21 and 35 and for the training of 1.2 million troops in just one year. There had been a military draft in the Civil War and World War I but only when the United States was officially at war. Isolationists strenuously opposed the peacetime draft, but they were now outnumbered as public opinion shifted away from strict neutrality.

Destroyers-for-Bases Deal In September 1940, Britain was under constant assault by German bombing raids. German submarine attacks threatened British control of the Atlantic. Roosevelt knew that selling U.S. destroyers to the British outright would outrage the isolationists. He therefore cleverly arranged a trade. Britain received 50 older but still serviceable U.S. destroyers and gave the United States the right to build military bases on British islands in the Caribbean.

The Election of 1940

Adding to suspense over the war was uncertainty over a presidential election. Might Franklin Roosevelt be the first president to break the two-term tradition and seek election to a **third term**? For months, the president gave an ambiguous reply, causing frenzied speculation in the press. At last, he announced that, in those critical times, he would not turn down the Democratic nomination if it were offered. Most Democrats were delighted to renominate their most effective campaigner. During the campaign, Roosevelt made the rash pronouncement: "Your boys are not going to be sent into any foreign wars."

Wendell Willkie The Republicans had a number of veteran politicians who were eager to challenge the president. Instead, they chose a newcomer to public office: **Wendell Willkie**, a lawyer and utility executive with a magnetic personality. Although he criticized the New Deal, Willkie largely agreed with Roosevelt on preparedness and giving aid to Britain short of actually entering the war. His strongest criticism of Roosevelt was the president's decision to break the two-term tradition established by George Washington.

Results Roosevelt won with 54 percent of the popular vote—a smaller margin than in 1932 and 1936. Important factors in the president's reelection were (1) a strong economic recovery enhanced by defense purchases and (2) fear of war, which caused voters to stay with the more experienced leader.

Arsenal of Democracy

Roosevelt viewed Germany's conquest of most of Europe as a direct threat both to U.S. security and to the future of democratic governments everywhere. After his reelection, he believed that he was in a stronger position to end the appearance of U.S. neutrality and give material aid to Britain. In a December 1940 fireside chat to the American people, he explained his thinking and concluded: "We must be the great arsenal of democracy."

Four Freedoms Addressing Congress on January 6, 1941, the president delivered a speech that proposed lending money to Britain for the purchase of U.S. war materials. He justified such a policy by arguing that the United States must help other nations defend **"four freedoms"**: freedom of speech, freedom of religion, freedom from want, and freedom from fear.

Lend-Lease Act Roosevelt proposed ending the cash-and-carry requirement of the Neutrality Act and permitting Britain to obtain all the U.S. arms it needed on credit. The president said it would be like lending a neighbor a garden hose to put out a fire. Isolationists in the America First Committee campaigned vigorously against the lend-lease bill. By now, however, majority opinion had shifted toward aiding Britain, and the **Lend-Lease Act** was signed into law in March 1941.

Atlantic Charter With the United States actively aiding Britain, Roosevelt knew that the United States might soon enter the war. He arranged for a secret meeting in August 1941 with British Prime Minister Winston Churchill aboard a ship off the coast of Newfoundland. The two leaders drew up a document known as the **Atlantic Charter** that affirmed that the general principles for a sound peace after the war would include self-determination for all people, no territorial expansion, and free trade.

Shoot-on-Sight In July 1941, the president extended U.S. support for Britain even further by protecting its ships from submarine attack. He ordered the U.S. Navy to escort British ships carrying lend-lease materials from U.S. shores as far as Iceland. On September 4, the American destroyer *Greer* was attacked by a German submarine it had been hunting. In response, Roosevelt ordered the navy to attack all German ships on sight. In effect, the United States was now fighting an undeclared naval war against Germany.

Disputes with Japan

Meanwhile, through 1940 and 1941, U.S. relations with Japan were becoming increasingly strained as a result of Japan's invasion of China and ambitions to extend its conquests to Southeast Asia. Beginning in 1940, Japan was allied with Germany and Italy as one of the Axis powers. Hitler's success in Europe enabled Japanese expansion into the Dutch East Indies, British Burma, and French Indochina—territories still held as European colonies.

U.S. Economic Action When Japan joined the Axis powers in September 1940, Roosevelt responded by prohibiting the export of steel and scrap iron to all countries except Britain and the nations of the Western Hemisphere. His action was aimed at Japan, which protested that it was an "unfriendly act." In July 1941, Japanese troops occupied French Indochina. Roosevelt then froze all Japanese credits in the United States and also cut off Japanese access to vital materials, including U.S. oil.

Negotiations Both sides realized that Japan needed oil to fuel its navy and air force. If the U.S. embargo on oil did not end, Japan would likely seize the oil resources in the Dutch East Indies. At the same time, Japan's invasion of China was a blatant violation of the Open Door policy, to which the United States was still committed. Roosevelt and Secretary of State Cordell Hull insisted that Japan pull its troops out of China, which Japan refused to do. The Japanese ambassador to the United States tried to negotiate a change in U.S. policy on oil. Agreement, however, seemed most unlikely. In October, a new Japanese government headed by General Hideki Tojo made a final attempt at negotiating an agreement. Neither side, however, changed its position.

U.S. military leaders hoped to delay armed confrontation with Japan until U.S. armed forces in the Pacific were strengthened. Japan, on the other hand, believed that quick action was necessary because of its limited oil supplies.

Pearl Harbor The U.S. fleet in the Pacific was anchored at **Pearl Harbor**, Hawaii. On Sunday morning, December 7, 1941, while most American sailors were still asleep in their bunks, Japanese planes from aircraft carriers flew over Pearl Harbor bombing every ship in sight. The surprise attack lasted less than two hours. In that time, Japan killed 2,400 Americans (including over 1,100 when the battleship *Arizona* sank), wounded almost 1,200 people, sank or severely damaged 20 warships, and destroyed approximately 150 airplanes.

Partial Surprise The American people were stunned by the attack on Pearl Harbor. High government officials, however, knew that an attack somewhere in the Pacific was imminent because they had broken the Japanese codes. They did not know the exact target and date for the attack, which many felt would be in the Philippines, the Dutch East Indies, or Malaya.

Declaration of War Addressing Congress on the day after Pearl Harbor, Roosevelt described December 7th as "a date which will live in infamy." He asked Congress to declare "that since the unprovoked and dastardly attack by Japan on December 7, 1941, a state of war has existed between the United States and the Japanese Empire." On December 8, Congress declared war, with only one dissenting vote. Three days later, Germany and Italy honored their treaty with Japan by declaring war on the United States.

The War in Europe in 1941–1942

By the time the United States entered the war in December 1941, Europeans had been fighting for two years. On June 22, 1941, Hitler had broken his nonaggression pact with Stalin and ordered his troops to invade the Soviet Union. This shifted the main battlefront in Europe from the west to the east. The principal Allies fighting Nazi Germany from 1942 to 1945, then, were Britain, the United States, and the Soviet Union. The three Allied leaders—Churchill, Roosevelt, and Stalin—agreed that they should concentrate on the European war against the aggressive militarism and fascism of the Nazis before shifting their resources to counter Japanese advances in the Pacific.

REFLECT ON THE LEARNING OBJECTIVE

1. Explain two similarities or differences in attitudes about the nation's proper role in the world during the 1920s and 1930s.

KEY TERMS BY THEME

Foreign Policy (WOR)
disarmament
Washington Conference (1921)
Five-Power (naval) Treaty
Nine-Power (China) Treaty
Kellogg-Briand Pact (1928)
war debts
reparations
Dawes Plan (1924)

Hoover-FDR Policies (WOR)
Good Neighbor policy
Pan-American conferences
recognition of the Soviet Union
Independence of the Philippines
reciprocal trade agreements

Militarist/Fascist Aggression (WOR)
Japanese aggression in Manchuria
Stimson Doctrine
Axis powers
Benito Mussolini
Fascist Party
fascism
Nazi Party
Adolf Hitler
Spanish Civil War
Francisco Franco
Ethiopia
Rhineland
Sudetenland
Munich
appeasement
Poland
blitzkrieg

Isolationist Response (WOR)
Gerald Nye
Neutrality Acts
America First Committee
Charles Lindbergh
isolationism

FDR's Response (WOR)
quarantine speech
"cash and carry"
Selective Training and Service Act (1940)
destroyers-for-bases deal
third term (FDR)
Wendell Willkie
"four freedoms"
Lend-Lease Act (1941)
Atlantic Charter
Pearl Harbor

Questions 1–3 refer to the cartoon below.

The Only Way We Can Save Her

1. Which of the following attitudes most directly contributed to the perspective of this cartoon?

   (A) The priority of Roosevelt to protect Latin American nations

   (B) The strong opposition to helping the Soviet Union under Stalin

   (C) The isolationist sentiment that developed after World War I

   (D) The antiwar policies of the Franklin Roosevelt administration

2. Which of the following events most directly conflicted with the perspective of this cartoon?

   (A) Congressional hearings into the U.S. entry into World War I

   (B) The Spanish Civil War between the fascist and the republican forces

   (C) Passage of laws prohibiting arms sales, bank loans, and travel to nations at war

   (D) Roosevelt's call for democracies to "quarantine" aggressive nations

3. Which of the following individuals and groups most strongly supported the perspective of this cartoon?

   (A) Henry Stimson and advocates of the Stimson Doctrine

   (B) Charles Lindbergh and many newspaper editors in rural areas

   (C) Franklin Roosevelt and other leaders of the Democratic Party

   (D) Wendell Willkie and the progressive wing of the Republican Party

SHORT-ANSWER QUESTIONS

Use complete sentences; an outline or bulleted list alone is not acceptable.

1. "Each of the tiny steps [Roosevelt] took was designed to keep the US out of the war... The only conclusion to be reached is [that] Britain in 1940 and 1941 survived with no significant outside help except that freely given by the Dominions, especially Canada. . . . The defender of liberal democracy in 1940–41 was not Britain along with the United States. . . . They fought freedom's battle while the largest democracy on earth occasionally threw them some crumbs."

    Robin Prior, historian, *When Britain Saved the West*, 2015

    "Roosevelt took the lead in educating Americans to this new perspective on world affairs. He has been criticized for his timidity. . . . But he had vivid memories of Wilson's defeat and feared getting too far out in front of public opinion. . . . Step by step between 1939 and 1941, he abandoned neutrality and, through aid to Britain and other nations fighting Hitler, took the United States to the brink of war. . . . He set forth the intellectual underpinnings for an American globalism that would take form in World War II and flourish in the postwar years."

    George C. Herring, historian, *From Colony to Superpower*, 2008

    Using the excerpts, answer (a), (b), and (c).

    (a) Briefly describe ONE major difference between Prior's and Herring's historical interpretation about Roosevelt's role in World War II.

    (b) Briefly explain how ONE specific historical event or development that is not explicitly mentioned in the excerpts could be used to support Prior's interpretation.

    (c) Briefly explain how ONE specific historical event or development that is not explicitly mentioned in the excerpts could be used to support Herring's interpretation.

2. Answer (a), (b), and (c).

    (a) Briefly explain ONE specific difference between the foreign policies of the Republican administrations and the Franklin Roosevelt administration during the 1920s and 1930s.

    (b) Briefly explain ONE specific similarity between the foreign policies of the Republican administrations and the Franklin Roosevelt administration during the 1920s and 1930s.

    (c) Briefly explain ONE specific similarity between the U.S. entry into World I and into World War II.

World War II Mobilization

*There is one front and one battle where everyone in the United States—
every man, woman, and child—is in action, and will be privileged to
remain in action throughout this war. That front is right here at home,
in our daily lives, and in our daily tasks.*

President Franklin D. Roosevelt, April 28th, 1942

Learning Objective: Explain how and why U.S. participation in World
War II transformed American society.

The success of U.S. and Allied armed forces depended on mobilizing
America's people, industries, and creative and scientific communities. The role
of the federal government expanded well beyond anything in World War I or
the New Deal.

The Federal Government Takes Action

As in World War I, the U.S. government organized a number of special agencies
to mobilize U.S. economic and military resources for the wartime crisis. Early
in 1942, the **War Production Board** (WPB) was established to manage war
industries. Later, the Office of War Mobilization (OWM) set production
priorities and controlled raw materials. The government used a cost-plus
system, in which it paid war contractors the costs of production plus a certain
percentage for profit. One federal agency, the **Office of Price Administration**
(OPA), regulated almost every aspect of civilians' lives by freezing prices,
wages, and rents, and by rationing such commodities as meat, sugar, gasoline,
and auto tires, primarily to fight wartime inflation. However, rationing led to a
black market, where people bought and sold these items illegally.

Deficit spending during the depression was dwarfed by the deficits incurred
during the war. **Federal spending** increased 1,000 percent between 1939 and
1945. As a result, the gross national product grew by 15 percent or more a year.
World War II proved what the New Deal did not, that the government could
spend its way out of a depression. By war's end, the national total **accumulated
debt** had reached the then staggering figure of $250 billion, five times what
it had been in 1941. This was 120 percent of the total economic output of the
country for 1946.

Business and Industry Stimulated by wartime demand and government
contracts, U.S. industries did a booming business, far exceeding their

production and profits of the 1920s. The depression was over, vanquished at last by the coming of war. By 1944, unemployment had practically disappeared.

War-related industrial output in the United States was astonishing. By 1944, it was twice that of all the Axis powers combined. Instead of automobiles, tanks and fighter planes rolled off the assembly lines. American factories produced over 300,000 planes, 100,000 tanks, and ships with a total capacity of 53 million tons. So efficient were production methods that Henry Kaiser's giant shipyard in California could turn out a new ship in just 14 days. The war concentrated production in the largest corporations, as smaller businesses lost out on government contracts to larger businesses with more capacity. The 100 largest corporations accounted for up to 70 percent of wartime manufacturing.

Research and Development Government worked closely not only with industries, but also universities and research labs to create and improve technologies that could be used to defeat the enemy. The Office of Research and Development was established to contract scientists and universities to help in the development of electronics such as radar and sonar, medicines such as penicillin, and military goods such as jet engines and rockets. It also ran the top-secret **Manhattan Project**, which produced the first atomic weapons. Ironically, many of the European scientists who fled Fascist persecution would contribute to fascism's defeat through their work in United States.

Workers and Unions Labor unions and large corporations agreed that while the war lasted, there would be no strikes. Workers became disgruntled, however, as their wages were frozen while corporations made large profits. John L. Lewis, therefore, called a few strikes by coal miner unions. The Smith-Connally Anti-Strike Act of 1943, passed over Roosevelt's veto, empowered the government to take over war-related businesses whose operations were threatened by a strike. In 1944, Roosevelt had occasion to use this law when he ordered the army to operate the nation's railroads for a brief period.

Financing the War The government paid for its huge increase in spending ($100 billion spent on the war in 1945 alone) by (1) increasing the income tax and (2) selling war bonds. For the first time, most Americans were required to pay an income tax, and in 1944, the practice was begun of automatically deducting a withholding tax from paychecks. Borrowing money by selling $135 billion in war bonds supplemented the tax increase. In addition, the shortage of consumer goods made it easier for Americans to save.

Wartime Propaganda Few people opposed the war, so the government's propaganda campaign of posters, songs, and news bulletins was primarily to maintain public morale, to encourage people to conserve resources, and to increase war production. The **Office of War Information** controlled news about troop movements and battles. Movies, radio, and popular music all supported and reflected a cheerful, patriotic view of the war. For example, Norman Rockwell's popular illustrations of the "Four Freedoms" captured the liberties and values at stake in the war. The unity of Americans behind the war's democratic ideals helped that generation remember it as **"the Good War."**

The Tuskegee Airmen created a distinguished record during World War II.
Source: Wikipedia.

The War's Impact on Society

Every group in the U.S. population adjusted to the unique circumstances of wartime. The increase in factory jobs caused millions to leave rural areas for industrial jobs in the Midwest and on the Pacific Coast, especially California. Entirely new communities arose around the construction of new factories and military bases. Many of the new defense installations were located in the South because of that region's warm climate and low labor costs. The wartime expansion set the stage for a postwar migration to the Sunbelt.

African Americans Attracted by jobs in the North and West, over 1.5 million African Americans left the South. In addition, a million young men left home to serve in the armed forces. During World War II, African Americans for the first time served as aviators in combat.

However, whether as soldiers or civilians, African Americans faced continued discrimination and segregation at home and in the armed forces. Dozens died in race riots in New York and Detroit during the summer of 1943 resulting from White resentment of Black families moving into their cities. **Civil rights** leaders encouraged African Americans to adopt the **"Double V"** slogan—victory over fascism abroad and the victory of equality at home.

Membership in the NAACP increased during the war, which continued to challenge unjust laws in court and advocate for civil rights legislation. Another civil rights organization, the Congress of Racial Equality (CORE), was formed in 1942 to work more militantly for African American interests. After Black leaders threatened a protest march on Washington, the Roosevelt administration issued an **executive order to prohibit discrimination** in government and in businesses that received federal contracts. One judicial victory was won in the Supreme Court case of *Smith v. Allwright* (1944). The Court ruled that it was unconstitutional to deny membership in political parties to African Americans as a way of excluding them from voting in primaries.

Mexican Americans Over 300,000 Mexican Americans served in the military and many others worked in defense industries. A 1942 agreement with Mexico allowed Mexican farmworkers, known as *braceros,* to enter the United States in the harvest season without going through formal immigration procedures. **Braceros** entered as temporary residents. They were not welcomed to stay permanently. The sudden influx of Mexican immigrants into Los Angeles stirred White resentment and led to the so-called zoot suit riots in the summer of 1943, in which Whites and Mexican Americans battled on the streets.

American Indians American Indians contributed to the war effort as both soldiers and workers. Approximately 25,000 served in the military, and thousands more worked in defense industries. Having discovered the opportunities off their reservations, more than half never returned.

Japanese Americans More than any ethnic group, Japanese Americans suffered special discrimination because of the war. Following the attack on Pearl Harbor, many people suspected that Japanese Americans were spies or saboteurs and that Japan would soon invade the West Coast. In 1942, these irrational fears, as well as racism, prompted the U.S. government to order more than 100,000 Japanese Americans on the West Coast to leave their homes and move to internment camps. The order did not apply to Japanese Americans living in Hawaii and other parts of the United States. In the case of ***Korematsu v. U.S.*** (1944), the Supreme Court upheld the government's internment policy as justified in wartime. Despite this discriminatory treatment, almost 20,000 Japanese Americans served in the military. In 1988, the federal government agreed the ruling was unjust and awarded financial compensation to those still alive who had been interned.

Women The war also changed the lives of women. Over 200,000 women served in uniform in the army, navy, and marines, but in noncombat roles. As in World War I, an acute labor shortage caused women to take jobs vacated by men in uniform. Almost 5 million women entered the workforce, many of them working in industrial jobs in the shipyards and defense plants. The number of married women in the workforce increased to 24 percent. A song about **"Rosie the Riveter"** was used to encourage women to take defense jobs. However, they received pay well below that of male factory workers. Women also became more independent as heads of the households and chief income earners while men served overseas.

Wartime Solidarity The New Deal helped immigrant groups feel more included, and serving together as "bands of brothers" in combat or working together for a common cause in defense plants helped to reduce prejudices based on nationality, ethnicity, and religion. The **wartime migrations** also helped to soften regional differences and open the eyes of many Americans to the injustice of racial discrimination.

REFLECT ON THE LEARNING OBJECTIVE

1. Explain two ways that U.S. participation in World War II transformed American society.

KEY TERMS BY THEME

Mobilization (SOC, WXT)
War Production Board
Office of Price Administration
federal spending
accumulated debt
business and industry
research and development
Manhattan Project
Office of War Information
"the Good War"

Home Front (SOC, MIG)
wartime migrations
civil rights
"Double V"
executive order to prohibit discrimination
Smith v. Allwright
braceros
internment camps
Korematsu v. U.S.
"Rosie the Riveter"
wartime solidarity

MULTIPLE-CHOICE QUESTIONS

Questions 1–2 refer to the excerpt below.

> "Rationing is a vital part of your country's war effort. Any attempt to violate the rules is an effort to deny someone his share and will create hardship and help the enemy. This book is our Government's assurance of your right to buy your fair share of certain goods made scarce by war. Price ceilings have also been established for your protection. Dealers must post these prices conspicuously. Don't pay more. Give your whole support to rationing and thereby conserve our vital goods. Be guided by the rule: "If you don't need it, DON'T BUY IT."
>
> IMPORTANT: When you used your ration, salvage the TIN CANS and WASTE FATS. They are needed to make munitions for our fighting men. Cooperate with your local Salvage Committee."
>
> *War Ration Books,* Office of Price Administration, 1943

1. Which of the following was the primary purpose of the message the above document was trying to communicate?

   (A) To control inflation caused by shortages of consumer goods

   (B) To boost the wartime economy by encouraging consumption

   (C) To discourage industries from making consumer products

   (D) To prevent workers and unions from demanding higher wages

2. Which of the following describes the most important historical situation in which the government issued the statement above?

(A) Governments wanted to control civilian behavior during wartime to reassure people that they were still in control.

(B) Industrial production was essential to successful modern warfare, and it required an effort by the entire nation.

(C) The increase in the size of the military meant that fewer people were available to work in recycling industries.

(D) Governments had to stop civilian hoarding during wartime so that people would not focus their anger on each other.

SHORT-ANSWER QUESTIONS

Use complete sentences; an outline or bulleted list alone is not acceptable.

1. "Whereas the successful prosecution of the war requires every possible protection against espionage and against sabotage to national-defense. . . . I hereby authorize and direct the Secretary of War . . . to prescribe military areas . . . from which any and all persons may be excluded, and with respect to which, the right of any person to enter, remain in, or leave shall be subject to whatever restrictions the Secretary of War or the appropriate Military Commander may impose in his discretion."

Executive Order 9066, February 19, 1942

Using the excerpt, answer (a), (b), and (c).

(a) Briefly explain ONE specific effect that this order had on Japanese Americans.

(b) Briefly explain ONE specific Constitutional issue that was raised by this order.

(c) Briefly explain ONE additional effect that the wartime experience had on the civil rights movement in the United States.

2. Answer (a), (b), and (c).

(a) Briefly explain ONE specific effect that federal mobilization policies had on the American economy during World War II.

(b) Briefly explain ONE specific effect that World War II had on opportunities for women.

(c) Briefly explain ONE specific example of how technological and scientific advances contributed to U.S. military victories.

World War II: Military

We knew the world would not be the same. . . . I remembered the line from the Hindu scripture, "Now I am become Death, the destroyer of worlds." I suppose we all thought that, one way or another.

J. Robert Oppenheimer, scientist upon seeing the first
atomic weapons explosion, from a 1965 interview

Learning Objective: Explain the causes and effects of the victory of the United States and its allies over the Axis powers.

The fighting of World War II was waged on two fronts, or "theaters of operation." In the Pacific, Japanese forces reached the height of their power in 1942, occupying islands throughout the western Pacific Ocean. In Europe, much of the fighting in the first year of war was between the Germans and the Soviets, as the latter fought desperately to prevent the conquest of Russia.

Fighting Germany

The high tide of the German advance ended in 1942, partly as a result of U.S. entry into the war but mainly because of a Soviet victory at Stalingrad in the winter of that year.

Defense at Sea, Attacks by Air Coordinating their military strategy, the British and Americans concentrated on two objectives in 1942: (1) overcoming the menace of German submarines in the Atlantic and (2) beginning bombing raids on German cities. The protracted naval war to control the shipping lanes was known as the **Battle of the Atlantic**. German submarines sank over 500 Allied ships in 1942. Gradually, however, the Allies developed ways of containing the submarine menace through the use of radar, sonar, and the bombing of German naval bases. The U.S. bombers carried out daylight **"strategic bombing"** raids on military targets in Europe, while the Germans and Britain attacked population centers. The lines between military and civilian targets became blurred as the war carried on, especially in Japan, when the United States started to fire bomb sections of large cities.

From North Africa to Italy The Allies had the daunting task of driving German occupying forces out of their advance positions in North Africa and the Mediterranean. They began their North Africa campaign, Operation Torch, in November 1942. Led by U.S. General **Dwight Eisenhower** and British

General Bernard Montgomery, Allied forces succeeded in taking North Africa from the Germans by May 1943.

The next U.S.–British target was the Mediterranean island of Sicily, which they occupied in the summer of 1943, preparatory to an invasion of Italy. Mussolini fell from power during the summer, but Hitler's forces rescued him and gave him nominal control of northern Italy. In fact, German troops controlled much of Italy at the time that the Allies invaded the peninsula in September 1943. The Germans put up a determined resistance to the Allied offensive, holding much of northern Italy until their final surrender in May 1945.

From D-Day to Victory in Europe The Allied drive to liberate France began on June 6, 1944, with the largest invasion by sea in history. On **D-Day**, as the invasion date was called, British, Canadian, and U.S. forces under the command of General Eisenhower secured several beachheads on the Normandy coast. After this bloody but successful attack, the Allied offensive moved rapidly to roll back German occupying forces. By the end of August, Paris was liberated. By September, Allied troops had crossed the German border for a final push toward Berlin. The Germans launched a desperate counterattack in Belgium in December 1944 in the Battle of the Bulge. After this setback, however, Americans reorganized and resumed their advance.

German Surrender and Discovery of the Holocaust Since 1942, Allied bombing raids over Germany had reduced that nation's industrial capacity and ability to continue fighting. Recognizing that the end was near, as the Russian army closed in on Berlin, Hitler committed suicide on April 30, 1945. The unconditional surrender of the Nazi armies took place a week later, on May 7.

As U.S. troops advanced through Germany, they came upon German concentration camps and witnessed the horrifying extent of the Nazis' program of genocide against the Jews and others. Americans and the world were shocked to learn that 6 million Jewish civilians and several million non-Jews had been systematically murdered by Nazi Germany.

Fighting Japan

In Europe, British, Soviet, and U.S. forces were jointly responsible for defeating Germany, but in the Pacific, it was largely the U.S. armed forces that challenged the Japanese. After the Pearl Harbor attack, Japan seized control of much of East Asia and Southeast Asia. By early 1942, Japanese troops occupied Korea, eastern China, the Philippines, the Dutch East Indies (Indonesia), British Burma and Malaya, French Indochina (Vietnam, Cambodia, and Laos), and most of the Pacific Islands west of Midway Island.

Turning Point, 1942 The war in the Pacific was dominated by naval forces battling over a vast area. Intercepting and decoding Japanese messages enabled U.S. forces to destroy four Japanese carriers and 300 planes in the decisive **Battle of Midway** on June 4–7. This battle ended Japanese expansion.

Island Hopping After the victory at Midway, the United States began a long campaign to get within striking distance of Japan's home islands by seizing strategic locations in the Pacific. Using a strategy called **island hopping**, commanders bypassed strongly held Japanese posts and isolated them with naval and air power. Allied forces moved steadily toward Japan.

Major Battles Early in 1942, the Japanese had conquered the Philippines. When General **Douglas MacArthur**, the commander of army units in the Southern Pacific, was driven from the islands, he famously vowed, "I shall return." The conflict that prepared the way for U.S. reoccupation of the Philippines was the largest naval battle in history. At the Battle of Leyte Gulf in October 1944, the Japanese navy was virtually destroyed. For the first time in the war, the Japanese used **kamikaze** pilots to make suicide attacks on U.S. ships. Kamikazes also inflicted major damage in the colossal Battle of Okinawa (April to June 1945). Before finally succeeding in taking this island near Japan, U.S. forces suffered 50,000 casualties and killed 100,000 Japanese.

Atomic Bombs After Okinawa, a huge invasion force stood ready to attack Japan. Extremely heavy casualties were feared. By this time, however, the United States had developed a frightfully destructive new weapon. The top-secret Manhattan Project under General Leslie Groves employed over 100,000 people and spent $2 billion to develop a weapon whose power came from the splitting of the atom. **J. Robert Oppenheimer**, director of the Los Alamos Laboratory, New Mexico, successfully tested the first **atomic bomb** on July 16, 1945.

The new president, Harry Truman, and his wartime allies called on Japan to surrender unconditionally or face "utter destruction." When Japan gave an unsatisfactory reply, Truman consulted with his advisers and decided to use the new weapon on two Japanese cities. On August 6, an A-bomb was dropped on **Hiroshima**, and on August 9, a second bomb was dropped on **Nagasaki**. About 250,000 Japanese died, either immediately or after a prolonged period of suffering, as a result of the two nuclear bombs.

War and Morality Nuclear weapons, by design, destroyed a much larger area than conventional weapons. When used on population centers, the new technology would cause tens or hundreds of thousands of deaths and injuries from the blast and radiation. The moral issue of killing civilians was raised in World War I by the German use of submarines against passenger ships. In World War II, the Germans and British bombed each other's cities based on the rationale that it would force the other side to sue for peace. Instead, research after the war concluded it did not have the desired effect. In fact, industrial output often went up because the bombing of urban centers released workers from their commercial jobs to work in well-hidden war plants.

Some would argue that in modern industrialized societies, civilians were part of the war effort and therefore legitimate targets. The United States in World War II first used "strategic bombing" of only military targets; however, it began to cross the line with the fire-bombing of Japanese cities, which caused thousands of civilian deaths. Today, people recognize that large-scale nuclear warfare could end most human life, if not most life of all kinds, on Earth.

Japan Surrenders Within a week after the second atomic bomb fell, Japan agreed to surrender if the Allies would allow the emperor to remain as a titular (powerless) head of state. General MacArthur received Japan's formal surrender on September 2, 1945, in Tokyo's harbor aboard the battleship USS *Missouri*. The diplomacy that led to the end of the war set the stage for the efforts to construct a more lasting peace (see Topic 7.14).

REFLECT ON THE LEARNING OBJECTIVE

1. Explain two significant causes for the victory of the United States and its allies over the Axis powers.

KEY TERMS BY THEME

Wartime Strategies (WOR)	island hopping
Battle of the Atlantic	Douglas MacArthur
"strategic bombing"	kamikaze
Dwight Eisenhower	J. Robert Oppenheimer
D-Day	atomic bomb
Holocaust	Hiroshima
Battle of Midway	Nagasaki

MULTIPLE-CHOICE QUESTIONS

Questions 1–3 refer to the following excerpt.

"I know that Japan is a terribly cruel and uncivilized nation in warfare but I can't bring myself to believe that, because they are beasts, we should ourselves act in the same manner. For myself, I certainly regret the necessity of wiping out whole populations because of the 'pigheadedness' of the leaders of a nation and, for your information, I am not going to do it unless it is absolutely necessary . . . My object is to save as many American lives as possible but I also have a humane feeling for the women and children in Japan."

> President Truman, letter to Senator Richard Russell of
> Georgia, August 9, 1945

1. Which of the following best reflects Truman's reason as stated in this letter for using the atomic bombs against Japan in August of 1945?

   (A) He sought revenge for Pearl Harbor and Japanese wartime atrocities.

   (B) He hoped to end the war before Britain and France became heavily involved.

   (C) He thought conventional fire-bombing of cities was unacceptable.

   (D) He wanted to avoid more U.S. military casualties.

2. One objection to the use of nuclear weapons that Truman seemed to be responding to in this letter was that the action would

   (A) lengthen the war because it would reinforce the refusal of Japan to surrender

   (B) cause the indiscriminate killing of tens of thousands of noncombatants

   (C) set off an arms race among countries as each tried to develop its own nuclear weapons

   (D) damage national security because it would justify later use of similar weapons against the United States

3. What was the historical situation before Truman made his decision on using atomic weapons?

   (A) U.S. forces had suffered 50,000 casualties in fighting on the Japanese island and *kamikaze* pilots were attacking U.S. ships.

   (B) The United States had just invaded the region of China controlled by Japan and was planning to send more troops there.

   (C) Japan had already publicly announced that it would stop fighting and that it was preparing to formally surrender.

   (D) The war in Europe was still going on, and the defeat of the Nazis was still uncertain.

SHORT-ANSWER QUESTION

1. Answer (a), (b), and (c).

   (a) Briefly explain ONE specific military strategy or tactic that contributed to the U.S. victory in World War II.

   (b) Briefly explain ONE example to support the argument that Allied cooperation helped win World War II.

   (c) Briefly explain ONE example to support the view that World War II was fought to preserve democracy and human rights against criminal regimes.

Topic 7.14

World War II and Postwar Diplomacy

Peace is never long preserved by weight of metal or by an armament race. Peace can be made tranquil and secure only by understanding and agreement fortified by sanctions. We must embrace international cooperation or international disintegration.

Bernard Baruch, U.S. representative to United Nations
Atomic Energy Commission, June 14, 1946

Learning Objective: Explain the consequences of U.S. involvement in World War II.

In order to defeat the Axis powers, the United States joined in alliance with unlikely partners such as the communist Soviet Union and former allies such as Great Britain and France that were trying to hold on to their colonial empires. Allied victory in World War II and the death of President Roosevelt exposed the contradictions in the Grand Alliance, and both caused and foreshadowed the conflicts of postwar diplomacy.

American Leadership

In 1944, President Roosevelt won the Democratic nomination for the fourth time. The Democrats made an important change, however, in their choice of a vice presidential running mate. Party leaders felt that Roosevelt's third-term vice president, Henry Wallace, was considered too radical and unmanageable. With Roosevelt's agreement, they replaced Wallace with **Harry S. Truman**, a Missouri senator with a national reputation for having conducted a much-publicized investigation of war spending. The Democrats won 53 percent of the popular vote and an overwhelming 432–99 victory in the Electoral College.

Although Roosevelt publicly denied medical problems, those near him recognized his poor health. As fate had it, FDR would live for less than three months after his inauguration. Harry Truman, who would serve the rest of the term, rarely met with Roosevelt. For example, Truman was told of the secret development of the atomic bomb only after Roosevelt's death. In retrospect, critics questioned the impact of Roosevelt's poor health and the changes in the administration on American diplomacy, especially with the Soviet Union.

Wartime Conferences

During the war, the **Big Three**—U.S. President Roosevelt, British Prime Minister Churchill, and Soviet Premier Stalin—arranged to confer secretly to coordinate military strategy and to lay the foundation for peace terms and postwar policies.

Casablanca The first conference, in January 1943, involved only Roosevelt and Churchill. They met in the North African city of Casablanca. They agreed on a grand strategy to win the war, including to invade Sicily and Italy and to demand **"unconditional surrender"** from the Axis powers.

Tehran The Big Three met for the first time in the Iranian city of Tehran in November 1943. They agreed that the British and Americans would begin their drive to liberate France in the spring of 1944 and that the Soviets would invade Germany and eventually join the war against Japan.

Yalta In February 1945, the Big Three conferred again at Yalta, a resort town on the Black Sea coast of the Soviet Union. Their agreement at Yalta would prove the most historic of the three meetings. They agreed on several policies to guide them after victory in Europe:

- The Allies would divide Germany into occupation zones. Germany would lose about 1/4 of its territories to Poland and the Soviet Union as their boundaries were moved westward.

- The liberated countries of Eastern Europe would hold **free elections**, even though Soviet troops controlled this territory.

- The Soviets would enter the war against Japan, which they did on August 8, 1945.

- The Soviets would control the southern half of Sakhalin Island and the Kuril Islands in the Pacific and have special concessions in Manchuria.

- Countries would hold a conference in San Francisco to form a new world peace organization (the future United Nations).

The Yalta Conference was the most important conference of the war because it largely determined the future map of Europe. After the war, President Roosevelt was criticized for "giving away" Eastern Europe to the Soviets. However, neither he nor the other Allies were in a position to stop the Soviet army from taking possession of these nations. At the time, before the successful test of the atomic bomb, Roosevelt also wanted Soviet help to defeat Japan.

Death of President Roosevelt When the president returned from Yalta and informed Congress of his agreement with Churchill and Stalin, people could see that his health had deteriorated. On April 12, 1945, while resting in a vacation home in Georgia, an exhausted Roosevelt died suddenly. News of his death shocked the nation almost as much as Pearl Harbor. Harry S. Truman entered the presidency unexpectedly to assume enormous responsibilities as commander in chief of a war effort that had not yet been won.

Seated, from left to right, are Winston Churchill of Great Britain, Franklin Roosevelt of the United States, and Joseph Stalin of the Soviet Union.
Source: National Archives and Records Administration. Wikipedia.

Potsdam In late July, after Germany's surrender, only Stalin remained as one of the Big Three. Truman was the new U.S. president, and Clement Attlee had just been elected the new British prime minister to replace Winston Churchill. The three leaders met in Potsdam, Germany (July 17–August 2, 1945) and agreed (1) to demand that Japan surrender unconditionally, and (2) Germany and Berlin would be divided into four zones of occupation. However, cracks in the Grand Alliance became more evident after the conference. Stalin wanted a harsher treatment of Germany and interpreted the use of the atomic bomb against Japan as a threat to the Soviet Union. Moreover, Truman wanted to get "tough" with the Soviets, especially for the takeover of Eastern Europe by Communist governments that proved to be puppets of the Soviet Union.

The War's Legacy

The most destructive war in the history of the world had profound effects on all nations, including the United States.

Human and Economic Costs The deadliest war ever conducted resulted in the deaths of 70 million to 80 million military personnel and civilians worldwide. About one-third of those were Soviet citizens. Fifteen million Americans served in uniform and approximately 400,000 Americans lost their lives and 800,000 others were wounded. Excluding the Civil War, more Americans died in World War II than in all other U.S. wars combined.

The war left the United States with a huge national debt. But while Europe and Japan lay in ruins, the United States had suffered no damage to its cities, factories, roads, universities, and farms. As a result, the United States emerged after the war far wealthier than any other country. Further, as the political leader of the victorious Allied coalition, it had shaped the postwar settlements and had influence around the globe. Few, if any, questioned that the United States was the most powerful nation on Earth in 1945.

The United Nations Unlike its rejection of the League of Nations following World War I, Congress readily accepted membership in the peacekeeping organization that was formed at the end of World War II. Meeting in 1944 at Dumbarton Oaks near Washington, D.C., Allied representatives from the United States, the Soviet Union, Great Britain, and China proposed an international organization to be called the **United Nations**. Then in April 1945, delegates from 50 nations assembled in San Francisco, where they took only eight weeks to draft a charter for the United Nations. The Senate quickly voted to accept U.S. involvement in the UN. On October 24, 1945, the UN came into existence when the majority of member-nations ratified its charter.

Expectations In a final speech, which he never delivered, Franklin Roosevelt wrote: "The only limit to our realization of tomorrow will be the doubts of today." Americans had concerns about what world order might emerge after World War II, but they also shared hopes that life would be more prosperous. Without a doubt, the United States in 1945 was the most prosperous and the most powerful nation in the world. It had played a major role in defeating the Fascist dictators. Now people looked forward with some optimism to both a more peaceful and more democratic world.

However, the specters of the Soviet Union dominating Eastern Europe and gaining the A-bomb would soon dim expectations for cooperation. In 1946, the United States presented a plan to the United Nations for the control of **atomic weapons** and disarmament, but the Soviet Union vetoed the plan and developed its own atomic weapons. The breakdown of cooperation with the Soviet Union ushered in a period (1945–1980) dominated by a Cold War between the democracies and capitalist economies of the "West" and the Communist political and economic ideologies of the "East."

REFLECT ON THE LEARNING OBJECTIVE

1. Explain two consequences of U.S. involvement in World War II.

KEY TERMS BY THEME

Wartime Diplomacy (WOR)
Harry S. Truman
Big Three
Casablanca
"unconditional surrender"
Tehran

Yalta
free elections
Potsdam
United Nations
atomic weapons

MULTIPLE-CHOICE QUESTIONS

Questions 1–2 refer to the following excerpt.

> "Mr. President (of the Senate), we still have two major wars to win. I said 'We.' That does not mean America alone. It means the continued and total battle fraternity of the United Nations. It must mean one for all and all for one. . . . President Roosevelt correctly said in his annual message that 'the nearer we come to vanquishing our enemies the more we become inevitably conscious of differences among the victors' . . . Since Pearl Harbor, World War II has put the gory science of mass murder into new and sinister perspective. Our oceans have ceased to be moats, which automatically protect our ramparts. . . . Let me put it this way for myself: I am prepared, by effective international cooperation, to do our full part in charting happier and safer tomorrows."
>
> Senator Arthur H. Vandenberg, Republican
> from Michigan, January 10, 1945

1. Which of the following actions would Vandenberg most likely have supported based on what he says in this passage?

   (A) The decision to replace Henry Wallace with Harry Truman

   (B) The membership of the Soviet Union in the United Nations

   (C) An "America First" view of the U.S. role in the world

   (D) A partisan fight over foreign policy after the end of World War II

2. Which of the following most clearly supported Roosevelt's belief that "the nearer we come to vanquishing our enemies the more we become inevitably conscious of differences among the victors" ?

   (A) The willingness of Britain and France to give up their colonies

   (B) The joint occupation by the Allies of Japan after the war

   (C) The decision to form the United Nations

   (D) The goal of the Soviet Union to control Eastern Europe for defense

SHORT-ANSWER QUESTION

1. Answer (a), (b), and (c).

   (a) Briefly explain ONE historical development that encouraged the involvement of the United States in the UN after World War II.

   (b) Briefly explain ONE historical effect of the dropping of the atomic bomb on the international community after World War II.

   (c) Briefly explain ONE development that contributed to the emergence of the United States as the most powerful nation after World War II.

Comparison in Period 7

Learning Objective: Compare the relative significance of major events of the first half of the 20th century in shaping American identity.

The reasoning process of *comparison* asks students to describe similarities and differences between specific historical developments. In studying Period 7, you can use comparison to make judgments about the relative significance of events that shaped the *American identity*. For example, a comparison of historical events, such as World War I and World War II, can also help one grasp the unique complexity of each. For example, after World War I, Congress and most voters rejected joining the League of Nations and committing to collective security. In contrast, after World War II, joining the United Nations had bipartisan support. The two wars provide other cases of *multiple variables*:

- **Political Conditions:** President Wilson was less willing to compromise than President Roosevelt was nearly three decades later.

- **Military Situation:** The entry into World War I was controversial, as people continued to question the need for U.S. involvement. The attack on Pearl Harbor unified the nation behind fighting World War II.

- **Diplomatic Relations:** The main allies of the United States in World War I were democracies. In World War II, the United States worked with non-democracies, such as the Soviet Union.

- **National Values:** Immediately after World War I, people believed the United States could go its own way in world affairs. By 1945, people had experienced the failure of isolationism to stop the aggression by Japan, Italy, and Germany, and the success of collective security in doing so.

The analysis of such variables will help you to develop a more complex and persuasive argument.

QUESTIONS ABOUT COMPARISON

1. Compare the significance of the 1920s with period from 1933 to 1945 in shaping beliefs about assimilation of migrants and minorities as part of the American national identity.

2. Compare the relative impact of the reforms of the Progressive era and the New Deal in shaping views on the economy and capitalism as part of the American national identity.

Which set of numbers is easier to remember in order: 2, 8, 10, 6, 4; or 2, 4, 6, 8, 10? They are the same numbers, but the first set lacks an obvious connection between one number and the next, while the second set has one. Recognizing and understanding the significance of connections between people, places, objects, and events in history helps you to better understand the importance of what you are studying. Here are the two ways of making connections that will help you on the AP® exam.

- **Identify patterns:** This means you notice when historical developments or processes have aspects in common.

- **Make connections:** This means you are able to identify and explain how one historical development or process relates to another.

Items related to contextualization may appear anywhere on the AP® exam. You can use various reasoning processes to help you see connections:

- **Causation:** This includes distinguishing between minor and major causes, and between short-term and long-term effects of a historical development.

- **Comparison:** This includes recognizing both similarities and differences among historical developments, either from the same era or different eras.

- **Continuity and change:** This includes evaluating how significant each continuity and each change is.

For each series of events below, identify the pattern they shared.

1. Purchase of Alaska, annexation of Hawaii, Spanish-American War

2. Commercial radio becomes popular, talking pictures debut, jazz music becomes widespread

3. Trail of Tears, Dawes Act, overthrow of Queen Liliuokalani

4. Jingoism, Cuban revolt of 1895, sinking of the *Maine*

5. Increasing power of big business, rise of an urban middle class, agitation for women's suffrage, opposition to Jim Crow laws

For each series of events below, explain the relationship that existed among them.

6. Harriet Beecher Stowe publishes *Uncle Tom's Cabin*, Frank Norris publishes *The Octopus*, Upton Sinclair publishes *The Jungle*

7. Secret ballots, direct primaries, direct election of U.S. senators

8. U.S. trade with Britain increases, submarine warfare, *Lusitania*, Zimmerman telegram

9. Segregation, destruction of cotton crops by boll weevil, economic opportunities in the northern United States

10. Langston Hughes publishes poetry, Bessie Smith sings the blues, Paul Robeson acts in plays

UNIT 7 — Period 7 Review: 1890–1945

WRITE AS A HISTORIAN: *WRITE THE SUPPORTING PARAGRAPHS*

The supporting paragraphs in your long essay will demonstrate your skill in using evidence. They will also demonstrate your ability to follow a reasoning process and develop a complex interpretation of the prompt.

Use of Evidence Suppose your thesis is that Progressive Era reforms were more focused on politics while New Deal reforms focused on economics. To earn any points, you need to provide two examples of evidence relevant to your thesis—that is, directly connected to your topic. For example, you might argue that the most important accomplishments of the Progressives were the amendments requiring the direct election of senators and allowing women to vote. In contrast, you might argue that most important accomplishments of the New Deal included a minimum wage, Social Security, and protection for union organizing.

To earn the maximum number of points, you need to show how your evidence *supports* your argument. The Progressives were often middle-class individuals for whom the economy was already working well. In contrast, many supporters of the New Deal were working-class individuals who wanted more government intervention in the economy. Using such terms as *because* and *for this reason* will help you link your evidence to your argument.

Historical Reasoning and Complexity Your supporting paragraphs also need to show that you used reasoning processes (causation, comparison, or continuity and change) to frame your argument. You can show this framing in your choice of words. Using terms such as *in contrast* and *on the other hand* will help you show the differences in two movements.

To earn the most points, however, your supporting paragraphs must demonstrate a complex understanding of the historical development that is the focus of the prompt. You could demonstrate this in various ways:

- Explain both similarities and differences or address multiple causes and effects. You might note how changes in technology shaped both sets of reforms.

- Note connections across geographic areas and time periods. You might add comparisons with reforms during Reconstruction.

- Use evidence from other sources to corroborate (verify), qualify (set limitations), or modify (revise) an argument. To qualify your argument, you might point to Progressive reforms that affected the economy (creating the Federal Reserve) and New Deal reforms that affected the political system (increasing federal government power).

Application: Review the sample scored essays on the College Board website. Explain why each received the score it did for the use of evidence, historical reasoning, and complexity.

For current free-response question samples, visit: https://apcentral.collegeboard.org/ courses/ap-united-states-history/exam

LONG ESSAY QUESTIONS

Directions: The suggested writing time for each question is 40 minutes. In your response, you should do the following:

- Respond to the prompt with a historically defensible thesis or claim that establishes a line of reasoning.
- Describe a broader historical context relevant to the prompt.
- Support an argument in response to the prompt using specific and relevant examples of evidence.
- Use historical reasoning (e.g., comparison, causation, continuity or change) to frame or structure an argument that addresses the prompt.
- Use evidence to corroborate, qualify, or modify an argument that addresses the prompt.

1. Evaluate the extent to which one of the wars fought by the United States between 1898 and 1945 had an effect on national identity.

2. Evaluate the extent to which a reform movement between 1900 and 1941 had an effect on the U.S. economic system.

3. Evaluate how the Progressive movement and World War I affected women compared to how the New Deal did.

4. Evaluate World War I's effect on American business and labor compared to World War II's effect.

5. Evaluate the extent to which technological innovations contributed to changes in American values during the period from 1890 to 1945.

6. Evaluate the extent to which federal wartime policies contributed to changes in American civil liberties during the period from 1890 to 1945.

7. Evaluate the extent to which immigration patterns in the United States changed in the period from 1900 to 1945.

8. Evaluate the extent to which internal migration patterns changed American culture in the period from 1900 to 1945.

Directions: Question 1 is based on the accompanying documents. The documents have been edited for the purpose of this exercise. You are advised to spend 15 minutes planning and 45 minutes writing your answer. In your response you should do the following:

- Respond to the prompt with a historically defensible thesis or claim that establishes a line of reasoning.
- Describe a broader historical context relevant to the prompt.
- Support an argument in response to the prompt using at least six documents.
- Use at least one additional piece of specific historical evidence (beyond that found in the documents) relevant to an argument about the prompt.
- For at least three documents, explain how or why the document's point of view, purpose, historical situation, and/or audience is relevant to an argument.
- Use evidence to corroborate, qualify, or modify an argument that addresses the prompt.

1. Evaluate the relative importance of long-standing American values in the decision for the United States' entry into World War I.

Document 1

> **Source:** Oswald Garrison Villard, writer and journalist, *Annals of the American Academy of Political and Social Science,* July 1916
>
> "Now, the real significance of this [campaign for preparedness] is that we have all at once, in the midst of a terrifying cataclysm, abjured our faith in many things American. We no longer believe, as for 140 years, in the moral power of an America unarmed and unafraid; we believe suddenly that the influence of the United States is to be measured only by the numbers of our soldiery and our dreadnoughts—our whole history to the contrary notwithstanding.
>
> Next, the preparedness policy signifies an entire change in our attitude toward the military as to whom we inherited from our forefathers' suspicions and distrust. A cardinal principle of our polity has always been the subordination of the miltary to the civil authority as a necessary safeguard for the republic."

Document 2

Source: U.S. Bureau of the Census. *Historical Statistics of the United States, Part 1, 1975.*

VALUE OF UNITED STATES IMPORTS AND EXPORTS, 1914 to 1919

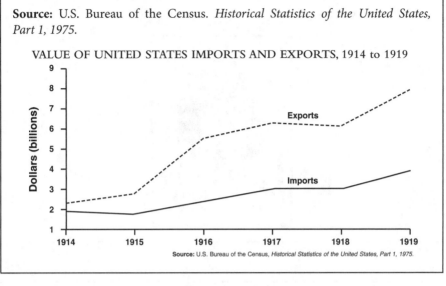

Source: U.S. Bureau of the Census, *Historical Statistics of the United States, Part 1, 1975.*

Document 3

Source: President Woodrow Wilson, War Message to Congress, April 2, 1917

We are glad, now that we see the facts with no veil of false pretense about them, to fight thus for the ultimate peace of the world and for the liberation of its peoples, the German peoples included: for the rights of nations great and small and the privilege of men everywhere to choose their way of life and of obedience. The world must be made safe for democracy. Its peace must be planted upon the tested foundations of political liberty. We have no selfish ends to serve. We desire no conquest, no dominion. We seek no indemnities for ourselves, no material compensation for the sacrifices we shall freely make. We are but one of the champions of the rights of mankind. We shall be satisfied when those rights have been made as secure as the faith and the freedom of nations can make them.

Document 4

Source: Senator George W. Norris, Speech in the U.S. Senate, April 4, 1917

We are taking a step today that is fraught with untold danger. We are going into war upon the command of gold. We are going to run the risk of sacrificing millions of our countrymen's lives in order that other countrymen may coin their lifeblood into money. . . . We are about to do the bidding of wealth's terrible mandate. By our act we will make millions of our countrymen suffer, and the consequences of it may well be that millions of our brethren must shed their lifeblood, millions of broken-hearted women must weep, millions of children must suffer with cold, and millions of babes must die from hunger, and all because we want to preserve the commercial right of American citizens to deliver munitions of war to belligerent nations.

Document 5

Source: Library of Congress

Document 6

Source: Norman Thomas, socialist and pacifist, *The New Republic,* May 26, 1917

Tolerance arises from the existence of varying types of doers, all willing to respect one another's special competence. It is not too extreme to assert that in wartime (as in peacetime) some of the most heroic deeds are performed by those who do not (and, if called upon, would not) take up arms in defense of the cause. There are other forms of bravery than the purely military one. Let us be reasonable.

In bringing the gift of freedom to the distant unemancipated, shall we betray so precious a cause by brute denial of freedom to those of our own blood and tradition, to our own freedom lovers within the gate? What a sorry, tragical miscarriage of wisdom!

Document 7

Source: Theodore Roosevelt, Pledge of Loyalty, September 11, 1917

We ask that good Americans . . . uphold the hands of the government at every point efficiently and resolutely against our foreign and domestic foes, and that they constantly spur the government to speedier and more effective action. Furthermore, we ask that, where government action cannot be taken, they arouse an effective and indignant public opinion against the enemies of our country, whether these enemies masquerade as pacifists, or proclaim themselves the enemies of our allies, or act through organizations such as the I.W.W. and the Socialist Party machine, or appear nakedly as the champions of Germany. Above all, we ask that they teach our people to spurn any peace save the peace of overwhelming victory in the war to which we have set our hands.

Topic 8.1

Contextualizing Period 8

Learning Objective: Explain the context for societal changes from 1945 to 1980.

In 1945, the United States emerged from World War II with the world's largest and strongest economy. Americans were happy to get back to civilian life. However, people feared that without the stimulus of wartime spending, the economic depression of the 1930s might return. What no one could predict with any confidence was how the economy at home, the migration to the suburbs and Sun Belt, the spread of communism, and the civil rights movements for African Americans and others would impact American lives in the future.

U.S.–Soviet Conflict The postwar struggle between the United States and the Soviet Union, between Western democracies and the Communist bloc nations, which became known as the *Cold War,* provided the context for many, if not most, events of the period from 1945 to 1980. This struggle showed up in U.S. involvement in wars both in Korea and Vietnam, and in the case of the Cuban Missile Crisis of 1962, a direct confrontation that brought the two nations to the brink of n   uclear war. The Cold War also had a pervasive effect on American society, from how we built schools (over bomb shelters) to the civil rights movement, as more Americans woke up to the glaring injustices of segregation, which mocked our democracy overseas and contradicted the basic principles of freedom and equal opportunity.

Concerns about Communism After World War II, the United States had a second *Red Scare*. Its context involved spies giving atomic bomb secrets to the Communists and hunting down Communists in the State Department, the military, Hollywood, schools, churches, and other American institutions, and at the height of the fear, neighbors. The Cold War also contributed to *public debates* over foreign policy issues, such as U.S. involvement in Vietnam, which led to massive protests by students and antiwar activists that deeply divided the nation and brought down a president. However, the Cold War fluctuated between periods of confrontation and *coexistence* or *détente*.

Economic Growth and Change At the same time, Americans enjoyed robust *economic growth* through the 1950s and 1960s. Part of the context that the country faced little overseas competition, as the rest of the world's economies recovered from the destruction of factories, roads, railways, and harbors during World War II. However, it also involved the pent-up demand for housing, autos, and other consumer goods following the austerity of the Great Depression and World War II. Veterans returning from war and their families changed the U.S. landscape by moving to the *Sun Belt* states and creating new *suburbs* across the nation with the help of the government's GI Bill.

Civil Rights and Liberal Reform If anything pushed the Cold War into the background it was the societal changes related to the *civil rights movement* of African Americans during the 1950s and 1960s, and then in the 1970s the issues of equality and social justice raised by women and ethnic minorities. The *liberalism* of the postwar era, which expanded the *role of government,* generated a range of responses from support to a growing backlash from both secular and religious conservatives.

Turn toward Conservatism By the late 1960s, frustration over the Vietnam War, opposition to civil rights reforms and other liberal domestic programs, and increased civil unrest weakened the Democratic majority. Postwar optimism and prosperity gave way to pessimism and a declining standard of living for many Americans, as many good-paying jobs in manufacturing went overseas to low-wage countries. People were losing confidence in government's ability to solve problems and in the effectiveness of American institutions, from the news media to colleges and universities. By the mid-1970s, as wage growth stagnated for average Americans, liberalism slowly gave way to a *conservative resurgence.*

ANALYZE THE CONTEXT

1. Explain a historical context for political debates and social anxieties about the Cold War during the period from 1945 to 1980.

2. Explain a historical context for the migration to the suburbs and the Sun Belt during the period from 1945 to 1980.

3. Explain a historical context for the civil rights movement of African Americans and other groups seeking equality and social justice during the period from 1945 to 1980.

LANDMARK EVENTS: 1945–1980

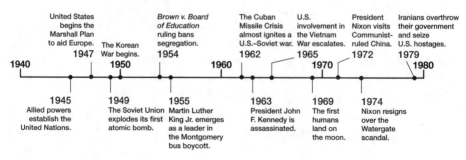

Topic 8.2

The Cold War from 1945 to 1980

Communism holds that the world is so deeply divided into opposing classes that war is inevitable. Democracy holds that free nations can settle differences justly and maintain lasting peace.

President Harry S. Truman, Inaugural Address, January 20, 1949

Learning Objective: Explain the continuities and changes in the Cold War policies from 1945 to 1980.

World War II dramatically changed the United States from an isolationist country into a military superpower and a leader in world affairs. After the war, most of the Americans at home and the millions coming back from military service wished to return to normal domestic life and enjoy the revitalized national economy. However, during the Truman presidency, the growing conflict between the Communist Soviet Union and the United States resulted in a long struggle that came to be known as the Cold War.

Origins of the Cold War

The **Cold War** dominated international relations from the late 1940s to the collapse of the Soviet Union in 1991. The conflict centered on the intense rivalry between two superpowers: the Communist **Soviet Union** and the leading Western democracy, the United States. They competed directly through diplomacy and indirectly through armed conflicts among allies, but rarely through direct military actions against each other. However, in several instances, the Cold War took the world dangerously near nuclear war.

Historians intensely debate how the Cold War began. Some see President Truman's (1945–1953) policies as a reasonable response to Soviet efforts to spread their influence. However, some critics argue that Truman misunderstood and overreacted to Russia's realistic need to secure its borders. Other critics have attacked his administration as being weak or "soft" on communism.

U.S.–Soviet Relations to 1945 The wartime alliance between the United States and the Soviet Union against the Axis powers was actually a temporary halt in their generally poor relations of the past. Since the Bolshevik Revolution that established a Communist government in Russia in 1917, Americans had viewed the Soviets as a threat to all capitalistic countries. In the United States, it led to the Red Scare of 1919. The United States refused to recognize the Soviet Union until 1933. Even then, after a brief honeymoon period, Roosevelt's advisers concluded that Joseph Stalin and the Communists could not be trusted. Confirming their view was the notorious Nonaggression Pact of 1939, in which Stalin and Hitler agreed to divide up Eastern Europe.

Allies in World War II In 1941, Hitler's surprise invasion of the Soviet Union and Japan's surprise attack on Pearl Harbor led to a U.S.–Soviet alliance of convenience—but not of mutual trust. Stalin bitterly complained that the British and Americans waited until 1944 to open a second front in France. Because of this wait, the Soviets bore the brunt of fighting the Nazis. By some estimates, half of all deaths in World War II were Soviets. The postwar conflicts over Central and Eastern Europe were already evident in the negotiations between Britain, the Soviet Union, and the United States at Yalta and Potsdam in 1945. Roosevelt hoped that personal diplomacy might keep Stalin in check, but when Truman came to power, he quickly became suspicious of the Soviets.

Postwar Cooperation and the United Nations The founding of the **United Nations** in the fall of 1945 provided one hopeful sign for the future. The General Assembly of the United Nations was created to provide representation to all member nations, while the 15-member **Security Council** was given the primary responsibility within the UN for maintaining international security and authorizing peacekeeping missions. The five major allies of wartime—the United States, Great Britain, France, China, and the Soviet Union—were granted permanent seats and veto power in the UN Security Council. Optimists hoped that these nations would be able to reach agreement on international issues. In addition, the Soviets went along with a U.S. proposal to establish an Atomic Energy Commission in the United Nations. They rejected, however, a plan proposed by Bernard Baruch for regulating nuclear energy and eliminating atomic weapons. American leaders interpreted rejection of the Baruch Plan as proof that Moscow did not have peaceful intentions.

The United States also offered the Soviets participation in the new International Bank for Reconstruction and Development (now commonly called the **World Bank**) created at the Bretton Woods Conference in 1944. The bank's initial purpose was to fund rebuilding of a war-torn world. The Soviets, however, declined to participate because they viewed the bank as an instrument of capitalism. The Soviets did join the other Allies in the 1945–1946 Nuremberg trials of 22 top Nazi leaders for war crimes and violations of human rights.

Satellite States in Eastern Europe Distrust turned into hostility beginning in 1946, as Soviet forces remained in occupation of the countries of Central and Eastern Europe. Elections were held by the Soviets—as promised by Stalin at Yalta—but the results were manipulated in favor of Communist candidates. One by one, from 1946 to 1948, Communist dictators, most of them loyal to Moscow, came to power in Poland, Romania, Bulgaria, Albania, Hungary, and Czechoslovakia. Apologists for the Soviets argued that Russia needed buffer states or **satellites** (nations under the control of a great power), as a protection against another Hitler-like invasion from the West.

The U.S. and British governments were alarmed by the Soviet takeover of Eastern Europe. They regarded Soviet actions there as a flagrant violation of self-determination, genuine democracy, and open markets. The British especially wanted free elections in Poland, whose independence had been the issue that started World War II.

Occupation Zones in Germany At the end of the war, the division of Germany and Austria into Soviet, French, British, and U.S. zones of occupation was meant to be only temporary. In Germany, however, the eastern zone under Soviet occupation gradually evolved into a new Communist state, the German Democratic Republic. The conflict over Germany was in part a conflict over differing views of national security and economic needs. The Soviets wanted a weak Germany for security reasons and large war reparations for economic reasons. The United States and Great Britain refused to allow reparations from their western zones because both viewed the economic recovery of Germany as important to the stability of Central Europe. The Soviets, fearing a restored Germany, tightened their control over East Germany. Also, since Berlin lay within their zone, they attempted to force the Americans, British, and French to give up their assigned sectors of the city.

Iron Curtain "I'm tired of babying the Soviets," Truman told Secretary of State James Byrnes in January 1946. News of a Canadian spy ring stealing atomic secrets for the Soviets and continued Soviet occupation of northern Iran further encouraged a get-tough policy in Washington.

In March 1946, in Fulton, Missouri, Truman was present on the speaker's platform as former British Prime Minister **Winston Churchill** declared: "An iron curtain has descended across the continent" of Europe. The **Iron Curtain** metaphor was later used throughout the Cold War to refer to the division between the U.S. allies in Western Europe and Soviet allies of Eastern Europe. Churchill's "iron curtain" speech called for a partnership between Western democracies to halt the expansion of communism. Did the speech anticipate the Cold War—or help to cause it? Historians still debate this question.

Containment in Europe

Early in 1947, Truman adopted a **containment policy** designed to prevent Soviet expansion without starting a war. The plan, which would guide U.S. foreign policy for decades, was formulated by three top advisers: Secretary of State General **George Marshall**, Undersecretary of State **Dean Acheson**, and an expert on Soviet affairs, **George F. Kennan**. In an influential article, Kennan had written that only "a long-term, patient but firm and vigilant containment of Russian expansive tendencies" would eventually cause the Soviets to back off their plan to spread communism and to live in peace with other nations.

Critics of the containment policy, such as journalist Walter Lippmann (who coined the term *Cold War*), argued that it was too ambitious. He considered some areas vital to U.S. security and others merely peripheral. Further, some governments deserved U.S. support but others did not. American leaders, however, had learned the lesson of Munich (when leaders had given into demands by Hitler for land in 1938): appeasing dictators did not work. They felt that Communist aggression, wherever it occurred, must be challenged.

The Truman Doctrine

Truman first implemented the containment policy in response to two threats: (1) a Communist-led uprising against the government in Greece, and (2) Soviet demands for some control of a water route in Turkey, the Dardanelles. In what became known as the **Truman Doctrine**, the president asked Congress in March 1947 for $400 million in economic and military aid to assist the "free people" of Greece and Turkey against "totalitarian" regimes. While Truman's alarmist speech might have oversimplified the situation in Greece and Turkey, it gained bipartisan support from Republicans and Democrats in Congress.

The Marshall Plan

After the war, Europe lay in ruins, short of food and deep in debt. The harsh winter of 1946–1947 further demoralized Europeans, who had already suffered through years of depression and war. Discontent encouraged the growth of the Communist Party, especially in France and Italy. The Truman administration feared that the Western democracies might vote the Communists into power.

In June 1947, George Marshall outlined an extensive program of U.S. economic aid to help European nations revive their economies and strengthen democratic governments. In December, Truman submitted to Congress a $17 billion European Recovery Program, better known as the **Marshall Plan**. In 1948, $12 billion in aid was approved for distribution to the countries of Western Europe over a four-year period. The United States offered Marshall Plan aid to the Soviet Union and its Eastern European satellites, but the Soviets refused it, fearing that it would lead to dependence on the United States.

Effects The Marshall Plan worked exactly as Marshall and Truman had hoped. The massive infusion of U.S. dollars helped Western Europe achieve self-sustaining growth by the 1950s and ended any real threat of Communist political successes in that region. It also bolstered U.S. prosperity by greatly increasing U.S. exports to Europe. At the same time, however, it deepened the rift between the non-Communist West and the Communist East.

The Berlin Airlift

A major crisis of the Cold War focused on Berlin. In June 1948, the Soviets cut off all access by land to the German city. Truman dismissed any plans to withdraw from Berlin, but he also rejected using force to open up the roads through the Soviet-controlled eastern zone. Instead, he ordered U.S. planes to fly in supplies to the people of West Berlin. Day after day, week after week, the massive airlift continued. At the same time, Truman sent 60 bombers capable of carrying atomic bombs to bases in England. The world waited nervously for the outbreak of war, but Stalin decided not to challenge the airlift. (Truman's stand on Berlin was partly responsible for his victory in the 1948 election.)

By May 1949, the Soviets finally opened up the highways to Berlin, thus bringing their 11-month blockade to an end. A major long-term consequence of the Berlin crisis was the creation of two Germanys: the Federal Republic of Germany (**West Germany**, a U.S. ally) and the German Democratic Republic (**East Germany**, a Soviet satellite). Berlin, located within the GDR, also divided into sectors allied with the United States and the Soviets.

NATO and National Security

Ever since Washington's farewell address of 1796, the United States had avoided permanent alliances with European nations. Truman broke with this tradition in 1949 by recommending that the United States join a military defense pact to protect Western Europe. The Senate readily gave its consent. Ten European nations joined the United States and Canada in creating the **North Atlantic Treaty Organization (NATO)**, a military alliance for defending all members from outside attack. Truman selected General Eisenhower as NATO's first Supreme Commander and stationed U.S. troops in Western Europe as a deterrent against a Soviet invasion. Thus, the containment policy led to a military buildup and major commitments abroad. The Soviet Union countered in 1955 by forming the **Warsaw Pact**, a military alliance for the defense of the Communist states of Eastern Europe.

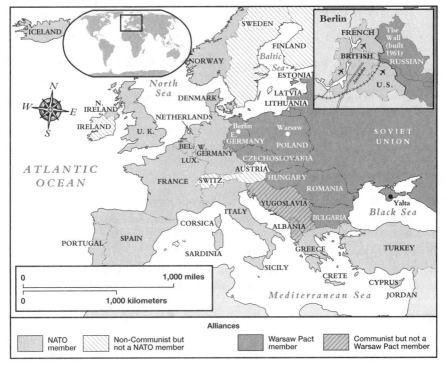

EUROPE AFTER WORLD WAR II: THE COLD WAR

National Security Act (1947) The United States had begun to modernize its military capability in 1947 by passing the **National Security Act**. It provided for (1) a centralized Department of Defense (replacing the War Department) to coordinate the operations of the army, navy, and air force; (2) the creation of the National Security Council (NSC) to coordinate the making of foreign policy; and (3) the creation of the Central Intelligence Agency (CIA) to gather information on foreign governments. In 1948, the Selective Service System and a peacetime military draft were instituted.

Atomic Weapons After the Berlin crisis, teams of scientists in both the Soviet Union and the United States were engaged in an intense competition— or **arms race**—to develop superior weapons systems. For a period of just four years (1945–1949), the United States was the only nation that had the atomic bomb. In this period it also developed a new generation of long-range bombers for delivering nuclear weapons.

The Soviets tested their first atomic bomb in the fall of 1949. Truman then approved the development of a bomb a thousand times more powerful than the A-bomb that had destroyed Hiroshima. In 1952, this hydrogen bomb (or H-bomb) was added to the U.S. arsenal. Earlier, in 1950, the National Security Council had recommended, in a secret report known as **NSC-68**, that the following measures were necessary to fight the Cold War:

- quadruple U.S. government defense spending to 20 percent of GNP

- convince the American public that a costly arms buildup was imperative for the nation's defense

- form alliances with non-Communist countries around the world

Evaluating U.S. Policy Critics of NATO and the defense buildup argued that the Truman administration intensified Russian fears and started an unnecessary arms race. Regardless, NATO became one of the most successful military alliances in history. In combination with the deterrent power of nuclear weapons, NATO effectively checked Soviet expansion in Europe and thereby maintained an uneasy peace until the Soviet Union collapsed in 1991.

Cold War in Asia

The successful containment policy in Europe was not duplicated in Asia. Following World War II, the old imperialist system in India and Southeast Asia crumbled, as former colonies became new nations. Because they had different cultural and political traditions and bitter memories of Western colonialism, they resisted U.S. influence. Ironically, the Asian nation that became most closely tied to the U.S. defense system was its former enemy, Japan.

Japan

Unlike Germany, Japan was solely under the control of the United States. General **Douglas MacArthur** took firm charge of the reconstruction of Japan. Seven Japanese generals, including Premier Hideki Tojo, were tried for war crimes and executed. Under MacArthur's guidance, the new constitution adopted in May 1947 set up a parliamentary democracy. It retained Emperor Hirohito as the ceremonial head of state, but the emperor gave up his claims to divinity. The new constitution also renounced war as an instrument of national policy and provided for only limited military capability. As a result, Japan depended on the military protection of the United States.

U.S.-Japanese Security Treaties With the signing of treaties in 1951, Japan gave up its claims to Korea and some Pacific islands. The United States ended its occupation of Japan, but U.S. troops remained in military bases in Japan for that country's protection against external enemies, particularly Communists. Japan became a strong ally and prospered under the American shield.

The Philippines and the Pacific

On July 4, 1946, in accordance with an act passed by Congress in 1934, the Philippines became an independent republic, but the United States retained important naval and air bases there throughout the Cold War. These bases, together with U.S. control of the UN trustee islands taken from Japan at the end of the war, began to make the Pacific Ocean look like an American lake.

China

Since coming to power in the late 1920s, **Chiang Kai-shek** (Jiang Jie-shi) had used his command of the Nationalist, or Kuomintang, party to control China's central government. During World War II, the United States had given massive military aid to Chiang to prevent all of China from being conquered by Japan. As soon as the war ended, a civil war dating back to the 1930s was renewed between Chiang's Nationalists and the Chinese Communists led by **Mao Zedong**. The Nationalists were losing the loyalty of millions of Chinese because of runaway inflation and widespread corruption, while the well-organized Communists successfully appealed to poor, landless peasants.

U.S. Policy The Truman administration sent George Marshall to China in 1946 to negotiate an end to the civil war, but his compromise fell apart in a few months. By 1947, Chiang's armies were in retreat. After ruling out a large-scale American invasion to rescue Chiang, Truman seemed unsure of what to do. In 1948, Congress voted to give the Nationalist government $400 million in aid, but 80 percent of the U.S. military supplies ended up in Communist hands because of corruption and the collapse of the Nationalist armies.

Two Chinas By the end of 1949, all of mainland China was controlled by the Communists. Chiang and the Nationalists had retreated to an island once under Japanese rule, Formosa (**Taiwan**). From there, Chiang still claimed to head the legitimate government for all of China. The United States continued to support Chiang and refused to recognize Mao Zedong's regime in Beijing (the **People's Republic of China**) until 30 years later, in 1979.

In the United States, Republicans blamed the Democrats for the "loss of China" to Communism. In 1950, Stalin and Mao signed a Sino-Soviet pact. This added to fears of a worldwide Communist conspiracy.

The Korean War

After the defeat of Japan, its former colony Korea was divided along the **38th parallel** by the victors. Soviet armies occupied Korean territory north of the line, while U.S. forces occupied territory to the south. By 1949, both armies were withdrawn, leaving the North in the hands of the Communist leader **Kim Il Sung** and the South under the conservative nationalist **Syngman Rhee**.

Invasion On June 25, 1950, the North Korean army surprised the world, possibly even Moscow, by invading South Korea. Truman took immediate action, applying his containment policy to this latest crisis in Asia. He called for a special session of the UN Security Council. Taking advantage of a temporary boycott by the Soviet delegation, the Security Council under U.S. leadership authorized a UN force to defend South Korea against the invaders. Although other nations participated in this force, U.S. troops made up most of the UN forces sent to help the South Korean army. Commanding the expedition was General Douglas MacArthur. Congress supported the use of U.S. troops in the Korean crisis but failed to declare war, accepting Truman's characterization of U.S. intervention as merely a "police action."

Counterattack At first the war in Korea went badly, as the North Koreans pushed the combined South Korean and U.S. forces to the tip of the peninsula. However, General MacArthur reversed the war with a daring amphibious assault at Inchon behind the North Korean lines. UN forces then proceeded to destroy much of the North Korean army, advancing northward almost as far as the Chinese border. MacArthur failed to heed China's warnings that it would resist threats to its security. In November 1950, masses of Chinese troops crossed the border into Korea, overwhelming UN forces and driving them out of North Korea.

Truman Versus MacArthur MacArthur stabilized the fighting near the 38th parallel. At the same time, he called for expanding the war, including bombing and invading mainland China. As commander in chief, Truman cautioned MacArthur about making public statements that suggested criticism of official U.S. policy. The general spoke out anyway. In April 1951, Truman, with the support of the Joint Chiefs of Staff, recalled MacArthur for insubordination.

MacArthur returned home as a hero. Most Americans understood his statement, "There is no substitute for victory," better than the president's containment policy and concept of "limited war." Critics attacked Truman and the Democrats as appeasers for not trying to destroy communism in Asia.

Stalemate In Korea, neither side seemed able to win. Fighting was stalled along a front just north of the 38th parallel. At the city of Panmunjom, peace talks began in July 1951.

Political Consequences From the perspective of the grand strategy of the Cold War, Truman's containment policy in Korea worked. It stopped Communist aggression without allowing the conflict to develop into a world war. The Truman administration used the **Korean War** as justification for dramatically expanding the military, funding a new jet bomber (the B-52), and stationing more U.S. troops in overseas bases.

However, Republicans were far from satisfied. The stalemate in Korea and the success of Mao in China led Republicans to characterize Truman and the Democrats as "soft on communism." They attacked leading Democrats as members of "Dean Acheson's Cowardly College of Communist Containment." (In 1949, Acheson had replaced George Marshall as secretary of state.) The Republicans went on to win the presidential race in 1952 with former General Dwight Eisenhower.

THE KOREAN WAR

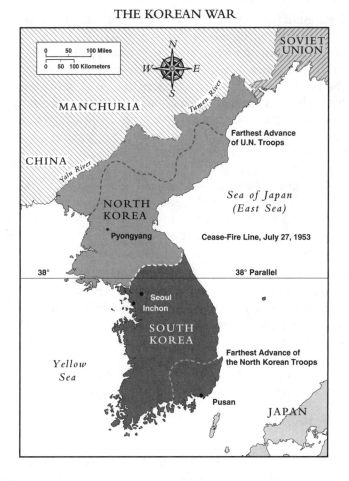

Eisenhower and the Cold War

President Dwight D. Eisenhower (1953–1961) focused in both his terms on foreign policy and the international crises arising from the Cold War. The experienced diplomat who helped to shape U.S. foreign policy throughout Eisenhower's presidency was Secretary of State **John Foster Dulles**.

Dulles's Diplomacy Dulles had been critical of Truman's containment policy as too passive. He advocated a "new look" to U.S. foreign policy that took the initiative in challenging the Soviet Union and the People's Republic of China. He talked of "liberating captive nations" of Eastern Europe and encouraging the Nationalist government of Taiwan to assert itself against "Red" (Communist) China. Dulles pleased conservatives—and alarmed many others—by declaring that, if the United States pushed Communist powers to the brink of war, they would back down because of American nuclear superiority. His hard line became known as **brinkmanship**. In the end, however, Eisenhower prevented Dulles from carrying his ideas to an extreme.

Massive Retaliation Dulles advocated relying more on nuclear weapons and air power and spending less on conventional military forces. This might save money ("more bang for the buck"), help balance the federal budget, and increase pressure on potential enemies. In 1953, the United States developed the hydrogen bomb, which could destroy the largest cities. Within a year, however, the Soviets caught up with a hydrogen bomb of their own. To some, the policy of **massive retaliation** looked more like a policy for mutual annihilation. Nuclear weapons indeed proved a powerful deterrent against the superpowers fighting an all-out war between themselves.

However, such weapons did not prevent superpower involvement in small "brushfire" wars in the developing nations of Southeast Asia, Africa, and the Middle East. With the United States and the Soviet backing opposing sides, these conflicts could expand, resulting in hundreds of thousands of casualties. But the superpowers, fearing escalation, refused to use even small nuclear weapons in these wars.

Korean Armistice Soon after taking office in 1953, Eisenhower kept his promise to go to Korea to visit UN forces and try to end the war. He understood that no quick fix was likely. Even so, diplomacy, the threat of nuclear war, and the death of Joseph Stalin in March 1953 finally moved China and North Korea to agree to an armistice and an exchange of prisoners in July 1953. The fighting stopped and most (but not all) U.S. troops were withdrawn. Korea remained divided near the 38th parallel, without a permanent peace treaty. More than 2.5 million people died in the Korean conflict, including 36,914 Americans.

U.S.-Soviet Relations

For U.S. security, nothing was more crucial than U.S. diplomatic relations with its chief political and military rival, the Soviet Union. Throughout Eisenhower's presidency, the relations between the two superpowers fluctuated between periods of relative calm and extreme tension.

Spirit of Geneva After Stalin's death, Eisenhower called for a slowdown in the arms race and presented to the United Nations an **"atoms for peace"** plan. The Soviets also showed signs of wanting to reduce Cold War tensions. They withdrew their troops from Austria (once that country had agreed to be neutral in the Cold War) and established peaceful relations with Greece and Turkey.

By 1955, a desire for improved relations on both sides resulted in a summit meeting in Geneva, Switzerland, between Eisenhower and the new Soviet premier, Nikolai Bulganin. At this conference, the U.S. president proposed an "**open-skies**" **policy** over each other's territory—open to aerial photography by the opposing nation—in order to eliminate the chance of a surprise nuclear attack. The Soviets rejected the proposal. Nevertheless, the "**spirit of Geneva**," as the press called it, produced the first thaw in the Cold War. Even more encouraging, from the U.S. point of view, was a speech by the new Soviet leader **Nikita Khrushchev** in early 1956 in which he denounced the crimes of Joseph Stalin and supported "**peaceful coexistence**" with the West.

Hungarian Revolt The relaxation in the Cold War encouraged workers in East Germany and Poland to demand reforms from their Communist governments. In October 1956, a popular uprising in Hungary actually succeeded in overthrowing a government backed by Moscow. The new, more liberal leaders wanted to pull Hungary out of the Warsaw Pact, the Communist security organization. This was too much for the Kremlin, and Khrushchev sent in Soviet tanks to crush the freedom fighters and restore control over Hungary. The United States took no action in the crisis. Eisenhower feared that sending troops to aid the Hungarians would touch off a major war in Europe. In effect, by allowing Soviet tanks to roll into Hungary, the United States gave de facto recognition to the Soviet sphere of influence in Eastern Europe and ended Dulles's talk of "liberating" this region. Soviet suppression of the **Hungarian revolt** also ended the first thaw in the Cold War.

Sputnik **Shock** In 1957, the Soviet Union shocked the United States by launching the first satellites, *Sputnik I* and *Sputnik II*, into orbit around the earth. Suddenly, the technological leadership of the United States was open to question. To add to American embarrassment, U.S. rockets designed to duplicate the Soviet achievement failed repeatedly.

What was responsible for this scientific debacle? Critics attacked American schools for their math and science instruction and failure to produce more scientists and engineers. In 1958, Congress responded with the National Defense and Education Act (NDEA), which authorized hundreds of millions of federal dollars for schools for math, science, and foreign language education.

Also in 1958, Congress created the **National Aeronautics and Space Administration (NASA)** to direct the U.S. efforts to build missiles and explore outer space. Billions were appropriated to compete with the Russians in the space race.

Fears of nuclear war were intensified by *Sputnik*. The missiles that launched the satellites could also deliver thermonuclear warheads anywhere in the world in minutes, and there was no defense against them.

Second Berlin Crisis "We will bury capitalism," Khrushchev boasted. With new confidence and pride based on *Sputnik*, the Soviet leader pushed the Berlin issue in 1958. He gave the West six months to pull its troops out of West Berlin before turning over the city to the East Germans. The United

States refused to yield. To defuse the crisis, Eisenhower invited Khrushchev to visit the United States in 1959. At the presidential retreat of Camp David in Maryland, the two agreed to put off the crisis and scheduled another summit conference in Paris for 1960.

U-2 Incident The friendly "spirit of Camp David" never had a chance to produce results. Two weeks before the planned meeting in Paris, the Russians shot down a high-altitude U.S. spy plane—the U-2—over the Soviet Union. The incident exposed a secret U.S. tactic for gaining information. After its open-skies proposals had been rejected by the Soviets in 1955, the United States had decided to conduct regular spy flights over Soviet territory to find out about its enemy's missile program. Eisenhower took full responsibility for the flights—*after* they were exposed by the **U-2 incident**—but his honesty proved to be a diplomatic mistake. Khrushchev denounced the United States and walked out of the Paris summit, temporarily ending the thaw in the Cold War.

Communism in Cuba

Perhaps more alarming than any other Cold War development during the Eisenhower years was the emergence of **Cuba** as a Communist country. A bearded revolutionary, **Fidel Castro**, overthrew the Cuban dictator Fulgencio Batista in 1959. At first, no one knew whether Castro's politics would be better or worse than those of his ruthless predecessor. Once in power, however, Castro nationalized American-owned businesses and properties in Cuba. Eisenhower retaliated by cutting off U.S. trade with Cuba.

Castro then turned to the Soviets for support. He also revealed that he was a Marxist and soon proved it by setting up a Communist totalitarian state. Fearing communism only 90 miles off the shores of Florida, Eisenhower authorized the Central Intelligence Agency to train anti-Communist Cuban exiles so they could invade the island and overthrow Castro. However, the decision to go ahead with the invasion would be the responsibility of the next president, John F. Kennedy.

Eisenhower's Legacy

After leaving the White House, Eisenhower claimed credit for checking Communist aggression and keeping the peace without the loss of American lives in combat. He also started the long process of relaxing tensions with the Soviet Union. In 1958, he initiated the first arms limitations by voluntarily suspending aboveground testing of nuclear weapons.

"Military-Industrial Complex" In his farewell address as president, Eisenhower spoke out against the negative impact of the Cold War on U.S. society. He warned the nation to "guard against the acquisition of unwarranted influence . . . by the **military-industrial complex**." He feared the arms race was taking on a momentum and logic all its own. It seemed to some Americans in the 1960s that the United States was in danger of going down the path of classical Rome by turning into a military, or imperial, state.

To the Brink of War and Back

In 1960, John F. Kennedy was elected president after attacking the Eisenhower administration for the recent recession and for permitting the Soviets to take the lead in the arms race. In reality, what Kennedy called a "missile gap" was actually in the U.S. favor, but his charges seemed plausible after *Sputnik*.

Bay of Pigs Invasion The youthful Kennedy made a major blunder shortly after entering office. He approved a plan to use Cuban exiles to overthrow Castro's regime. In April 1961, the CIA-trained force of Cubans landed at the **Bay of Pigs** in Cuba but failed to set off a general uprising as planned. Trapped on the beach, the anti-Castro Cubans surrendered after Kennedy rejected the idea of using U.S. forces to save them. Castro used the failed invasion to get more aid from the Soviet Union and to strengthen his grip on power.

Berlin Wall Trying to shake off the embarrassment of the Bay of Pigs defeat, Kennedy agreed to meet Soviet premier Khrushchev in Vienna in the summer of 1961. Khrushchev seized the opportunity to threaten the president by renewing Soviet demands that the United States pull its troops out of Berlin. Kennedy refused. In August, the East Germans, with Soviet backing, built a wall around West Berlin. Its purpose was to stop East Germans from fleeing to West Germany. As the wall was being built, Soviet and U.S. tanks faced off in Berlin. Kennedy called up the reserves, but he made no move to stop the completion of the wall. In 1963, the president traveled to West Berlin to assure its residents of continuing U.S. support. To cheering crowds, he proclaimed: "Freedom has many difficulties and democracy is not perfect, but we have never had to put up a wall to keep our people in. . . . As a free man, I take pride in the words, 'Ich bin ein Berliner' [I am a Berliner]." The **Berlin Wall** stood as a gloomy symbol of the Cold War until it was torn down by rebellious East Germans in 1989.

Cuban Missile Crisis (1962) The most dangerous moment in U.S.-Soviet relations came in October 1962. In response to the Bay of Pigs invasion, Castro invited the Soviets to build underground missile sites that could launch offensive missiles capable of reaching the United States in minutes. The Soviets agreed. U.S. reconnaissance planes soon discovered evidence of construction. Kennedy responded by announcing to the world that he was setting up a naval blockade of Cuba until the weapons were removed. If Soviet ships challenged the U.S. naval blockade, a full-scale nuclear war between the superpowers might result. After 13 days of tension, Khrushchev finally agreed to remove the missiles from Cuba in exchange for Kennedy's pledge not to invade the island nation and to later remove some U.S. missiles from Turkey.

The **Cuban missile crisis** had a sobering effect on both sides. They soon established a telecommunications hotline between Washington and Moscow so the countries' leaders could talk directly during a crisis. In 1963, the Soviet Union and the United States—along with nearly 100 other nations—signed the **Nuclear Test Ban Treaty** to end the testing of nuclear weapons in the atmosphere. This first step in controlling the testing of nuclear arms was offset by a new round in the arms race for developing missile and warhead superiority.

Flexible Response Many "brushfire wars" in Africa and Southeast Asia were a different Cold War challenge. Often, insurgent forces aided by Soviet arms and training challenged an existing government with ties to the United States. Such conflicts in the Congo in Africa and in Laos and Vietnam in Southeast Asia convinced the Kennedy administration to rethink Dulles's idea of massive retaliation and reliance on nuclear weapons. Kennedy and his Defense Secretary, Robert S. McNamara, wanted options less likely to escalate into global destruction. They increased spending on conventional (nonnuclear) arms and mobile military forces. While this **flexible-response policy** reduced the risk of using nuclear weapons, it also increased the temptation to send elite special forces, such as the Green Berets, into combat all over the globe.

Lyndon Johnson Becomes President

After less than three years in office, President Kennedy was assassinated during a visit to Texas (Topic 8.5). Kennedy's vice president, Lyndon Johnson, was a former leader of the Senate who was more interested in domestic reforms to further the New Deal than in foreign policy. However, Johnson (1963–1969) continued the containment policy that called upon the United States to block Communist expansion around the globe, including in Vietnam. His escalation of the Vietnam War (Topic 8.8) came to dominate the foreign policy of his administration. However, he continued to engage the Soviets on other fronts.

Despite the Vietnam War, President Johnson did negotiate agreements with the Soviet Union to control nuclear weapons. In the later 1960s, as a result of the costly arms race and its worsening relationship with China, the Soviet Union sought closer relations with the United States. The Johnson administration signed the Outer Space Treaty and laid the foundation for the Strategic Arms Limitation Talks. In July 1968, the United States, Britain, and the Soviet Union signed the **Non-Proliferation Treaty**, in which each signatory agreed not to help other countries develop or acquire nuclear weapons. A planned U.S.-Soviet nuclear disarmament summit was scuttled after Soviet forces violently suppressed the Prague Spring, an attempt to democratize Czechoslovakia. The ebbs and flows in the Cold War revealed that it was a complex chess game, and the next president proved a dedicated player.

Nixon's Detente Diplomacy

In his January 1969 inaugural address, President Richard M. Nixon (1969–1974) promised to bring Americans together after the turmoil of the 1960s. Nixon's first interest was international relations, not domestic policy. Together with his national security adviser, **Henry Kissinger** (who became secretary of state during Nixon's second term), Nixon fashioned a realist or pragmatic foreign policy that ended the war in Vietnam (Topic 8.8) and reduced the tensions of the Cold War.

Détente Nixon and Kissinger strengthened the U.S. position in the world by taking advantage of the rivalry between the two Communist giants, China and the Soviet Union. Their diplomacy was praised for bringing about **détente**—a deliberate reduction of Cold War tensions. Even after Watergate ended his presidency in disgrace, Nixon's critics would admit that his conduct of foreign affairs had enhanced world peace.

Visit to China Nixon had long been a fierce critic of communism. Because of this, he could stake the bold step of improving relations with Mao Zedong's Communist regime in "Red" China without being condemned as "soft" on communism. After a series of secret negotiations with Chinese leaders, Nixon astonished the world in February 1972 by traveling to Beijing to meet with Mao. His visit initiated diplomatic exchanges that ultimately led to U.S. recognition of the Communist government in 1979.

Arms Control with the U.S.S.R. Nixon used his new relationship with China to pressure the Soviets to agree to a treaty limiting **antiballistic missiles (ABMs)**, a new technology that would have expanded the arms race. After the first round of **Strategic Arms Limitations Talks** (SALT I), U.S. diplomats secured Soviet consent to a freeze on the number of ballistic missiles carrying nuclear warheads. While this agreement did not end the arms race, it was a significant step toward reducing Cold War tensions and bringing about détente.

Another Chill in the Cold War

The resignation of President Nixon (Topic 8.14) in August 1974 puzzled both allies and enemies. After Nixon's Watergate scandal and the fall of South Vietnam in 1975 many Americans lost trust in their government. Presidents faced strong opposition in Congress against further military interventions. During Ford's term (1974–1977), the Democratic Congress continued to investigate abuses in the executive branch, especially in the CIA. This intelligence agency was accused of engineering the assassinations of foreign leaders, among them the

Marxist president of Chile, Salvador Allende. Ford appointed a former member of Congress, George H. W. Bush, to reform the agency.

Soviets Invade Afghanistan President Jimmy Carter (1977–1981) attempted to continue the Nixon-Ford policy of détente with China and the Soviet Union. In 1979, the United States ended its recognition of the Nationalist government in Taiwan as the official government of China and completed the first exchange of ambassadors with the People's Republic of China. At first, détente also moved ahead with the Soviet Union with the signing in 1979 of the SALT II treaty, which provided for limiting the size of each superpower's nuclear delivery system. The Senate never ratified the treaty, however, as a result of a renewal of Cold War tensions over Afghanistan.

In December 1979, Soviet troops invaded Afghanistan—an aggressive action that ended a decade of improving U.S.–Soviet relations. The United States feared that the invasion might lead to a Soviet move to control the oil-rich Persian Gulf. Carter reacted by (1) placing an embargo on grain exports and the sale of high technology to the Soviet Union, and (2) boycotting the 1980 Olympics in Moscow. After having campaigned for arms reduction, Carter now had to switch to an arms buildup.

A Return to Tension At the end of Carter's administration, relations with the Soviet Union were back to a period of confrontation. Topic 9.3 will trace the arms race with the Soviet Union during the Reagan administration and the steps that led to the breakup of the Soviet Union and the end of the Cold War.

Views of the Cold War Among U.S. historians, the traditional view of the origins of the Cold War is that the Soviet government under Stalin started the conflict by subjugating the countries of Eastern Europe in the late 1940s. The United States was viewed as the defender of the free world.

In the 1960s, during the time of public unhappiness over the Vietnam War, revisionist historians began to argue that the United States contributed to starting the Cold War. They blamed Truman for antagonizing the Soviets with his blunt challenge of their actions in Poland and the Balkans. Gar Alperovitz (*The Decision to Use the Atomic Bomb,* 1995) concluded that Truman had dropped atomic bombs on Japan primarily to warn Stalin to remove his troops from Eastern Europe.

In the 21st century, John L. Gaddis (*The Cold War: A New History,* 2005), recognized by some as "the dean of Cold War historians," argued that the causes of the Cold War were rooted in the Big Three's failure "to reconcile divergent political objectives even as they pursued a common military task" during World War II. Gaddis suggested that objective observers would not have expected a different outcome given that great power rivalries are the normal pattern in history. Gaddis concluded that the most important aspect of the Cold War is what did not happen—a nuclear holocaust.

REFLECT ON LEARNING OBJECTIVE

1. Explain one example of continuity and one example of change in the United States' Cold War policies from 1945 to 1980.

KEY TERMS BY THEME

Origins of the Cold War (WOR)
Cold War
Soviet Union
Joseph Stalin
United Nations
Security Council
World Bank
satellites
Winston Churchill
Iron Curtain

Containment in Europe (WOR)
containment policy
George Marshall
Dean Acheson
George F. Kennan
Truman Doctrine
Marshall Plan
Berlin airlift
West Germany
East Germany
North Atlantic Treaty Organization (NATO)
Warsaw Pact
National Security Act
arms race
NSC-68

Cold War in Asia (WOR)
Douglas MacArthur
U.S.-Japanese security treaties
Chiang Kai-shek
Mao Zedong
Taiwan
People's Republic of China
38th parallel

Kim Il Sung
Syngman Rhee
Korean War

Eisenhower Foreign Policy (WOR)
John Foster Dulles
brinkmanship
massive retaliation
Korean armistice
atoms for peace
open-skies policy
spirit of Geneva
Nikita Khrushchev
peaceful coexistence
Hungarian revolt
Sputnik
National Aeronautics and Space
    Administration (NASA)
U-2 incident
Cuba
Fidel Castro
military-industrial complex

Kennedy-Johnson Foreign Policy (WOR)
Bay of Pigs
Berlin Wall
Cuban missile crisis
Nuclear Test Ban Treaty
flexible-response policy
Non-Proliferation Treaty

Nixon-Ford-Carter Foreign Policy (WOR)
Henry Kissinger
détente
antiballistic missiles (ABMs)
Strategic Arms Limitation Talks (SALT)

MULTIPLE-CHOICE QUESTIONS

Questions 1–3 refer to the excerpt below.

> "It is clear that the main element of any United States policy towards the Soviet Union must be that of a long-term, patient but firm and vigilant containment of Russian expansive tendencies. . . . It is clear that the United States cannot expect in the foreseeable future to enjoy political intimacy with the Soviet regime. It must continue to regard the Soviet Union as a rival, not a partner, in the political arena. It must continue to expect that Soviet policies will reflect no abstract love of peace and stability, no real faith in the possibility of a permanent happy coexistence of the Socialist and capitalist worlds, but rather a cautious, persistent pressure towards the disruption and weakening of all rival influence and rival power."

> Mr. X (George F. Kennan), State Department professional,
> "The Sources of Soviet Conduct," *Foreign Affairs,* July 1947

1. Which one of the following best reflects the policies advocated in the above excerpt?

   (A) The proposal to militarily roll back communism in Eastern Europe

   (B) General MacArthur's criticism of the concept of limited wars

   (C) The Truman Doctrine of aid to Greece and Turkey

   (D) George Marshall's negotiations to end the Chinese civil war

2. Which of the following actions would best implement the goals and strategy of George Kennan?

   (A) Offering economic aid to Eastern Europe and the Soviet Union

   (B) Using the U.S. Army to invade East Germany and liberate West Berlin

   (C) Reorganizing all military services under the Department of Defense

   (D) Using economic aid to block the appeal of communism in Western Europe

3. Implementing the policies based on this excerpt led the United States to change from earlier foreign policy traditions by

   (A) creating more peacetime military alliances with other countries

   (B) helping more European powers expand their influence in Central America

   (C) isolating itself from more economic involvement with the world

   (D) rejecting more participation in international organizations

SHORT-ANSWER QUESTIONS

Use complete sentences; an outline or bulleted list alone is not acceptable.

1. "I find it increasingly difficult, given what we know now, to imagine the Soviet Union or the Cold War without Stalin. . . . If one could have eliminated Stalin, alternative paths become quite conceivable. . . . And given his propensity for cold wars, a tendency firmly rooted long before he had even heard of Harry Truman. . . . It is equally clear that there was going to be a Cold War whatever the West did. Who then was responsible? The answer, I think, is authoritarianism in general, and Stalin in particular."

> John Lewis Gaddis, *We Know Now: Rethinking the Cold War,* 1997

"No one leader or nation caused the Cold War. . . . Nevertheless, from the Potsdam Conference through the Korean War, [President Truman] contributed significantly to the growing Cold War and the militarism of American foreign policy. . . . Throughout his presidency, Truman remained a parochial [narrow-minded] nationalist who lacked the leadership to move America away from conflict toward détente. Instead, he promoted an ideology and politics of Cold War confrontation that became the modus operandi [common method] of successor administrations and the United States for the next two generations."

> Arnold A. Offner, *Diplomatic History,* Spring 1999

Using the excerpts above, answer (a), (b), and (c).

(a) Briefly describe ONE specific difference between Gaddis's and Offner's historical interpretation of the origins of the Cold War.

(b) Briefly explain ONE specific historical event or development that is not explicitly mentioned in the excerpts that could be used to support Gaddis's interpretation of the origins of the Cold War.

(c) Briefly explain ONE specific historical event or development that is not explicitly mentioned in the excerpts that could be used to support Offner's interpretation of the origins of the Cold War.

2. Answer (a), (b), and (c).

(a) Briefly describe ONE specific difference between Cold War policies of the Truman and Eisenhower administrations.

(b) Briefly describe ONE specific similarity between Cold War policies of the Truman and Eisenhower administrations.

(c) Briefly explain ONE specific effect that resulted from the Cold War policies of either Truman or Eisenhower.

Topic 8.3

The Red Scare

There are today many Communists in America. They are everywhere—in factories, offices, butcher stores, on street corners, in private businesses. And each carries in himself the germ of death for society.

J. Howard McGrath, U.S. Attorney General, 1949–1952

Learning Objective: Explain the causes and effects of the Red Scare after World War II.

Just as a Red Scare had followed U.S. victory in World War I, a second Red Scare followed U.S. victory in World War II. The Truman administration's tendency to see a Communist conspiracy behind civil wars in Europe and Asia contributed to the belief that Communist conspirators and spies had infiltrated American society, including the U.S. State Department and the U.S. military.

Rooting Out Communists

In 1947, the Truman administration—under pressure from Republican critics—set up a **Loyalty Review Board** to investigate the background of more than 3 million federal employees. Thousands of officials and civil service employees either resigned or lost their jobs in a probe that went on for four years (1947–1951).

Prosecutions Under the Smith Act In addition, leaders of the American Communist Party were jailed for advocating the overthrow of the U.S. government. In the case of ***Dennis et al. v. United States*** (1951), the Supreme Court upheld the constitutionality of the **Smith Act** of 1940, which made it illegal to advocate or teach the overthrow of the government by force or to belong to an organization with this objective.

McCarran Internal Security Act (1950) Over Truman's veto, Congress passed the **McCarran Internal Security Act**, which (1) made it unlawful to advocate or support the establishment of a totalitarian government, (2) restricted the employment and travel of those joining Communist-front organizations, and (3) authorized the creation of detention camps for subversives.

Un-American Activities In the House of Representatives, the **House Un-American Activities Committee (HUAC)**, originally established in 1939 to seek out Nazis, was reactivated in the postwar years to find Communists. The committee not only investigated government officials but also looked for Communist influence in such organizations as the Boy Scouts and in the Hollywood film industry. Actors, directors, and writers were called before the committee to testify. Those who refused to testify were tried for contempt of Congress. Others were blacklisted from the industry, meaning no one would hire them.

Cultural Impact The second Red Scare had a chilling effect on freedom of expression. Creators of the gritty film noir crime dramas and playwrights such as Arthur Miller (*Death of a Salesman,* 1949) came under attack as anti-American. Rodgers and Hammerstein's musical *South Pacific* (1949) was criticized, especially by Southern politicians, as a Communistic assault on racial segregation. Loyalty oaths were commonly required of writers and teachers as a condition of employment. The American Civil Liberties Union and other opponents of these security measures argued that the First Amendment protected the free expression of unpopular political views and membership in political groups, including the Communist Party.

Artists and writers responded. Shirley Jackson's short story "The Lottery" (1948) is about a town whose citizens blindly accept a tradition even though it has deadly consequences. When called to testify before the HUAC in 1952, playwright Lillian Hellman refused, saying, "I cannot and will not cut my conscience to fit this year's fashions," for which she was blacklisted. Arthur Miller's play *The Crucible* (1953), about the Salem witch trials, was a thinly veiled metaphor for the government's persecution of suspected Communists.

Espionage Cases

The fear of a Communist conspiracy bent on world conquest was supported by a series of actual cases of Communist espionage in Great Britain, Canada, and the United States. The methods used to identify Communist spies, however, raised serious questions about whether the government was going too far and violating civil liberties in the process.

Hiss Case A star witness for the House Un-American Activities Committee in 1948 was **Whittaker Chambers**, who was a Communist. His testimony, along with the investigative work of a young member of Congress from California named Richard Nixon, led to the trial of **Alger Hiss**. Hiss was a prominent official in the State Department who had assisted Roosevelt at the Yalta Conference. He denied the accusations that he was a Communist and had given secret documents to Chambers. In 1950, however, he was convicted of perjury and sent to prison. Many Americans could not help wondering whether the highest levels of government were infiltrated by Communist spies.

Rosenberg Case When the Soviets tested their first atomic bomb in 1949, many Americans were convinced that spies had helped them to steal the technology from the United States. Klaus Fuchs, a British scientist who had worked on the Manhattan Project, admitted giving A-bomb secrets to the Russians. An FBI investigation traced another spy ring to **Julius and Ethel Rosenberg** in New York. After a controversial trial in 1951, the Rosenbergs were found guilty of treason and executed in 1953. Civil rights groups charged that anti-Communist hysteria was responsible for the conviction and execution of the Rosenbergs.

The Rise and Fall of Joseph McCarthy

Joseph McCarthy, a Republican senator from Wisconsin, used the growing concern over communism to advance his political career. In a speech in 1950, he claimed to have a list of 205 Communists who were working for the State Department. (In other speeches the number varied.) As the press publicized this sensational, though unproven, accusation, McCarthy became one of the most powerful leaders in America. Other politicians feared the damage McCarthy could do if he pointed his accusing finger toward them.

McCarthy's Tactics Senator McCarthy used a steady stream of unsupported accusations about Communists in government to keep the media focus on himself and to discredit the Truman administration. Working-class Americans at first loved his "take the gloves off" hard-hitting remarks, which were often aimed at the wealthy and privileged in society. While many Republicans disliked McCarthy's ruthless tactics, he was primarily hurting the Democrats before the election of Eisenhower to the presidency in 1952. He became so popular, however, that even Eisenhower would not dare to defend his old friend, George Marshall, against McCarthy's untruths.

Army-McCarthy Hearings In 1954, McCarthy's "reckless cruelty" was finally exposed on television. A Senate committee held televised hearings on Communist infiltration in the army, and McCarthy was seen as a bully by millions of viewers. In December, Republicans joined Democrats in a Senate censure of McCarthy. The "witch hunt" for Communists (**McCarthyism**) had played itself out. Three years later, McCarthy died a broken man.

Decline of the Red Scare The Red Scare after World War II ran out of steam as it became clear that the fear of a Communist takeover of the United States was overblown. Cooler heads, including President Eisenhower, gained control of the political dialogue. However, the language, tactics, and threats of McCarthyism remained a concern for democracy whenever politics became bitter and partisan. Americans also pushed the fear of communism into the background after the Korean War armistice as average Americans enjoyed the booming economy of the 1950s (Topic 8.4).

REFLECT ON THE LEARNING OBJECTIVE

1. Explain one cause and one effect of the Red Scare after World War II.

Second Red Scare (NAT)
Loyalty Review Board
*Dennis et al. v. United
   States*
Smith Act (1940)

McCarran Internal Security
   Act (1950)
House Un-American
   Activities Committee
   (HUAC)

Whittaker Chambers
Alger Hiss
Julius and Ethel Rosenberg
Joseph McCarthy
McCarthyism

MULTIPLE-CHOICE QUESTIONS

Questions 1–2 refer to the excerpt below.

"The United States Senate has long enjoyed the worldwide respect. . . . But recently that deliberative character has too often been debased to the level of a forum of hate and character assassination sheltered by the shield of congressional immunity.

The American people are sick and tired of being afraid to speak their minds lest they be politically smeared as 'Communists' or 'Fascists' by their opponents. Freedom of speech is not what it used to be in America. It has been so abused by some that it is not exercised by others. . . .

As an American, I am shocked at the way Republicans and Democrats alike are playing directly into the Communist design of 'confuse, divide and conquer.' As an American, I do not want a Democrat administration 'whitewash' or 'coverup' any more than I want a Republican smear or witch hunt."

> "Declaration of Conscience," Margaret Chase Smith,
> Republican Senator of Maine, June 1, 1950

1. Which of the following most directly contributed to the conditions that allowed members of the Senate to engage in what Smith called "character assassination" at this time?

   (A) The 1st Amendment guaranteed that all people, including senators, had the unrestricted right to say anything.

   (B) The Republicans controlled Congress and therefore could freely attack Democrats.

   (C) The president had been using unsupported allegations to lead attacks on the loyalty of members of Congress.

   (D) Members of the Senate and House were protected from legal actions against them for what they said while in Congress.

2. Which of the following best explains Smith's reason for delivering her "Declaration of Conscience" speech?

(A) She was attempting to get reelected in a solidly Republican state.

(B) She was concerned about how fear was corrupting American principles.

(C) She was defending herself from an attack by Senator McCarthy as a Communist.

(D) She felt that a cover-up was more dangerous than a witch hunt.

SHORT-ANSWER QUESTION

Use complete sentences; an outline or bulleted list alone is not acceptable.

1. "The reason why we find ourselves in a position of impotency is . . . because of the traitorous actions of those who have been treated so well by this Nation. It has not been the less fortunate or members of minority groups who have been selling this Nation out, but rather those who have had all the benefits that the wealthiest nation on earth has to offer—the finest homes, the finest college education, and the finest jobs in Government.

This is glaringly true in the State Department. There the bright young men who are born with silver spoons in their mouths are the ones who have been the worst. . . . In my opinion, the State Department . . . is thoroughly infested with Communists. I have in my hand 57 cases of individuals who would appear to be either card-carrying members or certainly loyal to the Communist Party, but who nevertheless are still helping to shape our foreign policy."

> Joseph R. McCarthy, Speech in Wheeling,
> West Virginia, February 1950

Using the excerpt above, answer (a), (b), and (c).

(a) Briefly explain ONE specific postwar event that would support the rhetoric of this excerpt.

(b) Briefly explain ONE specific tactic used by Joseph McCarthy that was condemned as a "witch hunt" or "McCarthyism."

(c) Briefly explain ONE specific cause of McCarthy's appeal to blue-collar Americans.

Topic 8.4

Economy after 1945

America at this moment stands at the summit of the world.

British Prime Minster Winton Churchill, 1945

Learning Objective 1: Explain the causes of economic growth in years after World War II.

Learning Objective 2: Explain causes and effects of the migrations of various groups of Americans after 1945.

The 15 million American military members returning to civilian life in 1945 and 1946 needed to find jobs and housing. Many feared that the war's end would bring back economic hard times. Happily, the fears were not realized because the war years had increased the per-capita income of Americans. Much of that income was tucked away in savings accounts, since wartime shortages meant there had been few consumer goods to buy. The pent-up consumer demand for autos and housing combined with government roadbuilding and other projects quickly overcame the economic uncertainty after the war and introduced an era of unprecedented prosperity and economic growth. By the 1950s, Americans enjoyed the highest standard of living achieved by any society in history.

Postwar Economy

President **Harry S. Truman** (1945–1953) was thrust into the presidency after Franklin Roosevelt's death in April 1945, Truman matured into a decisive leader whose basic honesty and unpretentious style appealed to average citizens. He attempted to continue the New Deal economic policies of his predecessor but faced growing conservative opposition.

Employment Act of 1946 In September 1945, in the same week that Japan formally surrendered, Truman urged Congress to enact a series of progressive measures. Among these were national health insurance, an increase in the minimum wage, and a government commitment to maintaining full employment. After much debate, a watered-down version of the full-employment bill was enacted as the **Employment Act of 1946**. It created the **Council of Economic Advisers** to advise the president and Congress on means of promoting national economic welfare. Over the next seven years, a coalition of Republicans and conservative Southern Democrats, combined with the beginning of the Cold War, hindered passage of Truman's domestic program.

GI Bill—Help for Veterans The **Servicemen's Readjustment Act** of 1944, popularly known as the **GI Bill of Rights** (or just GI Bill), proved powerful support during the transition of 15 million veterans to a peacetime economy. It helped more than 2 million GIs attend college and more than 5 million more receive other training, creating a postwar boom in post-high school education. The veterans also received more than $16 billion in low-interest, government-backed loans to buy homes and farms and to start businesses. By focusing on a better-educated workforce and also promoting new construction, the federal government stimulated the postwar economic expansion.

However, these government benefits helped White veterans far more than Black veterans. For example, most African Americans returned to their homes in the South. Since most universities in the region did not admit Black students, fewer could use the educational benefits. Further, many banks refused to make loans to African Americans. While the GI Bill helped the economy overall, it also increased the racial wealth gap.

Baby Boom One sign of the confidence among young people was an explosion in marriages and births. Earlier marriages and larger families resulted in 50 million babies entering the U.S. population between 1945 and 1960. As the **baby boom** generation gradually passed from childhood to adolescence to adulthood, it profoundly affected the nation's social institutions and economic life in the last half of the 20th century. Initially, the baby boom tended to focus women's attention on raising children and homemaking. Nevertheless, the trend of more women in the workplace continued. By 1960, one-third of all married women worked outside the home.

Suburban Growth The high demand for housing after the war resulted in a construction boom. William J. Levitt led in the development of postwar suburbia with his building and promotion of **Levittown**, a project of 17,000 mass-produced, low-priced family homes on Long Island, New York. Low interest rates on mortgages that were both government insured and tax deductible made the move from city to suburb affordable for even families of modest means. In a single generation, the majority of middle-class Americans became suburbanites.

Levittown, Long Island, New York, c. 1948.
Source: photos.com

However, Levittown was only for White families. African American families were not allowed to buy homes there. At that time, federal government policies, which subsidized loans for many people purchasing homes all over the country, supported segregation in housing.

For many older inner cities, the effect of the mass movement to suburbia was disastrous. By the 1960s, cities from Boston to Los Angeles became increasingly poor and racially divided.

Rise of the Sun Belt Uprooted by the war, millions of Americans moved more frequently in the postwar era. A warmer climate, lower taxes, and economic opportunities in defense-related industries attracted many GIs and their families to the **Sun Belt** states from Florida to California. By transferring tax dollars from the Northeast and Midwest to the South and West, military spending during the Cold War helped finance the shift of industry, people, and ultimately political power from one region to the other.

Inflation and Strikes Truman urged Congress to continue the price controls of wartime in order to hold inflation in check. Instead, Southern Democrats joined with Republicans to relax the controls of the Office of Price Administration. The result was an inflation rate of almost 25 percent during the first year and a half of peace.

Workers and unions wanted wages to catch up after years of wage controls. More than 4.5 million workers went on strike in 1946. Strikes by railroad and mine workers threatened the national safety. Truman took a tough approach to this challenge, seizing the mines and using soldiers to keep them operating until the United Mine Workers finally called off its strike.

Truman versus the Republican Congress

Unhappy with inflation and strikes, voters were in a conservative mood in the fall of 1946 when they elected Republican majorities in both houses of Congress. Under Republican control, the 80th Congress attempted to pass two tax cuts for upper-income Americans, but Truman vetoed both measures. More successful were Republican efforts to amend the Constitution and roll back some of the New Deal gains for labor.

Twenty-Second Amendment (1951) Reacting against the election of Roosevelt as president four times, the Republican-dominated Congress proposed a constitutional amendment to limit a president to a maximum of two full terms in office. The **22nd Amendment** was ratified by the states in 1951.

Taft-Hartley Act (1947) In 1947, Congress passed the probusiness **Taft-Hartley Act**. Truman vetoed the measure as a "slave-labor" bill, but Congress overrode his veto. The one purpose of the Republican-sponsored law was to check the growing power of unions. Its provisions included the following:

- outlawing the closed shop (requiring workers to join a union *before* being hired)

- permitting states to pass "right to work" laws outlawing the union shop (requiring workers to join a union *after* being hired)
- outlawing secondary boycotts (the practice of several unions supporting a striking union by joining a boycott of a company's products)
- giving the president the power to invoke an 80-day cooling-off period before a strike endangering the national safety could be called

For years afterward, unions sought unsuccessfully to repeal the Taft-Hartley Act. The act became a major issue dividing Republicans and Democrats in the 1950s.

The Election of 1948 Truman's popularity was at a low point as the 1948 presidential campaign began. Republicans were confident of victory, especially after both a liberal faction (Progressive Party) and a conservative faction (Dixiecrats) in the Democratic Party abandoned Truman to organize their own third parties. The Republicans once again nominated New York governor Thomas E. Dewey. Meanwhile, the man without a chance toured the nation by rail, attacking the "do-nothing" Republican 80th Congress with "give 'em hell" speeches. The feisty Truman confounded the polling experts with a decisive victory over Dewey, winning the popular vote by 2 million votes and winning the electoral vote 303 to 189.

The Fair Deal Truman launched an ambitious reform program, which he called the **Fair Deal**. In 1949, he urged Congress to enact national health insurance, federal aid to education, civil rights legislation, funds for public housing, and a new farm program. Conservatives in Congress blocked most of the proposed reforms, except for an increase in the minimum wage (from 40 to 75 cents an hour) and the inclusion of more workers under Social Security.

Most of the Fair Deal bills were defeated for two reasons: (1) Truman's political conflicts with Congress, and (2) the pressing foreign policy concerns of the Cold War. Nevertheless, liberal defenders of Truman praised him for at least maintaining the New Deal reforms of his predecessor and making civil rights part of the liberal agenda.

Eisenhower in the White House (1953–1961)

Much as Franklin Roosevelt dominated the 1930s, President **Dwight D. Eisenhower** ("Ike") personified the 1950s. The Republican campaign slogan, "I Like Ike," expressed the genuine feelings of millions of middle-class Americans. They liked his winning smile and trusted and admired the former general who had successfully commanded Allied forces in Europe in World War II.

The Election of 1952 The last year of Truman's presidency, Americans were looking for relief from the Korean War and an end to "the mess in Washington." Republicans looked forward with relish to their first presidential victory in 20 years, and nominated the leader of allied forces in Europe, General Dwight D. Eisenhower and Senator Richard Nixon of California as his running mate. The Democrats selected popular Illinois Governor Adlai Stevenson, who confronted McCarthyism. Eisenhower's pledge to go to Korea and end the war helped the Republicans win 55 percent of the popular vote and an Electoral College landslide of 442 to Stevenson's 89.

As president, Eisenhower adopted a style of leadership that emphasized the delegation of authority. He filled his cabinet with successful corporate executives who gave his administration a businesslike tone. His secretary of defense, for example, was Charles Wilson, the former head of General Motors. Eisenhower was often criticized by the press for spending too much time golfing and fishing and perhaps entrusting important decisions to others. However, later research showed that behind the scenes Eisenhower was in charge.

Modern Republicanism Eisenhower was a fiscal conservative whose first priority was balancing the budget after years of deficit spending. Although his annual budgets were not always balanced, he came closer to curbing federal spending than any of his successors.

As a moderate on domestic issues, he accepted most of the New Deal programs as a reality of modern life and even expanded some of them. During Eisenhower's two terms in office, Social Security was extended to 10 million more citizens, the minimum wage was raised, and additional public housing was built. In 1953, Eisenhower consolidated welfare programs by creating the **Department of Health, Education, and Welfare (HEW)** under Oveta Culp Hobby, the first woman in a Republican cabinet. For farmers, a **soil-bank program** was initiated as means of reducing farm production and thereby increasing farm income. On the other hand, Eisenhower opposed the ideas of federal health insurance and federal aid to education.

As the first Republican president since Hoover, Eisenhower called his balanced and moderate approach "**modern Republicanism**." His critics called it "the bland leading the bland."

Interstate Highway System The most permanent physical legacy of the Eisenhower years was the passage in 1956 of the **Highway Act**, which authorized the construction of 42,000 miles of **interstate highways** linking all the nation's major cities. When completed, the U.S. highway system became a model for the rest of the world. The justification for new taxes on fuel, tires, and vehicles was to improve national defense by facilitating movements of troops and weapons. At the same time, this immense public works project created jobs, promoted the trucking industry, accelerated the growth of the suburbs, and contributed to a more homogeneous national culture. The emphasis on cars, trucks, and highways, however, hurt railroads and the environment. Little attention was paid to public transportation, on which the old and the poor depended.

Prosperity Eisenhower's domestic legislation was modest. During his years in office, however, the country enjoyed a steady economic growth rate, with an inflation rate averaging a negligible 1.5 percent. Although the federal budget had a small surplus only three times in eight years, the deficits fell in relation to the national wealth. Between 1945 and 1960, the per-capita disposable income of Americans more than tripled. By the mid-1950s, the average American family had twice the real income of a comparable family during the boom years of the 1920s. The postwar economy gave Americans the highest standard of living in the world. For these reasons, some historians rate Eisenhower's economic policies the most successful of any modern president's.

Economy under the Democrats (1961–1969)

At 43, John F. Kennedy was the youngest candidate ever elected president. He was also the first Roman Catholic to serve in the White, winning despite fears among some Protestants that he would take directions from the pope. Kennedy's energy and sharp wit gave a new, personal style to the presidency. In his inaugural address, Kennedy spoke of "the torch being passed to a new generation" and promised to lead the nation into a "**New Frontier**." The Democratic president surrounded himself with both business executives such as Secretary of Defense Robert McNamara and academics such as economist John Kenneth Galbraith. For the sensitive position of attorney general, the president chose his younger brother, Robert.

Kennedy and his wife Jacqueline ("Jackie") brought style, glamour, and an appreciation of the arts to the White House. The press loved his news conferences, and some later likened his administration to the mythical kingdom of Camelot and the court of King Arthur, the subject of a then-popular Broadway musical.

New Frontier Programs The promises of the New Frontier proved difficult to keep. Kennedy called for aid to education, federal support of health care, urban renewal, and civil rights, but his domestic programs languished in Congress. While few of Kennedy's proposals became law during his thousand-day administration, most were passed later under President Johnson.

On economic issues, Kennedy had some success. He persuaded Congress to pass the **Trade Expansion Act** (1962), which authorized tariff reductions with the new European Economic Community (Common Market) of Western European nations. He faced down big steel executives over a price increase he charged was inflationary and achieved a price rollback. In addition, the economy was stimulated by increased spending for defense and space exploration, as the president committed the nation to land on the moon by the end of the decade.

Johnson's Domestic Reforms Upon Kennedy's assassination in 1963, Vice President Lyndon B. Johnson became president. Johnson knew how to pass legislation from his years in the House and Senate. He aggressively promoted the domestic programs that Kennedy had failed to get through Congress. Shortly after taking office, Johnson persuaded Congress to pass (1) an expanded version of Kennedy's civil rights bill, and (2) Kennedy's proposal for an income tax cut. The latter measure sparked an increase in consumer spending and jobs. The country enjoyed a long period of economic expansion in the 1960s.

President Johnson's other significant domestic programs, known as the "Great Society," will be explored in Topic 8.9. Johnson's programs to use the power of federal programs to attack the ills of society proved the high point of liberalism in the 20th century. Like the New Deal, some of Johnson's programs produced results, while others did not. Nevertheless, before being cut back to pay for the far more costly Vietnam War, the War on Poverty did significantly reduce the number of American families living in poverty.

Nixon's Domestic Policy

The election of Richard Nixon in 1968 and 1972 gave the Republicans control of the White House. However, the Democrats continued to hold majorities in both houses of Congress. The Republican president had to live with this reality and obtain some concessions from Congress through moderation and compromise. At the same time, Nixon laid the foundation for a shift in public opinion toward conservatism and for Republican gains that would challenge and overthrow the Democratic control of Congress in the 1980s and 1990s.

The New Federalism

Nixon tried to slow down the growth of Johnson's Great Society programs by proposing the Family Assistance Plan, which would have replaced welfare by providing a guaranteed annual income for working Americans. The Democratic majority in Congress easily defeated this initiative.

The Republican president did succeed, however, in shifting some responsibility for social programs from the federal to the state and local levels. In a program known as **revenue sharing**, or the **New Federalism**, Congress gave local governments $30 billion in block grants over five years to address local needs as they saw fit (instead of using federal money according to priorities set in Washington). Republicans hoped revenue sharing would check the growth of the federal government and return responsibility to the states, where it had rested before the New Deal.

Nixon attempted to bypass Congress by impounding (not spending) funds appropriated for social programs. Democrats protested that such action was an abuse of executive powers. The courts agreed with the president's critics, arguing that it was a president's duty to carry out the laws of Congress, whether or not the president agreed with them.

Nixon's Economic Policies

Starting with a recession in 1970, the U.S. economy throughout the 1970s faced the unusual combination of economic slowdown and high inflation—a condition referred to as **stagflation** (*stag*nation plus in*flation*). To slow inflation, Nixon at first tried to cut federal spending. However, when this policy contributed to a recession and unemployment, he adopted Keynesian economics and deficit spending so as not to alienate middle-class and blue-collar Americans. In August 1971, he surprised the nation by imposing a 90-day wage and price freeze. Next, he took the dollar off the gold standard, which helped to devalue it relative to foreign currencies, and imposed a 10-percent surtax on all imports. These actions cost consumers, but they made goods produced in the United States more competitive with those made in other countries.

By the election year of 1972, the recession was over. Also in that year, Congress approved automatic increases for Social Security benefits based on the annual rise in the cost of living. This measure protected seniors, the poor, and the disabled from the worst effects of inflation but also contributed to increasing costs for these programs in the future.

Ford and Carter Confront Inflation

In the 1970s, the biggest economic issue was the growing inflation rate. President Gerald Ford (1974–1977) urged voluntary measures on the part of businesses and consumers to fight inflation by minimizing price and wage increases, including the wearing of WIN (Whip Inflation Now) buttons. Not only did inflation continue, but the economy also sank deeper into recession, with the unemployment rate reaching more than 9 percent. Ford finally agreed to a Democratic package to stimulate the economy, but he vetoed most other Democratic bills.

At first President Jimmy Carter (1977–1981) tried to check inflation with measures aimed at conserving energy, particularly oil, and reviving the U.S. coal industry. However, the compromises that came out of Congress failed to reduce the consumption of oil or to check inflation. In 1979–1980, inflation seemed completely out of control and reached the unheard-of rate of 13 percent.

Troubled Economy Inflation slowed economic growth as consumers and businesses could no longer afford the high interest rates that came with high prices. Inflation also pushed middle-class taxpayers into higher tax brackets, which led to a "taxpayers' revolt." Government social programs that were indexed to the inflation rate helped to push the federal deficit to nearly $60 billion in 1980.

The chairman of the Federal Reserve Board, Paul Volcker, believed that breaking the back of inflation was more important than reducing unemployment. Under him, the Federal Reserve pushed interest rates on loans even higher, to 20 percent in 1980. The high interest rates especially hurt the automobile and building industries, which laid off tens of thousands of workers. The policy, though, worked to reduce inflation. By 1982, inflation was under 4 percent.

The Economic Shift in the 1970s The period of high inflation, high interest rates, and high unemployment in the 1970s changed how many Americans viewed the economy. The postwar economy of the 1940s and 1950s had benefited from a booming private sector, strong unions, high federal spending, the baby boom, and technological developments. However, the economic recovery of Japan, Germany, and other war-torn nations challenged the U.S. position as the strongest economy in the world. Less-expensive and often better-built automobiles and other consumer products from newer overseas factories competed successfully with American-made products. In addition, new technology required fewer workers. The combination of competition and technology undercut the high-paying manufacturing jobs that had expanded the middle class in the 1950s and early 1960s.

These new realities affected politics, society, and economic thinking from the 1970s well into the future. In the 1970s, Americans began to adjust to the harsh truth that, for the first time since World War II, their standard of living was on the decline.

REFLECT ON THE LEARNING OBJECTIVES

1. Explain two causes of economic growth in years after World War II.

2. Explain two effects of migration to the suburbs and the Sun Belt after 1945.

KEY TERMS BY THEME

Postwar Economy and Migration (WXT, MIG)
Harry S. Truman
Employment Act of 1946
Council of Economic Advisers
Servicemen's Readjustment Act (GI Bill of Rights or GI Bill)
baby boom
Levittown
Sun Belt
22nd Amendment
Taft-Hartley Act
Fair Deal

Dwight D. Eisenhower
Department of Health, Education, and Welfare (HEW)
soil-bank program
modern Republicanism
Highway Act
interstate highways
New Frontier
Trade Expansion Act
New Federalism
revenue sharing
stagflation

MULTIPLE-CHOICE QUESTIONS

Questions 1–3 refer to the excerpt below.

> "Truman found saving the free world easier than governing America. . . . By the time war broke out in Korea, the Fair Deal was over, Truman had tried to accomplish too much with too little, ending up with practically nothing. Without a liberal majority in Congress there could not be much in the way of liberal legislation.
>
> Through the Truman years domestic politics was a thing of rags and patches, a time when problems were ignored, programs shelved, and partisanship allowed to run rampant. Yet a recent history of the period 1945–1950 is called *The Best Years* because that is how they were remembered."

William L. O'Neill, historian, American High, 1986

1. One example that supports O'Neill's claim that "problems were ignored, programs shelved" under Truman was the debate over
   (A) number of terms for a president
   (B) the strength of unions
   (C) a national health insurance system
   (D) the minimum wage

2. Which of the following coalitions provided the strongest opposition to Truman's domestic programs?
   (A) Republicans and Roosevelt Democrats
   (B) Antiwar Progressives and Republicans
   (C) Dixiecrats and members of the Progressive Party
   (D) Republicans and Southern Democrats

3. Which of the following most advanced liberal domestic policies during the Truman administration?
   (A) The ratification of the 22nd Amendment
   (B) The inclusion of more workers under Social Security
   (C) The passage of the Taft-Hartley Act to outlaw closed shops
   (D) The successful implementation of wage and price controls

SHORT-ANSWER QUESTIONS

Use complete sentences; an outline or bulleted list alone is not acceptable.

1. Answer (a), (b), and (c).
   (a) Briefly describe ONE difference between the American economy of the 1950s and the economy of the 1970s.
   (b) Briefly describe ONE similarity between the American economy of the 1950s and the economy of the 1970s.
   (c) Briefly explain ONE specific reason for the difference between the American economies of the 1950s and the 1970s.

2. Answer (a), (b), and (c).
   (a) Briefly explain ONE specific cause for the expansion of higher education after 1945.
   (b) Briefly explain ONE specific effect of the expansion of higher education after 1945.
   (c) Briefly explain ONE cause for the population growth of the Sun Belt region after World War II.

Topic 8.5

Culture after 1945

*All you do is make a lot of dough and play golf and play bridge
and buy cars and drink Martinis and look like a hot-shot. . . .
How would you know you weren't being a phony?*

J. D. Salinger, *The Catcher in the Rye*, 1951

Learning Objective: Explain how mass culture has been maintained or challenged over time.

Among White suburbanites, the 1950s were marked by similarities in social norms. Consensus about political issues and conformity in social behavior were safe harbors for Americans troubled by worries about communism. Consensus and conformity were the hallmarks of a consumer-driven mass economy.

Consumer Culture and Conformity

Television, advertising, and the middle-class movement to the suburbs contributed mightily to the growing homogeneity of American culture.

Television Little more than a curiosity in the late 1940s, **television** suddenly became a center of family life in American homes. By 1961, there was one set for every 3.3 Americans. Programming was dominated by three national networks, which presented viewers with a bland menu of situation comedies, westerns, quiz shows, and professional sports. FCC chairman Newton Minnow criticized television as a "vast wasteland" and worried about the impact on children of a steady dose of five or more hours of daily viewing. The culture portrayed on television—especially for third and fourth generations of White ethnic Americans—provided a common content for their common language. Comedies like *The Adventures of Ozzie and Harriet*, *Father Knows Best*, and *Leave It to Beaver* reinforced conservative values by depicting a stereotype of a suburb. Families included a father working in a white-collar job and a mother who did not work outside the home, and everyone was white and middle class.

Advertising In all the media (television, radio, newspapers, and magazines), aggressive advertising by name brands promoted common material wants, and the introduction of suburban shopping centers and plastic **credit cards** in the 1950s provided a quick means of satisfying them. The phenomenal proliferation of chains of **fast food** restaurants on the roadside was one measure of success for the new marketing techniques and standardized products as the nation turned from "mom and pop" stores to franchise operations.

Paperbacks and Records Despite television, Americans read more than ever. **Paperback books**, an innovation in the 1950s, were selling almost a million copies a day by 1960. Popular music was revolutionized by the mass marketing of inexpensive long-playing (LP) record albums and stacks of 45 rpm records. Teenagers fell in love with **rock and roll** music, a blend of African American rhythm and blues sounds with White country music, popularized by the gyrating Elvis Presley.

Source: ©ClassicStock/Alamy

Corporate America In the business world, **conglomerates** with diversified holdings began to dominate such industries as food processing, hotels, transportation, insurance, and banking. For the first time in history, more American workers held white-collar jobs than blue-collar jobs. Working for one of *Fortune* magazine's top 500 companies seemed to be the road to success. Large corporations promoted teamwork and conformity, including a dress code for male workers of a dark business suit, white shirt, and conservative tie. Social scientist William Whyte documented this loss of individuality in his book *The Organization Man* (1956). A key point was that people believed that organizations could make better decisions than individuals, and thus serving an organization became preferable to developing one's individual creativity.

Big unions became more powerful after the merger of the American Federation of Labor and the Congress of Industrial Organizations into the AFL-CIO in 1955. They also became more conservative as blue-collar workers began to enjoy middle-class incomes.

For most Americans, conformity was a small price to pay for affluence, a home in the suburbs, a new automobile every few years, good schools, and maybe a vacation at the recently opened Disneyland (1955) in California.

Religion Organized religions expanded dramatically after World War II with the building of thousands of new churches and synagogues. Will Herberg's book *Protestant, Catholic, Jew* (1955) commented on the new religious tolerance of the times and the lack of interest in doctrine, as religious membership became a source of both individual identity and socialization.

Women's Roles

The baby boom and running a home in the suburbs made homemaking a full-time job for millions of women. The traditional view of a woman's role as caring for home and children was reaffirmed in the mass media and in the best-selling self-help book *Baby and Child Care* (1946) by Dr. Benjamin Spock.

At the same time, evidence of dissatisfaction was growing, especially among well-educated women of the middle class. More married women entered the workforce, especially as they reached middle age. Yet male employers in the 1950s saw female workers primarily as wives and mothers, and women's lower wages reflected this attitude.

Social Critics

Not everybody approved of the social trends of the 1950s. In *The Lonely Crowd* (1958), Harvard sociologist David Riesman criticized the replacement of "inner-directed" individuals in society with "other-directed" conformists. In *The Affluent Society* (1958), economist John Kenneth Galbraith wrote about the failure of wealthy Americans to address the need for increased social spending for the common good. (Galbraith's ideas were to influence the Kennedy and Johnson administrations in the next decade.) Sociologist C. Wright Mills portrayed dehumanizing corporate worlds in *White Collar* (1951) and threats to freedom in *The Power Elite* (1956).

Novels Some of the most popular novelists of the 1950s wrote about the individual's struggle against conformity. J. D. Salinger provided a classic commentary on "phoniness" as viewed by a troubled teenager in **The Catcher in the Rye** (1951). Joseph Heller satirized the rigidity of the military and the insanity of war in **Catch-22** (1961).

Beatniks A group of rebellious writers and intellectuals made up the Beat Generation of the 1950s. Led by Jack Kerouac (*On the Road,* 1957) and poet Allen Ginsberg ("Howl," 1956), the **beatniks** advocated spontaneity, use of drugs, and rebellion against societal standards. The beatniks would become models for the youth rebellion of the 1960s.

Assassination and the End of the Postwar Era

President Kennedy's "one brief, shining moment" of life was cut short on November 22, 1963, in Dallas, Texas, as two bullets from an assassin's rifle found their mark. After the shocking news of Kennedy's murder, millions of stunned Americans were fixed to their televisions for days and even witnessed the killing of the alleged assassin, Lee Harvey Oswald, just two days after the president's death. The **Warren Commission**, headed by Chief Justice Earl Warren, concluded that Oswald was the lone assassin. For years afterward, however, unanswered questions about the events in Dallas produced dozens of conspiracy theories pointing to possible involvement by organized crime, Fidel Castro, the Soviet Union, the CIA, and the FBI. For many Americans, the tragedy in Dallas and doubts about the Warren Commission marked the beginning of a loss of credibility in government.

In Retrospect Kennedy's presidency inspired many young Americans to take seriously his inaugural message and to "ask not what your country can do for you—ask what you can do for your country." In keeping with the patriotic sentiments of the postwar era, some volunteered for the Peace Corps or to fight in the Vietnam War. The war's failures, the conspiracy theories that multiplied after Kennedy's death, and conflicts over the civil rights movement and the shallow materialism of the 1950s raised doubts about American society and culture. Instead of the consensus of the 1950s, America had become by 1968 a country that was "coming apart." The counterculture had arrived.

HISTORICAL PERSPECTIVES: *A SILENT GENERATION?*

Among intellectuals, a commonly held view of the 1950s was that Americans had become complacent in their political outlook—a "silent generation" presided over by a grandfatherly and passive President Eisenhower. Liberal academics believed that McCarthyism had stopped any serious or critical discussion of the problems in American society. Eisenhower's policies and their general acceptance by most voters seemed a bland consensus of ideas that would bother no one. Critics contrasted the seeming calm of the 1950s with the more "interesting" social and cultural revolution of the next decade.

Eisenhower the Leader Over time, historians have treated the 1950s more positively. For example, William O'Neill's *American High: The Years of Confidence, 1945–1960* (1987) presents a more positive view of Eisenhower. Research into the Eisenhower papers has revealed a president who used a hidden-hand approach to leadership. Behind the scenes, he was an active and decisive administrator who was in full command of his presidency. His domestic policies achieved sustained economic growth, and his foreign policy relaxed international tensions. O'Neill argues that Eisenhower led a needed and largely successful economic and social postwar "reconstruction."

Liberal Victories Some historians have emphasized the liberal successes of the period. The strong economy featured strong unions and progressive taxes. The country made progress on civil rights issues, with African Americans organizing bus boycotts, marches, and other protests to draw attention to discrimination. Other historians emphasize that the 1950s prepared the way for the achievements of women and African Americans and other minorities in the following decades. Furthermore, the integration of Catholics, Jews, and other White ethnics into American society during the postwar years made it possible for Kennedy to be elected the first Roman Catholic president in 1960.

Conservative Foundations Some historians see the 1950s as laying the intellectual foundation for the conservative politics of the 1980s. Writers such as William F. Buckley and intellectuals such as economist Milton Friedman began arguing for limited government in the 1950s. Their ideas shaped the policies of President Ronald Reagan (1981–1989).

Supporting an Argument *Explain two perspectives on the 1950s.*

1. Explain two causes that influenced changes in mass culture after 1945.

KEY TERMS BY THEME

1950s Culture (ARC)	rock and roll	Catch-22
television	conglomerates	beatniks
credit cards	The Lonely Crowd	Warren Commission
fast food	The Affluent Society	
paperback books	The Catcher in the Rye	

MULTIPLE-CHOICE QUESTIONS

Questions 1–2 refer to the excerpt below.

"The fault is not in organization, in short; it is in our worship of it. It is in our vain quest for a Utopian equilibrium, which would be horrible if it ever did come to pass; it is in the soft-minded denial that there is a conflict between the individual and society. . . . There is little room for virtuoso performances. . . . Business is so complex, even in its non-technical aspects, that no one man can master all of it; to do his job, therefore, he must be able to work with other people. . . . Quite obviously to anyone who worked in a big organization, those who survived best were not necessarily the fittest but, in more cases than not, those who by birth and personal connections had the breaks."

William Whyte, *The Organization Man,* 1956

1. Which of the following trends in the United States during the mid-20th century most directly contributed to the perspective expressed in the excerpt?

   (A) The spreading influence of the military-industrial complex

   (B) The increasing domination of the economy by large corporations

   (C) The increasing diversity of middle-class suburbs

   (D) The rising percentage of inner-directed students graduating college

2. Which of the following best expresses the ideas of the author?

   (A) Corporations should encourage more teamwork among employees.

   (B) The business world rewards people who take risks.

   (C) The United States should encourage the growth of large companies.

   (D) Americans are trading individualism for lives of conformity.

SHORT-ANSWER QUESTIONS

Use complete sentences; an outline or bulleted list alone is not acceptable.

1. "In the 1950s critics launched a devastating attack on the consumer culture for fostering a docile, standardized nation. Wherever they looked—toward a woman's place in the home or antiseptic one-class suburb or the comatose campus—America seemed . . . routinized. One writer described the United States as 'The Packaged Society,' for we are all items in a national supermarket—categorized, processed, labeled, priced, and readied for merchandising.'"

> William E. Leuchtenburg, historian, *A Troubled Feast:*
> *American Society Since 1945*, 1973

"The Truman-Eisenhower period is regarded as conservative and backward looking. . . . But what this view obscures is the extent to which, without anyone realizing it, the preconditions for social change and reform were being established. . . . Before Selma there was Montgomery. . . . before the hippies were the Beats. . . . Withal, it had been a time of hope, a time of growth, and, in its best moments, even a time of glory."

> William L. O'Neill, historian, *American High: The Years of*
> *Confidence, 1945–1960*, 1986

Using the excerpts above, answer (a), (b), and (c).

(a) Briefly describe ONE major difference between Leuchtenburg's and O'Neill's historical interpretations of the 1950s.

(b) Briefly explain ONE specific historical event or development that is not explicitly mentioned in the excerpts that could be used to support Leuchtenburg's interpretation of the 1950s.

(c) Briefly explain ONE specific historical event or development that is not explicitly mentioned in the excerpts that could be used to support O'Neill's interpretation of the 1950s.

2. Answer (a), (b), and (c).

(a) Briefly explain how ONE specific innovation in communication positively influenced American society in the 1950s.

(b) Briefly explain how ONE specific innovation in communication negatively influenced American society in the 1950s.

(c) Briefly explain how innovations in communication affected the role of women in society in the 1950s.

Early Steps in the Civil Rights Movement, 1945–1960

We conclude that in the field of public education the doctrine of "separate but equal" has no place. Separate educational facilities are inherently unequal.

Chief Justice Earl Warren, *Brown v. Board of Education of Topeka*, May 17, 1954

Learning Objective: Explain how and why the civil rights movement developed and expanded from 1945 to 1960.

Baseball player **Jackie Robinson** had broken the color line in 1947 by being hired by the Brooklyn Dodgers as the first African American to play on a major league team since the 1880s. Robinson's breakthrough had a huge impact on many Americans. However, some argue that the origins of the modern civil rights movement can be traced back to the movement of millions of African Americans from the rural South to the urban centers of the South and the North. In the North, African Americans, who joined the Democrats during the New Deal, had a growing influence in politics in the 1940s and 1950s.

Origins of the Movement

African Americans had been fighting against racial discrimination since the 17th century. However, progress was slow until after World War II. As the 1950s began, African Americans in the South were still segregated by law from Whites in schools and in most public facilities. They were also kept from voting by poll taxes, literacy tests, grandfather clauses, and intimidation. Social segregation left most of them poorly educated, while economic discrimination kept them in a state of poverty.

Presidential Leadership Harry S. Truman (1945–1953) was the first modern president to use the powers of his office to challenge racial discrimination. Bypassing Southern Democrats who controlled key committees in Congress, the president used his executive powers to establish the **Committee on Civil Rights** in 1946. He also strengthened the civil rights division of the Justice Department, which aided the efforts of Black leaders to end segregation in schools. Most importantly, in 1948 he ordered the end of racial discrimination throughout the federal government, including the armed forces. The end of segregation changed life on military bases, many of which were in the South. Recognizing the odds against the passage of civil rights legislation, Truman nevertheless also urged Congress to create a Fair Employment Practices Commission that would prevent employers from discriminating against the hiring of African Americans. Southern Democrats blocked the legislation.

Changing Attitudes in the Cold War The Cold War also played an indirect role in changing both government policies and social attitudes. The U.S. reputation for freedom and democracy was competing against Communist ideology for the hearts and minds of the peoples of Africa and Asia. Against this global background, racial segregation and discrimination stood out as glaring wrongs that needed to be corrected.

Desegregating the Schools and Public Places

The **National Association for the Advancement of Colored People (NAACP)** had been working through the courts for decades trying to overturn the Supreme Court's 1896 decision in *Plessy v. Ferguson*, which allowed segregation as long as facilities were "separate but equal." In the late 1940s, the NAACP won a series of cases involving higher education.

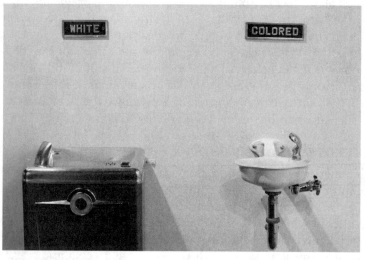

Source: Getty Images

Separate water fountains symbolized how strictly Jim Crow laws and customs tried to segregate people by race.

Brown Decision One of the great landmark cases in Supreme Court history was argued in the early 1950s by a team of NAACP lawyers led by **Thurgood Marshall.** In ***Brown v. Board of Education of Topeka,*** they argued that segregation of Black children in public schools was unconstitutional because it violated the 14th Amendment's guarantee of "equal protection of the laws." In May 1954, the Supreme Court agreed with Marshall and overturned the *Plessy* decision. Writing for a unanimous Court, Chief Justice **Earl Warren** ruled that (1) "separate facilities are inherently unequal" and hence unconstitutional, and (2) school segregation should end with "all deliberate speed."

Resistance in the South Opposition to the *Brown* decision erupted throughout the South. To start with, 101 members of Congress signed the "**Southern Manifesto**" condemning the Supreme Court for a "clear abuse of judicial power." States fought the decision several ways, including temporarily closing public schools and setting up private schools. The Ku Klux Klan made a comeback, and violence against African Americans increased.

In Arkansas in 1956, when a federal court ordered school desegregation, Governor Orval Faubus used the state's National Guard to prevent nine African American students from entering Little Rock Central High School. President Eisenhower then intervened. While the president did not actively support **desegregation** or the *Brown* decision, he understood his constitutional duty to uphold federal authority. Eisenhower ordered federal troops to stand guard in **Little Rock** and protect Black students. Resistance remained stubborn. In 1964, ten years after the Supreme Court decision, fewer than 2 percent of Black students in the South attended integrated schools.

Montgomery Bus Boycott In 1955, as a Montgomery, Alabama, bus took on more White passengers, the driver ordered a middle-aged Black woman to give up her seat to one of them. **Rosa Parks**, an active member of the local chapter of the NAACP, refused. The police were called and arrested her for violating the segregation law. This arrest sparked a massive African American protest in the form of a boycott of the city buses. The Reverend **Martin Luther King Jr.**, minister of a Montgomery Baptist church, soon emerged as the inspirational leader of a **nonviolent movement** to end segregation. The protest touched off by Rosa Parks and the **Montgomery bus boycott** resulted in the Supreme Court ruling that segregation laws were unconstitutional. The boycott also inspired other civil rights protests that reshaped America over the coming decades.

Nonviolent Protests In 1957, Martin Luther King Jr. formed the **Southern Christian Leadership Conference (SCLC)**, which organized ministers and churches in the South to get behind the civil rights struggle. In February 1960, college students in Greensboro, North Carolina, started the **sit-in movement** after being refused service at a Whites-only Woolworth's lunch counter. To call attention to the injustice of segregated facilities, students would deliberately invite arrest by sitting in restricted areas. Within a few months, young activists, including 23-year-old John Lewis, organized the **Student Nonviolent Coordinating Committee (SNCC)** to promote voting rights and to end segregation. In the 1960s, African Americans used sit-ins to integrate restaurants, hotels, libraries, pools, and transportation throughout the South.

The results of the boycotts, sit-ins, court rulings, and government responses to pressure marked a turning point in the civil rights movement. Progress was slow, however. In the 1960s, a growing impatience among many African Americans would be manifested in violent confrontations in the streets.

Federal Laws While President Eisenhower was skeptical about the *Brown* ruling, he did sign civil rights laws in 1957 and 1960. These were the first such laws to be enacted by the U.S. Congress since Reconstruction. They were modest in scope, providing for a permanent **Civil Rights Commission** and giving the Justice Department new powers to protect the voting rights of African Americans. Despite this legislation, southern officials still used an arsenal of obstructive tactics to discourage black citizens from voting.

The Court rulings and federal laws of the 1950s were only the beginning in the fight for racial justice. The movement for racial justice continued with decades of protests, legislation, and court decisions to win African Americans access to schools, public places, voting rights, housing, and employment. The effort took a state-by-state, county-by-county, city-by-city struggle against the entrenched traditions of segregation and discrimination in both the South and the North. These events will be further explored in Topic 8.10.

REFLECT ON THE LEARNING OBJECTIVE

1. Explain two specific examples of how and why the civil rights movements developed and expanded from 1945 to 1960.

KEY TERMS BY THEME

Civil Rights in the 1940s and 1950s (SOC)		
Jackie Robinson	*Brown v. Board of Education of Topeka*	Montgomery bus boycott
Harry S. Truman	Earl Warren	Southern Christian Leadership Conference (SCLC)
Committee on Civil Rights	Southern Manifesto	sit-in movement
National Association for the Advancement of Colored People (NAACP)	desegregation	Student Nonviolent Coordinating Committee (SNCC)
Thurgood Marshall	Little Rock	Civil Rights Commission
	Rosa Parks	
	Martin Luther King Jr.	
	nonviolent movement	

MULTIPLE-CHOICE QUESTIONS

Questions 1–2 refer to the excerpt below.

"Does segregation of children in public schools solely on the basis of race even though the physical facilities and other 'tangible' factors may be equal, deprive the children of the minority group of equal education opportunities? We believe that it does.

"[I]n finding that a segregated law school for Negroes could not provide them equal educational opportunities, this court relied in large part on 'those qualities which are incapable of objective measurement but which make for greatness in a law school.'

"Such considerations apply with added force to children in grade and high schools. To separate them from others of similar age and qualifications solely because of their race generates a feeling of inferiority as to their status in the community that may affect their hearts and minds in a way unlikely ever to be undone. . . .

"We conclude that in the field of public education the doctrine of 'separate but equal' has no place. Separate educational facilities are inherently unequal. Therefore, we hold that the plaintiffs . . . [are] deprived of the equal protection of the laws guaranteed by the 14th Amendment."

Supreme Court, Brown v. Board of Education of Topeka, May 17, 1954

1. Which of the following is the most important claim in the argument presented in this portion of the *Brown* verdict?
   (A) All-Black schools were not as well equipped as all-White schools.
   (B) Black and White students attended separate schools only because of residential patterns rather than required racial segregation.
   (C) Segregated schools existed in southern but not northern states.
   (D) Psychological research indicated the negative effects of segregation on African American children.

2. Which of the following best describes the initial reaction to the *Brown* decision?
   (A) Southern leaders supported the decision, but the voters did not.
   (B) President Eisenhower provided active support for the decision.
   (C) Resistance was widespread, and initially few schools were integrated.
   (D) It was implemented with little opposition in larger cities.

SHORT-ANSWER QUESTION

Use complete sentences; an outline or bulleted list alone is not acceptable.

1. Answer (a), (b), and (c).
   (a) Briefly explain how ONE specific action taken by the Truman administration attempted to end racial discrimination.
   (b) Briefly explain how ONE specific action taken by segregationists attempted to resist the *Brown* ruling.
   (c) Briefly explain how ONE specific action taken by African Americans attempted to fight racial segregation and discrimination during the 1950s.

Topic 8.7

America as a World Power

America was prone to its own illusions, one of which was that the independence movements of the developing world paralleled the American experience.

Henry Kissinger, *Diplomacy*, 1994

Learning Objective: Explain various military and diplomatic responses to international developments over time.

Decolonization, or the collapse of colonial empires, was among the most important developments of the era following World War II. Would people fighting for independence look to the anticolonial history of United States for inspiration or to the anticolonial ideology of the Communists?

Unrest in the "Third World"

Between 1947 and 1960, 37 new nations emerged from colonies in Asia, Africa, and the Middle East. Most were former subjects of European empires, such as Britain, France, and the Netherlands. In Asia, India and Pakistan became new nations in 1947, and the Dutch East Indies became the independent country of Indonesia in 1949. In Africa, Ghana threw off British colonial rule in 1957, and a host of other nations followed. These new developing nations of the "**Third World**" (in contrast to the industrialized nations of the Western bloc and the Communist bloc) often lacked stable political and economic institutions. Their need for foreign aid from either the United States or the Soviet Union often made them into pawns of the Cold War.

Foreign Aid The primary tool used by United States to win over the developing nations to its side during the Cold War was foreign aid. Until 1952, most of U.S. foreign aid went to Europe, but by 1960 more than 90 percent went to Third World nations. Some foreign aid was grant money with no strings attached. Often, though, the aid was in the form of low-interest loans and came with restrictions, which poorer nations came to resent. However, despite foreign aid many recipients, such as India and Egypt, refused to choose sides in the Cold War and followed a policy of "nonalignment."

The Middle East

In the Middle East, the United States tried to balance maintaining friendly ties with the oil-rich Arab states while at the same time supporting the new state of Israel. The latter nation was created in 1948 under UN auspices after a civil war in the British mandate territory of Palestine left the land divided between the Israelis and the Palestinians. Israel's neighbors, including Egypt, had fought unsuccessfully to prevent a Jewish state from being formed.

Covert Action President Eisenhower's administration's (1953–1961) conduct of U.S. foreign policy increased the use of **covert action**. Undercover intervention in the internal politics of other nations was less objectionable to voters than employing U.S. troops and proved less expensive. In 1953, the **CIA** helped overthrow a government in **Iran** that had tried to nationalize the holding of foreign oil companies. The overthrow of the elected government allowed for the return of Reza Pahlavi as shah (monarch) of Iran. In return the shah provided the West with favorable oil prices and made enormous purchases of American arms.

MIDDLE EAST AREAS OF CONFLICT, 1948–1990

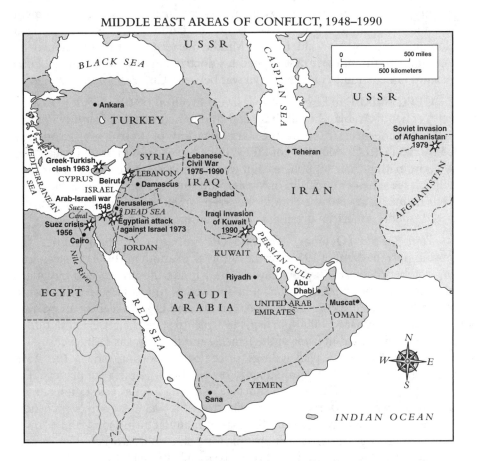

Suez Crisis Led by the Arab nationalist General Gamal Abdel Nasser, Egypt asked the United States for funds to build the ambitious Aswan Dam project on the Nile River. The United States refused, in part because Egypt threatened Israel's security. Nasser then turned to the Soviet Union to help build the dam. The Soviets agreed to provide limited financing for the project. Seeking another source of funds, Nasser precipitated an international crisis in July 1956 by seizing and nationalizing the British- and French-owned Suez Canal that passed through Egyptian territory. Loss of the canal threatened Western Europe's supply line to Middle Eastern oil. In response to this threat, Britain, France, and Israel carried out a surprise attack against Egypt and retook the canal.

Eisenhower, furious that he had been kept in the dark about the attack by his allies the British and French, sponsored a UN resolution condemning the invasion of Egypt. Under pressure from the United States and world public opinion, the invading forces withdrew.

Eisenhower Doctrine The United States quickly replaced Britain and France as the leading Western influence in the Middle East, but it faced a growing Soviet influence in Egypt and Syria. In a policy pronouncement later known as the **Eisenhower Doctrine**, the United States in 1957 pledged economic and military aid to any Middle Eastern country threatened by communism. Eisenhower first applied his doctrine in 1958 by sending 14,000 marines to Lebanon to prevent a civil war between Christians and Muslims.

OPEC and Oil In Eisenhower's last year in office, 1960, the Middle Eastern states of Saudi Arabia, Kuwait, Iraq, and Iran joined with the South American state of Venezuela to form the **Organization of Petroleum Exporting Countries (OPEC)**. Members of OPEC hoped to expand their political power by coordinating their oil policies. Oil was shaping up to be a critical foreign-policy issue. The combination of Western dependence on Middle Eastern oil, Arab nationalism, and the conflict between Israelis and Palestinian refugees would trouble American presidents in the coming decades.

Yom Kippur (October) War and Oil Embargo In world politics, the most important event of 1973 was the outbreak of another Middle Eastern war. On October 6, the Jewish holy day of Yom Kippur, the Syrians and Egyptians launched a surprise attack on Israel in an attempt to recover the lands lost in the Six-Day War of 1967. President Nixon ordered U.S. nuclear forces on alert and airlifted almost $2 billion in arms to Israel to stem the retreat. The tide of battle quickly shifted in favor of the Israelis, and the war was soon over.

The United States paid a huge price for supporting Israel. The Arab members of OPEC placed an embargo on oil sold to Israel's supporters. The embargo caused a worldwide oil shortage and long lines at gas stations in the United States. Even worse was the impact on the U.S. economy, which now suffered from runaway inflation, the loss of manufacturing jobs, and a lower standard of living. The hardest-hit people were blue-collar workers. Consumers switched from big American-made cars to smaller, more fuel-efficient Japanese cars, which cost U.S. automobile workers more than 225,000 jobs. Congress responded by enacting a 55-miles-per-hour speed limit to save gasoline and approving construction of a controversial oil pipeline to tap American oil reserves in Alaska. No government program, however, seemed to bolster the sluggish economy or stem high inflation rates, which continued until the end of the decade.

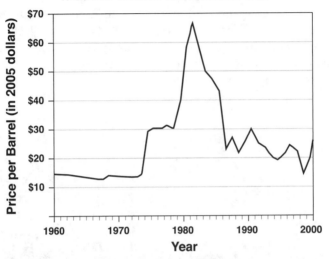

WORLD PRICE OF CRUDE OIL

Source: U.S. Energy Administration

Camp David Accords Perhaps President Carter's (1977–1981) single greatest achievement as president was arranging a peace settlement between Egypt and Israel. In 1977, Egyptian President Anwar Sadat took the first courageous step toward Middle East peace by visiting Israeli Prime Minister Menachem Begin in Jerusalem. President Carter followed this bold initiative by inviting Sadat and Begin to meet again at the presidential retreat in Camp David, Maryland. With Carter acting as an intermediary, the two leaders negotiated the **Camp David Accords** (September 1978), which provided a framework for a peace settlement between their countries.

Later, as a result of a peace treaty concluded in 1979, Egypt became the first Arab nation to recognize the nation of Israel. In return, Israel withdrew its troops from the Sinai territory taken from Egypt in the Six-Day War of 1967. The treaty was opposed by the Palestine Liberation Organization (PLO) and most of the Arab world, but it was a step toward a negotiated peace in the Middle East.

Iran and the Hostage Crisis The Middle East also provided Carter's greatest frustration. In Iran, anti-American sentiment had been strong since the United States had helped overthrow the country's democratically elected leader in 1953 and install a dictatorial government under a leader called a shah. The shah had kept the oil flowing for the West during the 1970s, but his autocratic rule and policy of westernization had alienated a large part of the Iranian population. In 1979, Islamic fundamentalists in Iran, led by the Ayatollah Khomeini, overthrew the shah. He escaped the country, but Iranians demanded his return to stand trials for crimes against his people.

With the ayatollah and fundamentalists in power, Iranian oil exports ground to a halt, causing the second worldwide oil shortage of the decade and another round of price increases. U.S. impotence in dealing with the crisis became more evident in November 1979. When the United States allowed the shah into the country for medical treatment, Iranian militants seized the U.S. embassy in Teheran and held more than 50 American staff members as prisoners and hostages. The hostage crisis dragged out through the remainder of Carter's presidency. In April 1980, Carter approved a rescue mission, but the breakdown of the helicopters over the Iranian desert forced the United States to abort the mission. For many Americans, Carter's unsuccessful attempts to free the hostages symbolized a failed presidency.

Source: U.S. Department of Defense, via pingnews

On January 27, 1981, the hostages returned to the United States after 14 months in captivity.

Latin America

In 1954, President Eisenhower (1953–1961) approved a CIA covert action to overthrow a leftist government in Guatemala that threatened American business interests. U.S. opposition to communism often drove Washington to support corrupt and often ruthless dictators, especially in Latin America. As in the case of Iran, this kind of intervention in Latin American politics also fueled anti-American feelings, which became evident in populist attacks on motorcades of U.S. Vice Presidents Richard Nixon and later Nelson Rockefeller during state visits in Latin America.

Kennedy's Policies After a close election, President John F. Kennedy (1961–1963) increasingly turned his attention to policies related to developing countries. In 1961, he set up the **Peace Corps**, an organization that recruited young American volunteers to give technical aid to developing countries. In 1961, Kennedy created the Alliance for Progress, a U.S. program that promoted land reform and economic development in Latin America. Kennedy's interest in Latin America and the **Alliance of Progress** were fondly remembered after his death. However, CIA operations fueled anti-American feelings in Latin America. These included the 1961 Bay of Pigs invasion that failed to overthrow Fidel Castro (Topic 8.2) and plots to assassinate Communist or leftist leaders, such as Fidel Castro of Cuba.

Return of the "Big Stick" President Johnson's administration (1963–1969) judged Western Hemisphere neighbors by their commitment against communism rather than their commitment to democracy. The Alliance for Progress, begun with such fanfare under Kennedy, was allowed to wither. Johnson's policy toward Latin America became increasingly interventionist, culminating in the deployment of U.S. soldiers to the Dominican Republic to prevent another Communist takeover in the Caribbean. In 1964, the administration backed a right-wing military coup in Brazil. When Panamanians rioted against U.S. control of the Panama Canal Zone, Johnson dealt firmly with the violence, although he later agreed to negotiations that eventually culminated in the return of the Canal Zone to Panama in 1999. Johnson's interventionist doctrine was that the United States would unilaterally prevent any Communist government from coming to power in the Western Hemisphere, reminding some of Theodore Roosevelt's "Big Stick" policy.

Panama Canal Promoting a human rights policy, the Carter administration attempted to correct inequities in the original Panama Canal Treaty of 1903 by negotiating a new treaty. In 1978, after long debate, the Senate ratified a treaty that would gradually transfer operation and control of the Panama Canal from the United States to the Panamanians, a process to be completed by the year 2000. Opponents criticized Carter's "giveaway" of the canal in the 1980 election.

Policies in Africa

The difficulties of nation building were especially challenging for newly created nations in Africa. Shortly after Belgium abruptly gave independence to the Congo in 1960, civil war broke out. Fearing a Communist victory, the United States helped the United Nations quell the insurrection. While the threat of a Communist takeover was overblown, the Kennedy administration's intervention into the shaky politics of the Congo caused resentment among African nationalists as another example of White colonialism.

Remnants of Colonialism Until the mid-1970s, Africa ranked low in President Richard Nixon's (1969–1974) list of priorities. The Nixon administration did strengthen ties with the White minority governments of Portuguese Angola, Rhodesia, and South Africa. When Black rebels tried to overthrow colonial control in Angola, the CIA spent tens of millions of dollars on covert actions to prevent the Communist-backed rebels from gaining power.

After Nixon resigned as president, Congress pulled funding from the scheme. In 1976, the Soviet- and Cuban-backed party took control of Angola. After the Angola experience, the United States decided to no longer back White minority governments with segregationist policies (*apartheid*) in Africa.

Human Rights Diplomacy The hallmark of President Carter's (1977–1981) foreign policy was human rights, which he preached fervently to the world's dictators. Carter appointed Andrew Young, an African American, to serve as U.S. ambassador to the United Nations. Carter and Young championed the cause of human rights around the world, especially by opposing the oppression of the Black majorities in South Africa and Rhodesia (Zimbabwe) by all-White governments. In Latin America, human rights violations by the military governments of Argentina and Chile caused Carter to cut off U.S. aid to those countries.

Limits of a Superpower

In 1969, television viewers around the world witnessed the astonishing sight of two American astronauts walking on the moon's surface. The United States had won the race to land men on the moon. This event, followed by a series of other successes for the U.S. space program, represented some of the high points of the 1970s. Offsetting these technological triumphs, however, were shocking revelations about White House participation in the Watergate break-in, a stagnant economy, and the fall of South Vietnam to communism (Topic 8.8).

Economic Challenges Increased foreign economic competition, oil shortages, rising unemployment, and high inflation made Americans aware that even the world's leading superpower would have to adjust to a fast-changing, less-manageable world. The United States was cutting back on its foreign aid to developing nations. Overall, in world economy the United States seemed to be losing its competitive edge, which had been the foundation of its unrivaled political and military strength since World War II.

REFLECT ON THE LEARNING OBJECTIVE

1. Explain two military and/or diplomatic responses of the United States to international developments in the Third World from 1945 to 1980.

KEY TERMS BY THEME

America in the World (WOR)	Iran	Yom Kippur (October) War
decolonization	Suez crisis	oil embargo
Third World	Eisenhower Doctrine	Camp David Accords
covert action	Organization of Petroleum	Peace Corps
CIA	Exporting Countries (OPEC)	Alliance for Progress

Questions 1–3 refer to the excerpt below.

> "The leaders of the independence movements were a different type than America's Founding Fathers. . . . The vast majority of them governed in an authoritarian manner. Many were Marxists. . . . However much America might dissociate from European colonialism, American leaders, to their chagrin, found themselves perceived in developing countries as useful auxiliaries from the imperialist camp rather than as genuine partners. . . . Above all, populist leaders like Nasser saw no future in being identified with the West. . . . Nonalignment was for them as much a domestic necessity as a foreign policy choice."
>
> Henry Kissinger, Secretary of State (1973–1977), *Diplomacy*, 1994

1. One claim that could be used to refute Kissinger's statement that "the leaders of the independence movements were a different type than America's Founding Fathers" would be that both groups
   (A) opposed efforts to protect civil liberties such as freedom of the press
   (B) wanted to avoid conflicts that involved more powerful countries
   (C) distrusted wealthy and highly educated individuals as political leaders
   (D) recognized the benefits of imperialism for small, weak countries

2. Which of the following best reflects Kissinger's criticism of the leaders of the developing countries?
   (A) The leaders were not as skilled as American political leaders.
   (B) Most leaders were not committed to democratic values.
   (C) Governments were auxiliaries of the imperialist camp.
   (D) Nonalignment was important for internal political reasons.

3. Which of the following best reflects the perspective of nonaligned nations according to Kissinger?
   (A) Former colonies did not want to join in alliances with imperialist nations.
   (B) Nonaligned nations had deeply held religious and cultural values.
   (C) People in these nations wanted to ally with the United States, but their governments did not.
   (D) Governments were not stable enough to cooperate with Western democracies.

Use complete sentences; an outline or bullet alone is not acceptable.

1.

Menachem Begin, Jimmy Carter, and Anwar Sadat at Camp David, Maryland, on September 7, 1978
Source: Jimmy Carter Library

Using the image above, answer (a), (b), and (c).

(a) Briefly describe ONE accomplishment of these three men from the meeting in 1978.

(b) Briefly explain ONE specific historical cause that led these three leaders to meet in 1978.

(c) Briefly explain ONE specific historical effect that resulted from the meeting of these leaders in 1978.

2. Answer (a), (b), and (c).

(a) Briefly explain how ONE specific covert action taken during the Eisenhower administration affected the image of the United States abroad.

(b) Briefly explain how ONE specific historical development involving oil supplies affected U.S. foreign policy in the 1950s, 1960s, or 1970s.

(c) Briefly explain how ONE specific act during the Carter administration affected human rights abroad.

The Vietnam War

Pouring money, material, and men into the jungle [of Vietnam] without at least a remote prospect of victory would be dangerously futile and self-destructive.

John F. Kennedy, speech in U.S. Senate, April 6, 1954

Learning Objective: Explain the causes and effects of the Vietnam War.

After losing their Southeast Asian colony of Indochina to Japanese invaders in World War II, the French made the mistake of trying to retake it. Wanting independence, native Vietnamese and Cambodians resisted. French imperialism had the effect of increasing support for nationalist and Communist leader Ho Chi Minh.

Eisenhower's Domino Theory

By 1950, the anticolonial war in Indochina became part of the Cold War rivalry between Communist and anti-Communist powers. Truman's government started to give U.S. military aid to the French, while China and the Soviet Union aided the Viet Minh guerrillas led by Ho Chi Minh. In 1954, a large French army at Dien Bien Phu was trapped and forced to surrender. After this disastrous defeat, the French tried to convince Eisenhower to send in U.S. troops, but he refused. At the Geneva Conference of 1954, France agreed to give up Indochina, which was divided into the independent nations of Cambodia, Laos, and Vietnam.

Division of Vietnam By the terms of the Geneva Conference, Vietnam was to be temporarily divided at the 17th parallel until a general election could be held. The new nation remained divided, however, as two hostile governments took power on either side of the line. In North Vietnam, Ho Chi Minh established a Communist dictatorship. In South Vietnam, a government emerged under **Ngo Dinh Diem**, whose support came largely from anti-Communist, Catholic, and urban Vietnamese, many of whom had fled from Communist rule in the North. The general election to unite Vietnam was never held, largely because South Vietnam's government feared that the Communists would win.

From 1955 to 1961, the United States gave over $1 billion in economic and military aid to South Vietnam in an effort to build a stable anti-Communist state. In justifying this aid, President Eisenhower made what became a famous analogy to a row of dominoes. According to this **domino theory**, if South Vietnam fell under Communist control, one nation after another in Southeast Asia would also fall, until Australia and New Zealand were in dire danger.

SEATO To prevent South Vietnam, Laos, and Cambodia from "falling" to communism, Secretary of State **John Foster Dulles** put together a regional defense pact called the **Southeast Asia Treaty Organization (SEATO)**. Agreeing to defend one another in case of an attack within the region, eight nations signed the pact in 1954: the United States, Great Britain, France, Australia, New Zealand, the Philippines, Thailand, and Pakistan.

Escalation of the Vietnam War in the 1960s

Vietnam was hardly mentioned in the election debates of 1960 between Nixon and Kennedy. U.S. involvement was minimal at that time, but every year thereafter, it loomed larger and eventually dominated the presidency of Lyndon Johnson and the thoughts of the nation. None of the divisive issues in the 1960s was as tragic as the war in Vietnam. Some 2.7 million Americans served in the conflict, and 58,000 died in a failed effort to prevent the takeover of South Vietnam by Communist North Vietnam. Total deaths from the war in Vietnam and related conflicts in Southeast Asia were probably between 2 million and 4 million.

Buildup under Kennedy President Kennedy adopted Eisenhower's domino theory that, if Communist forces overthrew South Vietnam's government, they would quickly overrun other countries of Southeast Asia— Laos, Cambodia, Thailand, Malaysia, and Indonesia. Kennedy therefore continued U.S. military aid to South Vietnam's regime and significantly increased the number of military "advisers," who trained the South Vietnamese army and guarded weapons and facilities. By 1963, more than 16,000 U.S. troops in South Vietnam served in support, but not combat, roles. They provided training and supplies for South Vietnam's armed forces and helped create "strategic hamlets" (fortified villages).

However, the U.S. ally in South Vietnam, Ngo Dinh Diem, was not popular. He and his government steadily lost the support of peasants in the countryside, while in the capital city of Saigon, Buddhist monks set themselves on fire in the streets to protest Diem's policies. Kennedy began to question whether the South Vietnamese could win "their war" against Communist insurgents. Just two weeks before Kennedy himself was assassinated in Dallas, Diem was overthrown and killed by South Vietnamese generals. Historians later learned that the generals acted with the knowledge of the Kennedy administration.

Tonkin Gulf Resolution Lyndon Johnson became president just as things began to fall apart in South Vietnam. The country had seven different governments in 1964. During the U.S. presidential campaign, Republican candidate Barry Goldwater attacked the Johnson administration for giving only weak support to South Vietnam's fight against the Vietcong (Communist guerrillas).

In August 1964, President Johnson and Congress took a fateful turn in policy. Allegedly, North Vietnamese gunboats had fired on U.S. warships in the Gulf of Tonkin off Vietnam's coast. The president persuaded Congress that this aggressive act was sufficient reason for a military response by the United States. Congress approved the **Tonkin Gulf Resolution**, which basically gave the president, as commander-in-chief, a blank check to take "all necessary measures" to protect U.S. interests in Vietnam. Johnson used this small, obscure naval incident to secure congressional authorization to send U.S. forces into combat.

Critics later called the full-scale use of U.S. forces in Vietnam an illegal war because Congress never declared war, as the Constitution requires. Congress, however, did not have this concern and did not withdraw its resolution. Until 1968, most Americans supported the effort to contain communism in Southeast Asia. Johnson was caught in a political dilemma to which there was no good solution. How could he stop the defeat of a weak and unpopular government in South Vietnam without making it into an American war—a war whose cost would doom his Great Society programs? If he pulled out, however, he would be seen as weak and lose public support.

THE VIETNAM WAR

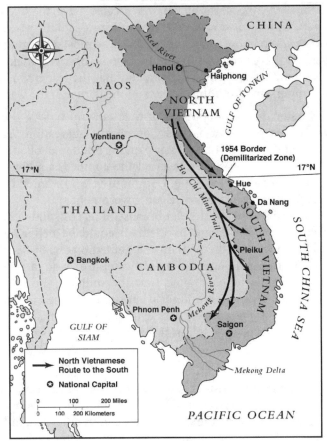

America's War

In 1965, the U.S. military and most of the president's foreign-policy advisers recommended expanding operations in Vietnam to save the Saigon government. After a Vietcong attack on the U.S. base at Pleiku in 1965, Johnson authorized Operation Rolling Thunder, a prolonged air attack using B-52 bombers against targets in North Vietnam. In April, the president decided to use U.S. combat troops for the first time to fight the Vietcong. By the end of 1965, more than 184,000 U.S. troops were in Vietnam, and most were engaged in a combat role. Johnson continued a step-by-step escalation of U.S. involvement in the war. Hoping to win a war of attrition, American generals used search-and-destroy tactics, which only further alienated the peasants. By the end of 1967, the United States had more than 485,000 troops in Vietnam (the peak was 540,000 in March 1969), and 16,000 Americans had already died in the conflict. Nevertheless, **General William Westmoreland**, commander of the U.S. forces in Vietnam, assured the American public that he could see "light at the end of the tunnel."

Credibility Gap Misinformation from military and civilian leaders combined with Johnson's reluctance to speak frankly to the American people about the scope and the costs of the war created what the media called a **credibility gap**. Johnson always hoped that a little more military pressure would bring the North Vietnamese to the peace table. The most damaging knowledge gap, however, may have been within the inner circles of government. Years later, Robert McNamara in his memoirs concluded that the leaders in Washington had failed to understand both the enemy and the nature of the war.

Hawks versus Doves Supporters of the war, or "**hawks**," believed that the war was an act of Soviet-backed Communist aggression against South Vietnam and that it was part of a master plan to conquer all of Southeast Asia. Opponents of the war, or "**doves**," viewed the conflict as a civil war fought by Vietnamese nationalists and some Communists who wanted to unite their country by overthrowing a corrupt Saigon government.

Some Americans opposed the war because of its costs in lives and money. They believed the billions spent in Vietnam could be better spent on the problems of the cities and the poor in the United States. By far the greatest opposition came from students on college campuses who, after graduation, would become eligible to be drafted into the military and shipped off to Vietnam. In November 1967, the antiwar movement gained a political leader when scholarly Senator Eugene F. McCarthy of Minnesota became the first antiwar advocate to challenge Johnson for the 1968 Democratic presidential nomination.

Tet Offensive On the occasion of their Lunar New Year (Tet) in January 1968, the Vietcong launched an all-out surprise attack on almost every provincial capital and American base in South Vietnam. Although the attack took a fearful toll in the cities, the U.S. military counterattacked, inflicted much heavier losses on the Vietcong, and recovered the lost territory. As a military attack, the **Tet Offensive** failed. Even so, it had tremendous impact in the United States. The millions of Americans who watched TV news footage of the destruction interpreted the attacks as a setback for Johnson's Vietnam policy. Victory was not imminent. Thus, for the Vietcong and North Vietnamese, Tet was a tremendous political victory in demoralizing the American public. In the New Hampshire primary in February, the antiwar McCarthy took 42 percent of the vote against Johnson.

Johnson Ends Escalation The Joint Chiefs of Staff responded to Tet by requesting 200,000 more troops to win the war. By this time, however, the group of experienced Cold War diplomats who advised Johnson had turned against further escalation of the war. On March 31, 1968, President Johnson went on television and told the American people that he would limit the bombing of North Vietnam and negotiate peace. He then surprised everyone by announcing that he would not run for reelection.

In May 1968, peace talks between North Vietnam, South Vietnam, and the United States started in Paris, but they were quickly deadlocked over minor issues. The war continued, and tens of thousands more died. But the escalation of the number of U.S. troops in Vietnam had stopped, and under the next administration it would be slowly reversed.

Coming Apart at Home, 1968

Few years in U.S. history outside of the Civil War were as troubled or violent as 1968. The Tet Offensive and the withdrawal of Johnson from the presidential race were followed by the murder of Martin Luther King Jr. and destructive riots in cities across the country. As the year unfolded, Americans wondered if their nation was coming apart from internal conflicts over the war issue, the race issue, and the generation gap between the baby boomers and their parents.

Election of 1968 In 1964, Kennedy's younger brother, **Robert F. Kennedy**, became a senator from New York. Four years later, he decided to enter the presidential race after McCarthy's strong showing in New Hampshire. Bobby Kennedy was more effective than McCarthy in mobilizing the traditional Democratic blue-collar and minority vote. On June 5, 1968, he won a major victory in California's primary, but immediately after his victory speech he was shot and killed by a young Arab nationalist who opposed Kennedy's support for Israel. After Robert Kennedy's death, the election of 1968 turned into a three-way race between two conservatives—**George Wallace** and **Richard Nixon**—and one liberal, Vice President Hubert Humphrey.

Democratic Convention in Chicago When the Democrats met in Chicago for their party convention, it was clear that **Hubert Humphrey** had enough delegates to win the nomination. As vice president, he had loyally supported Johnson's domestic and foreign policies. He controlled the convention, but the antiwar demonstrators were determined to control the streets. Chicago's mayor Richard Daley had the police out *en masse*, and the resulting violence was portrayed on television across the country as a "police riot." Humphrey left the convention as the nominee of a badly divided Democratic party, and early polls showed he was a clear underdog in a nation sick of disorder and protest.

White Backlash and George Wallace The growing hostility of many Whites to federal desegregation, antiwar protests, and race riots was tapped by Governor George Wallace of Alabama. Wallace was the first politician of late-20th-century America to marshal the general resentment against the Washington establishment ("pointy-head liberals," as he called them) and the two-party system. He ran for president as the self-nominated candidate of the American Independent Party, hoping to win enough electoral votes to throw the election into the House of Representatives.

Return of Richard Nixon Many observers thought Richard Nixon's political career had ended in 1962 after his unsuccessful run for governor of California. In 1968, however, a new, more-confident, and less-negative Nixon announced his candidacy and soon became the front-runner in the Republican primaries. The favorite of the party regulars, he had little trouble securing his nomination at the Republican convention. For his running mate, he selected Governor Spiro Agnew of Maryland, whose rhetoric was similar to that of George Wallace. Nixon was a "hawk" on the Vietnam War and ran on the slogans of "peace with honor" and "law and order."

Results Wallace and Nixon started strong, but the Democrats began to catch up, especially in northern urban centers, as Humphrey preached to the faithful of the old New Deal coalition. On election night, Nixon defeated Humphrey by a very close popular vote but took a substantial majority of the electoral vote (301 to 191), ending any threat that the three-candidate election would end up in the House of Representatives.

The significance of the 1968 election is clear in the combined total of Nixon's and Wallace's popular vote of almost 57 percent. Apparently, most Americans wanted a time-out to heal what they saw as the wounds inflicted on the national psyche by the upheavals of the 1960s. Supporters of Nixon and Wallace had had enough of protest, violence, permissiveness, the counterculture, drugs, and federal intervention in social institutions. Elections in the 1970s and 1980s would confirm that the tide was turning against New Deal liberalism in favor of the conservatives.

Richard Nixon's Vietnam Policy

In his January 1969 inaugural address, President Nixon promised to bring Americans together after the turmoil of the 1960s. However, suspicious and secretive by nature, Nixon soon began to isolate himself in the White House and create what Arthur Schlesinger Jr. called an "imperial presidency." Nixon's first interest was international relations, not domestic policy. Together with his national security adviser, **Henry Kissinger** (who became secretary of state during Nixon's second term), Nixon fashioned a pragmatic foreign policy that reduced the tensions of the Cold War.

U.S. FORCES IN VIETNAM, 1964 to 1973

Total Number of Troops

Deaths

1964 1965 1966 1967 1968 1969 1970 1971 1972 1973

■ Total Number of Troops (use scale on the left)
■ Deaths (use scale on the right)

Source: U.S. National Archives and Records Administration. Vietnam Conflict Extract Data File and other sources.

Vietnamization When Nixon took office, more than half a million U.S. troops were in Vietnam. His principal objective was to find a way to reduce U.S. involvement in the war while at the same time avoiding the appearance of conceding defeat. In a word, Nixon said the United States was seeking nothing less than "peace with honor." Almost immediately, the new president began the process called "**Vietnamization.**" He announced that he would gradually withdraw U.S. troops from Vietnam and give the South Vietnamese the money, the weapons, and the training that they needed to take over the full conduct of the war. Under this policy, U.S. troops in South Vietnam went from more than 540,000 in 1969 to under 30,000 in 1972. Extending the idea of disengagement to other parts of Asia, the president proclaimed the **Nixon Doctrine,** declaring that in the future Asian allies would receive U.S. support but without the extensive use of U.S. ground forces.

Opposition to Nixon's War Policies Nixon's gradual withdrawal of forces from Vietnam reduced the number of antiwar protests. However, in April 1970, the president expanded the war by using U.S. forces to invade Cambodia in an effort to destroy Vietnamese Communist bases in that country. A nationwide protest on college campuses against this action resulted in the killing of four youths by National Guard troops at **Kent State** University in Ohio and two students at Jackson State University in Mississippi. In reaction to the escalation of the war, the U.S. Senate (but not the House) voted to repeal the Gulf of Tonkin Resolution.

Also in 1970, the American public was shocked to learn about a 1968 massacre of women and children by U.S. troops in the Vietnamese village of

My Lai. Further fueling the antiwar sentiment was the publication by *The New York Times* of the **Pentagon Papers**, a secret government study documenting the mistakes and deceptions of government policymakers in dealing with Vietnam. The papers had been turned over, or "leaked," to the press by Daniel Ellsberg, a former Defense Department analyst.

Peace Talks, Bombing Attacks, and Armistice On the diplomatic front, Nixon had Kissinger conduct secret meetings with North Vietnam's foreign minister, Le Duc Tho. Kissinger announced in the fall of 1972 that "peace is at hand," but this announcement proved premature. When the two sides could not reach a deal, Nixon ordered a massive bombing of North Vietnam (the heaviest air attacks of the long war) to force a settlement. After several weeks of B-52 bomber attacks, the North Vietnamese agreed to an armistice, in which the United States would withdraw the last of its troops and get back more than 500 prisoners of war (POWs). The **Paris Accords** of January 1973 also promised a cease-fire and free elections. In practice, however, the armistice did not end the war between the North and the South and left tens of thousands of enemy troops in South Vietnam. Before the war ended, the death toll probably numbered more than a million.

The armistice finally allowed the United States to extricate itself from a war that had claimed more than 58,000 American lives. The $118 billion spent on the war began an inflationary cycle that racked the U.S. economy for years afterward.

War Powers Act Nixon was politically damaged by the news that he had authorized 3,500 secret bombing raids in Cambodia, a neutral country. Congress used the public uproar over this information to attempt to limit the president's powers over the military. In November 1973, after a long struggle, Congress finally passed the **War Powers Act** over Nixon's veto. This law required Nixon and any future president to report to Congress within 48 hours after taking military action. It further provided that Congress would have to approve any military action that lasted more than 60 days. After the long and unpopular war in Vietnam, Congress and the American people were ready to put the brakes on future presidents leading the nation into a war without a thorough debate.

Defeat in Southeast Asia

In 1974, South Vietnam continued to face strong attacks from Communist forces. However, President Ford was unable to get additional funds to support U.S. military involvement.

Fall of Saigon In April 1975, the U.S.-supported government in Saigon fell to the enemy, and Vietnam was reunified under the Communist government in Hanoi (North Vietnam's capital). Just before the final collapse, the United States was able to evacuate about 150,000 Vietnamese who had supported the United States and now faced certain persecution. The fall of South Vietnam marked a low point of American prestige overseas and confidence at home.

Genocide in Cambodia Also in 1975, the U.S.-supported government in Vietnam's neighbor, Cambodia, fell to the Khmer Rouge, a radical Communist faction that killed between 1 million and 2 million of its own people—perhaps one-quarter of the population—in a brutal relocation program to rid the country of Western influence. Together the wars in Southeast Asia created 10 million refugees, many of whom fled to the United States.

Future of Southeast Asia The fall of Cambodia seemed to fulfill Eisenhower's domino theory, but in fact the rest of Southeast Asia did not fall to communism. Instead, nations such as Singapore, Thailand, and Malaysia emerged as the "little tigers" of the vigorously growing Asian (Pacific Rim) economy. Some argued that U.S. support of South Vietnam was not a waste because it bought time for other nations of East Asia and Southeast Asia to develop and better resist communism.

REFLECT ON THE LEARNING OBJECTIVE

1. Explain the origins of the Vietnam War, the reasons for U.S. involvement, and the effects the war had on the United States.

KEY TERMS BY THEME

Vietnam War (WOR)	George Wallace
Ngo Dinh Diem	Richard Nixon
domino theory	Democratic Convention in Chicago
John Foster Dulles	Hubert Humphrey
Southeast Asia Treaty Organization (SEATO)	White backlash
	Henry Kissinger
Tonkin Gulf Resolution	Vietnamization
General William Westmoreland	Nixon Doctrine
credibility gap	Kent State
hawks	My Lai
doves	Pentagon Papers
Tet Offensive	Paris Accords
Robert F. Kennedy	War Powers Act

Questions 1–3 refer to the excerpt below.

"We will stay [in Vietnam] because a just nation cannot leave to the cruelties of its enemies a people who have staked their lives and independence on America's solemn pledge—a pledge which had grown through the commitment of three American Presidents.

We will stay because in Asia—and around the world—are countries whose independence rests, in large measure, on confidence in America's word and in American protection. To yield to force in Vietnam would weaken that confidence, would undermine the independence of many lands, and would whet the appetite of aggression. We would have to fight in one land, and then we would have to fight in another—or abandon much of Asia to the domination of Communists."

> Lyndon B. Johnson, State of the Union Message,
> January 12, 1966

1. Which foreign policy development supports the perspective presented in this excerpt?

   (A) The practice of brinkmanship

   (B) The process of decolonization

   (C) The belief in the domino theory

   (D) The principle of mutually assured destruction

2. In which way did Johnson most significantly depart from the policies of previous presidents regarding Vietnam?

   (A) He used a larger number of U.S. troops in combat roles.

   (B) He was more successful in negotiating with North Vietnam.

   (C) He set a lower limit on the number of U.S. troops sent to Vietnam.

   (D) He gave more decision-making authority to the generals.

3. Which of the following best characterizes the position of the president's antiwar critics?

   (A) The war threatened to cause an inflationary cycle.

   (B) The conflict was primarily a civil war between factions in Vietnam.

   (C) The containment policy would not work in Asia.

   (D) The continued involvement would weaken trust between the United States and its allies.

Use complete sentences; an outline or bulleted list alone is not acceptable.

1. "So it proved for the 1960's policymakers, whose ignorance and misconceptions of Southeast Asian history, culture and politics pulled America progressively deeper into the war. LBJ, Rusk, McNamara. . . . mistakenly viewed Vietnam through the simplistic prism of the Cold War. They perceived a deeply complex and ambiguous regional struggle, as a grave challenge to world order and stability. . . . Vietnam exposed the limitations and contradictions of this static doctrine in a world of flux. . . . Vietnam represented a failure not just of American foreign policy, but also of American statesmanship."

> Brian VanDemark, *Into the Quagmire: Lyndon Johnson and*
> *the Evolution of the Vietnam War,* 1991

"America's military bureaucracy depends on weapons, increasingly complex, difficult to maintain and expensive. . . . Our marvelously clever technology did not help us to understand the [Vietnam] war and, in fact, confused us even more because it created our unquestioning faith in our own power. . . . If we exploded enough bombs and fired enough rounds, we assumed the enemy would quit. . . . The utter failure of military tactics to utilize technology was not the fault of civilians. . . . By the sheer force of firepower the military won battles, but it could never have made these victories add up to victory."

> Leon Baritz, historian, *A History of How American Culture Led Us into*
> *Vietnam and Made Us Fight the Way We Did,* 1985

Using the excerpts above, answer (a), (b), and (c).

(a) Briefly describe ONE specific difference between VanDemark's and Baritz's historical interpretations of the U.S. policies in Vietnam.

(b) Briefly explain ONE specific historical event or development that is not explicitly mentioned in the excerpts that could be used to support VanDemark's interpretation of U.S. policies in Vietnam during the 1960s.

(c) Briefly explain ONE specific historical event or development that is not explicitly mentioned in the excerpts that could be used to support Baritz's interpretation of U.S. policies in Vietnam during the 1960s.

The Great Society

*The Great Society rests on abundance and liberty for all.
It demands an end to poverty and racial injustice, to which
we are totally committed in our time.*

Lyndon B. Johnson, Commencement Address
at the University of Michigan, May 1964

Learning Objective 1: Explain the causes and effects of continuing policy debates about the role of the federal government over time.

Learning Objective 2: Explain the contributions and changes in immigration patterns over time.

Two hours after the assassination of President Kennedy, **Lyndon Johnson** took the presidential oath aboard a plane in Dallas. A native of rural west Texas and a graduate of a little-known teacher's college, he seemed unsophisticated compared to the wealthy, Harvard-educated Kennedy. However, Johnson was a skilled politician who had started his career as a Roosevelt Democrat during the Great Depression. As the new president, Johnson was determined to expand the social reforms of the New Deal. He called his program the "**Great Society**." During his almost 30 years in Congress, he had learned how to get things done.

The War on Poverty

In his best-selling book on poverty, *The Other America* (1962), **Michael Harrington** helped focus national attention on the 40 million Americans still living in poverty. President Johnson responded by declaring in 1964 an "unconditional **war on poverty**." The Democratic Congress gave the president almost everything he asked for by creating the Office of Economic Opportunity (OEO) and providing this antipoverty agency with a billion-dollar budget. The OEO sponsored a wide variety of self-help programs for the poor, such as Head Start for preschoolers, the Job Corps for vocational education, literacy programs, and legal services. The controversial Community Action Program allowed the poor to run antipoverty programs in their own neighborhoods.

The Election of 1964

Johnson and his running mate, Senator Hubert Humphrey, went into the 1964 election with a clearly liberal agenda. In contrast, the Republicans nominated a staunch conservative, Senator **Barry Goldwater** of Arizona, who advocated ending the welfare state, including the Tennessee Valley Authority and Social Security. A television ad by the Democrats pictured Goldwater as a dangerous extremist who might ignite a nuclear war. However, the Goldwater campaign did energize young conservatives and introduced new conservative voices, such as former film actor and TV host Ronald Reagan of California.

Johnson won the election by a landslide, taking 61 percent of the popular vote—a higher figure than FDR's landslide of 1936. In addition, Democrats now controlled both houses of Congress by better than a two-thirds margin. A Democratic president and Congress were in a position to pass the economic and social reforms originally proposed by President Truman in the 1940s.

Great Society Reforms

Johnson's list of legislative achievements from 1963 to 1966 is long and includes new programs that would have lasting effects on U.S. society. Several of the most significant ones are listed in the table below.

GREAT SOCIETY PROGRAMS		
Title	**Year Passed**	**Program**
Food Stamp Act	1964	Expanded the federal program to help low-income people buy food
National Foundation on the Arts and Humanities	1965	Provided federal funding for the arts and for creative and scholarly projects
Medicare	1965	Provided health insurance for all people 65 and older
Medicaid	1965	Provided funds to states to pay for medical care for the poor and disabled
Elementary and Secondary Education Act	1965	Provided federal funds to poor school districts and funds for special education programs
Higher Education Act	1965	Provided federal scholarships for postsecondary education
Immigration Act	1965	Abolished discriminatory quotas based on national origins
Child Nutrition Act	1966	Added breakfast to the school lunch program

In addition to the programs listed in the table, Congress increased funding for mass transit, public housing, rent subsidies for low-income people, and crime prevention. Johnson also established two new cabinet departments: the **Department of Transportation (DOT)** and the **Department of Housing and Urban Development (HUD)**. In response to **Ralph Nader**'s book *Unsafe at Any Speed* (1965), Congress also passed automobile industry regulations that would save hundreds of thousands of lives in the following years. Clean air and water laws were enacted in part as a response to **Rachel Carson**'s exposé of pesticides, *Silent Spring* (1962). Federal parks and wilderness areas were expanded. President Johnson's wife, Lady Bird Johnson, helped improve the environment with her **Beautify America** campaign, which resulted in the Highway Beautification Act that removed billboards from federal highways.

Evaluating the Great Society Critics have attacked Johnson's Great Society for making unrealistic promises to eliminate poverty, for creating a centralized welfare state, and for being inefficient and very costly. Defenders point out that these programs gave vitally needed assistance to millions of Americans who had previously been forgotten or ignored—the poor, the disabled, and the elderly. Johnson himself would jeopardize his domestic achievements by escalating the war in Vietnam—a war that resulted in higher taxes and inflation.

Changes in Immigration

Before the 1960s, most immigrants to the United States had come from Europe and Canada. By the 1980s, 47 percent of immigrants were coming from Latin America, 37 percent from Asia, and fewer than 13 percent from Europe and Canada. In part, this dramatic shift was caused by the arrival of refugees leaving Cuba and Vietnam after the Communist takeovers of these countries. Of far greater importance was the impact of the **Immigration Act of 1965**, which ended the ethnic quota acts of the 1920s favoring Europeans and thereby opened the United States to immigrants from all parts of the world. Legal immigration increased sharply. In the 1970s, about 400,000 immigrants entered each year. In many years between 1990 and 2020, the number exceeded 1,000,000 people.

Undocumented Immigrants By the mid-1970s, as many as 12 million foreigners were in the United States illegally. The rise in the number of immigrants from Latin America and Asia led to the Immigration Reform and Control Act of 1986, which penalized employers for hiring immigrants who had entered the country illegally or had overstayed their visas while also granting amnesty to undocumented immigrants arriving by 1982. Even so, many Americans concluded that the nation had lost control of its own borders.

Political Impact of the Great Society President Johnson's Great Society programs also included legislation to end racial discrimination, which is explored in Topic 8.10. Johnson predicted that the Democratic Party would lose its Southern support because of its liberal social legislation. In fact, the mid-1960s did prove the high point for the use of the federal government to achieve racial equality at home. The conservative resurgence in the next decades was partly motivated to undo the Great Society legislation.

REFLECT ON THE LEARNING OBJECTIVES

1. Explain two causes and two effects of the War on Poverty and the Great Society programs.

2. Explain the impacts of the Immigration Act of 1965 on changes in immigration patterns over time.

Johnson: Domestic Programs (PCE, MIG)
Lyndon Johnson
Great Society
The Other America
Michael Harrington
war on poverty
Barry Goldwater

National Foundation on the Arts and Humanities
Medicare
Medicaid
Elementary and Secondary Education Act
Department of Transportation (DOT)

Department of Housing and Urban Development (HUD)
Ralph Nader
Unsafe at Any Speed
Rachel Carson
Silent Spring
Beautify America
Immigration Act of 1965

MULTIPLE-CHOICE QUESTIONS

Questions 1–4 refer to the excerpt below.

> "In your time we have the opportunity to move not only toward the rich society and the powerful society, but upward to the Great Society. The Great Society rests on abundance and liberty for all. It demands an end to poverty and racial injustice, to which we are totally committed in our time. . . . The Great Society is a place where every child can find knowledge to enrich his mind and to enlarge his talents."
>
> Lyndon B. Johnson, speech, May 1964

1. Which provides evidence to refute Johnson's argument in this source?

   (A) The information in Michael Harrington's 1962 book about poverty

   (B) The number of African Americans registered to vote in the South

   (C) The reaction to the *Brown v. Board of Education* decision

   (D) The hope of people in other nations to emigrate to the United States

2. Which of the following historical slogans or developments were most closely related to Johnson's plans as described in this source?

   (A) "Gilded Age," because it focused on material goods and wealth

   (B) "Square Deal," because it addressed business-labor relations

   (C) "Return to Normalcy," because it recalled a better time in the past

   (D) "New Deal," because it aimed to attack economic hardships

3. Johnson's primary purpose in giving this speech was to

   (A) present his goals for a second term in office

   (B) remind graduates to continue to enrich their minds

   (C) attack the rich and powerful supporters of his political opponent

   (D) separate himself from the policies of Kennedy and other Democrats

4. What is the relationship between this speech and Johnson's record as president?

(A) He ignored the goals expressed in this speech and focused on other priorities.

(B) He failed to get Congress to pass legislation to implement his policies.

(C) He made many compromises with Congress, so he accomplished only a little.

(D) He passed significant legislation that reflected the vision expressed in this speech.

SHORT-ANSWER QUESTIONS

Use complete sentences; an outline or bulleted list alone is not acceptable.

1.
IMMIGRATION TO THE UNITED STATES

Africa 1%

Americas 37%

Europe 56%

Asia and Oceania 6%

Total: 2,499,268
1950 to 1959

Africa 8%

Europe 13%

Americas 44%

Asia and Oceania 35%

Total: 10,299,430
2000 to 2009

Source: U.S. Census Bureau

Using the graphs above, answer (a), (b), and (c).

(a) Briefly explain ONE specific change in immigration patterns from the 1950s to the first decade of the 2000s.

(b) Briefly analyze ONE specific way the Immigration Act of 1965 contributed to the changes in immigration patterns.

(c) Briefly explain ONE additional cause for the changes in immigration patterns from the 1950s to the first decade of the 2000s.

2. Answer (a), (b), and (c).

(a) Briefly explain ONE specific way the Great Society attacked poverty.

(b) Briefly explain ONE specific way the Great Society tried to improve education.

(c) Briefly explain ONE specific way Johnson's health care programs had a lasting impact on American society.

The African American Civil Rights Movement in the 1960s

I have a dream my four little children will one day live in a nation where they will not be judged by the color of their skin but by the content of their character. I have a dream today!

Martin Luther King Jr., speech on steps of the Lincoln Memorial, August 23, 1963

Learning Objectives: Explain how and why various groups responded to calls for the expansion of civil rights from 1960 to 1980. Explain the various ways in which the federal government responded to the calls for the expansion of civil rights.

The civil rights movement gained momentum during the Kennedy and Johnson presidencies. A very close election in 1960 influenced President Kennedy not to press the issue of civil rights lest he alienate White voters. But the defiance of the governors of Alabama and Mississippi to federal court rulings on integration forced a showdown. In 1962, **James Meredith**, a young African American Air Force veteran, attempted to enroll at the University of Mississippi. A federal court guaranteed his right to attend. Supporting Meredith and the court order, Kennedy sent in 400 federal marshals and 3,000 troops to control mob violence and protect Meredith's right to attend class. A similar incident occurred in Alabama in 1963. Governor **George Wallace** tried to stop an African American student from entering the University of Alabama. Once again, Kennedy sent troops to the scene, and the student was admitted.

The Leadership of Dr. Martin Luther King Jr.

Civil rights activists and freedom riders who traveled through the South registering African Americans to vote and integrating public places were met with beatings, bombings, and murder by White extremists. Recognized nationally as the leader of the civil rights movement, Dr. **Martin Luther King Jr.** remained committed to nonviolent protests against segregation. In 1963, he and some followers were jailed in Birmingham, Alabama, for what local authorities maintained was an illegal march. The jailing of King, however, proved to be a milestone in the civil rights movement because most Americans believed King to have been jailed unjustly. From his jail cell, King wrote an essay, "**Letter from Birmingham Jail**," in which he argued:

[W]e need emulate neither the "do-nothingism" of the complacent nor the hatred and despair of the Black nationalist. For there is the more excellent way of love and nonviolent protest. I am grateful to God that, through the influence of the Negro church, the way of nonviolence became an integral part of our struggle. . . .

One day the South will know that when these disinherited children of God sat down at lunch counters, they were in reality standing up for what is best in the American dream and for the most sacred values in our Judeo-Christian heritage, thereby bringing our nation back to those great wells of democracy which were dug deep by the founding fathers in their formulation of the Constitution and the Declaration of Independence. . . .

King's letter moved President Kennedy to support a tougher civil rights bill.

March on Washington (1963) In August 1963, King led one of the largest, most successful demonstrations in U.S. history. About 200,000 Black and White people joined the peaceful **March on Washington** in support of jobs and the civil rights bill. The highlight of the demonstration was King's impassioned **"I Have a Dream" speech**, which appealed for the end of racial prejudice and ended with everyone in the crowd singing "We Shall Overcome."

Federal Civil Rights Acts of 1964 and 1965

Ironically, a Southern president succeeded in persuading Congress to enact the most important civil rights laws since Reconstruction. Even before the 1964 election, Johnson convinced both a majority of Democrats and some Republicans to pass the 1964 **Civil Rights Act**, which made segregation illegal in all public facilities, including hotels and restaurants, and gave the federal government more power to enforce school desegregation. This act also set up the **Equal Employment Opportunity Commission** to end discrimination in employment on the basis of race, religion, sex, or national origin.

Ending a Barrier to Voting Also in 1964, the **24th Amendment** was ratified. It abolished the practice of collecting a poll tax, one of the measures that, for decades, had discouraged poor people from voting.

March to Montgomery A voting rights march from Selma, Alabama, to the state capital of Montgomery in March 1965 was met with beatings and tear gas. Among those severely injured on "Bloody Sunday" was SNCC organizer John Lewis. He became known as the "conscience of Congress" for his leadership on civil rights as a member of the House of Representatives.

Televised pictures of the violence proved a turning point in the civil rights movement. The national outrage prompted Johnson to send federal troops to protect King and other marchers in another attempt to petition the state government. As a result, Congress passed the powerful **Voting Rights Act of 1965**. This act ended literacy tests and provided federal registrars in areas where African Americans had been kept from voting since Reconstruction. The impact was most dramatic in the Deep South.

Divisions in the Civil Rights Movement Laws such as the Civil Rights Act and the Voting Rights Act were hard-won victories. Nevertheless, young African Americans were losing patience with the slow progress toward equality and the continued violence by White extremists.

Black Muslims and Malcolm X

Seeking a new cultural identity based on Africa and Islam, the **Black Muslim** leader Elijah Muhammad preached Black nationalism, separatism, and self-improvement. The movement had already attracted thousands of followers by the time a young man named Malcolm Little became a convert while serving in prison. He adopted the name **Malcolm X**. Leaving prison in 1952, Malcolm X acquired a reputation as the movement's most controversial voice. He criticized King as "an Uncle Tom" (subservient to Whites) and advocated self-defense—using Black violence to counter White violence. He eventually left the Black Muslims and moved away from defending violence, but he was assassinated by Black opponents in 1965. *The Autobiography of Malcolm X* remains an engaging testimony to one man's development from a petty criminal into a major leader.

Race Riots and Black Power

The radicalism of Malcolm X influenced the thinking of young African Americans in civil rights organizations such as the **Student Nonviolent Coordinating Committee (SNCC)** and the **Congress of Racial Equality (CORE)**. **Stokely Carmichael**, the chairman of SNCC, repudiated nonviolence and advocated "black power" (especially economic power) and racial separatism. In 1966, the **Black Panthers** were organized by Huey Newton, Bobby Seale, and other militants as a revolutionary socialist movement advocating self-rule for American blacks.

Urban Riots Shortly after the passage of the Voting Rights Act of 1965, the arrest of a young black motorist by White police in the black neighborhood of **Watts** in Los Angeles sparked a six-day race riot that killed 34 people and destroyed more than 700 buildings.

For the following few summers through 1968, **race riots** continued to erupt in black neighborhoods of major cities, with increasing casualties and destruction of property. Rioters shouting slogans—"Burn, baby, burn" and "Get whitey"—made Whites suspect that Black extremists and revolutionaries were behind the violence. There was little evidence, however, that the small Black Power movement was responsible for the violence. A federal investigation of the many riots by the **Kerner Commission** concluded in late 1968 that racism and segregation were chiefly responsible and that the United States was becoming "two societies, one black, one white—separate and unequal."

By the mid-1960s, the issue of civil rights had spread far beyond *de jure* segregation practiced under the law in the South. It now included the **de facto segregation** and discrimination caused by racist attitudes in the North and West.

Murder in Memphis Martin Luther King Jr. received the Nobel Peace Prize in 1964, but his nonviolent approach was under increasing pressure from all sides. His effort to use peaceful marches in urban centers of the North, such as Chicago, met with little success. King also broke with President Johnson over the Vietnam War because that war was beginning to drain money from social programs. In April 1968, the nation went into shock over the news that King had been shot and killed by a White man while standing on a motel balcony in Memphis, Tennessee. Massive riots erupted in 168 cities across the country, leaving at least 46 people dead.

The violence did not reflect the ideals of the murdered leader, but it did reveal the anger and frustrations among African Americans in both the North and the South. The violence also fed a growing "White backlash" against the civil rights movement, especially among White blue-collar voters, which was soon reflected in national elections in November 1968 (Topic 8.14).

REFLECT ON THE LEARNING OBJECTIVES

1. Explain how and why two groups responded to calls for the expansion of civil rights from 1960 to 1980.

2. Explain two ways in which the federal government responded to calls for the expansion of civil rights from 1960 to 1980.

KEY TERMS BY THEME

Civil Rights Movement (SOC, PCE)
James Meredith
George Wallace
Martin Luther King Jr.
Letter from Birmingham Jail
March on Washington
"I Have a Dream" speech
Civil Rights Act
Equal Employment Opportunity
   Commission
24th Amendment
March to Montgomery

Voting Rights Act of 1965
Black Muslim
Malcolm X
Student Nonviolent Coordinating
   Committee (SNCC)
Congress of Racial Equality (CORE)
Stokely Carmichael
Black Panthers
Watts
race riots
Kerner Commission
de facto segregation

Questions 1–3 refer to the excerpt below.

"Last Sunday, more than eight thousand of us started on a mighty walk from Selma, Alabama. . . . Our whole campaign in Alabama has been centered around the right to vote. In focusing the attention of the nation and the world today on the flagrant denial of the right to vote, we are exposing the very origin, the root cause, of racial segregation in the Southland. . . . The segregation of the races was really a political stratagem employed by the emerging Bourbon [conservative] interests in the South to keep the southern masses divided and southern labor the cheapest in the land. . . . The threat of the free exercise of the ballot by the Negro and the white masses alike resulted in the establishment of a segregated society. . . .

Let us march on ballot boxes until brotherhood becomes more than a meaningless word in an opening prayer, but the order of the day on every legislative agenda. . . . How long? Not long, because the arc of the moral universe is long, but it bends toward justice."

Martin Luther King Jr., address at the conclusion of the Selma
to Montgomery March, March 25, 1965

1. Which of the following best explains the connection that King made with segregation and "the emerging Bourbon interests"?
   (A) Segregation can be traced back to the original founders of the Southern colonies.
   (B) Segregation was a natural result of hatred between the races after the Civil War.
   (C) After Reconstruction, the White ruling class used segregation to regain political control.
   (D) Both African Americans and poor Whites were the targets of voting restrictions.

2. Which of the following best explains the result of the 1965 march from Selma to Montgomery?
   (A) The marchers, along with Dr. King, were jailed for civil disobedience.
   (B) Under pressure, Congress passed the most effective voting rights legislation since Reconstruction.
   (C) There was White backlash against Blacks for demanding too much.
   (D) Race riots were sparked in cities across the nation.

3. Which of the following best reflects the loss of faith by younger African Americans in the established leadership of the civil rights movement after the March to Montgomery?

(A) The response to the passage of the Civil Rights Act of 1964

(B) The conversion of Malcolm X to the Black Muslims

(C) The shift in tactics of SNCC under Stokely Carmichael

(D) The reaction to the Kerner Commission's findings on racism

SHORT-ANSWER QUESTION

Use complete sentences; an outline or bulleted list alone is not acceptable.

1. "When he had entered the Oval Office for his conversation with Johnson, Wilkins (leader of the NAACP) had not much hope for the civil rights bill . . ., but by the time the conversation ended, he had been 'struck by the enormous difference between Kennedy and Johnson. . . . Kennedy had been polite and sympathetic . . . but as a legislator he was very green. . . . Johnson knew exactly what was possible. . . . Johnson made it plain he wanted the whole bill. If we could find the votes, we would win. . . . The problem was as simple as that.' Wilkins had entered the Oval Office without much hope; that wasn't the way he left it."

Robert A Caro, Passage of Power, 2012

Using the excerpt above, answer (a), (b), and (c).

(a) Briefly explain ONE specific example of how the federal government expanded civil rights during the 1960s.

(b) Briefly explain ONE specific example of how the leaders and supporters of the civil rights movement furthered their cause during the 1960s.

(c) Briefly explain the historical role of President Johnson in the civil rights movement of the 1960s.

Topic 8.11

The Civil Rights Movement Expands

I am woman, hear me roar/In numbers too big to ignore . . .
I am woman watch me grow/See me standing toe to toe . . .

Helen Reddy, "I Am Woman," 1971

Learning Objective: Explain how and why various groups responded to calls for expansion of civil rights from 1960 to 1980.

One aspect of the protest movements of the 1960s that continued into later decades was the movement by a variety of other groups to gain both relief from discrimination and recognition for their contributions to U.S. society, including women, Latinos, American Indians, and the gay community.

The Women's Movement

The increased education and employment of women in the 1950s, the civil rights movement, and the sexual revolution all contributed to a renewal of the **women's movement** in the 1960s. In addition, some feminists who participated in the countercultures of the 1960s rejected many of the social, economic, and political values of their parents' generation and advocated changes in sexual norms.

Betty Friedan's book *The Feminine Mystique* (1963) gave the movement a new direction by encouraging middle-class women to seek fulfillment in professional careers in addition to filling the roles of wife, mother, and homemaker. In 1966, Friedan helped found the **National Organization for Women (NOW)**, which adopted the activist tactics of other civil rights movements to secure equal treatment of women, especially for job opportunities. By this time, Congress had already enacted two antidiscrimination laws: the **Equal Pay Act of 1963** and the **Civil Rights Act of 1964**. These measures prohibited discrimination in employment and compensation on the basis of sex but had been poorly enforced.

In 1972, Congress also passed **Title IX**, a statute to end sex discrimination in schools that receive federal funding. Though far-reaching, the law is best known for its requirement that schools provide girls with equal athletic opportunities. Many believe that these new opportunities in athletics proved to be a key step in promoting women's equality.

Campaign for the Equal Rights Amendment Feminists achieved a major legislative victory in 1972 when Congress passed the **Equal Rights Amendment (ERA)**. This proposed constitutional amendment stated: "Equality of rights under the law shall not be denied or abridged by the United States or by any state on account of sex." Although NOW and other groups campaigned hard for the ERA, it just missed ratification by the required 38 states. It was defeated in part because of a growing reaction against feminism by conservatives who feared the movement threatened the traditional roles of women.

Achievements Even without the ERA, the women's movement accomplished fundamental changes in attitudes and hiring practices. In increasing numbers, women moved into professions previously dominated by men: business, law, medicine, and politics. Although women still experienced the "glass ceiling" in the corporate world, American society at the beginning of the 21st century was less and less a man's world.

Latino Americans

Most Latino Americans before World War II lived in the Southwestern states, but in the postwar years new arrivals from Puerto Rico, Cuba, and South and Central America increasingly settled in the East and Midwest. After suffering deportation during the Great Depression, Mexican workers returned to the United States in the 1950s and 1960s to take low-paying agricultural jobs. The farm workers were widely exploited before a long series of boycotts led by **César Chávez** and the **United Farm Workers Association** finally gained collective bargaining rights for them in 1975.

Latinos achieved goals in other areas as well. Mexican American activists also won a federal mandate for bilingual education requiring schools to teach Hispanic children in both English and Spanish. In the 1980s, a growing number of **Hispanic Americans** were elected to public office, including as mayors of Miami, San Antonio, and other large cities. The Census Bureau reported that, in 2000, Hispanics, including Cubans, Puerto Ricans, and other Latin Americans, had become the country's largest minority group.

American Indian Movement

In the 1950s, the Eisenhower administration had made an unsuccessful attempt to encourage American Indians to leave reservations and assimilate into urban America. American Indian leaders resisted the loss of cultural identity that would have resulted from such a policy. To achieve self-determination and revival of tribal traditions, the **American Indian Movement (AIM)** was founded in 1968. Militant actions soon followed, including AIM's takeover of the abandoned prison on Alcatraz Island in San Francisco Bay in 1969. AIM members also occupied Wounded Knee, South Dakota, in 1973, which was the site of the infamous massacre of American Indians by the U.S. cavalry in 1890.

AMERICAN INDIAN POPULATION OF THE UNITED STATES, 1950 TO 2010		
Year	Total	Percentage
1950	343,410	0.2
1960	508,675	0.3
1970	827,255	0.4
1980	1,420,400	0.6
1990	1,959,234	0.8
2000	2,475,956	0.9
2010	2,932,248	0.9

Source: U.S. Census Bureau. Figures include Alaska Natives.

American Indians had successes in the late 20st century. Congress passed the **Indian Self-Determination Act of 1975**, which gave reservations and tribal lands greater control over internal programs, education, and law enforcement. Federal courts supported efforts to regain property and compensation for treaty violations. American Indians attacked widespread unemployment and poverty on reservations by improving education through the Tribally Controlled Community College Assistance Act of 1978 and by building industries and gambling casinos on reservations under the self-determination legislation.

Interest in the cultural heritage of American Indians was also overcoming old prejudices. By the 2010 census, nearly 3 million people identified themselves as American Indian or Alaska Native, and more than 2 million more identified themselves as a combination of American Indian or Alaska Native and some other ethnic group.

Asian Americans

Americans of Asian descent had become the fastest growing ethnic minority by the 1980s. The largest group of **Asian Americans** were of Chinese ancestry, followed by Filipinos, Japanese, Indians, Koreans, and Vietnamese. A strong dedication to education resulted in Asian Americans being well represented in the best colleges and universities. However, at times, Asian Americans suffered from discrimination, envy, and Japan-bashing, while the less-educated immigrants earned well below the national average.

Gay Rights Movement

In 1969, a police raid on the Stonewall Inn, a gay bar in New York City, sparked both a riot and the **gay rights movement**. Gay activists urged homosexuals to be open about their identity and to work to end discrimination and violent abuse. By the mid-1970s, homosexuality was no longer classified as a mental illness, and the federal Civil Service dropped its ban on employment of homosexuals. In 1993, President Clinton attempted to end discrimination against gays and lesbians in the military, but settled for the compromise "don't ask, don't tell" policy. People would not be asked or expected to describe their sexual identity, but the military could still expel people for being gay or lesbian.

The Warren Court and Individual Rights

As chief justice of the Supreme Court from 1953 to 1969, Earl Warren had an impact on the nation comparable to that of John Marshall in the early 1800s. Warren's decision in the desegregation case of *Brown v. Board of Education of Topeka* (1954) was by far the most important case of the 20th century involving race relations. Then, in the 1960s, the **Warren Court** made a series of decisions that profoundly affected the criminal-justice system, state political systems, and the definition of individual rights. Before Warren's tenure as chief justice, the Supreme Court had concentrated on protecting property rights. During and after his tenure, the Court focused more on protecting individual rights.

Criminal Justice Several decisions of the Warren Court concerned defendants' rights. Four of the most important were the following:

- *Mapp v. Ohio* (1961) ruled that evidence seized illegally cannot be used against the accused in court.
- *Gideon v. Wainwright* (1963) required that state courts provide counsel (services of an attorney) for indigent (poor) defendants.
- *Escobedo v. Illinois* (1964) extended the ruling in *Gideon*, giving suspects the right to have a lawyer present during questioning by the police.
- *Miranda v. Arizona* (1966) extended the ruling in *Escobedo* to require the police to inform an arrested person of his or her right to remain silent.

Reapportionment Equality Before 1962, many states included at least one house of their legislatures (usually the senate) that had districts that strongly favored rural areas to the disadvantage of cities. In the landmark case of *Baker v. Carr* (1962), the Warren Court declared this practice unconstitutional. In *Baker* and later cases, the Court established the principle of "**one man, one vote**," meaning that election districts would have to be redrawn to provide equal representation for all citizens.

Freedom of Expression and Privacy Other rulings by the Warren Court extended the rights mentioned in the 1st Amendment to protect the actions of protesters, to permit greater latitude under freedom of the press, to ban religious activities sponsored by public schools, and to guarantee adults' rights to use contraceptives.

- *Yates v. United States* (1957) said that the 1st Amendment protected radical and revolutionary speech, even by Communists, unless it was a "clear and present danger" to the safety of the country.
- *Engel v. Vitale* (1962) ruled that state laws requiring prayers and Bible readings in the public schools violated the 1st Amendment's provision for separation of church and state.

- *Griswold v. Connecticut* (1965) ruled that, in recognition of a citizen's right to privacy, a state could not prohibit the use of contraceptives by adults. (This privacy case provided the foundation for later cases establishing a woman's right to an abortion.)

The Warren Court's defense of the rights of unpopular individuals, including people accused of crimes, provoked a storm of controversy. Critics called for Warren's impeachment. Both supporters and critics agreed that the Warren Court profoundly changed the interpretation of constitutional rights.

REFLECT ON THE LEARNING OBJECTIVE

1. Explain how and why various groups responded to calls for expansion of civil rights from 1960 to 1980.

KEY TERMS BY THEME

Civil Rights Movement Expands (SOC)	Equal Rights Amendment (ERA)	gay rights movement
women's movement	César Chávez	Warren Court
Betty Friedan	United Farm Workers Association	*Mapp v. Ohio*
The Feminine Mystique	Hispanic Americans	*Gideon v. Wainwright*
National Organization for Women (NOW)	American Indian Movement (AIM)	*Escobedo v. Illinois*
Equal Pay Act of 1963	Indian Self-Determination Act of 1975	*Miranda v. Arizona*
Civil Rights Act of 1964	Asian Americans	reapportionment
Title IX		*Baker v. Carr*
		one man, one vote
		Yates v. United States

MULTIPLE-CHOICE QUESTIONS

Questions 1–2 refer to the excerpt below.

"We, men and women who hereby constitute ourselves as the National Organization for Women, believe that the time has come for a new movement toward equality for all women in America, and towards a full equal partnership of the sexes. . . .

NOW Bill of Rights: Equal Rights Constitutional Amendment, Enforce Law Banning Sex Discrimination in Employment, Maternity Leave Rights in Employment and in Social Security Benefits, Tax Deduction for Home and Child Care Expenses for Working Parents, Child Care Centers, Equal and Unsegregated Education, Equal Job Training Opportunities and Allowances for Women in Poverty, Rights of Women to Control Their Reproductive Lives."

National Organization for Women, June 1966

1. The 1966 NOW statement most emphasized which of the following strategies to achieve its goals?
   (A) Passing laws and using public resources to give women equal opportunities with men
   (B) Going to court to protect freedom of speech for women
   (C) Electing women to political offices at local, state, and federal levels
   (D) Persuading individuals to change their cultural attitudes about the roles of women and men

2. Which of the following goals from the NOW Bill of Rights did the feminist movement most clearly fail to achieve?
   (A) Greater assistance with child care
   (B) New employment opportunities
   (C) Passage of the Equal Rights Amendment
   (D) Increased reproductive rights

SHORT-ANSWER QUESTIONS

Use complete sentences; an outline or bulleted list alone is not acceptable.

1. Answer (a), (b), and (c).
   (a) Briefly explain ONE specific historical event or development that helped to mobilize the American Indian Movement to address social and economic inequality or past injustices during the period from 1960 to 1980.
   (b) Briefly explain ONE specific historical event or development that helped to mobilize the Mexican-American movement to address social and economic inequality or past injustices during the period from 1960 to 1980.
   (c) Briefly explain ONE specific historical event or development that helped to mobilize the gay rights movement to address social and economic inequality or past injustices during the period from 1960 to 1980.

2. Answer (a), (b), and (c).
   (a) Briefly explain ONE specific ruling of the Warren Court that expanded the rights of defendants in the criminal justice system.
   (b) Briefly explain ONE specific ruling of the Warren Court that expanded the 1st Amendment.
   (c) Briefly analyze ONE specific impact of the Supreme Court's "one man, one vote" ruling on American politics.

Youth Culture of the 1960s

Hey, we're going to change everything.
We're going to stop the war tomorrow.

David Crosby, interview for *Woodstock: The Oral History,* 1989

Learning Objective: Explain how and why opposition to existing policies and values developed and changed over the course of the 20th century.

Many American youth in the 1960s were idealistic and desired to make the world a better place to live. When President Kennedy created the Peace Corps in 1961, there was a surge of volunteers. While most young Americans accepted the social order of the day, a growing number wanted more than the conformity and materialism they saw in the middle-class culture of the 1950s.

Baby Boom Generation

During the 1960s, the first of the baby boom generation were graduating from high school and going to college. Between 1945 and 1970, college and university enrollments had quadrupled. As many American institutions soon discovered, they were not ready for the large numbers of this generation that had not lived through the Great Depression and World War II. Instead they had been influenced by the civil rights movements of African Americans and other groups demanding justice, freedom, and equality.

Student Movement and the New Left

In the early and mid-1960s, various liberal groups began to identify with blacks' struggle against oppressive controls and laws. The first such group to rebel against established authority were college and university students. In 1962, a newly formed radical student organization called **Students for a Democratic Society (SDS)** held a meeting in Port Huron, Michigan. Following the leadership of Tom Hayden, the group issued a declaration of purposes known as the Port Huron Statement. It called for university decisions to be made through participatory democracy so that students would have a voice in decisions affecting their lives. Activists and intellectuals who supported Hayden's ideas became known as the **New Left**.

The first major student protest took place in 1964 on the Berkeley campus of the University of California. Calling their cause the **Free Speech Movement**, Berkeley students demanded an end to university restrictions on students' political activities. They also demanded a greater voice in the government of the university. By the mid-1960s, students across the country were protesting against everything from university rules against drinking and coed dorm visits to the right to organize and protest. However, their primary focus became opposition to the war in Vietnam and the draft.

Students Against the Vietnam War

Student demonstrations grew with the escalation of U.S. involvement in the Vietnam War and the dramatic increase in the draft of young men into the military. Students in college could usually claim a deferment but faced the draft after leaving school. Campuses across the nation were disrupted or closed down by antiwar protests. In the first six months of 1968, more than 40,000 students protested in more than 200 demonstrations on 100 campuses across the nation. Demonstrations included draft-card burning, sit-ins, and protests against military recruiters and ROTC programs. Students also protested against war-related companies trying to recruit graduates, such as Dow Chemical Company, which manufactured napalm. Several thousand young men also fled to Canada or Europe to avoid serving in what many thought was an immoral war.

The Vietnam War and the assassinations of Martin Luther King Jr. and Robert Kennedy made 1968 an especially bad year for protests. SDS members joined African American students in a sit-in and occupation of buildings on the campus of Columbia University in New York City to protest racial discrimination. After nearly a week, police were called in and some 150 protesters were injured and 700 arrested.

The Chicago Convention The best-known off-campus protest in 1968 was in Chicago during the **Democratic Convention**. A mix of peaceful and radical antiwar protesters, anarchists, and **Yippies** (members of the Youth International Party) damaged property, terrorized pedestrians, and taunted police. In response, Mayor Richard Daley ordered the police to break up the demonstrations in what some in the media called a "police riot."

The Weather Underground The most radical fringe of the SDS, known as the **Weather Underground**, embraced violence and vandalism in their attacks of "the system." Their methods escalated from riots to stealing weapons to bombings from 1969 through the 1970s. More than 280 Weathermen were arrested during the "Days of Rage" riots carried out in Chicago in 1969.

The Weather Underground was almost unique among radicals in that period in using dynamite bombs to protest government war policies, racial unfairness, and corporate greed. The Weathermen believed that the evil of these injustices warranted an extreme response, if not a revolution. They set off about 25 bombs during their seven years of existence, including bombs at the Capitol, Pentagon, and State Department, which landed them on the FBI's Most Wanted list. In the eyes of most Americans, the Weathermen's extremist acts and language discredited the early idealism of the New Left.

The Counterculture

The political protests of the New Left went hand in hand with a new youth **counterculture** that was expressed in rebellious styles of dress, music, drug use, and, for some, communal living. The apparent dress code of the "hippies" and "flower children" of the 1960s included long hair, beards, beads, and jeans. The **folk music** of Joan Baez and Bob Dylan gave voice to the younger generation's protests, while the **rock music** of the Beatles, the Rolling Stones, Jim Morrison, and Janis Joplin provided the beat and lyrics for the counterculture.

Woodstock In 1969, a gathering of hundreds of thousands of young people at the **Woodstock** Music Festival in upper New York State reflected the zenith of the counterculture. However, as a result of experimenting with hallucinogenic drugs such as LSD or becoming addicted to various other drugs, some young people destroyed their lives. The counterculture's excesses and the economic uncertainties of the times led to its demise in the 1970s.

Sexual Revolution One aspect of the counterculture that continued beyond the 1960s was a change in many Americans' attitudes toward sexual expression. Traditional beliefs about sexual conduct had originally been challenged in the late 1940s and 1950s by the pioneering surveys of sexual practice conducted by **Alfred Kinsey**. His research indicated that premarital sex, marital infidelity, and homosexuality were more common than anyone had suspected. Medicine (antibiotics for sexually transmitted diseases) and science (the introduction of the birth-control pill in 1960) also contributed to changing attitudes about engaging in casual sex with a number of partners. Moreover, overtly sexual themes in advertisements, magazines, and movies made sex appear to be just one more consumer product.

How deeply the so-called **sexual revolution** changed the behavior of the majority of Americans is open to question. There is little doubt, however, that premarital sex, contraception, abortion, and homosexuality became more visible and widely accepted. Later, in the 1980s, there was a general reaction against the loosened moral codes as many blamed it for an increase in illegitimate births, especially among teenagers, an increase in rape and sexual abuse, and the spread of a deadly new disease, AIDS (acquired immune deficiency syndrome).

In Retrospect

The generation of baby boomers that came of age in the 1960s believed fervently in the ideals of a democratic society. They hoped to slay the dragons of unresponsive authority, poverty, racism, and war. However, the impatience of some activists with change, the use of violence, and the spread of self-destructive behavior discredited their cause in the eyes of others, particularly older Americans. The mantra of the counterculture, "sex, drugs, and rock and roll," was rejected by the majority of Americans and helped to motivate the conservative resurgence in the late 1970s with an emphasis on order and traditional values (Topic 8.14).

1. Explain how and why opposition to existing policies and values changed over the course of the 20th century.

KEY TERMS BY THEME

Youth Culture (ARC)   counterculture
Students for a Democratic Society (SDS)   folk music
New Left   rock music
Free Speech Movement   Woodstock
Democratic Convention   Alfred Kinsey
Yippies   sexual revolution
Weather Underground

MULTIPLE-CHOICE QUESTIONS

Questions 1–2 refer to the following excerpt.

"We are people of this generation . . . looking uncomfortably to the world we inherit. When we were kids the United States was the wealthiest and strongest country in the world . . . an initiator of the United Nations that we thought would distribute Western influence throughout the world. Freedom and equality for each individual, government of, by, and for the people—these American values we found good, principles by which we could live as men . . .

As we grew, however, our comfort was penetrated by events too troubling to dismiss. First, the . . . fact of human degradation, symbolized by the Southern struggle against racial bigotry, compelled most of us from silence to activism. Second . . . the Cold War, symbolized by the presence of the Bomb, brought awareness that we ourselves, and our friends, and millions . . . might die at any time. . . .

Not only did tarnish appear on our image of American virtue, not only did disillusion occur when the hypocrisy of American ideals was discovered, but we began to sense that what we had originally seen as the American Golden Age was actually the decline of an era."

Students for a Democratic Society, Port Huron
Statement, June 15, 1962

1. The excerpt from the Port Huron Statement is most clearly an example of which of the following developments in the 1960s?

   (A) The essential role of colleges and universities in preserving Western civilization

   (B) The reaction by young civil rights workers to entrenched racial bigotry in the South

   (C) The alienation of the younger generation from contemporary American society

   (D) Increased anxiety in the younger generation that the Golden Age of America was over

2. The language used in the excerpt most directly reflects the influence of which of the following sets of beliefs?

   (A) The same principles expressed by the leaders of the civil rights movement

   (B) The anti-Communist studies popular in colleges and universities in the 1960s

   (C) The leadership of John F. Kennedy to abolish nuclear weapons and end the Cold War

   (D) The idealism of White upper- and middle-class students who rejected their privileged status

SHORT-ANSWER QUESTION

Use complete sentences; an outline or bulleted list alone is not acceptable.

1. Answer (a), (b), and (c).

   (a) Briefly describe ONE specific historical difference between the New Left and the counterculture movements.

   (b) Briefly describe ONE specific historical similarity between the New Left and the counterculture movements.

   (c) Briefly explain ONE reason for the difference between the New Left and the counterculture movements.

The Environment and Natural Resources from 1968 to 1980

Industrial vomit . . . fills our skies and seas . . .
Our technological powers increase, but the side effects
and potential hazards also escalate.

Alvin Toffler, *Future Shock*, 1970

Learning Objective: Explain how and why policies related to the environment developed and changed from 1968 to 1980.

The Progressive Era conservation movement was fairly small and led by politicians such as Theodore Roosevelt. In contrast, the modern environmental movement had widespread popular support. Some conservation measures, however, were driven by world events such as oil shortages and high prices.

Origins of the Environmental Movement

In the 1950s and 1960s, three biologists helped launch the modern environmental movement. Through their writings and activism, they made issues such as chemical pollution, nuclear fallout, and population growth a public concern.

Rachel Carson Many historians mark the beginning of the modern American environmental movement with the publication of biologist **Rachel Carson**'s *Silent Spring* in 1962. *Silent Spring* explained the negative environmental effects of DDT, a potent insecticide that had been used in American agriculture. Carson argued that unchecked industrial growth would destroy animal life and ultimately human life on earth. This best-selling book forced Americans to question whether "better living through chemistry" was the solution or the cause of the emerging environmental crisis.

Barry Commoner In the late 1950s, Barry Commoner and other researchers began finding high levels of a cancer-causing substance, strontium-90, in children's teeth. It came from nuclear weapons tests. Commoner led the political fight to end such testing. In 1963, the United States, the Soviet Union, and other countries agreed to stop testing weapons aboveground.

Paul Ehrlich In his book *The Population Bomb* (1968), biologist Paul Ehrlich argued that overpopulation was causing the world's environmental problems. The most frightening of his predictions, that starvation would increase dramatically, did not come to pass. Increases in agricultural productivity and anti-poverty programs moderated the effects of population growth. However, his book did spark a debate over how many people the earth could sustain.

Public Awareness

During the 1950s, 1960s, and 1970s, several environmental disasters raised the public awareness of damage to the environment caused by human behavior. Media coverage of industrial disasters increased public questioning of the benefits of industry and new technologies in what some called a "postmodern" culture.

Environmental accidents reinforced the fears of the deadly combination of human error and modern technology.

- In 1954, the 23-man crew of the Japanese fishing vessel *Lucky Dragon* was exposed to radioactive fallout from a hydrogen bomb test at Bikini Atoll, a chain of islands in the Pacific Ocean.

- In 1969, an oil well blowout in Santa Barbara Bay spilled more than 200,000 gallons of oil into the ocean. The widespread pollution of the California coastline forced the oil industry to reform its operations.

- Also in 1969, Ohio's Cuyahoga River burst into flames from all the oil and chemicals floating on the surface.

- In 1979, opinion also turned against building additional nuclear power plants after an accident at the **Three Mile Island** power plant in Pennsylvania.

Such events convinced many Americas that the United States had serious environmental problems.

Earth Day The first **Earth Day** in 1970 reflected the nation's growing concerns over air and water pollution and the destruction of the natural environment, including wildlife. In New York City, 100,000 people showed their support for protecting the earth. Organizers estimated that 1,500 colleges and 10,000 schools took part in Earth Day. *Time* magazine estimated that about 20 million Americans participated in some activity related to the event. The popularity of the environmental movement grew after 1970 and became an important political issue.

Pictures from Space The Apollo crew's first photographs of Earth from space in 1968 also raised awareness of humanity's home. These images portrayed a relatively small and fragile planet in the vast lifeless vacuum of space. The photograph, named "**Earthrise**," and variations of it, became iconic images for the environmental movement. They helped people around the world gain a new perspectiveson the human condition and better understand their shared but finite environment.

Source: Bill Anders, NASA

Environmental Activists The environmental movement grew and gained strength by the late 1960s. For example, membership in the Sierra Club expanded from 123,000 in 1960 to 819,000 in 1970. Building on the organization and tactics of the civil rights and antiwar movements, thousands of citizens, especially middle-class youth, men, and women, joined the environmental movement. During the 1970s, mainstream environmental organizations, such as the National Audubon Society, the Environmental Defense Fund, the National Wildlife Federation, the National Resources Defense Council, the National Parks Conservation Association, and the Sierra Club, established sophisticated operations in Washington, D.C. These groups served a watchdog function, monitoring whether environmental regulations were properly enforced by federal agencies. They hired lobbyists to advocate for environmental legislation, lawyers to enforce environmental standards in the courts, and scientists to help determine when new regulations were needed.

Government Environmental Protection

While the federal government was slow to develop environmental protection legislation, the state of California became a leader in auto emissions standards by mandating that engine gases be recycled to cut back on the pollution and smog choking its large cities. Congress had passed some air and water quality legislation during the postwar period but often left regulation and enforcement to the individual states.

In the 1960s, President Lyndon Johnson (1963–1969) signed almost 300 conservation and beautification bills, supported by more than $12 billion in authorized funds. The most significant was the **Wilderness Act**, which permanently set aside certain federal lands from commercial economic development in order to preserve them in their natural state. The federal government also took a new interest in controlling pollution.

During the Nixon administration, protecting the environment was a bipartisan issue, and the administration worked with a Democratic majority in Congress. President Nixon recognized the power of a popular movement and over the next few years proposed an ambitious program, including the Environmental Protection Agency, the foundation of the nation's modern environmental protection system.

Environmental Protection Agency To enforce federal regulations, Nixon created the **Environmental Protection Agency (EPA)** in 1970. An independent federal agency, the EPA was given responsibility for regulating and enforcing federal programs and policies on air and water pollution, radiation issues, pesticides, and solid waste. The agency began with a staff of 8,000 and a budget of $455 million, but by 1981 it had a staff of nearly 13,000 and a budget of $1.35 billion. Enforcing environmental regulations proved to be a difficult and complex task, particularly as new legislation gave the agency more responsibilities.

Clean Air and Water During the 1970s, the federal government took over responsibility for clean air and water. Growing concerns about the environmental and economic impact of polluted air and water came from growing cities as well as rural areas. The **Clean Air Act** of 1970 regulated air emissions from both stationary and mobile sources and authorized the EPA to set standards to protect public health by regulating emissions of hazardous air pollutants.

Other legislation followed, including the Marine Protection, Research, and Sanctuaries Act of 1972; the Safe Drinking Water Act (1974); the Resource Conservation and Recovery Act (1976); the Water Pollution Control Act Amendments of 1977, which became known as the **Clean Water Act**; and the **Superfund Act** (1980) to clean up toxic waste from former industrial sites.

Wildlife Protection The Endangered Species Act of 1973 was created to protect critically imperiled species such as the American bald eagle from extinction as a "consequence of economic growth and development untempered by adequate concern and conservation." The **Endangered Species Act** was created to also protect the ecosystems upon which wildlife depend. The habitat of wildlife became the source of contention between preservationists and land developers and industries. The Endangered Species Act of 1973 was called "the Magna Carta of the environmental movement."

The Oil Embargo and Fuel Economy As a result of the 1973 Yom Kippur War (Topic 8.7), the Arab members of the Organization of Petroleum Exporting Countries (OPEC) placed an embargo on oil sold to Israel's supporters, which included the United States. This caused a worldwide oil shortage and long lines at American gas pumps. In response, Congress reduced speed limits to save gasoline. And consumers switched from big American-made gas guzzlers to smaller, more fuel-efficient cars imported from Japan. In 1975 Congress first enacted standards for fuel economy, which resulted in more fuel-efficient American cars. More fuel-efficient cars meant fewer harmful **emissions**, bolstering the regulation of tailpipe emissions that was part of the Clean Air Act of 1970 and helping to reduce the **greenhouse gases** in the atmosphere that scientists blame for **climate change**.

Antinuclear Movement Antinuclear protests grew out of the environmental movement, peaking in the 1970s and 1980s. Public opinion also turned against building additional nuclear power plants after the accident at the Three Mile Island power plant in Pennsylvania. Besides the growing concerns over the safety of nuclear power plants, the issue of disposal of the radioactive waste became a major issue, as it needed to be safely stored somewhere for many generations. The **antinuclear movement** delayed construction or halted commitments to build new nuclear plants, and pressured the Nuclear Regulatory Commission to enforce and strengthen the safety regulations for nuclear power plants.

Backlash to Environmental Regulations

In the 1980s, President Ronald Reagan sought to curtail the scope of environmental protection. For example, by 1984 the EPA's budget was cut by 44 percent, and the number of enforcement cases submitted to the EPA declined by 56 percent. It turned out that the 1970s were a high point in the environmental movement as industrial and conservative groups fought back against federal regulations.

REFLECT ON THE LEARNING OBJECTIVE

1. Explain how and why policies related to the environment developed and changed from 1968 to 1980.

KEY TERMS BY THEME

Environmental Movement (GEO)	Environmental Protection Agency (EPA)
Rachel Carson	Clean Air Act
Silent Spring	Clean Water Act
Paul Ehrlich	Superfund Act
The Population Bomb	Endangered Species Act
Three Mile Island	emissions
Earth Day	greenhouse gases
"Earthrise"	climate change
Wilderness Act	antinuclear movement

MULTIPLE-CHOICE QUESTIONS

Questions 1–2 refer to the following excerpt.

"There was once a town in the heart of America where all life seemed to live in harmony with its surroundings. . . . Then a strange blight crept over the area and everything began to change. Some evil spell had settled on the community: mysterious maladies swept the flocks of chickens; the cattle and sheep sickened and died. . . . In the town the doctors had becomemore and more puzzled by new kinds of sickness. . . . There was a strange stillness. The birds, for example—where had they gone? . . . No witchcraft, no enemy action had silenced the rebirth of new life. . . . The people had done it themselves."

Rachel Carson, Silent Spring, 1962

1. Which of the following best explains why Rachel Carson wrote *Silent Spring?*
   (A) To explain the dangers of testing nuclear weapons in the atmosphere
   (B) To predict the effects of global warming on the environment
   (C) To warn about the impact of the chemicals made by humans on the environment
   (D) To argue for the preservation of open spaces and endangered species

2. Which of the following best explains the reaction to *Silent Spring* in the 1960s and 1970s?
   (A) Consumers and farmers should be more careful in the way they treat the environment.
   (B) Federal regulations were needed to protect the environment from human abuse.
   (C) American manufacturers and industries formed associations to protect the environment.
   (D) The dangers to the environment were a global problem that needed United Nations' action.

SHORT-ANSWER QUESTION

Use complete sentences; an outline or bulleted list alone is not acceptable.

1. Answer (a), (b), and (c).
   (a) Briefly explain ONE specific historical cause for the antinuclear movement of the 1960s and 1970s.
   (b) Briefly explain ONE specific historical reason for the creation of the Environmental Protection Agency.
   (c) Briefly explain ONE specific environmental protection law passed in the 1970s and its effects.

Society in Transition

My fellow Americans, our long national nightmare is over. Our Constitution works, our great Republic is a government of laws, not men.

President Gerald Ford, speech after Nixon's resignation, August 9, 1974

Learning Objectives: Explain the causes and effects of continuing policy debates about the role of the federal government over time. Explain the effects of religious movements over the course of the 20th century.

The 1970s was a decade many Americans wanted to forget, marked by losses in Vietnam and Cambodia, the Kent State shootings, the OPEC oil embargo, and the Watergate scandal, along with high unemployment, stagnant wages, hyperinflation, tax revolts, the polarization of politics, and the politicization of religion. The 1970s also marked the transition from the dominance of the more liberal Democratic Party to the more conservative Republican Party, each with a very different view on the role of the federal government.

American Society in Transition

Social changes in the 1970s had even greater potential significance than politics. By the end of the decade, half of all Americans lived in the fastest-growing sections of the country—the South and the West. Unlike the previous decade, which was dominated by the youth revolt, the 1970s was the decade when Americans became conscious that the population was aging. The fastest-growing age group consisted of senior citizens, people over age 65.

The country's racial and ethnic composition was also changing noticeably in the late 20th century. By 1990, minority groups made up 25 percent of the population. The Census Bureau predicted that by 2050 as much as half of the population would be Hispanic American, African American, or Asian American. Cultural pluralism was replacing the melting pot as the model for U.S. society, as diverse ethnic and cultural groups strove not only to end discrimination and improve their lives but also to celebrate their unique traditions.

The Nixon Presidency

Having received just 43 percent of the popular vote in 1968, President **Richard Nixon** (1969–1974) was well aware of being a minority president. He devised a political strategy to form a Republican majority by appealing to the millions of voters who had become disaffected by civil rights, liberal court rulings, antiwar protests, black militants, school busing to achieve racial balance, and the excesses of the youth counterculture. Nixon referred to these conservative Americans as the "**silent majority**." Many of them were Democrats, including southern Whites, northern Catholic blue-collar workers, and recent suburbanites who disagreed with the liberal drift of their party.

Nixon's Southern Strategy To win over the South, the president asked the federal courts in that region to delay integration plans and busing orders. He also nominated two Southern conservatives (Clement Haynsworth and G. Harold Carswell) to the Supreme Court. Though the courts rejected his requests and the Senate refused to confirm the two nominees, his strategy played well with southern White voters.

Nixon's **Southern strategy** proved a powerful tool for the Republican Party in future elections, as the party became more socially conservative and political power shifted to the Sun Belt and rural America. This also diminished prospects for further civil rights legislation far into the future.

The Election of 1972 The success of Nixon's Southern strategy became evident in the presidential election of 1972 when the Republican ticket won majorities in every Southern state. Nixon's reelection was practically assured by (1) his foreign policy successes in China and the Soviet Union (Topic 8.2), (2) the removal of George Wallace from the race by a would-be assassin's bullet that paralyzed the Alabama populist, and (3) the nomination by the Democrats of a very liberal antiwar, antiestablishment candidate, Senator George McGovern of South Dakota.

On election day, Nixon overwhelmed McGovern in a landslide victory that carried every state but Massachusetts and won 61 percent of the popular vote. The Democrats still managed to keep control of both houses of Congress. Nevertheless, the voting patterns for Nixon indicated the start of a major political realignment of Sun Belt and suburban voters, who were forming a new Republican majority. Nixon's electoral triumph in 1972 made the Watergate revelations and scandals of 1973 all the more surprising. For details about Richard Nixon's presidency, see Topics 8.2 (Cold War), 8.4 (Economy), and 8.8 (Vietnam).

Watergate Scandal

The tragedy of **Watergate** went well beyond the public humiliation of Richard Nixon and the conviction and jailing of 26 White House officials and aides. Watergate had a paralyzing effect on the political system in the mid-1970s, a critical time both at home and overseas, when the country needed respected, strong, and confident leadership.

White House Abuses In June 1972, a group of men hired by Nixon's reelection committee was caught breaking into the offices of the Democratic national headquarters in the Watergate complex in Washington, D.C. This break-in and attempted bugging were only part of a series of illegal activities and "dirty tricks" conducted by the Nixon administration and the Committee to Re-Elect the President (CREEP).

Earlier Nixon had ordered wiretaps on government employees and reporters to stop news leaks such as the one that had exposed the secret bombing of Cambodia. The president's aides created a group, called the "**plumbers**," to stop leaks as well as to discredit opponents. Before Watergate, the "plumbers" had burglarized the office of psychiatrist Daniel Ellsberg, the person behind the leaking of the Pentagon Papers, in order to obtain information to discredit Ellsberg. The White House had also created an "enemies list" of prominent Americans who opposed Nixon, the Vietnam War, or both. People on this list were investigated by government agencies, such as the IRS. The illegal break-in at Watergate reflected the attitude in the Nixon administration that any means could be used to promote national security—an objective that was often confused with protecting the Nixon administration from its critics.

Watergate Investigation No solid proof demonstrated that President Nixon ordered any of these illegal activities. However, after months of investigation, it became clear that Nixon did engage in an illegal cover-up to avoid scandal. Tough sentencing of the Watergate burglars by federal Judge John Sirica led to information about the use of money and a promise of pardons by the White House staff to keep the burglars quiet. A Senate investigating committee headed by Democrat Sam Ervin of North Carolina brought the abuses to the attention of Americans through televised hearings. A highlight of these hearings was the testimony of a White House lawyer, John Dean, who linked the president to the cover-up. Nixon's top aides, H. R. Haldeman and John Ehrlichman, resigned to protect him and were later indicted, as were many others, for obstructing justice.

The discovery of a taping system in the Oval Office led to a year-long struggle between Nixon, who claimed executive privilege for the tapes, and investigators, who wanted the tapes to prove the cover-up charges. The Nixon administration received another blow in the fall of 1973, when Vice President Agnew had to resign when the Justice Department discovered evidence of his political corruption, including accepting bribes as governor of Maryland and as vice president. Replacing him was Michigan Representative Gerald Ford.

Resignation of a President In 1974, Nixon made triumphal visits to Moscow and Cairo, but at home his reputation continued to slide. In October 1973, the president appeared to be interfering with the Watergate investigation when he fired Archibald Cox, the special prosecutor assigned to the case. In protest, the U.S. attorney general resigned. The House of Representatives began **impeachment** hearings, which caused Nixon to reveal transcripts of some of the Watergate tapes in April 1974. Still, it took a Supreme Court decision in July to force him to turn over the tapes to the courts and Congress. Included on one tape made just days after the Watergate burglary was an 18½-minute gap that had been erased. Meanwhile, the House Judiciary Committee voted three articles of impeachment: (1) obstruction of justice, (2) abuse of power, and (3) contempt of Congress.

Source: A 1974 Herblock cartoon, © The Herb Block Foundation

The conversations recorded on the tapes shocked friends and foes alike. The transcript of one such White House conversation clearly implicated Nixon in the cover-up only days after the Watergate break-in. Faced with certain impeachment in the House and a trial in the Senate, Richard Nixon chose to resign on August 9, 1974. Vice President Gerald Ford then took the oath of office as the first unelected president in U.S. history.

Significance To some, the final outcome of the Watergate scandal (Nixon leaving office under pressure) proved that the U.S. constitutional system of checks and balances worked as it was intended. For others, the scandal underlined the dangerous shift of power to the presidency that began with Franklin Roosevelt and had been expanded during the Cold War. Without a doubt, Watergate contributed to a growing loss of faith in the federal government.

Gerald Ford in the White House (1974–1977)

Before Nixon chose him to replace Vice President Agnew in 1973, **Gerald Ford** had served in Congress for years as a representative from Michigan and as the Republican minority leader of the House. Ford was a likable and unpretentious man, but many questioned his ability to be president. For details about Gerald Ford's presidency, see Topics 8.2 (Cold War), 8.4 (Economy), and 8.8 (Vietnam).

Pardoning of Nixon In his first month in office, President Ford lost the goodwill of many by granting Nixon a full and unconditional pardon for any crime that he might have committed. The pardon was extended even before any formal charges or indictment had been made by a court of law. Ford was accused of making a "corrupt bargain" with Nixon, but he explained that the purpose of the pardon was to end the "national nightmare," instead of prolonging it for months, if not years. Critics were angered that the full truth of Nixon's deeds never came out.

Investigating the CIA During Ford's presidency (1974–1977), the Democratic Congress continued to search for abuses in the executive branch, especially in the CIA. This intelligence agency was accused of engineering the assassinations of foreign leaders, among them the Marxist president of Chile, Salvador Allende. Ford appointed former Texas Congressman George H. W. Bush to reform the agency.

Bicentennial Celebration In 1976, the United States celebrated its 200th birthday. Americans' pride in their history helped to put Watergate and Vietnam behind them. Even the lackluster presidency of Gerald Ford served the purpose of restoring candor and humility to the White House.

The Election of 1976

Watergate still cast its gloom over the Republican Party in the 1976 elections. President Ford was challenged for the party's nomination by Ronald Reagan, a former actor and ex-governor of California, who enjoyed the support of the more conservative Republicans. Ford won the nomination in a close battle, but the conflict with Reagan hurt him in the polls.

A number of Democrats competed for their party's nomination, including a little-known former governor of Georgia, James Earl (Jimmy) Carter. With Watergate still on voters' minds, Carter had success running as an outsider against the corruption in Washington. His victories in open primaries reduced the influence of more experienced Democratic politicians. After watching his huge lead in the polls evaporate in the closing days of the campaign, Carter managed to win a close election (287 electoral votes to 241 for Ford) by carrying most of the South and getting an estimated 97 percent of the African American vote. In the aftermath of Watergate, the Democrats also won strong majorities in both houses of Congress.

An Outsider in the White House

The informal style of **Jimmy Carter** signaled an effort to end the **imperial presidency**. On his inauguration day, he walked down Pennsylvania Avenue to the White House instead of riding in the presidential limousine. Public images of the president carrying his own luggage may have impressed average Americans. However, veteran members of Congress always viewed Carter as an outsider who depended too much on his politically inexperienced advisers from Georgia. Even Carter's keen intelligence and dedication to duty may have been partly a liability in causing him to pay close attention to all the details of government operations. Critics observed that, when it came to distinguishing between the forest and the trees, Carter was a "leaf man." For details about Jimmy Carter's presidency, see Topics 8.2 (Cold War), 8.4 (Economy), and 8.7 (World Power).

Loss of Popularity The Iranian hostage crisis and worsening economic crisis hurt Carter in the opinion polls. In 1979, in what the press called Carter's **"national malaise"** speech, he blamed the problems of the United States on a "moral and spiritual crisis" of the American people. By that time, however, many Americans blamed the president for weak and indecisive leadership. By the 1980 election year his approval rating had fallen to only 23 percent. In seeking a second term, the unpopular president was clearly vulnerable to political challenges from both Democrats and Republicans.

The Burger Court

As liberal justices of the Supreme Court retired, Nixon had replaced them with more conservative members. However, like other presidents, Nixon found that his appointees did not always rule as he had hoped. In 1969, after Chief Justice Earl Warren resigned, Nixon appointed Warren E. Burger of Minnesota to replace him. The **Burger Court** was more conservative than the Warren Court, but several of its major decisions angered conservatives. For example, in 1971 the Court ordered busing to achieve racial balance in the schools, and in 1972 it issued strict guidelines that made carrying out the death penalty more difficult. Finally, in the last days of Nixon's Watergate agony, the Court that he had tried to shape denied his claims to executive privilege and ordered him to turn over the Watergate tapes (***United States v. Nixon***, 1974).

Abortion Rights The Court's most controversial ruling was ***Roe v. Wade*** (1973). In this 7–2 decision, the high court struck down many state laws prohibiting abortions as a violation of a woman's right to privacy. The decision to allow women access to abortions became a primary target for the conservative movement in the coming decades. Over time, opposition to abortion became a virtual political requirement for Republican candidates to either overturn or limit the *Roe* decision through legislation and conservative appointees to the federal courts.

PUBLIC OPINION ON ABORTION

Responses to the question: "Do you think abortions should be legal under any circumstances, legal, only under certain circumstances or illegal in all circumstances?

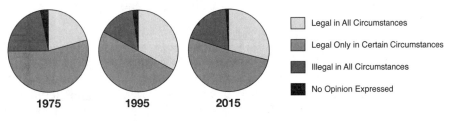

Source: Gallup Poll, Historical Trends

Conservative Resurgence

The protest movements by diverse groups in American society seemed to produce more social stress and fragmentation. Combined with a slowing economy and a declining standard of living, these forces left many Americans feeling angry and bitter. A conservative reaction to the liberal policies of the New Deal and the Great Society was gaining strength in the late 1970s and would prove a powerful force in the politics of the next decades.

Conservative Religious Revival Moral decay was a weekly theme of religious leaders on television such as Pat Robertson, Oral Roberts, and Jim Baker. By 1980, **televangelists** had a combined weekly audience of between 60 million and 100 million viewers.

Religion became an instrument of electoral politics when an evangelist from Virginia, Jerry Falwell, founded the **Moral Majority**, which financed campaigns to unseat liberal members of Congress. **Religious fundamentalists** attacked "secular humanism" as a godless creed taking over public education and also campaigned for the return of prayers and the teaching of the Biblical account of creation in public schools. The legalization of abortion in the *Roe v. Wade* (1973) decision sparked the right-to-life movement. This movement united many Catholics and fundamentalist Protestants who believed that human life begins at the moment of conception.

Deregulation of Business Starting in the 1970s, business interests launched a very successful campaign to mobilize and influence federal and state governments to curtail regulations, lower taxes, and weaken labor unions. Business donors created "**think tanks**," such as the American Enterprise Institute, the Heritage Foundation, and the Cato Institute, to promote free-market ideas, while the U.S. Chamber of Commerce lobbied for pro-business legislation.

Elimination of Racial Preferences In 1965, President Johnson had committed the U.S. government to a policy of affirmative action to ensure that underprivileged minorities and women would have equal access to education, jobs, and promotions. Suffering through years of recession and stagflation in the 1970s, many Whites blamed their troubles on affirmative action, calling it "**reverse discrimination**." In a landmark court case challenging the admissions policies of one medical school, *Regents of the University of California v. Bakke* (1978), the Supreme Court ruled that while race could be considered, the school had created racial quotas, which were unconstitutional. Using this decision, conservatives intensified their campaign to end all preferences based on race and ethnicity.

Taxpayers' Revolt In 1978, California voters led the revolt against increasing taxes by passing **Proposition 13**, a measure that sharply cut property taxes. Nationally, conservatives promoted economist **Arthur Laffer**'s belief that tax cuts would increase government revenues. Two Republican members of Congress, Jack Kemp and William Roth, proposed legislation to reduce federal taxes by 30 percent, which became the basis for President Ronald Reagan's tax cuts.

A New Era in American Politics

The rise of conservatism reshaped the political climate. Combined with the end of the Cold War, the rise of international terrorism, the impact of globalization, and a growing divide between a prosperous few and a stagnant standard of living for many, the country would become more divided in the four decades following 1980.

REFLECT ON THE LEARNING OBJECTIVES

1. Explain the causes and effects of continuing policy debates about the role of the federal government over time.

2. Explain the effects of religious movements over the course of the 20th century.

KEY TERMS BY THEME

Society in Transition (PCE)	Conservative Resurgence (ARC)
Richard Nixon	televangelists
silent majority	Moral Majority
Southern strategy	religious fundamentalists
Watergate	think tanks
"plumbers"	reverse discrimination
impeachment	*Regents of University of California v. Bakke*
Gerald Ford	Proposition 13
Jimmy Carter	Arthur Laffer
imperial presidency	
national malaise	
Burger Court	
United States v. Nixon	
Roe v. Wade	

Questions 1–3 refer to the following excerpt.

"Our people are losing faith, not only in government itself but in their ability as citizens to serve as the ultimate rulers and shapers of our democracy.

We were sure that ours was a nation of the ballot, not the bullet, until the murders of John Kennedy and Robert Kennedy and Martin Luther King Jr. We were taught that our armies were always invincible and our causes were always just, only to suffer the agony of Vietnam. We respected the Presidency as a place of honor until the shock of Watergate.

We remember when the phrase 'sound as a dollar' was an expression of absolute dependability, until ten years of inflation began to shrink our dollar and our savings. We believed that our Nation's resources were limitless until 1973, when we had to face a growing dependence on foreign oil."

Jimmy Carter, *Public Papers of the Presidents of the United States*, 1979

1. Which of the following was Carter referring to with the phrase "the shock of Watergate"?
   (A) The role of Watergate staff in aiding Nixon's reelection effort
   (B) The attempt by Nixon to cover up illegal campaign activities
   (C) The decision by Nixon to investigate the Watergate affair
   (D) The attempt by Nixon's campaign to rent offices in the Watergate

2. Which of the following actions would most strongly support Carter's contention that "our people are losing faith" in ideas such as "our armies were always invincible"?
   (A) The secret expansion of the Vietnam War into Cambodia
   (B) The killing of antiwar protesters at Kent State and Jackson State
   (C) The assassination of Chile's leader, Salvador Allende
   (D) The defeat of U.S. efforts by North Vietnam in 1975

3. Which of the following best identifies the effect of the speech from which the above excerpt is taken?
   (A) Consumers increased their efforts to conserve energy.
   (B) Americans saw Carter as a weak and ineffective leader.
   (C) Carter increased his approval ratings with his honesty.
   (D) The Federal Reserve raised interest rates to support the president.

Use complete sentences; an outline or bulleted list alone is not acceptable.

1. "Nixon defied simple political characterizations. . . . On most domestic issues he adopted centrist positions, bobbing and weaving in an effort to maintain support from both the liberal and conservative wings of the Republican Party. . . . Nixon hoped to win over some traditionally Democratic constituencies to ensure his reelection and to rebuild the Republican Party as a national party. To woo them, he supported the core of New Deal economic and social programs from which they benefited, even as he took conservative positions on other issues. Sometimes taken with thinking of himself as a Tory [a type of conservative] reformer, Nixon proved willing to take innovative steps most conservatives would blanch at."

Joshua B. Freeman, historian, American Empire, 2012

"At [Nixon's] funeral, Senator Bob Dole prophesied that 'the second half of the twentieth century will be known as the age of Nixon.' What Richard Nixon left behind was the very terms of our national self-image: a notion that there are two kinds of Americans. On the one side, that 'Silent Majority.' 'The 'nonshouters' . . . [the] coalition who call themselves, now 'Value voters,' 'people of faith,' 'patriots,' . . . who feel themselves condescended to by snobby opinion-making elites. . . . On the other side are 'liberals,' the 'cosmopolitans,' the 'intellectuals,' the 'professionals,' . . . who say shouting in opposition to injustice is a higher form of patriotism. . . . And both have learned to consider the other not quite Americans at all. The argument over Richard Nixon, pro and con, gave us the language for this war."

Rick Perlstein, historian and journalist, Nixonland, 2008

Using the excerpts above, answer (a), (b), and (c).

(a) Briefly describe ONE major difference between Freeman's and Perlstein's historical interpretations of the Nixon presidency.

(b) Briefly explain ONE specific historical event or development that is not explicitly mentioned in the excerpts that could be used to support Freeman's interpretation of the Nixon presidency.

(c) Briefly explain ONE specific historical event or development that is not explicitly mentioned in the excerpts that could be used to support Perlstein's interpretation of the Nixon presidency.

Topic 8.15

Continuity and Change in Period 8

Learning Objective: Explain the extent to which the events of the period from 1945 to 1980 reshaped national identity.

The Cold War tested Americans' image of themselves as the leaders of the free world. Hot wars in Korea and Vietnam challenged their resolve to bear the ongoing sacrifice of men and resources to stop the advances of communism. For example, by the 1970s it became clear that the involuntary military service through the Selective Service draft had become very unpopular with the younger generation. Under the Nixon Doctrine future allies would receive U.S. support but without U.S. ground forces. While the commitment to stop aggression remained largely unchanged, many Americans became unwilling to serve in future wars.

The Cold War also tested Americans' commitment to the Bill of Rights, especially during the Red Scare. Americans' tolerance of opposing views as an exercise of their freedom of speech rather than the work of traitors varied from case to case. The civil rights movements of the period also exposed differences in Americans' understanding of the Constitution and ideas about freedom, equality, and assimilation. Although the progress made in legal standing of women and minorities can be well documented or, as Dr. King argued, "the arc of the moral universe is long, but it bends toward justice," vestiges of bigotry and racism continued into the next period.

American identity as the economic powerhouse of the world also underwent change during this period as other nations recovered from World War II and modernized their industries. The identity of many American wage earners and others who became part of the middle class during the 1950s was also tested as their economic status stagnated or declined by the 1970s. The emergence of populist politicians such as George Wallace reflected the resentments of a working and middle class under pressure from competition from overseas and racial integration at home.

In addition to international, economic, and assimilation events, American identity was changed by the new generation of Americans born after World War II who not only had different ideas about music and dress, but also new definitions of status, work, and the freedom to live alternative lifestyles. Was there more continuity or change during the period from 1945 to 1980? The conclusion often depends on the topic and criteria used to measure change, but the period provides a wealth of contrasting points of view.

1. Evaluate the extent to which the Cold War reshaped the American national identity in the period from 1945 to 1980.

2. Evaluate the extent to which the African American civil rights movement changed the American national identity in the period from 1945 to 1980.

THINK AS A HISTORIAN: *ARGUMENTATION—SUPPORT AND REASONING*

Success on the AP® exam requires you to do much more than recall specific facts and details. You will also need to use and evaluate that information in various ways, including understanding that some pieces of evidence are more important and more convincing than others. The free-response questions on the exam will require you to think about what you have learned and then choose supporting evidence that is accurate and relevant to the argument.

Part of your task on the exam will be not only to cite evidence but also to explain how different pieces of evidence relate to one another. As discussed in the Think as a Historian feature in Unit 7, the exam will focus on the reasoning processes of causation, comparison, and continuity and change. Using these reasoning processes is particularly important in answering the document-based question and the long essay question.

Select one of the arguments below and answer the two questions that follow.

Argument 1: Actions such as Winston Churchill's "iron curtain" speech and Harry Truman's encouraging the United States to join NATO were meant to protect capitalist countries. However, these actions actually helped to bring about and intensify the Cold War.

Argument 2: The launch of the Soviet *Sputnik* satellites initially raised Cold War tensions but eventually led to significant technological achievements in the United States.

Argument 3: The completion of the Interstate Highway System led to economic progress and environmental destruction.

Argument 4: The Tet Offensive was a military failure but a political success for Communist forces in North Vietnam.

Argument 5: Although Lyndon Johnson's Great Society programs have been attacked as unrealistic and inefficient, many of them still affect Americans' daily lives.

1. What evidence for this argument can you describe and explain?

2. What relationships exist between these pieces of evidence? Do any of them share causation, comparison, or continuity? Explain your answer.

UNIT 8 — Period 8 Review: 1945–1980

WRITE AS A HISTORIAN: *WRITE THE CONCLUSION*

A strong conclusion helps create unity by circling back to the ideas in your introduction and thesis statement. The conclusion is also a good opportunity to extend and refine the complex understanding you have developed and woven throughout your essay.

Providing Unity While wrapping up your essay with a return to the ideas in your introduction helps provide unity, do more than restate your thesis. If your thesis is that the main cause of the end of the Cold War was technological change, avoid saying simply: "The Soviets lost the Cold War because they failed to adapt to new technology." Instead, you might say, "Although Gorbachev's efforts at reform and Reagan's willingness to negotiate arms deals weakened Soviet conservatives, the most basic problem the Soviets faced was that technology changed faster than the government did. The Soviets could neither afford new industrial technology nor keep out liberal ideas coming in through new communications technology." This change extends the thesis statement.

Demonstrating Complexity An extension of your thesis statement such as the one above also helps demonstrate a complex understanding of the topic by referring to multiple causes. The College Board identifies the following ways to demonstrate a complex understanding: "Corroborate, qualify, or modify an argument using diverse and alternative evidence in order to develop a complex argument." You might, for example, analyze multiple variables to arrive at a nuanced conclusion: You could point out that the Soviets continued to invest in new military technology and that the breakdown of the alliance with China hurt them diplomatically.

Other ways you can demonstrate a complex understanding are to consider the significance of a source's credibility and limitations and explain why a historical argument is or is not effective. Most of the development of your complex understanding must be done within the body of your essay for you to earn the point for complexity, but you can use the conclusion to summarize or extend that understanding.

Application: Review the sample scored essays on the College Board website. Evaluate the conclusion of each sample. For any that lack a conclusion, draft one that would provide unity to the essay and summarize a complex understanding of the historical development.

For current free-response question samples, visit: https://apcentral.collegeboard.org/ courses/ap-united-states-history/exam

LONG ESSAY QUESTIONS

Directions: The suggested writing time for each question is 40 minutes. In your response you should do the following:

- Respond to the prompt with a historically defensible thesis or claim that establishes a line of reasoning.
- Describe a broader historical context relevant to the prompt.
- Support an argument in response to the prompt using specific and relevant examples of evidence.
- Use historical reasoning (e.g., comparison, causation, continuity or change) to frame or structure an argument that addresses the prompt.
- Use evidence to corroborate, qualify, or modify an argument that addresses the prompt.

1. Evaluate the extent to which the Cold War shaped the role of the United States in the world during the period from 1945 to 1980.

2. Evaluate the extent to which connections with other world economies affected American workers during the period from 1945 to 1980.

3. Evaluate the extent to which the Great Society programs differed from the New Deal.

4. Evaluate the extent to which U.S. immigration policies of the 1960s differed from the U.S. immigration policies of the 1920s.

5. Evaluate the extent to which U.S. environmental policies changed during the period from 1945 to 1980.

6. Evaluate the extent to which the status of American women changed during the period from 1945 to 1980.

7. Evaluate the extent to which the civil rights movement had an impact on race relations in the United States during the period from 1945 to 1980.

8. Evaluate the extent to which federal government domestic programs had an impact on the American economy during the period from 1945 to 1980.

DOCUMENT-BASED QUESTION

Directions: Question 1 is based on the accompanying documents. The documents have been edited for the purpose of this exercise. You are advised to spend 15 minutes planning and 45 minutes writing your answer. In your response you should do the following:

- Respond to the prompt with a historically defensible thesis or claim that establishes a line of reasoning.
- Describe a broader historical context relevant to the prompt.
- Support an argument in response to the prompt using at least six documents.
- Use at least one additional piece of specific historical evidence (beyond that found in the documents) relevant to an argument about the prompt.
- For at least three documents, explain how or why each document's point of view, purpose, historical situation, and/or audience is relevant to an argument.
- Use evidence to corroborate, qualify, or modify an argument that addresses the prompt.

1. Evaluate the extent of similarities between the roles of civil rights activists and government officials in advancing the civil rights movement during the period from 1945 to 1980.

Document 1

> **Source:** Harry S. Truman, *Establishing the President's Committee on Equality of Treatment and Opportunity in the Armed Services,* July 1948
>
> "Whereas it is essential that there be maintained in the armed services of the United States the highest standards of democracy, with equality of treatment and opportunity for all those who serve in our country's defense:
> 1. It is hereby declared to be the policy of the President that there shall be equality of treatment and opportunity for all persons in the armed forces without regard to race, color, religion, or national origin. This policy shall be put into effect as rapidly as possible, having regard to the time required to effectuate any necessary changes without impairing efficiency or morale."

Document 2

Source: Jo Ann Gibson Robinson, civil rights organizer, *The Montgomery Bus Boycott and the Women Who Started It*, 1987

"The news [of Mrs. Parks' arrest] traveled like wildfire into every black home. Telephones jangled; people congregated on street corners and in homes and talked. But nothing was done. A numbing helplessness seemed to paralyze everyone. . . .

Lost in thought, I was startled by the telephone's ring. Black attorney Fred Gray. . . . had just gotten back and was returning the phone message I had left him about Mrs. Parks' arrest.

Fred was shocked by the news of Mrs. Parks' arrest. I informed him that I already was thinking that the WPC [Women's Political Council] should distribute thousands of notices calling for all bus riders to stay off the buses. . . . 'Are you ready?' he asked. Without hesitation, I assured him that we were. With that he hung up, and I went to work.

I made some notes on the back of an envelope: 'The Women's Political Council will not wait for Mrs. Parks' consent to call for a boycott of city buses. On Friday, December 1, 1955, the women of Montgomery will call for a boycott to take place on Monday, December 5.'"

Document 3

Source: Governor George C. Wallace, Proclamation at the University of Alabama, June 11, 1963

"I stand here today, as Governor of this sovereign State, and refuse to willingly submit to illegal usurpation of power by the Central Government. I claim today for all the people of the State of Alabama those rights reserved to them under the Constitution of the United States. Among those powers so reserved and claimed is the right of state authority in the operation of the public schools, colleges, and universities.

My action does not constitute disobedience to legislative and constitutional provisions. It is not defiance for defiance sake, but for the purpose of raising basic and fundamental constitutional questions. My action is raising a call for strict adherence to the Constitution of the United States as it was written—for a cessation of usurpation and abuses. My action seeks to avoid having state sovereignty sacrificed on the altar of political expediency."

Document 4

Source: March on Washington for Jobs and Freedom, August 28, 1963, Library of Congress

Document 5

Source: Malcolm X's Speech in Cleveland, Ohio, April 3, 1964

"The question tonight, as I understand it, is 'The Negro Revolt, and Where Do We Go From Here?', or 'What Next?'" In my little humble way of understanding it, it points toward either the ballot or the bullet. . . .

The black nationalists aren't going to wait. Lyndon B. Johnson is the head of the Democratic Party. If he's for civil rights, let him go into the Senate next week and declare himself. Let him go in there right now and declare himself. Let him go in there and denounce the Southern branch of his party. Let him go in there right now and take a moral stand—right now, not later. Tell him, don't wait until election time. If he waits too long, brothers and sisters, he will be responsible for letting a condition develop in this country which will create a climate that will bring seeds up out of the ground with vegetation on the end of them looking like something these people never dreamed of. In 1964, it's the ballot or the bullet."

Document 6

Source: Martin Luther King Jr., Acceptance Speech for the Nobel Peace Prize, December 10, 1964

"I accept the Nobel Prize for Peace at a moment when 22 million Negroes of the United States of America are engaged in a creative battle to end the long night of racial injustice. I accept this award on behalf of a civil rights movement which is moving with determination and a majestic scorn for risk and danger to establish a reign of freedom and a rule of justice. I am mindful that only yesterday in Birmingham, Alabama, our children, crying out for brotherhood, were answered with fire hoses, snarling dogs and even death. I am mindful that only yesterday in Philadelphia, Mississippi, young people seeking to secure the right to vote were brutalized and murdered. And only yesterday more than 40 houses of worship in the State of Mississippi alone were bombed or burned because they offered a sanctuary to those who would not accept segregation. I am mindful that debilitating and grinding poverty afflicts my people and chains them to the lowest rung of the economic ladder.

The tortuous road which has led from Montgomery, Alabama, to Oslo bears witness to this truth [nonviolence]. This is a road over which millions of Negroes are travelling to find a new sense of dignity. This same road has opened for all Americans a new era of progress and hope. It has led to a new Civil Rights Bill, and it will, I am convinced, be widened and lengthened into a super highway of justice as Negro and white men in increasing numbers create alliances to overcome their common problems."

Document 7

Source: President Lyndon B. Johnson, Speech to Congress and the Nation, March 15, 1965

"At times, history and fate meet at a single time in a single place to shape a turning point in man's unending search for freedom. So it was at Lexington and Concord. So it was a century ago at Appomattox. So it was last week in Selma, Alabama. There, long suffering men and women peacefully protested the denial of their rights as Americans. Many of them were brutally assaulted. One good man—a man of God—was killed. . . .

But I want to really discuss with you now briefly the main proposals of this legislation. This bill will strike down restrictions to voting in all elections—federal, state, and local—which have been used to deny Negroes the right to vote. . . .

But even if we pass this bill, the battle will not be over. What happened in Selma is part of a far larger movement, which reaches into every section and State of America. It is the effort of American Negroes to secure for themselves the full blessings of American life. Their cause must be our cause too. Because it is not just Negroes, but really it is all of us, who must overcome the crippling legacy of bigotry and injustice. And we shall overcome."

Topic 9.1

Contextualizing Period 9

Learning Objective: Explain the context in which the United States faced international and domestic challenges after 1980.

The election of Ronald Reagan in 1980 signaled the closing of the chapter on the postwar era. The United States now entered a more conservative political period. The political divide between rural and urban regions increased. Rural regions became older, Whiter, and more conservative. Urban regions became younger, multicultural, and more open to changing ideas about gender and ethnicity. This divide showed up clearly in bitterly fought presidential elections, contentious federal court nominations, and government shutdowns.

In Reagan's historic appearance at the Brandenburg Gate of the Berlin Wall in 1987, he challenged the Soviets to "tear down this wall."
Source: Ronald Reagan Presidential Library

In foreign affairs, President Reagan combined an aggressive anti-Communist foreign policy with a willingness to negotiate arms-reduction treaties with the Soviet Union, which collapsed in 1991. However, the end of the Cold War took away the 45-year focus of U.S. foreign policy and revealed the political, ethnic, and religious conflicts long suppressed in many countries during the Cold War that would explode in violence in the following decades. After the terrorists' attacks of September 11, 2001, the United States quickly became involved in seemingly endless wars in the Middle East, and terrorist threats and homeland security came to dominate American priorities.

The decline of faith in the federal government's ability to solve social and economic problems, and the championing of unregulated markets by American corporations, gave conservatism new life in both the Republican and Democratic Parties. Republicans were also strengthened by the increasing involvement of evangelical Christians in politics, the demographic growth of the Sun Belt, and the shift of Southern White conservative voters into their party. However, the economic problems of the era also opened the door to populist and autocratic movements.

After 1980, increased competition from globalization and financial mismanagement at home challenged American economic success. Corporate capitalism and tax cuts seemed to mainly benefit the top 5 percent, while the income of the lower and middle class stagnated. Industrial decline in many parts of America and downturns in the economy, such as the Great Recession of 2008, left many Americans living in or on the edge of poverty. Depression and drug use increased, and the average American life span declined for the first time in many decades.

ANALYZE THE CONTEXT

1. Explain the historical context for the international challenges faced by the United States after 1980.

2. Explain the historical context for the domestic challenges faced by the United States after 1980.

LANDMARK EVENTS: 1980–2020

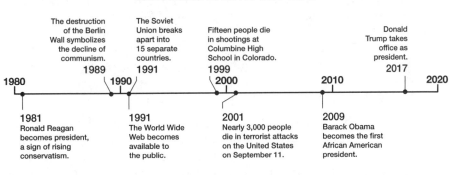

The destruction of the Berlin Wall symbolizes the decline of communism.
1989

The Soviet Union breaks apart into 15 separate countries.
1991

Fifteen people die in shootings at Columbine High School in Colorado.
1999

Donald Trump takes office as president.
2017

1980 — 1990 — 2000 — 2010 — 2020

1981
Ronald Reagan becomes president, a sign of rising conservatism.

1991
The World Wide Web becomes available to the public.

2001
Nearly 3,000 people die in terrorist attacks on the United States on September 11.

2009
Barack Obama becomes the first African American president.

Source: Justice for Jamar Response Action

Killings of African American by police led to marches for racial justice around the country beginning in 2014, an effort was known as the Black Lives Matter movement.

Topic 9.2

Reagan and Conservatism

In this present crisis, government is not the solution
to our problem; government is the problem.

President Ronald Reagan, inaugural address, January 20, 1981

Learning Objective: Explain the causes and effects of continuing debates about the role of the federal government.

The rebirth of the conservative movement can be traced back to the Goldwater campaign for president in 1964. The election of Ronald Reagan as president in 1980 signaled its arrival as a dominant force in American politics.

Ronald Reagan and the Election of 1980

Ronald Reagan, a well-known movie and television actor, gained fame among Republicans as an effective political speaker in the 1964 Goldwater campaign. He was soon elected the governor of California, the nation's most populous state. By 1976, Reagan was the party's leading spokesperson for conservative positions, and he almost defeated President Ford for the nomination. Handsome and vigorous in his late sixties, he proved a master of the media and was seen by millions as a likable and sensible champion of average Americans. In 1980, Reagan won the Republican presidential nomination.

Campaign for President As the Republican nominee, Reagan attacked the Democrats for expanding government and for undermining U.S. prestige abroad. (Throughout the campaign, American hostages remained in the hands of Iranian radicals.) Reagan also pointed to a "misery index" of 22 (the rate of inflation added to the rate of unemployment) and concluded his campaign by asking a huge television audience, "Are you better off now than you were four years ago?" The voters' rejection of Carter's presidency and the growing conservative mood gave Reagan 51 percent of the popular vote and almost 91 percent of the electoral vote. Carter received 41 percent of the popular vote. A third candidate, John Anderson, a moderate Republican running as an independent, received 8 percent.

Significance Reagan's election broke up a key element of the New Deal coalition by taking more than 50 percent of the blue-collar vote. The defeat of 11 liberal Democratic senators targeted by a political organization of conservative Christians called the Moral Majority gave the Republicans control of the Senate for the first time since 1954. The Republicans also gained 33 seats in the House. The combination of Republicans and conservative Southern Democrats formed a working majority on many key issues. The 1980 election ended a half century of Democratic dominance of Congress.

The Reagan Revolution

On the very day that Reagan was inaugurated, the Iranians released the 52 American hostages, giving his administration a positive start. Two months later, the president survived a serious gunshot wound from an assassination attempt. Reagan handled the crisis with such humor and charm that he emerged from the ordeal as an even more popular leader. He ran as a mainstream conservative whose goal was to reduce the size and scope of the federal government. Reagan pledged that his administration would lower taxes, reduce government spending on welfare, build up the U.S. Armed Forces, and create a more conservative federal court. He delivered on all four promises—but there were costs.

Reaganomics

The Reagan administration advocated **supply-side economics**, arguing that tax cuts and reduced government spending would increase investment by the private sector, which would lead to increased production, jobs, and prosperity. This approach, which became known as **"Reaganomics,"** contrasted with the Keynesian economics long favored by the Democrats, which relied on government spending during economic downturns to boost consumer income and demand. Critics of the supply-side theory compared it to the **"trickle-down" economics** of the 1920s, in which wealthy Americans prospered and some of their increased spending benefited the middle class and the poor.

Federal Tax Reduction The legislative activity early in Reagan's presidency reminded some in the media of FDR's Hundred Days. Congress passed the **Economic Recovery Tax Act** of 1981, which included a 25 percent decrease in personal income taxes over three years. Cuts in the corporate income tax, capital gains tax, and gift and inheritance taxes guaranteed that a large share of the tax relief went to upper-income taxpayers. Under Reagan, the top income tax rate was reduced to 28 percent. At the same time, small investors were also helped by a provision that allowed them to invest up to $2,000 a year in Individual Retirement Accounts (IRAs) without paying taxes on this money until they withdrew it.

Spending With the help of conservative Southern Democrats ("boll weevils"), the Republicans cut more than $40 billion from domestic programs, such as food stamps, student loans, and mass transportation. However, these savings were offset by a dramatic increase in military spending. Reagan pushed through no cuts in Medicare or Social Security, but he did support and sign into law a bipartisan bill to strengthen Social Security. The law increased what individuals paid into the system, raised the age at which they could get full benefits to 67, and taxed some benefits paid to upper-income recipients.

Deregulation Following up on the promise of "getting government off the backs of the people," the Reagan administration reduced federal regulations on business and industry—a policy of deregulation begun under Carter. Restrictions were eased on savings and loan institutions, mergers and takeovers by large corporations, and environmental protection. To help the struggling American auto industry, regulations on emissions and auto safety were also loosened. Secretary of the Interior James Watt opened federal lands for increased coal and timber production and offshore waters for oil drilling.

Labor Unions Despite having once been the president of the Screen Actors Guild, Reagan took a tough stand against unions. He fired thousands of striking federal air traffic controllers for violating their contract and he decertified their union (**PATCO**). Many businesses followed this action by hiring striker replacements in labor conflicts. These anti-union policies, along with the loss of manufacturing jobs, hastened the decline of union membership among nonfarm workers from more than 30 percent in 1962 to only 12 percent in the late 1990s. In addition, the recession of 1982 and foreign competition had a dampening effect on workers' wages.

Recession and Recovery In 1982, the nation suffered one of the worst recessions since the 1930s. Banks failed and unemployment reached 11 percent. However, the recession, along with a fall in oil prices, reduced the double-digit inflation rate of the late 1970s to less than 4 percent. With lower inflation, tax cuts, and ballooning federal deficits, the economy rebounded beginning in 1983. However, the recovery only widened the income gap between rich and poor. While upper-income groups, including well-educated workers and "yuppies" (young urban professionals), enjoyed higher incomes from lower taxes and a deregulated marketplace, the standard of living of the middle class remained stagnant or declined. Not until the late 1990s did the middle class gain back some of its losses.

Social Issues

President Reagan followed through on his pledge to appoint conservative judges to the Supreme Court. His nominations included **Sandra Day O'Connor**, the first woman on the court, as well as Antonin Scalia and Anthony Kennedy. Led by a new chief justice, **William Rehnquist**, the Supreme Court shifted to the right. It scaled back affirmative action in hiring and promotions and limited *Roe v. Wade* by allowing states to impose greater restrictions on abortion, such as requiring minors to notify their parents before having an abortion. However, the court did not end affirmative action or overturn the *Roe* decision.

The Election of 1984

The return of prosperity restored public confidence in the Reagan administration. At their convention in 1984, Republicans nominated their popular president by acclamation. Democrats nominated Walter Mondale, Carter's vice president, to be their presidential candidate. For vice president, they chose Representative Geraldine Ferraro of New York, the first woman to run on a major-party ticket.

President Reagan campaigned on an optimistic "It's Morning Again in America" theme. Reagan won every state except Mondale's home state of Minnesota. Two-thirds of White males voted for Reagan. Only two groups of voters favored the Democrats: African Americans and people earning less than $12,500 a year.

Budget and Trade Deficits

By the mid-1980s, Reagan's tax cuts, combined with large increases in military spending, were creating larger federal deficits. In 1979, the federal deficit was 1.5 percent of GDP. By 1986, it was 4.8 percent. Over the course of Reagan's two terms as president, the national debt tripled from about $900 billion to almost $2.7 trillion. The tax cuts, designed to stimulate investments, seemed only to increase consumption, especially of foreign-made luxury and consumer items. As a result, the U.S. trade deficit reached a then-staggering $150 billion a year. The cumulative trade imbalance of $1 trillion during the 1980s contributed to a dramatic increase in the foreign ownership of U.S. real estate and industry. In 1985, for the first time since the World War I era, the United States became a debtor nation.

Fearing that the federal deficit was getting too large, Congress passed and Reagan signed several bills to increase taxes. In 1985, Congress passed the Gramm-Rudman-Hollings Balanced Budget Act, which provided for across-the-board spending cuts. Court rulings and later congressional changes kept this legislation from achieving its full purpose. However, the combination of spending cuts, tax increases, and greater revenues from a stronger economy reduced the deficit to a manageable 2.9 percent of GDP in 1988.

Impact of President Reagan

During President Reagan's two terms, the government reduced restrictions on the economy and placed more money in the hands of investors and higher-income Americans. His policies also reduced the growth of the New Deal/Great Society welfare state. Another legacy of the Reagan years was greater concern about large federal deficits. Neither Democrats nor Republicans felt they could propose new social programs, such as universal health coverage. Instead of asking what new government programs might be needed, Reaganomics changed the debate to issues of which government programs to cut and by how much.

By the end of Reagan's second term in 1988, "the great communicator's" combination of style, humor, and expressions of patriotism had won over the electorate. He would leave office as one of the most popular presidents of the 20th century. In addition, he changed the politics of the nation for at least a generation by bringing many former Democrats into the Republican Party.

President George H. W. Bush

In the 1988 election, the Republican ticket consisted of Reagan's vice president, **George H. W. Bush**, and a young Indiana senator, Dan Quayle. Michael Dukakis, governor of Massachusetts, won the Democratic nomination and balanced the ticket geographically by selecting Senator Lloyd Bentsen of Texas as his running mate. Bush did not have Reagan's ease in front of the camera, but he quickly overtook a low-key Dukakis by charging that the Democrat was soft on crime (for furloughing criminals) and weak on national defense. Bush also appealed to voters by promising not to raise taxes: "Read my lips—**no new taxes.**"

The Republicans won a decisive victory in November by a margin of 7 million votes. Once again, the Democrats failed to win the confidence of most White middle-class voters. Nevertheless, the voters sent mixed signals by returning larger Democratic majorities to both the House and the Senate. Americans evidently believed in the system of checks and balances, but it often produced legislative gridlock in Washington.

President Bush faced a host of domestic problems. While some grew out of his decisions, others reflected larger economic changes. (See Topic 9.4.)

Nomination of Clarence Thomas The president's nomination of **Clarence Thomas** to the Supreme Court to replace the retiring Thurgood Marshall proved extremely controversial. Thomas faced strong opposition because of his conservative judicial philosophy, opposition to government efforts to combat racism, and the charges of sexual harassment against him. In the final Senate vote, a coalition of 41 Republicans and 11 Democrats approved his confirmation. He became only the second African American member of the Supreme Court.

Taxes and the Economy Americans were shocked to learn that the government's intervention to save weak savings and loan institutions (S&Ls) and to pay insured depositors for funds lost in failed S&Ls would cost the taxpayers more than $250 billion. Also disturbing were the federal budget deficits of more than $250 billion a year. In 1990, Bush, worried that federal deficits were growing too high and recognizing that most federal spending was for programs voters liked, such as defense, violated his campaign pledge of "no new taxes." He agreed to $133 billion in new taxes. Many Republicans felt betrayed. The unpopular tax law increased the top income tax rate to 31 percent and raised federal excise taxes on beer, wine, cigarettes, gasoline, luxury cars, and yachts. Most damaging of all for Bush's reelection prospects was a recession starting in 1990. The prosperity that began under Reagan ended as unemployment increased and average family income decreased.

Americans with Disabilities Act Bush's most significant accomplishment in domestic affairs was that he signed into law the **Americans with Disabilities Act** (ADA) in 1990. This act prohibited discrimination against citizens with physical and mental disabilities in hiring, transportation, and public accommodation. This act had a lasting change on the country, bringing individuals with disabilities into the mainstream of American life.

Political Inertia President Bush began his administration calling for "a kinder, gentler America" and declaring himself the "education president." However, dealing with budget issues and the declining trust in government allowed him little opportunity to change the direction of government. He tried to carry on Reagan's attempt to cut federal programs, but this was difficult in the midst of a recession. His administration seemed to offer little hope to the growing numbers of Americans who felt left behind by economic change and the "Reagan revolution."

Political Polarization

During most of this period the nation continued to become more divided between the conservative South, Great Plains, and Mountain States and the more moderate-to-liberal Northeast and West Coast. As a result of this division, a few swing states, such as Ohio and Florida, determined presidential elections. The more traditional, religious, and limited- or anti-government small towns and rural areas went Republican, while the more diverse large urban centers and internationally minded coasts voted Democratic.

The shift of Southern White conservatives that began in the 1960s from the Democratic to the Republican Party transformed American politics. In the 1990s, Southern conservatives took over the leadership of the Republican Party, making it more conservative and partisan. As the party of Lincoln became the party of Ronald Reagan, moderate Republicans lost influence and primary contests to conservatives. In the state legislatures, both parties gerrymandered congressional districts to create "safe seats," which rewarded partisanship and discouraged compromise in Congress. As the Republican Party became more ideologically conservative and Southern conservatives left the Democratic Party, the political split deepened. Close elections often created divided governments and legislative stagnation.

Divisions in the Federal Government The conservative resurgence starting with the election of Ronald Reagan in 1980 was most apparent in state legislatures and the control of Congress. In the post-World War II era, Democrats controlled the House and Senate with few exceptions until the 1980s, after which the control of the House and Senate has been closely contested, resulting in legislative stalemate and government shutdowns. However, the shift of Southern conservatives to the Republican Party gave the edge to the Republicans, especially in the Electoral College.

In the seven presidential elections after 1988, the Democrats won the popular vote for six times, but won the White House only four times. In 2000 and 2016, the Republican candidates won the electoral vote and hence the presidency. In often very close elections, Democratic Bill Clinton won the presidential elections of 1992 and 1996. Republican George W. Bush (son of George H. W. Bush) won the elections of 2000 and 2004. Democrat Barack Obama won the elections of 2008 and 2012 to become the first African American president. In 2016, Donald Trump, a one-time Democrat who became a Republican and reshaped the party, won the election for president.

POLITICAL CONTROL OF THE FEDERAL GOVERNMENT, 1980 TO 2018

Election Year	House of Rep.	Senate	Presidency	Election Year	House of Rep.	Senate	Presidency
1980	D	R	R	2000	R	D	R
1982	D	R		2002	R	R	
1984	D	R	R	2004	R	R	R
1986	D	D		2006	D	D	
1988	D	D	R	2008	D	D	D
1990	D	D		2010	R	D	
1992	D	D	D	2012	R	D	D
1994	R	R		2014	R	R	
1996	R	R	D	2016	R	R	R
1998	R	R		2018	D	R	

The Media Conservative versus liberal disagreements contributed to the growing partisan divide in Washington and across the nation. Changes in the media also intensified partisanship. CNN, television's first 24-hour all-news network in 1980, and the growth of cable television provided platforms that opened up American media to many different views and voices. The growth of talk radio in the late 1980s provided another outlet, especially for conservative opinions. Hosts such as Rush Limbaugh developed a large following. The media became more polarized after an FCC ruling in 1987 abolished the fairness doctrine. This doctrine had required broadcasters to present the news and issues of public debate in a manner the FCC considered honest, equitable, and balanced. Critics argued that the doctrine violated freedom of speech.

Abortion The Supreme Court's *Roe v. Wade* ruling in 1973 granted women the right to choose to have an abortion without excessive government restrictions. This ruling prompted a fierce, ongoing moral debate over abortion. Some argued that human beings came into existence at the moment of conception, so abortion was murder and should be illegal. Others argued that each woman had a right to control her own body, so whether to have an abortion was her choice and should be legal. In national politics, the issue produced a continual fight over appointment of federal judges, especially to the Supreme Court, who could uphold, restrict, or overturn the decision.

Gun Rights The assassination attempt on President Reagan renewed discussion for regulating gun ownership, especially for unstable persons. Congress in 1993 passed the **Brady Bill**, which mandated background checks and a five-day waiting period for the purchase of handguns. The **National Rifle Association (NRA)** mobilized its supporters to overturn the bill and helped to defeat politicians who supported it. In 2008, the Supreme Court ruled in *District of Columbia v. Heller* that the 2nd Amendment provides an individual the right to possess a firearm unconnected with service in a militia.

This created a new hurdle for the regulation of gun ownership, as some gun advocates argued that gun ownership was a constitutional right that allowed no, or only very limited, restrictions. The debate over guns grew more intense in the 21st century in response to mass shootings in schools, workplaces, clubs, and concerts. In general, conservatives and Republicans opposed new regulations on gun sales, background checks, and the ownership of semi-automatic military-style weapons, while liberals and Democrats were more supportive of these regulations.

Women's Equality and Safety Women during this period increased their participation in the labor force, narrowed the pay gap, and were more likely to be college educated than men. However, women still lagged in achieving pay equity and getting hired as top business leaders.

Women were also twice as likely as men to report gender discrimination on the job. It took the **#MeToo** movement in 2017 to roll back the curtain on the problem of sexual harassment and sexual abuse throughout society. In response, many businesses examined how they could improve their sexual harassment policies and end gender-based pay differences. A priority for the #MeToo movement was to change the laws surrounding sexual harassment and assault and to give survivors the ability to file complaints without retaliation. Many people with traditional views felt that the proposed reforms went too far.

African Americans and Justice The civil rights movement of the previous period opened up opportunities for many African Americans to move into the middle class and leadership positions in business and government. However, the legacy of segregation and ongoing discrimination was still evident in the poverty and incarceration rates, which for Black men was five times greater than Whites. Police beatings and killings of unarmed Black men and boys during arrests drew increasing attention during this period. The video of the severe beating of Rodney King in 1991 and the acquittal of the police involved ignited a national conversation about racial disparity in the justice system and the police use of force. The issue escalated as more videos captured police killing and beating Black men and boys. Starting in 2013, the **Black Lives Matter** movement began campaigning for reforms in police training and arrest procedures. The death of George Floyd in 2020 resulting from a police officer kneeling on his neck created international protests and deepened the divide between advocates for human rights and advocates for law and order.

LGBT Rights Equality related to sexual orientation continued to divide conservatives and liberals. President Clinton (1993–2001) failed to end discrimination against gays in the military and settled for the rule, **"Don't ask, don't tell."** In 2009, Congress made it a federal crime to assault someone because of sexual orientation or gender identity. Over several years, more than 30 states allowed same-sex marriage by legislation or by court order. Finally, in a 5–4 decision, the Supreme Court ruled in ***Obergefell v. Hodges*** (2015) that the Fourteenth Amendment protects the right of same-sex couples to marry. Some objected to same-sex marriage because of their religious beliefs or cultural values.

Immigration Demographic changes such as immigration from Latin America and Asia also contributed to political divisions during this period. (See Topic 9.5.) The divisions continued the long history of conflict over immigration between some native-born citizens who found fault with the newer arrivals because of their ethnic, racial, religious, or cultural traits. During this period, the issue of amnesty for those who had entered the country without authorization became a roadblock to immigration reform in Congress. Opponents argued that undocumented immigrants should be forced to leave the United States and, like other aspiring immigrants, apply to enter the country.

Economy and Health The growing income and wealth disparities between the wealthy and lower-income Americans and the domination of the economy by Wall Street and large corporations created debates, especially during recessions, when lower-income Americans tended to suffer the most, such as in the Great Recession of 2008. However, the issue of health care coverage for all Americans was an ongoing issue between those who argued that health care was a right and others who held it was a personal responsibility that should not involve the government. The Affordable Care Act of 2010 deeply divided Washington, with Republicans repeatedly trying to repeal it. The pandemic of 2020 also raised doubts about both the readiness of the health care system in the United States during a crisis and the disparity in health outcomes for the poor and minorities.

The problem of political polarization between liberals and conservatives, between Democrats and Republicans, became more critical during this period because it often prevented the political system from dealing with the challenges coming from within and from outside the nation. It caused former allies and observers around the world to question if the United States could carry on the leadership roles that it took on during the 20th century, or would that leadership pass on to others?

REFLECT ON THE LEARNING OBJECTIVE

1. Explain two causes and two effects of the debate about the role of the federal government during the period after 1980.

KEY TERMS BY THEME

Conservatism (PCE)		
Ronald Reagan	Sandra Day O'Connor	National Rifle Association (NRA)
supply-side economics ("Reaganomics")	William Rehnquist	*District of Columbia v. Heller*
"trickle down" economics	George H. W. Bush	LGBT rights
Economic Recovery Tax Act	"no new taxes"	"Don't ask, don't tell"
deregulation	Clarence Thomas	Black Lives Matter
PATCO	Americans with Disabilities Act	#MeToo
	political polarization	*Obergefell v. Hodges*
	Brady Bill	

Questions 1–3 refer to the excerpt below.

"In this present crisis, government is not the solution to our problem; government is the problem. From time to time we've been tempted to believe that society has become too complex to be managed by self-rule, that government by an elite group is superior to government for, by, and of the people. . . .

It is my intention to curb the size and influence of the Federal establishment and to demand recognition of the distinction between the powers granted to the Federal government and those reserved to the States or to the people. . . .

In the days ahead I will propose removing the roadblocks that have slowed our economy and reduced productivity. . . . It is time to reawaken this industrial giant, to get government back within its means, and to lighten our punitive tax burden. And these will be our first priorities, and on these principles there will be no compromise."

President Ronald Reagan, inaugural address,
January 20, 1981

1. Which of the following was an accomplishment by Reagan that fulfilled the pledges made in this excerpt?
   (A) Balancing the federal budget
   (B) Cutting military spending through greater efficiency
   (C) Strengthening environmental protections of federal lands
   (D) Reducing taxes for businesses and upper-income individuals

2. Ronald Reagan's philosophy was most similar to that of which of the following presidents?
   (A) William McKinley because he believed that privately owned corporations were the key to economic growth
   (B) Theodore Roosevelt because he believed that the country needed a strong federal government to regulate industries
   (C) Franklin Roosevelt because he believed that government spending was a useful tool to boost the economy and consumer demand
   (D) Lyndon Johnson because he supported using federal programs to reduce the income inequality among Americans

3. Which of the following would best support President Reagan's views on "removing roadblocks that have slowed our economy"?

(A) Cutting restrictions on financial institutions

(B) Improving mass transportation for workers

(C) Promoting college education with student loans

(D) Requiring older Americans to work longer

SHORT-ANSWER QUESTIONS

Use complete sentences; an outline or bulleted list alone is not acceptable.

1.

Source: Len Boro Rothco

Using the image above, which depicts a debate about the Reagan administration policies, answer (a), (b), and (c).

(a) Briefly describe ONE perspective of the artist expressed in the image.

(b) Briefly explain how ONE specific event or development during the Reagan administration contributed to the perspective depicted in the image.

(c) Briefly explain how ONE specific historical event or development during the Reagan administration challenged the perspective depicted in the image.

2. Answer (a), (b), and (c).

(a) Briefly explain ONE specific historical development that contributed to the conservative resurgence in the 1980s.

(b) Briefly explain ONE specific effect of this resurgence on federal government policy during the 1980s.

(c) Briefly explain ONE specific criticism of the Reagan administration.

Topic 9.3

The End of the Cold War

*General Secretary Gorbachev, if you seek peace, if you seek prosperity
for the Soviet Union and Eastern Europe, if you seek liberalization:
Come here to this gate! Mr. Gorbachev, open this gate! Mr. Gorbachev,
tear down this wall!*

Ronald Reagan, speech at Brandenburg Gate, West Berlin, June 12, 1987

Learning Objective: Explain the causes and effects of the end of the
Cold War and its legacy.

Historians debate the relative importance of the various causes for the end of
the Cold War, but the roles of Ronald Reagan of the United States and **Mikhail
Gorbachev** of the Soviet Union were pivotal. Today, Europeans, Russians, and
Americans continue to experience its long-lasting effects.

Foreign Policy During the Reagan Years

Reagan started his presidency determined to build the military might and
superpower prestige of the United States and to intensify the Cold War
competition with the Soviet Union. He called the Soviet Communists the **"evil
empire"** and "focus of evil in the modern world." Reagan was prepared to use
military force to back up his rhetoric. During his second term, however, he
proved flexible enough in his foreign policy to respond to significant changes
in the Soviet Union and its **satellites** in Eastern Europe.

Renewing the Cold War

Increased spending for defense and aid to anti-Communist forces in Latin
America marked Reagan's approach to the Cold War during his first term.

Military Buildup The Reagan administration spent billions to build
new weapons systems, such as the B-1 bomber and the MX missile, and to
expand the U.S. Navy from 450 to 600 ships. The administration also increased
spending on the **Strategic Defense Initiative (SDI)**, an ambitious plan for
building a high-tech system of lasers and particle beams to destroy enemy
missiles before they could reach U.S. territory. Critics called the SDI **"Star
Wars"** and argued that the costly program would only escalate the arms race
and could be overwhelmed by the Soviets building more missiles. Although

Congress made some cuts in the Reagan proposals, the defense budget grew from $171 billion in 1981 to more than $300 billion in 1985.

Central America In the Americas, Reagan supported "friendly" right-wing dictators to keep out communism. In **Nicaragua** in 1979, a Marxist movement known as the **Sandinistas** had overthrown the country's dictator. In response, the United States provided significant military aid to the **Contras** trying to dislodge the Sandinistas. In 1985, Democrats opposed to the administration's policies in Nicaragua passed the **Boland Amendment**, which prohibited further aid to the Contras.

In El Salvador, meanwhile, the Reagan administration spent nearly $5 billion to support the Salvadoran government against a coalition of leftist guerrillas. Many Americans protested the killing of more than 40,000 civilians, including American missionaries, by right-wing death squads with connections to the El Salvador army.

Grenada On the small Caribbean island of **Grenada**, a coup led to the establishment of a pro-Cuban regime. In October 1983, President Reagan ordered a small force of marines to invade the island in order to prevent the establishment of a strategic Communist military base in the Americas. The invasion quickly succeeded in reestablishing a pro-U.S. government in Grenada.

Iran-Contra Affair If Grenada was the notable military triumph of Reagan's presidency, his efforts to aid the Nicaraguan Contras involved him in a serious blunder and scandal. The so-called **Iran-Contra affair** had its origins in U.S. troubles with Iran. Since 1980, Iran and Iraq had been engaged in a bloody war. Reagan aides came up with the plan—kept secret from the American public—of selling U.S. antitank and antiaircraft missiles to Iran's government for helping to free the Americans held hostage by an Iranian-linked group in Lebanon. In 1986, another Reagan staff member had the "great idea" to use the profits of the arms deal with Iran to fund the Contras in Nicaragua.

President Reagan denied that he had knowledge of the illegal diversion of funds—illegal in that it violated both the Boland Amendment and congressional budget authority. The picture that emerged from a televised congressional investigation was of an uninformed, hands-off president who was easily manipulated by his advisers. Reagan suffered a sharp, but temporary, drop in the popularity polls.

Lebanon, Israel, and the PLO

Reagan suffered a series of setbacks in the Middle East. In 1982, Israel (with U.S. approval) invaded southern Lebanon to stop **Palestinian Liberation Organization (PLO)** fighters from raiding Israel. Soon the United States sent peacekeeping forces into Lebanon to contain that country's bitter civil war. In April 1983, an Arab suicide squad bombed the U.S. embassy in Beirut, killing 63 people. A few months later, another Arab terrorist drove a bomb-filled truck into the U.S. Marines barracks, killing 241 soldiers. Reagan soon pulled U.S. forces out of Lebanon, with little to show for the effort and loss of lives.

Secretary of State George Schultz pushed for a peaceful settlement of the Palestinian-Israeli conflict by setting up a homeland for the PLO in the West Bank territories occupied by Israel since the 1967 war. Under U.S. pressure, PLO leader **Yasser Arafat** agreed in 1988 to recognize Israel's right to exist.

Improved U.S.-Soviet Relations

The Cold War intensified in the early 1980s as a result of both Reagan's arms buildup and the Soviet deployment of more missiles against NATO countries.

Gorbachev In 1985, however, a dynamic reformer, Mikhail Gorbachev, became the new Soviet leader. Gorbachev attempted to change the troubled Communist political and economic system by introducing two major reforms: (1) *glasnost*, or openness, to end political repression and move toward greater political freedom for Soviet citizens, and (2) *perestroika*, or restructuring of the Soviet economy by introducing some free-market practices.

To achieve his reforms, Gorbachev wanted to end the costly arms race. However, Soviet conservatives fought efforts to reduce military spending. In 1987, President Reagan challenged the Soviet leader to follow through with the reforms he said he wanted. In front of Brandenburg Gate and the Berlin Wall, the most tangible symbol of the Cold War, Reagan ended his speech with the line, "Mr. Gorbachev, tear down this wall."

Reagan and Gorbachev held three summit meetings. The first, in November 1985, resulted in agreements on a range of issues, from cultural and scientific exchanges to environmental issues. A second meeting the following October in Reykjavik, Iceland, was less successful, since Reagan's commitment to a new missile defense system proved to be a major obstacle to talks on arms control. At their third summit in 1987, which took place in Washington, D.C., both sides were able to compromise on a range of arms-control issues. They agreed to remove and destroy all intermediate-range missiles (the **INF agreement**).

In 1988, Gorbachev further reduced Cold War tensions by starting the pullout of Soviet troops from Afghanistan. He also cooperated with the United States in putting diplomatic pressure on Iran and Iraq to end their war. By the end of Reagan's second term, superpower relations had so improved that the end of the Cold War seemed at hand.

Assessing Causes Multiple causes contributed to the decline in the Cold War. Some historians emphasize Gorbachev's desire for domestic reforms, which contributed to his willingness to negotiate. Others argue that Reagan's military buildup forced the Soviet Union to concede defeat in the Cold War. Reagan is also credited for his willingness to negotiate arms reductions with the Soviets. His actions relieved Russian domestic pressure on Gorbachev, who could then pursue his reform agenda. Historians also credit other leaders and thinkers besides Reagan and Gorbachev. For example, the opponents of communism in Eastern Europe, such as a Polish union leader, Lech Walesa, and a Polish pope, John Paul II, carried on a long struggle for freedom. In the United States, George Kennan's containment policy guided the United States through the Cold War without setting off a world war.

George H. W. Bush and the End of the Cold War

The Cold War threatened the existence of humankind. At the same time, it gave clear purpose to U.S. foreign policy. What would be the U. S. role in the world *after* the Cold War? George H. W. Bush, a former ambassador to the United Nations and director of the CIA (and the father of President George W. Bush), became the first president to define the country's role in the new era.

Persian Gulf War

President Bush's plans for a "new world order" of peace and democracy were challenged in August 1990 when Iraq's dictator, Saddam Hussein, invaded oil-rich but weak Kuwait. This move threatened Western oil sources in Saudi Arabia and the Persian Gulf. President Bush successfully built a coalition of United Nations members to pressure Hussein to withdraw from Kuwait. In January 1991, in a massive operation called Desert Storm, more than 500,000 Americans were joined by military units from 28 other nations. A brilliant invasion led by American forces took only 100 hours of fighting to defeat the Iraqi army. However, Saddam Hussein, though weakened, remained the dictator in Iraq.

The Collapse of Soviet Communism and the Soviet Union

The first years of the Bush administration were dominated by dramatic changes in the Communist world.

Tiananmen Square In China, during the spring of 1989, prodemocracy students and workers demonstrated for freedom in Beijing's **Tiananmen Square**. Television cameras from the West broadcast the prodemocracy movement around the world. Under the cover of night, the Chinese Communist government crushed the protest with tanks, killing hundreds and ending the brief flowering of an open political environment in China. The Chinese Communist Party, while promoting economic development and national pride, ruled its large population as an authoritarian one-party state.

Eastern Europe Challenges to communism in Eastern Europe produced more positive results. With the overwhelming electoral victory of the once-outlawed Solidarity movement led by **Lech Walesa**, the Communist Party fell from power in one country after another—Hungary, Czechoslovakia, Bulgaria, and Romania. The Communists in East Germany were forced out of power after protesters tore down the **Berlin Wall**, the hated symbol of the Cold War, in late 1989. In October 1990, the two Germanys, divided since 1945, were finally reunited with the blessing of both NATO and the Soviet Union.

Breakup of the Soviet Union The swift march of events and the nationalist desire for self-determination soon overwhelmed Gorbachev and the Soviet Union. In 1990, the Soviet Baltic republics of Estonia, Latvia, and Lithuania declared their independence. After a failed coup against Gorbachev by Communist hard-liners, the remaining republics dissolved the Soviet Union in December 1991, leaving Gorbachev a leader with no country. **Boris Yeltsin**, president of the **Russian Republic**, joined with nine former Soviet republics to form a loose confederation, the **Commonwealth of Independent States (CIS)**. Yeltsin disbanded the Communist Party in Russia and attempted to establish a democracy and a free-market economy.

End of the Cold War Sweeping agreements to dismantle their nuclear weapons were one piece of tangible proof that the Cold War had ended. Bush and Gorbachev signed the **START I** agreement in 1991, reducing the number of nuclear warheads to under 10,000 for each side. In late 1992, Bush and Yeltsin agreed to a **START II** treaty, which reduced the number of nuclear weapons to just over 3,000 each. The treaty also offered U.S. economic assistance to the troubled Russian economy.

EASTERN EUROPE AFTER THE FALL OF COMMUNISM

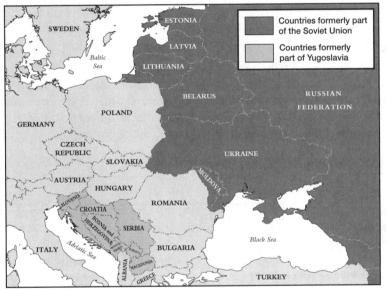

Even as Soviet communism collapsed, President Bush, a seasoned diplomat, remained cautious. Instead of celebrating final victory in the Cold War, Americans grew concerned about the outbreak of civil wars and violence in the former Soviet Union. In Eastern Europe, Yugoslavia started to disintegrate in 1991, and a civil war broke out in the province of Bosnia and Herzegovina in 1992. At home, the end of the Cold War raised questions about whether the United States still needed such heavy defense spending and so many U.S. military bases around the world.

Aftermath of the Cold War in Europe

In 2002, the **European Union (EU)** became a unified market of 15 nations, 12 of which adopted a single currency, the **euro**. The EU grew to include 27 European nations by 2007, including 10 former satellites of the USSR, such as **Poland**, Bulgaria, and Romania.

Russia Under President Boris Yeltsin, Russia struggled to reform its economy and to fight rampant corruption. In 2000, Yeltsin's elected successor, **Vladimir Putin**, took office. Relations with the United States were strained by Russia's brutal repression of the civil war in Chechnya, by NATO's admittance in 1999 of the Czech Republic, Hungary, and Poland, and by Russia's support of Serbia in the Balkan wars of the 1990s.

War in the Former Yugoslavia Serbian dictator Slobodan Milosevic violently suppressed independence movements in the former Yugoslav provinces of Slovenia, Croatia, Bosnia-Herzegovina, and Kosovo. Ethnic divisions were complicated by religious rivalries among Roman Catholics, Orthodox Christians, and Muslims. Hundreds of thousands of people, including many Muslims, were killed in **"ethnic cleansing."** A mix of diplomacy, bombing, and NATO troops, including U.S. troops, stopped the bloodshed in **Bosnia** in 1995 and then in Kosovo in 1999. These Balkan wars were Europe's bloodiest conflicts since World War II and reminded people of how World War I had started.

Difficult Times The path to democracy and prosperity for the former Communist bloc nations in Eastern Europe and Russia was hard. Years of economic stagnation under communism were difficult to overcome, and democracy was slow to take root in these newly independent states. These states became easy targets for corruption and autocratic rulers.

REFLECT ON THE LEARNING OBJECTIVE

1. Explain two causes and two effects of the end of the Cold War.

KEY TERMS BY THEME

Reagan Foreign Policy (WOR)	End of the Cold War (WOR)
Mikhail Gorbachev	Tiananmen Square
"evil empire"	Poland
satellites	Lech Walesa
Strategic Defense Initiative (SDI)	Berlin Wall
"Star Wars"	Boris Yeltsin
Nicaragua	Russian Republic
Sandinistas	Commonwealth of Ind-ependent States
Contras	(CIS)
Boland Amendment	START I
Grenada	START II
Iran-Contra affair	European Union (EU)
Palestine Liberation Organization (PLO)	euro
Yasser Arafat	Vladimir Putin
glasnost	Bosnia
perestroika	"ethnic cleansing"
INF agreement	

Questions 1–2 refer to the excerpt below.

[On the day after Solidarity had swept Poland's first open elections, ultimately winning 99 of 100 Senate seats, the Polish Communists met to discuss what to do.]

"Comrade W. Baka proposed to emphasize in the statement that we had taken into account the unfavorable result. We are consistent, we have no other alternative. Warn against attempts at destabilization, pointing at the situation in China. [Tiananmen occurred the same day as the Polish elections.] Comrade A. Kwasniewski emphasized that a matter extremely important after announcing the election results is to prevent spontaneous demonstrations, which neither side might be able to control. Comrade M.F. Rakowski—We had a false assessment of the situation. . . . The party are not connected with the masses. . . . There was a lack of awareness. . . . What has happened in Poland is going to have tremendous impact outside (USSR, Hungary, other countries). This may lead to upheavals in the whole camp, this must be driven to social awareness. We need to draw all conclusions from the fact that considerable part of the society said 'no'."

Transcript of the Central Committee Secretariat meeting of the Polish
United Workers [Communist] Party, June 5, 1989

1. Which of the following was the most direct catalyst for the political situation described in this excerpt?
   (A) Gorbachev had decided not to send in Soviet troops to support Communist governments.
   (B) President Bush took a cautious approach and would not help the Solidarity movement.
   (C) Most of the other Communist bloc governments in Eastern Europe had already fallen.
   (D) The Polish Communists wanted to keep the support of the Catholic Church in Poland.

2. Why was "the situation in China" an issue for Polish Communists?
   (A) Communist governments followed a similar economic model for their development.
   (B) Communist China had better relations with the United States than with the Soviet Union.
   (C) In 1989, the Polish Communists decided not to use suppression and violence to stay in power as the Chinese had.
   (D) The Polish Communists came to regret their support of Gorbachev.

1.

Source: Edmund S. Valtman / Library of Congress. 1991

Using the image above answer (a), (b), and (c). The image shows Karl Marx, Joseph Stalin, and Vladimir Lenin looking down from heaven as Mikhail Gorbachev leads a funeral procession. The casket says "COMMUNISM," and Stalin is saying, "I can't believe my eyes!"

(a) Briefly describe ONE historical perspective expressed in the image.

(b) Briefly explain how ONE specific event or development in the period from 1980 to 1991 contributed to the process depicted in the image.

(c) Briefly explain ONE specific historical effect in the period from 1980 to 2000 that resulted from the process depicted in the image.

2. Answer (a), (b), and (c).

(a) Briefly explain ONE specific historical event or development to support the position that the Reagan administration helped to end the Cold War.

(b) Briefly explain ONE specific historical event or development to support the position that political changes in the Soviet Union and Eastern Europe helped to end the Cold War.

(c) Briefly explain ONE specific historical foreign-policy challenge for the United States that resulted from the aftermath of the Cold War.

Topic 9.4

A Changing Economy

"We need a new approach to government. . . . A government that is leaner, not meaner; a government that expands opportunity, not bureaucracy; a government that understands that jobs must come from growth in a vibrant and vital system of free enterprise."

Bill Clinton, nomination acceptance speech, July 16, 1992.

Learning Objective: Explain the causes and effects of economic and technological change over time.

The Republicans nominated President George H. W. Bush in 1992 for a second term. After a long career in public service, the president seemed tired and out of touch with average Americans, such as when he was surprised by the use of barcode scanners in the check-out line at the supermarket. The Cold War was over, and America wanted to enjoy its economic benefits and the technological innovations of the period.

Election of 1992

A youthful governor of Arkansas, **Bill Clinton,** emerged from the Democratic primaries as the party's choice for president. The first member of the baby boom generation to be nominated for president, Clinton presented himself as a moderate "New Democrat" who focused on economic issues such as jobs, education, and health care, which were important to the "vital center" of the electorate. The strategy was, according to his political advisers, to focus on "the economy, stupid!" Clinton did well in the South and recaptured the majority of the elderly and blue-collar workers from the Republicans. Despite a serious third-party challenge from **Ross Perot**, a Texas billionaire, Clinton won with 370 electoral votes (and 43 percent of the popular vote) to 168 for Bush (37 percent of the popular vote).

Clinton's Focus on the Economy

During the first two years of the Clinton administration, Senate Republicans used filibusters and the threat of filibusters to prevent passage of the president's economic stimulus package, campaign finance reform, environmental bills, and health care reform. However, some "incremental" reforms did become law.

Early Accomplishments The Democratic Congress was able to pass the Family and Medical Leave Act, which required businesses to allow workers to take unpaid leave for specific medical reasons. It also passed the "motor voter" law that enabled citizens to register to vote as they got their driver's licenses. The **Brady Bill**, which mandated a five-day waiting period for the purchase of handguns, was enacted. In 1994, Congress enacted Clinton's **Anti-Crime Bill**, which provided $30 billion in funding for more police protection and crime-prevention programs. The legislation also banned the sale of most assault rifles, which angered the gun lobby led by the **National Rifle Association (NRA)**. After protracted negotiation and compromise, Congress passed a deficit-reduction budget that included $255 billion in spending cuts and $241 billion in tax increases. Incorporated in this budget were the president's requests for increased appropriations for education and job training.

Defeat and Adjustments In the midterm elections of November 1994, the Republicans gained control of both houses of Congress for the first time since 1954. Led by Representative **Newt Gingrich** of Georgia, who would become Speaker of the House, the phenomenon came to be known as the "**Republican Revolution**" or the "**Revolution of '94**." They benefited from a well-organized effort to promote a short list of policy priorities they called the "**Contract with America**." In addition, the Democratic Congress was unpopular because it had raised taxes and limited gun ownership. President Clinton adjusted to his party's defeat by declaring in his 1995 State of the Union address, "The era of big government is over."

Balanced Budget Finally, in the 1996 election year, Congress and the president compromised on a budget that left Medicare and Social Security benefits intact, limited welfare benefits to five years under the Personal Responsibility and Work Opportunity Act, set some curbs on immigration, increased the minimum wage, and balanced the budget. The spending cuts and tax increases made during Clinton's first term, along with strong economic growth, helped to eliminate the deficit in federal spending in 1998 and produced the first federal surplus since 1969. Unlike any other modern president, Clinton could point to a total $63 billion surplus during his two terms, if one adds up their four deficits and four surpluses.

Clinton Reelected In his battle with the Republican Congress, President Clinton tried to position himself as a moderate. He characterized the Republicans as extremists while at the same time he took over their positions that were popular, such as balancing the budget and reforming welfare. In the 1996 election, Clinton was aided by a fast-growing economy that had produced more than 10 million new jobs during his first term. Clinton became the first Democrat since Franklin Roosevelt to be reelected president. The Republicans could celebrate retaining control of both houses of Congress, which they had not done since the 1920s.

Tax Cuts Versus Social Security The prosperity of the late 1990s shifted the debate in Washington to what to do with the federal government's surplus revenues, projected to be $4.6 trillion over the first ten years of the 21st century. In 1997, Congress and the president did compromise on legislation that cut taxes on estates and capital gains and gave tax credits for families with children and for higher education expenses. The Republicans pressed for more tax cuts, such as the elimination of the estate tax (the "death tax") and taxes on two-income families (the "marriage penalty"). Clinton held out for using the projected surplus to support Social Security, expand Medicare, and reduce the national debt.

While Clinton could point to successful policies, his personal activities created problems for him. In 1999, the Republican House impeached President Clinton for lying under oath about sexual relations and related abuses of power, but he was not convicted. For his ability to get out of trouble, his critics nicknamed him "Slick Willie."

Technology and a Changing Economy

During President Clinton's two terms, the United States enjoyed the longest peacetime economic expansion in its history, with annual growth rates of more than 4 percent. Much of the economic boom resulted from increased productivity related to technological innovations.

Technological Innovations The use of the **Internet**, personal computers, software, and wireless mobile communications fueled increased national productivity (a gain of more than 5 percent in 1999) and made "e-commerce" (or electronic commerce) part of American life. GPS systems, digital photography, solar panels, and wind turbines brought more economic changes. High-tech companies, such as Apple, Intel, and Microsoft, were joined during the "dot-com" boom by the likes of Amazon, AOL, Yahoo, and Google.

Innovations in the medical field included DNA testing and sequencing, human genome mapping, magnetic resonance imaging (MRI), and robotic and noninvasive laser surgery. These new diagnostic tools and advances in surgery, along with drug development based on individual genetic factors, promoted the growth of the medical field and promises for the conquest of diseases.

Flattening of the Earth The technology of the period created new opportunities for growth and development across the globe. For example, cellular communication grew from zero to over four billion people with mobile devices that could connect them with other people and the latest knowledge all over the world. Technology leveled the playing field regardless of one's location. As Thomas Friedman explained in his book *The World is Flat*, the swift advances in technology and communications linked people all over Earth, creating new wealth in the developing world and flattening competition around the globe.

The Boom of the 1990s After years of heavy competition with Europe and Asia, American businesses had become proficient in cutting costs, which both increased their profitability and held down the U.S. inflation rate to below 3 percent a year. Investors were rewarded with record gains of more than 22 percent in the stock market. The number of households worth $1 million or more quadrupled in the 1990s to more than 8 million, or one in 14 households. The unemployment rate fell from 7.5 percent in 1992 to a 30-year low of 3.9 percent in 2000. The unemployment of African Americans and Hispanics was the lowest on record to that point. During the peak of prosperity from 1997 to 1999, middle- and lower-income Americans experienced the first gains in real income since 1973. However, the economic boom was over by 2001, and both investors and wage earners faced another recession.

Globalization The surging increases in trade and communications and the movement of capital around the world during this era were key parts of the process of **globalization**. Globalization promoted the development of global and regional economic organizations. During the Clinton administration, the **North American Free Trade Agreement (NAFTA)** was passed by Congress and signed by the president over objections from union leaders, who feared job losses to low-wage Mexico. It created a free-trade zone with Canada and Mexico. The **World Trade Organization (WTO)** was established in 1994 to oversee trade agreements, enforce trade rules, and settle disputes. The powerful **International Monetary Fund (IMF)** and the **World Bank** made loans to, and supervised the economic policies of, poorer nations with debt troubles.

The **Group of Eight (G8)**, the world's largest industrial powers (Canada, France, Germany, Italy, Japan, Russia, the United Kingdom, and the United States), which controlled two-thirds of the world's wealth, remained the leading economic powers in 2000. However, China, India, and Brazil would soon surpass many of the older industrial powers in the 21st century. The growing gap between the rich and poor nations of the world caused tensions, especially over the debts the poor nations owed to powerful banks and the richest nations. Workers and unions in the richest nations often resented globalization because they lost their jobs to cheaper labor markets in the developing world.

Digital Security and Privacy The use of wireless communications and the Internet raised the issue of privacy in the digital age. Domestic and foreign hacking of digital data and the use of social media to disrupt politics exposed failings and abuses by large Internet companies such as Facebook and Google. These companies became wealthy and powerful through the extraction and analysis of personal data of hundreds of millions of their users for focused advertisements and resale of data to third parties. Fearful of discouraging innovation, the government exercised little regulation of the industry. Congressional hearings exposed the failure of the Internet companies to monitor how the data was used or to protect it from cyber attacks. Some saw the rise of "surveillance capitalism" as a growing threat to Americans' privacy, security, and tradition of self-government.

Income and Wealth

In many ways, Americans were achieving the American dream. Homeownership continued to climb during the prosperity of the 1990s to 67.4 percent of all households. The economy was continuing to generate more and more wealth.

Per capita income in constant (inflation-adjusted) dollars rose dramatically, from $12,275 in 1970 to $22,199 in 2000. However, in 1999 the top fifth of American households received more than half of all income. The average after-tax income for the lowest three-fifths of households actually declined between 1977 and 1997. In addition, the distribution of income varied widely by race, sex, and education. For example, the median income in 2000 was $53,256 for White families, $35,054 for Hispanic families, and $34,192 for Black families. High school graduates earned only half the income of college graduates.

Concentration of Wealth In terms of wealth, which includes property and investments minus debts, data from 2007 show that wealth was concentrated in the hands of a few:

- the wealthiest 1 percent possessed 35 percent of the nation's wealth
- the next 19 percent possessed 50 percent
- the bottom 80 percent owned only about 15 percent

By the late 2010s, wealth was even more concentrated, with the **top 1 percent** holding 43 percent of the nation's financial wealth. The wealthy possessed greater financial opportunities that allowed their money to make more money. In contrast, one study found 62 percent of households headed by a single parent were without savings or other financial assets. The United States was the richest country in the world, but among industrialized nations, it had the largest gap between lowest and highest paid workers and the greatest concentration of wealth among the top-earning households. The economist Joseph Stiglitz argued that the decline of strong unions since the 1970s was related to the rise in the inequality of income and wealth in the United States.

This concentration of wealth reminded some of the Gilded Age of the late 19th century. Scholars and political leaders expressed concern that high levels of wealth inequality were incompatible with a democratic society and would result to a drift towards oligarchy and autocratic governments.

One debated cause of wage stagnation was the increase in immigration to the United States in the 1990s and 2000s. Topic 9.5 will explore the causes and effects of immigration and the shift of population growth to the South and West.

REFLECT ON THE LEARNING OBJECTIVE

1. Explain a cause and an effect of economic change after 1980.

2. Explain a cause and an effect of technological change after 1980.

Changing Economy (WXT)
election of 1992
Bill Clinton
Ross Perot
Brady Bill
Anti-Crime Bill
National Rifle Association (NRA)

Newt Gingrich
Republican Revolution
Revolution of '94
Contract with America
Internet
globalization
North American Free Trade Agreement (NAFTA)

World Trade Organization (WTO)
International Monetary Fund (IMF)
World Bank
Group of Eight (G8)
top 1 percent

MULTIPLE-CHOICE QUESTIONS

Questions 1–3 refer to the excerpt below.

> "Clinton was widely hailed, even by some of his detractors, as the most gifted politician of his generation—but the political task presented to him required continual bobbing and weaving, compromising and negotiation, retreating so as to advance. . . . Clinton was forced to establish a position independent of both the hostile Republican majority and the impotent Democratic minority. . . . Under siege, though, Clinton survived to become, by the end of his second term, a singularly admired if controversial leader."
>
> Sean Wilentz, *The Age of Reagan: A History 1974–2008,* 2008

1. Which of the following actions provides the strongest evidence to support the claim that Clinton's success was in "compromising and negotiation, retreating so as to advance"?
   (A) The bill ending all discrimination against gays in the military
   (B) The changes known as the Contract with America
   (C) The Brady Bill on the purchase of handguns
   (D) The actions on welfare and budget reform

2. Which of the following best explains the reason for the general popularity of the Clinton presidency?
   (A) Clinton survived an unpopular impeachment effort led by his political opponents.
   (B) Clinton presided over eight years of prosperity and improved middle-class incomes.
   (C) Clinton organized successful peacekeeping efforts in the former Yugoslavia.
   (D) Clinton negotiated a plan to stabilize Social Security and Medicare for seniors.

3. Which of the following best explains the reasons for the first budget surpluses in decades during the Clinton administration?

(A) Military savings as a result of the U.S. victory in the Cold War

(B) Republicans' ability to pass budget cuts over Clinton's opposition

(C) A compromise between Clinton and Republicans to cut Social Security

(D) A mixture of tax increases, budget cuts, and a growing economy

SHORT-ANSWER QUESTIONS

1.

DISTRIBUTION OF HOUSEHOLD INCOME, 1980 AND 2018		
Income Group	1980	2018
Wealthiest 5 Percent (Included in the highest 20 percent)	16.5	23.1
Highest 20 Percent	44.1	52.0
Fourth Highest 20 Percent	24.7	22.6
Middle 20 Percent	16.8	14.1
Second Lowest 20 Percent	10.2	8.3
Lowest 20 Percent	4.2	3.0

Source: U.S. Bureau of the Census.

Using the table above, answer (a), (b), and (c).

(a) Briefly explain ONE specific historical event or development that contributed to the increase in household income of the richest Americans after 1980.

(b) Briefly explain ONE specific historical event or development that contributed to the general stagnation of household income of the middle and poorest groups of Americans after 1980.

(c) Briefly explain ONE specific historical effect that resulted from the changes depicted in the table.

2. Answer (a), (b), and (c).

(a) Briefly explain ONE cause for increased productivity in the United States during the 1990s.

(b) Briefly explain ONE specific problem related to the Internet and wireless communications.

(c) Briefly explain ONE impact of globalization on the American economy after 1980.

Topic 9.5

Migration and Immigration in the 1990s and 2000s

"America has constantly drawn strength and spirit from wave after wave of immigrants. . . . They have proved to be the most restless, the most adventurous, the most innovative, the most industrious of people."

President Bill Clinton, speech at Portland (Oregon) State University, June 13, 1998

Learning Objective: Explain the causes and effects of domestic and international migration over time.

Anti-immigrant sentiment has risen and fallen throughout American history. Immigrants made up 13 percent to 15 percent of the nation's population in the decades before the passage of legislation restricting immigration in the 1920s. In the 2010s, the immigrant population again reached over 13 percent, and again restrictions on immigration gained a popular following. This was made evident in the 2016 national election, when supporters of the winning candidate opposed to undocumented immigration from Mexico chanted, "Build the wall!" The causes and effects of migration and immigration shaped many aspects of American life in the 1990s and early 2000s.

Changing Immigration Policies

The **Immigration and Nationality Act of 1965** did away with the racially based quota system of the 1920s. The new system gave preference to potential immigrants with relatives in the United States and with occupations deemed critical by the Department of Labor. It also opened up immigration from non-European countries. This change occurred as the recovery of Europe after World War II meant that fewer Europeans were interested in migrating, while Castro's takeover of Cuba and the war in Vietnam prompted people to flee those countries. The result of all of these changes was a dramatic change in the origins of immigrants to the United States. For example, the percentages of immigrants from Europe and Canada gradually dropped between 1970 and 2015 from 68 percent to 14 percent of the annual immigrant population. In contrast, the number of immigrants from South and East Asia increased from 7 percent to 27 percent, those from Mexico increased from 8 percent to 27 percent, and those from Latin America outside of Mexico increased from 11 percent to 24 percent.

By 2000, the Hispanic population was the fastest-growing segment of the population and emerged as the largest minority group in the nation, representing 13 percent of the population. The number of Asian Americans also increased sharply, exceeding 4 percent. Immigration accounted for 27.8 percent of the population increase in the 1990s and was a key stimulus to the economic growth during the decade. Without immigration, the United States was on a path to experience negative population growth by 2030.

Federal Legislation Undocumented entry into the United States became a growing political issue in the 1990s and 2000s. The **Immigration Reform and Control Act of 1986** attempted to create a fair entry process for immigrants, but it failed to stop people in search of work from entering the United States without authorization. The law was also criticized for granting amnesty to over three million undocumented immigrants from Mexico and the Americas.

During the Clinton administration, Congress passed the **Illegal Immigration Reform and Immigrant Responsibility Act of 1996** to reform the process for admitting or removing undocumented immigrants. It strengthened U.S. immigration laws, restructured immigration law enforcement, and limited immigration by addressing undocumented migration. However, these reforms did little to stop the flow of people. Private employers continued to hire undocumented workers, paying them far lower wages than they would have had to pay legal residents.

Executive Action In the 21st century, Congress discussed various plans for controlling immigration, but the Senate and House were unable to reach an agreement. The Obama administration had no more success than the Bush administration in getting immigration reform through Congress.

In 2012, President Obama took executive action to protect undocumented young people brought to the United States as children (known as "Dreamers") from deportation and to allow them to continue their education and apply for work permits. The **Deferred Action for Childhood Arrivals (DACA)** program was controversial. Further action to expand it in 2014 was challenged by lawsuits from 26 states and partially blocked by a federal judge. Anger at Obama's immigration policies increased, even though the number of border guards was increased, deportations of **undocumented immigrants** increased, and the total undocumented immigrant population decreased during his presidency.

Trump Immigration Policies As a presidential candidate in 2016, Donald Trump promised to be much tougher on immigration and asylum seekers than Obama had been. After his election, President Trump proposed policies to fulfill this promise. For example, he said he would force Mexico to build a 2,000-mile **border wall**, require Mexico and Central American countries to stop migrants at their borders to keep them from getting to the U.S. border, and use the courts to end the DACA program. Further, he would restrict legal immigration, limit the number of "**green cards**" granted legal residents and

asylum seekers, and prevent all immigrants from receiving welfare within the first five years of their arrival.

This broad attack on immigration did discourage the number of migrants trying to get into the United States by 2019. Many welcomed the changes as a needed pause after a period of dramatic increase in immigration, while others criticized these policies for abandoning an American tradition as a nation welcoming of, and built by, immigrants.

Influence of the American South and West

By 2000, almost 60 percent of Americans lived in the South or West. The increasing influence of the two regions was related to their growing economic and political power, which also affected their traditional cultures.

Economies By the 1980s, the Sun Belt was booming. The shift to the Sun Belt continued in the 1990s and 2000s because of its friendly business environment of small government, low taxes, weak labor unions, and low-wage economies. By the 1990s, these states had improved their communication and transportation systems to support growth. Southern states had also desegregated their public institutions to the extent that the region no longer discouraged the relocation of large corporations. Oil helped Texas grow economically, and military installations drew people, defense industries, and aerospace firms to the Southwest, while favorable weather led to increased tourism in Southern California, Las Vegas, and Florida.

Political Power In addition to economic growth, the South and West dramatically increased their political influence. As these mostly conservative states increased their populations, they gained more seats in the House of Representatives and more electoral votes in presidential elections. These population shifts, along with the movement of Southern conservatives from the Democratic to the Republican Party, played an important role in the Republican majorities in both houses of Congress for the first time in 40 years. By the 1990s, most U.S. political leadership came from the Sun Belt. Before the election of Barack Obama of Illinois in 2008, the previous seven U.S. presidents had come from the Sun Belt. Meanwhile, the more liberal Northeast and Midwest, which had been the most influential regions in U.S. politics since the Civil War, lost representation in Congress and some of their former political influence.

Cultural Change The culture of the South and West became more influential throughout the country. For example, country and western music became increasingly popular in all regions. Ideas once associated with these regions, such as evangelical Protestant Christianity, conservative attitudes toward gender issues, and opposition to regulations on gun ownership spread.

On the other hand, the cultures of these regions also changed. The growing Hispanic population made Mexican food, Roman Catholic Christianity, and the Spanish language more common. The migration of Americans from other regions to Southern states modified its traditional "Southern" culture and made the region more urban and cosmopolitan. In some cases, such as Virginia, the migration caused them to become politically liberal, with Democrats gaining control of the state government and even passing gun regulations.

Electoral Vote Shift, 1980–2020

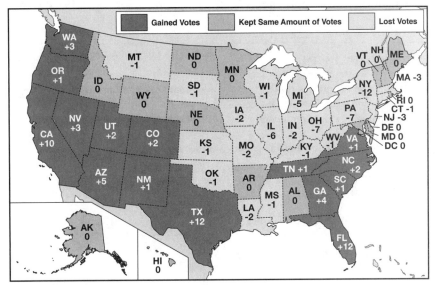

American Society in 2000

According to the 2000 census, the resident population of the United States was 281.4 million, making it the third most populous nation in the world, after China and India. The fastest-growing regions of the United States in the 1990s continued to be in the West and the South. The 2000 census reported that 50 percent of U.S. residents lived in suburbs, 30 percent in central cities, and only 20 percent in rural regions. Immigration was making the country more ethnically diverse.

A falling birthrate combined with an increase in life expectancy resulted in a population that was "graying." By 2000, 35 million people were over 65, but the fastest-growing segment of the population was those 85 and over. As the baby boom generation aged, concern about health care, prescription drugs, senior housing, and Social Security increased. In 2010, there were 2.9 workers for each beneficiary receiving Social Security. By 2035, the number of workers would decrease to 2.3.

The decline of the traditional family and the growing number of **single-parent families** was another national concern. The number of families headed by a female with no husband soared from 5.5 million in 1970 to 12.8 million in 2000. Single women headed 47.2 percent of Black families in 2000, but the same trend was also evident in White and Hispanic households with children under 18. Children in these families often grew up in poverty and without adequate support.

REFLECT ON THE LEARNING OBJECTIVE

1. Explain the causes and effects of international migration from 1980 to the present.

2. Explain the causes and effects of domestic migration from 1980 to the present.

KEY TERMS BY THEME

Immigration and Migration (MIG)
Immigration and Nationality Act of 1965
Immigration Reform and Control Act
   of 1986
Illegal Immigration Reform and Immigrant
   Responsibility Act of 1996

Deferred Action for Childhood Arrivals
   (DACA)
undocumented immigrants
border wall
green cards
asylum seekers
single-parent families

MULTIPLE-CHOICE QUESTIONS

Questions 1–2 refer to the excerpt below.

"The truth is, the central issue is not the needs of the 11 million illegal immigrants or however many. . . . Our government has no idea. . . . We will build a great wall along the southern border. . . .

AUDIENCE: Build the wall! Build the wall! Build the wall!

We've admitted 59 million immigrants to the United States between 1965 and 2015. Many of these arrivals have greatly enriched our country. So true. But we now have an obligation to them and to their children to control future immigration. . . . Within just a few years, immigration as a share of national population is set to break all historical records. . . . We take anybody. . . . Not anymore. . . .

We need a system that serves our needs, not the needs of others. Remember, under a Trump administration it's called America First. Remember that. . . . We will break the cycle of amnesty and illegal immigration. We will break the cycle. There will be no amnesty."

Donald J. Trump, campaign speech in Phoenix, September 1, 2016.

1. Which of the following best supports Trump's attack on previous administrations?
   (A) They had not built walls of any kind along the southern border.
   (B) They had not ended illegal immigration along the southern border.
   (C) They spent more money on welfare for illegal immigrants than for U.S. citizens.
   (D) They focused more on winning votes of immigrants than on the votes of native-born Americans.

2. Which of the following best explains the popularity of Trump's message expressed in this excerpt?
   (A) Trump had more experience and expertise than his opponents on national security issues.
   (B) Voters thought building a border wall would be part of a larger government jobs program.
   (C) Voters were influenced by their support for the America First movement of the 1930s.
   (D) Many working-class Americans blamed their wage stagnation on illegal immigration.

SHORT-ANSWER QUESTION

Use complete sentences; an outline or bulleted list alone is not acceptable.

1. Answer (a), (b), and (c).
   (a) Briefly explain ONE specific change in immigration patterns in the United States during and after the 1970s and its impact on diversity in America.
   (b) Briefly explain ONE specific effect of the growth of the Sun Belt on politics in the United States during the 1990s and 2000s.
   (c) Briefly explain ONE specific way that family structures were changing in the United States by the 2000s and its impact on society.

Challenges of the 21st Century

*There is not a Black America and a White America and Latino America
and Asian America—there's the United States of America.*

Barack Obama, Democratic National Convention keynote address, 2004

Learning Objective: Explain the causes and effects of the domestic and
international challenges the United States faced in the 21st century.

The United States entered the 21st century with unrivaled economic and
military dominance in the world. Few countries in history had been so
powerful. However, international terrorism, economic problems, and partisan
politics exposed the nation's vulnerabilities.

Disputed Election of 2000

The presidential election of 2000 was the closest since 1876 and the first ever to
be settled by the Supreme Court. President Clinton's vice president, **Al Gore**,
easily gained the nomination of the Democratic Party. Governor **George W.
Bush** of Texas, eldest son of former President George H. W. Bush, won the
nomination of the Republican Party. Both candidates fought over the moderate
and independent vote. Ralph Nader, the candidate for the Green Party, ran
a distant third, but he might have taken enough votes from Gore to make a
difference in Florida and other states.

Gore received over 500,000 more popular votes nationwide than Bush, but
victory hinged on who won Florida's 25 electoral votes. Bush led by only 537
popular votes in Florida after a partial recount. Then the Democrats asked for
manual recounts of the error-prone punch cards. The Supreme Court of Florida
ordered recounts of all the votes, as requested by the Gore campaign.

Then the Bush campaign appealed to the U.S. Supreme Court. In ***Bush v.
Gore,*** the U.S. Supreme Court issued a 5–4 decision that overruled the Florida
Supreme Court, making Bush the victory. The majority ruled that the varying
standards used in Florida's recount violated the Equal Protection Clause of the
14th Amendment, so the recount should be halted. The division on the Court
reflected the division in the country. The five justices appointed by Republican
presidents voted to end the recount. The four justices appointed by Democratic
presidents voted to let the recount go forward.

Al Gore ended the election crisis by accepting the ruling. Governor Bush
won with 271 electoral votes against Gore's 266. (One elector abstained.)

The War on Terrorism

George W. Bush entered the White House with no foreign policy experience. However, he surrounded himself with veterans of previous Republican administrations. For example, his vice president, Dick Cheney, had served as secretary of defense under Bush's father. General **Colin Powell** became his secretary of state, the first African American to hold the job. President Bush's confident and aggressive approach against terrorism won over many Americans, but his administration often alienated other nations.

Roots of Terrorism The United States was faulted by many in the Arab world, as well as in the non-Arab world, for siding with Israel in the deadly cycle of violence between Palestinians and Israel. However, the causes of anti-Americanism often went deeper. After World War I, the Ottoman Empire, the last of the Islamic empires, was replaced in the Middle East by Western-style, secular nation-states. Religious fundamentalists decried modernization, including equality for women, and the corruption of the "House of Islam," an ancient Islamic ideal of a realm governed by the precepts of the Quran (Koran) and Sharia (Islamic law). They saw the stationing of U.S. troops in the Middle East after the Gulf War as another violation of their lands. Islamic extremists, such as supporters of **Al-Qaeda** ("The Base"), preached jihad, which they defined as a holy war against the "Jews and Crusaders." The goal of Al-Qaeda and others was to restore an Islamic caliphate, or realm, from North Africa to East Asia. The restrictive economic and political conditions in the Middle East also provided a fertile breeding ground for recruiting extremists.

Early Terrorist Attacks The threat of terrorism and **"asymmetric" warfare** in which a small band of militants could inflict great damage on a more powerful country was brought home to the United through several attacks.

- In 1993, a truck bombing of the World Trade Center in New York City killed six people.

- In 1998, bombings of U.S. embassies in Kenya and Tanzania killed over 200 people, including 12 Americans. The United States responded by bombing Al-Qaeda camps in Afghanistan and the Sudan. Al-Qaeda leader **Osama bin Laden** had fled to **Afghanistan** and allied himself with the **Taliban**, Islamic fundamentalists who controlled Afghanistan.

- In 2000, two suicide bombers in a small rubber boat nearly sank a billion-dollar warship, the **USS *Cole***, docked in the Middle Eastern country of Yemen.

September 11 Terror Attacks The coordinated attacks by Al-Qaeda terrorists in commercial airliners on the twin towers of the **World Trade Center** in New York City and the Pentagon near Washington, D.C., and a fourth plane that crashed in Pennsylvania, claimed nearly 3,000 lives on **September 11, 2001**. The attacks galvanized public opinion as nothing had since the Japanese attack on Pearl Harbor in 1941, and they empowered the Bush administration to take action.

Source: World Trade Center, September 11, 2001. Wikimedia Commons/Michael Foran

War in Afghanistan President Bush declared that he wanted Osama bin Laden and other Al-Qaeda leaders "dead or alive." The Taliban refused to turn over bin Laden and his associates. In the fall of 2001, a combination of U.S. bombings, U.S. special forces, and Afghan troops in the anti-Taliban Northern Alliance quickly overthrew the Taliban government. American and Afghan forces continued to pursue the remnants of Al-Qaeda in the mountains bordering Pakistan but failed to capture bin Laden. With U.S. support, Hamid Karzai became head of the government in Kabul, but Afghanistan remained unstable and divided by the Taliban insurgency and tribal conflicts.

Homeland Security After the 9/11 attacks, most Americans accepted more extensive security measures such as background checks and airport searches. The **USA PATRIOT Act** of 2001 gave the U.S. government unparalleled powers to obtain information and to expand surveillance and arrest powers. However, many Americans were troubled by unlimited wiretaps and the collection of records about cell-phone calls and emails. Some also objected to the use of military tribunals to try suspects accused of terrorism and the indefinite imprisonment and alleged torture of suspects at a U.S. military prison in the Guantánamo Bay Naval Base in Cuba.

To better protect against terrorism, the Bush administration created a new **Department of Homeland Security** by combining more than 20 federal agencies with 170,000 employees. Among these were the Secret Service, the Coast Guard, and agencies dealing with customs and immigration. This was the largest reorganization of government since the creation of the Department of Defense after World War II. Many in Congress questioned why the FBI and CIA were left out of the new department. In 2004, a bipartisan commission on terrorism criticized the FBI and the CIA, as well as the Department of Defense, for failing to work together to "connect the dots" that might have uncovered the 9/11 plot. Congress followed up on the commission's recommendations, creating a **director of national intelligence** with the difficult job of coordinating the intelligence activities of all agencies.

Iraq War   In his 2002 State of the Union address, President Bush singled out Iraq, North Korea, and Iran as the **"axis of evil."** While U.S. intelligence agencies were finding no link between Iraq's **Saddam Hussein** and the September 11, 2001, attacks, the Bush administration publicly asserted there was. Furthermore, the Bush administration argued that Iraq was developing nuclear or biological **weapons of mass destruction (WMDs)** that it could use or sell to terrorists. Late in 2002, Secretary of State Powell negotiated an inspection plan with the UN Security Council, which Iraq accepted. UN inspectors would investigate Iraqi facilities to search for signs of weapon development. In the following months, the UN inspectors failed to find WMDs in Iraq.

Operation Iraqi Freedom   In early 2003, President Bush declared that Iraq had not complied with numerous UN resolutions and that "the game was over." Without support of the UN Security Council, the United States launched air attacks on Iraq on March 19. In less than four weeks, U.S. armed forces, with the support of the British and other allies, overran Iraqi forces, captured the capital city, Baghdad, and ended Hussein's dictatorship. When U.S. forces could not find WMDs in Iraq, criticism of the **"war of choice"** and the **"regime change"** mounted both at home and overseas.

The defeat of the Iraqi army and the capture of Saddam Hussein in late 2003 did not end the violence in Iraq. Diverse groups of insurgents (Sunni followers of the former dictator, Shiite militias, and foreign fighters, including Al-Qaeda) continued to attack U.S. and allied troops and one another. Millions of Iraqis fled the country or were displaced by the sectarian attacks. The Bush administration was widely criticized for going into Iraq without sufficient troops to control the country and for disbanding the Iraqi army. Photographs of the barbaric treatment of prisoners by U.S. troops at **Abu Ghraib** further diminished America's reputation in Iraq and around the world.

Elections of 2004 and a Bush Second Term

The Democrats approached the **elections of 2004** optimistic that they could unseat the incumbent president burdened by an increasingly unpopular war and limited economic recovery. Democratic voters selected Senator **John Kerry** of Massachusetts as their presidential candidate. The Republicans successfully energized their conservative base on issues such as the war against terrorism, more tax cuts, and opposition to abortion and gay marriage.

President Bush received 51 percent of the popular vote and captured 286 electoral votes to Kerry's 252. The Republicans also expanded their majorities in the Senate and House and continued to gain on the state level, especially in the South. This left the party in its strongest position since the 1920s.

Unresolved Wars The reconstruction of Iraq had made some headway by 2005, when the Iraqis held their first election, created a national assembly, and selected a prime minister and cabinet ministries, but the violence continued. On average, 100 Americans and 3,000 Iraqis were killed each month. In an attempt to reduce the violence, President Bush sent a "surge" of an additional 30,000 U.S. troops in early 2007. By late 2008, militia violence and American deaths were down in Iraq, and the United States had started to turn over control of the provinces to the Iraqi government.

In Afghanistan, the Taliban stepped up their attacks. For the first time, the number of Americans killed there outnumbered those killed in Iraq. President Bush turned over to the next president two unresolved wars and incomplete efforts to deal with nuclear threats from Iran and North Korea. The Bush administration, though, did have the satisfaction of knowing that there had not been another major terrorist attack in the United States since September 11, 2001.

Credit: Rockfinder

The war in Afghanistan began in 2001. By the time this photo was taken in 2013, the conflict was on its way to becoming the longest war in U.S. history.

Other Foreign Policies President Bush played an active role in selected global affairs. For example, he worked with European nations to expand the European Union and NATO, supported admission of China to the World Trade Organization, and brokered conflicts between India and Pakistan.

However, the Bush administration refused to join the **Kyoto Accord** to combat climate change, walked out of a UN conference on racism, abandoned the 1972 Anti-Ballistic Missile Treaty with Russia, and for years would not negotiate with North Korea or Iran. Critics questioned whether the administration valued cooperation with the nations of the world or instead followed a **unilateralist approach**. The president argued, in what became known as the "**Bush Doctrine**," that the old policies of containment and deterrence were no longer effective in a world of stateless terrorism. The president claimed that the United States was justified in protecting itself by using preemptive attacks to stop the acquisition of WMDs by terrorists and by nations that support terrorism.

Election of 2008

In 2008, the Democrats went through a long primary battle. The top candidates were former first lady and U.S. senator from New York **Hillary Clinton** and the charismatic 47-year-old African American junior senator from Illinois, **Barack Obama**. After winning the nomination, Obama chose as his running mate Joseph Biden of Delaware, an experienced member of the Senate. In the shadow of the unpopular Bush administration, the Republicans nominated Senator **John McCain** of Arizona, a Vietnam War hero and a political maverick who hoped to appeal to undecided voters.

Senator McCain briefly led in the polls, but Obama's message for change, his opposition to the Iraq War, and an economy on the brink of collapse helped the Democrats win in November. Obama received a decisive 364 electoral votes to McCain's 174 by taking eight states (including Florida, Ohio, Virginia, and North Carolina) that had been won by Bush in 2004. The Democrats also increased their majorities in the House and Senate well beyond their victories in 2006.

The election of the first African American president of the United States was historic. However, Barack Obama and the Democrats faced the country's worst economic crisis since the Great Depression, two unfinished U.S. wars, and a world increasingly skeptical of U.S. power and leadership. President Obama appointed his Democratic primary opponent, Hillary Clinton, as secretary of state and reappointed a Republican, Robert Gates, as secretary of defense to provide operational continuity in the Iraq and Afghanistan wars.

Foreign Policy of the Obama Presidency (2009–2017)

Barack Obama was elected in part because of his opposition to the Iraq War and his promise to end the unilateral approach overseas that had damaged the reputation of the United States during the Bush presidency. In general, the Obama administration was reluctant to use large-scale military actions that would put many U.S. troops on the ground. Instead, they opted for negotiations, targeted operations by special forces, and drone strikes. Critics attacked Obama for "leading from behind," but the issue remained unresolved whether more troops would solve or worsen conflicts in the Middle East and elsewhere.

Iraq In early 2009, the United States continued to wind down ground combat operations in Iraq. U.S. military support and air power helped the Iraqi forces battle insurgents through 2011, when the last of U.S. forces were withdrawn. However, sectarian violence between Sunni and Shiite Muslims erupted again.

Afghanistan The Obama campaign charged that the Bush administration had ignored Afghanistan in order to invade Iraq. As president, Obama made fighting Al-Qaeda and the Taliban in Afghanistan a priority. He approved adding 17,000 troops to the U.S. forces in Afghanistan in 2009 and then 30,000 more in 2010. The counterterrorism surge proved effective in Afghanistan, but the increased use of pilotless drone attacks on terrorists in Pakistan intensified anger against the United States. In 2012, President Obama and President Karzai of Afghanistan signed a long-term partnership agreement. After 2014, the new focus for U.S. forces was to train and support the Afghan military.

Death of Osama bin Laden In May 2011, Osama bin Laden, the leader of Al-Qaeda, was killed in Pakistan in a clandestine operation of the CIA and Navy SEALs. The death of bin Laden and other top leaders of Al-Qaeda raised the question of whether the U.S. role in the area was completed.

Arab Spring In June of 2009, President Obama traveled to Egypt and gave a speech at the University of Cairo calling for a "new beginning" in relations between the Islamic world and the United States. In 2010, Obama was soon tested by a wave of protests across the Middle East and North Africa, known as the "**Arab Spring**." Civil unrest and armed rebellion toppled governments in Tunisia, Libya (where the dictator, Muammar Gaddafi, was killed), Egypt (where the president, Hosni Mubarak, was imprisoned), and Yemen. However, the civil war in Syria created a greater humanitarian crisis as 12.5 million Syrian refugees tried to escape to safety, often to neighboring countries in the Middle East and Europe. President Obama was widely criticized for not intervening more effectively.

Rise of ISIS In Syria and Iraq, another terrorist movement, **ISIS** (Islamic State of Iraq and Syria, also known as ISIL) vowed to create a worldwide caliphate under strict Islamic law. This well-financed movement used social media to recruit fighters from around the world. Former members of the Iraqi military, driven from power in the U.S. invasion of Iraq in 2003, also joined ISIS. President Obama, while reluctant to return American soldiers to fight in Iraq and Syria, did commit American air power and trainers to help Iraq regain lost territories. By 2016, the United States had around 5,000 military personnel in Iraq.

Iran The Obama Administration joined other world powers in a 2015 agreement with Iran that would prevent Iran from developing and producing nuclear bombs for at least 15 years. Republicans opposed the agreement because it released the frozen assets of Iran, which it could use for conventional weapons and terrorism.

Asia Events in the Middle East limited President Obama's planned "pivot" to Asia. The administration understood that America's economic and strategic future was closely tied to the Pacific Rim. The United States and 11 other Pacific countries (excluding China) negotiated the Trans-Pacific Partnership (TPP) trade agreement in 2016. However, American public opinion turned against globalization, and the U.S. Senate did not ratify the TPP.

U.S. relations with China and North Korea also became more difficult under Obama. China's attempts to claim islands in the South China Sea threatened Southeast Asian nations and free passage through international waters guarded by the U.S. Navy. The most immediate threat to U.S. interests in Asia came from North Korea, which was developing nuclear weapons and long-range missiles.

Europe After the Great Recession of 2008, the European Union struggled with a debt crisis, especially in countries with weaker economies, such as Greece. The crisis passed, but the resulting fiscal austerity programs and the EU open-borders policies alienated many working-class people. This promoted a resurgence of nationalism among people who worried that they were losing their jobs and national identities.

Russia In 2014, **Ukraine**'s pro-Russian government was overthrown by a popular pro-Western movement. Russia, under **Vladimir Putin**, responded by orchestrating a revolt of pro-Russian partisans in eastern Ukraine and annexing the militarily strategic Crimea peninsula. The United States and European nations retaliated by placing economic sanctions on Russia and its leaders. A resurgent Russia also intervened in Syria's civil war, making it a player in Middle Eastern politics once again. By the end of the Obama administration, relations between the United States and Russia were at their lowest point since the end of the Cold War.

Cuba President Obama started a slow normalization of relations with **Cuba**. In 2015, the two countries agreed to open embassies in Havana and Washington and to resume direct flights for the first time since the Eisenhower administration. Against some Republican opposition, American travelers and businesses took advantage of the thaw in relations with the former Cold War enemy.

Cyber Attacks The greatest new threats to the nation's security in the 21st century were electronic. Cybercrime, such as stealing digital data, and cyber warfare, such as incapacitating the computerized networks that operate another country's electric power grid, threatened to be very destructive. Russians, Chinese, Iranians, and others used **cyber attacks** to steal U.S. private and governmental digital data, including credit card and personnel records. In 2016, Russian agents hacked documents and emails from Hillary Clinton's presidential campaign and released the information through the anti-secrecy group **WikiLeaks** in an effort to disrupt the U.S. election.

Domestic Policy of the George W. Bush Years (2001–2009)

On the domestic front, President George W. Bush aggressively pushed his conservative agenda: tax cuts, deregulation, federal aid to faith-based organizations, antiabortion legislation, school choice, privatization of Social Security and Medicare, drilling for oil and gas in the Alaskan wildlife refuge, and voluntary environmental standards for industry.

Republican Tax Cuts In 2001, Congress, enjoying a rare budget surplus, passed a $1.35 trillion-dollar tax cut spread over ten years. The bill lowered the top tax bracket, gradually eliminated estate taxes, increased the child tax credit and limits for IRA and 401(k) contributions, and gave all taxpayers an immediate tax rebate. In 2003, President Bush pushed through another round of tax cuts for stock dividends, capital gains, and married couples. Democrats criticized the tax cuts for giving most of the benefits to the richest 5 percent of the population and for contributing to the doubling of the national debt during the Bush presidency from about $5 trillion to $10 trillion. By the time Bush left office, the deficit was approaching 10 percent of GDP, about triple what economists thought was manageable.

Education and Health Reform President Bush championed the bipartisan **No Child Left Behind Act**. It aimed to improve student performance and close the gap between well-to-do and poor students in the public schools through testing of all students nationwide, granting students the right to transfer to better schools, funding stronger reading programs, and training high-quality teachers. Republicans also passed laws to give seniors enrolled in Medicare the option to enroll in private insurance companies. Congress also fulfilled a campaign promise by President Bush to provide prescription drug coverage for seniors. Democrats criticized the legislation as primarily designed to profit insurance and drug companies.

Economic Bubbles and Corruption The technology boom of the 1990s peaked in 2000 and was over by 2002. The stock market crashed; the Dow Jones Industrial Average fell by 38 percent. The unemployment rate climbed to 6 percent, and the number of people living in poverty increased for the first time in eight years.

Fraud and dishonesty committed by business leaders also hurt the stock market and consumer confidence in the economy. For example, the large corporations **Enron** and WorldCom had "cooked their books" (falsified stated earnings and profits) with the help of accounting companies.

The Federal Reserve fought the recession by cutting interest rates to 1.25 percent, the lowest in 50 years. The end of the technology boom-bust cycle (1995–2002) encouraged many investors to move their money into real estate, which created another speculative "bubble" (2002–2007) that would burst with even more tragic consequences in Bush's second term.

Washington Politics After his reelection victory in 2004, President Bush pushed Congress without success to **privatize Social Security** by encouraging Americans to invest part of their Social Security payroll deductions in various market investments. His administration also argued for immigration reform, which was blocked by conservatives who criticized it as "amnesty" for undocumented immigrants. President Bush did, however, leave a lasting impact on the federal courts by appointing two conservatives to the Supreme Court—**John Roberts** (as Chief Justice) and **Samuel Alito**—and increasing conservative majorities in the federal appellate courts.

When **Hurricane Katrina** hit the Gulf Coast hard and flooded New Orleans in August 2005, the Federal Emergency Management Agency (FEMA) failed both to anticipate and respond to the crisis. More than 1,000 people died, and tens of thousands of others (mostly poor people) were left in desperate conditions. Public dissatisfaction with the Katrina response, the Iraq War, and a variety of Republican congressional scandals involving bribery, perjury, and obstruction of justice helped the Democrats win control of both houses of Congress in 2006.

The Great Recession The housing boom of 2002–2007 was fueled by fraudulent mortgage lending and runaway real-estate speculation, particularly by nonbank financial institutions that worked with little government regulation. Wall Street firms packaged these high-risk loans into a variety of complex investments (**securitization**) and sold them to unsuspecting investors around the world.

However, as soon as housing prices started to dip, the bubble burst. Prices collapsed, foreclosures climbed, and investments worth trillions of dollars lost value. Investors panicked, which caused many banks and financial institutions at home and overseas to face failure. This resulted in a credit, or liquidity, crisis because banks either lacked funds or were afraid to make the loans to businesses and consumers that were necessary for the day-to-day functioning of the economy.

As the crisis within credit markets deepened, Americans were also hit with soaring gas prices (well over $4 a gallon), stock market declines of more than 40 percent, and rising unemployment. In early 2008, the federal government tried a $170 billion stimulus package and took over a few critical financial institutions, such as quasigovernmental mortgage institutions **Fannie Mae** and **Freddie Mac**.

However, the crisis was not over. In September, the bankruptcy of the large Wall Street investment bank **Lehman Brothers** led to panic in the financial industry. This persuaded the Bush administration to ask Congress for additional funds to help U.S. banks and restore the credit markets. Congress passed the controversial Economic Stabilization Act of 2008, creating a $700 billion **Troubled Assets Relief Program (TARP)** to purchase from financial institutions failing assets that included mortgages and mortgage-related securities. Some conservatives attacked TARP as "socialism," while some liberals attacked it as a bailout of the Wall Street executives who had caused the problems.

As with the Great Depression of 1929, the causes of this crash will be debated for years. Some blamed the Federal Reserve for keeping interest rates too low. Others criticized excessive deregulation of the financial industry. And others saw the cause in government efforts to promote home ownership. Moreover, real-estate bank fraud and Ponzi schemes that cost investors tens of billions of dollars in losses also helped to destroy investor confidence. Whatever its causes, the crisis significantly affected the 2008 election.

Domestic Policy of the Obama Presidency (2009–2017)

The rapidly growing economic crisis dominated the transition between President Bush and President Obama. Congress approved the use of the second half of the controversial TARP funding—$350 billion. At Obama's request, Bush used more than $10 billion of TARP funds to support the failing automakers General Motors (GM) and the Chrysler Corporation. Republicans largely rejected the president's efforts at bipartisanship legislation.

However, during Obama's first term, Democrats controlled the House and briefly had enough Senate votes to stop filibusters and so could pass legislation with little Republican support. Several Republicans did vote to confirm the appointments of **Sonia Sotomayor** and **Elena Kagan** to the Supreme Court. Since the new justices replaced other liberals, Justice Anthony Kennedy remained the swing vote in many 5–4 decisions.

Economic Stimulus The **Great Recession** of 2008 started in the United States. During the downturn, the stock market lost half of its value and unemployment peaked at more than 10 percent. Relying on Keynesian economic ideas to avoid a greater depression, Obama and the Democrats enacted a number of programs to promote recovery and financial reform.

The **American Recovery and Reinvestment Act** of 2009 provided a $787 billion economic stimulus package designed to create or save 3.5 million jobs. Included was $288 billion for tax cuts to stimulate spending and $144 billion to help state and local governments maintain services. The balance of the package was for construction projects, health care, education, and renewable energy. The **Federal Reserve**, under the leadership of economist and scholar of the Great Depression Ben Bernanke, also promoted recovery. It lowered interest rates and injected $600 billion dollars into the banking system.

With the domestic auto industry near collapse, the federal government became deeply involved in its recovery. The government temporarily took over General Motors ("Government Motors") while the company went through bankruptcy and guided the sale of Chrysler to Fiat, an Italian automaker. The popular "Cash for Clunkers" program provided $3 billion in incentives to U.S. residents to scrap old cars in order to promote sales and to purchase new, more fuel-efficient vehicles.

Financial Reforms The Great Recession revealed serious flaws in the federal oversight of financial institutions after the deregulation that began in the 1970s. The comprehensive **Dodd-Frank Wall Street Reform and Consumer Protection Act** (2010) was designed to improve regulation of banking and investment firms and to protect taxpayers from future bailouts of businesses that were "too big to fail." The act also set up a new **Consumer Financial Protection Bureau (CFPB)** to regulate consumer products, such as mortgages and credit cards. Some criticized the act for not breaking up the big banks that contributed to the meltdown of the economy and needed the bailouts.

By late 2016, the economy looked far stronger than in 2010. It had added 15 million jobs, the unemployment rate had fallen to 4.6 percent, and the

Dow Jones Industrial Average was up 210 percent. The new CFPB had already investigated nearly one million consumer banking and credit card complaints and provided $11.7 billion in relief for more than 27 million consumers. However, the Obama administration was still criticized for a slow recovery, and a lower percentage of Americans were working than before the recession.

Environment and Climate Change The Obama administration used the stimulus bill to reduce reliance on oil and increase development of alternative energy sources, such as solar and wind power. Auto manufacturers were encouraged to produce more hybrid and electric cars. In 2015, the United States joined 195 other nations in the **Paris Agreement** to reduce global carbon emissions. However, many in Congress disagreed with the science behind climate change and opposed tighter controls of greenhouse gases caused by the use of fossil fuels, making the environment another partisan issue.

Education In the stimulus package, Obama promoted reforms in early childhood and K–12 education (Race to the Top), including more private-public partnerships and more use of charter schools. Democrats attacked the growing college loan debt crisis by cutting out private banks in the federal college-loan program. The bipartisan **Every Student Succeeds Act** was signed into law in 2015 to replace No Child Left Behind, which had been attacked for excessive testing and for supporting efforts to develop common curriculum standards across the country. The new law placed more emphasis on local and state flexibility.

Budget Deficits The recession decreased federal tax receipts, increased federal spending to avoid a depression, and shrank the overall economy. As a result, total national debt initially ballooned under Obama. Congressional efforts to reduce deficit spending were stymied by Democrats who opposed cuts to social services and by Republicans who fought tax increases: *compromise* had become a dirty word in Washington. Despite the stalemate in Congress, renewed economic growth reduced the burden of the annual deficit. It declined from almost 10 percent of GDP at the depth of the recession to under 3 percent in 2016, a level most economists thought the government could afford.

Health Care The U.S. "fee for service" medical system was the most expensive in the world but produced mixed results. It promoted innovation but left more than 45 million people outside the system to seek medical care in emergency rooms. The Patient Protection and **Affordable Care Act** of 2010 ("**Obamacare**") aimed to extend affordable health insurance to an additional 25 million Americans through combinations of subsidies, mandates, insurance exchanges, and expansion of Medicaid while introducing medical and insurance reforms to control health care costs. The act required insurance companies to accept patients regardless of preexisting conditions, allowed children to remain on their parents' insurance until age 26, and funded wellness exams and women's medical needs. Republicans opposed the law for its regulations and costs, but after a slow rollout, nearly 20 million Americans gained coverage through private health insurance or Medicaid.

Other Presidential Initiatives President Obama signed a number of executive orders to overturn actions of the Bush administration. He placed a formal ban on torture by requiring that army field manuals be used as the guide for interrogating terrorist suspects. The new president expanded stem cell research and ended restrictions on federal funding of overseas health organizations. One of the first bills passed by Congress that Obama signed was the Lilly Ledbetter Fair Pay Act that strengthened protection of equal pay for female employees. He had promised to close the U.S. prison at Guantánamo Bay, Cuba, but failed to win needed congressional support.

The Tea Party The opposition to government spending and to "Obamacare" coalesced in a loosely united conservative and libertarian movement known as the **Tea Party**. While many in the movement focused on debt and health care, others emphasized expanding gun rights, outlawing abortions, and preventing undocumented immigration. Fueled by Tea Party energy, the Republicans in 2010 took control of the House with a 242 to 193 majority. In the Senate, the Republicans reduced the Democrats' majority to 53 votes, which consisted of 51 Democrats and 2 independents who caucused with them.

Elections and Money In 2010, the Supreme Court ruled in *Citizens United v. Federal Election Commission* that corporations were "legal persons" and had the same rights as individuals to buy ads to influence political elections. This ruling opened a flood of new money into politics from wealthy donors. As individual donors replaced traditional party fundraising, the parties became weaker.

Election of 2012 The presidential election of 2012 was dominated by issues related to the Great Recession, the Affordable Care Act, immigration, and the long-term fiscal health of the United States. Republicans conducted a long, hard-fought battle for their party's nomination before selecting **Mitt Romney**, former governor of Massachusetts. President Obama defeated Romney 332 to 206 in the Electoral College and by five million popular votes. The president ran strongly among Hispanics, winning 71 percent of their votes.

In Congress, Republicans could celebrate after the election of 2012 by keeping their strong majority in the House of Representatives, while the Democrats retained control of the Senate. However, the election of 2014 again proved the strength of the Republican turnout in nonpresidential elections as the Republicans took control of both the House and Senate.

Government in Deadlock During Obama's first term, the divisions between the Democratic president and the Republican-controlled Congress were so serious that Standard & Poor's downgraded the government's credit rating. These differences continued through the last four years of Obama's presidency. Compromise was difficult and rare, and as a result, little significant legislation was signed into law. The sharply divided government produced one one budget stalemate after another and even a Republican threat to default on the national debt.

One high-profile point of conflict was the Affordable Care Act. After Republicans regained control of the House, they unsuccessfully tried more than 50 times to overturn or defund the ACA.

The two parties did pass one major tax compromise in January 2013. It preserved the Bush tax cuts for incomes of $400,000 and less and allowed the top tax rate to rise to 39.6 percent for higher incomes. However, Congress was unable to compromise on the annual budget, so **sequestrations** (automatic cuts) went into effect across both domestic and defense spending. Neither party liked the impact on military and domestic programs, but the deep divisions prevented compromise. In October 2013, Republicans carried out their threat to shut down the federal government, which remained closed for 16 days.

The unexpected death of Justice Antonin Scalia in February 2016 opened a new arena for conflict. Senate Republicans refused to hold hearings for Obama's Supreme Court nominee, Merrick Garland. As a result, the Supreme Court had only eight members for 13 months. When the Court deadlocked 4–4, it could not rule on decisions made in the lower federal courts.

The Trump Presidency and the Election of Biden

The flood of refugees and immigrants into Europe from the Middle East and Africa fueled a worldwide backlash against immigration and globalization. In the United States, the unsolved issues of 11 million undocumented immigrants and the loss of manufacturing jobs to new technology and to lower-wage countries in Asia and Latin America set the stage for a dramatic political upset.

2016 Election The most vocal U.S. leader against globalization was Donald J. Trump, a well-known real estate developer and reality TV show personality. He became a prominent political figure by fueling the false belief that Obama was not born in the United States. He criticized Washington politicians ("drain the swamp"), unwanted immigration ("build the wall"), and international trade deals (such as NAFTA). Trump's effective use of slogans ("Make America Great Again"), social media (Twitter), and large rallies won him the Republican Party's presidential nomination. In the Democratic Party, Hillary Clinton, former secretary of state, U.S. senator, and first lady, became the first woman nominated for president by a major party. She vowed to build on Obama's achievements by expanding access to health care and continuing U.S. leadership globally.

Early polls favored Clinton. However, Trump's bold attacks energized some working-class voters, adding them to the traditional Republican base. Though Trump lost the popular vote by three million votes, he won the closely contested "swing" states of Pennsylvania, Ohio, Michigan, Wisconsin, and Florida. As a result, he received 306 electoral votes against Clinton's 232 votes, giving him a solid victory. The Republican Party held control of the House and Senate.

Trump's Domestic Policy President Trump emphasized tax cuts, deregulation of the private sector, trade protection, and immigration control. In 2017, he signed the Tax Cuts and Jobs Act, which cut the corporate tax rate from 35 to 21 percent, temporarily lowered personal tax brackets, and raised the threshold for estate taxes to $11 million per individual. The cuts mostly benefitted wealthy Americans and resulted in a sharp increase in the federal deficit. The Republicans dismantled parts of the Dodd-Frank Act that regulated banks and consumer borrowing and overturned Obama era regulations to control greenhouse gases.

Trump used executive orders to weaken Obama's Affordable Care Act by eliminating the mandate to buy health insurance and to overturn DACA, an Obama program that stopped deportation of individuals who had entered the country with their families as children. His administration discouraged illegal immigration with get-tough policies at the border and cooperation with Mexico and Central American countries to restrict people leaving them.

President Trump fulfilled another campaign promise by filling over 200 vacancies in the federal courts with conservative judges, including three Supreme Court justices: Neil Gorsuch, Brett Kavanaugh and Amy Coney Barrett. By 2019, President Trump enjoyed the lowest unemployment rate (3.5 percent) in decades, steady business growth, and a booming stock market.

However, Trump failed to deliver on his pledges to propose a replacement for the ACA and to persuade Mexico to pay for a border wall. In addition, Trump's term was marked by frequent firings and resignations of top officials, and the president was repeatedly cited by fact-checking services for making false statements.

Trump's Foreign Policy On the international front, Trump pledged to follow an "America First" policy. He pulled the United States out of the Intermediate-Range Nuclear Forces Treaty with Russia, the Paris Agreement to curb climate change, the Trans-Pacific Partnership, the UN Human Rights Council, and UNESCO, and he announced that the U.S. would withdraw from the World Health Organization. Further, he threatened to leave NATO and the World Trade Organization. Trump placed tariffs on China with mixed results, including increased prices for U.S. consumers, difficulties for U.S. manufacturers that relied on parts imported from China, and reduced agricultural exports to China. However, the tariffs led to a "Phase 1" trade agreement that softened the impact of the trade war.

With Iran, Trump withdrew the United States from the six-nation agreement to restrict Iran's development of nuclear weapons and ordered the assassination of a top Iranian general who had been involved in terrorist attacks. In a strategy to isolate Iran, the administration brokered Arab-Israel peace agreements with UAE, Bahrain, Sudan, and Morocco, which some of his critics supported.

Investigation and Impeachment In 2017, the Justice Department appointed Robert Mueller to lead an investigation into the Russian government's interference in the 2016 election. The investigation resulted in 34 indictments and 8 convictions of Trump campaign staff. However, following Justice Department guidelines against indicting a sitting president, Mueller did not make an explicit recommendation to indict Trump.

After the Democrats gained control of the House in the 2018 elections, they impeached President Trump for abuse of power and obstruction of Congress for withholding military aid to Ukraine in exchange for evidence against the Biden family. In February 2020, the Republican majority in the Senate found Trump not guilty. Democrats generally saw Trump's actions as a threat to the rule of law. Some Republicans labeled Mueller's investigation as a "witch hunt" based on unproven charges. Others argued that what Trump did was not an impeachable offense.

2020 Pandemic The virus COVID-19 was first identified in China in December 2019. The first case in the United States was confirmed on January 20, 2020. While the Trump administration restricted travel from China and later from Europe, he consistently rejected the warnings of his advisors and downplayed the significance of the disease. With a lack of federal leadership, the United States was slow in testing for the virus and in manufacturing critical medical supplies, and policies across the 50 states were inconsistent. Many American refused to wear masks or practice social distancing, seeing these actions as violations of their personal liberties. Together, these factors contributed to the United States having one of the poorest records among advanced nations in its initial response to the crisis. By early 2021, over 500,000 Americans had died.

The pandemic caused many schools and all but essential businesses to close. Tens of millions of people lost their jobs and many businesses failed. The economic disruption did benefit Internet and e-commerce companies. Congress and the Federal Reserve responded with a series of aid programs costing over $7 trillion to help the unemployed, small businesses, and industries. President Trump's Operation Warp Speed, a $10 billion government program to help pharmaceutical companies develop COVID-19 vaccines at a record pace, proved successful, with the first shots given in December 2020.

Election of 2020 The pandemic curtailed large political rallies and promoted voting by mail. The government's response to the pandemic and economic stress contributed to President Trump's decline in the polls. The Democrats nominated 78-year-old Joseph Biden, Barack Obama's former vice president. He picked California Senator Kamala Harris as his vice president, the first person of color for the position.

In a historic turnout of more than 66 percent of eligible voters, Biden and Harris won by seven million votes, receiving 306 electoral votes to Trump's 232. Yet President Trump, without evidence, claimed he had won. After months of recounts and court rulings, no serious fraud was found. However, Trump continued to energize his followers to "Stop the Steal."

Attack on the Capitol and a Second Impeachment Finally, on January 6, 2021, the date the Senate was to accept the electoral votes from the 50 states, Trump held a rally near the White House, encouraging his supporters to march to the Capitol. That march turned into an attack on the Capitol, the first since

Source: Wikimedia

On January 6, a mob vowing to overturn the election attacked the Capitol.

the British invasion in 1814. Five people died and hundreds were injured, as lawmakers and their staff members fled for their lives. After troops overcame the mob, the Senate finally confirmed Biden as president.

Trump's actions before and during the attack on the Capitol resulted in his becoming the first president ever to be impeached twice by the House of Representatives. In the Senate, the vote to convict him won bipartisan, majority support but not the two-thirds needed to pass.

Biden's Administration Speaking to a deeply divided nation, President Biden called for unity in his inaugural address: "Every disagreement doesn't have to be a cause for total war." His priority was to end the suffering from the pandemic, in part through a $1.9 trillion aid package for struggling Americans and by vaccinating every American against COVID-19 by the fall of 2021.

HISTORICAL PERSPECTIVES: *WHAT DOES FREEDOM MEAN?*

Freedom is a major theme of American history, but people have always disagreed on what "freedom" means. The most dramatic example of this was the Civil War. Both sides fought in the name of freedom, but for Confederates the right to enslave others was a "freedom."

Contests over Freedom In *The Story of American Freedom* (1999), Eric Foner traced America's thoughts about freedom from the struggle for independence through the Reagan era. The Reconstruction, Progressive, New Deal, and Civil Rights eras enlarged the meaning of freedom to include equal rights for more people, often by expanding the power of government to protect individuals. During the Reagan Revolution, freedom was frequently defined as reducing the power of "big government" by cutting federal regulations. Foner attributed this change to reactions against federal court rulings promoting desegregation, equality, privacy, abortion rights, and other issues.

Diverse Expressions of Freedom David Hackett Fischer, in *Liberty and Freedom* (2005), pursued its meaning through American visual expressions, customs, and what Tocqueville called "habits of the heart." Fischer's analysis of the images and symbols from the Liberty Trees of the American Revolution through the protest posters of the late 20th century revealed the rich diversity of traditions about freedom that eluded abstract definitions. Hackett concluded that the United States remains free because of its diversity of traditions about freedom. He believes that the gravest threat to freedom comes from those incapable of imagining any vision of freedom except their own.

Develop an Argument *Explain two perspectives on the meaning of "freedom."*

REFLECT ON LEARNING OBJECTIVE

1. Explain the causes and effects of two international challenges the United States faced in the 21st century.

2. Explain the causes and effects of two domestic challenges the United States faced in the 21st century.

KEY TERMS BY THEME

Bush Foreign Policy (WOR)
George W. Bush
Al Gore
Bush v. Gore
Colin Powell
Al-Qaeda
Osama bin Laden
Afghanistan
Taliban
"asymmetric" warfare
USS *Cole*
World Trade Center
September 11, 2001
USA PATRIOT Act
Department of Homeland Security
director of national intelligence
Saddam Hussein
"axis of evil"
weapons of mass destruction (WMDs)
Operation Iraqi Freedom
"war of choice"
"regime change"
Abu Ghraib
Kyoto Accord
Bush Doctrine
unilateralist approach

Obama Foreign Policy (WOR)
Hillary Clinton

Barack Obama
John McCain
Arab Spring
ISIS
Ukraine
Vladimir Putin
Cuba
cyber attacks
WikiLeaks

Bush Domestic Policy (PCE)
No Child Left Behind Act
Enron
elections of 2004
John Kerry
privatize Social Security
Hurricane Katrina
John Roberts
Samuel Alito

Great Recession (WXT)
securitization
Fannie Mae
Freddie Mac
Lehman Brothers
Troubled Assets Relief Program (TARP)
Great Recession
American Recovery and Reinvestment Act
Federal Reserve

Dodd-Frank Wall Street Reform and Consumer Protection Act
Consumer Financial Protection Bureau

Obama Domestic Policy (PCE)
Sonia Sotomayor
Elena Kagan
Paris Agreement
Every Student Succeeds Act
Affordable Care Act
"Obamacare"
Tea Party
Mitt Romney
sequestrations

Trump Presidency (PCE)
"Brexit"
undocumented immigrants
Donald J. Trump
"Make America Great Again"
Tax Cuts and Jobs Act
Neil Gorsuch
Brett Kavanaugh
border wall
Robert Mueller
impeachment
"America First"
United States-Mexico-Canada Agreement (USMCA)

MULTIPLE-CHOICE QUESTIONS

Questions 1–3 refer to the excerpt below.

"These militants are not just the enemies of America or the enemies of Iraq. They are the enemies of Islam, and they're the enemies of humanity. . . .

[I]t is cowardice that seeks to kill children and the elderly with car bombs, and cuts the throat of a bound captive, and targets worshipers leaving a mosque. It is courage that liberated more than 50 million people from tyranny. And it is courage in the cause of freedom that will once again destroy the enemies of freedom!

Islamic radicalism, like the ideology of communism, contains inherent contradictions that doom it to failure. By fearing freedom, by distrusting human creativity, and punishing change, and limiting the contributions of half a population, this ideology undermines the very qualities that make human progress possible and human societies successful. The only thing modern about the militants' vision is the weapons they want to use against us. The rest of their grim vision is defined by a warped image of the past, a declaration of war on the idea of progress itself."

George W. Bush, Veterans Day speech, November 11, 2005

1. Which of the following was the most direct cause for this speech by President Bush?

   (A) The attack on the Twin Towers in New York

   (B) The resurgence of the Taliban in Afghanistan

   (C) The challenge to control the violence in Iraq

   (D) The breakdown of relations with Iran

2. President Bush's comparison of Islamic radicalism to communism is best supported by the claim that both opposed

   (A) education for all children as a path to progress

   (B) basic human rights for all individuals

   (C) government efforts to promote cultural change

   (D) modern advances in technology such as personal communications

3. Bush's comment about "limiting the contributions of half a population" is a reference to

   (A) the divide between Muslims and non-Muslims in many countries

   (B) the struggle between Sunni and Shiite factions for power in Iraq

   (C) the conflict between ISIS and its rivals in the Middle East

   (D) the denial of equal rights for women by many militants

SHORT-ANSWER QUESTIONS

Use complete sentences; an outline or bulleted list alone is not acceptable.

1.

Source: Otherwords.org

Using the image above, answer (a), (b), and (c).

(a) Briefly describe ONE historical perspective expressed in the image.

(b) Briefly explain how ONE specific event or development in the Middle East after 2000 contributed to the perspective depicted in the image.

(c) Briefly explain ONE specific historical effect of increased U.S. involvement in the Middle East after 2000.

2. Answer (a), (b), and (c).

(a) Briefly explain ONE specific historical event or development that contributed to the Great Recession of 2008.

(b) Briefly explain ONE specific political impact of the Great Recession of 2008.

(c) Briefly explain ONE specific program created by the George W. Bush or Barack Obama administration to deal with the Great Recession.

Causation in Period 9

Learning Objective: Explain the relative significance of the effects of change in the period after 1980 on American national identity.

One way to evaluate effects on the national identity is to look at who Americans were becoming in this period after 1980. The significant shift of migration to the Sun Belt affected how many Americans thought about the nation. The norms of the urban and more liberal Northeast and Midwest were challenged in the South, where people favored less government, little regulation of business, and a more active role for religion. One could argue that the culture wars fought over these differences left Americans with deeply divided views of the national identity. The change in immigration patterns from predominantly ethnic European countries to Asian, Latin American, and African countries also sparked fears among older White majorities about what was happening to the national identity, and the identity of America in 2050 and beyond.

Economic Division The economic changes after 1980 were particularly negative for many lower- and middle-class Americans. In previous decades, they had won prosperity and security from industrial growth, strong unions, and the social safety net policies of the New Deal and Great Society. However, new technology, globalization, and pro-business public policies meant that the benefits of economic growth were distributed unequally. The identity of the United States as the land of opportunity suffered in both the old industrial centers of the Rust Belt and in the new low-wage economy of the Sun Belt.

At the same time, the American dream and entrepreneurial opportunities remained strong for well-educated people in urban centers. The result caused deeper divisions between rural and urban regions and between working-class and upper-class Americans. Critics wondered if America's democracy would survive the inequality caused by the concentration of wealth.

Foreign Affairs The end of the Cold War and the rise of terrorism also left Americans with a less clear mission of how to use the country's military power. Formerly, the country could focus on a single foe, such as the Soviet Union, that could be deterred by a large military. Replacing it were stateless terrorists scattered around the world with access to powerful explosives. After 2001, the large-scale use of American troops in the Middle East, a region with deep-rooted conflicts, seemed inappropriate to many. These challenges again left Americans divided over the U.S. role in the world. Would it be a partner in collective security pacts with other nations, a superpower that would take unilateral action for its own purposes, or a bystander in a type of isolationism?

QUESTIONS ABOUT CAUSE AND EFFECT

1. Evaluate the extent to which changes in immigration and migration after 1980 contributed to changes in American national identity.

2. Evaluate the extent to which changes in the American economy after 1980 contributed to changes in American national identity.

THINK AS A HISTORIAN: *ARGUMENTATION—DEVELOPING COMPLEXITY*

To do well on the AP® exam, you will need to develop and support complex arguments, ones that are detailed and demonstrate four skills:

- **Explain the nuance.** Nuance means subtlety or precision. A nuanced argument analyzes multiple variables related to that argument.
- **Explain connections.** These connections should be relevant, which means related to the argument. They should also be insightful, which means you understand why they are important on a deep level.
- **Explain significance.** Beyond merely citing names and dates, you should describe the argument's credibility, signficance, and possible limitations.
- **Explain effectiveness.** Is this evidence solid enough, relevant enough, and important enough to strengthen the argument? Why or why not?

Being able to write a complex argument is one of the most challenging tasks for many students. Mastering it takes practice.

Choose one of the arguments below and answer the questions that follow.

Argument 1: After 1980, the United States became increasingly polarized between rural and urban regions.

Argument 2: Passage of the Americans with Disabilities Act in 1990 affected U.S. employment, transportation, and architecture in ways that still exist today.

Argument 3: The political philosophy of the United States is a struggle between proponents of "freedom to" have equal rights and participation and "freedom from" government regulations and restrictions.

1. How can you make this argument more nuanced? Describe details related to this argument that make it more precise or subtle.

2. What connections can you make, either within one historical period or across periods, that will help strengthen this argument?

3. What details can you add that are significant to this argument? Significant details should be closely connected to the argument and should help to illuminate it in some way.

4. How effective is the evidence you have provided to support the argument? Explain why your evidence is relevant, trustworthy, important, or persuasive.

UNIT 9 — Period 9 Review: 1980–Present

You can learn how to best use the 40 minutes allotted for the long essay by writing several timed essays. Allowing time to understand the task and gather your evidence before you start writing will likely result in a stronger essay. Leave time at the end of the 40 minutes to reread and evaluate your essay. As you evaluate your essay, start at the basic level: Did you fulfill the task the prompt requires? Check the key terms of the question and the key terms you use in your response, and be sure they align.

For an easy reminder of what else you should look for, remember this sentence: The clearest essays require care. The first letter of each word, T, C, E, R, and C, can remind you of the key elements your essay must contain:

1. **Thesis/claim:** The thesis must make a historically defensible claim that responds to the prompt and lays out a line of reasoning. It must also consist of one or more sentences located in one place, either in the introduction or the conclusion.

2. **Contextualization:** Place your thesis in historical context, relating the topic of the prompt to broader historical events, developments, or processes that occur before, occur during, or continue after the time frame of the question.

3. **Evidence:** Provide a number of specific and relevant pieces of evidence, and clearly show how they support your thesis.

4. **Reasoning:** Use the historical reasoning process of comparison, continuity and change, or causation to frame your argument. Use an organizational strategy appropriate to the reasoning process.

5. **Complexity:** Check that you have woven a complex understanding throughout your essay (or fully developed it in one place). Look for an explanation of multiple variables and both causes and effects, similarities and differences, and continuities and changes; connections across and within periods; the significance of a source's credibility and limitations; and the effectiveness of a historical claim.

Application: After answering one or more of the long essay questions on the next page, use "The clearest essays require care" to evaluate your essay. Make revisions where you believe you can make your essay stronger, clearer, or more aligned with the rubric expectations.

For current free-response question samples, visit: https://apcentral.collegeboard.org/ courses/ap-united-states-history/exam

LONG ESSAY QUESTIONS

In your response you should do the following:

- Respond to the prompt with a historically defensible thesis or claim that establishes a line of reasoning.
- Describe a broader historical context relevant to the prompt.
- Support an argument in response to the prompt using specific and relevant examples of evidence.
- Use historical reasoning (e.g., comparison, causation, continuity or change) to frame or structure an argument that addresses the prompt.
- Use evidence to corroborate, qualify, or modify an argument that addresses the prompt.

1. Evaluate the extent to which the conservative resurgence changed the political and policy goals of the United States government after 1980.

2. Evaluate the extent to which new developments in science and technology enhanced the economy and transformed society while manufacturing decreased.

3. Evaluate the extent to which the interventionist foreign policy of the Reagan administration continued in later administrations, even after the Cold War ended.

4. Evaluate the extent to which immigration and migration patterns changed in the United States after 1980.

5. Evaluate the causes of the growing divide between conservatives and liberals in American politics after 1980.

6. Evaluate the U.S. government's response to environmental concerns and the challenges of climate change since 1980.

U.S. History
Practice Examination

Section 1

Part A: Multiple Choice—55 minutes, 55 questions

Directions: *Two to four questions are in sets that focus on a primary source, secondary source, or other historical issue. Each question has four answers or completions. Select the best one for each question or statement.*

Questions 1–4 refer to the following excerpt.

> "Part of the myth about the first Americans is that all of them . . . had one culture . . . the white man turned everything upside down. Three elements were important in the early influence: the dislodgement of eastern tribes, the introduction of the horse, and metal tools and firearms.
>
> "The British invaders of the New World, and to lesser degree the French, came to colonize. They came in thousands to occupy the land. They were, therefore, in direct competition with the Indians and acted accordingly, despite their verbal adherence to fine principles of justice and fair dealing. The Spanish came quite frankly to conquer, to Christianize. . . . They came in small numbers. . . . and the Indian labor force was essential to their aims. Therefore they did not dislodge or exterminate the Indians. . . .
>
> "The Spanish, then, did not set populations in motion. That was done chiefly from the east. The great Spanish contribution was the horse."
>
> Oliver LaFarge, anthropologist, "Myths That Hide the American Indian," *The American Indian: Past and Present,* 1971

1. During the early years of colonization, French policy in North America was based primarily on which of the following?

   (A) Settling on lands controlled by American Indians

   (B) Controlling the fur trade

   (C) Farming in the Mississippi River Valley

   (D) Establishing a series of Catholic missions

2. United States policy toward the American Indians in the 19th century was most similar to the colonial Indian policy of the

   (A) British

   (B) Dutch

   (C) French

   (D) Spanish

3. Which of the following best describes something Europeans introduced in the Americas that helped American Indians survive colonization?

(A) New farming methods, which enabled American Indians to maintain their agricultural heritage

(B) Metal tools, which led to increased trade and better relationships with Europeans

(C) Horses, which transformed the cultures of American Indians on the Great Plains

(D) Christianity, which brought unity among American Indians

4. Which of the following generalizations best describes a similarity among European nations who colonized North America?

(A) All wanted to convert American Indians to Roman Catholicism.

(B) All included extensive marriage between Europeans and American Indians.

(C) All attempted to dominate American Indians in some way.

(D) All intended to exterminate or remove American Indians.

"Instructions to you, Vicente de Zaldivar. . . . of the expedition to New Mexico. . . . for the punishment of the pueblo of Acoma for having killed . . . soldiers. . . .

"Since the good success of the undertaking depends on the pleasure of God our Lord in directing you to appropriate and effective methods, it is right that you should seek to prevent public or private offenses to Him in the expedition. . . . You will proceed over the shortest route. . . . At the places and pueblos that you pass through on the way you will treat the natives well and not allow harm to be done them. . . .

"If God shall be so merciful as to grant us victory, you will arrest all of the people, young and old, without sparing anyone. Inasmuch as we have declared war on them without quarter, you will punish all those of fighting age as you deem best, as a warning to everyone in this kingdom."

Don Juan de Oñate, Spanish colonial official in New Mexico, 1599

5. The excerpt provides evidence to support the general claim that the Spanish who colonized America
   (A) viewed Native Americans as criminals who deserved no mercy
   (B) considered Native Americans as partners in serving the king
   (C) respected Native Americans as their equals in the eyes of God
   (D) treated some groups of Native Americans better than others

6. Which of the following best explains why Native Americans became so important to the Spanish empire?
   (A) Native Americans quickly filled powerful positions in the Spanish colonial government.
   (B) Native Americans provided most of the labor on Spanish-owned land.
   (C) Native Americans often joined the Spanish military.
   (D) Native Americans were primarily trading partners of the Spanish.

7. Officials in the Spanish colonies such as the writer of this excerpt received their authority to act from which of the following?
   (A) The joint-stock companies that began as trading ventures
   (B) A governor elected by residents of the colonies
   (C) The king of Spain who claimed control over the Spanish empire
   (D) The pope who led the Roman Catholic Church

Questions 8–10 refer to the following excerpt.

"Now we all found the loss of Captain Smith; yea, his greatest maligners could now curse his loss. As for corn provision and contribution from the savages, we had nothing but mortal wounds, with clubs and arrows. . . .

"Nay, so great was our famine that a savage we slew and buried, the poorer sort took him up again and ate him; and so did diverse one another boiled and stewed with roots and herbs. . . .

"This was that time, which still to this day, we called the starving time [1609–1610]. It were too vile to say, and scarce to be believed, what we endured; but the occasion was our own for want of providence, industry, and government, and not the barrenness and defect of the country. . . . For till then in three years, for the numbers were landed us, we have never from England provision sufficient for six months."

John Smith, *Works*, 1608–1631

8. The group most directly responsible for governing the colony and responding to the experience described in the excerpt were
   (A) the members of an assembly elected by colonists
   (B) the representatives who served in Parliament in England
   (C) the religious leaders who controlled the colony
   (D) the shareholders of a joint-stock company

9. The reference to Native Americans in the excerpt indicate that the relationship between them and the English settlers in the Chesapeake region was characterized by
   (A) frequent intermarriage between the two groups
   (B) shared suffering because of a lack of food in the region
   (C) conflicts over land and other resources
   (D) trade based primarily on gold and silver

10. One similarity between the colony described in the excerpt and the colony founded by the Pilgrims in Plymouth was that by 1620, both would
   (A) protect equal rights for all people
   (B) welcome settlers of all religious beliefs
   (C) have peaceful relations with Native Americans
   (D) develop a type of representative government

"I, Francis Daniel Pastorius . . . . laid out and planned a new town. . . . we called Germantown. . . . in a very fine and fertile district, with plenty of springs of fresh water, being supplied with oak, walnut, and chestnut trees, and having besides excellent and abundant pasturage for the cattle. . . .

"The air is pure and serene. . . . and we are cultivating many kinds of fruits and vegetables, and our labors meet with rich reward.

"Our surplus of grain and cattle we trade to Barbados for rum, syrup, sugar, and salt. The furs, however, we export to England for other manufactured goods. We are also endeavoring to introduce the cultivation of the vine, and also the manufacture of woolen cloths and linen, so as to keep our money as much as possible in the country. . . .

"William Penn is one of the sect of Friends. . . . Still he will compel no man to belong to his particular society."

Francis D. Pastorius, German colonist, *A Particular Geographical Description of the Lately Discovered Province of Pennsylvania,* 1700

11. Based on this excerpt, what does Pastorius think will cause people to settle in his community?

    (A) A desire to flee political persecution and have equal rights

    (B) A desire to escape poverty and find greater economic opportunity

    (C) A desire to move away from rural life and live in an urban area

    (D) A desire to leave Germany and become part of an English colony

12. The work done by colonists described in the excerpt supports the interpretation that the leaders of Pennsylvania had

    (A) rejected the emphasis on increasing the amount of gold in England

    (B) resisted the development of an agricultural economy

    (C) attempted to use American Indians as a labor force

    (D) planned to create a joint-stock company

13. Which of the following conditions could best be used to support the argument made in the last sentence of the excerpt?

    (A) Pennsylvania had its religious leaders serve as its political leaders.

    (B) Pennsylvania was a proprietary colony, so it was independent of English control.

    (C) Pennsylvania allowed settlers to practice religious faiths other than Quakerism.

    (D) Pennsylvania prohibited slavery while it was governed by Penn.

"I like much the general idea of framing a government into Legislative, Judiciary and Executive. . . . . I will now add what I do not like. First the omission of a bill of rights . . . .

"The second feature I dislike, and greatly dislike, is the abandonment in every instance of the necessity of rotation in office and most particularly in the case of [the] President. . . .

"I own that I am not a friend to very energetic government. . . .

"I think our governments will remain virtuous for many centuries; as long as they are chiefly agricultural; and this will be as long as there shall be vacant lands in any part of America. . . .

"Above all things I hope the education of the common people will be attended to; convinced that on their good sense we may rely with the most security for the preservation of a due degree of liberty."

Thomas Jefferson, letter to James Madison, December 1787

14. Jefferson's feelings about "rotation in office" were at least partially resolved by which of the following later actions?
    (A) The decision by George Washington not to run for a third term as president
    (B) The development by political parties of nominating conventions
    (C) The impeachment of Andrew Johnson for violating the Tenure of Office Act
    (D) The ratification of the 17th Amendment requiring the direct election of U.S. senators

15. Which of the following government actions did the most to make possible Jefferson's belief that "our governments will remain virtuous . . . as long as they [the citizens] are chiefly agricultural"?
    (A) Agreeing to the Louisiana Purchase
    (B) Passing the Embargo Act
    (C) Funding internal improvements
    (D) Establishing a national bank

16. Based on this excerpt, which of the following would Jefferson most likely have supported?

    (A) Expansion of voting rights to women, African Americans, and 18-year-olds

    (B) Establishment of publicly supported land-grant universities

    (C) Creation of an income tax

    (D) Prohibition of the sale of alcohol

17. Which statement best describes the context for understanding Jefferson's concern about a bill of rights?

    (A) Enlightenment ideas emphasized the importance of individual liberty.

    (B) Federalists refused to compromise on the issue of adding a bill of rights.

    (C) The debate over adding a bill of rights would continue until the Civil War.

    (D) Few states included a bill of rights in their own constitutions.

"I have now to perform the most pleasing task of exhibiting . . . the existing state of the unparalleled prosperity of the country. . . .

"The greatest prosperity which this people have enjoyed since the establishment of their present constitution, it would be exactly that period of seven years which immediately followed the passage of the tariff of 1824.

"This transformation of the condition of the country from gloom and distress to brightness and prosperity, has been mainly the work of American legislation, fostering American industry. . . .

"When gentlemen have succeeded in their design of an immediate or gradual destruction of the American system, what is their substitute? . . . . Free trade!

"Gentlemen are greatly deceived as to the hold which this system [the American system] has. . . . They represent that it is the policy of New England. . . . and most determined in its support is Pennsylvania. . . . Maryland was against it; now the majority is for it. . . . The march of public sentiment is to the South."

Henry Clay, "Defense of the American System," 1832

18. Which leader most clearly expressed ideas on trade and economic development similar to those held by Clay?

   (A) Alexander Hamilton when arguing in support of his financial plan

   (B) Thomas Jefferson while debating with the Federalists in the 1790s

   (C) James Madison during the War of 1812

   (D) James Monroe in response to foreign intervention in Latin America

19. The economic philosophy expressed in this excerpt was a response to a desire

   (A) to connect the American West with the East to create national self-sufficiency

   (B) to persuade European countries to reduce tariffs on imported American goods

   (C) to reverse the declines in the exports of cotton to Great Britain and France

   (D) to acquire lands from Mexico that would become slave states

20. Which of the following later groups would strongly oppose the ideas about trade expressed in this excerpt?

(A) Owners of manufacturing companies during the Civil War

(B) Leaders of the Republican Party in the late 1800s

(C) Most Populists and Progressives

(D) Supporters of the Hawley-Smoot Tariff

21. The most persistent opposition to Clay's ideas in this excerpt came from which of the following groups?

(A) Industrialists who faced competition from British companies

(B) Politicians who opposed to the expansion of slavery into the territories

(C) Judges who thought the Constitution supported a strong federal government

(D) Plantation owners who primarily raised cotton for export

Questions 22–25 refer to the following excerpt.

"We. . . . declare that this act on our part implies no sanction of, nor promise of voluntary obedience to such of the present laws of marriage, as refuse to recognize the wife as an independent, rational being. . . .

"We believe that personal independence and equal human rights can never be forfeited, except for crime; that marriage should be an equal and permanent partnership, and so recognized by law; that until it is so recognized, married partners should provide against the radical injustice of present laws, by every means in their power.

"We believe that where domestic difficulties arise, no appeal should be made to legal tribunals under existing laws, but that all difficulties should be submitted to the equitable adjustment of arbitrators mutually chosen.

"Thus reverencing law, we enter our protest against rules and customs which are unworthy of the name, since they violate justice, the essence of law."

Lucy Stone, speech at her marriage, 1855

22. Which of the following groups would be most likely to support the views expressed by Stone in this excerpt?

(A) Participants in the Second Great Awakening

(B) Members of the American Party

(C) Supporters of the Liberty Party

(D) Individuals who attended the Seneca Falls Convention

23. The words and ideals expressed in the excerpt fostered which of the following later reforms in U.S. history?

(A) The union movement in the late 19th century

(B) The antiwar movement in World War I

(C) The rise of isolationism in the 1920s

(D) The feminist movement that began in the 1960s

24. At the time this excerpt was written, which of the following activities were women legally able to do in most states?

(A) Work in factories

(B) Vote in federal elections

(C) Hold political office

(D) Serve on juries

25. What does Stone mean by "marriage should be an equal and permanent partnership"?

   (A) In the 19th century, wives and husbands did not have the same legal rights.

   (B) Until the Civil War, marriage was a religious ceremony rather than a government one.

   (C) One of the reforms of the Jacksonian era was to outlaw divorce.

   (D) In 1855, most people thought of marriage as a business arrangement.

Questions 26–28 refer to the following excerpt.

"We want peace and good order at the South; but it can only come by the fullest recognition of the rights of all classes. . . .

"We simply demand the practical recognition of the rights given us in the Constitution and laws. . . .

"The vicious and exceptional political action had by the White League in Mississippi has been repeated in other contests and in other states of the South, and the colored voters have been subjected therein to outrages upon their rights similar to those perpetrated in my own state at the recent election . . . and we ask such action as will not only protect us in the enjoyment of our constitutional rights but will preserve the integrity of our republican institutions."

Senator Blanche K. Bruce, African American U.S. senator
from Mississippi, speech to the Senate, 1876

26. Which of the following developments had the clearest influence in eventually overcoming the issue raised by Senator Bruce in the excerpt?

   (A) The formation of the NAACP in 1909

   (B) The decision in *Brown v. Board of Education* in 1954

   (C) The March on Washington in 1963

   (D) The passage of civil rights legislation in 1964 and 1965

27. One response to Bruce's call for action in the excerpt was Booker T. Washington's program based on which of the following?

   (A) Participation in the Republican Party to gain political power

   (B) Migration of African Americans to Africa

   (C) Development of job skills that promote economic self-help

   (D) Creation of an agriculture-based society

28. The end of Senator Bruce's senate career and the reduction of African American political power in the South were the result of the

   (A) removal of federal troops from the South

   (B) success of the radical wing of the Republican Party

   (C) election of a Republican as president

   (D) rebirth of the Ku Klux Klan

Questions 29–31 refer to the following excerpt.

"That evening there was a general discussion in regard to the main subject in hunters' minds. Colorado had passed stringent laws that were practically prohibitory against buffalo-hunting; the Legislature of Kansas did the same. . . .

"General Phil Sheridan was then in command of the military department of the Southwest. . . . when he heard of the nature of the Texas bill for the protection of the buffaloes. . . . He told them that instead of stopping the hunters they ought to give them a hearty, unanimous vote of thanks. . . . 'These men . . . will do more in the next year to settle the vexed Indian question . . . they are destroying the Indians' commissary. . . .'

"But there are two sides to the question. It is simply a case of the survival of the fittest. Too late to stop and moralize now. And sentiment must have no part in our thoughts from this time on."

> John R. Cook, soldier, hunter, and author,
> *The Border and the Buffalo,* 1877

29. Which of the following ideas provided the base of Cook's point of view and government policies toward American Indians in the 1870s?
    (A) Finding ways for the U.S. government to protect traditional tribal cultures
    (B) Establishing new reservations in order to separate American Indians and Whites
    (C) Removing Indians to lands west of the Great Plains
    (D) Forcing American Indians to assimilate into White culture

30. Cook's perspective on buffalo hunting and the future of American Indians shows the influence of which of the following ideas?
    (A) The gospel of wealth
    (B) Laissez-faire principles
    (C) Social Darwinism
    (D) Protectionism

31. Opposition to the policies expressed in the excerpt came from which of the following movements?
    (A) Grange members who were eager for new farmland
    (B) Conservationists who wanted to preserve natural areas and habitat
    (C) Industrialists who hoped to open factories in western states.
    (D) National Labor Union members who saw American Indians as rivals for jobs

"There is not among these three hundred bands of Indians one which has not suffered cruelly at the hands of either the Government or of white settlers. . . .

"It makes little difference, however, where one opens the record of the history of the Indians. . . . every page and every year has its dark stain. . . . but neither time nor place makes any difference in the main facts. Colorado is as greedy and unjust in 1880 as was Georgia in 1830, and Ohio in 1795. . . .

"President after president has appointed commission after commission to inquire into and report upon Indian affairs. . . . These reports are bound up. . . . and that is the end of them. . . .

"All judicious plans and measures for their safety and salvation must embody provisions for their becoming citizens as fast as they are fit. . . .

"Cheating, robbing, breaking promises—these three are clearly things which must cease to be done."

> Helen Hunt Jackson, writer and activist for American Indians,
> *A Century of Dishonor,* 1881

32. The actions referred to in the excerpt about Georgia in 1830 are strongly associated with which of the following actions?

(A) Massacres of Native Americans in their homes and villages

(B) Removal of Native Americans to lands farther west

(C) Establishment of reservations in Georgia for Native Americans

(D) Use of Native Americans as troops in conflicts with Mexico

33. Jackson's statement that policies toward American Indians "must embody provisions for their becoming citizens as fast as they are fit" is most similar to

(A) the widespread treatment of Tories after the Revolutionary War

(B) the Jim Crow laws regarding Black Americans in the late 1800s

(C) the melting pot concept regarding immigrants in the early 1900s

(D) the executive order about Japanese Americans during World War II

34. The ideas expressed in this excerpt supported which development?

(A) Legislation to establish a clearer policy of assimilation

(B) Legislation to grant Native Americans the lands of their ancestors

(C) Recognition of the cultural identities of the Native American tribes

(D) Recognition that Native American tribes had the same status as foreign nations

Questions 35–37 refer to the following excerpt.

"They were begging for workers. They didn't care whether you were black, white, young, old. . . . I got caught up in that patriotic 'win the war,' 'help the boys.' The patriotism that was so strong in everyone then. . . .

"The first paycheck I got in aircraft was more money than I'd ever seen in my life. I didn't even know what to do with it. I didn't have a bank account. You couldn't buy anything much. . . .

"Soap was rationed, butter, Kleenex, toilet paper, toothpaste, cigarettes, clothing, shoes. And you saw people making a lot of money and not doing anything for the war effort. . . .

"By 1944 a lot of people were questioning the war. . . . I think when we actually began to see boys come home in late 1943, 1944—those that had been injured. . . .—then the rumbles grew into roars, and the young people thought maybe they were being led into this."

Juanita Loveless, African American worker in a war plant,
Rosie the Riveter Revisited, 1988

35. Which of the following groups of people does Loveless imply had their lives improved during World War II?

    (A) Soldiers who returned home who were treated as heroes

    (B) Producers of common consumer products such as soap and shoes

    (C) Women working in factories who received equal pay with men

    (D) African Americans who moved to jobs in the North and West

36. Loveless provides evidence that indicates which of the following changed in the U.S. economy?

    (A) Factory jobs paid higher wages, but rationing limited spending.

    (B) Taxes increased so much that people could not afford to buy much.

    (C) The sale of war bonds increased the amount of money circulating in the economy.

    (D) Union demands for higher wages caused prices to increase dramatically.

37. During World War II, the U.S. government took stronger actions than in previous wars to

    (A) lower taxes so that people could afford to pay for needed goods

    (B) avoid borrowing money to pay for the costs of fighting

    (C) give companies flexibility so they could increase production

    (D) regulate wages and prices throughout the economy

MEAN CENTER of POPULATION for the UNITED STATES, 1790 to 2010

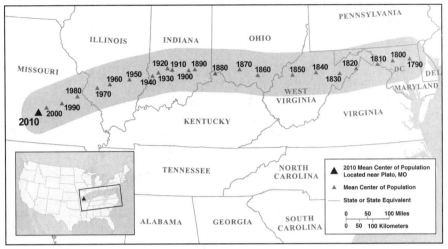

38. Which of the following contributed most to the slight northward movement shown in the map between 1860 and 1870?

(A) Completion of the Erie Canal

(B) Start of the California gold rush

(C) End of the Civil War

(D) Purchase of Alaska

39. The slowing of the westward movement of the center of population in the first decades of the 20th century is best explained by which of the following?

(A) Many people were moving to rural areas after World War I ended.

(B) Farmers from western states were returning to farms in the Midwest.

(C) African Americans were moving from southern states to northern states.

(D) European immigrants were moving to cities in eastern states.

40. Which of the following changes in the United States during and immediately after World War II most directly contributed to the shift shown in the map?

(A) Conflicts between younger and older generations caused people to move.

(B) Decreasing prosperity pushed people to move to other regions.

(C) The expansion of the defense industry created jobs in certain regions.

(D) Climate changes made some regions easier to live in than they had been.

Questions 41–43 refer to the graph below.

U.S. BIRTH RATE, 1909 to 2009

41. The graph above provides evidence of a population change following World War II that is commonly referred to as the

(A) cult of domesticity

(B) generation gap

(C) baby boom

(D) population bomb

42. Which of the following generalizations about the birth rate between 1949 and 2009 is best supported by this graph?

(A) It generally increased as immigration increased.

(B) It generally increased during the civil rights movement.

(C) It generally decreased whenever the economy got worse.

(D) It generally decreased when more women entered the workforce.

43. Which of the following government policies contributed most to the changes in the birth rate in the decade following World War II?

(A) Containing communism around the world

(B) Reducing the power of labor unions

(C) Encouraging steps toward racial equality

(D) Helping GIs attend college and buy homes

Questions 44–46 refer to the photograph below.

Source: Madison, Wisconsin, 1967. AP Photo/Neal Ulevich

44. Which of the following groups provided the most consistent and active support for the position on the Vietnam War portrayed in the photo?

(A) Members of conservative religious denominations

(B) Members of labor unions

(C) Supporters of funding the Great Society programs

(D) University students opposed to the draft

45. This photo provides support for the claim that one problem faced by the U.S. government during the Vietnam War was that it

(A) failed to maintain strong public support for its policies

(B) did not employ enough experts on Southeast Asia to advise it

(C) placed too many restrictions on the military

(D) suffered from weak presidential leadership under Johnson

46. The movement most similar to the one portrayed above was the

(A) American Indian Movement, because both had deep hisorical roots

(B) labor union movements, because both suffered from hundreds of protesters being killed

(C) civil rights movement, because both used mass marches effectively

(D) Populist movement, because both founded strong new political parties

Questions 47–49 refer to the following excerpt.

"Monday, January 3, 1983

"A tough budget meeting & how to announce the deficits we'll have—they are horrendous & yet the Dems. in Cong. are saying there is no room for budget cuts. . . . Newt Gingrich has a proposal for freezing the budget at the 1983 level. It's a tempting idea except that it would cripple our defense program. . . .

"Monday, October 24, 1983

"Opened with NSC brf. [brief] on Lebanon & Grenada. Lebanon gets worse as the death toll climbs. . . . Ambas. Hartman [Russia] came by. He confirms what I believe: the Soviets won't really negotiate on arms reductions until we deploy the Pershing II's [missiles] & go forward with MX [another missile program]. . . .

"Then at 8 P.M., Tip, Jim Wright, Bob Byrd, Howard Baker, Bob Michel [five congressional leaders] & our gang met upstairs in the W.H. [White House] & told them of the Grenada operation that would take place in the next several hours."

Ronald Reagan, *The Reagan Diaries*, published in 2007

47. On which topic mentioned in this excerpt did Reagan make the most progress in achieving his goals during his presidency?
   (A) Freezing the budget for the defense program
   (B) Approving a peace agreement between Lebanon and its neighbors
   (C) Reducing the threat of nuclear war with the Soviet Union
   (D) Stopping the Grenada operation

48. The change in federal spending that had the most impact on the overall budget balance during the Reagan administration was on
   (A) nutrition programs
   (B) Social Security
   (C) welfare benefits
   (D) the military

49. Reagan's goal for the federal budget implied in this source would be achieved during
   (A) his second term in office
   (B) the administration of George H. W. Bush
   (C) the administration of Bill Clinton
   (D) the administration of George W. Bush

"Besides being political to the core, Clinton is notable for his intelligence, energy, and exceptional articulateness. He is also marked by a severe lack of self-discipline that leads to difficulties, and a resiliency and coolness under pressure. . . . The most damaging blow of the year for Clinton was the failure of his most ambitious policy initiative, a bill guaranteeing health care to all Americans. . . .

"Clinton's first two years in the White House were marked by such legislative successes as NAFTA, the creation of a youth volunteer corps, a major deficit-reduction measure, and a law permitting family members to take unpaid leave to attend to children and sick relatives. . . . Clinton seems certain to be recognized for moving the Democratic Party to the center of the political spectrum and for many incremental policy departures."

> Fred I. Greenstein, political scientist,
> *The Presidential Difference*, 2000

50. Which of the following developments provides the most significant context for economic change during the Clinton presidency?
   (A) Technological innovations in communication systems and data transmission
   (B) Reductions in social services spending by the federal government
   (C) Significant declines in budget allocations for the military
   (D) Foreign policy initiatives in Eastern Europe and the Middle East

51. The primary reason many Americans viewed Clinton's presidency as a success was his
   (A) personal behavior as a leader for the country
   (B) economic policies that promoted growth
   (C) domestic policies such as support for medical insurance reform
   (D) foreign policy in the Balkans and the Middle East

52. Based on Clinton's actions as president, which of the following most accurately describes his basic views as president as portrayed by Greenstein?
   (A) Conservative, because his policies often were similar to those of Reagan
   (B) Moderate, because his policies often tried to appeal to people in both parties
   (C) Progressive, because his policies often anticipated future problems
   (D) Radical, because his policies often called for far-reaching political changes

Questions 53–55 refer to the following excerpt.

The second half of the 1990s marked the longest sustained stretch of economic growth in U.S. history. Unlike other periods of long-term economic expansion reversed by rising inflation, growth continued and even accelerated as inflation declined. The combination of rapid technological change, rise of the services sector, and emergence of the global marketplace had experts convinced that the United States was in the midst of 'a second industrial revolution.' . . .

"Economists attributed these developments to a restructuring of companies and an economy abetted by such government policies as the North American Free Trade Agreement. . . . Many economists pointed to the breakup of AT&T (1995) and the deregulation of the telecommunications industry as enhancing opportunities for competition, innovation, and growth. . . . A decline in the influence of organized labor, for better or worse, enabled firms to exercise greater flexibility."

"The American Economy," *American Decades,*
1900–1999, 2001

53. The causes of economic change described in the excerpt were most similar to causes of economic change in which of the following periods?

(A) The post-Revolutionary War era

(B) The mid- and late-19th century

(C) The 1920s

(D) The 1950s

54. The changes described in this excerpt most directly affected politics in the 1990s by

(A) increasing the popularity of the Democratic presidential administration

(B) causing conservative Christians to gain more power in the Republican Party

(C) strengthening the power of state and local governments

(D) prompting additional regulations on banks and other financial institutions

55. Which of the following did not share in the economic growth of the 1990s as much as other groups did?

(A) Large corporations

(B) College graduates

(C) Southern states

(D) Labor unions

Section 1

Part B: Short Answer—40 minutes, 3 questions

Use complete sentences; an outline or bulleted list alone is not acceptable.

Question 1 is based on the following excerpts.

1. "By the fall of 1963 the Kennedy administration, though still worried about its ability to push legislation through a recalcitrant Congress, was preparing initiatives on civil rights and economic opportunity. . . .

   "John F. Kennedy cautiously eased tensions with the Soviet Union, especially after Kennedy found himself on the brink of nuclear war over the presence of Soviet weapons in Cuba in 1962.

   "Although Kennedy did not rush to deal with domestic issues—in large part because he believed that foreign policy needed precedence—the press of events gradually forced his administration to use government power to confront racial discrimination and advance the cause of equality at home."

   John M. Murrin, et al., historians,
   Liberty, Equality and Power, 1996

   "Chopped down in his prime after only slightly more than a thousand days in the White House, Kennedy was acclaimed more for the ideals he enunciated and the spirit he had kindled than for the concrete goals he had achieved. He had laid one myth to rest forever—that a Catholic could not be trusted with the presidency of the United States.

   "In later years revelation about Kennedy's womanizing and allegations about his involvement with organized crime figures tarnished his reputation. But despite those accusations, his apparent vigor, charisma, and idealism made him an inspirational figure for the generation of Americans who came of age in the 1960s."

   David M. Kennedy, et al., historians,
   The American Pageant, 2006

   Using the excerpts above, answer (a), (b), and (c).

   (a) Briefly explain ONE major difference between Murrin and Kennedy's interpretations of the impact of the Kennedy presidency.

   (b) Briefly explain how ONE event, development, or circumstance from the period 1960 to 1963 that is not explicitly mentioned in the excerpts supports Murrin's view.

   (c) Briefly explain how ONE event, development, or circumstance from the period 1960 to 1963 that is not explicitly mentioned in the excerpts supports Kennedy's view.

Question 2 is based on the following painting.

2.

Source: Benjamin West, *American Commissioners of the Preliminary Peace Negotiations with Great Britain*, London, England, 1783. Winterthur Museum, gift of Henry Francis du Point, 1957.856

Using the image above, which depicts the peace negotiations of 1783, answer (a), (b), and (c).

(a) Briefly describe one historical perspective expressed in the image.

(b) Briefly describe one specific historical event or development in the period from 1754 to 1783 that contributed to the process depicted in the image.

(c) Briefly explain one historical effect in the period 1783 to 1812 that resulted from the process depicted in the image.

Question 3. Answer (a), (b), and (c).

(a) Briefly describe ONE specific historical difference between American society and culture in the mid-18th century and the mid-19th century.

(b) Briefly describe ONE specific historical similarity between American society and culture in the mid-18th century and the mid-19th century.

(c) Briefly explain ONE specific historical effect of American society and culture in either the mid-18th century or the mid-19th century.

Question 4. Answer (a), (b), and (c).

(a) Briefly describe ONE specific historical similarity between the women's rights movement in the period from 1900 to the 1920s and in the period from the 1960s to the 1970s.

(b) Briefly describe ONE specific historical difference between the women's rights movement in the period from 1900 to the 1920s and in the period from the 1960s to the 1970s.

(c) Briefly explain ONE reason for the difference in the two movements for women's rights in 1900 to the 1920s and 1960s to 1970s.

Section 2

Part A: Document-Based Question—60 minutes, 1 question

Directions: Question 1 is based on the accompanying documents. The documents have been edited for the purpose of this exercise. You are advised to spend 15 minutes planning and 45 minutes writing your answer. In your response you should do the following:

- Respond to the prompt with a historically defensible thesis or claim that establishes a line of reasoning.
- Describe a broader historical context relevant to the prompt.
- Support an argument in response to the prompt using at least six documents.
- Use at least one additional piece of specific historical evidence (beyond that found in the documents) relevant to an argument about the prompt.
- For at least three documents, explain how or why the document's point of view, purpose, historical situation, and/or audience is relevant to an argument.
- Use evidence to corroborate, qualify, or modify an argument that addresses the prompt.

1. Evaluate the extent to which the reform efforts of the Progressive Era were aimed at maintaining the existing society rather than bringing about radical changes.

Document 1

Source: Progressive Party Platform, August 5, 1912

The conscience of the people, in a time of grave national problems, has called into being a new party, born of the nation's sense of justice. We of the Progressive Party here dedicate ourselves to the fulfillment of the duty laid upon us by our fathers to maintain the government of the people, by the people and for the people whose foundations they laid. . . .

Political parties exist to secure responsible government and to execute the will of the people. . . . Instead of instruments to promote the general welfare, they have become the tools of corrupt interests which use them impartially to serve their selfish purposes. Behind the ostensible government sits enthroned an invisible government owing no allegiance and acknowledging no responsibility to the people.

To destroy this invisible government, to dissolve the unholy alliance between corrupt business and corrupt politics is the first task of statesmanship of the day.

Document 2

Source: President Woodrow Wilson, First Inaugural Address, March 4, 1913

No one can mistake the purpose for which the Nation now seeks to use the Democratic Party. It seeks to use it to interpret a change in its own plans and point of view. Some old things. . . . as we have latterly looked critically upon them. . . . have dropped their disguises and shown themselves alien and sinister. Some new things, as we look frankly upon them. . . . have come to assume the aspect of things long believed in and familiar, stuff of our own convictions.

We have itemized. . . . the things that ought to be altered. . . . A tariff which makes the Government a facile instrument in the hands of private interests; a banking and currency system perfectly adapted to concentrating cash and restricting credits; an industrial system which restricts labor, and exploits natural resources; a body of agriculture never served through science or afforded the facilities of credit best suited to its practical needs.

Document 3

Source: Senator Elihu Root, former secretary of state and secretary of war, "Experiments in Government," lecture at Princeton University, April 1913

The recognition of shortcomings or inconveniences in government is not by itself sufficient to warrant a change of system. There should be also an effort to estimate and compare the shortcomings and inconveniences of the system to be substituted, for although they may be different, they will certainly exist.

Document 4

Source: Library of Congress

Document 5

Source: W. E. B. Du Bois, sociologist and civil rights activist, "An Open Letter to Woodrow Wilson," September 1913

Sir, you have now been President of the United States for six months and what is the result? It is no exaggeration to say that every enemy of the Negro race is greatly encouraged; that every man who dreams of making the Negro race a group of menials and pariahs is alert and hopeful.

A dozen worthy Negro officials have been removed from office, and you have nominated but one black man for office, and he, such a contemptible cur, that his very nomination was an insult to every Negro. . . .

To this negative appearance of indifference has been added positive action on the part of your advisers, with or without your knowledge, which constitutes the gravest attack on the liberties of our people since emancipation. Public segregation of civil servants in government employ. . . . has for the first time in history been made the policy of the United States government.

Document 6

Source: Mary Harris "Mother" Jones, labor and community organizer, Miners' Magazine, April 1915

When one starts to investigate conditions the result is appalling. . . . For instance, it is a fact that although this country is in its infancy, and has gained in wealth more in fifty years than any other country has in 700 years, still we have more poverty in comparison with any of those old countries.

I have always felt that no true state of civilization can ever be realized as long as we continue to have two classes of society. But that is a tremendous problem. . . . I think myself that we are bound to have a revolution here before these questions are straightened out. We were on the verge of it in the Colorado strike and the reason we did not have it then was not due to the good judgement of public officials, but to that of labor officials, who worked unceasingly to prevent it.

Document 7

Source: George Grantham Bain Collection, Library of Congress

Part B: Long Essay Question—40 minutes, 1 question

LONG ESSAY QUESTIONS

Directions: *Choose Question 2 OR Question 3 OR Question 4. The suggested writing time for each question is 40 minutes. In your response you should do the following:*

- Respond to the prompt with a historically defensible thesis or claim that establishes a line of reasoning.
- Describe a broader historical context relevant to the prompt.
- Support an argument in response to the prompt using specific and relevant examples of evidence.
- Use historical reasoning (e.g., comparison, causation, continuity, or change) to frame or structure an argument that addresses the prompt.
- Use evidence to corroborate, qualify, or modify an argument that addresses the prompt.

2. Evaluate the extent of similarity in American views concerning the British following the Seven Years' War and the American Revolution.

3. Evaluate the extent of similarity in American views concerning the role of the United States in North America between 1800–1850 and 1860–1910.

4. Evaluate the extent of similarity in American views concerning the role of the United States in the world following World War I and World War II.

Index

Axis of evil, 729
Azores, 10
Aztecs, 3

B

Baby boom, 606, 639
Baby boom generation, 663, 665
Back-to-Africa movement, 511
Backwoods utopias, 224
Bacon, Nathaniel, 55
Bacon's Rebellion, 55–56
Baez, Joan, 665
Bailey, Thomas B., 459
Bailyn, Bernard, 99
Baker, Jim, 680
Baker v. Carr (1962), 660
Bank holiday, 527
Bank of the United States, 171, 316
    Jackson and rechartering, 214–215, 219
    Second, 171, 176, 177, 178
Bank veto, 214
Banneker, Benjamin, 154
Baptists, 230
Barbary pirates, 182
Barbed wire, 351
Baritz, Leon, 645
Barnburners, 278
Bartram, John, 69
Baruch, Bernard, 491
Baseball, 405, 621
Bay of Pigs, 593
Beard, Charles A., 134
Bear Flag Republic, 272
Beatniks, 617
Beautify America campaign, 647
Beckwourth, James, 266
Begin, Menachem, 634
Bell, Alexander Graham, 371
Bellamy, Edward (*Looking Backward,* 1888) 408
Bell, John, 298
Benton, Thomas Hart, 509
Berkeley, John, 44
Berkeley, William, 55
Berlin airlift, 584–585
Berlin, Irving, 502
Berlin Wall, 593, 708
Bernanke, Ben, 736
Bessemer, Henry, 371
Beverly, Robert, 37
B-52 bombers, 638
Bicycling, 405
Big-city political machines, 422
Big Four, 485
"Big stick" policy, 631

Bill, Brady, 700
Bill of Rights, 84, 127, 131–132
Bingham, George Caleb, 225, 226
Black abolitionists, 238
Black Codes, 261, 334
Blacklist, 384
Black Lives Matter movement, 693, 701
Black Muslim, 653
Black Panthers, 653
Black Star Steamship line, 511
Black Thursday, 519
Black Tuesday, 519
Bland-Allison Act, 418
"Bleeding Kansas," 290
"Bloody shirt" (waving the), 324, 329, 422
Bloomer, Amelia, 238
Blues music, 405
Blumin, Stuart M., 407
Boland Amendment, 706
Bolden, Buddy, 405
Bonaparte, Napoleon, 167
Bonus March, 522
Books, 464–465
Boone, Daniel, 151
Booth, John Wilkes, 317
Border wall, 740
Bosnia, 710
Boston Massacre, 95
Boston Tea Party, 95
Boxer Rebellion (1900), 451
Braceros, 559
Bradford, William, 40
Brady Bill, 714
Breckinridge, John C., 298
Brereton, John, 28
Brexit, 739
Bridger, Jim, 266
Brinkley, Alan, 296
British colonies, 36
    British-French wars, 84
    colonial tensions, 90
    corporate, 38
    demand for independence by, 96
    demand for labor in, 59–60
    development of New England, 41–42
    early settlements, 38–41
    early political institutions, 46
    effect of Seven Years' War on, 88–89
    institution of slavery, 60–61
    proprietary, 38
    Restoration, 43–46
    royal, 38
    taxation, 92
British East India Company, 95

Grant, Ulysses S., 271, 308, 512
Great American Desert, 265, 349
Great Awakening, 67–68
Great Basin, Native Americans of, 4–5
Great Britain
    Embargo Act and, 183
    espionage in, 601
    Guiana and, 443
    Jay Treaty (1794) with, 137
    mercantilism, 50–51
    Oregon boundary dispute with, 264
    Seven Years' War and, 87–90
    World War I, 479–480
    World War II, 569, 570
Great Depression, 494, 507, 525, 542, 658, 735
    African Americans during, 537
    American Indians during, 537
    causes of, 518–529
    depression mentality, 536
    drought, 536
    dust bowl, 536
    effects of, 520–521
    Hoover's policies, 521–523
    life during, 536–538
    Mexican Americans during, 538
    Okies, 536
    social effects of, 521
    women during, 536–537
Great Migration of African Americans, 494
Great Migration of Puritans, 40
Great Plains, 349, 351, 348–349
    Native Americans, 4–5, 217
Great Railroad Strike (1877), 385
Great Recession, 735, 736
Great Seal, 146
Great Society, 646–648
Great White Fleet, 454
Greece, 732
Greenback Party, 417–418
Greenbacks, 316
Green cards, 721
Greenhouse gases, 672
Gregg, William, 252
Grenada, 706
Griffith, D. W.
    The Birth of a Nation, 335
Grimké, Angelina, 237
Grimké, Sarah, *Letters on the Equality of the*
    Sexes, and the Condition of Women, 237
Griswold v. Connecticut (1965), 661
Gross national product, 520
Group of Eight (G8), 716
Growth of leisure time, 404
Gulf of Mexico, 35

Gunpowder, 8
Gun rights, 700–701

H

Habeas corpus, 313
Hahn, Steven, 270
Haitian Revolution (1791–1804), 113
Hakluyt, Richard, 12
Halfway covenant, 42
Hamilton, Alexander, 110, 121, 123, 124,
    133, 135
    duel with Burr, 169
    financial program, 136–137
Hancock, John, 124
Hanna, Mark, 426
Harding, Warren, 512, 541, 543
Hard money, 417
Harlem Renaissance, 510–511
Harpers Ferry, 297
Harrington, Michael, 646
Harrison, William Henry, 263
Hartford Convention, 188
Hawley-Smoot Tariff (1930), 521
Hawthorne, Nathaniel, 224, 226
Hayes, Rutherford B., 334
Haymarket bombing, 385–386
Hays, Samuel L., 477
Headright system, 60
Hearst, William Randolph, 404
Hell-and-brimstone revivals, 230
Heller, Joseph
    Catch-22, 1961, 617
Helper, Hinton R., 286
    Impending Crisis of the South, 286
Hemingway, Ernest, 509
Henry, Patrick, 70, 93, 124, 127
Henry the Navigator, 9
Herberg, Will
    Protestant, Catholic, Jew, 616
Herring, George C., 459, 555
High protective tariff, 425
Highsmith, Carol M., 501
Highway Act, 609
Hillbillies, 249
Hispanic Americans, 658
Hiss, Alger, 601
Hiss Case, 601
Hitler, Adolf, 582, 584
Hofstadter, Richard, 134, 429
Hohokam, 4
Holding company, 378
Holmes Jr., Oliver Wendell, 404
Home Owners Loan Corporation (HOLC), 528
Homer, Winslow, 411

Homestead Act (1862), 317, 351
Homestead strike, 386
Hoover, Herbert, 491, 512
    election of 1928, 513
    foreign policy, 543–544
    Great Depression and, 521–523
    as "lame-duck" president, 525–526
    Latin America and, 543
Hopi, 56, 358
Hopper, Edward, 509
Horizontal integration, 378
Horwitz, Tony, 303
Hostage crisis, 629–630
House of Burgesses, 72
House of Islam, 727
House Un-American Activities Committee
    (HUAC), 600
Houston, Sam, 263
Howe, Elias, 284
Hudson, Henry, 35
Hughes, Charles Evans, 512
Hughes, Langston, 511
Huguenots, 12
Humphrey, Hubert, 639
Hussein, Saddam, 729
Hutchinson, Anne, 42
Hydrogen bomb (H-bomb), 586, 590, 669

I

Ickes, Harold, 528
Idaho, 350
Illegal Immigration Reform and Immigrant
    Responsibility Act (1996), 721
Illinois, 193, 206
Immigrants, 60, 63, 178, 260
    American society in 2000, 723
    from Asia, 390
    Chinese, 348, 391, 395
    discrimination against, 261
    historical perspectives, 396–397
    restrictions on Chinese and other, 395
    undocumented, 648, 721, 739
    voter, 422
Immigration, 201, 282–283
    cities and, 390–391
    growth of, 389–390
    historical perspectives, 396–397
    Nativist opposition to, 283, 394–395,
        507–508
    push and pull factors, 389–390
    during World War I, 493
Immigration Act (1965), 648
Immigration and Nationality Act (1965),
    720

Immigration Reform and Control Act (1986),
    721
Imperialism, 440
    conflict over, 443
    expansion after the Civil War, 440–441
    Monroe Doctrine and, 443
    "new imperialism," 441–442
    opposition to, 442
    Pan-American diplomacy, 443
Imperial presidency, 640
Imports and exports, 50, 125, 267
Impressionism techniques, 411
Incas, 3
Income tax, 424, 470
Indentured servants, 59
Indiana, 193, 206
Indian Intercourse Act (1790), 149
Indian Removal Act (1830), 212
Indian Reorganization (Wheeler-Howard) Act
    (1934), 360, 537–538
Indian Self-Determination Act (1975),
    659
Indian, Plains, 358–360
Individual rights, definition of, 660
Industrial design, 501
Industrialization
    effect on families and women's role in,
        236–237
    during the Gilded Age, 405
    impact of, 284
    market revolution and, 299
    in the North, 317
    railroads and, 284–285
    in the South, 365–366
    urbanization and, 347, 390–391
Industrial warfare, 384–385
Industry
    conditions in 1900, 387
    controversy over corporate power,
        378–379
    growth of, 195–197, 365–366
    oil, 378
    steel, 377–378
    strikes and strikebreaking, 386–387
    during World War I, 491–492
INF agreement, 707
Inflation, 66
Influenza outbreak (1918 pandemic), 495
Initiative, 466
Institution of slavery, 60–61
Insular (island) Cases, 449
Interchangeable parts, 196
Interlocking directorates, 376
International Monetary Fund (IMF), 716

Interstate Commerce Act (1887), 376, 416
Interstate highways, 609
Intolerable Acts, 96
Inventions, 8, 193, 196, 284, 371–372
Iran, 732
    Contra affair, 706
    hostage crisis and, 629–630
    Obama and, 732
    overthrow of government, 627
Iran-Contra affair, 706
Iraq, 708, 729–732, 735
Iraq War, 729, 730, 735
Irish immigrants, 282
Iron Curtain, 583
Iron law of wages, 383
Iroquois Confederation, 6
Iroquois (Haudenosaunee), 25
Irreconcilable faction, 487
Irving, Washington, 225
Isabella, Queen, 9, 10, 14, 19
Islamic State of Iraq and Syria (ISIS or ISIL), 732
Island hopping, 564
Israel, 627, 629, 706–707
Italy, 546

J

Jackson, Andrew, 164, 219
    Democrats and Whigs, 215
    election of 1824, 210
    and expanding democracy, 207–208
    Kitchen cabinet, 212
    military campaign, 189–190
    presidency of, 211–214, 215–216
    spoils system and, 207
Jackson, Helen Hunt, 360
Jackson, Shirley, 601
Jackson, Thomas (Stonewall), 306
James I, King, 39
James II, King, 44, 52
Japan
    aggression in Manchuria, 543–544
    and China, 548
    Cold War and, 585–586
    "Gentlemen's Agreement," 453
    nationalists and militarists in, 546
    Pearl Harbor, 552
    Russo-Japanese War, 553
    Second Sino-Japanese War, 546
    World II and, 552–553
    World War II and, 563–565
Japanese Americans, 559
Jay, John, 124, 137
Jay Treaty (1794), 137

Jazz, 405
Jazz Age, 511
Jeffersonian tradition, 422
Jefferson, Thomas, 69, 106, 124, 135, 136, 149, 165, 173, 175, 181, 254, 259
    election of 1800, 165–166
    foreign policy, 182–183
    presidency of, 166–169
    reelection, 169
Jews, 422, 509, 563
Jim Crow laws, 367
John Paul II, Pope, 707
Johns Hopkins University, 403
Johnson, Andrew, 316
    impeachment of, 325
    Reconstruction Policy of, 322
Johnson, James Weldon, 511
Johnson, Lyndon B., 691
    domestic reforms under, 610–611
    election of 1964, 646–647
    Great Society of, 646–648
    presidency of, 594–595
    Tonkin Gulf Resolution, 636–637
    Vietnam War and, 636–637
    War on Poverty, 646
Johnson, Paul, 517
Johnson, Reverend Samuel, 86
Johnson, Tom L., 466
Joint Committee, 324
Joint-stock company, 15
Jolliet, Louis, 35
Jones, Samuel M. "Golden Rule," 466
    "golden rule," 466
Joplin, Scott, 405
Judicial impeachments, 169
Judiciary Act (1789), 136
Juneteenth, 320

K

Kagan, Elena, 736
Kanagawa Treaty, 268
Kansas-Nebraska Act (1854), 290
Kavanaugh, Brett, 740
Kearney, Stephen, 271
Kelley, Florence, 467
Kellogg-Briand Pact, 542
Kelly, William, 371
Kennan, George F., 583, 598
Kennedy, David M., 539
Kennedy, John F., 610
    assassination of, 617–618, 654
    Bay of Pigs invasion, 593–594
    Latin America and, 630–631
    Vietnam War and, 639–640

"Log Cabin and Hard Cider" (campaign of 1840), 216
London, Jack, 411
Longhorn cattle, 350
Longhouses, 6
Long, Huey, 533
Louisiana, 35, 88
Louisiana Purchase, 166–169
L'ouverture, Toussaint, 113, 167
Lowell System, 196
Loyalty Review Board, 600
Lusitania crisis, 479, 480, 481
Lutherans, 422
Lyceum lecture societies, 236
Lynch mobs, 367
Lyon, Mary, 236

M

MacArthur, Douglas, 586
    Japan and, 586–587
    Korean War and, 588
Machine politics, 395
Macon's Bill No. 2 (1810), 184
Macy, R. H., 373
Madeira, 10
Madison, James, 112, 123
    at Annapolis Convention, 123
    at Constitution Convention, 125
    drafting of the Constitution, 124
    foreign policy, 183–184
    New York newspaper by, 127
    presidency of, 172
    as slaveowner, 151
Magazines, 464
Mahican Indians, 54
Maine, sinking of, 447
Malaria, 448
Malcolm X, 653, 690
Manifest Destiny, 262
    annexing Texas, 265
    boundary dispute, 263–264
    conflicts over Texas, Maine, and Oregon, 262–263
    conflict with Mexico, 271–272
    consequences of the Mexican-American War, 272–273
    dividing Oregon, 265
    election of 1844, 264–265
    expansion after the Civil War, 268
    historical perspectives, 273
    settlement of the Western Territories, 265–268
Mann-Elkins Act (1910), 470
Mann, Horace, 236

Mao Zedong, 587
Mapp v. Ohio (1961), 660
Marbury v. Madison (1803), 170
March on Washington, 652, 690
March to Montgomery, 652
March to Washington, 424
Marketing consumer goods, 373
Market revolution, 193
    advertising, 373
    commercial agriculture, 197
    communication, 195
    cotton and the South, 197
    development of the Northwest, 193–194
    economic and social mobility, 201
    growth of industry, 195–197
    organized labor, 202
    population growth and change, 201–202
    transportation, 194
    women's role, 200–201
Marquette, Jacques, 35
Marshall, George, 583
Marshall, John, as Chief Justice of the Supreme Court, 170–172
Marshall Plan, 584
Marshall, S. L. A., 364
Marshall, Thurgood, 622
Martin v. Hunter's Lease (1816), 171
Maryland, 40–41
Maryland Act of Toleration, 47
Maslin, Mark A., 18
Mason, George, 127
Massachusetts Bay Colony, 40, 46
Massachusetts Bay Company, 40
Massachusetts 54th Regiment, 314
Massachusetts Government Act (1774), 96
Mass-circulation newspapers, 404
Mass media, 426, 439, 502
Mather, Cotton, 69
Mayas, 3
May Day labor movement, 385
Mayflower, 40, 46
Mayflower Compact (1620), 80
McAdoo, William, 491
McCain, John, 730
McCarran Internal Security Act (1950), 600
McCarthy, Joseph R., 602, 604
McCauley, Mary (Molly Pitcher)
    in battle of Monmouth, 111
McClellan, George B., 306
McClure, Samuel Sidney, 464
McCormick, Richard L., 477
McCulloch v. Maryland (1819), 171
McDougall, Walter A., 29
McElroy, William, 428

Montana, 350
Montgomery bus boycott, 623
Moody, Dwight, 409
Moral education, 236
Moral majority, 680
Morgan, J. Pierpont, 376, 378, 480
Morrill Land Grant Acts (1862, 1890), 317, 402
Morrill Tariff Act (1861), 317
Morris, Gouverneur, 124
Morris, Jeffrey B., 211
Morris, Richard B., 211
Morse, Samuel F. B., 284
Morton, Jelly Roll, 405
Motor-voter law, 714
Mott, Lucretia, 237
Mountain people, 249
Mount, William S., 225
Mt. Vernon, 130
Movie business, 502
Mubarak, Hosni, 731
Muckrakers, 463–465
Mueller, Robert, 740
Muir, John, 362
Muller v. Oregon (1908), 467
Municipal reforms, 466
Munn v. Illinois (1877), 353
Murray, Judith Sargent, 111
Musical theatre, 509
Mussolini, Benito, 546
My Lai, 641–642

N

Nader, Ralph, 726
Nagasaki, 564
Napoleonic wars, 169, 182, 222
    Challenges to U.S. neutrality, 182–183
    fall of Napoleon, 190
    France and Britain during, 182
    Napoleon's deception, 184
Narragansett Bay, 42
Nasser, Gamal Abdel, 628
Nast, Thomas, 328
National Aeronautics and Space Administration (NASA), 591
National American Woman Suffrage Association (NAWSA), 410, 474
National Association for the Advancement of Colored People (NAACP)
    founding, 473
    desegregation, 622–623
National Bank, 136–137, 316
National Broadcasting Company (NBC), 502

National Defense Act (1916), 481
National Defense and Education Act (NDEA), 591
National Grange Movement, 353
National Industrial Recovery Act, 534
National Labor Relations (Wagner) Act (1935), 530
National Labor Union, 385
National malaise speech, 679
National Organization for Women (NOW), 657
National Recovery Administration (NRA), 528–529
National Rifle Association (NRA), 700, 714
National Security Act (1947), 586
National Urban League, 473
National Woman's Party, 474
National Youth Administration (NYA), 530
Nation, Carry A., 410
Nation-states, 10
Native Americans. *See* American Indians
Nativism, 283, 508
Naturalism, 411
Naturalization Act, 142
Natural laws, 70
Naval battles, 187
Naval operations, 483
Navigation Acts, 50–51
Nazi Party, 546
Neutrality Acts, 547
Nevada, 350
New birth of freedom, 260
New Deal, 525–538
    election of 1936 and the, 531–532
    first hundred days of, 527–529
    labor unions and workers' rights, 534–535
    opponents of, 532–533
    philosophy of, 526–527
    programs of, 529
    Second New Deal, 529–531
    Social Security Act, 531
New England, 39
    conflict in, 54–55
    development of, 41–42
    Dominion of, 52
    trade tensions, 52
New England Confederation (1643), 54, 81
New England Emigrant Aid Company (1855), 290
New Federalism, 611
New Freedom, 455, 471
New Frontier, 610
New governments, organization of, 117–118
New Hampshire, 42

New Harmony, 224
New Haven, 42
"New" immigrants, 390
New imperialism, 441–442
New Jersey, 44
New Jersey Plan, 125
Newlands Reclamation Act, 469
New Laws of 1542, 24
New Left, 663–665
New Orleans, battle of, 211
"New South," 365–368
Newspapers, 70
New York, 44
New York Female Moral Reform Society, 236
Niagara Movement, 473
Nicaragua, 454
Nine-Power Treaty, 542
Nineteenth Amendment (1920), 474
Ninth Amendment, 132
Nixon Doctrine, 641
Nixon, Richard M., 539
    detente diplomacy, 595
    domestic policy, 611–612
    economic policies, 611–612
    election debates of 1960, 636
    election of 1952, 608–609
    election of 1968, 639
    election of 1972, 675
    impeachment of, 676
    pardoning of, 678
    presidency of, 674–675
    resignation of, 595, 676–677
    return of, 640
    Southern strategy, 675
    Vietnam policy of, 640–642
    visit to China, 595
    Watergate Scandal and, 675–677
No Child Left Behind Act, 734
Nonintercourse Act (1809), 183
Nonviolent movement, 623
Normalcy, 496
Norris, Frank, 464
Norris, George W., 577
North, the
    advantages in the Civil War, 285
    African Americans in, 107, 242
    black abolitionists in, 238
    Civil War and, 272–273
    modernization of, 317
    political dominance of, 316
    slavery in, 151–152
North America
    colonization in, 32–33
    control of land, claims for, 10–12

    cultures of, 4–6
    early settlements, 32–33
    European colonization in, 34–36
    social structures in, 4
    sources of labor in, 33
North American Free Trade Agreement (NAFTA), 716
North Atlantic Treaty Organization (NATO), 585
North Carolina, 44
Northeast, Native Americans of the, 6
North, Lord Frederick, 94
Northwest, Native Americans of the, 4
Northwest Ordinance (1787), 119, 153. 193
Novels, see Literature
Noyes, John Humphrey, 224
NSC-68, 586
Nuclear Test Ban Treaty, 593
Nueces River, 271
Nullification crisis, 213–214
Nunn, Nathan, 18
Nye, Gerald, 547

O

Oakley, Annie, 404
Obama, Barack
    domestic policy of, 736–739
    election of 2008, 730–731
    executive action of, 721
    financial reforms by, 736–737
    foreign policy of, 731–733
Obamacare, 737
Obergefell v. Hodges (2015), 701
Ocala platform, 353–354
Occupation zones, 583
O'Connor, Sandra Day, 696
Office of Economic Opportunity (OEO), 646
Office of Price Administration (OPA), 556
Office of War Mobilization (OWM), 556
Offner, Arnold A., 599
Oglethorpe, James, 45
Ohio, 193
Ohio River, 6
Oil embargo, 628–629, 671–672
Okinawa, battle of, 564
"Old Hickory," 211
"Old" immigrants, 390
Olmsted, Frederick Law, 402, 412
Olney, Richard, 383, 443
Omaha platform, 422
"On Civil Disobedience," 223
Oneida community, 224
O'Neill, Eugene, 509
O'Neill, William L., 613, 620

Taiwan. *See* Formosa
Tallmadge Amendment, 179–180
Tammany Hall, 283, 395
Tampico incident, 456
Taney, Roger, 293
Tarbell, Ida, 464
Tariff
 of 1816, 176
 of Abominations, 211–214
 Dingley Tariff, 426
 election of 1800 and, 165
 Fordney-McCumber Tariff (1922) 512, 542
 graph of, 418
 Hamilton and, 136
 Hawley-Smoot Tariff (1930), 521
 issues in the 1870s and 1880s, 416–418
 Morrill Tariff (1861) 317
 Payne-Aldrich Tariff (1909), 470
 reduction in under Wilson, 471–472
 reform, 424
 Trump and, 741
 Underwood Tariff, 471–472
 Wilson-Gorman Tariff, 424
Tax cuts
 American Recovery and Reinvestment
  Act, 736
 Economic Recovery and Tax Act, 695
 Tax Cuts and Jobs Act, 740
 under Barack Obama, 736
 under Bill Clinton, 714–715
 under Donald Trump, 740
 under George W. Bush, 734
 under Ronald Reagan, 695
Taxpayers' revolt, 680–681
Taylor, Zachary, 271, 471
 election of 1848, 278
Tea Act (1773), 95
Tea Party
 Boston, 95
 movement in 21st century, 738
Technology, 284, 501–502, 715
 innovations, 8, 371–372, 499–500, 715
 and growth of cities, 372–373
Tehran, 568
Telegraph, 195
Telephone, 371
Televangelists, 680
Television, 615
Teller Amendment, 447
Temperance, 410, 422, 467
Tenant farmers, 366
Tenement apartments, 391
Tennessee Valley Authority (TVA), 528
Tennis, 405

Tenth Amendment, 132
Tenure of Office Act, 325
Terrorism
 roots of, 727
 September 11, 2001, 727
 war on, 726–729
Tet offensive, 638–639
Think tanks, 680
Third Amendment, 131
Third World, unrest in, 626
Thirteenth Amendment, 323
Thomas, Clarence, 698
Thomas, John L., 233
Thomas, Norman, 578
Thoreau, Henry David (1817–1862), 222,
 223, 227
 Walden (1854), 223
Three Mile Island power plant, 669
Tiananmen Square, 708
Tilden, Samuel J., 335
Time zones, 375
Tippecanoe, 216
Title IX, 657
Tocqueville, Alexis de, 205
Tojo, Premier Hideki, 586
Tonkin Gulf Resolution, 636–637
Tories, 107–108
Townsend, Francis E., 533
Townshend Acts, 94–95
Trade Expansion Act (1962), 610
Trail of Tears, 212, 216
Transatlantic cable, 371
Transatlantic exchange, 1
Transatlantic trade, 49
Transcontinental railroads, 348–349
Transportation, 67, 178, 194, 372, 647
Treaty of 1818, 189
Treaty of Ghent (1814), 187–188
Treaty of Guadalupe Hidalgo (1848), 272
Treaty of Paris (1783), 109, 120
Treaty of Paris (1899) 448–449
Treaty of Tordesillas (1494), 10
Treaty of Versailles (1919), 485–487
Triangle Shirtwaist fire (1911), 467
Triangular trade, 49
"Trickle-down" economics, 695
Troubled Assets Relief Program (TARP), 735
Truman Doctrine, 584
Truman, Harry S., 605, 688
 civil rights movement and, 621–622
 Cold War and, 581–590
 election of 1948, 608
 Employment Act (1946), 605
 Fair Deal of, 608

W

Wineapple, Brenda, 296
Winthrop, John, 40
Winthrop, Robert C., 269
Wisconsin, 193
Wolfe, James, 88
Woman's Christian Temperance Union
(WCTU), 235, 410
Women
in the American Revolution, 111–112
in the colonies, 66
campaign for suffrage, 474
changing roles for, 329
effects of the market revolution on, 200–201
equality and safety of, 701
and the progressive movement, 474
reforms in women's rights, 237
in the 1920s, 509–510
in the 1930s, 536–537
voting rights for, 410
on the western frontier, 217
in the workforce, 617
Women's movement, 657–658
Wood, Gordon S., 99, 113, 115
Wood, Grant, 509
Woodland mound builders, 6
Woodstock Music Festival, 665
Workingmen's Party, 206
Works Progress Administration (WPA), 530
World Bank, 582
World Trade Center, 727, 728
World Trade Organization (WTO), 716
World War I debate, 481
World War I
armed forces in, 493–494
casualties of, 484
civil liberties, 493
debate over, 481
decision for, 482–483
declaration of, 483
economic links with Britain and France,
479–480
effects on American society, 494
election of 1916, 481–482
fighting of, 483–484
lesson of, 547
mobilization for, 491–492
neutrality in, 478–479
opposition to, 481
partisanship after, 485–486
peace efforts during, 482, 484–485
postwar agreements, 541–542
postwar problems, 495–496
public opinion about, 480–481, 492
ratification of peace treaty, 486–487

submarine warfare, 479
Treaty of Versailles, 485–487
World War II
D-Day, 563
declaration of, 553
in Europe, 553
financing, 557
impact on society, 558–559
invasion of Poland, 549
legacy, 569–570
mobilization for, 556–557
and morality, 564
outbreak of, 548–549
Pearl Harbor, 552
Potsdam, 569
prelude to, 547–548
preparedness for, 548
propaganda, 557
solidarity, 559
U.S. economic action in, 552
wartime conferences, 568–569
women after, 559
Worldwide depression, 520, 521, 546
Wright, Frank Lloyd, 412

X

Xenophobia, 451, 495
XYZ Affair, 141–142

Y

Yachting, 405
Yale University, 379
Yalta Conference, 568, 601
Yates v. United States (1957), 660
Yellow-dog contract, 384
Yellow journalism (yellow press), 447
Yellowstone, 361
Yeltsin, Boris, 708–709
Yom Kippur (October) War, 628–629, 671
Yorktown, battle of, 109
Yosemite Valley, 361
Yucatán Peninsula, 3
Yugoslavia, 710

Z

Zenger case, 70
Zenger, John Peter, 70
Zimmermann, Arthur, 482, 488
Zimmermann Telegram, 482–483, 488
Zinn, Howard, 540
Zoot suit riots, 559
Zuni, 56, 358